LOYALISTS OF AMERICA

AND

THEIR TIMES:

THE

LOYALISTS OF AMERICA

AND

THEIR TIMES:

FROM 1620 TO 1816.

BY EGERTON RYERSON, D.D., LL.D.,

*Chief Superintendent of Education for Upper Canada
from 1844 to 1876.*

IN TWO VOLUMES.

VOL. I.

SECOND EDITION

HASKELL HOUSE PUBLISHERS LTD.
Publishers of Scarce Scholarly Books
NEW YORK. N. Y. 10012
1970

First Published 1880

HASKELL HOUSE PUBLISHERS Ltd.
Publishers of Scarce Scholarly Books
280 LAFAYETTE STREET
NEW YORK, N. Y. 10012

Library of Congress Catalog Card Number: 68–31273

Standard Book Number 8383-0195-9

Printed in the United States of America

DEDICATED, BY PERMISSION, TO

THE QUEEN.

MOST GRACIOUS SOVEREIGN,—*I have written the History of* THE LOYALISTS OF AMERICA AND THEIR TIMES *in obedience to the requests of public men and the newspaper press of all parties, urged upon me more than twenty years since; but not less prompted by my own filial feelings of traditional affection.*

The first edition of my work having received the general approbation of the Canadian public, and been disposed of in a few months, and having been brought under the favourable notice of your Majesty by your Representative in Canada, I have the additional pleasure and honour of issuing the Second Edition of my work under ROYAL PATRONAGE, BY BEING PERMITTED TO DEDICATE IT TO YOUR MAJESTY.

The satisfaction of being able, after the lapse of more than fifty years of public life, to pay a filial tribute to the character and merits of the fathers and founders of my native country, is greatly enhanced by the patronage of a Sovereign whose praise is in all lands and the love of whom dwells in all Canadian and British hearts, and under whose benign reign the unity of the Empire has become a sentiment of intense affection, as well as of loyal obligation, among all classes, both in the Parent State and in the Colonies.

Such have been the life-long efforts, and such is the latest and fervent prayer of your Majesty's devoted Canadian subject,

THE AUTHOR.

TORONTO, *November, 1880.*

PREFACE.

As no Indian pen has ever traced the history of the aborigines of America, or recorded the deeds of their chieftains, their "prowess and their wrongs"—their enemies and spoilers being their historians; so the history of the Loyalists of America has never been written except by their enemies and spoilers, and those English historians who have not troubled themselves with examining original authorities, but have adopted the authorities, and in some instances imbibed the spirit, of American historians, who have never tired in eulogizing Americans and everything American, and deprecating everything English, and all who have loyally adhered to the unity of the British Empire.

I have thought that the other side of the story should be written; or, in other words, the true history of the relations, disputes, and contests between Great Britain and her American colonies and the United States of America.

The United Empire Loyalists were the losing party; their history has been written by their adversaries, and strangely misrepresented. In the vindication of their character, I have not opposed assertion against assertion; but, in correction of unjust and untrue assertions, I have offered the records and documents of the actors themselves, and in their own words.

To do this has rendered my history, to a large extent, *documentary*, instead of being a mere popular narrative. The many fictions of American writers will be found corrected and exposed in the following volumes, by authorities and facts which cannot be successfully denied. In thus availing myself so largely of the proclamations, messages, addresses, letters, and records of the times when they occurred, I have only followed the example of some of the best historians and biographers.

No one can be more sensible than myself of the imperfect manner in which I have performed my task, which I commenced more than a quarter of a century since, but I have been prevented from completing it sooner by public duties—pursuing, as I have done from the beginning, an untrodden path of historical investigations. From the long delay, many supposed I would never complete the work, or that I had abandoned it. On its completion, therefore, I issued a circular, an extract from which I hereto subjoin, explaining the origin, design, and scope of the work :—

"I have pleasure in stating that I have at length completed the task which the newspaper press and public men of different parties urged upon me from 1855 to 1860. In submission to what seemed to be public opinion, I issued, in 1861, a circular addressed to the United Empire Loyalists and their descendants, of the British Provinces of America, stating the design and scope of my proposed work, and requesting them to transmit to me, at my expense, any letters or papers in their possession which would throw light upon the early history and settlement in these Provinces by our U. E. Loyalist forefathers. From all the British Provinces I received answers to my circular ; and I have given, with little abridgment, in one chapter of my history, these intensely interesting letters and papers—to which I have been enabled to add considerably from two large quarto manuscript volumes of papers relating to the U. E. Loyalists in the Dominion Parliamentary Library at Ottawa, with the use of which I have been favoured by the learned and obliging librarian, Mr. Todd

"In addition to all the works relating to the subject which I could collect in Europe and America, I spent, two years since, several months in the Library of the British Museum, employing the assistance of an amanuensis, in verifying quotations and making extracts from works not to be found elsewhere, in relation especially to unsettled questions involved in the earlier part of my history.

"I have entirely sympathized with the Colonists in their remonstrances, and even use of arms, in defence of British constitutional rights, from 1763 to 1776 ; but I have been compelled to view the proceedings of the Revolutionists and their treatment of the Loyalists in a very different light.

"After having compared the conduct of the two parties during the Revolution, the exile of the Loyalists from their homes after the close of the War, and their settlement in the British Provinces, I have given a brief account of the government of each Province, and then traced the alleged and real causes of the War of 1812-1815, together with the courage, sacrifice, and patriotism of Canadians, both English and French, in defending our country against eleven successive American invasions, when the population of the two Canadas was to that of the United States as one to twenty-seven, and the population of Upper Canada (the chief scene of the War) was as one to one hundred and six. Our defenders, aided by a few English regiments, were as handfuls, little Spartan bands, in comparison of the hosts of the invading armies ; and yet at the end of two years, as well as at the end of the third and last year of the War, not an invader's foot found a place on the soil of Canada.

"I undertook this work not self-moved and with no view to profit ; and if I receive no pecuniary return from this work, on which I have expended no small labour and means, I shall have the satisfaction of having done all in my power to erect an historical monument to the character and merits of the fathers and founders of my native country."

E. RYERSON.

"Toronto, Sept. 24th, 1879."

CONTENTS.

CHAPTER I.

CHAPTER III.

PART FIRST.

PART SECOND.

PART THIRD.

CHAPTER V.

CHAPTER VII.

CHAPTER VIII.

CHAPTER IX.

CHAPTER X.

APPENDIX "A" TO CHAPTER X.

APPENDIX "B" TO CHAPTER X.

CHAPTER XI.

CHAPTER XII.

CHAPTER XIII.

CHAPTER XIV.

b

CHAPTER XV.

CHAPTER XVI.

CHAPTER XVII.

CHAPTER XVIII.

CHAPTER XIX.

CHAPTER XX.

CHAPTER XXII.

(1775, Continued.)

CHAPTER XXIII.

(1775, Continued.)

CHAPTER XXIV.

(THE YEAR 1775 AND BEGINNING OF 1776.)

CHAPTER XXV.

CHAPTER XXVI.

THE

LOYALISTS OF AMERICA

AND

THEIR TIMES.

CHAPTER I.

INTRODUCTION.—TWO CLASSES OF EMIGRANTS—TWO GOVERNMENTS FOR
SEVENTY YEARS—THE "PILGRIM FATHERS"—THEIR PILGRIMAGES AND
SETTLEMENT.

IN proceeding to trace the development and characteristics of
Puritanism in an English colony, I beg to remark that I write,
not as an Englishman, but as a Canadian colonist by birth and
life-long residence, and as an early and constant advocate of
those equal rights, civil and religious, and that system of government in the enjoyment of which Canada is conspicuous.

In tracing the origin and development of those views and
feelings which culminated in the American Revolution, in the
separation of thirteen colonies from Great Britain, it is necessary
to notice the early settlement and progress of those New England
colonies in which the seeds of that revolution were first sown
and grew to maturity.

The colonies of New England resulted from two distinct
emigrations of English Puritans; two classes of Puritans; two
distinct governments for more than sixty years. The one class
of these emigrants were called "Pilgrim Fathers," having first
fled from England to Holland, and thence emigrated to New
England in 1620, in the *Mayflower*, and called their place of
settlement "New Plymouth," where they elected seven Governors

1

in succession, and existed under a self-constituted government for seventy years. The other class were called "Puritan Fathers;" the first instalment of their emigration took place in 1629, under Endicot; they were known as the Massachusetts Bay Company, and their final capital was Boston, which afterwards became the, capital of the Province and of the State.

The characteristics of the separate and independent government of these two classes of Puritans were widely different. The one was tolerant and non-persecuting, and loyal to the King during the whole period of its seventy years' existence; the other was an intolerant persecutor of all religionists who did not adopt its worship, and disloyal from the beginning to the Government from which it held its Charter.

It is essential to my purpose to compare and contrast the proceedings of these two governments in relation to religious liberty and loyalty. I will first give a short account of the origin and government of the "*Pilgrim* Fathers" of New Plymouth, and then the government of the "*Puritan* Fathers" of Massachusetts Bay.*

In the later years of Queen Elizabeth, a "fiery young clergyman," named Robert Brown, declared against the lawfulness of both Episcopal and Presbyterian Church government, or of fellowship with either Episcopalians or Presbyterians, and in favour of the absolute independence of each congregation, and the ordination as well as selection of the minister by it. This was the origin of the Independents in England. The zeal of Brown, like that of most violent zealots, soon cooled, and he returned and obtained a living again in the Church of England, which he possessed until his death ; but his principles of separation and independence survived. The first congregation was formed about the year 1602, near the confines of York, Nottingham, and Leicester, and chose for its pastor John Robinson. They gathered for worship secretly, and were compelled to change their places of meeting in order to elude the pursuit of spies and soldiers. After enduring many cruel sufferings,

* From the nature of the facts and questions discussed, the following history is largely *documentary* rather than popular ; and the work being an *historical argument* rather than a popular narrative, will account for repetitions in some chapters, that the vital facts of the whole argument may be kept as constantly as possible before the mind of the reader.

Robinson, with the greater part of his congregation, determined to escape persecution by becoming *pilgrims* in a foreign land. The doctrines of Arminius, and the advocacy and sufferings of his followers in the cause of religious liberty, together with the spirit of commerce, had rendered the Government of Holland the most tolerant in Europe; and thither Robinson and his friends fled from their persecuting pursuers in 1608, and finally settled at Leyden. Being Independents, they did not form a connection with any of the Protestant Churches of the country. Burke remarks that "In Holland, though a country of the greatest religious freedom in the world, they did not find themselves better satisfied than they had been in England. There they were tolerated, indeed, but watched; their zeal began to have dangerous languors for want of opposition; and being without power or consequence, they grew tired of the indolent security of their sanctuary; they chose to remove to a place where they should see no superior, and therefore they sent an agent to England, who agreed with the Council of Plymouth for a tract of land in America, within their jurisdiction, to settle in, and obtained from the King (James) permission to do so."*

During their twelve years' *pilgrimage* in Holland they were good citizens; not an accusation was brought against any one of them in the courts; they were honourable and industrious, and took to new trades for subsistence. Brewster, a man of property, and a gentleman in England, learned to be a printer at the age of forty-five. Bradford, who had been a farmer in England, became a silk-dyer. Robinson became noted as a preacher and controversialist against Arminianism.

Bradford, the historian of their colony and its Governor for eleven years, gives the chief reasons for their dispute in Holland and of their desire to remove to America.†

As to what particular place these Pilgrims should select for settlement in America, some were for Guiana, some for Virginia; but they at length obtained a patent from the second or Northern Virginia Company for a settlement on the northern

* Burke's (the celebrated Edmund) Account of European Settlements in America. Second Edition, London, 1758, Vol. II., p. 143.

† Bradford's History of Plymouth Plantation, pp. 22—24. Massachusetts Historical Collection, 4th Series, Vol. III.

part of their territory, which extended to the fortieth degree of North latitude—Hutchinson Bay. "The Dutch laboured to persuade them to go to the Hudson river, and settle under the West India Company; but they had not lost their affection for the English, and chose to be under their government and protection."* Bancroft, after quoting the statement that "upon their talking of removing, sundry of the Dutch would have them go under them, and made them large offers, remarks: "But the Pilgrims were attached to their nationality as Englishmen, and to the language of their times. A secret but deeply-seated love of their country led them to the generous purpose of recovering the protection of England by enlarging her dominions. They were restless with the desire to live once more under the government of their native land."† It appears from Bradford's History, as well as from his Letter Book, and other narratives, that there were serious disputes and recriminations among the Pilgrim exiles and their friends in England, before matters could be arranged for their departure. But only "the minor part [of Robinson s congregation], with Mr. Brewster, their elder, resolved to enter upon this great work." They embarked at Delft Haven, a seaport town on the River Maaser, eight miles from Delft, fourteen miles from Leyden, and thirty-six miles from Amsterdam. The last port from which they sailed in England was Southampton; and after a tempestuous passage of 65 days, in the *Mayflower*, of 181 tons, with 101 passengers, they spied land, which proved to be Cape Cod—about 150 miles north of their intended place of destination. The pilot of the vessel had been there before and recognised the land as Cape Cod; "the which," says Bradford, "being made and certainly known to be it, they were not a little joyful."‡ But though the Pilgrims

---

* History of Massachusetts, Vol. I., pp. 11, 12.

† History of the United States, Vol. I., p. 304.

‡ Many American writers and orators represent the Pilgrims as first finding themselves on an unknown as well as inhospitable coast, amidst shoals and breakers, in danger of shipwreck and death. But this is all fancy; there is no foundation for it in the statement of Governor Bradford, who was one of the passengers, and who says that they were "not a little joyful" when they found certainly that the land was Cape Cod; and afterwards, speaking of their coasting in the neighbourhood, Bradford says, "They hasted to a place that their pilot (one Willm. Coppin, *who had been there before*) did assure them was a good harbour, which he had been in." (History of Ply-

were "not a little joyful" at safely reaching the American coast, and at a place so well known as Cape Cod; yet as that was not their intended place of settlement, they, without landing, put again to sea for Hudson river (New York), but were driven back by stress of weather, and, on account of the lateness of the season, determined not to venture out to sea again, but to seek a place of settlement within the harbour.

As the Pilgrims landed north of the limits of the Company from which they received their patent, and under which they expected to become a "body politic," it became to them "void and useless." This being known, some of the emigrants on board the *Mayflower* began to make "mutinous speeches," saying that "when they came ashore they would use their own liberty, for none had power to command them." Under these circumstances it was thought necessary to "begin with a combination, which might be as firm as any patent, and in some respects more so." Accordingly, an agreement was drawn up and signed in the cabin of the *Mayflower* by forty-one male passengers, who with their families constituted the whole colony of one hundred and one.* Having thus provided against disorder and

mouth Plantation, p. 86.) They did not even go ashore on their first entrance into Cape Cod harbour; but, as Bradford says, "after some deliberation among themselves and with the master of the ship, they *tacked about* and resolved to stand for the *southward, to find some place about Hudson river for their habitation.*" (*Ib.*, p. 117.) "After sailing southward half a day, they found themselves suddenly among shoals and breakers" (a ledge of rocks and shoals which are a terror to navigators to this day); and the wind shifting against them, they scud back to Cape Cod, and, as Bradford says, "thought themselves happy to get out of those dangers before night overtook them, and the next day they got into the Cape harbour, where they rode in safety. Being thus arrived in a good harbour, and brought safe to land, they fell upon their knees and blessed the God of heaven," etc.

The selection, before leaving England, of the neighbourhood of the Hudson river as their location, showed a worldly sagacity not to be exceeded by any emigrants even of the present century. Bancroft designates it "the best position on the whole coast." (History of the United States, Vol. I., p. 209.)

* The agreement was as follows:—"In the name of God, Amen. We whose names are underwritten, the loyal subjects of our dread Sovereign Lord, King James, by the grace of God, of Great Britain, France and Ireland, King, Defender of the Faith, &c., having undertaken, for the glory of God and advancement of the Christian faith, and honour of our King and country, a voyage to plant the first colony in the northern parts of [then called] Virginia, do by these presents, solemnly and mutually, in the presence of

faction, the Pilgrims proceeded to land, when, as Bradford says, they "fell upon their knees and blessed the God of heaven who had brought them over the vast and furious ocean, and delivered them from all the perils and miseries thereof, again to set their

God and of one another, covenant and combine ourselves together into a civil body politic, for our better ordering and preservation, and furthermore of the ends aforesaid ; and by virtue hereof to enact, constitute, and frame such just laws, ordinances, acts, constitutions, and offices, from time to time, as shall be thought most mete and convenient for the general good of the colony, unto which we promise all due submission and obedience. In witness whereof we have hereunder subscribed our names at Cape Cod, the 11th of November, in the 18th year of the reign of our Sovereign Lord King James, of England, France, and Ireland the eighteenth, and of Scotland the fifty-fourth. Anno Dom. 1620." Mr. John Carver was chosen Governor for one year.

This simple and excellent instrument of union and government, suggested by apprehensions of disorder and anarchy, in the absence of a patent for common protection, has been magnified by some American writers into an almost supernatural display of wisdom and foresight, and even the resurrection of the rights of humanity. Bancroft says, " This was the birth of popular constitutional liberty. The middle ages had been familiar with charters and constitutions ; but they had been merely compacts for immunities, partial enfranchisements, patents of nobility, concessions of municipal privileges, or the limitations of sovereign in favour of feudal institutions. In the cabin of the *Mayflower* humanity recorded its rights, and instituted a government on the basis of 'equal laws' for the 'general good.'" (History of the United States, Vol. I., p. 310.)

Now, any reader of the agreement will see that it says not a word about "popular constitutional liberty," much less of the "rights of humanity." It was no Declaration of Independence. Its signers call themselves "loyal subjects of the King of England," and state one object of their emigration to be the "honour of our King and country." The Pilgrim Fathers did, in the course of time, establish a simple system of popular government ; but from the written compact signed in the cabin of the *Mayflower* any form of government might be developed. The good sense of the following remarks by Dr. Young, in his *Chronicles of the Pilgrims of Plymouth*, contrast favourably with the fanciful hyperboles of Bancroft : " It seems to me that a great deal more has been discovered in this document than the signers contemplated. It is evident that when they left Holland they expected to become a body politic, using among themselves civil government, and to choose their own rulers from among themselves. Their purpose in drawing up and signing this compact was simply, as they state, to restrain certain of their number who had manifested an unruly and factious disposition. This was the whole philosophy of the instrument, whatever may have since been discovered and deduced from it." (p. 120.)

feet on the firm and stable earth, their proper element."* Of the manner of their settlement, their exposures, sufferings, labours, successes, I leave the many ordinary histories to narrate, though they nearly all revel in the marvellous.†

I will therefore proceed to give a brief account of the Plymouth government in relation to religious liberty within its limits and loyalty to the Mother Country.

---

* Bradford's History of the Plymouth Plantation, p. 78. "The 31st of December (1620) being Sabbath, they attended Divine service for the first time on shore, and named the place *Plymouth*, partly because this harbour was so called in Capt. John Smith's map, published three or four years before, and partly in remembrance of very kind treatment which they had received from the inhabitants of the last port of their native country from which they sailed." (Moore's Lives of the Governors of Plymouth, pp. 37, 38.)

The original Indian name of the place was *Accomack;* but at the time the Pilgrims settled there, an Indian informed them it was called *Patuxet,* Capt. John Smith's Description of New England was published in 1616. He says, "I took the description as well by map as writing, and called it New England." He dedicated his work to Prince Charles (afterwards King Charles I.), begging him to change the "barbarous names." In the list of names changed by Prince Charles, *Accomack* [or Patuxet] was altered to *Plymouth.* Mr. Dermer, employed by Sir F. Gorges and others for purposes of discovery and trade, visited this place about four months before the arrival of the Pilgrims, and significantly said, "I would that Plymouth [in England] had the like commodities. I would that the first plantation might here be seated if there come to the number of fifty persons or upwards."

† See following Note :—

Note on the Inflated American Accounts of the Voyage and Settlement of the Pilgrim Fathers.—Everything relating to the character, voyage, and settlement of the Pilgrims in New England has been invested with the marvellous, if not supernatural, by most American writers. One of them says, " God not only sifted the three kingdoms to get the seed of this enterprise, but sifted that seed over again. Every person whom He would not have go at that time, to plant the first colony of New England, He sent back even from mid-ocean in the *Speedwell.* (Rev. Dr. Cheever's Journal of the Pilgrims.)

The simple fact was, that the *Mayflower* could not carry any more passengers than she brought, and therefore most of the passengers of the *Speedwell,* which was a vessel of 50 tons and proved to be unseaworthy, were compelled to remain until the following year, and came over in the *Fortune;* and among these Robert Cushman, with his family, one of the most distinguished and honoured of the Pilgrim Fathers. And there was doubtless as good "seed" in "the three kingdoms" after this "sifting" of them for the New England enterprise as there was before.

In one of his speeches, the late eloquent Governor Everett, of Massachusetts, describes their voyage as the "long, cold, dreary autumnal passage, in that one solitary, adventurous vessel, the *Mayflower* of forlorn hope, freighted with prospects of a future state, and bound across the unknown sea, pursuing, with a thousand misgivings, the uncertain, the tedious voyage, suns rise and set, and winter surprises them on the deep, but brings them not the sight of the wished-for shore. The awful voice of the storm howls through the rigging. The labouring masts seem straining from their base ; the dismal sound of the pumps is heard ; the ship leaps, as it were, madly from billow to billow ; the ocean breaks, and settles with engulfing floods over the floating deck, and beats with deadening, shivering weight against the staggering vessel."

It is difficult to imagine how "winter" could surprise passengers crossing the ocean between the 6th of September and the 9th of November—a season of the year much *chosen* even nowadays for crossing the Atlantic. It is equally difficult to conceive how that could have been an "unknown sea" which had been crossed and the New England coasts explored by Gosnold, Smith, Dermer and others (all of whom had published accounts of their voyage), besides more than a dozen fishing vessels which had crossed this very year to obtain fish and furs in the neighbourhood and north of Cape Cod. Doubtless often the "suns rose and set" upon these vessels without their seeing the "wished-for shore ;" and probably more than once "the awful voice of the storm howled through their rigging," and "the dismal sound of their pumps was heard," and they "madly leaped from billow to billow," and "staggered under the deadening, shivering weight of the broken ocean," and with its "engulfing floods" over their "floating decks." The *Mayflower* was a vessel of 180 tons burden—more than twice as large as any of the vessels in which the early English, French, and Spanish discoverers of America made their voyages—much larger than most of the vessels employed in carrying emigrants to Virginia during the previous ten years—more than three times as large as the ship *Fortune*, of 53 tons, which crossed the ocean the following year, and arrived at Plymouth also the 9th of November, bringing Mr. Cushman and the rest of the passengers left by the *Speedwell* the year before. Gosnold had crossed the ocean and explored the eastern coasts of America in 1602 in a "small bark ;" Martin Pring had done the same in 1603 in the bark *Discovery*, of 26 tons ; Frobisher, in northern and dangerous coasts, in a vessel of 25 tons burden ; and two of the vessels of Columbus were from 15 to 30 tons burden, and without decks on which to "float" the "engulfing floods" under which the *Mayflower* "staggered" so marvellously. All these vessels long preceded the *Mayflower* across the "unknown ocean ;" but never inspired the lofty eloquence which Mr. Everett and a host of inferior rhapsodists have bestowed upon the *Mayflower* and her voyage. Bancroft fills several pages of his elaborate history to the same effect, and in similar style with the passages above quoted. I will give a single sentence, as follows :—"The Pilgrims having selected for their settlement the country near the Hudson, the best position on the whole coast, were conducted to the most barren and inhospitable part of Massachusetts." (History of the United States, Vol. I., p. 309.)

There was certainly little self-abnegation, but much sound and worldly wisdom, in the Pilgrims selecting "the best position on the whole coast" of

America for their settlement ; and there is as little truth in the statement, though a good antithesis—the delight of Mr. Bancroft—that the Pilgrims were conducted to "the most barren and inhospitable part of Massachusetts" for "actual settlement," as appears from the descriptions given of it by Governors Winslow and Bradford and other Pilgrim Fathers, written after the first and during the subsequent years of their settlement. I will give but two illustrations. Mr. Winslow was one of the passengers in the *Mayflower*, and was, by annual election, several years Governor of the Plymouth colony. It has been stated above that the ship *Fortune*, of 53 tons burden, brought in the autumn of 1621 the Pilgrim passengers who had been left in England the year before by the sea-unworthiness of the *Speedwell*. The *Fortune* anchored in Plymouth Bay the 9th of November—just a year from the day on which the *Mayflower* spied the land of Cape Cod. Mr. Winslow prepared and sent back by the *Fortune* an elaborate "Relation" of the state and prospects of the colony, for the information of the merchant adventurers and others in England. He describes the climate, soil, and all the resources of the colony's means of support, together with the process and result of the first year's labour. I will simply give his account of the manner in which they celebrated what in England would be called a "Harvest Home." He says : "Our harvest being got in, our Governor sent four men on fowling, that so we might, after a more special manner, rejoice together after we had gathered the fruit of our labours. They four in a day killed as much fowl as, with little help besides, served the company almost a week ; at which time, amongst other recreations, we exercised our arms. Many of the Indians came amongst us, and amongst the rest their greatest king, Massasoit, with some ninety men, whom for three days we entertained and feasted ; and they went out and killed fine deer, which they brought to the Plantation, and bestowed them on our Governor, and upon the Captain and others ; and although it be not always so plentiful with us, we are so far from want that we *often wish you partakers of our plenty.*"

Governor Bradford, writing in 1646, twenty-five years after this feast, and referring to it, says : " Nor has there been any general want of food amongst us since to this day." (Morton's Memorials, p. 100.)

Such was the result of the first year's experience in this chosen place of settlement by the first New England colony, as stated by the most distinguished of its founders. During the winter of this year more than half the pioneer settlers had died of a prevalent sickness,—not owing to the climate, but their sea voyage, their want of experience, and to temporary circumstances, for not a death occurred amongst them during the three succeeding years. As great as was the mortality amongst the noble colonists of New England, it was far less, comparatively, than that which fell upon the first colonists of Virginia, who were, also, more than once almost annihilated by the murderous incursions of the Indians, but from whom the Pilgrim Fathers did not suffer the loss of a life.

In his "true and brief Relation," Mr. Winslow says : " For the temper of the air here, it agreeth well with that in England ; and if there be any difference at all, this is somewhat hotter in summer. Some think it colder in winter, but I cannot out of experience say so. The air is very clear and foggy, not as hath been reported. I never in my life remember a more seasonable year than we have here enjoyed."

Mr. Winslow's doubt as to whether the cold of his first winter in New England exceeded that of the ordinary winters which he had passed in England, refutes the fictitious representations of many writers, who to magnify the virtues and merits of the Plymouth colonists, describe them as braving, with a martyr's courage, the appalling cold of an almost Arctic winter—a winter which enabled the new settlers to commence their gardens the 16th of March, and they add in their Journal : " Monday and Tuesday, March 19th and 20th, proved fair days. We digged our grounds and *sowed our garden seeds.*"

Not cne of the American United Empire Loyalists—the Pilgrim Fathers of Canada, Nova Scotia, and New Brunswick—could tell of a winter in the countries of their refuge, so mild, and a spring so early and genial, as that which favoured the Pilgrim Fathers of New England during their first year of settlement ; nor had any settlement of the Canadian Pilgrim Fathers been able to command the means of celebrating the *first* " Harvest Home" by a week's festivity and amusements, and entertaining, in addition, ninety Indians for three days.

CHAPTER II.

THE GOVERNMENT OF THE PILGRIM* FATHERS DURING SEVENTY YEARS, FROM 1620 TO 1692, AS DISTINCT FROM THAT OF THE PURITAN FATHERS.

TWO GOVERNMENTS.—*Difference between the Government of the Pilgrims and that of the Puritans.*—Most historians, both English and American, have scarcely or not at all noticed the fact that within the present State of Massachusetts two separate governments of Puritan emigrants were established and existed for seventy years—two governments as distinct as those of Upper and Lower Canada from 1791 to 1840—as distinct as those of any two States of the American Republic. It is quite natural that American historians should say nothing of the Pilgrim government, beyond the voyage and landing of its founders, as it was a standing condemnation of the Puritan government, on which they bestow all their eulogies. The two governments were separated by the Bay of Massachusetts, about forty miles distant from each other by water, but still more widely different from each other in spirit and character. The government of the Pilgrims was marked from the beginning by a full and hearty recognition of franchise rights to all settlers of the Christian faith; the government of the Puritans denied those rights to all but Congregational Church members for sixty years, and until they were compelled to do otherwise by Royal Charter in 1692. The government of the Pilgrims was just and kind to the Indians, and early made a treaty with the neighbouring tribes, which remained inviolate on both sides during half a century, from 1621 to 1675; the government of the

---

* "The term PILGRIMS belongs exclusively to the Plymouth colonists." (Young's Chronicles of the Pilgrims, p. 88, note.)

Puritans maddened the Indians by the invasion of their rights, and destroyed them by multitudes, almost to entire extermination. The government of the Pilgrims respected the principles of religious liberty (which they had learned and imbibed in Holland), did not persecute those who differed from it in religious opinions,* and gave protection to many who fled from the persecutions of neighbouring Puritans' government, which was more intolerant and persecuting to those who differed from it in religious opinions than that of James, and Charles, and Laud had ever been to them. The government of the Pilgrims was frank and loyal to the Sovereign and people of England; the government of the Puritans was deceptive and disloyal to the Throne and Mother Country from the first, and sedulously sowed and cultivated the seeds of disaffection and hostility to the Royal government, until they grew and ripened into the harvest of the American revolution.

These statements will be confirmed and illustrated by the facts of the present and following chapters.

The compact into which the Pilgrims entered before landing from the *Mayflower*, was the substitute for the body politic which would have been organized by charter had they settled, as first intended, within the limits of the Northern Virginia Company. The compact specified no constitution of government beyond that of authority on the one hand, and submission on the other; but under it the Governors were elected annually, and the local laws were enacted during eighteen years *by the general meetings of the settlers*, after which a body of elected representatives was constituted.

The first *official record* of the election of any Governor was in 1633, thirteen years after their settlement at Plymouth; but, according to the early history of the Pilgrims, the Governors were elected annually from 1620. The Governors of the colony were as follows:—

* The only exception was by Prince, when elected Governor in 1657. He had imbibed the spirit of the Boston Puritans against the Quakers, and sought to infuse his spirit into the minds of his assistants (or executive councillors) and the deputies; but he was stoutly opposed by Josias Winslow and others. The persecution was short and never unto death, as among the Boston Puritans. It was the only stain of persecution upon the rule of the Pilgrims during the seventy years of their separate government, and was nobly atoned for and effaced by Josias Winslow, when elected Governor in the place of Prince.

1. John Carver, in 1620, who died a few months afterwards;
2. William Bradford, 1621 to 1632, 1635, 1637, 1639 to 1643, 1645 to 1656;
3. Edward Winslow, 1633, 1636, 1644;
4. Thomas Prince, 1634, 1638, 1657 to 1672;
5. Josiah Winslow, 1673 to 1680;
6. Thomas Hinckley, 1681 to 1692;*

when the colony of Plymouth† (which had never increased in population beyond 13,000) was incorporated with that of Massachusetts Bay, under the name of the Province of Massachusetts, by Royal Charter under William and Mary, and by which religious liberty and the elective franchise were secured to all freeholders of forty shillings per annum, instead of being confined to members of the Congregational Churches, as had been the case down to that period under the Puritans of Massachusetts Bay—so that equal civil and religious liberty among all classes was established in Massachusetts, not by the Puritans, but by Royal Charter, against the practice of the Puritans from 1631 to 1692.

The government of the Pilgrims was of the most simple kind. At first the Governor, with one assistant, was elected annually by general suffrage; but in 1624, at the request of Governor Bradford, a Council of five assistants (increased to seven in 1633) was annually elected. In this Court, or Executive Council, the Governor had a double vote. In the third year, 1623, trial by jury was established. During eighteen years, from 1620 to 1638, the legislative body, called the General Court, or Court of Associates, was composed of the whole body of freemen. It was not until 1639 that they established a House of Representatives. The qualifications of a *freeman* were, that he " should be twenty-one years of age, of sober, peaceable conversation, orthodox in religion [which included belief in God and the Holy Scriptures, but did not include any form of Church government], and possess rateable estate to the value of twenty pounds."

---

* Massachusetts Historical Collections, 3rd Series, Vol. II., p. 226.

† " The colony of Plymouth included the present counties of Plymouth, Barnstaple, and Bristol, and a part of Rhode Island. All the Providence Plantations were at one time claimed by Plymouth. The boundaries between Plymouth and Massachusetts were settled in 1640 by commissioners of the united colonies." (*Ib.*, p. 267.)

In 1636—sixteen years after their landing at New Plymouth —the laws which they had enacted were first collected, prefaced by a declaration of their right to enact them, in the absence of a Royal Charter. Their laws were at various times revised and added to, and finally printed in 1671, under the title of "Their Great Fundamentals." They recognized the general laws of England, and adopted local statutes or regulations according to what they considered their needs.* Of their sense of duty as British subjects, and of the uniform mutual relations of friendship existing between them and their Sovereigns, their records and history furnish abundant proofs. The oath required of their Governors commenced in the following words: 'You shall swear to be truly loyal to our Sovereign Lord King Charles, his successors and heirs." "At the Court held," (says the record,) "at Plymouth, the 11th of June, 1664, the following was added, and the Governor took the oath thereunto: 'You shall also attend to what is required by His Majesty's Privy Council of the Governors of the respective colonies in reference unto an Act of Parliament for the encouraging and increasing of shipping and navigation, bearing date from the 1st of December, 1660.'"

The oath of a freeman commenced with the same words, as did the oath of the "Assistants" or Executive Councillors, the oath of constables and other officers in the colony. It was likewise ordered, "That an oath of allegiance to the King and fidelity to the Government and to the several colonies [settlements] therein, be taken of every person that shall live within or under the same." This was as follows: "You shall be truly loyal to our Sovereign Lord the King and his heirs and suc-

---

* The laws they intended to be governed by were the laws of England, the which they were willing to be subject unto, though in a foreign land, and have since that time continued of that mind for the general, adding only some particular municipal laws of their own, suitable to their constitution, in such cases where the common laws and statutes of England could not well reach, or afford them help in emergent difficulties of place." (Hubbard's "General History of New England, from the Discovery to 1680." Massachusetts Historical Collection, 2nd Series, Vol. I., p. 62.)

Palfrey says: "All that is extant of what can properly be called the legislation of the first twelve years of the colony of Plymouth, suffices to cover in print only two pages of an octavo volume." (History of New England, Vol. I., pp. 340, 341.)

cessors : and whereas you make choice at present to reside within
the government of New Plymouth, you shall not do or cause to be
done any act or acts, directly or indirectly, by land or water, that
shall or may tend to the destruction or overthrow of the whole
or any of the several colonies [settlements] within the said government that are or shall be orderly erected or established ; but
shall, contrariwise, hinder, oppose and discover such intents and
purposes as tend thereunto to the Governor for the time being,
or some one of the assistants, with all convenient speed. You
shall also submit unto and obey such good and wholesome laws,
ordinances and officers as are or shall be established within the
several limits thereof. So help you God, who is the God of
truth and punisher of falsehood."

The Government of Plymouth prefaced the revised collection
of their laws and ordinances as follows :

"A form to be placed before the records of the several
inheritances granted to all and every of the King's subjects
inhabiting with the Government of New Plymouth :

"Whereas John Carver, William Bradford, Edward Winslow,
William Brewster, Isaack Alliston and divers others of the subjects of our late Sovereign Lord James, by the Grace of God,
King of England, Scotland, France and Ireland, Defender of the
Faith, &c., did in the eighteenth year of his reigne of England,
France and Ireland, and of Scotland the fifty-four, which was
the year of our Lord God 1620, undertake a voyage into that
part of America called Virginia or New England, thereunto
adjoining, there to erect a plantation and colony of English,
intending the glory of God and the enlargement of his Majesty's
dominions, and the special good of the English nation."

Thus the laws and ordinances of the Plymouth Government,
and the oaths of office from the Governor to the constable, freeman and transient resident, recognize their duty as British subjects, and breathe a spirit of pure loyalty to their Sovereign.
The only reference I find in their records to the Commonwealth
of England is the following declaration, made in 1658, the last
year of Cromwell's government. It is the preface to the collection of the General Laws, revised and published Sept. 29, 1658,
and is as follows :

"We, the associates of New Plymouth, coming hither as freeborn subjects of the State of England, endowed with all the

privileges belonging to such, being assembled, do ordain, constitute and enact that no act, imposition, laws or ordinances be
made or imposed on us at present or to come, but such as shall
be made and imposed by consent of the body of the associates
or their representatives legally assembled, which is according to
the free libertie of the State of England."

At the first annual meeting of the Plymouth House of
Representatives after the restoration of Charles the Second, the
following declaration and order was made:

"Whereas we are certainly informed that it hath pleased God
to establish our Sovereign Lord King Charles the Second in the
enjoyment of his undoubted rights to the Crowns of England,
Scotland, France and Ireland, and is so declared and owned by
his good subjects of these kingdoms; We therefore, his Majesty's
loyal subjects, the inhabitants of the jurisdiction of New Plymouth, do hereby declare our free and ready concurrence with
such other of his Majesty's subjects, and to his said Majesty, his
heirs and successors, we do most humbly and faithfully submit
and oblige ourselves for ever.   God save the King.

"June the fifth, Anno Dom. 1661.

"The fifth day of June, 1661, Charles the Second, King of
England, Scotland, France and Ireland, &c., was solemnly pro-
claimed at Plymouth, in New England, in America." (This the
Puritan Government of Massachusetts Bay refused to do.)

On the accession of James the Second we find the following
entry in the Plymouth records: "The twenty fourth of April,
1685, James the Second, King of England, Scotland, France and
Ireland, &c., was solemnly proclaimed at Plymouth according to
the form required by his Majesty's most honourable Privy
Council."

After the Revolution of 1688 in England, there is the following record of the proceedings of the Legislature of the Plymouth
colony—proceedings in which testimony is borne by the colonists
of the uniformly kind treatment they had received from the
Government of England, except during a short interval under
the three years' reign of James the Second:

"At their Majesties' General Court of Election, held at Plymouth on the first Tuesday in June, 1689.

"Whereas, through the great changes Divine Providence hath
ordered out, both in England and in this country, we the loyal

subjects of the Crown of England are left in an unsettled estate, destitute of government and exposed to the ill consequences thereof : and *having heretofore enjoyed a quiet settlement of government in this their Majesties' colony of New Plymouth for more than threescore and six years, without any interruptions ; having also been by the late kings of England from time to time, by their royal letters, graciously owned and acknowledged therein:* whereby, notwithstanding our late unjust interruption and suspension therefrom by the illegal arbitrary power of Sir Edmond Andros, now ceased, the General Court held there in the name of their present Majesties William and Mary, King and Queen of England, &c., together with the encouragement given by their said Majesties' gracious declarations and in humble confidence of their said Majesties' good liking: do therefore hereby resume and declare their reassuming of their said former way of government, according to such wholesome constitutions, rules and orders as were here in force in June, 1686, our title thereto being warranted by prescription and otherwise as aforesaid ; and expect a ready submission thereunto by all their Majesties' good subjects of this colony, until their Majesties or this Court shall otherwise order ; and that all our Courts be hereafter held and all warrants directed and officers sworn in the name of their Majesties William and Mary, King and Queen of England, &c.

" The General Court request the Honourable Governor, Thomas Hinckley, Esq., in behalf of said Court and Colony of New Plymouth, to make their address to their Majesties the King and Queen of England, &c., for the re-establishment of their former enjoyed liberties and privileges, both sacred and civil."

We have thus the testimony of the Plymouth colony itself that there was no attempt on the part of either Charles the First or Second to interfere with the fullest exercise of their own chosen form of worship, or with anything which they themselves regarded as their civil rights. If another course of proceedings had to be adopted in regard to the Puritan Government of Massachusetts Bay, it was occasioned by their own conduct, as will appear hereafter. Complaints were made by colonists to England of the persecuting and unjust conduct of the Puritan Government, and inquiries were ordered in 1646, 1664, 1678, and afterwards. The nature and result of these inquiries will be

2

noticed hereafter. At present I will notice the first Commission
sent out by Charles the Second, in 1664, and which was made
general to the several colonies, to avoid invidious distinction,
though caused by complaints against the conduct of the Puritan
Government of Massachusetts Bay. The Commissioners proposed
four questions to the Governments of the several colonies of New
England. I will give the questions, or rather propositions, and
the answers to them on the part of the Pilgrim Government of
Plymouth, as contained in its printed records :—

"*The Propositions made by His Majesty's Commissioners to the
General Court of (New Plymouth), held at Plymouth, for the
jurisdiction of New Plymouth, the 22nd of February, Anno
Dom. 1665.*

"1. That all householders inhabiting in the colony take the
oath of allegiance, and the administration of justice be in his
Majesty's name.

"2. That all men of competent estates and civil conversation,
though of different judgments, may be admitted to be freemen,
and have liberty to choose and to be chosen officers, both civil
and military.

"3. That all men and women of orthodox opinions, competent
knowledge and civil lives (not scandalous), may be admitted to
the sacrament of the Lord's Supper, and their children to
baptism if they desire it; either by admitting them into the
congregation already gathered, or permitting them to gather
themselves into such congregations, where they may have the
benefit of the sacraments.

"4. That all laws and expressions in laws derogatory to his
Majesty, if any such have been made in these late troublesome
times, may be repealed, altered, and taken off from the file."

THE COURT'S ANSWER.

"1. To the first we consent, it *having been the practice of this
Court,* in the first place, *to insert in the oath of fidelity required
of every householder, to be truly loyal to our Sovereign Lord the
King, his heirs and successors. Also to administer all acts of
justice in his Majesty's name.*

"2. To the second we also consent, *it having been our constant
practice to admit men of competent estates and civil conversation, though of different judgments, yet being otherwise orthodox,*

to be freemen, and to have liberty to choose and be chosen officers, both civil and military.

" 3. To the third, we cannot but acknowledge it to be a high favour from God and from our Sovereign, that we may enjoy our consciences in point of God's worship, the main end of transplanting ourselves into these remote corners of the earth, and should most heartily rejoice that all our neighbours so qualified as in that proposition would adjoin themselves to our societies, according to the order of the Gospel, for enjoyment of the sacraments to themselves and theirs ; but if, through different persuasions respecting Church government, it cannot be obtained, we could not deny a liberty to any, according to the proposition, that are truly conscientious, although differing from us, especially where his Majesty commands it, they maintaining an able preaching ministry for the carrying on of public Sabbath worship, which we doubt not is his Majesty's intent, and withdrawing not from paying their due proportions of maintenance to such ministers as are orderly settled in the places where they live, until they have one of their own, and that in such places as are capable of maintaining the worship of God in two distinct congregations, we being greatly encouraged by his Majesty's gracious expressions in his letter to us, and your Honours' further assurance of his Royal purpose to continue our liberties, that where places, by reason of our paucity and poverty, are incapable of two, it is not intended, that such congregations as are already in being should be rooted out, but their liberties preserved, there being other places to accommodate men of different persuasions in societies by themselves, which, by our known experience, tends most to the preservation of peace and charity.

" 4. To the fourth, we consent that all laws and expressions in laws derogatory to his Majesty, if any sect shall be formed amongst us, which at present we are not conscious of, shall be repealed, altered, and taken off from the file.

" By order of the General Court
" For the jurisdiction of New Plymouth,
" Per me, NATHANIEL MORTON, *Secretary.*"

" The league between the four colonies was not with any intent, that ever we heard of, to cast off our dependence upon England, a thing which we utterly abhor, intreating your Honours to believe us, for we speak in the presence of God."

"NEW PLYMOUTH, May 4th, 1665.

"The Court doth order Mr. Constant Southworth, Treasurer, to present these to his Majesty's Commissioners, at Boston, with all convenient speed."

The above propositions and answers are inserted, with some variations, in Hutchinson's History of Massachusetts, Vol. I., p. 214. The remark respecting the union between the colonies is not on the colony records—it was inserted at the close of the copy delivered to the Commissioners, in conformity to a letter from the Commissioners, written to Governor Prince after they had left Plymouth. The conditions expressed in the answer to the third proposition appeared so reasonable to the Commissioners, that when they afterward met the General Assembly of Connecticut, in April, 1665, their third proposition is qualified, in substance, conformably to the Plymouth reply. (Morton's Memorial, Davis' Ed., p. 417.)

It is thus seen that there was not the least desire on the part of. King Charles the Second, any more than there had been on the part of Charles the First, to impose the Episcopal worship upon the colonists, or to interfere in the least with their full liberty of worship, according to their own preferences. All that was desired at any time was toleration and acknowledgment of the authority of the Crown, such as the Plymouth colony and that of Connecticut had practised from the beginning, to the great annoyance of the Puritans of Massachusetts.

Several letters and addresses passed between Charles the Second and the Pilgrim Government of Plymouth, and all of the most cordial character on both sides; but what is given above supersedes the necessity of further quotations.*

It was an object of special ambition with the Government of Plymouth to have a Royal Charter like those of Massachusetts Bay, Connecticut, and Rhode Island, instead of holding their land, acting under a Charter from the Plymouth Council (England)

---

* "Their residence in Holland had made them acquainted with the various forms of Christianity ; a wide experience had emancipated them from bigotry ; and they were never betrayed into the excesses of religious persecution, though they sometimes permitted a disproportion between punishment and crime." (Bancroft's History of the United States, Vol. I., p. 322.)

"The Plymouth Church is free from blood." (Elliott's History of New England, Vol. I., p. 133.)

and Charles the Second. In his last address to Mr. Josiah Winslow, their Governor promised it to them in most explicit terms; but there was a case of *quo warranto* pending in the Court of King's Bench against the Puritan Government for the violation of their Charter, which delayed the issuing of a Royal Charter to Plymouth. Charles died soon after;[*] the Charter of the Massachusetts Corporation was forfeited by the decision of the Court, and James the Second appointed a Royal Governor and a Royal Commissioner, which changed for the time being the whole face of things in New England.

It, however, deserves notice, that the Massachusetts Puritans, true to their instinct of encroaching upon the rights of others, whether of the King or of their neighbours, white or tawny, did all in their power to prevent the Pilgrims of Plymouth— the pioneers of settlement and civilization in New England— from obtaining a Royal Charter. This they did first in 1630, again in the early part of Charles the Second's reign, and yet again towards its end. Finally, after the cancelling of the Massachusetts Charter, and the English Revolution of 1688, the agents of the more powerful and populous Massachusetts colony succeeded in getting the colony of Plymouth absorbed into that of Massachusetts Bay by the second Royal Charter granted by William and Mary in 1692. "The junction of Plymouth with Massachusetts," says Moore, "destroyed all the political consequence of the former. The people of Plymouth shared but few favours which the new Government had to bestow, and it was seldom indeed that any resident of what was termed the old colony obtained any office of distinction in the Provisional Government, or acquired any influence in its councils."[†]

This seems a melancholy termination of the Government of the

---

[*] "Charles the Second, with a spirit that does honour to his reign, at that time meditated important plans for the reformation of New England." (Annals of the Colonies, pp. 88, 89.)

[†] Moore's Lives of the Governors of New Plymouth, p. 228.

The contest between the Pilgrims of Plymouth and the Puritans of Massachusetts, in regard to granting a separate charter to the former, was severe and bitter. The Plymouth Government, by its tolerance and loyalty, had been an "eyesore" to the other intolerant and disloyal Puritans of Massachusetts. Perhaps the Imperial Government of the day thought that the fusion of the two Governments and populations into one would render the new Government more liberal and loyal; but the result proved otherwise.

Pilgrims—a princely race of men, who voluntarily braved the sufferings of a double exile for the sake of what they believed to be the truth and the glory of God; whose courage never failed, nor their loyalty wavered amidst all their privations and hardships; who came to America to enjoy religious liberty and promote the honour of England, not to establish political independence, and granted that liberty to others which they earned and had suffered so much to enjoy themselves; who were honourable and faithful to their treaty engagements with the aborigines as they were in their communications with the Throne; who never betrayed a friend or fled from an enemy; who left imperishable footprints of their piety and industry, as well as of their love of liberty and law, though their self-originated and self-sustained polity perished at length, by royal forgetfulness and credulity, to the plausible representations and ambitious avarice of their ever aggressive Massachusetts Puritan neighbours.

While the last act of the Pilgrims before leaving the *May-flower*, in the harbour of Cape Cod, was to enter into a compact of local self-government for common protection and interests, and their first act on landing at New Plymouth was, on bended knees, to commend themselves and their settlement to the Divine protection and blessing, it is a touching fact that the last official act of the General Assembly of the colony was to appoint a day of solemn fasting and humiliation on the extinction of their separate government and their absorption into that of Massachusetts Bay.

It was among the sons and daughters of the Plymouth colony that almost the only loyalty in New England during the American Revolution of the following century was found. Most of the descendants of Edward Winslow, and of his more distinguished son, Josiah Winslow, were loyalists during that revolution.* In the councils of the mother country, the merits of the posterity of the Pilgrims have been acknowledged; as in her service some of them, by their talents and courage, have won their way to eminence. Among the proudest names in the British navy are the descendants of the original purchaser of Mattapoisett, in Swansey (William Brenton, afterwards Governor

* "Most of his descendants were loyalists during the American Revolution. One of them was the wife of John S. Copley, the celebrated painter, and father of the late Lord Lyndhurst." (Moore.)

of Rhode Island);* to the distinguished title of one of the English peerage is attached the name of one of the early settlers of Scituate, in the Plymouth colony (William Vassall, who settled there in 1635.)†

"In one respect," says Moore, "the people of the Old Colony present a remarkable exception to the rest of America. They are the purest English race in the world; there is scarcely an intermixture even with the Scotch or Irish, and none with the aboriginals. Almost all the present population are descended from the original English settlers. Many of them still own the lands which their early ancestors rescued from the wilderness; and although they have spread themselves in every direction through this wide continent, from the peninsula of Nova Scotia to the Gulf of Mexico, some one of the family has generally remained to cultivate the soil which was owned by his ancestors. The fishermen and the navigators of Maine, the children of Plymouth, still continue the industrious and bold pursuits of their forefathers. In that fine country, beginning at Utica, in the State of New York, and stretching to Lake Erie, this race may be found on every hill and in every valley, on the rivers and on the lakes. The emigrant from the sandbanks of Cape Cod revels in the profusion of the opulence of Ohio. In all the Southern and South-Western States, the natives of the "Old Colony," like the Arminians of Asia, may be found in every place where commerce and traffic offer any lure to enterprise; and in the heart of the peninsula of Michigan, like their ancestors they have commenced the cultivation of the wilderness—like them originally, with savage hearts and savage men, and like them patient in suffering, despising danger, and animated with hope."‡

* Jahleel Brenton, grandson of Governor Wm. Brenton, had twenty-two children. His fourth son, born Oct. 22, 1729, entered the British navy when a youth, distinguished himself and rose to the rank of Admiral. He died in 1802. His son Jahleel was bred to the sea, rose to be an Admiral, and was knighted in 1810." (Moore's Lives of the Governors of New Plymouth, p. 229.)

† In 1650 he removed to the West Indies, where he laid the foundation of several large estates, and where he died, in Barbadoes, in 1655. (Moore, p. 126.) "Thomas Richard, the third Lord Holland, married an heiress by the name of Vassall, and his son, Henry Richard Fox Vassall, is the present Lord Holland, Baron Holland in Lincolnshire, and Foxley in Wilts." (Playfair's British Family Antiquities, Vol. II., p. 182.)

‡ Moore's Lives of the Governors of New Plymouth, pp. 228—230.

CHAPTER III.

THE PURITANS OF THE MASSACHUSETTS BAY COMPANY AND THEIR GOVERNMENT, COMMENCING IN 1629.

PART I.

FIRST SETTLEMENT—ROYAL CHARTER GRANTED.

ENGLISH Puritanism, transferred from England to the head of Massachusetts Bay in 1629, presents the same characteristics which it developed in England. In Massachusetts it had no competitor; it developed its principles and spirit without restraint; it was absolute in power from 1629 to 1689, and during that sixty years it assumed independence of the Government to which it owed its corporate existence; it made it a penal crime for any emigrant to appeal to England against a local decision of Courts or of Government; it permitted no oath of allegiance to the King, nor the administration of the laws in his name; it allowed no elective franchise to any Episcopalian, Presbyterian, Baptist, Quaker, or Papist. Every non-member of the Congregational Churches was compelled to pay taxes and bear all other Puritan burdens, but was allowed no representation by franchise, much less by eligibility for any office.

It has been seen that the "*Pilgrim* Fathers" commenced their settlement at New Plymouth in 1620—nine years before the "*Puritan* Fathers" commenced their settlement on the opposite side of Massachusetts Bay, making Boston their ultimate seat of government. The Pilgrim Fathers and their descendants were professedly congregational separatists from the Church of England; they had fled by stealth, under severe sufferings, from persecution in England to Holland, where they had resided eleven years and upwards, and where they had learned the principles of religious toleration and liberty—the fruit of Dutch

Arminian advocacy and suffering. The Puritans of the Massachusetts Bay Company emigrated directly from England, on
leaving which they professed to be members of the Church of
England; their emigration commenced in 1628, the very year
that Charles the First, having quarrelled with and dissolved the
last of three Parliaments in less than four years, commenced his
eleven years' rule without a Parliament. During that eleven
years a constant current of emigration flowed from England to
Massachusetts Bay, to the extent of 13,000, including no less
than seventy clergymen of the Church of England, and many
men of rank, and wealth to the amount of some £300,000. All
these emigrants, or "adventurers," as they were called, left
England with a stinging sense of royal and episcopal despotism,
and with a corresponding hatred of royalty and episcopacy, but
with no conception of the principles of religious toleration or
liberty beyond themselves.

During the eight years' interval between the settlement of
the Pilgrims at New Plymouth to that of the Puritans at Salem
and Boston, trade had largely increased between England and
Massachusetts Bay,* and the climate, fisheries, furs, timber, and
other resources of northern New England became well known,
and objects of much interest in England.

King James had divided all that part of North America, 34°
and 45° of North latitude, into two grand divisions, bestowing
the southern part upon a London Company, and the northern
part upon a Company formed in Plymouth and Bristol. The
Northern Company resolved to strengthen their interests by
obtaining a fresh grant from the King. A new patent was
issued reorganizing the Company as the Council for the Affairs
of New England, the corporate power of which was to reside
at Plymouth, west of England, under the title of the "Grand
Council of Plymouth," with a grant of three hundred square
miles in New England. The Company formed projects on

---

* Two years after the Plymouth settlement, "Thirty-five ships sailed this
year (1622) from the west of England, and two from London, to fish on the
New England coasts, and made profitable voyages." (Holmes' Annals of
America, Vol. I., p. 179.) In a note on the same page it is said: "Where in
Newfoundland they shared six or seven pounds for a common man, in New
England they shared fourteen pounds; besides, six Dutch and French ships
made wonderful returns in furs."

too large a scale, and did not succeed; but sold that portion of its territory which constituted the first settlements of the Massachusetts Bay Company to some merchants in the west of England, who had successfully fished for cod and bartered for furs in the region of Massachusetts Bay, and who thought that a plantation might be formed there. Among the most active encouragers of this enterprise was the Rev. John White, a clergyman of Dorchester, a maritime town, which had been the source of much commercial adventure in America.* One special object of Mr. White was to provide an asylum for the ministers who had been deprived and silenced in England for non-conformity to the canons and ceremonies imposed by Laud and his associates. Through Mr. White the guarantees became acquainted with several persons of his religious sympathies in London, who first associated with them, and afterwards bought rights in their patent. Among these was Matthew Cradock, the largest stockholder in the Company, who was appointed its first president, with eighteen associates, including John Winthrop, Isaac Johnson, Sir Richard Saltunstall, and other persons of "like quality." The chief object of these gentlemen in promoting a settlement in New England was to provide a retreat where their co-religionists of the Church of England could enjoy liberty in matters of religious worship and discipline. But the proposed undertaking could not be prosecuted with success without large means; in order to secure subscriptions for which the commercial aspect of it had to be prominently presented.

The religious aspect of the enterprise was presented under the idea of connecting and civilizing the idolatrous and savage Indian tribes of New England. There was no hint, and I think no intention, of abolishing and proscribing the worship of the Church of England in New England; for Mr. White himself, the projector and animating spirit of the whole enterprise, was

---

* "The Council of New England, on the 19th of March (1627), sold to Sir Henry Rowsell, Sir John Young, and four other associates, [Thomas South-wood, John Humphrey, John Endicot, and Simeon Whitcombe,] in the vicinity of Dorchester, in England, a patent for all that part of New England lying between three miles to the northward of Merrimack River, and three miles to the southward of Charles River, and in length within the described breadth from the Atlantic Ocean to the South Sea." (Holmes' Annals, Vol. I., p. 193.)

a conformist clergyman.* It was professedly a religio-commercial undertaking, and combined for its support and advancement the motives of religion and commerce, together with the enlargement of the Empire.

For greater security and more imposing dignity, the " adventurers" determined to apply for a Royal Charter of incorporation. Their application was seconded by Lord Dorchester and others near the Throne ; and Charles the First, impressed with the novel idea of at once extending religion, commerce, and his Empire, granted a Royal Patent incorporating the Company under the name of " The Governor and Company of Massachusetts Bay, in New England." But several months before the Royal Charter was obtained, or even application for it made, Endicot, one of the stockholders, was sent out with a ship of one hundred emigrants, and, in consequence of his favourable report, application was made for a Royal Charter.†

It was the conduct of Endicot, a few months after his arrival at Massachusetts Bay—first condemned and afterwards sustained and justified by the Directors of the Corporation in London— that laid the foundation of the future Church history of New

---

* The zeal of White soon found other powerful associates in and out of London—kindred spirits, men of religious fervour, uniting emotions of enthusiasm with unbending perseverance in action—Winthrop, Dudley, Johnson, Pynchon, Eaton, Saltunstall, Bellingham, so famous in colonial annals, besides many others, men of fortune and friends to colonial enterprise.   Three of the original purchasers parted with their rights ; Humphrey and Endicot retained an equal interest with the original purchasers. (Bancroft's United States, Vol. I., pp. 368, 369.)

† Bancroft says : " Endicot, a man of dauntless courage, and that cheerfulness which accompanies courage, benevolent though austere, firm though choleric, of a rugged nature, which the sternest forms of Puritanism had not served to mellow, was selected as a fit instrument for this wilderness work." .(History of the United States, Vol. I., pp. 369, 370.)

" When the news reached London of the safe arrival of the emigrants [under Endicot], the number of the adventurers had already enlarged.   The Puritans throughout England began to take an interest in the efforts which invited the imagination to indulge in delightful visions.   Interest was also made to obtain a Royal Charter, with the aid of Bellingham and White, an eminent lawyer, who advocated the design.   The Earl of Warwick had always been a friend to the Company ; and Lord Dorchester, then one of the Secretaries of State, is said to have exerted a powerful influence in behalf of it. At last [March 4th, 1629], after much labour and large expenditures, the patent for the Company of Massachusetts Bay passed the seals." (Ib., p. 379.)

England, and of its disputes with the mother country. Endicot and his one hundred emigrant adventurers arrived in the summer of 1628, and selected Naumkeag, which they called Salem, as their place of settlement, the 6th of September. Endicot was sent, with his company, by the Council for New England, "to supersede Roger Conant at Naumkeag as local manager."* "The colony, made up of two sources, consisted of not much above fifty or sixty persons, none of whom were of special importance except Endicot, who was destined to act for nearly forty years a conspicuous part in New England history."† The Royal Charter passed the seals the 4th of March, 1629, with Mr. Cradock as the first Governor of the Company. "The first step of the new Corporation was to organize a government for its colony. It determined to place the local administration in the hands of thirteen councillors, to retain their office for one year. Of these, seven, besides the Governor (in which office Endicot was continued), were to be appointed by the Company at home; these eight were to choose three others; and the whole number was to be made up by the addition of such as should be designated by the persons on the spot at the time of Endicot's arrival, described as "old planters."‡ A second embarkation of planters and servants was ordered by the Company at a meeting, April 30, 1629, shortly after its incorporation by Royal Charter. Five ships were provided for this embarkation; and four ministers were provided—Francis Higginson, Samuel Skelton, Francis Bright,

---

* The precursor of this Company was a Joint Stock Association, established at Dorchester under the auspices of the Rev. Mr. White, "patriarch of Dorchester," and called the "Dorchester Adventurers," with a view to fishing, farming, and hunting; but the undertaking was not successful, and an attempt was made to retrieve affairs by putting the colony under a different direction. The Dorchester partners heard of some religious and well-affected persons that were lately removed out of New Plymouth, out of dislike of their principles of rigid separation, of which Mr. Roger Conant was one—a religious, sober, and prudent gentleman. (Hubbard's History of New England, Chap. xviii.) The partners engaged Conant to be their Governor, with the charge of all their affairs, as well fishing as planting. The change did not produce success. The Association sold its land, shipping, &c.; and Mr. Endicot was appointed under the new *regime*. (Palfrey's Hist. of New England, Vol. I., pp. 285—8.)

† Palfrey, Vol. I., p. 289.

‡ *Ib.*, p. 292.

and Ralph Smith.*   Mr. Higginson says in his journal that he
sailed from the Isle of Wight the 11th of May, and arrived at
Cape Ann the 27th of June, and at Naumkeag (Salem) the
29th.   They found at Naumkeag about one hundred planters
and houses, besides a fair house built for Mr. Endicot.   The
old and new planters together were about three hundred, of
whom one hundred removed to Charlestown, where there was a
house built; the rest remained at Salem.

"Mr. Endicot had corresponded with the settlers at Plymouth,
who satisfied him that they were right in their judgments of the
outward form of worship, being much like that of the Reformed
Churches of France, &c.   On the 20th of July, Mr. Higginson
and Mr. Skelton, after fasting and prayer, were first elected by
the Company for their ministers—the first, teacher; the other,
pastor.   Each of them, together with three or four grave members,
lay their hands on each and either, with solemn prayer.   Nothing
is said of any Church being formed; but on the 6th of August,
the day appointed for the choice and ordination of elders and
deacons, thirty persons entered into a covenant in writing, which
is said to be the beginning of the Church, and that the ministers
were ordained or instituted anew.   The repetition of this form
they probably thought necessary, because the people were not
in a Church state before.   It is difficult to assign any other
reason.   Messengers or delegates from the Church of Plymouth
were expected to join with them, but contrary winds hindered
them, so that they did not arrive until the afternoon, but time
enough to give the right hand of fellowship.

"Two of the company, John and Samuel Brown, one a lawyer,
the other a merchant, both men of good estates, and of the first
patentees of the Council, were dissatisfied.   They did not like
that the Common Prayer and service of the Church of England

---

* Mr. Bright, one of these ministers, is said by Hubbard to have been a
Conformist.   He went, soon after his arrival, to Charlestown, and tarried
about a year in the country, when he returned to England.   Ralph Smith
was required to give a pledge, under his hand, that he would not exercise his
ministry within the limits of the patent, without the express leave of the
Governor on the spot.   Mr. Smith seems to have been of the separation in
England, which occasioned the caution to be used with him.   He was a little
while in Nantasket, and went from thence to Plymouth, where he was their
minister for several years."   (Hutchinson's History of Massachusetts Bay,
Vol. I., pp. 10, 11.)

should be wholly laid aside, and therefore drew off, with as many as were of their sentiments, from the rest, and set up a separate society. This offended the Governor, who caused the two members of his Council to be brought before him; and judging that this practice, together with some speeches they had uttered, tended to sedition, he sent them back to England. The heads of the party being removed, the opposition ceased."*

PART II.

THE QUESTION INVOLVING THE PRIMARY CAUSE OF THE AMERICAN REVOLU-
TION, THE SETTING UP OF A NEW FORM OF WORSHIP, AND ABOLISHING
AND PROSCRIBING THAT OF THE CHURCH OF ENGLAND ; THE FACTS
ANALYZED AND DISCUSSED ; INSTRUCTIONS AND OATHS OF ALLEGIANCE
ORDERED BY THE LONDON COMPANY AND DISREGARDED BY THE GOV-
ERNOR AND COUNCIL AT MASSACHUSETTS BAY.

As the whole question of the future Church-state in Massachusetts, and the future relations of the colony to England, is involved in and resulted from this proceeding, it is necessary to examine it thoroughly in relation both to the state of things in the mother country and in the colony, as well as the provisions of the Royal Charter. To do this, several things are to be considered: 1. With what views was the Royal Charter granted, and with what professed views did the first Governor and his associates leave England under the provisions of the Charter, and carrying it with them to Massachusetts Bay? 2. What were the provisions of the Charter itself on the subject of religion? 3. What were the powers claimed and exercised under it by the Massachusetts Puritans? 4. How far the proceedings of the Massachusetts Puritans were consistent with their original professions, with good faith towards the Mother Country, and with the principles of civil and religious liberty in the colony?

A careful recollection of the collateral events in England and those of the colony, at the time and after granting the Royal Charter, is requisite to a correct understanding of the question, and for the refutation of those statements by which it was misrepresented and misunderstood.

1. The first question is, with what views was the Royal Charter granted, and with what professed views did the Governor and his associates leave England under the provisions of the Charter, and carrying it with them to Massachusetts Bay?

* Hutchinson's History of Massachusetts Bay, Vol. I., pp. 11, 12.

The theory of some New England historians is, that Puritanism in England was opposed to the Church of England, and especially to its Episcopal government—a theory true as respects the Puritanism of the Long Parliament after the second year of its existence, and of the Commonwealth and Cromwell, but which is entirely at variance with facts in respect to the Puritanism professed in England at the time of granting the Royal Charter to the Massachusetts Company in 1629, and for twelve years afterwards. In the Millenary Petition presented by the Puritan party in the Church to James the First, on his coming to the throne, presbytery was expressly disclaimed; and in the first three Parliaments of Charles the First, during which all the grievances complained of by the Puritans were stated and discussed in the Commons, not the slightest objection was made to Episcopacy, but, on the contrary, reverence and fidelity in regard to it was professed without exception; and when the Long Parliament first met, eleven years after the granting of the Royal Charter to the Massachusetts Bay Company, every member but one professed to be an Episcopalian, and the Holy Communion, according to the order of the Church, was, by an unanimous vote of the Commons, ordered to be partaken by each member. In all the Church, as well as judicial and political, reforms of this Parliament during its first session, Episcopacy was regarded and treated as inviolate; and it was not until the following year, under the promptings of the Scotch Commissioners, that the "root and branch" petition was presented to Parliament against Episcopacy and the Prayer Book, and the subject was discussed in the Commons. The theory, therefore, that Puritanism in England was hostile to the Church at the period in question is contradicted by all the "collateral" facts of English history, as it is at variance with the professions of the first Massachusetts Puritans themselves at the time of their leaving England.

This is true in respect to Endicot himself, who was appointed manager of the New England Company, to succeed Roger Conant, and in charge of one hundred "adventurers" who reached Naumkeag (which they called Salem) in September, 1628 —seven months before the Royal Charter granted by Charles the First passed the seals. Within two months after the Royal Charter was granted, another more numerous party of "adven-

turers" embarked for New England, and among these two
gentlemen, original patentees and members of the Council—John
and Samuel Brown, and four ministers—Higginson, Skelton,
Bright, and Smith. During the winter of 1628-9 much sickness
prevailed among the emigrants who accompanied Endicot, who
sent for a physician to the Plymouth settlement of the Pilgrim
Fathers. A Doctor Fuller was sent, who, while he prescribed
medicine for the sick of the newly-arrived emigrants, converted
Endicot from Episcopalianism to Congregationalism—at least
from being a professed Churchman to being an avowed Congregationalist. This is distinctly stated by all the historians of the
times.*

It is therefore clear that Endicot had imbibed new views of
Church government and form of worship, and that he determined not to perpetuate the worship of the Church of England,
to which he had professed to belong when he left England, but
to form a new Church and a new form of worship. He seems to
have brought over some thirty of the new emigrants to his new
scheme; and among these were the newly-arrived ministers,
Higginson and Skelton. They were both clergymen of the
Puritan school—professing loyalty to the Church, but refusing
to conform to the novel ceremonies imposed by Laud and his
party.† But within two months after their arrival, they

---

* "How much of the Church system thus introduced had already been resolved upon before the colonists of the Massachusetts Company left England,
and how long a time, if any, previous to their emigration such an agreement
was made, are questions which we have probably not sufficient means to
determine. Thus much is certain—that when Skelton and Higginson
reached Salem, they found Endicot, who was not only their Governor, but
one of the six considerable men who had made the first movement for a
patent, fully prepared for the ecclesiastical organization which was presently
instituted. In the month before their arrival, Endicot, in a letter [May 11,
1629] to Bradford thanking him for the visit of Fuller, had said: 'I rejoice
much that I am by him satisfied touching your judgments of the outward
form of God's worship.'"—Collections of the Massachusetts Historical Society,
First Series, Vol. III., p. 65.

† Cotton Mather relates that, "taking the last look at his native shore,
Higginson said, 'We will not say, as the Separatists say, "Farewell, Babylon;
farewell, Rome;" but we will say, "Farewell, dear England; farewell, Church
of God in England, and all the Christian friends there.' We do not go to New
England as separatists from the Church of England, though we cannot but
separate from the corruptions of it. But we go to practise the positive part

entered into the new views of Endicot to found a new Church
on the Congregational system.   Their manner of proceeding to
do so has been stated above (p. 29.)   Mr. Hutchinson remarks—
" The New England Puritans, when at full liberty, went the full
length which the Separatists did in England.   It does not follow
that they would have done so if they had remained in England.
In their form of worship they universally followed the New
Plymouth Church."*

The question is naturally suggested, could King Charles the
First, in granting the Charter, one declared object of which was
converting the Indians, have intended or contemplated the superseding the Church for whose episcopacy he perished on the
scaffold, by the establishment of Congregationalism in New
England?   The supposition is absurd, and it is equally unreasonable to suppose that those who applied for and obtained the
Charter contemplated anything of the kind, as will appear
presently.

It can hardly be conceived that even among the newly-arrived
emigrants on the shores of Massachusetts, such a revolution as
the adoption of a new form of worship could be accomplished
without doing violence to the convictions and endeared associations of some parties.   However they might have objected to the
ceremonies and despotic acts of the Laudian school in England,
they could not, without a pang and voice of remonstrance, renounce the worship which had given to England her Protestantism and her liberties, or repudiate the book which embodied that
form of worship, and which was associated with all that had
exalted England, from Cranmer and Ridley to their own day.

---

of Church reformation, and propagate the gospel in America."''—Magnalia,
Book III., Part II., Chap. i., quoted by Palfrey, Vol. I., p. 297, in a note.

" They were careful to distinguish themselves from the Brownist and
other Separatists.   Had they remained in England, and the Church been
governed with the wisdom and moderation of the present day, they would
have remained, to use their own expression, 'in the bosom of the Church where
they had received their hopes of salvation.'"—Hutchinson's History of Massachusetts Bay, Vol. I., p. 417.

Note by Mr. Hutchinson : " The son of one of the first ministers, in a preface to a sermon preached soon after the Revolution, remarks that 'if the
bishops in the reign of King Charles the First had been of the same spirit as
those in the reign of King William, there would have been no New England.'"

* History of Massachusetts Bay, Vol. I., Chap. iv., p. 418.

3

Congregationalism had done nothing for the Protestantism or liberties of England, and it would have been strange indeed had there not been some among the emigrants who would not consider their change of latitude and longitude as destroying their Church membership, and sundering the additional ties which connected them with their forefathers and the associations of all their past life. Endicot, therefore, with all his authority as local Governor, and all his energy and zeal, and canvassing among the two or three hundred new emigrants for a new Church, had not been able to get more than thirty of them, with the aid of the two newly-arrived ministers, to unite in the new Covenant Confession ; but he had got the (if not coerced) majority of the local Councillors to join with him, and therefore exercised absolute power over the little community, and denounced and treated as mutinous and factious all who would not renounce the Church of their fathers and of their own profession down to that hour, and adopt the worship of his new community.

As only thirty joined with Endicot in the creation of his new. Church organization and Covenant, it is obvious that a majority of the emigrants either stood aloof from or were opposed to this extraordinary proceeding. Among the most noted of these adherents to the old Church of the Reformation were two brothers, John and Samuel Brown, who refused to be parties to this new and locally-devised Church revolution, and resolved, for themselves, families, and such as thought with them, to continue to worship God according to the custom of their fathers and nation.

It is the fashion of several American historians, as well as their echoes in England, to employ epithets of contumely in regard to those men, the Browns—both of them men of wealth—the one a lawyer and the other a private gentleman—both of them much superior to Endicot himself in social position in England—both of them among the original patentees and first founders of the colony—both of them Church reformers, but neither of them a Church revolutionist. It is not worthy of Dr. Palfrey and Mr. Bancroft to employ the words "faction" and "factionists" to the protests of John and Samuel Brown.*

---

* "The Messrs. Brown went out with the second emigration, at the same time as Messrs. Higginson and Skelton, a few months after Endicot, and while he was the local Governor, several months before the arrival of the third emigration of eleven ships with Governor Winthrop. In the Company's

What is stated by Dr. Palfrey and Mr. Bancroft more than refutes and condemns the opprobrious epithets they apply to the Browns. On pages 29 and 30 I have given, in the words of Mr. Hutchinson, the account of the formation of the new Church, and the expulsion of the Browns for their refusal to conform to it. Dr. Palfrey states the transaction between Endicot and the Browns in the following words:

"The transaction which determined the religious constitution of New England gave offence to two of the Councillors, John and Samuel Brown. Considering the late proceedings, *as well they might do*, to amount to a *secession from the national Establishment*, they, with some others of the same mind, set up a separate worship, conducted according to the Book of Common Prayer. Endicot and his friends were in no mood to tolerate this schism. The brothers, brought before the Governor, said that the ministers 'were Separatists, and would be Anabaptists.' The ministers replied that 'they came away from the Common Prayer and ceremonies, and had suffered much for their non-conformity in their native land, and therefore, being placed where they might have their liberty, they neither could nor would use them, because they judged the imposition of these things to be sinful corruptions of God's worship.' There was no composing such strife, and 'therefore, finding these two brothers to be of high spirits, and their speeches and practice tending to mutiny and faction, the Governor told them that New England was no place for such as they, and therefore he sent them both back for England at the return of the ships the same year.' "*

first letter of instructions to Endicot, dated the 17th of April, 1629, they speak of and commend the Messrs. Brown in the following terms:

" 'Through many businesses we had almost forgot to recommend to you two brethren of our Company, Mr. John and Mr. Samuel Brown, who though they be no adventurers in the general stock, yet are they men we do much respect, being fully persuaded of their sincere affections to the good of our Plantation. The one, Mr. John Brown, is sworn assistant here, and by us chosen one of the Council there ; a man experienced in the laws of our kingdom, and such an one as we are persuaded will worthily deserve your favour and furthermore, which we desire he may have, and that in the first division of lands there may be allotted to either of them two hundred acres.' " (Young's Chronicles of the First Planters of the Colony of Massachusetts Bay from 1623 to 1636, p. 168.)

* History of New England, Vol. I., p. 298.

Mr. Bancroft says: "The Church was self-constituted. It did not ask the assent of the King or recognize him as its head; its officers were set apart and ordained among themselves; it used no Liturgy, and it rejected unnecessary ceremonies; and reduced the simplicity of Calvin to a still plainer standard." "There existed even in this little company a few individuals to whom the new system was unexpected; and in John and Samuel Brown they found able leaders. Both were members of the Colonial Council, and they had been favourites of the Corporation in England; and one of them, an experienced and meritorious lawyer, had been a member of the Board of Assistants in London. They declared their dissent from the Church of Higginson; and at every risk of union and tranquillity, they insisted upon the use of the English Liturgy." "Finding it to be a vain attempt to persuade the Browns to relinquish their resolute opposition, and *believing* that their speeches *tended* to produce *disorder* and dangerous feuds, Endicot sent them back to England in the returning ships; and *faction*, deprived of its leaders, died away."*

It is clear from these statements—partial as they are in favour of Endicot and against the Browns—that Endicot himself was the innovator, the Church revolutionist and the would-be founder of a new Church, the real schismatic from the old Church, and therefore responsible for any discussions which might arise from his proceedings; while the Browns and their friends were for standing in the old ways and walking in the old paths, refusing to be of those who were given to change. Mr. Bancroft says that "the *new system* was *unexpected*" to them. Mr. Palfrey says that "John and Samuel Brown, considering the late proceedings, *as well they might*, to amount to a *secession from the national Establishment*, they, with some others of the same mind, set up a separate worship conducted according to the Book of Common Prayer." Or, more properly, they *continued* the worship according to the Book of Common Prayer, which they and their fathers had practised, as well as Endicot and Higginson themselves up to that day, refusing to leave the old Church of the Reformation, and come into a new Church founded by joining of hands of thirty persons, in a new covenant,

* Bancroft's History of the United States, Vol. I., p. 379.

walking around the place of the old town-pump of Salem. Mr. Endicot is sent from England as the manager of a trading Company, and invested with powers as their local temporary Governor, to manage their business and remove persons that might disturb or interfere with its operations; and he becomes acquainted with a Doctor Fuller, a deacon of a Congregational Church at New Plymouth, and imbibes his views; and forthwith sets himself to abolish the old Church, and found a new one, and proceeds at length to banish as seditious and mutinous those who would not forsake the old way of worship and follow him in his new way of worship.

Some of the above quoted language of Dr. Palfrey and Mr. Bancroft implies improper conduct on the part of the brothers Brown, and for which they were banished. Even if that were so, their position of unchangeable loyalty to their post and of good faith to their Company might be pleaded in justification of the strongest language on their part. But such was not the fact; it was their *position*, and not their language or tempers. Mr. Bancroft himself says, in the American edition of his History, that "the Browns were banished *because they were Churchmen. Thus was Episcopacy professed in Massachusetts, and thus was it exiled. The blessings of the promised land were to be kept for Puritan dissenters.*"* This statement of Mr. Bancroft is confirmed and the conduct of Endicot more specifically stated by earlier New England historians. In the "Ecclesiastical History of Massachusetts," reprinted by the Massachusetts Historical Society, the whole affair is minutely related. The following passages are sufficient for my purpose:

"An opposition of some consequence arose from several persons of influence, who had been active in promoting the settlement of the place. At the head of this were Mr. Samuel Brown and Mr. John Brown, the one a lawyer and the other a merchant, who were attached to the form and usage of the Church of England. The ministers [Higginson and Skelton], assisted by Mr. Endicot, endeavoured to bring them over to the practice of the Puritans, but without success." "These gentlemen, with

* History of the United States, Am. Ed. 8vo, Vol. I., p. 350. These three sentences are not found in the British Museum (English) Edition of Mr. Bancroft's History, but are contained in Routledge's London reprint of the American Edition.

others, were conscientious Churchmen, and desired to use the Liturgy, and for this purpose met in their own houses. The magistrates, or rather Mr. Endicot, sent to demand a reason for their separation. They answered, that as they were of the Church established by law in their native country, it was highly proper they should worship God as the Government required, from whom they had received their Charter. Surely they might be allowed that *liberty of conscience* which all conceived to be reasonable when they were on the other side of the water. But these arguments were called *seditious* and *mutinous.*"

" Mr. Bentley imputes the errors of the ministers to the temper of Endicot, who was determined to execute his own plan of Church government. Inexperienced in the passions of men, and unaccustomed to consult even his friends, he was resolved to suffer no opposition; and as the Salem Church had disdained the authority of the Church of England, his feelings were hurt and his temper raised against those who preferred a Liturgy, and whose object might be, as he conceived, to cause a schism in the community."*

The Mr. Bentley referred to above was the historian of the town of Salem, in a book entitled "Description and History of Salem, by the Rev. William Bentley," and reprinted in the "Collection of the Massachusetts Historical Society," Vol. VI., pp. 212—277. Referring to Endicot's conduct to the Browns, Mr. Bentley says:

"Endicot had been the cause of all the rash proceedings against the Browns. He was determined to execute his own plan of Church government. Inexperienced in the passions of men, and unaccustomed to consult even his friends, he was resolved to admit of no opposition. They *who could not be terrified into silence* were *not commanded to withdraw, but they were seized and banished as criminals.* The fear of injury to the colony induced its friends in England to give private satisfaction, and then to write a reproof to him who had been the cause of the outrages; and Endicot never recovered his reputation in England." (p. 245.)

It is thus clear beyond reasonable doubt that the sole offence of the Browns, and those who remained with them, was that

---

* "Ecclesiastical History of Massachusetts," in the Collection of the Massachusetts Historical Society, Vol. IX., pp. 3—5.

they adhered to the worship which they had always practised, and which was professed by all parties when they left England, and because they refused to follow Mr. Endicot in the new Church polity and worship which he adopted from the Congregational Plymouth physician, after his arrival at Salem, and which he was determined to establish as the only worship in the new Plantation. It was Endicot, therefore, that commenced the change, the innovation, the schism, and the power given him as Manager of the trading business of the Company he exercised for the purpose of establishing a Church revolution, and banishing the men who adhered to the old ways of worship professed by the Company when applying for the Royal Charter, and still professed by them in England. It is not pretended by any party that the Browns were not interested in the success of the Company as originally established, and as professed when they left England; it is not insinuated that they opposed in any way or differed from Endicot in regard to his management of the general affairs of the Company ; on the contrary, it is manifest by the statement of all parties that the sole ground and question of dispute between Endicot and the Browns was the refusal of the latter to abandon the Episcopal and adopt the Congregational form of worship set up by Endicot and thirty others, by joining of hands and subscribing to a covenant and confession of faith around the well-pump of Naumkeag, then christened Salem.

The whole dispute, then, narrowed to this one question, let us inquire in what manner the Browns and their friends declined acting with Endicot in establishing a new form of worship instead of that of the Church of England ?

It does not appear that Endicot even consulted his local Council, much less the Directors of the Company in England, as to his setting up a new Church and new form of worship in the new Plantation at Salem. Having with the new accession of emigrants received the appointment of Governor, he appears to have regarded himself as an independent ruler. Suddenly raised from being a manager and captain to being a Governor, he assumed more despotic power than did King Charles in England, and among the new emigrants placed under his control, and whom he seems to have regarded as his subjects—himself their absolute sovereign, in both Church and State. In his conferences with Fuller, the Congregational doctor from New Plymouth, he found the Congregational worship to answer to his aspirations, as in it he could on the one hand gratify his hatred of King and Church, and on the other hand become the founder of the new Church in a new Plantation.   He paused not to consider whether the manager of a trading Company of adventurers had any authority to abolish the worship professed by the Company under whose authority he was acting; how far fidelity required him to give effect to the worship of his employers in carrying out their instructions in regard to the religious instruction of their servants and the natives; but he forthwith resolved to adopt a new confession of faith and to set up a new form of worship.   On the arrival of the first three chaplains of the Company, in June of 1629, several months after his own arrival, Endicot seems to have imparted his views to them, and two of them, Higginson and Skelton, fell in with his scheme; but Mr. Bright adhered to his Church.   It was not unnatural for Messrs. Higginson and Skelton to prefer becoming the fathers and founders of a new Church than to remain subordinate ministers of an old Church.   The Company, in its written agreement with them, or rather in its instructions accompanying them to Endicot, allowed them discretion in their new mission field as to their mode of teaching and worship; but certainly no authority to ignore it, much less authority to adopt a new confession of faith and a new form of worship.

Within three months after the arrival of these chaplains of the Company at Salem, they and Endicot matured the plan of setting up a new Church, and seemed to have persuaded thirty-one of the two hundred emigrants to join with them—a minority of less than one-sixth of the little community; but in that minority was the absolute Governor, and against whose will a majority was nothing, even in religious matters, or in liberty of conscience.   Government by majorities and liberty of conscience are attributes of freedom.

Let it be observed here, once for all, that Endicot and his friends are not, in my opinion, censurable for changing their professed religious opinions and worship and adopting others, if they thought it right to do so.   If, on their arrival at Massachusetts Bay, they thought and felt themselves in duty bound to renounce their old and set up a new form of worship and Church discipline, it was doubtless their right to do so; but in doing so it was unquestionably their duty not to violate their previous engagements and the rights of others. They were not the original owners and occupants of the country, and were not absolutely free to choose their own form of government and worship; they were British subjects, and were commencing the settlement of a territory granted them by their Sovereign; they were sent there by a Company existing and acting under Royal Charter; Endicot was the chief agent of that Company, and acting under their instructions. As such, duty required him to consult his employers before taking the all-important step of setting aside the worship they professed and establishing a new one, much less to proscribe and banish those who had adventured as settlers upon the old professed worship, and declined adopting the new. And was it not a violation of good faith, as well as liberty of conscience, to deny to the Browns and their friends the very worship on the profession of which by all parties they had embarked as settlers in New England? To come to New England as Churchmen, and then abolish the worship of the Church and set up a new form of worship, without even consulting his employers, was what was done by Endicot; and to come as Churchmen to settle in New England, and then to be banished from it for being Churchmen, was what was done to the Browns by Endicot.

This act of despotism and persecution—apart from its relations to the King, and the Company chartered by him—is the more reprehensible from the manner of its execution and the circumstances connected with it.

It appears from the foregoing statements and authorities, that the Browns were not only gentlemen of the highest respectability, Puritan Churchmen, and friends of the colonial enterprise, but that when Endicot resolved upon founding a new Church and worship, they did not interfere with him; they did not interrupt, by objection or discussion, his proceedings around the well-pump of Salem in organizing a new Church and in heretofore professing clergymen of the Church of England, and with its vows upon them, and coming as chaplains of a Church of England Corporation, submitting to a new ordination in order to exercise ecclesiastical functions. The Browns and their friends seem to have been silent spectators of these proceedings

—doubtless with feelings of astonishment if not of grief—but determined to worship in their families and on the Sabbath in their old way. But in this they were interrupted, and hailed before the new Governor, Endicot, to answer for their not coming to his worship and abandoning that which they and their fathers, and Endicot himself, had practised; were called "Separatists," for not acting as such in regard to their old way of worship; and were treated as "seditious and mutinous," for justifying their fidelity to the old worship before the new "Star Chamber" tribunal of Endicot. The early New England ecclesiastical historian above quoted says: "The magistrates, or rather Endicot, *sent to demand a reason** for their separation. They *answered* that as they were of the Church established by law in their native country, it was highly proper they should worship God as the Government required from whom they had received their Charter. Surely they might be allowed that liberty of conscience which all conceived to be reasonable when they were on the other side of the water. But their arguments were called "seditious and mutinous." The first Congregational historian of Salem, above quoted, says: "Endicot had been the cause of all the rash proceedings against the Browns. He was determined to execute his plan of Church government. Inexperienced in the passions of men, and unaccustomed to consult even his friends, he was resolved to admit of no opposition· They who could not be terrified into silence *were not commanded to withdraw*, but were *seized* and *transported as criminals*."†

Such are the facts of the case itself, as related by the New

* It is clear, from these and other corresponding statements, that the Messrs. Brown had had no controversy with Endicot ; had not in the least interfered with *his* proceedings, but had quietly and inoffensively pursued their own course in adhering to the old worship ; and only stated their objections to his proceedings by giving the reasons for their own, when arraigned before his tribunal to answer for their not coming to his worship, and continuing in that of their own Church. The reasonings and speeches thus drawn from them were deemed "seditious and mutinous," and for which they were adjudged "criminals'" and banished. Looking at all the facts of the case—including the want of good faith to the Browns and those who agreed with them—it exceeds in inquisitorial and despotic proscriptive persecution that which drove the Brownists from England to Holland in the first years of James the First.

† Collection of the Massachusetts Historical Society.

Mr. F. M. Hubbard, in his new edition of Belknap's American Biography,

England Puritan writers themselves. I will now for a short
time cross the Atlantic, and see what were the professions and
proceedings of the Council or " Grand Court" of the Company
in England in regard to the chief objects of establishing the
Plantation, their provision for its religious wants, and their
judgment afterwards of Endicot's proceedings. In the Company's
first letter of instructions to Endicot and his Council, dated
the 17th of April, 1629, they remind him that the propagation
of the Gospel was the primary object contemplated by them ;
that they had appointed and contracted with three ministers to
promote that work, and instructed him to provide accommodation and necessaries for them, according to agreement. They
apprise him also of his confirmation as " Governor of *our*
Plantation," and of the names of the Councillors joined with
him.* In their letter to Endicot, they call the ministers sent
by them " your ministers," and say : " For the manner of exer-

iii. 166, referring to Endicot, says : " He was of a quick temper, which the
habit of military command had not softened ; of strong religious feelings,
moulded on the sternest features of Calvinism ; resolute to uphold with the
sword what he had received as gospel truth, and fearing no enemy so much
as a gainsaying spirit. Cordially disliking the English Church, he banished
the Browns and the Prayer Book ; and averse to all ceremonies and symbols,
the cross on the King's colours was an abomination he could not away with.
He cut down the Maypole on Merry Mount, published his detestation of long
hair in a formal proclamation, and set in the pillory and on the gallows the
returning Quakers."

    * The words of the Company's letter are as follows :
" And for that the propagating of the Gospel is the thing we do profess
above all to be our aim in settling this Plantation, we have been careful to
make plentiful provision of godly ministers, by whose faithful preaching,
godly conversation, and exemplary life, we trust not only those of our own
nation will be built up in the knowledge of God, but also the Indians may,
in God's appointed time, be reduced to the obedience of the Gospel of Christ.
One of them, viz., Mr. Skelton, whom we have rather desired to bear a part
in this work, for that we have been informed yourself formerly received much
good by his ministry. Another is Mr. Higgeson [Higginson], a grave man,
and of worthy commendations. The third is Mr. Bright, sometimes trained
up under Mr. Davenport. We pray you, accommodate them all with necessaries as well as you may, and in convenient time let there be houses built
for them, according to the agreement we have made with them, copies whereof,
as of all others we have entertained, shall be sent you by the next ships, time
not permitting now. We doubt not these gentlemen, your ministers, will
agree lovingly together ; and for cherishing of love betwixt them, we pray
you carry yourself impartially to all. For the manner of exercising their

cising their ministry, and teaching both our own people and the
Indians, we leave that to themselves, hoping they will make
God's Word the rule of their actions, and mutually agree in
the discharge of their duties." Such instructions and directions
have doubtless been given by the Managing Boards of many
Missionary Societies to missionaries whom they sent abroad;
but without the least suspicion that such missionaries could, in
good faith, on arriving at their destination, ignore the Church
and ordination in connection with which they had been employed,
and set up a new Church, and even be parties to banishing from
their new field of labour to which they had been sent, the
members of the Church of which they themselves were professed ministers when they received their appointment and
stipulated support.

Six weeks after transmitting to Endicot the letter above
referred to, the Company addressed to him a second general
letter of instructions. This letter is dated the 28th of May,
1629, and encloses the official proceedings of the Council or
" General Court" appointing Endicot as Governor, with the
names of the Councillors joined with him, together with the
form of *oaths* he and the other local officers of the Company
were to take.* The oath required to be taken by Endicot and

ministry, and teaching both our own people and the Indians, we leave that
to themselves, hoping they will make God's Word the rule of their actions,
and mutually agree in the discharge of their duties.

" We have, in prosecution of that good opinion we have always had of you,
confirmed you Governor of our Plantation, and joined in commission with
you the three ministers—namely, Mr. Francis Higginson, Mr. Samuel Skelton,
and Mr. Francis Bright; also Mr. John and Samuel Brown, Mr. Thomas Groves,
and Mr. Samuel Sharpe."—The Company's First General Letter of Instructions
to Endicot and his Council, the 17th of April, 1629. (Young's Chronicles
of the First Planters of the Colony of Massachusetts Bay, pp. 142—144.)

" A form of an oath for a Governor beyond the seas, and of an oath for the
Council there, was drawn and delivered to Mr. Humphrey to show to the
[Privy] Council." (Company's Records, Young, &c., p. 69.)

* The following is an extract of the Company's Second General Letter of
Instructions to Endicot and his Council, dated London, 28th May, 1629:

" We have, and according as we then advised, at a full and ample Court
assembled, elected and established you, Captain John Endicot, to the place
of Governor in our Plantation there, as also some others to be of the
Council with you, as more particularly you will perceive by an Act of
Court herewith sent, confirmed by us at a General Court, and sealed with
our common seal, to which Act we refer you, desiring you all punctually

each local Governor is very full and explicit.* It is also to be observed that these two letters of instructions, with forms of oaths and appointments of his Council, were sent out three months before Endicot, Higginson, and Skelton proceeded to ignore and abolish the Church professed by the Company and themselves, and set up a new Church.

to observe the same, and that the *oaths* we herewith send you (which have been penned by learned counsel, to be administered to each of you in your several places) may be administered in such manner and form as in and by our said order is particularly expressed ; and that yourselves do frame such other oaths as in your wisdom you shall think fit to be administered to your secretary or other officers, according to their several places respectively." (Young's Chronicles, &c., p. 173.)

* The form of oath, which had been prepared under legal advice, submitted to and approved of by the King's Privy Council, was as follows :

"Oaths of Office for the Governor, Deputy Governor, and Council in New England (ordered May 7th, 1620).

"The Oath of the Governor in New England." [The same to the Deputy Governor.]

"You shall be faithful and loyal unto our Sovereign Lord the King's Majesty, and to his heirs and successors. You shall support and maintain, to the best of your power, the Government and Company of Massachusetts Bay, in New England, in America, and the privileges of the same, having no singular regard to yourself in derogation or hindrance of the Commonwealth of this Company ; and to every person under your authority you shall administer indifferent and equal justice. Statutes and Ordinances shall you none make without the advice and consent of the Council for Government of the Massachusetts Bay in New England. You shall admit none into the freedom of this Company but such as may claim the same by virtue of the privileges thereof. You shall not bind yourself to enter into any business or process for or in the name of this Company, without the consent and agreement of the Council aforesaid, but shall endeavour faithfully and carefully to carry yourself in this place and office of Governor, as long as you shall continue in it. And likewise you shall do your best endeavour to draw the natives of this country called New England to the knowledge of the true God, and to conserve the planters, and others coming hither, in the same knowledge and fear of God. And you shall endeavour, by all good unions, to advance the good of the Plantations of this Company, and you shall endeavour the raising of such commodities for the benefit and encouragement of the adventurers and planters as, through God's blessing on your endeavours, may be produced for the good and service of the kingdom of England, this Company, and the Plantations. All these premises you shall hold and keep to the uttermost of your power and skill, so long as you shall continue in the place of Governor of this fellowship ; so help you God." [The same oath of allegiance was required of each member of the Council.] (Young's Chronicles of First Planters of the Colony of Massachusetts Bay, from 1623 to 1636, pp. 201, 202.)

PART III.

EVASIONS AND DENIALS OF THE ABOLITION OF EPISCOPAL, AND ESTABLISH-
MENT OF CONGREGATIONAL WORSHIP AT MASSACHUSETTS BAY; PROOFS
OF THE FACTS, THAT THE COMPANY AND FIRST SETTLERS OF MASSA-
CHUSETTS BAY WERE PROFESSED EPISCOPALIANS WHEN THE LATTER
LEFT ENGLAND; LETTERS OF THE LONDON COMPANY AGAINST THE
INNOVATIONS WHICH ABOLISHED THE EPISCOPAL, AND ESTABLISHED
CONGREGATIONAL WORSHIP BY THE "ADVENTURERS" AFTER CROSSING
THE ATLANTIC; THIS THE FIRST SEED OF THE AMERICAN REVOLUTION,
AND OF CRUEL PERSECUTIONS.

When the Browns arrived in England as banished "criminals"
from the Plantation to which they had gone four months before
as members of the Council of Government, and with the highest
commendation of the London General Court itself, they naturally
made their complaints against the conduct of Endicot in superseding the Church of England by the establishment of a new
confession of faith and a new form of worship. It is worthy of
remark, that in the Records of the Company the specific subjects of complaint by the Browns are carefully kept out of
sight—only that a "dispute" or "difference" had arisen between
them and "Governor Endicot;" but what that difference was is
nowhere mentioned in the Records of the Company. The
letters of Endicot and the Browns were put into the hands of
Goffe, the Deputy Governor of the Company; were never published; and they are said to have been "missing" unto this day.
Had the real cause and subject of difference been known in
England, and been duly represented to the Privy Council, the
Royal Charter would undoubtedly have been forthwith forfeited
and cancelled; but the Puritan-party feeling of the Browns seems
to have been appealed to not to destroy the Company and their
enterprise; that in case of not prosecuting their complaints before
a legal tribunal, the matter would be referred to a jointly selected
Committee of the Council to arbitrate on the affair; and that
in the meantime the conduct of Endicot in making Church
innovations (if he had made them) would be disclaimed by
the Company. To render the Browns powerless to sustain
their complaints, their letters were seized* and their statements
were denied.

* The Company's Records on the whole affair are as follows :—

Nevertheless, the rumours and reports from the new Plantation of Massachusetts produced a strong impression in England, and excited great alarm among the members and friends of the

"Sept. 19, 1629.

"At this Court letters* were read from Mr. Endicot and others of New England. And whereas a difference hath fallen out betwixt the Governor there and John and Samuel Brown; it was agreed by the Court that, for the determination of those differences, John and Samuel Brown might choose out any three of the Company on their behalf to hear the said differences, the Company choosing as many."

From the Records of the Company, September 29, 1629 :

"The next thing taken into consideration was the letters from John and Samuel Brown to divers of their private friends here in England, whether the same should be delivered or detained, and whether they should be opened and read, or not. And for that it was to be doubted by probable circumstances that they had defamed the country of New England, and the Governor and Government there, it was thought fit that some of the said letters should be opened and publicly read, which was done accordingly ; and the rest to remain in the Deputy's house (Goffe's), and the parties to whom they are directed to have notice ; and Mr. Governor and Mr. Deputy, Mr. Treasurer, and Mr. Wright, or any two of them, are entreated to be at the opening and reading thereof, to the end that the Company may have notice if aught be inserted prejudicial to their Government or Plantation in New England. And it is also thought fit that none of the letters from Mr. Samuel Brown shall be delivered, but to be kept for use against him as occasion shall be offered." (Young's Chronicles, &c., pp. 91, 92.)

"Upon the desire of John and Samuel Brown it is thought fit that they should have a copy of the accusation against them, to the end they may be better prepared to make answer thereto."

The accusation against the Browns seems to have been simply for sedition and seditious speeches—a charge brought by persecutors for religion against the persecuted since the days of our Lord and his Apostles—a charge for being the victims of which the Puritans in England had loudly complained in the reigns of James and Charles.

There is but one other record of the Company on the affair of Endicot and the Browns, but the suppression of their letters shows clearly that the publication of them would have been damaging to the Company.

The intercepting and seizure of private letters, after the example of the Company in seizing private letters of the Browns and punishing their authors, was reduced to a system by the Government of Massachusetts Bay, whose officers were commanded to inspect all letters sent by each vessel leaving their port, and to seize all suspected letters, which were opened, and,

* Note by the compiler of the Records—" Those letters are unfortunately missing."

Company, who adopted three methods of securing themselves and their Charter, and of saving the Plantation from the consequences of Endicot's alleged innovations and violent conduct. Firstly—The Governor of the Company, Mr. Cradock, wrote to Endicot, Higginson, and Skelton, professing doubts of the truth of the charges made against them—disclaiming and warning them against the reported innovations—thus protecting themselves in case of charge from all participation in or responsibility for such proceedings. Secondly—They positively denied the statements of the Browns as to Endicot's alleged "innovations," and used every means to depreciate the trustworthiness and character of the Browns, notwithstanding their former commendation of them and their acknowledged respectability. Thirdly—They prepared and published documents declaring their adherence to the Church of England, and the calumny of the charges and rumours put forth against them as being disaffected to it.

1. Their Governor, Mr. Cradock, wrote to Endicot in the name of the Company. This letter, dated October 16, 1629, is given

if found to contain any complaint or statement against the local authorities, were retained and the authors arraigned and punished. Thus the Government and public in England were kept in perfect ignorance of what was transpiring at Massachusetts Bay, except what the local Government chose to communicate ; and aggrieved persons in the Plantations were deprived of all means of appealing to the higher tribunals in England, and were condemned and punished for sedition in attempting to do so. This practice continued (as will be shown hereafter) until the death of King Charles and the usurpation of the regicides in England.

The following extract from the Company's Records seems to explain the manner in which the further proceedings of the Browns was stayed. In order to get some compensation for their losses, they seem to have agreed to the stipulations of the Company. But previous to this meeting of the Company, their Governor had written to Endicot, Higginson, and Skelton, in letters dated Oct. 18, 1629. These letters will be found in a note on a subsequent page. The extract from the Company's Records, dated February 10, 1630, is as follows :

"A writing of grievances of Samuel and John Brown was presented to the Court, wherein they desire recompense for loss and damage sustained by them in New England ; and which this Assembly taking into consideration, do think fit upon their submitting to stand to the Company's *final order for ending all differences between them (which they are to signify under their hands)*. Mr. Wright and Mr. Eaton are to hear their complaint, and to set down what they in their judgments shall think requisite to be allowed them for their pretended damage sustained, and so to make a final end with them accordingly." (Young's Chronicles, &c., p. 123.)

at length in a note.*   It will be seen by this letter how strongly the Company condemned the innovations charged against Endicot by the Browns, and how imperatively they direct him to correct them, while they profess to doubt whether he could have been a party to any such proceedings.   In this letter is also

---

* The Company's letter to the Governor, dated October 16, 1629:—

"Sir,—We have written at this time to Mr. Skelton and Mr. Higginson touching the rumours of John and Samuel Brown, spread by them upon their arrival here, concerning some unadvised and scandalous speeches uttered by them in their public sermons or prayers, so have we thought meet to advertise you of what they have reported against you and them, concerning some rash innovations (a) begun and practised in the civil and ecclesiastical government. We do well to consider that the Browns are likely to make the worst of anything they have observed in New England, by reason of your sending them back, against their wills, for their *offensive behaviour*, expressed in a *general letter* from the Company there; (b) yet—for we likewise do consider that you are in a government newly formed, and want that assistance which the weight of such a business doth require—we may have leave to think it is possible some *indigested counsels have too suddenly been put in execution, which may have ill construction with the State here, and make us obnoxious to any adversary.* Let it therefore seem good unto you to be *very sparing in introducing any laws or commands which may render yourself or us distasteful to the State here, to which we must and will have an obsequious eye. And as we make it our care to have the Plantation so ordered as may be most to the honour of God and of our gracious Sovereign, who hath bestowed many large privileges and royal favours upon this Company, so we desire that all such as shall by word or deed do anything to detract from God's glory or his Majesty's honour, may be duly corrected, for their amendment and the terror of others.* And to that end, if you know anything which hath been spoken or done, either by the ministers (whom the Browns do seem tacitly to blame for some things uttered in their sermons or prayers) or any others, we require you, if any such there be, that you form due process against the offenders, and send it to us by the first, that we may, as our duty binds us, use means to have them duly punished.

"So not doubting but we have said enough, we shall repose ourselves upon your wisdom, and do rest

                                 "Your loving friends.

"To the Governor, Capt. Endicot."

(a) These innovations, I suppose, had reference principally to the formation of the Church at Salem, the adoption of a confession of faith and covenant by the people, and their election and ordination of the ministers. Endicot, we know, sympathized fully with the Separatists of New Plymouth.—*Note by the Editor of the Records.*

(b) This letter has always been missing.

4

the most explicit testimony by the Company of the King's kindness and generosity to them, as well as a statement of the clear understanding between the King and the Company as to the intentions and spirit of the Royal Charter, and which the Company in London expressed their determination to observe in good faith—a good faith which was invariably and even indulgently observed by both Charles the First and Second, but which was as constantly violated by the Government of Massachusetts Bay, as will appear hereafter from the transfer of the Charter there in 1630, to the cancelling of the Charter under James the Second, in 1687. Endicot, confident in his ability to prevent the transmission of any evidence to England that could sustain the statements of the Browns, paid no heed to the instructions of the Company, and persisted in his course of Church revolution and proscription.

The letter addressed to Higginson and Skelton was signed not only by the Governor, but by the chief members of the Company; and among others by John Winthrop, who took the Royal Charter to Massachusetts Bay, and there, as Governor, administered it by maintaining all that Endicot was alleged to have done, continued to proscribe the worship of the Church of England, allowed its members no elective franchise as well as no eligibility for office, and persecuted all who attempted to worship in any other form than that of the Church of Endicot, Higginson, and Skelton—a course in which he persevered until his energies began to fail; for Mr. Bancroft says: "The elder Winthrop had, I believe, relented before his death, and, it is said, had become weary of banishing heretics; the soul of the younger Winthrop [who withdrew from the intolerance of the Massachusetts Puritans, and was elected Governor of Connecticut] was incapable of harbouring a thought of intolerant cruelty; but the rugged Dudley was not mellowed by old age."*

The letter addressed to Higginson and Skelton expressed a hope that the report made in England as to their language and proceedings were "but shadows," but at the same time apprised them of their duty to vindicate their innocency or acknowledge and reform their misdeeds, declaring the favour of the Government to their Plantation, and their duty and determination not

* History of the United States, Vol. I., pp. 486, 487.

to abuse the confidence which the State had reposed in them. This letter is given entire in a note.*

Nothing can be more clear, from the letters addressed by the Company both to Endicot and the ministers Higginson and Skelton, that renunciation of the worship of the Church of England was at variance with the intentions and profession of all parties in granting and receiving the Royal Charter, and that the only defence set up in England of Endicot, Higginson, and Skelton was a positive denial that they had done so. Dudley himself, Deputy Governor, who went to Massachusetts Bay in the same fleet of eleven ships with Governor Winthrop, wrote to his patroness, the Countess of Lincoln, several months after his arrival, and in his letter, dated March 12, 1630, explicitly denies the existence of any such changes in their

---

* The Company's letter to the Ministers:

"REVEREND FRIENDS,—

"There are lately arrived here, being sent from the Governor, Mr. John Endicot, as men of faction and evil-conditioned, John and Samuel Brown, being brethren who since their arrival have raised rumours (as we hear) of divers scandalous and intemperate speeches passed from one or both of you in your public sermons and prayers in New England, as also of some innovations attempted by you. We have reason to hope that their reports are but slanders; partly, for your godly and quiet conditions are well known to some of us; as also, for that these men, your accusers, seem to be embittered against Captain Endicot for injuries which they have received from some of you there. Yet, for that we all know that the best advised may overshoot themselves, we have thought good to inform you of what we hear, and if you be innocent you may clear yourselves; or, if otherwise, you may be intreated to look back upon your miscarriage with repentance; or at least to notice that we utterly disallow any such passages, and must and will take order for the redress thereof, as shall become us. But hoping, as we said, of your unblamableness herein, we desire only that this may testify to you and others that we are tender of the least aspersion which, either directly or obliquely, may be cast upon the State here; to whom we owe so much duty, and from whom we have received so much favour in this Plantation where you reside. So with our love and due respect to your callings, we rest,

"Your loving friends,

"R. SALTONSTALL,   "THO. ADAMS,
"ISA JOHNSON,   "SYM WHITCOMBE,
"MATT. CRADOCK, Governor,   "WM. VASSAL,
"THOS. GOFFE, Deputy,   "WM. PYNCHION,
"GEO. HARWOOD, Treasurer,   "JOHN REVELL,
"JOHN WINTHROP,   "FRANCIS WEBB

"London, 16th October, 1629."

worship as had been alleged; that they had become "Brownists
[that is, Congregationalists] in religion," etc., and declaring all
such allegations to be "false and scandalous reports;" appealing
to their friends in England to "not easily believe that we are
so soon turned from the profession we so long have made at
home in our native land;" declaring that he knew "no one
person who came over with us last year to be altered in judgment or affection, either in ecclesiastical or civil respects, since
our coming here;" acknowledging the obligations of himself
and friends to the King for the royal kindness to them, and
praying his friends in England to "give no credit to such
malicious aspersions, but be more ready to answer for us than
we hear they have been." Dudley's own words are given in
note.* The only escape from the admission of Dudley's statements being utterly untrue is resort to a quibble which is
inconsistent with candour and honesty—namely, that the
Brownist or Congregational worship had been adopted by

* Extract from Deputy Governor Dudley's letter to the Countess of
Lincoln, dated November 12th, 1631 :

"To increase the heap of our sorrows, we received from our friends in
England, and by the reports of those who came hither in this ship [the
Charles] to abide with us (who were about twenty-six), that they who went
discontentedly from us last year, out of their evil affections towards us, have
raised many false and scandalous reports against us, affirming us to be
Brownists in religion, and ill affected to our State at home, and that these
vile reports have won credit with some who formerly wished us well. But
we do desire and cannot but hope that wise and impartial men will at length
consider that such malcontents have ever pursued this manner of casting
dirt, to make others seem as foul as themselves, and that our godly friends,
to whom we have been known, will not easily believe that we are so soon
turned from the profession we so long have made in our native country.
And for our further clearing, I truly affirm that I know no one person, who
came over with us last year, to be altered in judgment and affection, either
in ecclesiastical and civil respects, since our coming hither. But we do continue to pray daily for our Sovereign Lord the King, the Queen, the Prince,
the Royal blood, the Council and whole State, as duty binds us to do, and
reason persuades us to believe. For how ungodly and unthankful should
we be if we should not do thus, who came hither by virtue of his Majesty's
letters patent and under his gracious protection; under which shelter we
hope to live safely, and from whose kingdom and subjects we now have
received and hereafter expect relief. Let our friends therefore give no credit
to such malicious aspersions, but be more ready to answer for us than we
hear they have been." (Young's Chronicles, &c., pp. 331, 332.)

Endicot and his party before the arrival of Dudley; but the scope and evident design of his letter was to assure the Countess of Lincoln and his friends in England that no new Church worship had been established at Massachusetts Bay, when the reverse must have been known to Dudley, and when he, in support of the new Brownist or Congregational worship, became a fierce persecutor, even to old age, of all who would not conform to it; for, as Mr. Bancroft says, "the rugged soul of Dudley was not mellowed by old age."

But while Dudley, in Massachusetts, was denying to his English friends the existence of ecclesiastical changes there which all history now declares to have taken place, the "Patriarch of Dorchester," the father of the whole enterprise—the Rev. John White, a conformist clergyman of the Church of England, even under Archbishop Laud—wrote and published a pamphlet called "The Planters' Plea,"* in which he denied also that any ecclesiastical changes, as alleged, had taken place in the Massachusetts Plantation, and denounces the authors of such allegations in no measured terms. This pamphlet contains a "Brief Relation of the Occasion of the Planting of this Colony." After referring to the third, or "great emigration under Winthrop,"† the author proceeds:

"This is an impartial though brief relation of the occasion of planting the colony; the particulars whereof, if they could be entertained, were clear enough to any indifferent judgment, that

---

* "'The Planters' Plea' was printed in London in 1630, soon after the sailing of Winthrop's fleet [with Dudley]. It has generally been ascribed to the Rev. John White, of Dorchester, England. 'The Planters' Plea' appears to have been unknown to our historians. Neither Mather, Prince, Hutchinson, Bancroft, nor Graham make any allusion to it." (Young's Chronicles of the First Planters of the Colony of Massachusetts, from 1623 to 1636, pp. 15, 16, in a note.)

† The *first* emigration under the authority of the Massachusetts Company was that under "Master Endicot, who was sent over Governor, assisted with a few men, and arriving in safety there in September, 1628, and uniting his own men with those who were formerly planted there into one body, they made up in all not much above fifty or sixty persons."

The second emigration was under Higginson, who says: "We brought with us about two hundred passengers and planters more," arriving in June, 1629.

The third, or "great emigration," was under Winthrop, arriving in May, 1630.

the suspicious and scandalous reports raised upon these gentlemen and their friends (as if, under the colour of planting a colony,
they intended to raise a seminary of faction and separation), are
nothing than the fruits of jealousy of some distempered mind
or, which is worse, perhaps savour of a desperate malicious plot
of men ill affected to religion, endeavouring, by casting the
undertakers into the jealousy of the State, to shut them out of
those advantages which otherwise they might expect from the
countenance of authority. Such men would be entreated to
forbear that base and unchristian course of traducing persons
under these odious names of Separatists, and enemies of Church
and State, for fear lest their own tongues fall upon themselves
by the justice of His hand who will not fail to clear the innocency of the just, and to cast back into the bosom of every
slanderer the filth that he rakes up to throw into other men's
faces. As for men of more indifferent and better minds, they
would be seriously advised to beware of entertaining or admitting,
much more countenancing and crediting, such uncharitable persons as discover themselves by their carriage, and that in this
particular to be men ill affected towards the work itself, if not
to religion, at which it aims, and consequently unlikely to report
any truths of such as undertake it."*

This language is very severe, not to say scurrilous; but it is
the style of all Puritan historians and writers in regard to those
who complained of the Puritan Government of Massachusetts.
Not even Messrs. Bancroft and Palfrey have thought it unworthy
of their eloquent pages. But imputation of motives and
character is not argument, is most resorted to for want of argument, much less is it a refutation of statements now universally
known to be true. The venerable author of this "Planters'
Plea" denied in indignant terms that Endicot and his friends
had become "Separatists" or "enemies of the Church" (he had
doubtless been so assured); the very thing in which Endicot
gloried—setting up a "Separatist" worship, forbidding the worship
of "the Church," and banishing its members who resolved to
continue the use of its Prayer Book, in public or in private.

This, however, is not all. Not only did the Company, in their
letters to Endicot, Higginson, and Skelton, disdain to forbid any-

* Young's Chronicles, &c., pp. 15, 16.

thing like abolishing the Church of England and setting up a
new Church, and the use of language offensive to their Sovereign
and the Established Church; not only were there the most
positive denials on both sides of the Atlantic that anything of
the kind had been done by Endicot; but on the appointment of
Winthrop to supersede Endicot as Governor, and on his departure
with a fleet of eleven ships and three hundred "Adventurers"
and "Planters," as they were called, a formal and affectionate
address to their "Fathers and Brethren of the Church of
England" was published by Winthrop from his ship *Arabella*,
disclaiming any acts of some among them (evidently alluding to
what Endicot had been alleged to have done) hostile to the
Church of England, declaring their obligation and attachment
to it, their prayers for it, and entreating the prayers of its
members for the success of their undertaking. This address is
said to have been written by the Rev. John White, the "Patriarch of Dorchester," and prime mover of the whole Plantation
enterprise. It is an imputation upon the integrity of the author,
and upon all parties concerned in the address, and absurd in
itself, to suppose that the prayers of the Church in England
were solicited with a view to the abolition of its worship in
Massachusetts, and the establishment there of a "Separatist"
Church. This address—not to be found in any modern history
of the Massachusetts Puritans—speaks for itself, and is given
in a note as originally published.* It will be recollected that

* This address is called "The humble Request of his Majesties loyall subjects, the Governour and the Company late gone for New England; to the
rest of their Brethren in and of the Church of England," and is as follows:
    "REVEREND FATHERS AND BRETHREN,—
    "The generall rumor of this solemne enterprise, wherein ourselves, with
others, through the providence of the Almightie, are engaged, as it may spare
us the labour of imparting our occasion unto you, so it gives us the more
incouragement to strengthen ourselves by the procurement of the prayers and
blessings of the Lord's faithful servants: For which end wee are bold to have
recourse unto you, as those whom God hath placed nearest his throne of
mercy; which, as it affords you the more opportunitie, so it imposeth the
greater bond upon you to intercede for his people in all their straights. We
beseech you, therefore, by the mercies of the Lord Jesus, to consider us as
your Brethren, standing in very great need of your helpe, and earnestly
imploring it. And howsoever your charitie may have met with some occasion
of discouragement through the misreport of our intentions, or through the
disaffection or indiscretion of some of us, or rather amongst us, for wee are

Winthrop and the other signers of this address had the Royal Charter with them, and now constituted the "principals" of the

not of those that dreame of perfection in this world ; yet we desire you would be pleased to take notice of the principals and body of our Company, as those who esteeme it an honour to call the Church of England, from whence we rise, our deare Mother, and cannot part from our native countrie, where she specially resideth, without much sadness of heart and many tears in our eyes, ever acknowledging that such hope and part as we have obtained in the common salvation, we have received it in her bosome, and suckt it from her breasts : Wee leave it not, therefore, as loathing the milk wherewith wee were nourished there ; but blessing God for the parentage and education, as members·of the same body shall always rejoice in her good, and unfeignedly grieve for any sorrow that shall ever betide her ; and, while we have breath, sincerely desire and endeavour the continuance and abundance of her welfare, with the enlargement of her bounds in the kingdome of Christ Jesus.

"Be pleased, therefore, Reverend Fathers and Brethren, to helpe forward this worke now in hand ; which, if it prosper, you shall be the more glorious ; howsoever, your judgment is with the Lord, and your reward with your God. It is an usuall and laudable exercise of your charity to recommend to the prayers of your congregations the necessities and straights of your private neighbours. Doe the like for a Church springing out of your owne bowels. Wee conceive much hope that this remembrance of us, if it be frequent and fervent, will bee a most prosperous gale in our sailes, and provide such a passage and welcome for us from the God of the whole earth, as both we which shall finde it, and yourselves with the rest of our friends who shall heare of it, shall be much enlarged to bring in such daily returns of thanksgivings, as the specialties of his Providence and Goodnes may justly challenge at all our hands. You are not ignorant that the Spirit of God stirred up the Apostle Paul to make continuall mention of the Church of Philippi (which was a colonie of Rome) ; let the same Spirit, we beseech you, put you in mind, that are the Lord's Remembrancers, to pray for us without ceasing (who are a weake Colony from yourselves), making continuall request for us to God in all your prayers.

"What we entreat of you, that are the ministers of God, that we crave at the hands of all the rest of our Brethren, that they would at no time forget us in their private solicitations at the throne of grace.

"If any there be, who, through want of clear intelligence of our course, or tendernesses of affection towards us, cannot conceive so well of our way as we could desire, we would entreat such not to despise us, nor to desert us in their prayers and affections ; but to consider rather that they are so much the more bound to expresse the bowels of their compassion towards us ; remembering alwaies that both Nature and Grace doth binde us to relieve and rescue, with our utmost and speediest power, such as are deare unto us, when we conceive them to be running uncomfortable hazards.

"What goodness you shall extend to us, in this or any other Christian kindnesse, wee, your Brethren in Christ Jesus, shall labour to repay, in what

Company, whose authority in England now ceased, and was henceforth to be exercised at Massachusetts Bay. They beg that the "disaffection or indiscretion" of some of the Company —evidently alluding to what Endicot was reported to have done —might not be imputed to "the principals and body of the Company." Their words are, addressing their Fathers and Brethren of the Church of England: "And howsoever your charity may have met with some occasional discouragement through the misreport of our intentions, or through the disaffection or indiscretion of some of us, or rather amongst us (for we are not of those who dream of perfection in this world); yet we desire you would look at the *principals and body of* our *Company, as those who esteem it an honour to call the Church of England, whence we rise, our dear Mother,"* &c.

It is passing strange that any man who respects himself could say, in the face of these words and of the whole address, that Mr. Winthrop and the "principals and body of the Company" did not profess to be members of the Church of England, and did not assure their "Fathers and Brethren in England" of their intention to remain so, and implore the prayers of their Fathers and Brethren for their success. No darker stigma could be inflicted upon the character of Winthrop and his Company, than the assertion that at the very moment of making and publishing these professions in England they intended to extinguish their "dear Mother" in Massachusetts, and banish every one from their Plantation who should use her Prayer Book, or worship as the "dear Mother" worshipped. Yet such is the theory, or fallacy, of some Puritan writers.

dutie wee are or shall be able to performe ; promising, so farre as God shall enable us, to give him no rest on your behalfes, wishing our heads and hearts may be as fountains of tears for your everlasting welfare, when wee shall be in our poore cottages in the wildernesse, over-shadowed with the spirit of supplication, through the manifold necessities and tribulations which may, not altogether unexpectedly nor we hope unprofitably, befall us.

"And so commending you to the Grace of God in Christ, we shall ever rest

"Your assured Friends and Brethren."

Signed by JOHN WINTHROP, *Governor* ;

Charles Fines, George Philips, Richard Saltonstall, Isaac Johnson, Thomas Dudley, William Coddington, &c., and was dated " From Yarmouth, aboard the *Arabella,* April 7, 1630."

It has also been pretended that there was no Church of
England in Massachusetts, and therefore the planters were free
to set up what form of worship they pleased. It may be asked
in reply, what makes a Church but the presence of members of
it ? An early Christian writer says that "wherever there are
two or three believers there is a Church." But were not Endicot,
and Higginson, and Skelton as much members of the Church of
England on their arrival at Massachusetts Bay as when they left
England ? And were not the two latter as much clergymen of
the Church of England when they met Endicot at Naumkeag,
or Salem, as when they engaged with the Company in England
to go out as ministers to the new Plantation ? Does crossing
the sea change or annihilate the churchmanship of the missionary, or the passenger, or the emigrant ? There may not be a
place of worship, or a minister, but there are the members of the
Church. Is a missionary or agent of a Committee or Board of a
particular Church in London, no longer a member of that Church
when he reaches the foreign land to which he is sent because he
finds no Church worship there, much less if he finds members of
his own Church already there ? Yet such are the pretences on
which some Puritan writers, and even historians, attempt to
justify the conduct of Endicot, Higginson, and Skelton ! But, be
it remembered, I make no objection to their renouncing their
Church, and establishing for themselves and those who chose to
follow them, a new Church confession and worship. The points
of discussion are: 1. Was it honest for them to do so without
consulting those who employed and settled them there, and provided for their religious instruction by clergymen of the Church
of England ? 2. Was it right or lawful, and was it not contrary
to the laws of England, for them to abolish the worship of the
Church of England and banish its members from the Plantation,
as settlers, for continuing to worship according to the Church of
England ? 3. And can they be justified for denying to their
friends in England, and their friends denying to the public and
to the King, on their behalf and on their authority, what they
had done, and what all the world now knows they had done, at
Massachusetts Bay ? 4. And finally, was it not a breach of
faith to their Sovereign, from whom they had received their
Charter, and, as they themselves acknowledged, most kind treatment, to commence their settlement by abolishing the established

religion which both the King and they professed when the Charter was granted, and when they left England, and banish from the territory which the King had granted them all settlers who would not renounce the form of worship established in England from the Reformation, and adopt a new form of worship, which was not then lawful in England?

The foregoing pages bear witness that I have not taken a sentence from any writer adverse to the Puritans. I have adhered to their own statements in their own words, and as printed in their Records. Their eloquent apologist and defender, Mr. Bancroft, says: "The Charter confers on the colonists the rights of English subjects; it does not confer on them new and greater rights. On the contrary, they are strictly forbidden to make laws or ordinances repugnant to the laws or statutes of the realm of England. The express concession of power to administer the oath of supremacy demonstrates that universal toleration was not designed; and the freemen of the Corporation, it should be remembered, were not at that time Separatists. Even Higginson, and Hooker, and Cotton were still ministers of the Church of England."*

From this accumulation of evidence—which might be greatly increased—I think it is as clear as day that the abolition of the worship of the Church of England, and the establishment of a new form of worship, and a new confession of faith, and a new ordination to the ministry at Massachusetts Bay in 1629, was a violation of the Charter, an insult to the King, and a breach of faith with him, notwithstanding his acknowledged kindness to

---

* History of the United States, Vol. I., p. 273.

In a note, Mr. Bancroft says :—"The Editor of Winthrop did me the kindness to read to me *unpublished letters* which are in his possession, and *which prove that the Puritans in England were amazed as well as alarmed at the boldness of their brethren in Massachusetts." (Ib.)*

Why have these letters remained unpublished, when every line from any opposed to Endicot and his party, however private and confidential, has been published to the world? The very fact that all the letters of Endicot and the Browns, and of the Puritans who wrote on the subject, according to Mr. Bancroft, have been suppressed, affords very strong ground to believe that the Massachusetts Puritans violated the acknowledged objects of the Charter and the terms of their settlement, and committed the first breach of faith to their Sovereign, and inculcated that spirit and commenced that series of acts which resulted in the dismemberment of the British Empire in America.

them, and a renunciation of all the professions which were made by the Company in England.

This was the first seed sown, which germinated for one hundred and thirty years, and then ripened in the American Revolution; it was the opening wedge which shivered the transatlantic branches from the parent stock. It was the consciousness of having abused the Royal confidence and broken faith with their Sovereign, of having acted contrary to the laws and statutes of England, that led the Government of Massachusetts Bay to resist and evade all inquiries into their proceedings—to prevent all evidence from being transmitted to England as to their proceedings, and to punish as criminals all who should appeal to England against any of their proceedings—to claim, in short, independence and immunity from all responsibility to the Crown for anything that they did or might do. Had Endicot and his party not done what they knew to be contrary to the loyal Charter and the laws of England, they would have courted inquiry, that the light of their fair and loyal acts might be manifest to all England, in refutation of all statements made against them. Had the Browns and their Church friends been permitted to worship after the manner of their fathers and of their childhood, while Endicot and his converts elected to worship in a new manner, there would have been no cause of collision, and no spirit of distrust and hostility between the Massachusetts settlement and the King, any more than there was between either Charles the First or Second, and the settlements and separate Governments of Plymouth, Rhode Island, or Connecticut. But Endicot, in the spirit of tyranny and intolerance, would allow no liberty of worship not of his own establishment; and to maintain which in the spirit of proscription and persecution, caused all the disputes with the parent Government and all the persecutions and bloodshed on account of religion in Massachusetts which its Government inflicted in subsequent years, in contradistinction to the Governments of Plymouth, Rhode Island, Connecticut, and even Maryland.*

---

* The General Assembly of the Province of Maryland passed an Act in 1649 containing the following provision:

"No person whatsoever, in this province, professing to believe in Jesus Christ, shall from henceforth be anywise troubled or molested for his or her

PART IV.

It is well known that the Puritans in England objected to the ceremonies enforced by Laud, as "corrupt and superstitious," and many ministers were ejected from their benefices for nonconformity to them; but none of the nonconformists who refused compliance with such "corrupt and superstitious" ceremonies ever professed that the *polity* and *worship* of the Church was "corrupt and superstitious," and should therefore be renounced, much less abolished, as did Endicot and his party at Massachusetts Bay, and that twenty years before the death of Charles the First and the usurpation of Cromwell.*

religion, or in the free exercise thereof, or any way compelled to the belief or exercise of any other religion against his or her consent."

Mr. Bancroft says : "Christianity was made the law of the land [in Maryland], and no preference was given to any sect, and equality in religious rights, no less than civil freedom, was assured.

* It appears that the cause of dissatisfaction among the Puritan clergy of the Church, and of the emigration of many of them and of their lay friends to New England, was not the Prayer Book worship of the Church (abolished by Endicot at Massachusetts Bay), but the enforced reading of the Book of Sports, in connection with "the rigorous proceedings to enforce ceremonies;"

It might be confidently expected that Mr. Winthrop, after an address of loyalty and affection to his "Fathers and Brethren of the Church of England," from the very ship on which he left his native land, would, on his arrival at Massachusetts Bay and assuming its government, have rectified the wrongs of Endicot and his party, and have secured at least freedom of worship to the children of his "dear Mother." But he seems to have done nothing of the kind; he seems to have fallen in with the very proceedings of Endicot which had been disclaimed by him in his address to his "Fathers and Brethren of the Church of England," on embarking at Yarmouth for his new government. American historians are entirely silent on the subject. It is very clear that Mr. Winthrop had correspondence with his English friends on these matters, as intimated by Mr. Bancroft in words quoted on page 59. If this suppressed correspondence were published, it would doubtless show how it was that Mr. Winthrop, like Endicot, and to the astonishment of his Puritan friends in England, changed from and suppressed the worship of his "dear Mother" Church, on changing from one side of the Atlantic to the other. Mr. Hutchinson, referring to the address of Governor Winthrop to his "Fathers and Brethren of the Church of England," to remove suspicions and misconstructions, says: "This paper has occasioned a dispute, whether the first settlers in Massachusetts were of the Church of England or not. However problematical it may be what they were while they remained in England, they left no room to doubt after they arrived in America."*

for Rushworth, Vol. II., Second Part, page 460, Anno 1636, quoted by the American antiquarian, Hazard, Vol. I., p. 440, states as follows :

"The severe censures in the *Star Chamber*, and the greatness of the fines and the rigorous proceedings to impose ceremonies, the suspending and silencing of multitudes of ministers, for not reading in the Church the Book of Sports to be exercised on the Lord's Day, caused many of the nation, both ministers and others, to sell their estates, and set sail for New England (a late Plantation in America), where they held a Plantation by patent from the Crown."

* History of the Colony of Massachusetts Bay, Vol. I., pp. 19, 20. It appears, however, that within a month after Mr. Winthrop's arrival at Massachusetts Bay, both he and the Deputy-Governor Dudley joined the new Endicot and Higginson Church ; for Mr. Holmes in his Annals says : "A fleet of 14 sail, with men, women and children, and provisions, having been prepared early in the year to make a firm plantation in New England,

But though the Editor of Winthrop has suppressed the letters which would explain how Mr. Winthrop changed from Episcopalianism to Congregationalism on his assuming the government of Massachusetts Bay, we are at no loss to know the character of his proceedings, since, in less than a year after his arrival there, the worship of his "dear Mother" Church not only continued to be suppressed, but its members were deprived of the privilege of even becoming "freemen" or electors in the new "Commonwealth," as it forthwith begun to call itself, and the privileges of citizenship were restricted to members of the new established Congregational Churches; for on May 18th, 1631, the newly organized Legislature, or "General Court," as it was called, enacted that, "To the end the body of the commons may be preserved of honest and good men, it was ordered and agreed that for time to come, no man shall be admitted to the freedom of this body politic but such as are members of some of the churches within the limits of the same."

Mr. Bancroft, after quoting this extraordinary and unprecedented enactment, remarks—"The principle of universal suffrage was the usage of Virginia; Massachusetts, resting for its defence on its unity and its enthusiasm, gave all power to the select band of religious votaries, into which the avenues could be opened only by the elders [ministers]. The elective franchise was thus confined to a small proportion of the whole population, and the Government rested on an essentially aristocratic foundation. But it was not an aristocracy of wealth; the polity was a sort of theocracy; the servant of the bondman, if he were a member of the Church, might be a freeman of the Company."— "It was the reign of the Church; it was a commonwealth of the chosen people in covenant with God."*

12 of the ships arrived early in July [1630] at Charlestown. In this fleet came Governor Winthrop, Deputy Governor Dudley, and several other gentlemen of wealth and quality. In this fleet came about 840 passengers." "On the 30th of July, a day of solemn prayer and fasting was kept at Charlestown; when Governor Winthrop, Deputy Governor Dudley, and Mr. Wilson first entered into Church covenant; and now was laid the foundation of the Church of Charlestown, and the first Church in Boston. (Vol. I., pp. 202, 203.)

* History of the United States, Vol. I., pp. 390, 391.

Referring to this order, May 18, 1631—not a year after Mr. Winthrop's arrival—Mr. Hutchinson says: "None may now be a freeman of that Company unless he be a Church member among them. None have voice in

It thus appears that the new Congregationalists of Massachusetts were far behind the old Episcopalians of Virginia in the first principle of civil liberty; for while among the latter the Episcopal Church alone was the recognized Church, the elective franchise was not restricted to the members of that Church, but was universal; while in the new Government of Massachusetts, among the new Puritan Congregationalists, none but a Congregational Church member could be a citizen elector, and none could be a Church member without the consent and recommendation of the minister; and thus the Commonwealth of Massachusetts Bay, at the very beginning, became, in the words of Mr. Bancroft, "the reign of the Church"—not indeed of the Church of England, but of the new Congregational Church established by joining of hands and covenant around the well-pump of Naumkeag—then christened Salem.

The New England historians assure us that on the settlement of the Puritans at Massachusetts Bay, the connection between Church and State ceased. It is true that the connection of the Church of England with the State ceased there; it is true that there was not, in the English sense of the phrase, connection between the Church and State there; for there was no State but the Church; the "Commonwealth" was not the government of free citizens by universal suffrage, or even of property citizens, but was "the reign of the Church," the members of which, according to Mr. Bancroft himself, constituted but "a small proportion of the whole population"—this great majority (soon five-sixths) of the population being mere helots, bound to do the work and pay the taxes imposed upon them by the "reigning Church," but denied all eligibility to any office in the "Commonwealth," or even the elective franchise of a citizen! It was indeed such a "connection between Church and State" as had never existed, and has never existed to this day, in any

the election of Governor, or Deputy, or assistants—none are to be magistrates, officers, or jurymen, grand or petit, but freemen. The ministers give their votes in all the elections of magistrates. Now the most of the persons at New England are not admitted to their Church, and therefore are not freemen; and when they come to be tried there, be it for life or limb, name or estate, or whatsoever, they must be tried and judged too by those of the Church, who are, in a sort, their adversaries. How equal that hath been or may be, some by experience do and others may judge."—In a note, quoted from the lawyer Lichford. Vol. I., p. 26.

Protestant country. "The reign of the Church"—the small minority over the great majority of the "Commonwealth;" and this system of "the reign of the Church" over the State—of the government of a Church minority of one-sixth over a whole population of five-sixths—continued for sixty years (as will hereafter appear), until suppressed by a second Royal Charter, which placed all citizens upon equal footing before the law, and in respect to the elective franchise. Though the Congregational Puritans of Massachusetts Bay may have been the fathers of American independence of England, they were far from being the fathers or even precursors of American liberty. They neither understood nor practised the first principles of civil and religious liberty, or even the rights of British subjects as then understood and practised in England itself.

It is admitted on all sides, that, according to the express words of the Royal Charter, the planter emigrants of Massachusetts Bay should enjoy all "the privileges of British subjects," and that no law or resolution should be enacted there "contrary to the laws and statutes of England." Was it not, therefore, perfectly natural that members of the Church of England emigrating to Massachusetts Bay, and wishing to continue and worship as such after their arrival there, should complain to their Sovereign in Council, the supreme authority of the State, that, on their arrival in Massachusetts, they found themselves deprived of the privilege of worshipping as they had worshipped in England, and found themselves subject to banishment the moment they thus worshipped? And furthermore, when, unless they actually joined one of the new Congregational Churches, first established at Massachusetts Bay, August 6th, 1629, five months after granting the Royal Charter (March 4th, 1629), they could enjoy none of the rights of British subjects, they must have been more or less than men had they not complained, and loudly complained, to the highest authority that could redress their grievances, of their disappointments, and wrongs as British subjects emigrating to Massachusetts. And could the King in Council refuse to listen to such complaints, and authorize inquiry into their truth or falsehood, without violating rights which, even at that period of despotic government, were regarded as sacred to even the humblest British subject? And the leading complainants were men of the most respectable position in

5

England, and who had investments in New England—not only
the Messrs. Brown, but Capt. John Mason and Sir Ferdinand
Gorges, who complained that the Massachusetts Company had
encroached upon the territory held by them under Royal
Charter—territory which afterwards constituted portions of New
Hampshire and Maine.   Were the King and Privy Council to be
precluded from inquiring into such complaints?   Yet New
England historians assail the complainants for stating their
grievances, and the King and Council for listening to them even
so far as to order an inquiry into them.   The petitioners are
held up as slanderers and enemies, and the King and Council
represented as acting tyrannically and as infringing the rights
of the Massachusetts Puritans, and seeking the destruction of
their liberties and enterprise even by inquiring into complaints
made.   The actual proceedings of the King in Council prove
the injustice and falsity of such insinuations and statements.

The pretence set up in Massachusetts was that the authority
of the Local Government was *supreme;* that to appeal from it to
the King himself was sedition and treason ;* and the defence
set up in England was that the allegations were untrue, and
that the Massachusetts Corporation was acting loyally according
to the provisions of the Charter and for the interests of the
King.   The account of these proceedings before the King's
Privy Council is given in a note from Mr. Palfrey himself.†

---

* Examples of such pretensions and imputations will be given in future
pages.

† The malcontents had actually prevailed to have their complaints entertained by the Privy Council. "Among many truths misrepeated," writes
Winthrop, "accusing us to intend rebellion, to have cast off our allegiance,
and to be wholly separate from the Church and laws of England, that our
ministers and people did continually rail against the State, Church, and
Bishops there, etc." Saltonstall, Humphrey, Cradock (Ratcliff's master)
appeared before the Committee of the Council in the Company's behalf, and
had the address or good fortune to vindicate their clients, so that on the termination of the affair, the King said *"he would have them severely punished who
did abuse his Governor and Plantation ;"* and from members of the Council it
was learned, says Winthrop, *"that his Majesty did not intend to impose the
ceremonies of the Church of England upon us, for that it was considered that
it was freedom from such things that made the people come over to us ; and it
was credibly informed to the Council that this country would be beneficial to
England for masts, cordage, etc., if the Sound* [the passage to the Baltic]

In regard to these proceedings, the reader's attention is directed to the following facts: 1. The principal charges of the complainants were denied—resting to be proved by parties that must be called from that place [Massachusetts], which required long, expensive time, "and were in due time further to be inquired into;" and the Massachusetts Corporation took effectual precaution against any documentary evidence being brought thence, or "parties" to come, unless at the expense of their all, even should the complainants be able and willing to incur the expense of bringing them to England. The Privy Council therefore deferred further inquiry into these matters, and in the meantime gave the accused the benefit of the doubt and postponement. 2. The nominal Governor of the Company in England, Mr. Cradock, Sir R. Saltonstall, &c., "appeared before the Committee of Council on the Company's behalf, and had the address on good fortune to vindicate their clients," &c. This they did so effectually as to prejudice the King and Council against the complainants, and excite their sympathies in favour of the Company, the King saying "he would have them severely punished who did abuse his Governor and Plantations." But the question arises, And by what sort of "address or good fortune" were Messrs. Cradock and Company able to vindicate their clients

---

should be debarred." "The reason for dismissing the complaint was alleged in the Order adopted by Council to that effect: '*Most of the things informed being denied, and resting to be proved by parties that must be called from that place, which required a long expense of time,* and at the present their Lordships finding that the adventurers were upon the despatch of men, victuals, and merchandise for that place, all which would be at a stand if the adventurers should have discouragement, or take suspicion that the State there had no good opinion of that Plantation,—their Lordships not laying the fault, or fancies (if any *be,*) *of some particular men upon the general government, or principal adventurers,* which in *due time is* further to be inquired into, have thought fit in the meantime to declare that *the appearances were so fair, and the hopes so great, that the country would prove both beneficial to this country and to the particular adventurers, as that the adventurers had cause to go on cheerfully with their undertakings, and rest assured, if things were carried as was pretended* when the patents were granted, and accordingly as by the patents is appointed, his Majesty would not only maintain the liberties and privileges heretofore granted, but supply anything further that might tend to the good government of the place, and prosperity and comfort of his people there."— Palfrey's History of New England, Vol. I., Chap. ix., pp. 364, 365.

"to the King's satisfaction and their complete triumph?" Must it not have been by denying the charges which all the world now knows to have been true? Must it not have been by appealing to the address of Mr. Winthrop and Company to their "Fathers and Brethren of the Church of England," declaring their undying attachment to their "dear Mother?" and also by appealing to the letter of Deputy Governor Dudley to the Countess of Lincoln, declaring in 1630 that no such Church innovations as had been alleged had taken place at Massachusetts Bay? Must it not have been by their assuring the King's Council that the worship of the Church of England had not been abolished in Massachusetts, much less had any one been banished thence for continuing to worship according to the Prayer Book of that Church? Must it not have been by their declaring that they were faithfully and loyally carrying out the intentions and provisions of the Charter, according to the statutes and laws of England? 3. Let it be further observed that the King, according to the statements of the very party who was imposing upon his confidence in their sincerity, that throughout this proceeding he evinced the same good-will to the Massachusetts Bay colony that he had done from the granting of the Charter, and which they had repeatedly acknowledged in their communications with each other, as quoted above. Yet the Puritan historians ascribe to Charles jealous hostility to their colony from the commencement, and on that ground endeavour to justify the deceptive conduct of the Company, both in England and at Massachusetts Bay. Had Charles or his advisers cherished any hostile feelings against the Company, there was now a good opportunity of showing it. Had he been disposed to act the despot towards them, he might at once, on a less plausible pretext than that now afforded him, have cancelled his Charter and taken the affairs of the colony into his own hands.

It is a singular concurrence of circumstances, and on which I leave the reader to make his own comments, that while the representatives of the Company were avowing to the King the good faith in which their clients were carrying out his Majesty's royal intentions in granting the Charter, they at that very time were not allowing a single Planter to worship as the King worshipped, and not one who desired so to worship to enjoy the privilege of a British subject, either to vote or even to remain in the colony.   As Mr. Bancroft says in the American, but not in the English edition of his History, men "were banished because they were Churchmen.   Thus was Episcopacy first professed in Massachusetts, and thus was it exiled.   The blessings of the promised land were to be kept for Puritan dissenters."

But while the King and Privy Council were showering kindness and offers of further help, if needed, to advance the Plantation, believing their statements "that things were carried there as was pretended when the patents were granted," complaints could not fail to reach England of the persecution of members of the Church of England, and of the disfranchisement of all Planters who would not join the Congregational Church, in spite of the efforts of the dominant party in Massachusetts to intercept and stifle them; and it at length came to the knowledge of the King and Privy Council that the Charter itself had been, as it was supposed, "surreptitiously" carried from England to Massachusetts, new councillors appointed, and the whole government set up at Massachusetts Bay instead of being administered in England, as had been intended when the Charter was granted. This had been kept a profound secret for nearly four years; but now came to light in 1634.

It has been contended that this transfer of the Charter was lawful, and was done in accordance with the legal opinion of an able lawyer, Mr. John White, one of the party to the transfer. I enter not into the legal question; the more important question is, Was it honourable?   Was it loyal?   Was it according to the intention of the King in granting it?   Was there any precedent, and has there ever been one to this day, for such a proceeding? And when they conceived the idea of transferring the management of the Company from London to Massachusetts, and Mr. Winthrop and his friends refused to emigrate except on the condition of such transfer of the Charter, did not fairness and duty dictate application to the King, who granted the Charter, for permission to transfer it as the best means of promoting the original objects of it?   And is there not reason to believe that their application would have been successful, from the kind conduct of the King and Privy Council towards them, as stated above by themselves, when complaints were made against them? Was their proceeding straightforward?   Was not the secrecy of it suspicious, and calculated to excite suspicion, when, after more

than three years of secrecy, the act became known to the King
and Privy Council ?*

* The Congregational Society of Boston has published, in 1876, a new book
in justification of the "Banishment of Roger Williams from the Massachusetts Plantation," by the Rev. Dr. Henry M. Dexter, of Boston. It is a book
of intense bitterness against Roger Williams, and indeed everything English ;
but his account of the origin and objects of the Massachusetts Charter suggests,
stronger than language can express, the presumption and lawlessness of Endicot's
proceedings in establishing a new Church and abolishing an old one ; and Dr.
Dexter's account of the removal of the Charter, and its secrecy, is equally
suggestive. It is as follows :
"Let me here repeat and emphasize that it may be remembered by and
by that this 'Dorchester Company,' originally founded on the transfer of a
portion of the patent of Gorges, and afterwards enlarged and re-authorized
by the Charter of Charles the First, as the 'Governor and Company of Massachusetts Bay,' was in its beginning, and in point of fact, neither more nor less
than a private corporation chartered by the Government for purposes of
fishing, real estate improvement, and general commerce, for which it was to
pay the Crown a fifth part of all precious metals which it might unearth. It
was then more than this only in the same sense as the egg, new-laid, is the
full-grown fowl, or the acorn the oak. It was not yet a State. It was not,
even in the beginning, in the ordinary sense, a colony. It was a plantation
with a strong religious idea behind it, on its way to be a colony and a state.
In the *original intent*, the Governor and General Court, and therefore the
Government, *were to be and abide in England.* When, in 1628, Endicot and
his little party had been sent over to Salem, his authority was expressly
declared to be 'in subordination to the Company here' [that is, in London].
And it was only when Cradock [the first Governor of the Company] found
that so many practical difficulties threatened all proceedings upon that basis,
as to make it unlikely that Winthrop, and Saltonstall, and Johnson, and
Dudley, and other men whose co-operation was greatly to be desired, would
not consent to become partners in the enterprise unless a radical change were
made in that respect, that he proposed and the Company consented, 'for the
advancement of the Plantation, the inducing and encouraging persons of
worth and quality to transplant themselves and families thither, and for other
weighty reasons therein contained, to transfer the government of the Plantation to those that shall inhabit there,' &c. It was even a grave question of
law whether, under the terms of the Charter, this transfer were possible."
* * "They took the responsibility—so quietly, however, that the Home
Government seem to have remained in ignorance of the fact for more than
four years thereafter." (pp. 12, 13.)
In a note Dr. Dexter says : "I might illustrate by the Hudson Bay
Company, which existed into our time with its original Charter—strongly
resembling that of the Massachusetts Company—and which has always been
rather a corporation for trade charterers in England than a colony of England
on American soil." (*Ib.*, p. 12.)

The complainants against the Company in 1632, who found themselves so completely overmatched before the Privy Council by the denials, professions, and written statements produced by Mr. Cradock, Sir R. Saltonstall, and others, could not but feel exasperated when they knew that their complaints were well-founded; and they doubtless determined to vindicate the truth and justice of them at the first opportunity. That opportunity was not long delayed. The discovery that the Charter and government of the Company had been secretly transferred from London to Massachusetts Bay excited suspicion and curiosity; rumors and complaints of the proscriptions and injustice of the Colonial Government began to be whispered on all sides; appeal was again made to the King in Council; and the further inquiry indicated in the proceedings of the Privy Council two years before, was decided upon; a Royal Commission was appointed to inquire into these and all other complaints from the colonies, and redress the wrongs if found to exist; the appointment of a Governor-General over all the New England colonies, to see justice done to all parties, was contemplated.

The complainants against the conduct of the government of Endicot and Winthrop are represented by their historians as a few individuals of malicious feelings and more than doubtful character; but human nature at Massachusetts Bay must have been different from itself in all civilized countries, could it have been contented or silent when the rights of citizenship were denied, as Mr. Bancroft himself says, to " by far the larger proportion of the whole population," and confined to the members of a particular denomination, when the only form of worship then legalized in England was proscribed, and its members banished from the land claimed as the exclusive possession of Puritan dissenters. The most inquisitorial and vigilant efforts of the Local Government to suppress the trans-mission of information to England, and punish complainants,

It is evident from the Charter that the original design of it was to constitute *a corporation in England* like that of the East India and other great Companies, with powers to settle plantations within the limits of the territory, under such forms of government and magistracy as should be fit and necessary. The first step in sending out Mr. Endicot, and appointing him a Council, and giving him commission, instructions, etc., was agreeable to this constitution of the Charter. (Hutchinson's History of Massachusetts Bay, Vol. I., pp. 12, 13.)

could not prevent the grievances of the proscribed and oppressed being wafted to England, and commanding attention, and especially in connection with the startling fact now first discovered, that the Royal Charter had been removed from England, and a government under its authority set up at Massachusetts Bay.

Mr. Bancroft ascribes the complaints on these subjects as originating in "revenge," and calls them "the clamours of the malignant," and as amounting to nothing but "marriages celebrated by civil magistrates," and "the system of Colonial Church discipline;" confined, as he himself says elsewhere, "the elective franchise to a small proportion of the whole population," and "established the reign of the [Congregational] Church." Mr. Bancroft proceeds: "But the greater apprehensions were raised by a requisition that the Letters Patent of the Company should be produced in England—a requisition to which the emigrants returned no reply."

"Still more menacing," says Mr. Bancroft, "was the appointment of an arbitrary Special Commission [April 10, 1634] for all the colonies.*

"The news of this Commission soon reached Boston [Sept. 19, 1634;] and it was at the same time rumoured that a Governor-General was on his way. The intelligence awakened the most intense interest in the whole colony, and led to the boldest measures. Poor as the new settlements were, six hundred pounds were raised towards fortifications; 'and the assistants and the deputies discovered their minds to one another,' and the fortifications were hastened. All the ministers assembled in Boston [Jan. 19, 1635]; it marks the age, that their opinions were consulted; it marks the age still more, that *they unanimously declared against the reception of a General Governor.* 'We ought,' said the fathers of Israel, 'to defend our lawful possessions if we are able; if not, *to avoid and protract.*'"

The rumour of the appointment of a Governor-General over all the New England colonies was premature; but it served to develop the spirit of the ruling Puritans of Massachusetts Bay in their determining to resist the appointment of a general officer to which no other British colony had, or has, ever

* History of the United States, Vol. I., pp. 439, 440.

objected.*   The decision in their behalf by the King in Council,
in regard to the complaints made against them in 1632, deserved
their gratitude; the assurance in the recorded Minutes of the
Privy Council, that the King had never intended to impose
upon them those Church ceremonies which they had objected to
in England, and the liberty of not observing which they went
to New England to enjoy, should have produced corresponding
feelings and conduct on their part.   In their perfect liberty of
worship in New England, there was no difference between them
and their Sovereign.   In the meeting of the Privy Council
where the Royal declaration is recorded that liberty of worship,
without interference or restriction, should be enjoyed by all the
settlers in New England, Laud (then Bishop of London) is reported as present.   Whatever were the sins of King Charles and
Laud in creating by their ceremonies. and then punishing, nonconformists in England, they were not justly liable to the charge
of any such sins in their conduct towards the Puritans of New
England.   Throughout the whole reign of either Charles the
First or Second, there is no act or intimation of their interfering,
or intending or desiring to interfere, with the worship which the
Puritans had chosen, or might choose, in New England.   In
Plymouth the Congregational worship was adopted in 1620, and
was never molested; nor would there have been any interference
with its adoption nine years afterwards at Massachusetts Bay,
had the Puritans there gone no further than their brethren at
Plymouth had gone, or their brethren afterwards in Rhode
Island and Connecticut.   But the Puritans at Massachusetts
Bay assumed not merely the liberty of worship for themselves,

---

* The New England historians represent it as a high act of tyranny for
the King to appoint a Governor-General over the colonies, and to appoint
Commissioners with powers so extensive as those of the Royal Commission
appointed in 1634.   But they forget and ignore the fact that nine years afterwards, in 1643, when the Massachusetts and neighbouring colonies were much
more advanced in population and wealth than in 1634, the Parliament, which
was at war with the King and assuming all his powers, passed an Ordinance
appointing a Governor-General and Commissioners, and giving them quite as
extensive powers as the proposed Royal Commission of 1634.   This Ordinance
will be given entire when I come to speak of the Massachusetts Bay Puritans, under the Long Parliament and under Cromwell.   It will be seen that
the Long Parliament, and Cromwell himself, assumed larger powers over the
New England colonies than had King Charles.

but *the liberty of prohibiting any other form of worship, and of proscribing and banishing all who would not join in their worship ;* that is, doing in Massachusetts what they complained so loudly of the King and Laud doing in England. This was the cause and subject of the whole contest between the Corporation of Massachusetts Bay and the authorities in England. If it were intolerance and tyranny for the King and Laud to impose and enforce one form of worship upon all the people of England, it was equal intolerance and tyranny for the Government of Massachusetts Bay to impose and enforce one form of worship there upon all the inhabitants, and especially when their Charter gave them no authority whatever in the matter of Church organization.* They went to New England avowedly for liberty of worship ; and on arriving there they claimed the right to persecute and to banish or disfranchise all those who adhered to the worship of the Church to which they professed to belong, as did their persecutors when they left England, and which was the only Church then tolerated by the laws of England.

When it could no longer be concealed or successfully denied that the worship of the Church of England had been forbidden at Massachusetts Bay and its members disfranchised ; and when it now came to light that the Charter had been secretly transferred from England to Massachusetts, and a new Governor and Council appointed to administer it there ; and when it further became known that the Governor and Council there had actually prepared to resist by arms the appointment of a General Governor and Royal Commission, and had not only refused to produce the Charter, but had (to "avoid and protract") not even deigned to acknowledge the Privy Council's letter to produce it, the King was thrown upon the rights of his Crown, either to maintain them or to have the Royal authority exiled from a part of his dominions. And when it transpired that a large and increasing emigration from England was flowing to the very Plantation where the Church had been abolished and the King's authority

---

* "The Charter was far from conceding to the patentees the privilege of freedom of worship. Not a single line alludes to such a purpose ; nor can it be implied by a reasonable construction from any clause in the Charter." (Bancroft's History of the United States, Vol. I., pp. 271, 272.)

set at defiance,* it became a question of prudence whether such emigration should not be restricted; and accordingly a Royal Order in Council was issued forbidding the conveyance of any persons to New England except those who should have a Royal license.

This Order has been stigmatized by New England writers as most tyrannical and oppressive. I do not dispute it; but it was provided for in the Royal Charter, and the writers who assail King Charles and his Council for such an Act should remember that Cromwell himself and his Rump Parliament passed a similar Act eighteen years later, in 1653, as will hereafter appear; and it is a curious coincidence, that the same year, 1637, in which the King ordered that no person should be conveyed to New England without first obtaining a certificate that they had taken the oath of allegiance and supremacy, and conformed to the worship of the Church of England, the Massachusetts General Court passed an ordinance of a much more stringent character, and interfering with emigration and settlement, and even private hospitality and business to an extent not paralleled in Colonial history. It was enacted " That none shall entertain a stranger who should arrive with intent to reside, or shall allow the use of any habitation, without liberty from the Standing Council."†

The Charter having been transferred to Massachusetts, a new Council appointed to administer it there, and no notice having been taken of the Royal order for its production, the Commissioners might have advised the King to cancel the Charter forthwith and take into his own hands the government of the obstreperous colony; but instead of exercising such authority towards the colonists, as he was wont to do in less flagrant cases in England, he consented to come into Court and submit his own authority, as well as the acts of the resistant colonists, to

---

* It has been seen, p. 45, that the London Company had transmitted to Endicot in 1630 a form of the oath of allegiance to the King and his successors, to be taken by all the officers of the Massachusetts Bay Government. This had been set aside and a new oath substituted, leaving out all reference to the King, and confining the oath of allegiance to the local Government.

† Historians ascribe to this circumstance a remarkable change in the political economy of that colony; a cow which formerly sold for twenty pounds now selling for six pounds, and every colonial production in proportion. (Chalmers' Annals, pp. 265, 266. Neal's History of New England, Vol. I., Chap. ix., pp. 210—218.)

judicial investigation and decision. The Grand Council of Plymouth, from which the Massachusetts Company had first procured their territory, were called upon to answer by what authority and at whose instigation the Charter had been conveyed to New England. They disclaimed any participation in or knowledge of the transaction, and forthwith surrendered their own patent to the King. In doing so they referred to the acts of the new patentees at Massachusetts Bay, "whereby they did rend in pieces the foundation of the building, and so framed unto themselves both new laws and new conceits of matter of religion, forms of ecclesiastical and temporal orders of government, and punishing divers that would not approve them," etc. etc., and expressed their conviction of the necessity of his Majesty "taking the whole business into his own hands."*

After this surrender of their Charter by the Grand Council of Plymouth (England), the Attorney-General Bankes brought a *quo warranto* in the Court of King's Bench against the Governor, Deputy-Governor, and Council of the Corporation of the Massachusetts Bay, to compel the Company to answer to the complaints made against them for having violated the provisions of the patent.† The patentees residing in England disclaiming all responsibility for the acts complained of at Massachusetts

---

* Hazard, Vol. I.

† "At the trial, 'In Michas. T. XI^mo Carl Primi,' and the patentees, T. Eaton, Sir H. Rowsell, Sir John Young, Sir Richard Saltonstall, John Ven, George Harmood, Richard Perry, Thomas Hutchins, Nathaniel Wright, Samuel Vassall, Thomas Goffe, Thomas Adams, John Brown pleaded a disclaimer of any knowledge of the matters complained of, and that they should not 'for the future intermeddle with any the liberties, privileges and franchises aforesaid, but shall be for ever excluded from all use and claim of the same and every of them."

"Matthew Cradock [first Governor of the Company] comes in, having had time to interplead, etc., and on his default judgment was given, that he should be convicted of the usurpation charged in the information, and that the said liberties, privileges and franchises should be taken and seized into the King's hands; the said Matthew not to intermeddle with and be excluded the use thereof, and the said Matthew to be taken to answer to the King for the said usurpation."

" The rest of the patentees stood outlawed, and no judgment entered against them."

Collection of Original Papers relative to the Colony of Massachusetts Bay (in the British Museum), by T. Hutchinson, Vol. I., pp. 114—118.

(except Mr. Cradock), and no defence having been made of those acts, nor the authors of them appearing either personally or by counsel, they stood outlawed, and judgment was entered against the Company in the person of Mr. Cradock for the usurpation charged in the information.

The Lords Commissioners, in pursuance of this decision of the Court of King's Bench, sent a peremptory order to the Governor of Massachusetts Bay, to transmit the Charter to England, intimating that, in case of "further neglect or contempt," "a strict course would be taken against them."[*] They were now brought face to face with the sovereign authority; the contempt of silence; nor did they think it prudent to renew military preparations of resistance, as they had done in 1634; their policy now was to "avoid and protract," by pleading exile, ignorance, innocence, begging pardon and pity, yet denying that they

---

[*] The following is a copy of the letter sent by appointment of the Lords of the Council to Mr. Winthrop, for the patent of the Plantations to be sent to them :

"At Whitehall, April 4th, 1638 :—

"This day the Lords Commissioners for Foreign Plantations, taking into consideration the petitions and complaints of his Majesty's subjects, planters and traders in New England, grew more frequent than heretofore for want of a settled and orderly government in those parts, and calling to mind that they had formerly given order about two or three years since to Mr. Cradock, a member of that Plantation (alleged by him to be there remaining in the hands of Mr. Winthrop), to be sent over hither, and that notwithstanding the same, the said letters patent were not as yet brought over ; and their Lordships being now informed by Mr. Attorney-General that a *quo warranto* had been by him brought, according to former order, against the said patent, and the same was proceeded to judgment against so many as had appeared, and that they which had not appeared were outlawed : 'Their Lordships, well approving of Mr. Attorney-General's care and proceeding therein, did now resolve and order, that Mr. Meawtis, clerk of the Council attendant upon the said Commissioners for Foreign Plantations, should, in a letter from himself to Mr Winthrop, inclose and convey this order unto him; and their Lordships hereby, in his Majesty's name and according to his express will and pleasure, strictly require and enjoin the said Winthrop, or any other in whose power and custody the said letters patent are, that they fail not to transmit the said patent hither by the return of the ship in which the order is conveyed to them, it being resolved that in case of any further neglect or contempt by them shewed therein, their Lordships will cause a strict course to be taken against them, and will move his Majesty to resume into his hands the whole Plantation.'" (*Ib.*, pp. 118, 119.)

had done anything wrong, and insinuating that if their Charter should be cancelled, their allegiance would be forfeited and they would remove, with the greater part of the population, and set up a new government. I have not met with this very curious address in any modern history of the United States—only glosses of it. I give it entire in a note.* They profess a willingness

* "To the Right Honourable the Lords Commissioners for Foreign Plantations.

"The humble Petition of the Inhabitants of the Massachusetts Bay, in New England, of the Generall Court there assembled, the 6th day of September, in the 14th year of the Reigne of our Soveraigne Lord King Charles.

"Whereas it hath pleased your Lordships, by order of the 4th of April last, to require our patent to be sent unto you, wee do hereby humbly and sincerely professe, that wee are ready to yield all due obedience to our Soveraigne Lord the King's majesty, and to your Lordships under him, and in this minde wee left our native countrie, and according thereunto, hath been our practice ever since, so as wee are much grieved, that your Lordships should call in our patent, there being no cause knowne to us, nor any delinquency or fault of ours expressed in the order sent to us for that purpose, our government being according to his Majestie's patent, and we not answerable for any defects in other plantations, etc.

"This is that which his Majestie's subjects here doe believe and professe, and thereupon wee are all humble suitors to your Lordships, that you will be pleased to take into further consideration our condition, and to afford us the liberty of subjects, that we may know what is layd to our charge ; and have leaive and time to answer for ourselves before we be condemned as a people unworthy of his Majestie's favour or protection. As for the *quo warranto* mentioned in the said order, wee doe assure your Lordships wee were never called to answer it, and if we had, wee doubt not but wee have a sufficient plea to put in.

"It is not unknowne to your Lordships, that we came into these remote parts with his Majestie's license and encouragement, under the great seale of England, and in the confidence wee had of that assurance, wee have transported our families and estates, and here have wee built and planted, to the great enlargement and securing of his Majestie's dominions in these parts, so as if our patent should now be taken from us, we shall be looked up as renegadoes and outlaws, and shall be enforced, either to remove to some other place, or to returne into our native country againe ; either of which will put us to unsupportable extremities ; and these evils (among others) will necessarily follow. (1.) Many thousand souls will be exposed to ruine, being laid open to the injuries of all men. (2.) If wee be forced to desert this place, the rest of the plantations (being too weake to subsist alone) will, for the most part, dissolve and goe with us, and then will this whole country fall into the hands of the French or Dutch, who would speedily embrace such an opportunity. (3.) If we should loose all our labour and costs, and be

to "yield all *due* obedience to their Soveraigne Lord the King's Majesty," but that they "are much grieved, that your Lordships should call in our patent, there being no cause knowne to us, nor any delinquency or fault of ours expressed in the order sent to us for that purpose, our government being according to his Majestie's patent, and wee not answerable for any defects in other plantations. This is that which his Majestie's subjects here doe believe and professe, and thereupon wee are all humble suitors to your Lordships, that you will be pleased to take into *further consideration* our condition, and to afford us the *liberty of subjects, that we may know what is laid to our charge;* and have leaive and time to *answer for ourselves before* we be condemned as a people unworthy of his Majestie's favour or protection."

This profession and these statements are made in presence of the facts that three years before the Royal Commissioners had in like manner demanded the production of the patent in England, giving the reasons for it, and the present "humble suitors to their Lordships" had "avoided and protracted," by not even acknowledging the reception of the order, much less

deprived of those liberties which his Majestie hath granted us, and nothing layd to our charge, nor any fayling to be found in us in point of allegiance (which all our countrymen doe take notice of, and will justify our faithfulness in this behalfe), it will discourage all men hereafter from the like undertakings upon confidence of his Majestie's Royal grant. Lastly, if our patent be taken from us (whereby wee suppose wee may clayme interest in his Majestie's favour and protection) the common people here will conceive that his Majestie hath cast them off, and that, heereby, they are freed from their allegiance and subjection, and, thereupon, will be ready to confederate themselves under a new Government, for their necessary safety and subsistence, which will be of dangerous example to other plantations, and perillous to ourselves of incurring his Majestie's displeasure, which wee would by all means avoyd.

"Wee dare not question your Lordships' proceedings ; wee only desire to open our griefs where the remedy is to be expected. If in any thing wee have offended his Majesty and your Lordships, wee humbly prostrate ourselves at the footstool of supreme authority ; let us be made the object of his Majestie's clemency, and not cut off, in our first appeal, from all hope of favour. Thus with our earnest prayers to the King of kings for long life and prosperity to his sacred Majesty and his Royall family, and for all honour and welfare to your Lordships, we humbly take leave.

" EDWARD RAWSON, *Secretary.*"

(Hutchinson's History of the Colony of Massachusetts Bay, Vol. I., Appendix V., pp. 507, 508, 509.)

answering the charges of which they were informed, but rather preparing military fortifications for resisting a General Governor and Royal Commissioners of Inquiry, and "for regulating the Plantations." Yet they profess not to know "what is laid to their charge," and are "grieved that their Lordships should now demand the patent," as if the production of it had never before been demanded. It will be seen by the letter of their Lordships, given in a note on p. 77, that they refer to this treatment of their former order, and say, in the event of "further *neglect and contempt*," a strict course would be taken against them.

The authors of the Address profess that the cancelling of their Charter would involve the loss of their labours, their removal from Massachusetts, the exposure of the country to the invasions of the French and Dutch, the forfeiture of their allegiance, and their setting up a new government. It was a mere pretext that the Plantation becoming a Crown colony, as it would on the cancelling of the Charter, would not secure to the planters the protection of the Crown, as in the neighbouring Plymouth settlement, which had no Royal Charter. They knew that, under the protection of the King and laws of England, their liberties and lives and properties would be equally secure as those of any other of his Majesty's subjects. They twice repeat the misstatement that "nothing had been laid to their charge," and "no fault found upon them;" they insinuate that they would be causelessly denied the protection of British subjects, that their allegiance would be renounced, and they with the greater part of the population would establish a new government, which would be a dangerous precedent for other colonies. These denials, professions, insinuations, and threats, they call "opening their griefes," and conclude in the following obsequious, plaintive, and prayerful words:

"If in any thing wee have offended his Majesty and your Lordships, wee humbly prostrate ourselves at the footstool of supreme authority; let us be made the objects of his Majestie's clemency, and not cut off, in our first appeal, from all hope of favour. Thus with our earnest prayers to the King of kings for long life and prosperity to his sacred Majesty and his Royall family, and for all honour and welfare to your Lordships."

The Lords Commissioners replied to this Address through Mr. Cradock, pronouncing the jealousies and fears professed in the

Address to be groundless, stating their intentions to be the regulation of all the Colonies, and to continue to the settlers of Massachusetts Bay the privileges of British subjects.   They repeated their command upon the Corporation to transmit the Charter to England, at the same time authorising the present Government to continue in office until the issuing of a new Charter. Mr. Cradock transmitted this letter to the Governor of Massachusetts Bay, the General Court of which decided not to acknowledge the receipt of it, pronouncing it "unofficial" (being addressed to Mr. Cradock,. who, though the Governor mentioned in the Charter, and the largest proprietor, was not now Governor); that the Lords Commissioners could not "proceed upon it," since they could not prove that it had been delivered to the Governor; and they directed Mr. Cradock's agent not to mention Lords Commissioners' letter when he wrote to Mr. C.

At this juncture the whole attention of the King was turned from Massachusetts to Scotland, his war with which resulted ultimately in the loss of both his crown and his life.

In view of the facts stated in this and the preceding chapters, I think it must be admitted that during the nine years which elapsed between granting the first Charter by Charles and the resumption of it by *quo warranto* in the Court of King's Bench, the aggression and the hostility was on the side of the Puritans of Massachusetts Bay.   Their first act was one of intolerance, and violation of the laws of England in abolishing the worship of the Church of England, and banishing its members for adhering to its worship.   Their denials of it were an admission of the unlawfulness of such acts, as they were also dishonourable to themselves.   Their maxim seems to have been, that the end sanctified the means—at least so far as the King was concerned; and that as they distrusted him, they were exempt from the obligations of loyalty and truth in their relations to him; that he and his were predestined reprobates, while they and theirs were the elected saints to whom, of right, rule and earth belonged.   They were evidently sincere in their belief that they were the eternally elected heirs of God, and as such had a right to all they could command and possess, irrespective of king or savage.   Their brotherhood was for themselves alone—everything for themselves and nothing for others; their religion partook more of Moses than of Christ—more of law

6

than of Gospel—more of hatred than of love—more of antipathy
than of attractiveness—more of severity than of tenderness.
In sentiment and in self-complacent purpose they left England
to convert the savage heathen in New England; but for more
than twelve years after their arrival in Massachusetts they
killed many hundreds of Indians, but converted none, nor
established any missions for their instruction and conversion.

The historians of the United States laud without stint the
Puritans of Massachusetts Bay; and they are entitled to all
praise for their industry, enterprise, morality, independence. But
I question whether there are many, if any, Protestants in the
United States who would wish the views and spirit of those
Puritans to prevail there, either in religion or civil government—
a denial of the liberty of worship to Episcopalians, Presbyterians,
Baptists, or Quakers; a denial of eligibility to office or of
elective franchise to any other than members of the Congregational Churches; compulsory attendance upon Congregational
worship, and the support of that worship by general taxation,
together with the enforcement of its discipline by civil law and
its officers.

Had the Puritans of Massachusetts Bay understood the
principles and cherished the spirit of civil and religious liberty,
and allowed to the Browns and their Episcopalian friends the
continued enjoyment of their old and venerated form of
worship, while they themselves embraced and set up a new
form of worship, and not made conformity to it a test of loyalty
and of citizenship in the Plantation, there would have been no
local dissensions, no persecutions, no complaints to England, no
Royal Commissions of Inquiry or Regulation, no restraints upon
emigration, no jealousies and disputes between England and the
colony; the feelings of cordiality with which Charles granted
the Charter and encouraged its first four years' operations,
according to the testimony of the Puritans themselves, would
have developed into pride for the success of the enterprise, and
further countenance and aid to advance it; the religious toleration in the new colony would have immensely promoted the
cause of religious toleration in England; and the American
colonies would have long since grown up, as Canada and
Australia are now growing up, into a state of national independence, without war or bloodshed, without a single feeling

other than that of filial respect and affection for the Mother Country, without any interruption of trade or commerce— presented an united Protestant and English nationality, under separate governments, on the great continents of the globe and islands of the seas.

I know it has been said that, had Episcopal worship been tolerated at Massachusetts Bay, Laud would have soon planted the hierarchy there, with all his ceremonies and intolerance. This objection is mere fancy and pretence. It is fancy—for the Corporation, and not Laud, was the chartered authority to provide for religious instruction as well as settlement and trade in the new Plantation, as illustrated from the very fact of the Company having selected and employed the first ministers, as well as first Governor and other officers, for the two-fold work of spreading religion and extending the King's dominions in New England. The objection is mere pretence, for it could not have been dread of the Church of England, which dictated its abolition and the banishment of its members, since precisely the same spirit of bigotry, persecution, and proscription prevailed, not only against Roger Williams, Mrs. Hutchinson and her brother Wright and their friends, but in 1646 against the Presbyterians, and in 1656 against the Baptists, as will hereafter appear.

Their iron-bound, shrivelled creed of eternal, exclusive election produced an iron-hearted population, whose hand was against every man not of their tribal faith and tribal independence; but at the same time not embodying in their civil or ecclesiastical polity a single element of liberty or charity which any free State or Church would at this day be willing to adopt or recognize as its distinctive constitution or mission.

It was the utter absence of both the principles and spirit of true civil and religious liberty in the Puritans of Massachusetts Bay, and in their brethren under the Commonwealth and Cromwell in England, that left Nonconformists without a plea for toleration under Charles the Second, from the example of their own party on either side of the Atlantic, and that has to this day furnished the most effective argument to opponents against dissenters' pretensions to liberality and liberty, and the strongest barrier against their political influence in England. They were prostrate and powerless when the liberal Churchmen, guided by the views of Chillingworth, Burnet, and Tillotson, under William and Mary, obtained the first Parliamentary enactment for religious toleration in England.   It is to the same influence that religious liberty in England has been enlarged from time to time; and, at this day, it is to the exertions and influence of liberal Churchmen, both in and out of Parliament, more than to any independent influence of Puritan dissenters, that civil and religious liberty are making gradual and great progress in Great Britain and Ireland—a liberty which, I believe, would ere this have been complete but for the proscriptive, intolerant and persecuting spirit and practice of the Puritans of the seventeenth century.

CHAPTER IV.

THE GOVERNMENT OF MASSACHUSETTS BAY UNDER THE LONG PARLIAMENT,
THE COMMONWEALTH, AND CROMWELL.

CHARLES THE FIRST ceased to rule after 1640, though his death did not take place until January, 1649. The General Court of Massachusetts Bay, in their address to the King's Commissioners in September, 1637, professed to offer "earnest prayers for long life and prosperity to his sacred Majesty and his royal family, and all honour and welfare to their Lordships;" but as soon as there was a prospect of a change, and the power of the King began to decline and that of Parliament began to increase, the Puritans of Massachusetts Bay transferred all their sympathies and assiduities to the Parliament. In 1641, they sent over three agents to evoke interest with the Parliamentary leaders—one layman, Mr. Hibbins, and two ministers, Thomas Weld and Hugh Peters, the latter of whom was as shrewd and active in trade and speculations as he was ardent and violent in the pulpit. He made quite a figure in the civil war in England, and was Cromwell's favourite war chaplain. Neither he nor Weld ever returned to New England.

As the persecution of Puritans ceased in England, emigration to New England ceased; trade became depressed and property greatly depreciated in value; population became stationary in New England during the whole Parliamentary and Commonwealth rule in England, from 1640 to 1660—more returning from New England to England than emigrating thither from England.*

* Neal says: "Certainly never was country more obliged to a man than New England to Archbishop Laud, who by his cruel and arbitrary proceed-

The first success of this mission of Hugh Peters and his colleagues soon appeared. By the Royal Charter of 1629, the King encouraged the Massachusetts Company by remitting all taxes upon the property of the Plantations for the space of seven years, and all customs and duties upon their exports and imports, to or from any British port, for the space of twenty-one years, except the five per cent. due upon their goods and merchandise, according to the ancient trade of merchants ; but the Massachusetts delegates obtained an ordinance of Parliament, or rather an order of the House of Commons, complimenting the colony on its progress and hopeful prospects, and discharging all the exports of the natural products of the colony and all the goods imported into it for its own use, from the payment of any custom or taxation whatever.*

On this resolution of the Commons three remarks may be made : 1. As in all previous communications between the King and the Colony, the House of Commons termed the colony a

---

ings drove thousands of families out of the kingdom, and thereby stocked the Plantations with inhabitants, in the compass of a very few years, which otherwise could not have been done in an age." This was the sense of some of the greatest men in Parliament in their speeches in 1641. Mr. Tienns [afterwards Lord Hollis] said that "a certain number of ceremonies in the judgment of some men unlawful, and to be rejected of all the churches ; in the judgment of all other Churches, and in the judgment of our own Church, but indifferent ; yet what difference, yea, what distraction have those indifferent ceremonies raised among us? What has deprived us of so many thousands of Christians who desired, and in all other respects deserved, to hold communion with us? I say what has deprived us of them; and scattered them into I know not what places and corners of the world, but these indifferent ceremonies."—[Several other speeches to the same effect are quoted by Neal.]—History of New England, Vol. I., pp. 210—212.

* "Veneris, 10 March, 1642 :

"Whereas the plantations in New England have, by the blessing of the Almighty, had good and prosperous success, without any public charge to the State, and are now likely to prove very happy for the propagation of the gospel in those parts, and very beneficial and commodious to this nation. The Commons assembled in Parliament do, for the better advancement of those plantations and the encouragement of the planters to proceed in their undertaking, ordain that all merchandising goods, that by any person or persons whatsoever, merchant or other, shall be exported out of the kingdom of England into New England to be spent or employed there, or being of the growth of that kingdom [colony], shall be from thence imported thither, or shall be laden or put on board any ship or vessel for necessaries in passing to

" Plantation," and the colonists "Planters." Two years afterwards the colony of Massachusetts Bay assumed to itself (without Charter or Act of Parliament) the title and style of "a Commonwealth." 2. While the House of Commons speaks of the prospects being "very happy for the propagation of the Gospel in those parts," the Massachusetts colony had not established a single mission or employed a single missionary or teacher for the instruction of the Indians. 3. The House of Commons exempts the colony from payment of all duties on articles exported from or imported into the colony, *until the House of Commons shall take further order therein to the contrary,*"—clearly implying and assuming, as beyond doubt, the right of the House of Commons to impose or abolish such duties at its pleasure. The colonists of Massachusetts Bay voted hearty thanks to the House of Commons for this resolution, and ordered it to be entered on their public records as a proof to posterity of the gracious favour of Parliament.*

The Massachusetts General Court did not then complain of the Parliament invading their Charter privileges, in assuming its right to tax or not tax their imports and exports, but rebelled against Great Britain a hundred and thirty years afterwards, because the Parliament asserted and applied the same principle.

The Puritan Court of Massachusetts Bay were not slow in reciprocating the kind expressions and acts of the Long Parliament, and identifying themselves completely with it against the King. In 1644 they passed an Act, in which they allowed perfect freedom of opinion, discussion, and action on the side of Parliament, but none on the side of the King; the one party in the colony could say and act as they pleased (and many of them went to England and joined Cromwell's army or got places in public departments); no one of the other party was allowed to give expression to his opinions, either "directly or indirectly," without being "accounted as an offender of a high

---

and fro, and all and every the owner or owners thereof shall be freed and discharged of and from paying and yielding any custom, subsidy, taxation, or other duty for the same, either inward or outward, either in this kingdom or New England, or in any port, haven, creek or other place whatsoever, until the House of Commons shall take further order therein to the contrary."— Hutchinson's History of Massachusetts Bay, Vol. I., pp. 114, 115.

* Hutchinson's History of Massachusetts Bay, Vol. I., p. 114.

nature against this Commonwealth, and to be prosecuted, capitally or otherwise, according to the quality and degree of his offence."*

The New England historians have represented the acts of Charles the First as arbitrary and tyrannical in inquiring into the affairs of Massachusetts Bay, and in the appointment of a Governor-General and Commissioners to investigate all their proceedings and regulate them; and it might be supposed that the Puritan Parliament in England and the General Court of Massachusetts Bay would be at one in regard to local independence of the colony of any control or interference on the part of the Parent State. But the very year after the House of Commons had adopted so gracious an order to exempt the exports and imports of the colony from all taxation, both Houses of Parliament passed an Act for the appointment of a Governor-General and seventeen Commissioners—five Lords and twelve Commoners—with unlimited powers over all the American colonies. Among the members of the House of Commons composing this Commission were Sir Harry Vane and Oliver Cromwell. The title of this Act, in Hazard, is as follows:

"An Ordinance of the Lords and Commons assembled in Parliament: whereby Robert Earl of Warwick is made Governor-in-Chief and Lord High Admiral of all those Islands and Plantations inhabited, planted, or belonging to any of his Majesty the King of England's subjects, within the bounds and upon the coasts of America, and a Committee appointed to be assisting unto him, for the better government, strengthening

---

* The following is the Act itself, passed in 1644 : "Whereas the civil wars and dissensions in our native country, through the seditious words and carriages of many evil affected persons, cause divisions in many places of government in America, some professing themselves for the King, and others for the Parliament, not considering that the Parliament themselves profess that they stand for the King and Parliament against the malignant Papists and delinquents in that kingdom. It is therefore ordered, that what person whatsoever shall by word, writing, or action endeavour to disturb our peace, directly or indirectly, by drawing a party under pretence that he is for the King of England, and such as join with him against the Parliament, shall be accounted as an offender of a high nature against this Commonwealth, and to be proceeded with, either *capitally* or *otherwise*, according to the quality and degree of his offence." (Hutchinson's History of Massachusetts Bay, Vol. I., pp. 135, 136.)

and preservation of the said Plantations; but chiefly for the advancement of the true Protestant religion, and further spreading of the Gospel of Christ* among those that yet remain there, in great and miserable blindness and ignorance."†

* It was not until three years after this, and three years after the facts of the banished Roger Williams' labours in Rhode Island (see note V. below), that the *first* mission among the Indians was established by the Puritans of Massachusetts Bay—seventeen years after their settlement there; for Mr. Holmes says: "The General Court of Massachusetts passed the *first* Act [1646] to encouraging the carrying of the Gospel to the Indians, and recommended it to the ministers to consult on the best means of effecting the design. By their advice, it is probable, the first Indian Mission was undertaken; for on the 28th of October [1646] Mr. John Eliot, minister of Roxbury, commenced those pious and indefatigable labours among the natives, which procured for him the title of The Indian Apostle. His first visit was to the Indians at Nonantum, whom he had apprised of his intention." (Annals of America, Vol. I., p. 280.)

† Hazard, Vol. I., pp. 533, 534. The provisions of this remarkable Act are as follows:

"Governours and Government of Islands in America.—November 2nd, 1643:

"I. That Robert Earl of Warwick be Governour and Lord High Admirall of all the Islands and other Plantations inhabited, planted, or belonging unto any of his Majestie's the King of England's subjects, or which hereafter may be inhabited, planted, or belonging to them, within the bounds and upon the coasts of America.

"II. That the Lords and others particularly named in the Ordinance shall be Commissioners to joyne in aid and assistance of the said Earl, Chief Governour and Admirall of the said Plantations, and shall have power from Time to Time to provide for, order, and dispose of all things which they shall think most fit and advantageous for the well governing, securing, strengthening and preserving of the sayd Plantations, and chiefly for the advancement of the true Protestant Religion amongst the said Planters and Inhabitants, and the further enlarging and spreading of the Gospel of Christ amongst those that yet remain there in great Blindness and Ignorance.

"III. That the said Governour and Commissioners, upon all weighty and important occasions which may concern the good and safety of the Planters, Owners of Lands, or Inhabitants of the said Islands, shall have power to send for, view, and make use of all Records, Books, and Papers which may concern the said Plantations.

"IV. That the said Earl, Governour in Chief, and the said Commissioners, shall have power to nominate, appoint, and constitute, as such subordinate Commissioners, Councillors, Commanders, Officers, and Agents, as they shall think most fit and serviceable for the said Islands and Plantations: and upon death or other avoidance of the aforesaid Chief Governour and Admirall, or other the Commissioners before named, to appoint such other Chief Governour

This Act places all the affairs of the colonies, with the appointment of Governors and all other local officers, under the direct control of Parliament, through its general Governor and Commissioners, and shows beyond doubt that the Puritans of the Long Parliament held the same views with those of Charles the First, and George the Third, and Lord North a century afterwards, as to the authority of the British Parliament over the American colonies. Whether those views were right or wrong, they were the views of all parties in England from the beginning for more than a century, as to the relations between the British Parliament and the colonies. The views on this subject held and maintained by the United Empire Loyalists, during the American Revolution of 1776, were those which had been held by all parties in England, whether Puritans or Churchmen, from the first granting of the Charter to the Company of Massachusetts Bay in 1629. The assumptions and statements of American historians to the contrary on this subject are at variance with all the preceding facts of colonial history.*

Mr. Bancroft makes no mention of this important ordinance

or Commissioners in the roome and place of such as shall be void, as also to remove all such subordinate Governours and Officers as they shall judge fit.

"V. That no subordinate Governours, Councillors, Commanders, Officers, Agents, Planters, or Inhabitants, which now are resident in or upon the said Islands or Plantations, shall admit or receive any new Governours, Councillors, Commanders, Officers, or Agents whatsoever, but such as shall be allowed and approved of under the hands and seals of the aforesaid Chief Governour and High Admirall, together with the hands and seals of the said Commissioners, or six of them, or under the hands of such as they shall authorize thereunto.

"VI. That the Chief Governour and Commissioners before mentioned, or the greater number of them, are authorized to assign, ratifie, and confirm so much of their aforementioned authority and power, and in such manner, to such persons as they shall judge fit, for the better governing and preserving the said Plantations and Islands from open violence and private distractions.

"VII. That whosoever shall, in obedience to this Ordinance, do or execute any thing, shall by virtue hereof be saved harmless and indemnified."

* In 1646 the Parliament passed another ordinance, exempting the colonies for three years from all tollages, "except the excise," provided their productions should not be "exported but only in English vessels." While this Act also asserted the parliamentary right of taxation over the Colonial plantations, it formed a part of what was extended and executed by the famous Act of Navigation, first passed by the Puritan Parliament five years afterwards, in 1651, as will be seen hereafter.

passed by both Houses of the Long Parliament;* nor does Hutchinson, or Graham, or Palfrey. Less sweeping acts of

* Mr. Bancroft must have been aware of the existence of this ordinance, for he makes two allusions to the Commission appointed by it. In connection with one allusion to it, he states the following interesting facts, illustrative of Massachusetts exclusiveness on the one record, and on the other the instruments and progress of religious liberty in New England. "The people of Rhode Island," says Mr. Bancroft, "*excluded from the colonial union*, would never have maintained their existence as a separate state, had they not sought the interference and protection of the Mother Country ; and the founder of the colony [Roger Williams] was chosen to conduct the important mission. Embarking at Manhattan [for he was not allowed to go to Boston], he arrived in England not long after the death of Hampden. *The Parliament had placed the affairs of the American Colonies under the Earl of Warwick, as Governor-in-Chief, assisted by a Council of five peers and twelve commoners.* Among these commoners was Henry Vane, a man who was ever true in his affections as he was undeviating in his principles, and who now welcomed the American envoy as an ancient friend. The favour of Parliament was won by his [Roger Williams'] incomparable 'printed Indian labours, the like whereof was not extant from any part of America ;' and his merits as a missionary induced both houses of Parliament to grant unto him and friends with him a free and absolute charter(*a*) of civil government for those parts of his abode.' Thus were the places of refuge for 'soul-liberty' on the Narragansett Bay incorporated 'with full power and authority to rule themselves.' To the Long Parliament, and especially to Sir Harry Vane, Rhode Island owes its existence as a political State."—History of the United States, Vol. I., pp. 460, 461.

The other allusion of Mr. Bancroft to the Parliamentary Act and Commission of 1643 is in the following words : "*The Commissioners appointed by Parliament, with unlimited authority over the Plantations*, found no favour in Virginia. They promised indeed freedom from English taxation, but this immunity was already enjoyed. They gave the colony liberty to choose its own Governor, but it had no dislike to Berkeley ; and though there was a party for the Parliament, yet the King's authority was maintained. The sovereignty of Charles had ever been mildly exercised."—*Ib.*, p. 222.

(*a*) This is not quite accurate. The word "absolute" does not occur in the patent. The words of the Charter are: "A *free* Charter of civil incorporation and government ; that they may order and govern their Plantations in such a manner as to maintain justice and peace, both among themselves, and towards all men with whom they shall have to do "—"Provided nevertheless that the said laws, constitutions, and punishments, for the civil government of said plantations, be conformable to the laws of England, so far as the nature and constitution of the place will admit. And always reserving to the said Earl and Commissioners, and their successors, power and authority for to dispose the general government of that, as it stands in relation to the

authority over the colonies, by either of the Charters, are por-
trayed by these historians with minuteness and power, if not
in terms of exaggeration.   The most absolute and comprehensive
authority as to both appointments and trade in the colonies
ordered by the Long Parliament and Commonwealth are referred
to in brief and vague terms, or not at all noticed, by the historical eulogist of the Massachusetts Bay Puritans,* who, while
they were asserting their independence of the royal rule of
England, claimed and exercised absolute rule over individual
consciences and religious liberty in Massachusetts, not only
against Episcopalians, but equally against Presbyterians and
Baptists ; for this very year, says Hutchinson, " several persons
came from England in 1643, made a muster to set Presbyterian
government under the authority of the Assembly of Westminster ; but the New England Assembly, the General Court,
soon put them to the rout."†   And in the following year, 1644,
these " Fathers of American liberty" adopted measures equally
decisive to " rout " the Baptists.   The ordinance passed on this
subject, the " 13th of the 9th month, 1644," commences thus :
" Forasmuch as experience hath plentifully and often proved
that since the first arising of the Anabaptists, about one hundred
years since, they have been the incendaries of the Commonwealths and the infectors of persons in main matters of religion,
and the troubles of churches in all places where they have been,
and that they who have held the baptizing of infants unlawful,
have usually held other errors or heresies therewith, though they

rest of the Plantations in America, as they shall conceive from time to time
most conducing to the general good of the said Plantations, the honour of his
Majesty, and the service of the State."—(Hazard, Vol. I., pp. 529—531, where
the Charter is printed at length.)

   * But Mr. Holmes makes explicit mention of the parliamentary ordinance
of 1643 in the following terms :—"The English Parliament passed an
ordinance appointing the Earl of Warwick Governor-in-Chief and Lord High
Admiral of the American Colonies, with a Council of five Peers and twelve
Commoners. It empowered him, in conjunction with his associates, to
examine the state of affairs ; to send for papers and persons, to remove
Governors and officers, and appoints other in their places ; and to assign over
to these such part of the powers that were now granted, as he should think
proper." (Annals of America, Vol. I., p. 273.)

   † History of Massachusetts Bay, Vol. I., p. 117 ; Massachusetts Laws, pp.
140—145.

have (as other heretics used to do) concealed the same till they spied out a fit advantage and opportunity to vent them by way of question or scruple," etc.: "It is ordered and agreed, that if any person or persons within this jurisdiction shall either openly condemn *or* oppose the baptizing of infants, *or* go about secretly to seduce others from the approbation or use thereof, *or* shall purposely depart the congregation at the ministration of the ordinance, *or* shall deny the ordinance of magistracy, or their lawful right and authority to make war, *or* to punish the outward breakers of the first Table, and shall appear to the Court to continue therein after the due time and means of conviction, *shall be sentenced to banishment.*"*

In the following year, 1646, the Presbyterians, not being satisfied with having been "put to the rout" in 1643, made a second attempt to establish their worship within the jurisdiction of Massachusetts Bay. Mr. Palfrey terms this attempt a "Presbyterian cabal," and calls its leaders "conspirators." They petitioned the General Court or Legislature of Massachusetts Bay, and on the rejection of their petition they proposed to appeal to the Parliament in England. They were persecuted for both acts. It was pretended that they were punished, not for petitioning the local Court, but for the expressions used in their petition—the same as it had been said seventeen years before, that the Messrs. Brown were banished, not because they were Episcopalians, but because, when called before Endicot and his councillors, they used offensive expressions in justification of their conduct in continuing to worship as they had done in England. In their case, in 1629, the use and worship of the Prayer Book was forbidden, and the promoters of it banished, and their papers seized; in this case, in 1646, the Presbyterian worship was forbidden, and the promoters of it were imprisoned and fined, and their papers seized. In both cases the victims of religious intolerance and civil tyranny were men of the highest position and intelligence. The statements of the petitioners in 1646 (the truth of which could not be denied, though the petitioners were punished for telling it) show the state of bondage and oppression to which all who would not join the

---

* Hazard, Vol. 1., p. 538 ; Massachusetts Records. The working of this Act, and the punishments inflicted under it for more than twenty years, will be seen hereafter.

Congregational Churches—that is, five-sixths of the population —were reduced under this system of Church government—the Congregational Church members alone electors, alone eligible to be elected, alone law-makers and law administrators, alone imposing taxes, alone providing military stores and commanding the soldiery; and then the victims of such a Government were pronounced and punished as "conspirators" and "traitors" when they ventured to appeal for redress to the Mother Country. The most exclusive and irresponsible Government that ever existed in Canada in its earliest days never approached such a despotism as this of Massachusetts Bay. I leave the reader to decide, when he peruses what was petitioned for—first to the Massachusetts Legislature, and then to the English Parliament— who were the real "traitors" and who the "conspirators" against right and liberty: the "Presbyterian cabal," as Mr. Palfrey terms the petitioners, or those who imprisoned and fined them, and seized their papers. Mr. Hutchinson, the best informed and most candid of the New England historians, states the affair of the petitioners, their proceedings and treatment, and the petition which they presented, as follows:

"A great disturbance was caused in the colony this year [1646] by a number of persons of figure, but of different sentiments, both as to civil and ecclesiastical government, from the people in general. They had laid a scheme for petition of such as were non-freemen to the courts of both colonies, and upon the petitions being refused, to apply to the Parliament, pretending they were subjected to arbitrary power, extra-judicial proceedings, etc. The principal things complained of by the petitioners were:

"1st. That the fundamental laws of England were not owned by the Colony, as the basis of their government, according to the patent.

"2nd. The denial of those civil privileges, which the freemen of the jurisdiction enjoyed, to such as were not members of Churches, and did not take an oath of fidelity devised by the authority here, although they were freeborn Englishmen, of sober lives and conversation, etc.

"3rd. That they were debarred from Christian privileges, viz., the Lord's Supper for themselves, and baptism for their children, unless they were members of some of the particular

Churches in the country, though otherwise sober, righteous, and godly, and eminent for knowledge, not scandalous in life and conversation, and members of Churches in England.

"And they prayed that civil liberty and freedom might be forthwith granted to all truly English, and that all members of the Church of England or Scotland, not scandalous, might be admitted to the privileges of the Churches of New England; or if these civil and religious liberties were refused, that they might be freed from the heavy taxes imposed upon them, and from the impresses made of them or their children or servants into the war; and if they failed of redress there, they should be under the necessity of making application to England, to the honourable Houses of Parliament, who they hoped would take their sad condition, etc.

"But if their prayer should be granted, they hoped to see the then contemned ordinances of God highly prized; the Gospel, then dark, break forth as the sun; Christian charity, then frozen, wax warm; jealousy of arbitrary government banished; strife and contention abated; and all business in Church and State, which for many years had gone backward, successfully thriving, etc.

"The Court, and great part of the country, were much offended at this petition. A declaration was drawn up by order of the Court, in answer to the petition, and in vindication of the Government—a proceeding which at this day would not appear for the honour of the supreme authority. The petitioners were required to attend the Court. They urged their right of petitioning. They were told they were not accused of petitioning, but of contemptuous and seditious expressions, and were required to find sureties for their good behaviour, etc. A charge was drawn up against them in form; notwithstanding which it was intimated to them, that if they would ingenuously acknowledge their offence, they should be forgiven; but they refused, and were fined, some in larger, some in smaller sums, two or three of the magistrates dissenting, Mr. Bellingham,* in particular, desiring his dissent might be entered. The petitioners

---

* "Mr. Winthrop, who was then Deputy-Governor, was active in the prosecution of the petitioners, but the party in favour of them had so much interest as to obtain a vote to require him to answer in public to the complaint against him. Dr. Mather says: ' He was most irregularly called forth to an

claimed an appeal to the Commissioners of Plantations in England; but it was not allowed. Some of them resolved to go home with a complaint. Their papers were seized, and among them was found a petition to the Right Honourable the Earl of Warwick, etc., Commissioners, from about five and twenty non-freemen, for themselves and many thousands more in which they represent that from the pulpits* they had been reproached and branded with the names of destroyers of Churches and Commonwealths, called Hamans, Judases, sons of Korah, and the Lord entreated to confound them, and the people and magistrates stirred up against them by those who were too forward to step out of their callings, so that they had been sent for to the Court, and some of them committed for refusing to give two hundred pounds bond to stand to the sentence of the Court, *when all the crime was a petition to the Court,* and they had been publicly used as malefactors, etc.

"Mr. Winslow, who had been chosen agent for the colony to answer to Gorton's complaint, was now instructed to make defence against these petitioners; and by his prudent management, and the credit and esteem he was in with many members of the Parliament and principal persons then in power, he prevented any prejudice to the colony from either of these applications."†

ignominious hearing before a vast assembly, to which, " with a sagacious humility," he consented, although he showed he might have refused it. The result of the hearing was that he was honourably acquitted,' etc."

* This refers to a sermon preached by Mr. Cotton on a fast day, an extract of which is published in the Magnalia, B. III., p. 29, wherein he denounces the judgments of God upon such of his hearers as were then going to England with evil intentions against the country.

† Hutchinson's History of Massachusetts Bay, Vol. I., pp. 145—149.

Mr. Palfrey, under the head of " Presbyterian Cabal," states the following facts as to the treatment of Dr. Child, Mr. Dand, and others who proposed to make their appeal to the English Parliament :

"Child and Dand, two of the remonstrants, were preparing to go to England with a petition to the Parliament from a number of the non-freemen. Informed of their intention, the magistrates ordered a seizure of their papers. The searching officers found in their possession certain memorials to the Commissioners for Plantations, asking for ' settled Churches according to the [Presbyterian] Reformation in England ;' for the establishment in the colony of the laws of the realm ; for the appointment of ' a General Governor, or some honourable Commissioner,' to reform the existing state of things. For

Mr. (Edward) Winslow, above mentioned by Mr. Hutchinson, had been one of the founders and Governors of the *Plymouth* colony; but twenty-five years afterwards he imbibed the persecuting spirit of the Massachusetts Bay colony, became their agent and advocate in London, and by the prestige which he had acquired as the first narrator and afterwards Governor of the Plymouth colony, had much influence with the leading men of the Long Parliament. He there joined himself to Cromwell, and was appointed one of his three Commissioners to the West Indies, where he died in 1655. Cromwell, as he said when he first obtained possession of the King, had "the Parliament in his pocket;" he had abolished the Prayer Book and its worship; he had expurgated the army of Presbyterians, and filled their places with Congregationalists; he was repeating the same process in Parliament; and through him, therefore (who was also Commander-in-Chief of all the Parliamentary forces), Mr. Winslow had little difficulty in stifling the appeal from Massachusetts Bay for liberty of worship in behalf of both Presbyterians and Episcopalians.

But was ever a petition to a local Legislature more constitutional, or more open and manly in the manner of its getting up, more Christian in its sentiments and objects? Yet the petitioners were arraigned and punished as "conspirators" and "disturbers of the public peace," by order of that Legislature, for openly petitioning to it against some of its own acts. Was ever appeal to the Imperial Parliament by British subjects more justifiable than that of Dr. Child, Mr. Dand, Mr. Vassal (progenitor of British Peers), and others, from acts of a local Government which deprived them of both religious rights of worship and civil rights of franchise, of all things earthly most valued by enlightened men, and without which the position of man is little better than that of goods and chattels? Yet the respectable men who appealed to the supreme power of the realm for the attainment of these attributes of Christian and

this further offence, such of the prominent conspirators as remained in the country were punished by additional fines. Child and Dand were mulcted in the sum of two hundred pounds; Mauerick, in that of a hundred and fifty pounds; and two others of a hundred pounds each."—Palfrey's History of New England [Abridged edition], Vol. I., pp. 327, 328.

7

British citizenship were imprisoned and heavily fined, and their private papers seized and sequestered!

In my own native country of Upper Canada, the Government for nearly half a century was considered despotic, and held up by American writers themselves as an unbearable tyranny. But one Church was alleged to be established in the country, and the government was that of a Church party; but never was the elective franchise there confined to the members of the one Church; never were men and women denied, or hailed before the legal tribunals and fined for exercising the privilege of Baptism, the Lord's Supper, or public worship for themselves and families according to the dictates of their own consciences never was the humblest inhabitant denied the right of petition to the local Legislature on any subject, or against any governmental acts, or the right of appeal to the Imperial Government or Parliament on the subject of any alleged grievance. The very suspicion and allegation that the Canadian Government did counteract, by influences and secret representations, the statements of complaining parties to England, roused public indignation as arbitrary and unconstitutional. Even the insurrection which took place in both Upper and Lower Canada in 1837 and 1838 was professedly against alleged partiality and injustice by the *local* Government, as an obstruction to more liberal policy believed to be desired by the Imperial Government.

But here, in Massachusetts, a colony chartered as a Company to distribute and settle public lands and carry on trade, in less than twenty years assumes the powers of a sovereign Commonwealth, denies to five-sixths of the population the freedom of citizenship, and limits it to the members of one Church, and denies Baptism, the Lord's Supper, and worship to all who will not come to the one Church, punishes petitioners to itself for civil and religious freedom from those who were deprived of it, and punishes as "treason" their appeal for redress to the English Parliament. Though, for the present, this unprecedented and unparalleled local despotism was sustained by the ingenious representations of Mr. Winslow and the power of Cromwell; yet in the course of four years the surrender of its Charter was ordered by the regicide councillors of the Commonwealth, as it had been ordered by the beheaded King Charles and his Privy Council thirteen years before. In the meantime tragical events

in England diverted attention from the colonies. The King
was made prisoner, then put to death; the Monarchy was
abolished, as well as the House of Lords; and the Long Parliament became indeed Cromwell's "pocket" instrument.

It was manifest that the government of Massachusetts Bay
as a colony was impossible, with the pretensions which it had
set up, declaring all appeals to England to be "treason," and
punishing complainants as "conspirators" and "traitors." The
appointment by Parliament in 1643 of a Governor-General and
Commissioners had produced no effect in Massachusetts Bay
Colony; pretensions to supremacy and persecution were as rife
as ever there. Dr. Child and his friends were punished for
even asking for the administration that appointed the Governor-
General and those Commissioners; and whether the Government
of England were a monarchy or republic, it was clear that the
pretensions to independence of the Puritans of Massachusetts
Bay must be checked, and their local tyranny restrained. For
this purpose the Long Parliament adopted the same policy in
1650 that King Charles had done in 1637; demanded the
surrender of the Charter; for that Parliament sent a summons
to the local Government ordering it to transmit the Charter to
England, to receive a new patent from the Parliament in all its
acts and processes.

This order of Parliament to Massachusetts Bay Colony to
surrender its Charter was accompanied by a proclamation prohibiting trade with Virginia, Barbadoes, Bermuda, and Antigua,
because these colonies continued to recognize royal authority,
and to administer their laws in the name of the King. This
duplicate order from the Long Parliament was a double blow
to the colony of Massachusetts Bay, and produced general consternation; but the dexterity and diplomacy of the colony
were equal to the occasion. It showed its devotion to the
cause of the Long Parliament by passing an Act prohibiting
trade with the loyal, but by them termed rebel colonies;* and

---

* Mr. Bancroft, referring to the petition of Dr. Child and others, quoted
on page 94, says: "The document was written in the spirit of wanton
insult;" then refers to the case of Gorton, who had appealed to the Earl of
Warwick and the other Parliamentary Commissioners against a judicial
decision of the Massachusetts Bay Court in regard to land claimed by him.
From Mr. Bancroft's statement, it appears that the claim of Gorton, friendless

it avoided surrendering the Charter by repeating its policy of
delay and petition, which it had adopted on a similar occasion

as he was, was so just as to commend its. to the favourable judgment of an
impartial and competent tribunal of the Parliamentary Commissioners,
whose authority his oppressors expressly denied, and then, in their address to
Parliament in reference to its order, denied any authority of Parliament over
their proceedings. Mr. Bancroft's words are as follows :

" Gorton had carried his complaints to the Mother Country ; and, though
unaided by personal influence or by powerful friends, had succeeded in all
his wishes. At this very juncture an order respecting his claims arrived in
Boston ; and was couched in terms *which involved an assertion of the right of
Parliament to reverse the decisions and control the Government of Massachusetts.*
The danger was imminent ; it struck at the very life and foundation of the
rising Commonwealth. *Had the Long Parliament succeeded in revoking the
patent of Massachusetts,* the Stuarts, on their restoration, would have found
not one chartered government in the colonies ; and the tenor of American
history would have been changed. The people (a) rallied with great unanimity
in support of their magistrates.

" At length the General Court assembled for the discussion of *the usurpations of Parliament* and the *dangers from domestic treachery.* The elders
[ministers] did not fail to attend in the gloomy season. One faithless
deputy was desired to withdraw ; and then, *with closed doors,* that the consultation might remain in the breast of the Court, the *nature of the relation
with England* was made the subject of debate. After much deliberation it
was agreed that Massachusetts owed the same allegiance to England as the
free Hanse Towns had rendered to the Empire ; as Normandy, when its
dukes were kings in England, had paid to the monarchs of France. It was
also resolved not to accept a new Charter from Parliament, for that would
imply a surrender of the old. Besides, Parliament granted none but by way
of ordinance, and always made for itself an express preservation of a supreme
power in all things. The *elders* [ministers], after a day's consultation,
confirmed the decisions.

" The colony proceeded to exercise the *independence* which it claimed.
The General Court replied to the petition in a State paper, written with
great moderation ; and the disturbers of the public security were summoned
into its presence. Robert Child and his companions appealed to the Commissioners in England. *The appeal was not admitted.*" " To the Parliament
of England the Legislature remonstrated with the noblest frankness *against
any assertion of permanent authority of that body.*"—Hist. U. S., Vol. I., pp.
475—477.

(a) By the "people" here Mr. Bancroft must mean the members of the
Congregational Churches (one-sixth of the whole population), for they alone
were *freemen,* and had all the united powers of the franchise—the *sword,* the
legislation—in a word, the whole civil, judicial, ecclesiastical, and military
government.

in 1638 to King Charles; and its professions of loyalty to
Charles, and prayers for the Royal Family, and the success of
the Privy Council, it now repeated for the Long Parliament and
its leaders, supporting its petition by an appeal to its ten years'
services of prayers and of men to the cause of the Long
Parliament against the King. I will, in the first place, give in
a note Mr. Bancroft's own account of what was claimed and
ordered by the Long Parliament, and the pretensions and proceedings of the Legislature of Massachusetts Bay, and then
will give the principal parts of their petition to the Long
Parliament in their own words. The words and statements of
Mr. Bancroft involve several things worthy of notice and
remembrance: 1. The Congregational Church rulers of Massachusetts Bay denied being British subjects, admitting no other
allegiance to England than the Hanse Towns of Northern
Germany to the Empire of Austria, or the Normandy ducal
kings of England to the King of France; or, as Mr. Palfrey
says, "the relations which Burgundy and Flanders hold to
France." 2. Mr. Bancroft calls the petitioners "disturbers of
the public security," and Mr. Palfrey calls them "conspirators"—
terms applied to the Armenian remonstrants against the persecuting edicts of the Synod of Dort—terms applied to all the
complainants of the exclusive and persecuting policy of the
Tudor and Stuart kings of England—terms applied to even
the first Christians—terms now applied to pleaders of religious
and civil freedom by the advocates of a Massachusetts Government as intolerant and persecuting as ever existed in Europe.
The petition of these impugned parties shows that all they
asked for was equal religious and civil liberty and protection
with their Congregational oppressors. Opprobrious names are
not arguments; and imputations of motives and character are
not facts, and are usually resorted to for want of them. 3. Mr.
Bancroft designates as "usurpations of Parliament" the proceedings of the Long Parliament in appointing a Governor-General
and Commissioners for the colonies, and in exercising its right
to receive and decide upon appeals from the colonies; and terms
the support of the Parliament in the colony "domestic treachery;"
and the one member of the Legislature who had the courage to
maintain the supremacy of the Mother Country is called the
"faithless deputy," who was forthwith turned out of the House,

which then proceeded, " with closed doors," to discuss in secret conclave its relations to England, and concluded by declaring " against any assertion of paramount authority" on the part of the English Parliament. This was substantially a " Declaration of Independence ;" not, indeed, against an arbitrary king, as was alleged sixteen years before, and a hundred and thirty years afterwards, but against a Parliament which had dethroned and beheaded their King, and abolished the House of Lords and the Episcopal Church! All this Mr. Bancroft now treats as maintaining the *Charter*, of which he himself had declared, in another place, as I have quoted above : " The Charter on which the freemen of Massachusetts succeeded in erecting a system of independent representative liberty did not secure to them a single privilege of self-government, but left them as the Virginians had been left, without any valuable franchise, at the mercy of the Corporation within the realm." Who then were the " usurpers," and had been for twenty years, of power which had not been conferred on them—the new Church and the persecuting Government of Massachusetts Bay, or the supreme authority of England, both under a King and under a professed republican commonwealth ? 4. Mr. Bancroft says : " Had the Long Parliament succeeded in revoking the patent of the Massachusetts Bay,* the tenor of American history would have been changed." I agree with him in this opinion, though probably not in his application of it. I believe that the " tenor of American history" would have led to as perfect an independence of the American States as they now enjoy—as free, but a better system of government, and without their ever having made war and bloodshed against Great Britain.

The facts thus referred to show that there were *Empire Loyalists* in America in the seventeenth, as there were afterwards in the eighteenth century; they then embraced all the colonies of New England, except the ruling party of Massachusetts Bay; they were all advocates of an equal franchise,

---

* But Mr. Bancroft seems to forget that in less than forty years after this the Charter was revoked, and that very system of government was established which the General Court of Massachusetts Bay now deprecated, but under which Massachusetts itself was most prosperous and peaceful for more than half a century, until the old spirit was revived, which rendered friendly government with England impossible.

and equal religious and civil liberty for all classes—the very reverse of the Massachusetts Government, which, while it denied any subordination to England, denied religious and civil liberty to all classes except members of the Congregational Churches.

It is a curious and significant fact, stated by Mr. Bancroft, that these intolerant and persecuting proceedings of the Massachusetts Bay Legislature were submitted to the Congregational ministers for their approval and final endorsement. The Long Parliament in England checked and ruled the Assembly of Westminster divines; but in Massachusetts the divines, after a day's consideration, "approved the proceedings of the General Court." No wonder that such divines, supported by taxes levied by the State and rulers of the State, denounced all toleration of dissent from their Church and authority.

Before leaving this subject, I must notice the remarks of Mr. Palfrey,—the second, if not first in authority of the historians of New England.

Mr. Palfrey ascribes what he calls "the Presbyterian Cabal" to Mr. William Vassal, who was one of the founders and first Council of the colony of Massachusetts Bay, whose brother Samuel had shared with Hampden the honour of having refused to pay ship-money to Charles, and who was now, with the Earl of Warwick,* one of the Parliamentary Commissioners for the colonies. It appears that Mr. Vassal opposed from the beginning the new system of Church and proscriptive civil government set up at Massachusetts Bay, and therefore came under Mr. Bancroft's category of "disturbers of the public security," and Mr. Palfrey's designation of "conspirators;" but was in reality a liberal and a loyalist, not to King Charles indeed, but to the Commonwealth of England. I give Mr. Palfrey's statements, in his own words, in a note.†

---

* Mr. Hutchinson says : " The Earl of Warwick had a patent for Massachusetts Bay about 1623, but the bounds are not known." (History of Massachusetts Bay, Vol. I., p. 7.)

† Mr. Palfrey says : " While in England the literary war against Presbytery was in great part conducted by American combatants, their attention was presently required at home. William Vassal, a man of fortune, was one of the original assistants named in the Charter of the Massachusetts Company. He came to Massachusetts with Winthrop's fleet in the great emigration ; but for some cause—*possibly from dissatisfaction with the tendencies to Separatism*

The spirit and sentiments of Mr. Palfrey are identical with those which I have quoted of Mr. Bancroft; but while Mr. Bancroft speaks contemptuously of the authors of the petition

which he witnessed—he almost immediately returned. He crossed the sea again five years after, but then it was to the colony of Plymouth. Establishing his home at Scituate, he there conducted himself so as to come under the reproach of being 'a man of a busy, factious spirit, and always opposite to the civil government of the country and the way of the Churches.'" (Winthrop, II., p. 261.) His disaffection occasioned the more uneasiness, because his brother Samuel, also formerly an assistant of the Massachusetts Company, was now one of the Parliament's Commissioners for the government of Foreign Plantations.

In the year when the early struggle between the Presbyterians and Independents in England had disclosed the importance of the issues depending upon it, and the obstinate determination with which it was to be carried on, Vassal " practised with " a few persons in Massachusetts " to take some course, first by petitioning the Courts of Massachusetts and of Plymouth, *and if that succeeded not*, then to the Parliament of England, that the distinctions which were maintained here, both in civil and church state, might be done away, and that we might be wholly governed by the laws of England." In (*a*) a " Remonstrance and Humble Petition," addressed by them to the General Court [of Massachusetts], they represented—1. That they could not discern in that colony " a settled form of government according to the laws of England ; " 2. That " many thousands in the plantation of the English nation were debarred from civil employments," and not permitted " so much as to have any vote in choosing magistrates, captains, or other civil and military officers ; " and, 3. " That numerous members of the Church of England, * * not dissenting from the latest reformation in England, Scotland, etc., were detained from the seals of the covenant of free grace, as it was supposed they will not take these Churches' covenants." They prayed for relief from each of these grievances ; and they gave notice that, if it were denied, they should " be necessitated to apply their humble desires to the honourable Houses of Parliament, who, they hoped, would take their sad condition into their serious consideration."

After describing the social position of the representative petitioners, Mr. Palfrey proceeds : " But however little importance the movement derived from

(*a*) Winthrop, II., 261. " The movement in Plymouth was made at a General Court in October, 1645, as appears from a letter of Winslow to Winthrop (Hutchinson's Collection, 154) ; though the public record contains nothing respecting it. I infer from Winslow's letter, that half the assistants (namely, Standish, Hatherly, Brown, and Freeman) were in favour of larger indulgence to the malcontents." (Note by Mr. Palfrey.)

[The majority of the General Court were clearly in favour of the movement ; and knowing this, the Governor, Prince (the only persecuting Governor of the Plymouth Colony), refused to put the question to vote.]

for equal civil and religious rights, Mr. Palfrey traces the movement to Mr. William Vassal, one of the founders and first
Council of the Massachusetts Colony, and progenitor of the
famous Whig family of Holland House.　Nor does Mr. Palfrey
venture to question the doctrine or one of the statements of the
petitioners, though he calls them " conspirators."

Mr. Palfrey—very unfairly, I think—imputes to the petitioners a design to subvert the Congregational worship and
establish the Presbyterian worship in its place; and to give
force to his imputations says that a numerous party in the

the character or position of the agitators, it was essentially of a nature to create
alarm.　It proposed nothing less than an abandonment of institutions, civil
and ecclesiastical, which the settlers and owners of Massachusetts had set up,
for reasons impressing their own minds as of the greatest significance and
cogency.　The demand was enforced by considerations which were not without plausibility, and were presented in a seductive form.　*It was itself an
appeal to the discontent of the numerical majority, not invested with a share in
the government.*　And it frankly threatened an appeal to the English Parliament—an authority always to be dreaded for encroachment on colonial rights,
and especially to be dreaded at a moment when the more numerous party
among its members were bent on setting up a Presbytery as the established
religion of England and its dependencies, determined on a severe suppression
of dissent from it, and keenly exasperated against that Independency which
New England had raised up to torment them in their own sphere, and which,
for herself, New England cherished as her life."

" It being understood that two of the remonstrants, Fowle and Smith,
were about to embark for England, to prosecute their business, the Court
stopped them with a summons to appear and ' answer *to the matter of the
petition.*'　They replied ' to the Gentlemen Commissioners for Plantations ;' and the Court committed them to the custody of the Marshal till
they gave security to be responsible to the judgment of the Court.　The
whole seven were next arraigned as authors of divers false and scandalous
statements in a certain paper * * * against the Churches of Christ and the
civil government here established, derogating from the honour and authority
of the same, and tending to sedition.　Refusing to answer, and ' appealing
from this government, they disclaimed the jurisdiction thereof.'　This was
more than Presbyterian malcontents could be indulged in at the present
critical time in Massachusetts.　The Court found them all deeply blamable,
and punished them by fines, which were to be remitted on their making ' an
ingenuous and public acknowledgment of their misdemeanours ;' a condition
of indemnity which they all refused, probably in expectation of obtaining
both relief and applause in England."—" Four deputies opposed the sentence ;
three magistrates—Bellingham, Saltonstall, and Bradstreet—also dissented."—
Palfrey's History of New England, Vol. I., pp. 166—170.

English Parliament " were bent on setting up Presbytery as the established religion in England and *its dependencies.*" There is not the slightest ground for asserting that any party in the Long Parliament, any more than in Massachusetts, designed the setting up of Presbytery as *the* established worship in the "*dependencies* of England." King Charles the First, on his first sitting in judgment on complaints against the proceedings of the Massachusetts Bay Council, declared to his Privy Council, in 1632, that he had never intended to impose the Church ceremonies, objected to by the Puritan clergy of the time, upon the colonists of Massachusetts. Charles the Second, thirty years afterwards, declared the same, and acted upon it during the quarter of a century of his reign. The Long Parliament acted upon the same principle. There is not an instance, during the whole sixty years of the first Massachusetts Charter, of any attempt, on the part of either King or Commonwealth, to suppress or interfere with the Congregational worship in New England; all that was asked by the King, or any party in Massachusetts, was *toleration* of other forms of Protestant worship as well as that of the Congregational. The very petition, whose promoters are represented as movers of sedition, asked for no exclusive establishment of Presbyterianism, but for the toleration of both the Episcopal and Presbyterian worship, and the worship of other Protestant Churches existing in England; and their petition was addressed to a Legislature of Congregationalists, elected by Congregationalists alone; and it was only in the event of their reasonable requests not being granted by the local Legislature that they proposed to present their grievances to the Imperial Parliament. The plea of fear for the safety of Congregational worship in Massachusetts was a mere pretence to justify the proscription and persecution of all dissent from the Congregational establishment. The spirit of the local Government and of the clergy that controlled it was *intolerance.* Toleration was denounced by them as the doctrine of devils; and the dying lines of Governor Dudley are reported to have been—

> " Let men of God, in Court and Church, watch
> O'er such as do a toleration hatch."*

There is one other of Mr. Palfrey's statements which is of

---

* Hutchinson's History of Massachusetts Bay, Vol. I., Chap. v., p. 75.

special importance; it is the admission that a majority of the population of Massachusetts were excluded from all share in the Government, and were actually opposed to it. Referring to the petition to the local Legislature, he says: "The demand was enforced by considerations which were not without plausibility, and were presented in a seductive form. It was itself an appeal to the *discontent of the numerical majority not invested with a share in the government.*"*

* History of New England, Vol. II. p. 169. In another case mentioned by Mr. Palfrey, it is clear the public feeling was not with the local Government, which pretended to absolute independence of Parliament, and called the entrance of a parliamentary war vessel into its harbour, and action there, a "*foreign* encroachment." A Captain Stagg arrived at Boston from London, in a vessel carrying twenty-four guns, and found there a merchant vessel from Bristol (which city was then held for the King), which he seized. Governor Winthrop wrote to Captain Stagg "to know *by what authority* he had done it in *our* harbour." Stagg produced his commission from the Earl of Warwick to capture vessels from ports in the occupation of the King's party, as well in harbours and creeks as on the high seas. Winthrop ordered him to carry the paper to Salem, the place of the Governor's residence, there to be considered at a meeting of the magistrates. *Of course the public feeling was with the Parliament and its officers;* but it was not so heedless as to forget its jealousy of *foreign encroachment* from whatever quarter. "Some of the elders, the last Lord's Day, had in their sermons reproved this proceeding, and exhorted magistrates to maintain the people's liberties, which were, they said, *violated by this act,* and that a commission could not supersede a patent. And at this meeting some of the magistrates and some of the elders were of the same opinion, and that the captain should be forced to restore the ship." The decision, however, was different; and the reasons for *declining to defy the Parliament,* and allowing its officer to retain possession of his prize, are recorded. The following are passages of this significant manifesto: "This could be no precedent to bar us from opposing any commission or other foreign power that might indeed tend to our hurt or violate our liberty; for the Parliament had taught us that *salus populi* is *suprema lex.*" (a) "If

(a) This maxim, that *the safety of the people is the supreme law,* might, by a similar perversion, be claimed by any mob or party constituting the majority of a city, town, or neighbourhood, as well as by the Colony of Massachusetts, against the Parliament or supreme authority of the nation. They had no doubt of their own infallibility; they had no fear that they "should hereafter be of a malignant spirit;" but they thought it very possible that the Parliament might be so, and then it would be for them to fight if they should have "strength sufficient." But after the restoration they thought it not well to face the armies and fleets of Charles the Second, and made as humble, as loyal, and as laudatory professions to him—calling him "the best of kings"—as they had made to Cromwell.

It is thus admitted, and clear from indubitable facts, that professing to be republicans, they denied to the great majority of the people any share in the government. Professing hatred of the persecuting intolerance of King Charles and Laud in denying liberty of worship to all who differed from them, they now deny liberty of worship to all who differ from themselves, and punish those by fine and imprisonment who even petition for equal religious and civil liberty to all classes of citizens. They justify even armed resistance against the King, and actually decapitating as well as dethroning him, in order to obtain, professedly, a government by the majority of the nation and liberty of worship; and they now deny the same principle and right of civil and religious liberty to the great majority of the people over whom they claimed rule. They claim the right of resisting Parliament itself by armed force if they had the power, and only desist from asserting it, to the last, as the *salus populi* did not require it, and for the sake of their "godly friends in England," and to not afford a pretext for the "rebellious course" of their fellow-colonists in Virginia and the West Indies, who claimed the same independence of Parliament that the Government of Massachusetts claimed, but upon the ground which was abhorrent to the Congregational Puritans of Massachusetts— namely, that of loyalty to the king.

I will now give in a note, in their own words, the principal parts of their petition, entitled "General Court of Massachusetts Bay, New England, in a Petition to Parliament in 1651,"*

Parliament should hereafter be of a malignant spirit, then, *if we have strength sufficient*, we may make use of *salus populi* to withstand any authority from thence to our hurt." "If we who have so openly declared our affection to the cause of Parliament by our prayers, fastings, etc., should now oppose their authority, or do anything that would make such an appearance, it would be laid hold on by those in Virginia and the West Indies to confirm them in their rebellious course, and it would grieve all our godly friends in England, or any other of the Parliament's friends."—Palfrey's History of New England, Vol. II., pp. 161—163.

Note.—It is plain from these words, as well as from other words quoted elsewhere, how entirely and avowedly the Massachusetts Court identified themselves with the Parliament and Cromwell against the King, though they denied having done so in their addresses to Charles the Second.

* They say: "Receiving information by Mr. Winslow, our agent, that it is the Parliament's pleasure that we should take a new patent from them, and keep our Courts and issue our warrants in their names, which we have

together with extracts of two addresses to Cromwell, the one
enclosing a copy of their petition to Parliament, when he was
Commander-in-Chief of the army, and the other in 1654, after
he had dismissed the Rump Parliament, and become absolute—
denying to the whole people of England the elective franchise,
as his admiring friends in Massachusetts denied it to the great

not used in the late King's time or since, not being able to discern the need
of such an injunction,—these things make us doubt and fear what is
intended towards us. Let it therefore please you, most honourable, we
humbly entreat, to take notice hereby what were our orders, upon what
conditions and with what authority we came hither, and what we have done
since our coming. We were the first movers and undertakers of so great an
attempt, being men able enough to live in England with our neighbours, and
being helpful to others, and not needing the help of any for outward things.
About three or four and twenty years since, seeing just cause to fear the
persecution of the then Bishops and High Commissioners for not conforming
to the ceremonies then pressed upon the consciences of those under their
power, we thought it our safest course to get to this outside of the world,
out of their view and beyond their reach. Yet before we resolved upon so
great an undertaking, wherein should be hazarded not only all our estates,
but also the lives of ourselves and our posterity, both in the voyage at sea
(wherewith we were unacquainted), and in coming into a wilderness unin-
habited (unless in some few places by heathen, barbarous Indians), we
thought it necessary to procure a patent from the late King, who then ruled
all, to warrant our removal and prevent future inconveniences, and so did.
By which patent liberty and power was granted to us to live under the
government of a Governor, magistrates of our own choosing, and under laws
of our own making (not being repugnant to the laws of England), according
to which patent we have governed ourselves above this twenty years, we
coming hither at our proper charges, without the help of the State, an
acknowledgment of the freedom of our goods from custom," etc. "And for
our carriage and demeanour to the honourable Parliament, for these ten
years, since the first beginning of your differences with the late King, and
the war that after ensued, we have constantly adhered to you, not withdrawing
ourselves in your weakest condition and doubtfullest times, but by our
fasting and prayers for your good success, and our thanksgiving after the
same was attained, in days of solemnity set apart for that purpose, as also by
our sending over useful men (others also going voluntarily from us to help
you), who have been of good use and done acceptable services to the army,
declaring to the world hereby that such was the duty and love we bear unto
the Parliament, that we were ready to rise and fall with them ; for which
we have suffered the hatred and threats of other English colonies now in
rebellion against you, as also the loss of divers of our ships and goods, taken
by the King's party that is dead, by others commissioned by the King of
Scots [Charles II.], and by the Portugalls." "We hope that this most

majority of the people within their jurisdiction. Chalmers says they "outfawned and outwitted Cromwell." They gained his support by their first address, and thanked him for it in their second. Having "the Parliament in his pocket" until he threw even the rump of it aside altogether, Cromwell caused Parliament to desist from executing its own order.

It will be seen in the following chapter, that ten years after these laudatory addresses to Parliament and Cromwell, the same General Court of Massachusetts addressed Charles the Second in words truly loyal and equally laudatory, and implored the continuance of their Charter upon the ground, among other reasons, that they had never identified themselves with the

honourable Parliament will not cast such as have adhered to you and depended upon you, as we have done, into so deep despair, from the fear of which we humbly desire to be speedily freed by a just and gracious answer ; which will freshly bind us to pray and use all lawful endeavours for the blessing of God upon you and the present Government." (Appendix viii. to the first volume of Hutchinson's History of Massachusetts Bay, pp. 516—518.

The "General Court" also sent a letter to Oliver Cromwell, enclosing a copy of the petition to Parliament, to counteract representations which might be made against them by their enemies, and intreat his interest in their behalf. This letter concludes as follows :

"We humbly petition your Excellence to be pleased to shew us what favour God shall be pleased to direct you unto on our behalf, to the most honourable Parliament, unto whom we have now presented a petition. The copy of it, *verbatim*, we are bold to send herewith, that, if God so please, we be not hindered in our comfortable proceedings in the work of God here in this wilderness. Wherein, as for other favours, we shall be bound to pray, that the Captain of the Host of Israel may be with you and your whole army, in all your great enterprises, to the glory of God, the subduing of his and your enemies, and your everlasting peace and comfort in Jesus Christ." (*Ib.*, Appendix ix., p. 522.)

In August (24th), 1654, the General Court addressed another letter to Oliver Cromwell, commencing as follows :

"It hath been no small comfort to us poor exiles, in these utmost ends of the earth (who sometimes felt and often feared the frowns of the mighty), to have had the experience of the good hand of God, in raising up such, whose endeavours have not been wanting to our welfare : amongst whom we have good cause to give your Highness the first place : who by a continued series of favours, have obliged us, not only while you moved in a lower orb, but since the Lord hath called your Highness to supreme authority, whereat we rejoice and shall pray for the continuance of your happy government, that under your shadow not only ourselves, but all the Churches, may find rest and peace." (*Ib.*, Appendix x., p. 523.)

Parliament against his Royal father, but had been "passive" during the whole of that contest. Their act against having any commerce with the colonies who adhered to the King indicated their neutrality; and the reader, by reading their addresses to the Parliament and Cromwell, will see whether they did not thoroughly identify themselves with the Parliament and Cromwell against Charles the First. They praise Cromwell as raised up by the special hand of God, and crave upon him the success of "the Captain of the Lord's hosts;" and they claim the favourable consideration of Parliament to their request upon the ground that they had identified themselves with its fortunes to rise or fall with it; that they had aided it by their prayers and fastings and by men who had rendered it valuable service. The reader will be able to judge of the agreement in their *professions* and *statements* in their addresses to Parliament and Cromwell and to King Charles the Second ten years afterwards. In their addresses to Parliament and Cromwell they professed their readiness to *fall* as well as rise with the cause of the Parliament; but when that *fell*, they repudiated all connection with it.

In the year 1651, and during the very Session of Parliament to which the General Court addressed its petition and narrated its sacrifices and doings in the cause of the Parliament, the latter passed the famous Navigation Act, which was re-enacted and improved ten years afterwards, under Charles the Second, and which became the primary pretext of the American Revolution. The Commonwealth was at this time at war with the Dutch republic, which had almost destroyed and absorbed the shipping trade of England. Admiral Blake was just commencing that series of naval victories which have immortalized his name, and placed England from that time to this at the head of the naval powers of the world. Sir Henry Vane, as the Minister of the Navy, devised and carried through Parliament the famous Navigation Act—an Act which the colony of Massachusetts, by the connivance of Cromwell (who now identified himself with that colony), regularly evaded, at the expense of the American colonies and the English revenue.* Mr. Palfrey says:

* "1651.—The Parliament of England passed the famous Act of Navigation. It had been observed with concern, that the English merchants for several years past had usually freighted the Hollanders' shipping for bring-

"The people of Massachusetts might well be satisfied with their condition and prospects. Everything was prospering with them. They had established comfortable homes, which they felt strong enough to defend against any power but the power of the Mother Country; and that was friendly. They had always the good-will of Cromwell. In relation *to them*, he allowed the Navigation Law, *which pressed on the Southern colonies, to become* A DEAD LETTER, and they received the commodities of all nations free of duty, and sent their ships to all the ports of continental Europe."*

But that in which the ruling spirits of the Massachusetts General Court—apart from their ceaseless endeavours to monopolise trade and extend territory—seemed to revel most was in searching out and punishing *dissent* from the Congregational Establishment, and, at times, with the individual liberty of citizens in sumptuary matters. No Laud ever equalled them in this, or excelled them in enforcing uniformity, not only of doctrine, but of opinions and practice in the minutest particulars. When a stand against England was to be taken, in worship, or

ing home their own merchandise, because their freight was at a lower rate than that of the English ships. For the same reason the Dutch ships were made use of even for importing American products from the English colonies into England. The English ships meanwhile lay rotting in the harbours, and the English mariners, for want of employment, went into the service of the Hollanders. The Commonwealth now turned its attention towards the most effectual mode of retaining the colonies in dependence on the parent State, and of securing to it the benefits of their increasing commerce. With these views the Parliament enacted, 'That no merchandise, either of Asia, Africa, or America, including the English Plantations there, should be imported into England in any but English-built ships, and belonging either to English or English Plantation subjects, navigated also by an English commander, and three-fourths of the sailors to be Englishmen; excepting such merchandise as should be imported directly from the original place of their growth, manufactured in Europe solely: and that no fish should thenceforward be imported into England or Ireland, nor exported thence to foreign parts, nor even from one of their own ports, but what should be caught by their own fishers only." (Holmes' Annals of America, Anderson, ii., 415, 416; Robertson, B. 9, p. 303; Janes' edit. Vol. I., p. 294.) Mr. Holmes adds in a note: "This Act was evaded at first by New England, which still traded to all parts, and enjoyed a privilege peculiar to themselves of importing their goods into England free of customs." (History Massachusetts Bay, Vol. I., p. 40.)

* Palfrey's History of New England, Vol. II., p. 393.

inquisition into matters of religious dissent, and woman's apparel, Endicot became Governor (according to the "advice of the Elders " in such matters), and Winthrop was induced to be Deputy Governor, although the latter was hardly second to the former in the spirit and acts of religious persecution. He had been a wealthy man in England, and was well educated and amiable ; but after his arrival at Massachusetts Bay he seems to have wanted firmness to resist the intolerant spirit and narrow views of Endicot. He died in 1649. Mr. Palfrey remarks : " Whether it was owing to solicitude as to the course of affairs in England after the downfall of the Royal power, or to the absence of the moderating influence of Winthrop, or to sentiments engendered, on the one hand by the alarm from the Presbyterians in 1646, and on the other by the confidence inspired by the [Congregational] Synod in 1648, or to all these causes in their degree, the years 1650 and 1651 appear to have been years of more than common sensibility in Massachusetts to danger from *Heretics*."*

In 1650, the General Court condemned, and ordered to be publicly burnt, a book entitled " The Meritorious Price of our Redemption, Justification, etc., Clearing of some Common Errors," written and published in England, by Mr. Pynchion, " an ancient and venerable magistrate." This book was deficient in ortho doxy, in the estimation of Mr. Endicot and his colleagues, was condemned to be burnt, and the author was summoned to answer for it at the bar of the inquisitorial court. His explanation was unsatisfactory ; and he was commanded to appear a second time, under a penalty of one hundred pounds ; but he returned to England, and left his inquisitors without further remedy.

" About the same time," says Mr. Palfrey, " the General Court had a difficulty with the Church of Malden. Mr. Marmaduke Matthews having ' given offence to magistrates, elders, and many brethren, in some unsafe and unsound expressions in his public teaching,' and the Church of Malden having proceeded to ordain him, in disregard of remonstrances from ' both magistrates, ministers, and churches,' Matthews was fined ten pounds for assuming the sacred office, and the Church was summoned to make its defence" (Massachusetts Records, III., 237) ; which

---

* Palfrey's History of New England, Vol. II., p. 397, in a note.

8

" failing to do satisfactorily, it was punished by a fine of fifty
pounds—Mr. Hathorne, Mr. Leverett, and seven other Deputies
recording their votes against the sentence." (*Ibid.* 252 ; compare
276, 289.)

But these reputed fathers of civil and religious liberty not
only held inquisition over the religious writings and teachings
of magistrates and ministers, and the independence of their Congregational Churches, but even over the property, the income,
and the apparel of individuals ; for in this same year, 1651, they
passed a Sumptuary Act.   Mr. Holmes justly remarks :   " This
sumptuary law, for the matter and style, is a curiosity."   The
Court, lamenting the inefficacy of former " Declarations and
Orders against excess of apparel, both of men and women," proceed to observe :   " We cannot but to our grief take notice, that
intolerable excess and bravery hath crept in upon us, and especially among people of mean condition, to the dishonour of God, the
scandal of our profession, the consumption of estates, and altogether unsuitable to our poverty.   The Court proceed to order,
that no person whose visible estate should not exceed the true
and indifferent sum of £200, shall wear any gold or silver
lace, or gold and silver buttons, or have any lace above two
shillings per yard, or silk hoods or scarves, on the penalty of ten
shillings for every such offence."   The select men of every town
were required to take notice of the apparel of any of the inhabitants, and to assess such persons as " they shall judge to exceed
their ranks and abilities, in the costliness or fashion of their
apparel in any respect, especially in wearing of ribbands and
great boots," at £200 estates, according to the proportion which
some men used to pay to whom such apparel is suitable and
allowed.   An exception, however, is made in favour of public
officers and their families, and of those " whose education and
employment have been above the ordinary degree, or whose
estates have been considerable, though now decayed."*

---

* Hutchinson's History of Massachusetts Bay, Vol. I., p. 152 ; Holmes'
Annals, Vol. I., p. 294.   Note xxxi., p. 579.

This law was passed in 1651, while Endicot was Governor.   Two years
before, shortly after Governor Winthrop's death, Governor Endicot, with
several other magistrates, issued a declaration against men wearing long hair,
prefaced with the words, " Forasmuch as the wearing of long hair, after the
manner of the ruffians and barbarous Indians, has begun to invade New

It will be recollected by the reader that in 1644 the Massachusetts Bay Court passed an act of banishment, etc., against Baptists; that in 1643 it put to "the rout" the Presbyterians, who made a move for the toleration of their worship; that in 1646, when the Presbyterians and some Episcopalians petitioned the local Court for liberty of worship, and in the event of refusal expressed their determination to appeal to the English Parliament, they were punished with fines and imprisonment, and their papers were seized. The above acts of censorship over the press, and private opinions in the case of Mr. Pinchion, and their tyranny over the organization of new Churches and the ordinations of ministers—fining both Church and ministers for exercising what is universally acknowledged to be essential to *independent* worship—are but further illustrations of the same spirit of intolerance. It was the intolerance of the Massachusetts Bay Government that caused the settlement of Connecticut, of New Haven, as well as of Rhode Island. The noble minds of the younger Winthrop, of Eaton, no more than that of Roger Williams, could shrivel themselves into the nutshell littleness of the Massachusetts Bay Government—so called, indeed, by courtesy, or by way of accommodation, rather than as conveying a proper idea of a Government, as it consisted solely of Congregationalists, who alone were eligible to office and eligible as electors to office, and was therefore more properly a Congregational Association than a civil government ; yet this association assumed the combined powers of legislation, administration of government and law, and of the army—absolute censorship of the press, of worship, of even private opinions—and punished as criminals those who even expressed their griefs in petitions; and when punished they had the additional aggravation of being told that they were not punished for petitioning, but for what the petitions contained, as if they could petition without using words, and as if they could express their griefs and wishes without using words for that purpose. Yet under such pretexts was a despotism established and maintained for sixty years without a parallel in the annals of colonial history, ancient or

England," and declaring "their dislike and detestation against wearing of such long hair as a thing uncivil and unmanly, whereby men do deform themselves, and offend sober and modest men, and do corrupt good manners," etc.—*Ib.*

modern; under which five-sixths of the population had no more
freedom of worship, of opinion, or of franchise, than the slaves
of the Southern States before the recent civil war. It is not
surprising that a Government based on no British principle,
based on the above principle of a one Church membership,
every franchise under which was granted, or cancelled, or
continued at the pleasure of Elders and their Courts—such a
Government, un-British in its foundation and elements, could
not be expected to be loyal to the Royal branch of the constitution.

It is not surprising that even among the Puritan party themselves, who were now warring against the King, and who were
soon to bring him to the block, such unmitigated despotism and
persecutions in Massachusetts should call forth, here and there,
a voice of remonstrance, notwithstanding the argus-eyed watch-
fulness and espionage exercised by the Church government at
Massachusetts Bay over all persons and papers destined for
England, and especially in regard to every suspected person or
paper. One of these is from Sir Henry Vane, who went to
Massachusetts in 1636, and was elected Governor; but he was
in favour of toleration, and resisted the persecution against
Mrs. Anne Hutchinson and her brother, Mr. Wheelwright. The
persecuting party proved too strong for him, and he resigned
his office before the end of the year. He was succeeded as
Governor by Mr. Winthrop, who ordered him to quit Massachusetts. He was, I think, the purest if not the best statesman
of his time;* he was too good a man to cherish resentment
against Winthrop or against the colony, but returned good for
evil in regard to both in after years. Sir Henry Vane wrote to
Governor Winthrop, in regard to these persecutions, as follows:

"HONOURED SIR,—

"I received yours by your son, and was unwilling to let him
return without telling you as much. The exercise of troubles
which God is pleased to lay upon these kingdoms and the
inhabitants in them, teaches us patience and forbearance one
with another in some measure, though there be no difference in
our opinions, which makes me hope, that from the experience

* Such was the opinion of the late Mr. John Forster, in his beautiful Life
of Sir Henry Vane, in his Lives of the Puritan Statesmen of the Commonwealth.

here, it may also be derived to yourselves, lest while the Congregational way amongst you is in its freedom, and is backed with power, it teach its oppugners here to extirpate it and roote it out, and from its own principles and practice. I shall need say no more, knowing your son can acquaint you particularly with our affairs.

"&c., &c.,

"H. VANE.*

"June 10, 1645."

Another and more elaborate remonstrance of the same kind was written by Sir Richard Saltonstall, one of the original founders, and of the first Council of the Company—one who had appeared before the King in Council in 1632, in defence of Endicot and his Council, in answer to the charges of Church innovation, of abolishing the worship of the Church of England, and banishing the Browns on account of their adhering to the worship which all the emigrants professed on their leaving England. Sir R. Saltonstall and Mr. Cradock, the Governor of the Company, could appeal to the address of Winthrop and his eleven ships of emigrants, which they had delivered to their "Fathers and Brethren of the Church of England" on their departure for America, as to their undying love and oneness with the Church of England, and their taking Church of England chaplains with them; they could appeal to the letter of Deputy Governor Dudley to Lady Lincoln, denying that any innovations or changes whatever had been introduced; they could appeal to the positive statements of the Rev. John White, "the Patriarch of Dorchester," a Conformist clergyman, and the first projector of the colony, declaring that the charges of innovations, etc., were calumnies. Doubtless all these parties believed what they said; they believed the denials and professions made to them; and they repeated them to the King's Privy Council with such earnestness as to have quite captivated the Judges, to have secured even the sympathies of the King,

---

* Hutchinson's Collection of Original Papers, etc.; Publication of the Prince Society.

Note by Mr. Hutchinson : "Mr. Winthrop had obliged Mr. Vane to leave Massachusetts and return to England. The letter was written when Mr. Vane's interest in Parliament was very great. It shows a good spirit, and the reproof is decent as well as seasonable."

who was far from being the enemy of the colony represented by his enemies. Accordingly, an order was made in Council, January 19, 1632, "declaring the fair appearances and great hopes which there then were, that the country would prove beneficial to the kingdom, as profitable to the particular persons concerned, and that the *adventurers might be assured* that if things should be carried as was pretended when the patents were granted, and according as by the patent is appointed, his Majesty would not only maintain the liberties and privileges heretofore granted, but supply anything further which might tend to the good government, prosperity, and comfort of the people there." According to the statement of some of the Privy Council, the King himself said "he would have severely punished who did abuse his Governor and Plantation."

Mr. Palfrey well observes: "Saltonstall, Humphrey, and Cradock appeared before a Committee of the Council on the Company's behalf, and had the *address or good fortune* to vindicate their clients."* It was certainly owing to their "address or good fortune," and not to the justice of their case, that they succeeded in deceiving the King and Council. The complainants had unwisely mixed the charge of disloyal speeches, etc., with Church innovations. It was to parry the former, by assuming the statements to be *ex parte*, and at any rate uttered by private individuals, who should be called to account for their conduct, and for whose words the Company could not be justly held responsible. On the main charge of Church innovations, or Church revolution, and proscription of the worship of the Church of England, positive denials were opposed—the profession of Winthrop with his company and chaplains on leaving England, the positive statement of the "Patriarch of Dorchester," and that of Deputy Governor Dudley, who went to Massachusetts with Winthrop, and wrote to the Countess of Lincoln the year after his arrival, denying that any innovations had been made. To all this the complainants had only to oppose their own words—their papers having been seized. They were overwhelmed by the mass of authority arrayed against them. But though they were defeated for the time, they were not silenced; and the following two years were pro-

---

* History of New England, Vol. I. p. 364.

ductive of such a mass of rumours and statements, all tending
to prove the Church revolutionary and Church proscriptive
proceedings of the Massachusetts Corporation, that the King
and Council found it necessary to prosecute those inquiries
which they had deferred in 1632, and to appoint a Royal Commission to proceed to Massachusetts Bay and inquire into the
disputed facts, and correct all abuses, if such should be found,
on the spot.   This was what the Massachusetts Bay persecutors
most dreaded.   As long as the inquiry should be conducted in
London, they could, by intercepting papers and intimidating
witnesses, and with the aid of powerful friends in England—
one or two of whom managed to retain their place in office
and in the Privy Council, even when Charles ruled without a
Parliament—with such advantages they could laugh to scorn
the complaints of the persecuted, and continue their prescrip
tions and oppressions with impunity.   But with a Royal Commission sitting on the spot, these acts of concealment and
deception would be impossible.   They therefore changed their
ground ; they now denied the right of the King to inquire into
their proceedings ; they invoked, as was their wont, the counsel
of their ministers, or " Elders," who preached warlike sermons
and gave warlike advice—" to resist if they were strong
enough ;" but if not strong enough to fight, " to avoid and
delay."   For the former purpose they forthwith raised £800 to
erect a fort to protect the entrance of their harbour, and organized and armed companies ; and in pursuance of the latter,
they delayed a year even to acknowledge the receipt of the
Royal orders to answer the charges preferred against them, and
then, when a more imperative and threatening Royal demand
was sent, they pleaded for another year to prepare for their
defence, and thus " avoided and delayed " from time to time,
until the King, getting so entangled with his Scottish subjects
and Parliament, became unable to pursue his inquiries into the
proceedings of the Massachusetts Bay Plantation ; and the Congregational Church rulers there had, for more than twenty years,
the luxury of absolute rule and unrestricted persecution of all
that dissented from their newly set up Church polity and
worship.

Sir Richard Saltonstall, as well as Sir Henry Vane, and
doubtless many others of the Puritan party in England, could

not endure in silence the outrageous perversions of the Charter, and high-handed persecutions by the Congregational rulers of Massachusetts Bay.*   Sir R. Saltonstall therefore wrote to Cotton and Wilson, who, with Norton, were the ablest preachers among the "Elders," and were the fiercest persecutors.   The letter is without date, but is stated by Mr. Hutchinson, in his Collection of Massachusetts State Papers, to have been written "some time between 1645 and 1653."   Sir R. Saltonstall's indignant and noble remonstrance is as follows:

"Reverend and deare friends, whom I unfaynedly love and respect:

"It doth not a little grieve my spirit to heare what sadd things are reported day by day of your tyranny and persecutions in New England as that you fine, whip and imprison men for their consciences.   First, you compell such to come to your

---

* Mr. Neal gives the following account of certain Baptists—Clarke, Holmes and Crandall—who "were all apprehended upon the 20th July this year, [1651], at the house of one William Witters, of Lin.   As they were worshipping God in their own way on a Lord's-day morning, the constable took them into custody.   Next morning they were brought before the magistrate of the town, who sent them in custody to Boston, where they remained in prison a fortnight, when they were brought to trial, convicted and fined : John Clarke, twenty pounds or to be well whipped ; John Crandall, five pounds or to be whipped ; Obadiah Holmes, thirty pounds for several offences."   Mr. Neal adds : "The prisoners agreed not to pay their fines but to abide the corporal punishment the Court had sentenced them to ; but some of Mr. Clarke's friends paid the fine without his consent ; and Crandall was released upon the promise to appear at the next Court ; but Holmes received thirty lashes at the whipping-post.   Several of his friends were spectators of his punishment ; among the rest John Spear and John Hazell, who, as they were attending the prisoner back to prison, took him by the hand in the market-place, and, in the face of all the people, praised God for his courage and constancy ; for which they were summoned before the General Court the next day, and were fined each of them forty shillings, or to be whipped.   The prisoners refused to pay the money, but some of their friends paid it for them."

Mr. Neal adds the following just and impressive remarks : " *Thus the Government of New England, for the sake of uniformity in divine worship, broke in upon the natural rights of mankind, punishing men, not for disturbing the State, but for their different sentiments in religion,* as appears by the following Law :" [Then Mr. Neal quotes the law passed against the Baptists seven years before, in 1644, and given on page 92.]   (Neal's History of New England, Vol. I., pp. 299, 300, 302, 303.)

assemblys as you know will not joyne, and when they show their dislike thereof or witness against it, then you stirre up your magistrates to punish them for such (as you conseyve) their publicke affronts. Truly, friends, this your practice of compelling any in matters of worship to do that whereof they are not fully persuaded, is to make them sin, for so the apostle (Rom. xiv. 23) tells, and many are made hypocrites thereby, conforming in their outward man for feare of punishment. We pray for you and wish you prosperity every way; we hoped the Lord would have given you so much light and love there, that you might have been eyes to God's people here, and not to practise those courses in the wilderness, which you went so far to prevent. These rigid ways have laid you very lowe in the hearts of the saints. I do assure you I have heard them pray in the public assemblies that the Lord would give you meeke and humble spirits, not to strive so much for uniformity as to keepe the unity of the spirit in the bond of peace."

Addressed: "For my reverend and worthyly much esteemed friends, Mr. Cotton and Mr. Wilson, preachers to the Church which is at Boston, in New England."*

---

* Hutchinson's Collection of State Papers, etc., pp. 401, 402.

Mr. Cotton wrote a long letter in reply to Sir R. Saltonstall, denying that he or Mr. Wilson had instigated the complaints against the Baptists, yet representing them as *profane* because they did not attend the established worship, though they worshipped God in their own way. Cotton, assuming that the Baptist worship was no worship, and that the only lawful worship was the Congregational, proceeds to defend compulsory attendance at the established worship upon the ground of preventing Sabbath profaneness (which was a perversion of Sir R. Saltonstall's letter), the same as compulsory attendance at the established worship was justified in the time of Elizabeth and James the First, and against which the whole army of Puritan writers had contended. Some of Cotton's words were as follows: "But (you say) it doth make men hypocrites to compel men to conforme the outward men for fear of punishment. If it did so, yet better be hypocrites than profane persons. Hypocrites give God part of his due, the outward man; but the profane person giveth God neither the outward or inward man."—" If the magistrate connive at his absenting himself from the Sabbath duties, the sin will be greater in the magistrate than can be the other's coming."

Mr. Hutchinson, referring to Sir R. Saltonstall's letter, says:—" It discovers a good deal of that catholic spirit which too many of our first settlers were destitute of, and confirms what I have said of Mr. Dudley's zeal in the first volume of the Massachusetts History."

It is seen that Sir R. Saltonstall's letter was addressed to the two principal Congregational ministers of Boston. It has been shown that the preachers were the counsellors and prompters of all violent measures against dissenting Baptists, Presbyterians, Episcopalians, and Quakers—a fact further illustrated and confirmed by Mr. Bancroft, who, under the date of 1650 and 1651, says: "Nor can it be denied, nor should it be concealed, that the Elders, especially Wilson and Norton, instigated and sustained the Government in its worst cruelties."*

During this first thirty years of the Massachusetts Bay Government, it evinced, in contrast with all the other British American colonies, constant hostility to the authorities in England, seizing upon every possible occasion for agitation and dispute; perverting and abusing the provisions of the Royal Charter to suppress the worship of the Church of England, and banishing its adherents; setting up a new Church and persecuting, by whipping, banishment and death, those who refused to conform to it; seeking its own interests at the expense of the neighbouring colonies; sacrificing the first principles of civil and religious liberty in their legislation and government; basing eligibility to office, and even the elective franchise, upon the condition of membership in a Congregational Church—a condition without a precedent or a parallel in any Protestant country.

I cannot better conclude this review of the first three decades of the Massachusetts Bay Puritan Government, than in the words of the celebrated Edmund Burke, who, in his account of the European settlements in America, after describing the form of government established at Massachusetts Bay, remarks that: "From such a form as this, great religious freedom might, one would have imagined, be well expected. But the truth is, they

---

* History of the United States, Vol. I., p. 484.

"I believe," says Mr. Bancroft, "that the elder Winthrop had relented before his death, and, it is said, became weary of banishing heretics. The soul of the younger Winthrop was incapable of harbouring a thought of intolerant cruelty; but the rugged Dudley was not mellowed by old age." Cotton affirmed: "Better tolerate hypocrites and tares than thorns and briers." "Religion," said Norton, from the pulpit, "admits of no eccentric motions." (*Ib.*, pp. 486, 487.)

had no idea at all of such freedom. The very doctrine of any sort of toleration was so odious to the greater part, that one of the first persecutions set up here was against a small party which arose amongst themselves, who were hardy enough to maintain that the civil magistrate had no lawful power to use compulsory measures in affairs of religion. After harassing these people by all the vexatious ways imaginable, they obliged them to fly out of their jurisdiction." "If men, merely for the moderation of their sentiments, were exposed to such severe treatment, it was not to be expected that others should escape unpunished. The very first colony had hardly set its foot in America, when, discovering that some amongst them were false brethren, and ventured to make use of the Common Prayer, they found means to make the country so uneasy to them, that they were glad to fly back to England. As soon as they began to think of making laws, I find no less than five about matters of religion; all contrived, and not only contrived, but executed in some respects with a rigour that the persecution which drove the Puritans out of England, might be considered lenity and indulgence in the comparison. For, in the first of these laws, they deprive every man who does not communicate with their Established Church, of the right to his freedom, or a vote in the election of their magistrates. In the second, they sentence to banishment any who should oppose the fourth commandment, or deny the validity of infant baptism, or the authority of the magistrates. In the third, they condemn Quakers to banishment, and make it capital for them to return; and not stopping at the offenders, they lay heavy fines upon all who should bring them into the province, or even harbour them for an hour. In the fourth, they provide banishment, and death in case of return, for Jesuits and Popish priests of every denomination. In the fifth, they decree death to any who shall worship images. After they had provided such a complete code of persecution, they were not long without opportunities of reading bloody lectures upon it." "In short, this people, who in England could not bear to be chastised with rods, had no sooner got free from their fetters than they scourged their fellow-refugees with scorpions; though the absurdity as well as injustice of such proceeding in them might stare them in the face!"*

* Burke, Vol. II., Second London Edition, 1758, pp. 148—152.

Mr. Palfrey observes, that " the death of the Protector is not so much as referred to in the public records of Massachusetts." If this silence even as to the fact of Cromwell's death was intended to disclaim having had any connection or sympathy with the Protector, it was a deception ; if it was intended as preparatory to renouncing the worship of the setting sun of Cromwell, and worshipping the rising sun of Charles the Second, it was indeed characteristic of their siding with the stronger party, if they could thereby advance their own interests. But I think every candid man in this age will admit, that there was much more dignity of sentiment and conduct of those loyal colonies who adhered to their Sovereign in his adversity as well as in his prosperity, who submitted to compulsory subjection to the Cromwell power without acknowledging its legitimacy, and were the first to recognize and proclaim the restored king.*

The reader will be better able to appreciate the professions of the Massachusetts Bay Government, in regard to the restored king, after reviewing its professions and relations to the Government of the Long Parliament and of Cromwell.

* " In October, 1650, the Commons passed a memorable ordinance, prohibiting trade with Barbadoes, Virginia, Antigua, and the Bermudas, because they had adhered to the fortunes of their late Sovereign. It declared such persons ' notorious robbers and traitors ;' it forbade every one to confederate with them ; it prohibited all foreign vessels from sailing thither, and it empowered the Council of State to compel all opponents to obey the authority of Parliament. Berkley's defence of Virginia against the fortunate invaders gained him the approbation of his prince and the applause of his countrymen. When he could no longer fight, he delivered up the government, upon such favourable terms as the English Commissioners were willing to grant. He retired to a private station, to wait with patience for favourable events. Virginia changed the various rulers which the revolutions of the age imposed on England, with the reluctance that acknowledged usurpation generally incites. But with the distractions that succeeded the death of Cromwell, she seized the opportunity to free herself from the dominion of her hated masters by recalling Berkley from his obscurity, and proclaiming the exiled king ; and she by this means acquired the unrivalled honour of being the last dominion of the State which submitted to that unjust exercise of government, and the first which overturned it." —Chalmers' History of the Revolt of the American Colonies, Vol. I., pp. 74, 75 (Boston Collection).

It has been shown above, that when obstinate silence could not prevent the inquiry by a Royal Commission into the oppressive and disloyal proceedings complained of, and that resistance was fruitless, the Massachusetts Bay Government, September 1638, transmitted to the Lords Commissioners for the Colonies a petition in which it professed not to question the authority of their Lordships' proceedings, but only to open their griefs; that if they had offended in anything, they prostrated themselves at the foot of authority. They begged for time to answer, before condemnation, professed loyalty to the King and prayers for his long life, and the happiness of his family, and for the success of the Lords of his Council. Two years after, when the King's power began to wane, the Massachusetts Bay Government sent home a Commission, headed by the notorious Hugh Peters,* to conciliate the support of the leading members of the Commons against the King's commission, and to aid the opposition to the King. In 1644, the General Court of Massachusetts Bay enacted, "that what person so ever shall draw a party to the King, against the Parliament, shall be accounted a high offender against this Commonwealth, and shall be punished capitally." (See this Act, quoted at large in a previous page.) This proceeding was as decisive as possible against the King and all who adhered to the monarchy.

Again, in the Massachusetts General Court's address to Parliament, in 1651, occur the following words:

"And for our carriage and demeanour to the honourable Parliament, for these *ten years*, since the first beginning of your differences with the late king, and the war that after ensued, *we have constantly adhered to you*, not withdrawing ourselves in your weakest condition and doubtfullest times, but by our fasting and prayers for your good success, and our thanksgiving after the same was attained, in days of solemnity set apart for that purpose, *as also by our over-useful men* (others going voluntarily from us to help you), *who have been of good use and*

---

* It was proved on Hugh Peters' trial, twenty years afterwards, that he had said his work, out of New England, was, "to promote the interest of the Reformation, *by stirring up the war and driving it on.*" He was Cromwell's favourite chaplain, and preached before the Court that tried King Charles I., urging the condemnation and execution of the King.

done good acceptable service to the army, declaring to the world hereby that such was the duty and love we bear unto the Parliament that we were ready to rise and fall with them; for which we have suffered the hatred and threats of other English colonies, now in rebellion against you, as also the loss of divers of our ships and goods, taken by the King's party that is dead, by others commissioned by the King of Scots [Charles II.] and by the Portugalls."*

An address of the same General Court, in the same year, 1651, and on the same occasion (against the order of Parliament to recall the old and grant the new Charter), to Oliver Cromwell, concludes in the following words:

"We humbly petition your Excellence to be pleased to show

---

* Hutchinson's History of Massachusetts Bay, Vol. I., Appendix viii., pp. 517, 518.

"The 'other English Colonies' with which Massachusetts, by her attachment to the new Government, had been brought into unfriendly relations, were 'Barbadoes, Virginia, Bermudas, and Antigua.' Their persistent loyalty had been punished by an ordinance of Parliament forbidding Englishmen to trade with them—a measure which the General Court of Massachusetts seconded by a similar prohibition addressed to masters of vessels belonging to that jurisdiction. The rule was to remain in force 'until the compliance of the aforesaid places with the Commonwealth of England, or the further order of this Court;' and the penalty of disobedience was to be a confiscation of ship and cargo. In respect to Virginia, it may be presumed that this step was not the less willingly taken, on account of a grudge of some years' standing. At an early period of the civil war, that colony had banished nonconformist ministers who had gone thither from Massachusetts [1643]; and the offence had been repeated five years afterwards."—Palfrey's History of New England, Vol. II., pp. 402, 403.

But Mr. Palfrey omits to remark that the Act of the Virginia Legislature, in forbidding the Congregational Ministers of Massachusetts Bay from propagating their system in Virginia, was but a *retaliation* upon the Government of Massachusetts Bay, which had not only forbidden Episcopal worship, but denied citizenship to Episcopalians. The Virginia Legislature, while it established the Episcopal Church, had never, like the Legislature of Massachusetts Bay, disqualified all except the members of one Church from either holding office or exercising the elective franchise. The Massachusetts Bay Government, like that of the Papacy, would tolerate only their own form of worship; would allow no Episcopalian, Presbyterian, or Baptist worship within their jurisdiction; yet complain of and resent it as unjust and persecuting when they are not permitted to propagate their system in other colonies or countries.

us what favour God shall be pleased to direct you unto on our behalf, to the most honourable Parliament, unto whom we have now presented a petition. The copy of it, *verbatim,* we are bold to send herewith, that if God please, we may not be hindered in our comfortable work of God here in this wilderness. Wherein, as for other favours, we shall be bound to pray, that the Captain of the host of Israel may be with you and your whole army, in all your great enterprises, to the glory of God, the subduing of his and your enemies, and your everlasting peace and comfort in Jesus Christ."

Likewise, August 24th, 1654, after Cromwell had not only put the King to death, but abolished the House of Lords, excluded by his soldiers 154 members of Parliament, then dismissed the remaining "rump" of the Parliament itself and become sole despot, the General Court of Massachusetts Bay concluded an address to him as follows :

"We shall ever pray the Lord, your protector in all your dangers, that hath crowned you with honour after your long service, to lengthen your days, that you may long continue Lord Protector of the three nations, and the Churches of Christ Jesus."*

---

* Hutchinson's History of Massachusetts Bay, Vol. I., Appendix ix., p. 522.

To these extraordinary addresses may be added a letter from the Rev. John Cotton, a chief Congregational minister in Boston, to "Lord General Cromwell," dated Boston, N. E., May 5th, 1651.

There are three things in this letter to be specially noticed.

The *first* is, the terms in which Cromwell is addressed and complimented.

The *second* is, the indication here given of the manner in which the Scotch prisoners taken at the battle of Dunbar (while fighting in their own country and for their King) were disposed of by Cromwell, and with what complacency Mr. Cotton speaks of the slavery into which they were sold not being " perpetual servitude," but limited to " 6 or 7, or 8 years."

The *third* thing noteworthy in this letter, in which Mr. Cotton compliments Cromwell for having cashiered from the army every one but his own partizans, thus placing the army beneath his feet, to support his absolutism in the State, having extinguished the Parliament itself, and with it every form of liberty dear to the hearts of all true Englishmen.

The chief passages of Mr. Cotton's letter are as follows :

" Right Honourable,—For so I must acknowledge you, not only for the eminency of place and command to which the God of power and honour hath called you ; but also for that the Lord hath set you forth as a vessel of

The documentary evidence which I have adduced, shows, I think, beyond reasonable doubt, that the rulers of Massachusetts Bay Colony were disaffected to the King from the beginning, and so displayed that feeling on every occasion except one, in 1638, when they professed humiliation and loyalty in order to avert the investigation which they dreaded into their proceedings; that the King, whatever may have been his misdoings towards his subjects in England, treated his subjects in the colonies, and especially in Massachusetts Bay, with a kindness and consideration which should have secured their gratitude; that the moment, in the matters of dispute between the King and his Parliament (and in which the colonies had no concern), the scale appeared to turn in favour of the Parliament, the rulers of Massachusetts Bay renounced their allegiance to the King, and identified themselves as thorough partizans of the war against the King—that they suppressed, under the severest penalties, every expression of loyalty to the King within their jurisdiction —offered prayers for and furnished men in aid of the Parliamentary army—denounced and proscribed all recognition, except as enemies, the other American colonies who adhered to their

honour to his name, in working many and great deliverances for his people, and for his truth, by you ; and yet helping you to reserve all the honour to him, who is the God of salvation and the Lord of hosts, mighty in battell."

"The Scots, whom God delivered into your hand at Dunbarre, and whereof sundry were sent hither, we have been desirous (as we could) to make their yoke easy. Such as were sick of the scurvy or other diseases have not wanted physick or chyrurgery. They have not been sold for slaves to perpetual servitude, but for 6 or 7, or 8 years, as we do our owne ; and he that bought the most of them (I heare) buildeth houses for them, for every 4 an house, layeth some acres of ground thereto, which he giveth them as their owne, requiring three dayes in the weeke to worke for him (by turnes), and 4 dayes for themselves, and promiseth, as soon as they can repay him the money he layed out for them, he will set them at liberty."

"As for the aspersion of factious men, I hear, by Mr. Desborough's letter [Cromwell's brother-in-law], last night, that you have well vindicated yourselfe therefrom *by cashiering sundry corrupt spirits* out of the army. And truly, Sir, better a few and faithfull, than many and unsound. The army on Christ's side (which he maketh victorious) are called chosen and faithfull, Rev. 17. 14—a verse worthy your Lordship's frequent and deepe meditation. Go on, therefore (good Sir), to overcome yourselfe (Prov. 16. 32), to overcome your army (Deut. 29. 9, with v. 14), and to vindicate your orthodox integrity to the world." (Hutchinson's Collection of Original Papers relative to the History of Massachusetts Bay, pp. 233—235.)

oaths of allegiance to the King; that when Cromwell had obliterated every landmark of the British constitution and of British liberty—King, Lords, and Commons, the freedom of election and the freedom of the press, with the freedom of worship, and transformed the army itself to his sole purpose—doing what no Tudor or Stuart king had ever presumed to do—even then the General Court of Massachusetts Bay bowed in reverence and praise before him as the called and chosen of the Lord of hosts.*

But when Cromwell could no longer give them, in contempt to the law of Parliament, a monopoly of trade against their fellow-colonists, and sustain them in their persecutions; when he ceased to live, they would not condescend to record his demise, but, after watching for a while the chances of the future, they turned in adulation to the rising sun of the restored Charles the Second.

The manner in which they adjusted their denials and professions to this new state of things, until they prevailed upon the kind-hearted King not to remember their past transgressions, and to perpetuate their Charter on certian conditions; how they evaded those conditions of toleration and administering the government, and resumed their old policy of hostility to the Sovereign and of persecution of their Baptist and other brethren who differed from them in worship, and in proscribing them from the elective franchise itself, will be treated in the following chapter.

---

* In view of the documents which I have quoted, it seems extraordinary to see Mr. Hutchinson, usually so accurate, so far influenced by his personal prejudices as to say that the government of the Massachusetts Bay Colony "prudently acknowledged subjection to Parliament, and afterwards to Cromwell, *so far as was necessary to keep upon terms, and avoid exception, and no farther.* The addresses to the Parliament and Cromwell show this to have been the case."—History of Massachusetts Bay, Vol. I., p. 209.

The addresses to Parliament and to Cromwell prove the very reverse—prove that the rulers of the Massachusetts Bay Colony avowedly identified themselves with the Parliament and afterwards with Cromwell, when he overthrew the Parliament, and even when he manipulated the army to his purpose of absolutism.

CHAPTER V.

GOVERNMENT OF MASSACHUSETTS BAY AND OTHER COLONIES, DURING
TWENTY YEARS, UNDER CHARLES THE SECOND.

THE restoration of Charles the Second to the throne of his
ancestors was received in the several American colonies with
very different feelings; the loyal colonies, from the Bermudas
to Plymouth, hailed and proclaimed the restored King without
hesitation; Virginia proclaimed him before he was proclaimed
in England;* the rulers of the Massachusetts Bay Colony alone
stood in suspense; hesitated, refused to proclaim him for a year,

---

* The captain of a ship brought the news from England in July, that the
King had been proclaimed, but a false rumour was circulated that the
Government in England was in a very unsettled state, the body of the people
dissatisfied ; that the Scotch had demanded work ; that Lord Fairfax
was at the head of a great army, etc.   Such a rumour was so congenial to the
feelings of the men who had been lauding Cromwell, that when it was proposed in the General Court of Massachusetts Bay, in the October following,
to address the King, the majority refused to do so.   They awaited to see
which party would prevail in England, so as to pay court to it.   On the 30th
of November a ship arrived from Bristol, bringing news of the utter falsity
of the rumours about the unsettled state of things and popular dissatisfaction
in England, and of the proceedings of Parliament ; and letters were received
from their agent, Mr. Leverett, that petitions and complaints were preferred
against the colony to the King in Council.   Then the Governor and assistants
called a meeting of the General Court, December 9th, when a very loyal
address to the King was presently agreed upon, and another to the two
Houses of Parliament.   Letters were sent to Sir Thomas Temple, to Lord
Manchester, Lord Say and Seal, and to other persons of note, praying them to
intercede in behalf of the colony.   A most gracious answer was given to the
address by the King's letter, dated February 15, 1660 (1661, new style),
which was the first public act or order concerning them after the restoration."
(Hutchinson's History of Massachusetts Bay, Vol. I., pp. 210, 211.)

until ordered to do so. When it was ascertained that the restoration of the King, Lords, and Commons had been enthusiastically ratified by the people of England, and was firmly established, the General Court of Massachusetts Bay adopted a most loyal address to the King, and another to the two Houses of Parliament, notwithstanding the same Court had shortly before lauded the power which had abolished King, Lords, and Commons. The Court also thought it needful to give practical proof of the sincerity of their new-born loyalty to the monarchical government by condemning a book published ten years before, and which had been until now in high repute among them, written by the Rev. John Eliot, the famous apostle to the Indians. This book was entitled "The Christian Commonwealth," and argued that a purely republican government was the only Christian government, and that all the monarchical governments of Europe, especially that of England, was anti-Christian. It appears that this book had been adduced by the complainants in England against the Massachusetts Bay Government as a proof of their hostility to the system of government now restored in England. To purge themselves from this charge, the Governor and Council of Massachusetts Bay, March 18, 1661, took this book into consideration, and declared "they find it, on perusal, full of seditious principles and notions relative to all established governments in the Christian world especially against the government established in their native country." Upon consultation with the Elders, their censure was deferred until the General Court met, "that Mr. Eliot might have the opportunity in the meantime of public recantation." At the next sessions, in May, Mr. Eliot gave into the Court the following acknowledgment under his hand :

"Understanding by an Act of the honoured Council, that there is offence taken at a book published in England by others, the copy whereof was sent over by myself about nine or ten years since, and that the further consideration thereof is commended to this honoured Court now sitting in Boston : Upon perusal thereof, I do judge myself to have offended, and in way of satisfaction not only to the authority of this jurisdiction, but also to any others that shall take notice thereof, I do hereby acknowledge to this General Court, that such expressions as do too manifestly scandalize the Government of England, by King,

Lords and Commons, as anti-christian, and justify the late
innovators, I do sincerely bear testimony against, and acknowledge it to be not only a lawful but eminent form of government.

" 2nd. All forms of civil government, deduced from Scripture,
I acknowledge to be of God, and to be subscribed to for conscience sake ; and whatsoever is in the whole epistle or book
inconsistent herewith, I do at once and most cordially disown.

"JOHN ELIOT."*

It must have been painful and humiliating to John Eliot to
be brought to account for and compelled to recant the sentiments of a book which had been in circulation eight or nine
years, and much applauded by those who now arraigned and
made a scapegoat of him, to avert from themselves the consequence and suspicion of sentiments which they had held and
avowed as strongly as Eliot himself.

It has been said that the Government of Massachusetts Bay
had desisted from acknowledging and addressing Charles the
Second as King, until they found that their silence endangered
their interests.   Mr. Holmes, in his Annals, speaking under the
date of May, 1661 (a year after Charles had entered London as
King), says : " Charles II., had not yet been proclaimed by the
colony.   The Governor (Endicot), on receiving intelligence of
the transactions that were taking place in England to the
prejudice of the colony, judged it inexpedient longer to delay
that solemnity.   Calling the Court together, a form of proclamation was agreed to, and Charles was acknowledged to be their
sovereign Lord, and proclaimed to be the lawful King of Great
Britain, France and Ireland, and all other territories thereto
belonging."   An address to the King was agreed to, and ordered
to be sent to England.†

* Hutchinson's History of Massachusetts Bay, Vol. I., pp. 211, 212.

† Holmes' Annals of America, Vol. I., p. 318.   Hutchinson, Vol. I., p. 216.
Hazard, Vol. II., pp. 593—595.   The address is a curiosity in its way, and a
strange medley which I must leave the reader to characterize in view of
the facts involved.   The following are the principal passages of it :

Extracts from the Massachusetts General Court—Address to the King,
dated 19th December, 1660 :

" To the High and Mighty Prince, Charles the Second, by the grace of God,
    King of Great Britain, France and Ireland, Defender of the Faith.

  " Most gracious and dread Sovereign :

" May it please your Majesty—In the day wherein you happily say you know

In this remarkable address (given in a note) the reader will be struck with several things which appear hardly reconcilable with words of sincerity and truth.

First, the reason professed for delaying nearly a year to recognise and address the King after his restoration. Nearly thirty years before, they had threatened the King's Royal father with resistance, since which time they had greatly increased in wealth and population; but now they represent themselves as "poor exiles," and excuse themselves for not acknowledging the King because of their Mephiboseth lameness of distance—as if they were more distant from England than the other American colonies. Their "lameness" and "ineptness" and "impotence" plainly arose from disinclination alone. It is amusing to hear

you are King over your British Israel, to cast a favourable eye upon your poore Mephiboseth now, and by reason of lameness in respect of distance, not until now appearing in your presence, we mean upon New England, kneeling with the rest of your subjects before your Majesty as her restored King. We forget not our ineptness as to those approaches; we at present owne such impotence as renders us unable to excuse our impotency of speaking unto our Lord the King; yet contemplating such a King, who hath also seen adversity, that he knoweth the hearts of exiles, who himself hath been an exile, the aspect of Majesty extraordinarily influenced animateth exanimated outcasts, yet outcasts as we hope for the truth, to make this address unto our Prince, hoping to find grace in your sight. We present this script, the transcript of our loyall hearts, wherein we crave leave to supplicate your Majesty for your gracious protection of us in the continuance both of our civill and religious liberties (according to the grantees known, and of suing for the patent) conferred on this Plantation by your royal father. This, viz., our libertie to walk in the faith of the gospell, was the cause of our transporting ourselves, with our wives, little ones, and our substances, from that over the Atlantick ocean, into the vast wilderness, choosing rather the pure Scripture worship with a good conscience in this remote wilderness among the heathen, than the pleasures of England with submission to *the impositions* of the *then* so disposed and so far *prevailing hierarchy*, which we could not do without an evil conscience." "Our witness is in heaven that we left not our native country upon any dissatisfaction as to the constitution of the civil state. Our lot after the good old nonconformists hath been only to *act a passive part throughout these late vicissitudes* and successive turnings of States. Our separation from our brethren in this desert hath been and is a sufficient bringing to mind the afflictions of Joseph. But providentiall exemption of us hereby from the late warres and temptations of *either party* we account as a favour from God; the former cloathes us with sackcloth, the latter with innocency.

(Signed)   " JOHN ENDICOT, *Governor.*
" In the name and by order of the *General Court of Massachusetts.*"

them speak of themselves as "exanimated outcasts," hoping to be animated by the breath of Royal favour. Their "script" was no doubt "the transcript of their loyal hearts" when they supplicated the continuance of the Royal Charter, the first intentions and essential provisions of which they had violated so many years.

Secondly. But what is most suspicious in this address is their denial of having taken any part in the civil war in England—professing that their lot had been the good old nonconformists',* "only to act a passive *part* throughout these late vicissitudes," and ascribed to the favour of God their "exemption from the temptations of *either party*." Now, just ten years before, in their address to the Long Parliament and to Cromwell, they said:

"And for our carriage and demeanour to the honourable Parliament for these ten years, since the first beginning of your differences with the late King, and the war that after ensued, we have constantly adhered to you, notwithstanding ourselves in your weakest condition and doubtfullest times, but by our fasting and prayers for your good success, and our thanksgiving after the same was attained, in days of solemnity set apart for that purpose, as also by our sending over useful men (others also going voluntarily from us to help you) who have been of good use and have done good acceptable service to the army, declaring to the world hereby that such was the duty and love we bear unto the Parliament that we were ready to rise and fall with them: for which we suffered the hatred and threats of other English colonies now in rebellion against you," etc.†

Whether this address to Parliament (a copy of it being enclosed with an address to Cromwell) had ever at that time been made public, or whether King Charles the Second had then seen it, does not appear; but it is not easy to conceive statements and words more opposite than those addressed by the General Court of Massachusetts Bay to the Parliament in 1651, and to the King, Charles the Second, in 1661.

* It is known that the "*old* nonconformists" did not fight against the king, denounced his execution, suffered for their "nonconformity" to Cromwell's despotism, and were among the most active restorers of Charles the Second.

† See above, in a previous page.

On the contrasts of acts themselves, the reader will make his own remarks and inferences. The King received and answered their address very graciously.* They professed to receive it gratefully; but their consciousness of past unfaithfulness and transgressions, and their jealous suspicions, apprehended evil from the general terms of the King's reply, his reference to his Royal predecessors and religious liberty, which above all things they most dreaded, desiring religious liberty for themselves alone, but not for any Episcopalian, Presbyterian, Baptist, or Quaker. They seem, however, to have been surprised at the kindness of the King's answer, considering their former conduct towards him and his Royal father, and towards the colonies that loyally adhered to their King; and professed to have been excited to an ectasy of inexpressible delight and gratitude at the gracious words of the best of kings.† Their

---

* Letter from Charles II. to Governor Endicot :

" CHARLES R.

" Trusty and well beloved —Wee greet you well. It having pleased Almighty God, after long trialls both of us and our people, to touch their hearts at last with a just sense of our right, and by their assistance to restore us, peaceably and without blood, to the exercise of our legall authority for the good and welfare of the nations committed to our charge, we have made it our care to settle our lately distracted kingdom at home, and to extend our thoughts to increase the trade and advantages of our colonies and plantations abroad, amongst which as wee consider New England to be one of the chiefest, having enjoyed and grown up in a long and orderly establishment, so wee shall not be behind any of our royal predecessors in a just encouragement and protection of all our loving subjects there, whose application unto us, since our late happy restoration, hath been very acceptable, and shall not want its due remembrance upon all seasonable occasions ; neither shall wee forget to make you and all our good people in those parts equal partakers of those promises of liberty and moderation to tender consciences expressed in our gracious declarations ; which, though some persons in this kingdom, of desperate, disloyal, and unchristian principles, have lately abused to the public disturbance and their own destruction, yet wee are confident our good subjects in New England will make a right use of it, to the glory of God, their own spiritual comfort and edification. And so wee bid you farewell. Given at our Court of Whitehall, the 15th day of February, 1660 (1661, new style), in the thirteenth year of our reigne.

(Signed)   " WILL. MORRICE."

† The following are extracts from the reply of the General Court of Massachusetts Bay to the foregoing letter of Charles the Second :

" ILLUSTRIOUS SIR,—

" That majestie and benignitie both sate upon the throne whereunto

address presented a curious mixture of professed self-abase-
ment, weakness, isolation, and affliction, with fulsome adulation
not surpassed by anything that could have been indited by the
most devout loyalist.   But this honeymoon of adulation to the

your outcasts made their former addresse ; witness this second eucharistical
approach unto the best of kings, who to other titles of royaltie common to
him with other gods amongst men, delighteth herein more particularily to
conforme himselfe to the God of gods, in that he hath not despised nor
abhorred the affliction of the afflicted, neither hath he hid his face from him,
but when he heard he cried.

"Our petition was the representation of exiles' necessities ; this script,
congratulatory and lowly, is the reflection of the gracious rayes of Christian
majestie.   There we besought your favour by presenting to a compassionate
eye that bottle full of tears shed by us in this Teshimon : here we acknowledge the efficacie of regal influence to qualify these salt waters.   The mission
of ours was accompanied with these Churches sitting in sack-cloth ; the
reception of yours was as the holding forth the scepter of life.   The truth
is, such were the impressions upon our spirits when we received an answer
of peace from our gracious Sovereigne as transcends the facultie of an
eremitical scribe.   Such, as though our expressions of them neede pardon,
yet the suppression of them seemeth unpardonable."

The conclusion of their address was as follows :

"ROYAL SIR,—

"Your just Title to the Crown enthronizeth you in our consciences, your
graciousness in our affections : That inspireth us unto Duty, this naturalizeth
unto Loyalty : Thence we call you Lord ; hence a Savior.   Mephibosheth,
how prejudicially soever misrepresented, yet rejoiceth that the King is come
in Peace to his own house.   Now the Lord hath dealt well with our Lord the
King.   May New England, under your Royal Protection, be permitted still
to sing the Lord's song in this strange Land.   It shall be no grief of Heart
for the Blessing of a people ready to perish, daily to come upon your
Majesty, the blessings of your poor people, who (not here to alledge the
innocency of our cause, touching which let us live no longer than we subject
ourselves to an orderly trial thereof), though in the particulars of subscriptions and conformity, supposed to be under the hallucinations of weak
Brethren, yet crave leave with all humility to say whether the voluntary
quitting of our native and dear country be not sufficient to expiate so innocent a mistake (if a mistake) let God Almightie, your Majesty, and all good
men judge.

"Now, he in whose hands the times and trials of the children of men are,
who hath made your Majesty remarkably parallel to the most eminent of
kings, both for space and kind of your troubles, so that vere day cannot be
excepted, wherein they drove him from abiding in the inheritance of the
Lord, saying, 'Go, serve other gods ; make you also (which is the crown of
all), more and more like unto him, in being a man after God's own heart, to
do whatsoever he will.'   Yea, as the Lord was with David, so let him be with

restored King was not of long duration; the order of the King,
September 8, 1661, to cease persecuting the Quakers, was
received and submitted to with remonstrance; and obedience
to it was refused as far as sending the accused Quakers to
England for trial, as that would bring the Government of
Massachusetts Bay before the English tribunals.*

But petitions and representations poured in upon the King
and Council from Episcopalians, Presbyterians, Baptists, etc.,
from Massachusetts Bay, and their friends in England, complaining that they were denied liberty of worship, the ordinance
of Baptism and the Lord's Supper to their families and themselves, that they were deprived of even the elective franchise
because of their not being members of the Congregational
Church, and praying for the redress of their grievances.†

your most excellent Majesty, and make the Throne of King Charles the
Second both greater and better than the Throne of King David, or than the
Throne of any of your Royal Progenitors. So shall always pray,
"Great Sir,
"Your Majesty's most humble and loyal subjects.
"JOHN ENDICOT, *Governor.*"
(Hutchinson's Collection of Original Papers, etc., pp. 341, 342. Massa-
chusetts Records, August 7, 1661.)

* The Government of New England received a letter from the King,
signifying his pleasure that there should be no further prosecution of the
Quakers who were condemned to suffer death or other corporal punishment,
or who were imprisoned or obnoxious to such condemnation; but that they be
forthwith sent over to England for trial. The Massachusetts General Court,
after due consideration of the King's letter, proceeded to declare that the
necessity of preserving religion, order, and peace had induced the enactment
of laws against the Quakers, etc., and concluded by saying, "All this, notwithstanding their restless spirits, have moved some of them to return, and
others to fill the royal ear of our Sovereign Lord the King with complaints
against us, and have, by their unwearied solicitations, in our absence, so far
prevailed as to obtain a letter from his Majesty to forbear their corporal
punishment or death; although we hope and doubt not but that if his
Majesty were rightly informed, he would be far from giving them such favour,
or weakening his authority here, so long and orderly settled : Yet that we may
not in the least offend his Majesty, this Court doth hereby order and declare
that the execution of the laws in force against Quakers as such, so far as they
respect corporal punishment or death, be suspended until this Court take
further order." Upon this order of the Court twenty-eight Quakers were
released from prison and conducted out of the jurisdiction of Massachusetts.
(Holmes' Annals, Vol. I., pp. 318, 319.)

† "Upon the Restoration, not only Episcopalians, but Baptists, Quakers,

The leaders of the colony had, however, warm and influential advocates in the Council of the King: the Earl of Manchester, formerly commander of the Parliamentary army against Charles the First, until supplanted by Cromwell; Lord Say, a chief founder of Connecticut; and Mr. Morrice, Secretary—all Puritans.* Under these influences the King sent a letter to the colony,

etc., preferred complaints against the colony; and although, by the interest of the Earl of Manchester and Lord Say, their old friends, and Secretary Morrice, all Puritans, King Charles confirmed their Charter, yet he required a toleration in religion, and an alteration in some civil matters, neither of which were fully complied with." (Hutchinson's History of Massachusetts Bay, Vol. II., p. 3.)

    * "In the Earl of Manchester and Lord Say; in Annesley, created Earl of Anglesea; in Denzil Hollis, now Lord Hollis; and in Ashley Cooper, now Lord Ashley, the expectant cavaliers saw their old enemies raised to the place of honour. Manchester had not taken any part in public affairs since the passing of the self-denying ordinances. He was still a Presbyterian, but had favoured the return of the King. Lord Say, also, had long since withdrawn from public life, and though of a less pliant temper than Manchester, his new friends had no reason to doubt his steady adherence to the new order of things. Annesley was an expert lawyer. Hollis had been the leader of the Presbyterians in the Long Parliament, until the crisis which turned the scale in favour of the Independents.

    "Lord Ashley, better known as the Earl of Shaftesbury, had been devoted successively to the King, the Parliament, and the Protector. Nichols and Morrice were the two Secretaries of State."—Dr. R. Vaughan's Revolutions in English History, Vol. III., B. 14, Chap. i., pp. 430, 431.

    "Totally devoid of resentment, as well from natural lenity as carelessness of his temper, Charles the Second ensured pardon to the most guilty of his enemies, and left hopes of favour to his most violent opponents. From the whole tenor of his actions and discourse, he seemed desirous of losing the memory of past animosities, and of making every party in affection to their prince and their native country.

    "Into his Council he admitted the most eminent men of the nation, without regard to former distinctions; the Presbyterians equally with the Royalists shared this honour. Annesley was created Earl of Anglesea; Ashley Cooper, Lord Ashley; Denzil Hollis, Lord Hollis; the Earl of Manchester was appointed Lord Chamberlain; and Lord Say, Privy Seal. Calamy and Baxter, Presbyterian clergymen, were even made chaplains to the King; Admiral Montague, created Earl of Sandwich, was entitled from his recent services to great favour, and he obtained it. Monk, created Duke of Albemarle, had performed such signal services that according to a vulgar and inelegant observation, he ought rather to have expected hatred and ingratitude, yet was he ever treated by the King with great marks of distinction. Charles' disposition was free from jealousy; and the prudent conduct

which had been avowedly at war in connection with Cromwell, against his royal father and himself (and by which they had justly forfeited the Charter, apart from other violations of it), pardoning the past and assuring them he would not cancel but restore and establish their Charter, provided they would fulfil certain conditions which were specified. They joyously accepted the pardon of the past, and the promised continuance of the Charter as if unconditional, without fulfilling the conditions of it, or even mentioning them ; just as their fathers had claimed the power given them in the Royal Charter by Charles the First in 1628, to make laws and regulations for order and good government of the Massachusetts Bay Plantation, concealing the Charter, claiming absolute power under it, and wholly ignoring the restrictive condition that such laws and regulations were not to be "contrary to the laws of England"—not only concealing the Charter, but not allowing their laws and regulations to be printed until after the fall of Charles the First, and resisting all orders for the production of their proceedings, and all Commissions of Inquiry to ascertain whether they had not made laws or regulations and performed acts "contrary to the laws of England." So now, a generation afterwards, they claimed and contended that Charles the Second had restored their Charter, as if done absolutely and unconditionally without their recognising one of the five conditions included in the proviso of the King's letter. Nothing could have been more kindly and generously conceived than the terms of the King's letter, and nothing could be more reasonable than the conditions contained in its proviso— conditions with which all the other British colonies of America readily complied, and which every province of the Dominion of Canada has assumed and acted upon as a duty and pleasure from the first establishment of their respective Governments. Of all the colonies of the British Empire for the last three centuries, that of Massachusetts Bay is the only one that ever refused to acknowledge this allegiance to the Government from which it derived its existence and territory. The conditions

of the General, who never overrated his merits, prevented all State disgusts which naturally arise in so delicate a situation. Morrice, his friend, was created Secretary of State, and was supported more by his patron's credit than by his own abilities and experience."—Hume's History of England, Vol. VII., Chap. xliii., pp. 338, 339.

which Charles the Second announced as the proviso of his consenting to renew and continue the Charter granted by his Royal father to the Company of Massachusetts Bay, were the following :

" 1. That upon a review, all such laws and ordinances that are now, or have been during these late troubles, in practice there, and which are contrary or derogatory to the King's authority and government, shall be repealed.

" 2. That the rules and prescriptions of the said Royal Charter for administering and taking the oath of allegiance, be henceforth duly observed.

" 3. That the administration of justice be in the King's name.

" 4. That since the principle and formation of that Charter was and is the freedom of liberty of conscience, we do hereby charge and require you that freedom of liberty be duly admitted and allowed, so that they that desire to use the Book of Common Prayer and perform their devotion in the manner that is established here, be not denied the exercise thereof, or undergo any prejudice or disadvantage thereby, they using the liberty peaceably, without any disturbance to others.

" 5. That all persons of good and honest lives and conversations be admitted to the sacrament of the Lord's Supper, according to the said Book of Common Prayer, and their children to Baptism."*

---

* Letter of King Charles the Second to the General Court at Massachusetts (June 28, 1662) :

" CHARLES REX.

" Trusty and well beloved, We greete you well :

" Whereas we have lately received an humble address and petition from the General Court of our colony of Massachusetts, in New England, presented to us by Simon Bradstreet and John Norton : We have thought it agreeable to our princely grace and justice to let you know that the same have been very acceptable unto us, and that we are satisfied with your expressions of loyalty, duty and good affection made to us in the said address, which we doubt not proceeds from the hearts of good and honest subjects, and We are therefore willing that all our good subjects of that Plantation do know that We do receive them into our gracious protection, and will cherish them with our best encouragement, and that We will preserve and do hereby confirme the patent and charter heretofore granted to them by our royall father of blessed memory, and that they shall freely enjoy all the priviledges and libertys granted to them in and by the same, and that We will be ready to renew the same charter to them under our great seale of England, whenever they shall desire it. And because the licence of these late ill times has like-

Nothing could be more kind and assuring than the terms of the King's letter, notwithstanding the former hostility of the Massachusetts Bay rulers to him and his Royal father,* and

wise had an influence upon our colony, in which they have swerved from the rules prescribed, and even from the government instituted by the charter, which we do graciously impute rather to the iniquity of the time than to the evil intents of the hearts of those who exercised the government there. And we do therefore publish and declare our free and gracious pardon to all our subjects of that our plantation, for all crimes and offences committed against us during the late troubles, except any persons who stand attainted by our parliament here of high treason, if any such persons have transported themselves into these parts ; the apprehending of whom and delivering them into the hands of justice, we expect from the dutiful and affectionate obedience of those of our good subjects in that colony, if they be found within the jurisdiction thereof. Provided always, and be it our declared expectation, that upon a review of all such laws and ordinances that are now or have been during these late troubles in practice there, and which are contrary or derogatory to our authority and government, the same may be annulled and repealed, and the rules and prescriptions of the said charter for administering and taking the oath of allegiance be henceforth duly observed, and that the administrations of justice be in our name. And since the principle and foundation of that charter was and is the freedom of liberty of conscience, We do hereby charge and require you that freedom and liberty be duly admitted and allowed, so that they that desire to use the book of common prayer and performe their devotion in that manner that is established here be not denied the exercise thereof, or undergoe any prejudice or disadvantage thereby, they using their liberty peaceably without any disturbances to others ; and that all persons of good and honest lives and conversations be admitted to the sacrament of the Lord's Supper, according to the said Book of Common Prayer, and their children to baptism."

* Indeed, so conscious were they that they had justly forfeited all consideration from the King, that the first address extracted from them when they found the monarchy firmly established, expressed deep humiliation and confession, and implored the forgiveness and favour of their Sovereign ; and being sensible of the many and well-founded complaints made against them by the victims of their persecuting intolerance, they appointed two of their ablest and most trusted members—Simon Bradstreet, an old magistrate, and John Norton, a minister of Boston—to proceed to England to present their address, to intercede for them, and secure the interest of those of their old friends who might have influence with the King and his councillors. But as Bradstreet and Norton had both been persecutors of their Episcopalian, Presbyterian, and Baptist brethren, and were conspicuous in promoting the bloody persecutions of the Quakers (now getting a favourable hearing for their sufferings at the English Court), they were unwilling to undertake so difficult and hazardous a mission without formal provision being made by the Massachusetts Court for indemnity for all the damage they might incur

nothing could be more reasonable than the five conditions on
which he assured them of the oblivion of the past and the continuance of the Royal Charter ; but with not one of these
conditions did they take a step to comply for several months,
under the pretext of affording time, after publishing it, that
"all persons might have opportunity to consider what was
necessary to be done," though the "all persons" referred to included only one-sixth of the population : for the term "Freeman
of Massachusetts" was at that time, and for thirty years before
and afterwards, synonymous with member of one of the Congregational Churches. And it was against their disloyalty and
intolerance that the five conditions of the King's pardon were
chiefly directed. With some of these conditions they never
complied ; with others only as they were compelled, and even
complained of them afterwards as an invasion of their chartered
privileges,* though, in their first order for public thanksgiving

---

"At length," says their historian, "the Committee appointed to do everything
for their dispatch in the recess of the Court, 'engaged to make good all
damages they might sustain by the detention of their persons in England, or
otherwise.' They departed the 10th of February (1662.)

"Their reception in England was much more favourable than was expected ;
their stay short, returning the next autumn with the King's most gracious
letter, some parts of which cheered the hearts of the country ; and they then
looked upon and afterwards recurred to them as a confirmation of their
charter privileges, and an amnesty of all past errors. The letter was ordered
to be published (as the King had directed), and in an order for public thanksgiving, particular notice is taken of 'the return of the messengers, and the
continuance of the mercies of peace, liberties, and the Gospel.'"

The early New England historian, Hubbard, says : "They returned like
Noah's dove, with an olive branch of peace in their mouths."

"There were some things, however, in the King's letter hard to comply
with ; and though it was ordered to be published, yet it was with this
caution, that 'inasmuch as the letter hath influence upon the Churches as
well as the civil state, all manner of acting in relation thereto shall be
suspended until the next General Court, that all persons may have opportunity to consider what was necessary to be done, in order to know his
Majesty's pleasure therein.'" (Hutchinson's History of Massachusetts Bay,
Vol. I., pp. 221, 222.)

* So dissatisfied were these Congregational "freemen" with the conditions
which were intended to put an end to their persecutions of their brethren
and their disloyal practices, that they denounced their old friends and
representatives to England, Messrs. Bradstreet and Norton, for those conditions which they could not prevent, and upon which they might well be

for the King's letter, they spoke of it as assuring "the continuance of peace, liberties and the gospel." Though the agent of Rhode Island met the agents of Massachusetts Bay Colony before the King, and challenged them to cite, in behalf of Massachusetts, one act of duty or loyalty to the kings of England, in support of their present professions as loyal subjects; yet the King was not disposed to punish them for the past, but continue to them their privileges, as they desired and promised they would act with loyalty and tolerance in the future.*

thankful to preserve the Charter and obtain pardon for their past offences. Their historian says: "The agents met with the fate of most agents ever since. The favours they obtained were supposed to be no more than might well have been expected, and their merits were soon forgot; the evils which they had it not in their power to prevent, were attributed to their neglect or unnecessary concessions. Mr. Bradstreet was a man of more phlegm and not so sensibly touched, but Mr. Norton was so affected that he grew melancholy; and died suddenly soon after his return (April 5, 1663)." (Hutchinson's History of Massachusetts Bay, Vol. I., p. 223.)

In a note the historian quotes the remark of Mr. Norton to the Massachusetts Court, that "if they complied not with the King's letter, the blood that should be spilt would lie at their door."

"Dr. Mather says upon this occasion: 'Such has been the jealous disposition of our New Englanders about their dearly bought privileges, and such also has been the various interpretations of the people about the extent of their privileges, that of all the agents sent over to the Court of England for now forty years together, I know of not one who did not, at his return, meet with some froward entertainment among his countrymen.'" (Ib., p. 222.)

* Mr. Hildreth gives the following account of this mission and its results upon the state of society in Massachusetts Bay Colony and its agents to England:

"The Massachusetts' agents presently returned, bearers of a royal letter, in which the King recognized the Charter and promised oblivion of past offences. But he demanded the repeal of all laws inconsistent with his due authority; an oath of allegiance to the royal person, as formerly in use, but dropped since the commencement of the late civil war; the administration of justice in his name; complete toleration for the Church of England; the repeal of the law which restricted the privilege of voting, and tenure of office to Church members, and the substitution of property qualification instead; finally, the admission of all persons of honest lives to the sacraments of Baptism and the Lord's Supper.

"The claimants for toleration, formerly suppressed with such prompt severity, were now encouraged, by the King's demands in their favour, again to raise their heads. For the next thirty years the people of Massachusetts (Bay) were divided into three parties, a very decided, though gradually

The King's promised oblivion of the past and recognition of the Charter was hailed and assumed as *unconditional,* while the King's conditions were ignored and remained a dead letter. The elective franchise and eligibility for office were still, as heretofore, the exclusive prerogative of Congregational Church members; the government of the colony was still in the hands alone of Congregational ministers and magistrates, and which they cleaved to as for life; their persecutions of those who did not worship as they did, continued without abatement; they persisted in their theocratic independence, and pretended to do all this under a Royal Charter which forbade their making laws or regulations contrary to the laws of England, acting also in the face of the King's conditions of pardoning their past offences, and perpetuating their Charter privileges.

The King's letter was dated the 28th of June, 1662, and was presented by Mr. Bradstreet and Mr. Norton to the Governor and General Court at Boston, 8th of October, 1662;* but it was not until a General Court called in August, 1664, that "the said letter was communicated to the whole assembly, according

diminishing majority (of the Congregationalists, the only "freemen") sustaining with ardour the theocratic system, and, as essential to it, entire independence of external control. At the opposite extreme, a party, small in numbers and feeble in influence (among the "freemen"), advocated religious toleration—at least to a limited extent—and equal civil rights for all inhabitants. They advocated, also, the supremacy of the Crown, sole means in that day of curbing the theocracy, and compelling it to yield its monopoly of power. To this party belonged the Episcopalians, or those inclined to become so; the Baptists, Presbyterians, the Quakers, and other sectaries who feared less the authority of a distant monarch than the present rule of their watchful and bitter spiritual rivals. In the intermediate was a third party, weak at first but daily growing stronger, and drawing to its ranks, one after another, some former zealous advocates of the exclusive system, convinced that a *theocracy,* in its stricter form, was no longer tenable, and some of them, perhaps, beginning to be satisfied that it was not desirable. Among the earliest of these were Norton and Bradstreet, the agents who came back from England impressed with the necessity of yielding. But the avowal of such sentiments was fatal to their popularity (among the Congregational "freemen"), and Norton, accustomed to nothing but reverence and applause, finding himself now looked at with distrust, soon died of melancholy and mortification." (Hildreth's History of the United States, Vol. I., Chap. xiv., pp. 455, 456.)

* Collection of Massachusetts, etc., Civil Society, Vol. VIII., Second Series, p. 53.

to his Majesty's command, and copies thereof spread abroad.* In the meantime they boasted of their Charter being recognised by the King, according, of course, to their own interpretation of it, while for *twenty-two months* they withheld the King's letter, against his orders, from being published; concealing from the victims of their proscription and persecution the toleration which the King had announced as the conditions of his perpetuating the Charter.

It is not surprising that those proscribed and persecuted parties in Massachusetts Bay Colony should complain to the King's Government that the local Government had denied them every privilege which his Majesty had assured to them through their friends in England, and by alleged orders to the Government of Massachusetts Bay, and therefore that the King's Government should determine to appoint Commissioners to proceed to the New England colonies to investigate the complaints made, and to regulate the affairs of the colonies after the disorders of the then recent civil war, during which the Massachusetts Bay Government had wholly identified itself with Cromwell, and acted in hostility to those other American colonies which would not renounce their allegiance to the Throne, and avow allegiance to the usurper.

It was not till the Government of Massachusetts Bay saw that their silence could no longer be persisted in with safety, and that a Royal Commission was inevitable,† that they even published the King's letter, and then, as a means of further procrastination and delay, they appended their order that the conditions prescribed in the Royal letter, which "had influence upon the Churches as well as the civil state, should be suspended until the Court should take action thereon"—thus

---

* Collections of Massachusetts, etc., Civil Society, Vol. VIII., Second Series, pp. 59, 60.

† From the representations made respecting the state of affairs in the New England colonies, the appointment of this Commission was decided upon after the restoration of the King, and the agents of those colonies were informed of it. Col. Nichols, the head of the Commission, stated in his introductory address to the Massachusetts Bay Court, May 2, 1665, that "The King himself and the Lord Chancellor (Clarendon) told Mr. Norton and Mr. Bradstreet of this colony, and Mr. Winthrop of Connecticut, Mr. Clarke of Rhode Island, and several others now in these countries, that he intended shortly to send over Commissioners." (*Ib.*, p. 56.)

10

subordinating the orders of the King to the action of the Massachusetts Bay Court.

From the Restoration, reports were most industriously circulated in the Bay Colony, designed to excite popular suspicion and hostility against the Royal Government, such as that their constitution and Church privileges were to be suppressed, and superseded by a Royal Governor and the Episcopal hierarchy, etc.; and before the arrival of the Royal Commissioners the object of their appointment was misrepresented and their character assailed; it was pretended their commission was a bogus one. prepared "under an old hedge,"* and all this preparatory to the intended resistance of the Commissioners by the Governor and Council of Massachusetts Bay.

The five conditions of continuing the Charter, specified in the King's letter of the 28th of June, 1662, the publication of which

* It was in refutation of such reports that Col. Nichols made the statements quoted on a previous page; in the course of which, referring to the slanders circulated by persons high in office under the Court, he said: "Some of them are these: That the King hath sent us over here to raise £5,000 *a year out of the colony* for his Majesty's use, and 12d. for every acre of improved land besides, and to take from this colony many of their civil liberties and ecclesiastical privileges, of which particulars we have been asked the truth in several places, all of which reports we did, and here do, disclaim as false; and protest that they are diametrically contrary to the truth, as ere long we shall make it appear more plainly."

"These personal slanders with which we are calumniated, as private men we slight; as Christians we forgive and will not mention; but as persons employed by his Sacred Majesty, we cannot suffer his honour to be eclipsed by a cloud of black reproaches, and some seditious speeches, without demanding justice from you against those who have raised, reported, or made them." (*Ib.*, p. 56.)

These reports were spread by some of the chief officers of the Council, and the most seditious of the speeches complained of was by the commander of their forces; but they were too agreeable to the Court for them even to contradict, much less investigate, although Col. Nichols offered to give their names.

Hubbard, the earliest and most learned of the New England historians, says:

"The Commissioners were but four in number, the two principal of whom were Colonel Nichols and Colonel Cartwright, who were both of them eminently qualified, with abilities fit to manage such a concern, nor yet wanting in resolution to carry on any honourable design for the promotion of his Majesty's interest in any of those Plantations whither they were sent." (Massachusetts History Collection, Vol. V., Second Series, p. 577.)

was suppressed by the Massachusetts Bay Court for nearly two years, and the intolerance and proscription which it was intended to redress being still practised, were doubtless among the causes which led to the appointment of the Royal Commissioners; but that Commission had reference to other colonies as well as Massachusetts Bay, and to other subjects than the intolerant proscriptions of that colony.*

* The following is a copy of the Royal Commission, in which the reasons and objects of it are explicitly stated :

"Copy of a Commission from King Charles the Second to Col. Nichols and others, in 1664.

"Charles the 2nd, by the Grace of God, King of England, Scotland, France, and Ireland, Defender of the Faith, etc.

"To all to whom these presents shall come, Greeting : Whereas we have received several addresses from our subjects of several colonies in New England, all full of duty and affection, and expressions of loyalty and allegiance to us, with their humble desires that we would renew their several Charters, and receive them into our favourable opinion and protection ; and several of our colonies there, and other our loving subjects, have likewise complained of differences and disputes arisen upon the limits and bounds of their several Charters and jurisdictions, whereby unneighbourly and unbrotherly contentions have and may arise, to the damage and discredit of the English interest ; and that all our good subjects residing there, and being Planters within the several colonies, do not enjoy the liberties and privileges granted to them by our several Charters, upon confidence and assurance of which they transported themselves and their estates into those parts ; and we having received some addresses from the great men and natives of those countries in which they complain of breach of faith, and acts of violence, and injustice which they have been forced to undergoe from our subjects, whereby not only our Government is traduced, but the reputation and credit of the Christian religion brought into prejudice and reproach with the Gentiles and inhabitants of those countries who know not God, the reduction of whom to the true knowledge and feare of God is the most worthy and glorious end of all those Plantations : Upon all which motives, and as an evidence and manifestation of our fatherly affection towards all our subjects in those several colonies of New England (that is to say, of the Massachusetts, Connecticut, New Plimouth, Rhode Island, and Providence Plantations, and all other Plantations within that tract of land known under the appelation of New England), and to the end we may be truly informed of the state and condition of our good subjects there, that so we may the better know how to contribute to the further improvement of their happiness and prosperity : Know ye therefore, that we, reposing special trust and confidence in the fidelity, wisdome and circumspection of our trusty and well-beloved Colonel Richard Nichols, Sir Robert Carre, Knt., George Cartwright, Esq., and Samuel Maverick, Esq., of our special grace, certain knowledge, and mere motion,

All the New England colonies except that of Massachusetts Bay respectfully and cordially received the Royal Commissioners, and gave entire satisfaction in the matters which the Commissioners were intended to investigate.* The Congregational rulers of

have made, ordained, constituted and appointed, and by these presents do make, ordain, constitute and appoint the said Colonel Richard Nichols, Sir Robert Carre, George Cartwright, and Samuel Maverick, our Commissioners, and do hereby give and grant unto them, or any three or two of them, or of the survivors of them, of whom we will the said Colonel Richard Nichols, during his life, shall be alwaies one, and upon equal divisions of opinions, to have the casting and decisive voice, in our name to visit all and every the several colonies aforesaid, and also full power and authority to heare and receive and to examine and determine all complaints and appeals in all causes and matters, as well military as criminal and civil, and proceed in all things for the providing for and settling the peace and security of the said country, according to their good and sound discretion, and to such instructions as they or the survivors of them have, or shall from time to time receive from us in that behalfe, and from time to time, as they shall find expedient, to certify us or our Privy Council of their actings or proceedings touching the premises ; and for the doing thereof, or any other matter or thing relating thereunto, these presents, or the enrolment thereof, shall be unto them a sufficient warrant and discharge in that behalf. In witness whereof we have caused these our letters to be made patent. Witness ourselfe at Westminster, the 25th day of April, in the sixteenth yeare of our reigne." (Hutchinson's History of Massachusetts Bay, Vol. I., Appendix xv., pp. 535, 536.)

* The following are extracts from the report of the Commissioners who were appointed to visit the several colonies of New England in 1666:

" *The Colony of Connecticut* returned their thanks to his Majesty for his gracious letters, and for sending Commissioners to them, with promises of their loyalty and obedience ; and they did submit to have appeals made to his Majesty's Commissioners, who did hear and determine some differences among them. All forms of justice pass only in his Majesty's name ; they admit all that desire to be of their corporation ; they will not hinder any from enjoying the sacraments and using the Common Prayer Book, provided that they hinder not the maintenance of the public minister. They will amend anything that hath been done derogatory to his Majesty's honour, if there be any such thing, so soon as they shall come to the knowledge of it."

" *The Colony of Rhode Island and Providence* Plantations returned their humble thanks to his Majesty for sending Commissioners, and made great demonstration of their loyalty and obedience. They approved as most reasonable, that appeals should be made to his Majesty's Commissioners, who, having heard and determined some cases among them, referred other some in civility to their General Court, and some to the Governor and others ; some of which cases they again remitted to the Commissioners to determine. All proceedings are in his Majesty's name ; they admit all to be freemen who

Massachusetts Bay alone rejected the Royal Commissioners, denied their authority, and assailed their character. In the early history of Upper Canada, when one Church claimed to

desire it ; they allow liberty of conscience and worship to all who live civilly ; and if any can inform of anything in their laws or practices derogatory to his Majesty's honour, they will amend it."

" *The Colony of New Plymouth* did submit to have appeals made to the Commissioners, who have heard but one plaint made to them, which was that the Governor would not let a man enjoy a farm four miles square, which he had bought of an Indian. The complainant soon submitted to the Governor when he understood the unreasonableness of it."

" *The Colony of Massachusetts Bay* was the hardest to be persuaded to use his Majesty's name in the forms of justice. In this colony, at the first coming of the Commissioners, were many untruths raised and sent into the colonies, as that the King had to raise £15,000 yearly for his Majesty's use, whereupon Major Hawthorne made a seditious speech at the head of his company, and the late Governor (Bellingham) another at their meeting house at Boston, but neither of them were so much as questioned for it by any of the magistrates." * * " But neither examples nor reasons cou'l prevail with them to let the Commissioners hear and determine so much as those particular cases (Mr. Deane's and the Indian Sachems), which the King had commanded them to take care of and do justice in ; and though the Commissioners, who never desired that they should appear as delinquents, but as *defendants*, either by themselves or by their attorneys, assured them that if they had been unjustly complained of to his Majesty, their false accusers should be severely punished, and their just dealing made known to his Majesty and all the world ; yet they proclaimed by sound of trumpet that the General Court was the supremest judiciary in all the province ; that the Commissioners pretending to hear appeals was a breach of the privileges granted by the King's royal father, and confirmed to them by his Majesty's own letter, and that they would not permit it ; by which they have for the present silenced above thirty petitioners which desired justice from them and were lost at sea.

" To elude his Majesty's desire for admitting men of civil and competent estates to be freemen, they have an Act whereby he that is 24 years old, a housekeeper, and brings a certificate of his civil life, another of his being orthodox in matters of faith, and a third of his paying ten shillings besides head-money, at a single rate, *may then have the liberty to make his desires known to the Court,* and then it shall be put to vote. The Commissioners examined many townships, and found that scarce three in a hundred pay ten shillings at a single rate ; yet if this rate were general it would be just ; but he that is *a church member, though* he be a servant, and pay not *twopence, may be a freeman.* They do not admit any who is not a Church member to communion, nor their children to baptism, yet they will marry their children to those whom they will not admit to baptism, if they be rich. They did imprison and barbarously use Mr. Jourdan for baptising children, as himself

be established above every other, and the local Government
sustained its pretensions as if authorized by law, it is known
with what tenacity and denunciation the Canadian ecclesiastic-

complained in his petition to the Commissioners. Those whom they will not
admit to the communion, they compel to come to their sermons by forcing
from them five shillings for every neglect ; yet these men thought their paying
one shilling for not coming to prayers in England was an unsupportable
tyranny." * * " They have made many things in their laws derogatory to his
Majesty's honour, of which the Commissioners have made and desired that
they might be altered, but they have done nothing of it (a). Among others,
whoever keeps Christmas Day is to pay a fine of five pounds."
  " They caused at length a map of the territories to be made; but it was
made in a Chamber by direction and guess ; in it they claim Fort Albany,
and beyond it all the land to the South Sea. By their South Sea line they
entrench upon the colonies of New Plymouth, Rhode Island and Connecticut ;
and on the east they usurped Capt. Mason's and Sir Ferdinardo Gorges'
patents, and said that the Commissioners had nothing to do betwixt them
and Mr. Gorges, because his Majesty neither commanded them to deliver
possession to Mr. Gorges or to give his Majesty reason why they did not." * *
  " They of this colony say that King Charles the First granted to them a
Charter as a warrant against himself and his successors, and that so long as
they pay the fifth part of the gold and silver ore which they get, they shall
be free to use the privileges granted them, and that they are not obliged to the
King except by civility ; they hope by writing to tire the King, Lord Chancellor, and Secretaries too ; seven years they can easily spin out by writing,
and before that time a change may come ; nay, some have dared to say,
who knows what the event of this Dutch war will be ?"
  " This colony furnished Cromwell with many instruments out of their
corporation and college; and those that have retreated thither since his
Majesty's happy return, are much respected, and many advanced to be magistrates. They did solicit Cromwell by one Mr. Winslow to be declared a free
State, and many times in their laws declaring themselves to be so."
  (Hutchinson's Collection of Original Papers relative to the History of Massa
chusetts Bay, pp. 412—420.)

  (a) The Commissioners specify upwards of twenty anomalies in the book
entitled the " Book of the General Laws and Liberties concerning the Inhabitants of Massachusetts," which should be altered to correspond with the
Charter, and the relations of the colony to England. A few specimens may
be given : That the writs and forms of justice be issued and performed in his
Majesty's name ; that his Majesty s arms be set up in the courts of justice
within the colony, and that the masters of vessels and captains of foot
companies do carry the colours of England, by which they may be known to
be British subjects ; that in the 12th capital law, if any conspire against our
Commonwealth, *Commonwealth* may be expunged, and "against the peace of
his Majesty's colony" be inserted instead of the other ; that at p. 33, " none be

civil government resisted all appeals, both to the Local Legislature and to England, for a liberal government of equal laws
and equal rights for all classes of the King's subjects in Canada.
But the excluded majority of the Canadians had little to complain of in comparison of the excluded majority of his Majesty's
subjects of the Massachusetts Bay Colony, where the only
avenue to office, or even the elective franchise, was membership
in the Congregational Church, and where no dissenter from
that Church could have his children baptized, or worship God
according to his conscience, except under pain of imprisonment,
fine, banishment, or death itself.

The " Pilgrim Fathers" crossed the Atlantic to Plymouth in
1620, and the " Puritan Fathers" to Massachusetts Bay in 1628,
professedly for the same purpose, namely, liberty to worship God
without the imposition of ceremonies of which they disapproved.
The " Pilgrim Fathers," as true and consistent friends of liberty,
exercised full liberty of worship for themselves, and left others
to enjoy the same liberty of worship which they enjoyed; but
the " Puritan Fathers" exercised their liberty not only by
abandoning the Church and worship which they professed when
they left England, and setting up a Congregational worship,
but by prohibiting every other form of worship, and its adherents
with imprisonment, fine, exile, and death. And under this pretext of liberty of worship for themselves, they proscribed and
persecuted all who differed from them in religious worship for
fifty years, until their power to do so was taken from them
by the cancelling of the Charter whose provisions they had so
persistently and so cruelly abused, in contradistinction to
the tolerant and liberal conduct of their brethren and neighbours
of the Plymouth, Rhode Island, and Connecticut colonies. In
note on page 148, I have given extracts of the Report of the Royal
Commissioners relative to these colonies and their conduct and

admitted freemen but members of some of the Churches within the limits of
their jurisdiction," be made to comprehend " other than members of the Congregational Churches ;" that on the same page, the penalty for keeping
Christmas so directly against the law of England, be repealed ; that page 40,
the law for settling the Indians' title to land, be explained, for it seems as
if they were dispossessed of their land by Scripture, which is both against the
honour of God and the justice of the King. In 115th Psalm, 16, " Children
of men" comprehend Indians as well as English ; and no doubt the country
is theirs till they give it up or sell it, though it be not improved."

treatment of the Commissioners; and in the lengthened extract of the report relative to Massachusetts Bay Colony, it is seen how different was the spirit and government of the rulers of that colony, both in respect to their fellow-colonists and their Sovereign, from that of the rulers of the other New England colonies, which had, indeed, to seek royal protection against the oppressions and aggressions of the more powerful domineering Government of Massachusetts Bay. The rulers of this colony alone rejected the Royal Commissioners. For nearly two years the King's letter of the 28th of June, 1662 (given in note on page 140), pardoning their acts of disloyalty and assuring them of the continuance of their Charter on certain conditions, remained unpublished and unnoticed; but on the appointment of the Royal Commissioners, in 1664, they proceeded to acknowledge the kindness of the King's letter of 1662, and other Royal letters; then changing their tone, they protest against the Royal Commission. They sent a copy of their address to the King, to Lord Chancellor Clarendon, who, in connection with the Earl of Manchester and Lord Say, had befriended them. They also wrote to others of their friends, and among others to the Hon. and celebrated Robert Boyle, than whom no man had shown himself a warmer or more generous friend to their colony. I will give, not in successive notes, but in the text, their address to the King, the King's reply, Lord Clarendon's and the Hon. Robert Boyle's letters to them on the subject of their address to the King, and their rejection and treatment of the Royal Commission. I will then give the sentiments of what is called the "Petition of the minority" of their own community on the subject, and their own answers to the chief propositions of the Royal Commissioners. From all this it will appear that the United Empire Loyalists were the true liberals, the advocates of universal toleration and of truly liberal government; while the rulers of Massachusetts Bay were the advocates of religious intolerance and persecution of a government by a single religious denomination, and hostile to the supreme authority of England, as well as to their more tolerant and loyal fellow-colonists.

I will first give their characteristic address, called "Petition" or "Supplication," to the King. I do so without abridgment, long as it is, that I may not be chargeable with unfairness. It is as follows:—

Copy of the Address of the Massachusetts Colony to King Charles the Second, in 1664:

"To the King's Most Excellent Majestie.—The humble Supplication of the General Court of the Massachusetts Colony, in New England.

"DREAD SOVEREIGN,

"Iff your poor subjects, who have removed themselves into a remote corner of the earth to enjoy peace with God and man, doe, in this day of their trouble, prostrate themselves at your Royal feet, and beg your favour, we hope it will be graciously accepted by your Majestie, and that as the high place you sustain on earth doth number you here among the gods, for you well imitate the God of heaven, in being ready to maintain the cause of the afflicted, and the right of the poor,* and to receive their cries and addresses to that end. And we humbly beseech your Majestie with patience and clemency to heare and accept our plain discourse, tho' of somewhat greater length than would be comely in other or lesser cases. We are remote,† and can speake but seldom, and therefore crave leave to speake the more at once. Wee shall not largely repeat how that the first undertakers for this Plantation, having by considerable summs purchased the right thereof granted to the Council established at Plimouth by King James, your Royal grandfather, did after obtain a patent given and confirmed to themselves by your Royal father, King Charles the First, wherein it is granted to them, and their heirs, assigns and associates for ever, not only the absolute use and propriety of the tract of land therein mentioned, but also full and absolute power of governing‡ all the people of this place, by men chosen from among themselves, and according to such lawes as they shall from time to time see meet to make and establish, being not

---

* They were not so poor as when, just 30 years before, they, by the advice of their ministers, prepared to make armed resistance against the rumoured appointment over them of a Governor General of New England.

† They were not more "remote' than when they wrote to their friends in England as often as they pleased, or than when they addressed the Long Parliament four years before, and twice addressed Cromwell, stating their services to him in men and prayers against Charles the First, and asking his favours.

‡ The words "full and absolute power of governing" are not contained in the Royal Charter.

repugnant to the laws of England (they paying only the fifth part of the ore of gold and silver that shall here be found, for and in respect of all duties, demands, exactions, and service whatsoever), as in the said patent is more at large declared. Under the encouragement and security of which Royal Charter this people did, at their own charges,* transport themselves, their wives and families, over the ocean, purchase the lands of the natives, and plant this colony, with great labour, hazards, cost and difficulties, for a long time wrestling with the wants of a wilderness and the burdens of a new plantation; having, also, now above 30 years enjoyed the aforesaid power and priviledge of government within themselves, as their un-doubted right in the sight of God and man,† and having had, moreover, this further favour from God and from your Majes-tie, that wee have received several gracious letters from your Royal selfe, full of expressions tending to confirme us in our enjoyments, viz., in your Majestie's letter bearing date the 15th day of February, 1660, you are pleased to consider New England as one of the chiefest of your colonies and plantations abroad, having enjoyed and grown up in a long and orderly establishment, adding this royal promise : ' Wee shall not come behind any of our royal predecessors in a just encouragement and protection of all our loving subjects there.' In your Majestie's letter of the 28th of June, 1662, sent us by our messengers, besides many other gracious expressions, there is this : ' Wee will preserve and do hereby confirme the patent and Charter heretofore granted unto them by our Royal father of blessed memory, and they shall freely enjoy all the privileges and liberties granted unto them in and by the same.'‡ As for

* Emigrants generally transport themselves from one country to another, whether across the ocean or not, at their own charges.

† It is shown in this volume that they never had the " undoubted right" by the Charter, or the " undoubted right in the sight of God and man," to abolish one form of worship and set up another; to imprison, fine, banish, or put to death all who did not adopt their newly set up form of worship; to deny the rights of citizenship to four-fifths of their citizens on religious grounds, and tax them without representation. How far they invaded the " undoubted right" of others, " in the sight of God and man," and exceeded their own lawful powers, is shown on the highest legal authority in the 6th and 7th chapters of this volume.

‡ These references are acknowledgments on the part of the Massachusetts

such particulars, of a civil and religious nature, as are subjoined in the said letter, we have applyed ourselves to the utmost to satisfy your Majesty, so far as doth consist with conscience, of our duty toward God and the just liberties and privileges of our patent.* Wee are further bound, with humble thankfulness, to acknowledge your Majestie's gracious expressions in your last letter we have received, dated April 23, 1664, as (besides other instances thereof) that your Majestie hath not the least intention or thought of violating, or in the least degree infringing, the Charter heretofore granted by your Royal father with great wisdom, and upon full deliberation, etc.

"But what affliction of heart must it needs be unto us, that our sins have provoked God to permit our adversaries to set themselves against us by their misinformations, complaints and solicitations (as some of them have made it their worke for many years), and thereby to procure a commission under the great seal, wherein four persons (one of them our knowne and professed enemy) are impowered to hear, receive, examine and determine all complaints and appeals, in all causes and matters as well military as criminal and civil, and to proceed in all things, for settling this country according to their good and sound discretion, etc., whereby, instead of being governed by rulers of our owne choosing (which is the fundamental privilege of our patent), and by lawes of our owne, wee are like to be subjected to the arbitary power of strangers, proceeding not by any established law, but by their own discretion.   And whereas our patent gives a sufficient royal warrant and discharge to all officers and persons for executing the lawes here made and published, as is therein directed, we shall now not be discharged, and at rest from further molestation, when wee have so

Bay Court, that they had been kindly and liberally treated by both Charles the First and Charles the Second.

* They here limit their compliance with the six conditions on which the King proposed to continue the Charter which they had violated, to their "conscience" and "the just liberties and privileges of their patent." But according to their interpretation of these, they could not in "conscience" grant the "toleration" required by the King, or give up the sectarian basis of franchise and eligibility to office, or admit of appeals from their tribunals to the higher courts or the King himself in England. They seize upon and claim the promise of the King to continue the Charter, but evade and deny the fulfilment of the conditions on which he made that promise.

executed and observed our lawes, but be liable to complaints
and appeales, and to the determinations of new judges, whereby
our government and administrations will be made void and of
none effect. And though we have yet had but a little taste of
the words or actings of these gentlemen that are come over
hither in this capacity of Commissioners, yet we have had enough
to confirm us in our feares that their improvement of this
power, in pursuance of their commission (should the same proceed), will end in the subversion of our all. We should be glad
to hope that your Majesty's instructions (which they have not
been pleased to impart to us) may put such limitations to their
business here as will take off our fear; but according to the
present appearance of things, we thus speak.

"In this case (dread Sovereign), our refuge under God is
your royal selfe, whom we humbly address ourselves unto, and
are the rather emboldened therein because your Majesty's last
gracious letter doth encourage us to suggest what, upon the
experience we have had, and observations we have made, we
judge necessary or convenient for the good and benefit of this
plantation, and because we are well persuaded that had your
Majestie a full and right information of the state of things here,*
you would find apparent reason to put a stop to these proceedings, which are certainly discervient to your Majesty's interest
and to the prosperity and welfare of this place.

"If these things go on (according to the present appearance),
your subjects here will either be forced to seek new dwellings,
or sink and faint under burdens that will to them be intolerable.
The rigour of all new endeavours in the several callings and
occupations (either for merchandise abroad or for subduing this
wilderness at home) will be enfeebled, as we perceive it already
begins to be, the good of converting the natives obstructed, the
inhabitants driven to we know not what extremities, and this
hopeful plantation in the issue ruined. But whatever becomes
of us, we are sure the adversary cannot countervail the King's
damages.

"It is indeed a grief to our hearts to see your Majesty put

---

* But they rejected the King's commission of inquiry, refused the information required ; and they modestly pray the King to accept as proof of their
innocence and right doings their own professions and statements against the
complaints made of their proscriptions and oppressions.

upon this extraordinary charge and cost about a business the product whereof can never reimburse the one half of what will be expended upon it. Imposed rulers and officers will have occasion to expend more than can be raised here, so as nothing will return to your Majesty's exchequer; but instead thereof, the wonted benefit of customs, exported and imported into England from hence, will be diminished by discouragement and diminution of men's endeavours in their several occupations ; or if the aim should be to gratify some particular by livings and revenues here that will also fail, where nothing is to be had, the King himself will be loser, and so will the case be formed here; for such is the poverty and meanness of the people (by reason of the length and coldness of the winters, the difficulty of subduing a wilderness, defect of staple commodity, the want of money, etc.), that if with hard labour men get a subsistence for their families, 'tis as much as the generality are able to do, paying but very small rates towards the public charges ; and yet if all the country hath ordinarily raised by the year for all the charges of the whole government were put together and then doubled or trebled, it would not be counted, for one of these gentlemen, a considerable accommodation.*

"It is true, that the estates men have in conjunction with hard labour and vigorous endeavours in their several places do bring in a comfortable subsistence for such a mean people (we do not diminish our thankfulness to God, that he provides for us in a wilderness as he doth), yet neither will the former stand or the latter be discouraged, nor will both ever answer the ends of those that seek great things.

"We perceive there have been great expectations of what is to be had here raised by some men's informations. But those informations will prove fallacious, disappointing them that have

---

* The threat at the beginning of this, and also in the following paragraph, is characteristic ; it was tried, but without effect, on other occasions. The insinuations and special pleading throughout these paragraphs are amply answered in the letters of Lord Clarendon and the Hon. R. Boyle, which follow this extraordinary address, which abounds alternately and successively in affected helplessness and lofty assumptions, in calumnious statements and professed charity, in abject flattery and offensive insinuations and threats, in pretended poverty amidst known growing wealth, in appeals to heaven and professed humility and loyalty, to avoid the scrutiny of their acts and to reclaim the usurpation of absolute power.

relied upon them ; and if the taking of this course should drive the people out of the country (for to a coalition therein they will never come), it will be hard to find another people that will stay long or stand under any considerable burden in it, seeing it is not a country where men can subsist without hard labour and great frugality.

" There have also been high representations of great divisions and discontents among us, and of a necessity of sending commissioners to relieve the aggrieved, etc.; whereas it plainly appears that the body of this colony are unanimously satisfied in the present government, and abhorrent from change, and that what is now offered will, instead of relieving, raise up such grievances as are intolerable. We suppose there is no government under heaven wherein some discontented persons may not be found ; and if it be a sufficient accusation against a government that there are some such, who will be innocent ? Yet, through the favour of God, there are but few amongst us that are malcontent, and fewer that have cause to be so.

" Sir, the all-knowing God knows our greatest ambition is to live a poor and quiet life, in a corner of the world, without offence to God or man. We came not in this wilderness to seek great things for ourselves ; and if any come after us to seek them here, they will be disappointed. We keep ourselves within our line, and meddle not with matters abroad ; a just dependence upon and subjection to your Majesty, according to our Charter, it is far from our hearts to disacknowledge. We so highly prize your favourable aspect (though at so great a distance), as we would gladly do anything that is within our power to purchase the continuance of it. We are willing to testify our affection to your Majesty's service, by answering the proposal of your honourable Commissioners, of which we doubt not but that they have already given your Majesty an account. We are carefully studious of all due subjection to your Majesty, and that not only for wrath, but for conscience sake ; and should Divine Providence ever offer an opportunity wherein we might, in any righteous way, according to our poor and mean capacity, testify our dutiful affection to your Majesty, we hope we should most gladly embrace it. But it is a great unhappiness to be reduced to so hard a case, as to have no other testimony of our subjection and loyalty offered us but this, viz., to destroy our own

being, which nature teacheth us to preserve.; or to yield up our
liberties, which are far dearer to us than our lives, and which,
had we had any fears of being deprived of, we had never
wandered from our fathers' houses into these ends of the earth,
nor laid our labours or estates therein; besides engaging in a
most hazardous and difficult war, with the most warlike of the
natives, to our great charge and the loss of some of the lives of
our dear friends. Neither can the deepest invention of man
find out a more certain way of consistence than to obtain a
Royal donation from so great a prince under his great seal,
which is the greatest security that may be had in human
affairs.

"Royal Sir, it is in your power to say of your poor people in
New England, they shall not die. If we have found favour in
the sight of our King, let our life be given us at our petition
(or rather that which is dearer than life, that we have ventured
our lives, and willingly passed through many deaths to obtain),
and our all at our request. Let our government live, our
patent live, our magistrates live, our laws and liberties live, our
religious enjoyments live; so shall we all yet have further cause
to say from our hearts, let the King live for ever. And the blessing of them that were ready to perish shall come upon your
Majesty; having delivered the poor that cried, and such as had
none to help them. It was an honour to one of your royal
ancestors that he was called the poor man's king. It was Job's
excellency that he sat as king among his people—that he was a
father to the poor. They are a poor people (destitute of outward favour, wealth and power) who now cry to their lord the
King. May your Majesty please to regard their cause and
maintain their right. It will stand among the marks of lasting
honour to after generations. And we and ours shall have lasting cause to rejoice, that we have been numbered among your
Majesty's most humble servants and suppliants.

        "25th October, 1664."

As the Massachusetts Governor and Council had endorsed a
copy of the foregoing petition to the Earl of Clarendon, then
Lord Chancellor (who had dictated, with the Puritan ministers
of the King, his generous letter of the 28th of June, 1662), I
will here insert Lord Clarendon's reply to them, in which he
vindicates the appointment of the Commissioners, and exposes

the unreasonableness of the statements and conduct of the Massachusetts Court. The letter is as follows :

Copy of a letter from the Earl of Clarendon to the Massachusetts Colony in 1664 :—

"MR. GOVERNOR AND GENTLEMEN,

" I have received yours of the 7th of November, by the hands of Mr. Ashurst, a very sober and discreet person, and did (by his communicating it to me) peruse the petition you had directed to his Majesty ; and I do confess to you, I am so much a friend to your colony that if the same had been communicated to nobody but myself, I should have dissuaded the presenting the same to his Majesty, who I doubt will not think himself well treated by it, or the singular care he hath expressed of his subjects in those parts sufficiently acknowledged ; but since I found by your letter to my Lord Chamberlaine and Mr. Boyle, that you expect some effect from your petition, upon conference with them wee all agreed not to hinder the delivery of it, though I have read to them and Mr. Ashurst every word of the instructions the Commissioners have ; and they all confessed that his Majesty could not expresse more grace and goodness for that his plantation, nor put it more out of their power in any degree to invade the liberties and privileges granted to you by your Charter ; and therefore wee were all equally amazed to find that you demand a revokation of the Commission and Commissioners, without laying the least matter to their charge of crymes or exorbitances. What sense the King hath of your address to him, you will, I presume, heare from himself, or by his direction. I shall only tell you that as you had long cause to expect that the King would send Commissioners thither, so that it was absolutely necessary he should do so, to compose the differences amongst yourselves of which he received complaint, and to do justice to your neighbours, which they demand from his royall hands. I know not what you mean by saying, the Commissioners have power to exercise government there altogether inconsistent with your Charter and privileges, since I am sure their commission is to see and provide for the due and full observation of the Charter, and that all the privileges granted by that Charter may be equally enjoyed by all his Majesty's subjects there. I know they are expressly inhibited from intermeddling with or obstructing the administra-

tion of justice, according to the formes observed there ; but if
in truth, in any extraordinary case, the proceedings there have
been irregular, and against the rules of justice, as some particular
cases particularily recommended to them by his Majesty, seeme
to be, it cannot be presumed that his Majesty hath or will leave
his subjects of New England without hope of redresse by any
appeale to him, which his subjects of all his other kingdoms
have free liberty to make.   I can say no more to you but that it
is in your owne power to be very happy, and to enjoy all that
hath been granted to you ; but it will be absolutely necessary that
you perform and pay all that reverence and obedience which is
due from subjects to their king, and which his Majesty will
exact from you, and doubts not but to find from the best of that
colony both in quality and in number.   I have no more to add
but that I am,

" Gentlemen,

" Your affectionate servant,

" CLARENDON, C.

" Worcester House, 15 March, 1665.

To Lord Clarendon's letter I will add the letter of the Honourable Robert Boyle to Governor Endicot.   The Hon. Robert
Boyle was not only distinguished as the first philosopher of his
age, but as the founder of the Royal Society and the President
of the Society for the Propagation of the Gospel in New
England—the Society which supported John Eliot, the apostle
to the Indians of New England—for the Massachusetts Bay
Government neither established nor supported his mission to
the Indians.   New England never had a warmer and more
benevolent friend than the celebrated Robert Boyle, who, in a
letter dated March 17th, 1665, and addressed to the Governor
Endicot and the Massachusetts Court, after acknowledging their
resolution of thanks, through Mr. Winthrop, to him for his
exertions on their behalf, proceeds as follows :

" I dealt very sincerely with Mr. Winthrop in what I informed him concerning the favourable inclinations I had found
both in his Majesty and in my Lord Chancellor toward the
united colonies of New England ; and though his lordship again
repeats and confirms the assurances he had authorized me to give
to your friends in the city, yet I cannot but acquaint you with
this, observing that in your last addresses to his Majesty, and

11

letters to his lordship, there are some passages that were much more unexpected than welcome; insomuch that not only those who are unconcerned in your affairs, but the most considerable persons that favour you in England, have expressed to me their being unsatisfied in some of the particulars I am speaking of. And it seems generally unreasonable that when the King had so graciously remitted all that was past, and upon just and important inducements, sent Commissioners to promote the welfare of your colony, you should (in expressions not over manly or respectfully worded) be importunate with him to do an action likely to blemish his wisdom or justice, or both, as immediately to recall public ministers from so remote a part of the world before they or any of them be so much as accused of any one crime or miscarriage.

"And since you are pleased I should concern myself in this business, I must deal so ingenuously with you as to inform you, that hearing about your affairs, I waited upon my Lord Chancellor (and finding him, though not satisfied with your late proceedings, yet neither your enemy, nor indisposed to be your favourer as before). His lordship was pleased, with a condescending and unexpected freedom, to read himself, not only to me, but to another good friend of yours that I brought along with me, the whole instructions and all the other papers that were delivered to the Commissioners, and by the particulars of those it appeared to us both that they had been so solicitous, viz., in the things that related to your Charter, and especially to the liberty of your consciences, that I could not but wonder at it, and add to the number of those that cannot think it becomes his Majesty to recall Commissioners sent so far with no other instructions than those, before they have time to do any part of the good intended you by themselves, and before they are accused of having done any one harmful thing, even in your private letters either to me or (as far as I know) to any of your friends here, who will be much discouraged from appearing on your behalf; and much disabled to do it successfully so long as such proceedings as these that relate to the Commissioners supply others with objections which those that wish you well are unable to answer.

"I should not have taken this liberty, which the honour of your letter ought to have filled with little less than acknow-

ledgment, if the favourable construction you have made of my
former endeavours to do you good offices did not engage me to
continue them, though in a way which (in my poor apprehension)
tends very directly to serve you, whether I do or no to please
you; and as I presume you will receive, both from his Majesty
and my Lord Chancellor, express assurances that there is nothing
intended in violation to your Charter, so if the Commissioners
should break their instructions and endeavour to frustrate his
Majesty's just and favourable intentions towards you, you may
find that some of your friends here were not backward to accuse the Commissioners upon general surmises that may injure
you, than they will be ready to represent your grievances, in
case they shall actually oppress you; which, that they may
never do, is not more the expectation of them that recommended
them to you than it is the hearty wish of a person who, upon
the account of your faithfulness and care of so good a work as
the conversion of the natives among you, is in a peculiar manner concerned to shew himself, honoured Sir, your most affectionate and most humble servant,*

"Ro. Boyle."

But in addition to the benevolent and learned Robert Boyle
and their other friends in England, besides Lord Clarendon and
the King, who disapproved of their pretentious spirit and proceedings, there were numbers of their own fellow-colonists who
equally condemned the assumptions and conduct of Governor
Endicot and his Council. It has been shown in a previous
chapter that in connection with the complete suppression of the
freedom of the press, petitioners to the Governor and Court
were punished for any expressions in their petitions which complained of the acts or proceedings of the Court. It therefore
required no small degree of independence and courage for any
among them to avow their dissent from the acts of rulers so
despotic and intolerant. Yet, at this juncture of the rejection
of the Royal Commission, and the denial of the King's authority,
there were found United Empire Loyalists and Liberals, even
among the Congregational "freemen" of Massachusetts Bay,
who raised the voice of remonstrance against this incipient
separation movement. A petition was prepared and signed by

---

* Collections of the Massachusetts Historical Society, Vol. VIII., Second
Series, pp. 49—51.

nearly two hundred of the inhabitants of Boston, Salem, Newbury, and Ipswich, and presented to the Court. The compiler
of the "Danforth Papers," in the Massachusetts Historical
Collection, says: "Next follows the petition in which the
minority of our forefathers have exhibited so much good sense
and sound policy." The following is an extract of the Boston
petition, addressed "To the Honourable General Court now
assembled in Boston:"

"May it please the Hon. Court:

"Your humble petitioners, being informed that letters are
lately sent from his Majesty to the Governor and Council, expressive of resentment of the proceedings of this colony
with his Commissioners lately sent hither, and requiring also
some principal persons therein, with command upon their
allegiance to attend his Majesty's pleasure in order to a final
determination of such differences and debates as have happened
between his Majesty's Commissioners and the Governor here,
and which declaration of his Majesty, your petitioners, looking
at as a matter of the greatest importance, justly calling for the
most serious consideration, that they might not be wanting,
either to yourselves in withholding any encouragement that
their concurrence might afford in so arduous a matter, nor to
themselves and the country in being involved by their silence
in the dangerous mistakes of (otherwise well united) persons
inclining to disloyal principles, they desire they may have
liberty without offence to propose some of their thoughts and
fears about the matter of your more serious deliberation.

"Your petitioners humbly conceive that those who live in this
age are no less than others concerned in that advice of the wise
man, to keep the King's commandment, because of the oath of
God, and not to be tardy to go out of his sight that doth whatever pleaseth him; wherefore they desire that seeing his
Majesty hath already taken no little displeasure against us, as
if we disowned his Majesty's jurisdiction over us, effectual care
be taken, lest by refusing to attend his Majesty's order for
clearing our pretences unto right and favour in that particular,
we should plunge ourselves into great disfavour and danger.

"The receiving of a Charter from his Majesty's royal pre-
decessor for the planting of this colony, with a confirmation of
the same from his royal person, by our late address, sufficiently

declares this place to be part of his dominions and ourselves his subjects. In testimony of which, also, the first Governor, Mr. Matthew Cradock (as we are informed), stands recorded *juratus de fide et obedientia*, before one of the Masters in Chancery; whence it is evident that if any proceedings of this colony have given occasion to his Majesty to say that we believe he hath no jurisdiction over us, what effectual course had need be taken to free ourselves from the incurring his Majesty's future displeasure by continuance in so dangerous an offence ? And to give his Majesty all due satisfaction in that point, such an assertion would be no less destructive to our welfare than derogatory to his Majesty's honour. The doubtful interpretations of the words of a patent which there can be no reason to hope should ever be construed to the divesting of the sovereign prince of his Royal power over his natural subjects and liege people, is too frail a foundation to build such transcendent immunity and privilege upon.

" Your petitioners earnestly desire that no part will so irresistibly carry on any design of so dangerous a consequence as to necessitate their brethren equally engaged with them in the same undertaking to make their particular address to his Majesty, and declaring to the world, to clear themselves from the least imputation of so scandalous an evil as the appearance of disaffection or disloyalty to the person and government of their lawful prince and sovereign would be.

" Wherefore your petitioners do here humbly entreat that if any occasion hath been given to his Majesty so to resent any former actings as in his last letter is held forth, that nothing of that nature be further proceeded in, but contrariwise that application be made to his Majesty, immediately to be sent for the end to clear the transactions of them that govern this colony from any such construction, lest otherwise that which, if duly improved, might have been a cloud of the latter rain, be turned into that which, in the conclusion, may be found more terrible than the roaring of a lion.

" Thus craving a favourable interpretation of what is here humbly presented, your petitioners shall ever be obliged to, etc."*

* Collections of Massachusetts Historical Society, Vol. VIII., Second Series, pp. 103—105.

The following is the King's letter, referred to by Lord Clarendon, evidently written on the advice of the Puritan Councillors, whom the King retained in his government, and to whom the management of New England affairs seems to have been chiefly committed, with the oversight of the Lord Chancellor Clarendon. This letter, in addition to a previous letter from the King of the same kind, together with the letters of Lord Clarendon and the Hon. Robert Boyle, left them not a shadow of pretext for the inflammatory statements they were putting forth, and the complaints they were making, that their Charter privileges and rights of conscience were invaded, and was a reply to the petition of the Massachusetts Bay Governor and Council (inserted above at length, pages 153—159), and shows the utter groundlessness of their statements; that what they contended for under the pretext of conscience was the right of persecuting and proscribing all who did not conform to the Congregational worship; and that what they claimed under the pretence of Charter rights was absolute independence, refusing to submit even to inquiry as to whether they had not encroached upon the rights and territories of their white and Indian neighbours, or made laws and regulations and performed acts contrary to the laws of England and to the rights of other of the King's subjects. This letter breathes the spirit of kindness and forbearance, and contends for *toleration,* as did all the loyal colonists of the time, appealing to the King for protection against the intolerance, persecution and proscription of the Massachusetts Bay Congregational Government. The letter is as follows :

Copy of a Letter from Secretary Morrice to the Massachusetts Colony:

"Sirs,

"His Majesty hath heard this petition* read to him, and hath well weighed all the expressions therein, and the temper and spirit of those who framed it, and doth not impute the same to his colony of Massachusetts, amongst whom he knows the major part consists of men well affected to his service and

* The petition entire is inserted above, pp. 153—159. Mr. Hutchinson gives this petition in the Appendix to the first volume of his History of Massachusetts Bay, No. 16, pp. 537—539 ; but he does not give the King's reply.

obedient to his government, but he hath commanded me to let
you know that he is not pleased with this petition, and looks
upon it as the contrivance of a few persons who have had too
long authority there, and who use all the artifices they can to
infuse jealousies into his good subjects there, and apprehensions,
as if their Charter were in danger, when it is not possible for
his Majesty to do more for the securing it, or to give his subjects
there more assurance that it shall not in any degree be in-
fringed, than he hath already done, even by his late Commission
and Commissioners sent thither, who are so far from having the
least authority to infringe any clause in the said Charter, that
it is the principal end of their journey, so chargeable to his
Majesty, to see that the Charter be fully and punctually observed.
His Majesty did expect thanks and acknowledgments from that
his colony, of his fatherly care in sending his Commissioners
thither, and which he doubts not he shall receive from the rest
of the colonies in those parts, and not such unreasonable and
groundless complaint as is contained in your petition, as if he
had thereby intended to take away your privileges and to drive
you from your habitations, without the least mention of any
misdemeanour or miscarriage in any one of the said Commissioners or in any one particular.   Nor can his Majesty comprehend
(except you believe that by granting your Charter he hath
parted with his sovereign power over his subjects there) how
he could proceed more graciously, or indeed any other way, upon
so many complaints presented to him by particular persons of
injustice done contrary to the constitution of that government :
from the other colonies, for the oppression they pretend to
undergo by the conduct of Massachusetts, by extending their
bounds and their jurisdiction further than they ought to do,
as they pretend ; from the natives, for the breach of faith and
intolerable pressures laid upon them, as they allege, contrary
to all kind of justice, and even to the dishonour of the English
nation and Christian faith, if all they allege be true.   I say, his
Majesty cannot comprehend how he could apply proper remedies
to these evils, if they are real, or how he could satisfy himself
whether they are real or no by any other way or means than by
sending Commissioners thither to examine the truth and grounds
of all the allegations, and for the present to compose the differences the best they can, until, upon a full and clear representa-

tion thereof to his Majesty, who cannot but expect the same from them, his Majesty's own final judgement and determination may be had. And it hath pleased God so far already to bless that service that it's no small benefit his Majesty and his English colonies in those parts have already received by the said Commissioners in the removal of so inconvenient neighbours as the Dutch have been for these late years, and which would have been a more spreading and growing mischief in a short time if it had not been removed. To conclude, I am commanded by his Majesty to assure you again of your full and peaceable enjoyment of all the privileges and liberties granted to you by his Charter, which he hath heretofore and doth now again offer to renew to you, if you sha'l desire it; and that you may further promise yourselves all the protection, countenance, and encouragement that the best subjects ever received from the most gracious Prince; in return whereof he doth only expect that duty and cheerful obedience that is due to him, and that it may not be in the power of any malicious person to make you miserable by entertaining any unnecessary and unreasonable jealousies that there is a purpose to make you so. And since his Majesty hath too much reason to suspect that Mr. Endicot,* who hath during all the late revolutions continued the govern-

---

* Mr. Endicot died before the next election. He was the primary cause of the disputes between the Massachusetts Bay Colony and the Parent Government, and the unrelenting persecutor of all who differed from him in religious worship. He was hostile to monarchy and all English authority from the beginning; he got and kept the elective franchise, and eligibility to office, in the hands of the Congregationalists alone, and became of course their idol. The King's suggesting the election of a Governor other than Endicot was a refutation of their statements that he intended to deprive them of their local self-government. The following is Neal's notice of the death of Mr. Endicot: "On the 23rd of March, 1665, died Mr. John Endicot, Governor of the Jurisdiction of Massachusetts. He arrived at Salem in the year 1628, and had the chief command of those that first settled there, and shared with them in all their hardships. He continued at Salem till the magistrates desired him to remove to Boston for the more convenient administration of justice, as Governor of the Jurisdiction, to which he was frequently elected for many years together. He was a great enemy of the Sectaries, and was too severe in executing the penal laws against the Quakers and *Anabaptists* during the time of his administration. He lived to a good old age, and was interred at Boston with great honour and solemnity."—Neal's History of New England, Vol. II., p. 346.

ment there, is not a person well affected to his Majesty's person or his government, his Majesty will take it very well if at the next election any other person of good reputation be chosen in the place, and that he may no longer exercise that charge. This is all I have to signify unto you from his Majesty, and remain,

"Your very humble servant,

"WILL. MORRICE.

"Whitehall, February 25th, 1665."

But this courteous and explicit letter had no effect upon the Governor and Council of Massachusetts Bay in allaying opposition to the Royal Commissioners, whose authority they refused to acknowledge, nor did it prevent their persecution of their brethren whom they termed "Sectaries"—the "Dissenting party." The Commissioners having executed the part of their commission relative to the Dutch and Indians, and finding their authority resisted by the Governor and Council of Massachusetts Bay, reported the result to the King's Government, which determined to order the attendance of representatives of the Massachusetts Bay Government, to answer in England the complaints prepared against them, and for their conduct to the Commissioners. The letter which the King was advised to address to that pretentious and persecuting Government speaks in a more decisive but kindly tone, and is as follows :

Copy of a letter from King Charles II. to the Massachusetts Colony, April, 1666:

"CHARLES R.

"His Majesty having received a full information from his Commissioners who were sent by him into New England, of their reception and treatment in the several colonies and provinces of that plantation, in all which they have received great satisfaction but only that of Massachusetts; and he having likewise been fully informed of the account sent hither by the Counsell of the Massachusetts, under the hand of the present Governor, of all the passages and proceedings which have been there between the said Commissioners and them from the time of their first coming over; upon all which it is very evident to his Majesty, notwithstanding many expressions of great affection and duty, that those who govern the Colony of Massachusetts do believe that the commission given by his Majesty to those Commissioners, upon so many and weighty reasons, and after so long deliberation, is an apparent violation of their Charter, and tending to the dissolution of it, and that in truth they do, upon the matter, believe that his Majesty hath no jurisdiction over them, but that all persons must acquiesce in their judgments and determinations, how unjust soever, and cannot appeal to his Majesty, which would be a matter of such a high consequence as every man discernes where it must end. His Majesty, therefore, upon due consideration of the whole matter, thinks fit to recall his said Commissioners which he hath at this present done, to the end he may receive from them a more particular account of the state and condition of those his plantations, and of the particular differences and debates they have had with those of the Massachusetts, that so his Majesty may pass his final judgment and determination thereupon. His Majesty's express command and charge is, that the Governor and Counsell of the Massachusetts do forthwith make choice of five or four persons to attend upon his Majesty, whereof Mr. Richard Bellingham and Major Hathorn are to be two, both which his Majesty commands upon their allegiance to attend, the other three or two to be such as the Counsell shall make choice of; and if the said Mr. Bellingham be the present Governor, another fit person is to be deputed to that office till his return, and his Majesty will then, in person, hear all the allegations, suggestions, or pretences to right or favour that can be made on the behalf of the said colony, and will then make it appear how far he is from the least thought of invading or infringing, in the least degree, the Royal Charter granted to the said colony. And his Majesty expects the appearance of the said persons as soon as they can possibly repair hither after they have notice of this his Majesty's pleasure. And his further command is, that there be no alterations with reference to the government of the Province of Maine till his Majesty hath heard what is alledged on all sides, but that the same continue as his Majesty's Commissioners have left the same, until his Majesty shall further determine. And his Majesty further expressly charges and commands the Governor and Counsell there, that they immediately set all such persons at liberty who have been or are imprisoned only for petitioning or applying themselves to his Majesty's Commissioners. And for the better prevention of all differences and disputes upon the bounds and limits of the several colonies, his Majesty's pleasure is, that all determinations made by his and limits may still continue to be observed, till, upon a full representation of all pretences, his Majesty shall make his own final determination; and particularly the present temporary bounds set by the Commissioners between the colonies of New Plymouth and Rhode Island, until his Majesty shall find cause to alter the same. And his Majesty expects that full obedience be given to this signification of his pleasure in all particulars.

"Given at the Court at Whitehall, the 10th day of April, 1666, in the eighteenth year of his Majesty's reign.

"WILL. MORRICE."

Before noticing the proceedings of the Massachusetts Bay Court in reference to this letter of the King, it may be proper to pause a little and retrospect past transactions between the two Charleses and the Congregational rulers of Massachusetts Bay, and the correspondence of the latter with the Royal Commissioners, so prominently referred to in the above letter.

The foregoing documents which I have so largely quoted evince the Royal indulgence and kindness shown to the Massachusetts Bay Colony after the conduct of its rulers to the King and his father during the twenty years of the civil war and Commonwealth; the utter absence of all intention on the part of Charles the Second, any more than on the part of Charles the First, to limit or interfere with the exercise of their own conscience or taste in their form or manner of worship, only insisting upon the enjoyment of the same liberty by those who preferred another form and manner of worship, However intolerant and persecuting the Governments of both Charles the First and Second were to all who did not conform to the established worship and its ceremonies in England, they both disclaimed enforcing them upon the New England colonies; and I repeat, that it may be kept in mind, that when the first complaints were preferred to Charles the First and the Privy Council, in 1632, against Endicot and his Council, for not only not conforming to, but abolishing, the worship of the Church of England, the accused and their friends successfully, though falsely, denied having abolished the Episcopal worship; and the

King alleged to his Council, when Laud was present, that he had never intended to enforce the Church ceremonies objected to upon the New England colonists. The declarations of Charles the Second, in his letters to them, confirmed as they were by the letters of the Earl of Clarendon and the Honourable Robert Boyle, show the fullest recognition on the part of the Government of the Restoration to maintain their perfect liberty of worship. Their own address to the King in 1664 bears testimony that for upwards of thirty years liberty of worship had been maintained inviolate, and that King Charles the Second had himself invariably shown them the utmost forbearance, kindness, and indulgence.*

---

* The same year, 1662, in which Charles the Second sent so gracious a letter to the Governor and Council of Massachusetts Bay, he granted Charters to the colonies of Connecticut and Rhode Island, in both of which perfect liberty of conscience and religious liberty was encouraged and provided for, evincing the settled policy of the Government of the Restoration in regard to the New England colonies. The annalist Holmes says :

" 1662.—The Charter of Connecticut was granted by Charles II. with most ample privileges, under the great seal of England. It was ordained by the Charter that all the King's subjects in the colony should enjoy all the privileges of free and natural born subjects within the realm of England." (Holmes' Annals, etc., Vol. I., pp. 320, 321.)

So liberal were the provisions of this Charter, that as Judge Story says : " It continued to be the fundamental law of the State of Connecticut until the year 1818, when a new constitution of government was framed and adopted by the people." (Commentaries on the Constitution of the United States, Vol. I., Sec. 88.)

Rhode Island.—Rhode Island had two English Charters, the circumstances connected with both of which were very peculiar. Its founder, Roger Williams, had been banished from the jurisdiction of Massachusetts Bay.

" Rhode Island," says Judge Story, " was originally settled by emigrants from Massachusetts, fleeing hither to escape from religious persecution, and it still boasts of Roger Williams as its founder and as the early defender of religious freedom and the rights of conscience. One body of them purchased the island which gave name to the State, and another the territory of the Providence Plantations from the Indians, and began their settlements at the same period, in 1636 and 1638. They entered into separate associations of government. But finding their associations not sufficient to protect them *against the encroachments of Massachusetts,* and having no title under any royal patents, they sent Roger Williams to England in 1643 to procure a surer foundation both of title and government. He succeeded in obtaining from the Earl of Warwick (in 1643) a Charter of incorporation of Providence Plantations ; and also in 1644 a Charter from the two Houses of Parliament

Yet they no sooner felt their Charter secure, and that the King had exhausted the treasury of his favours to them, than they deny his right to see to their fulfilment of the conditions on which he had promised to continue the Charter. The Charter itself, be it remembered, provided that they should not make

(Charles the First being driven from his capital) for the incorporation of the towns of Providence, Newport, and Portsmouth, for the absolute government of themselves, but according to the laws of England."

But such was the hostility of the rulers of Massachusetts Bay that they refused to admit Rhode Island into the confederacy of the New England colonies formed in 1643 to defend themselves against the Indians, the Spanish, the Dutch, and the French; yet they had influence enough with Cromwell to get the Charter of Rhode Island suspended in 1652. "But," says Dr. Holmes, "that colony, taking advantage of the distractions which soon after ensued in England, resumed its government and enjoyed it without further interruption until the Restoration." (Holmes' Annals, etc., Vol. I., p. 297.)

"The restoration of Charles the Second," says Judge Story, "seems to have given great satisfaction to these Plantations. They immediately proclaimed the King and sent an agent to England; and in July, 1663, after some opposition, they succeeded in obtaining a Charter from the Crown."

"The most remarkable circumstance in the Charter, and that which exhibits the strong feeling and spirit of the colony, is the provision for *religious freedom.* The Charter, after reciting the petition of the inhabitants, 'that it is much in their hearts (if they may be permitted) to hold forth a lively experiment, that a most flourishing civil state may stand, and be *best maintained, and that among English subjects with full liberty* in religious concernments, and that true piety, rightly grounded upon Gospel principles, will give the least and greatest security to sovereignty,' proceeds to declare:

"'We being willing to encourage the hopeful undertaking of our said loyal and loving subjects, and to secure them in the free exercise of all their civil and religious rights appertaining to them as our loving subjects, and to preserve to them that liberty in the true Christian faith and worship of God which they have sought with so much travail and with peaceful minds and loyal subjection to our progenitors and ourselves to enjoy; and because some of the people and inhabitants of the same colony cannot, in their private opinion, conform to the public exercise of religion according to the liturgy, form, and ceremonies of the Church of England, or take or subscribe to the oaths and articles made and established in that behalf; and for that the same, by reason of the remote distances of these places, will, as we hope, be no breach of the unity and uniformity established in this nation, have therefore thought fit, and do hereby publicly grant and ordain and declare, that our royal will and pleasure is, that *no person within the said colony,* at any time hereafter, shall be any wise molested, punished, disquieted, or called in question for any

any laws or regulations contrary to the laws of England, and that all the settlers under the Charter should enjoy all the rights and privileges of British subjects. The King could not know whether the provisions of the Royal Charter were observed or violated, or whether his own prescribed conditions of continuing the Charter were ignored or fulfilled, without examination ; and how could such an examination be made except by a Committee of the Privy Council or special Commissioners ? This was what the King did, and what the Governor and Court of Massachusetts Bay resisted. They accepted with a profusion of thanks and of professed loyalty the King's pardon and favours, but denied his rights and authority. They denied any other allegiance or responsibility to the King's Government than the payment of five per cent. of the proceeds of the gold and silver mines. The absurdity of their pretensions and of their resistance to the Royal Commission, and the injustice and unreasonableness of their attacks and pretended suspicions, are well exposed in the documents above quoted, and especially in the petition of the " minority" of their own fellow-colonists. But all in vain; where they could not openly deny, they evaded so as to render nugatory the requirements of the King as the conditions of continuing the Charter, as will appear from their correspondence with the Royal Commissioners. I will give two or three examples.

They refused to take the oath of allegiance according to the form transmitted to them by the King's order, or except with limitations that neutralized it. The first Governor of their

differences in opinion on matters of religion, but that all and every person and persons may, from time to time, and at all times hereafter, freely and fully have and enjoy his and their own judgment and conveniences in matters of religious concernment throughout the tract of land hereafter mentioned, they behaving themselves peaceably and quietly, and not using this liberty to licentiousness and profaneness, nor to the civil injury or outward disturbance of others.'" (Hazard's Collection, p. 613.)

Judge Story, after quoting this declaration of the Royal Charter, justly remarks, " This is a noble declaration, worthy of any Prince who rules over a free people. It is lamentable to reflect how little it comports with the domestic persecutions authorized by the same monarch during his profligate reign. It is still more lamentable to reflect how little a similar spirit of toleration was encouraged, either by precept or example, in other of the New England Colonies." (Commentaries, etc., Vol. I., Chap. viii., Section 97.)

Corporation, Matthew Cradock, took the oath of allegiance as other officers of the Crown and British subjects, and as provided in the Royal Charter; but after the secret conveyance of the Charter to Massachusetts Bay and the establishment of a Government there, they, in secret deliberation, decided that they were not British subjects in the ordinary sense; that the only allegiance they owed to the King was such as the homage the Hanse Towns paid to Austria, or Burgundy to the Kings of France; that the only allegiance or obligation they owed to England was the payment of one-fifth per cent. of the produce of their gold and silver mines; that there were no appeals from their acts or decisions to the King or Courts of England; and that the King had no right to see whether their laws or acts were according to the provisions of the Charter. When the King, after his restoration, required them to take the oath of allegiance as the first condition of continuing the Charter, they evaded it by attaching to the oath the Charter *according to their interpretation of it.* Any American citizen could at this day take the oath of allegiance to the Sovereign of England if it were limited to the Constitution of the United States. First of all, they required of every freeman the oath of fidelity to the local Government; and then, after three years' delay and debating about the oath of allegiance to the King, the Massachusetts Bay Court adopted the following order:

"May 16th, 1665.

"It is ordered by this Court and by the authority thereof, that the following oath be annexed unto the oaths of every freeman, and oath of fidelity, and to the Governor, Deputy Governor and Assistants, and to all other public officers as followeth. The oaths of freemen and of fidelity to run thus: 'Whereas, I, A. B., an inhabitant within this jurisdiction, considering how I stand to the King's Majesty, his heirs and successors, *by our Charter,* and the Government established thereby, do swear *accordingly,* by the great and dreadful name of the ever living God, that I will bear faithful and true allegiance to our Sovereign Lord the King, his heirs and successors; and so proceed *as in the printed oaths of freemen and fidelity.*'"*

* Collections of the Massachusetts Historical Society, Vol. VIII., Second Series, p. 74.

On this, Col. Nichols, Chairman of the Royal Commission, addressing the Court, remarks as follows:

"You profess you highly prize the King's favour, and that offending him shall never be imputed to you; and yet you, in the same paper, refuse to do what the King requires should be done—that all that come into this colony to dwell should take the oath of allegiance here. Your Charter commands it; yet you make promises not therein expressed, and, in short, would curtail the oath, as you do allegiance, refusing to obey the King. It is your duty to administer justice in the King's name; and the King acknowledgeth in his letter, April 23, that it is his duty to see that justice be administered by you to all his subjects here, and yet you will not give him leave to examine by his Commissioners."

Referring to this subject again, Col. Nichols remarks:

"Touching the oath of allegiance, which is exactly prescribed in your Charter, and no faithful subject will make it less than according to the law of England. The oath mentioned by you was taken by Mr. Matthew Cradock, as Governor, which hath a part of the oath of allegiance put into it, and ought to be taken in that name by all in public office; also in another part of the Charter it is expressly spoken of as the oath of allegiance; and how any man can make that in fewer words than the law of England enjoins, I know not how it can be acceptable to his Majesty."*

As a sect in the Jewish nation made void the law by their traditions, so the sect of Congregational rulers in Massachusetts Bay thus made void the national oath of allegiance by their additions. On the subject of liberty of worship according to the Church of England, these sectarian rulers express themselves thus:

"Concerning the use of the Common Prayer Book and ecclesiastical privileges, our humble addresses to his Majesty have fully declared our ends, in our being voluntary exiles from our dear native country, which we had not chosen at so dear a rate, could we have seen the word of God warranting us to perform our devotions in that way; and to have the same set

* Collections of the Massachusetts Historical Society, Vol. VIII., Second Series, pp. 76—78.

up here, we conceive it is apparent, that it will disturb our peace in our present enjoyments; and we have commended to the ministry and people here the word of the Lord for their rule therein, as you may find by your perusal of our law book, title 'Ecclesiastical,' p. 25."

To this the King's Commissioners reply as follows:

" The end of the first Planters coming hither was (as expressed in your address, 1660), the enjoyment of the liberty of your own consciences, which the King is so far from taking away from you, that by every occasion he hath promised and assured the full enjoyment of it to you. We therefore advise that you should not deny the liberty of conscience to any, especially where the King requires it; and that upon a vain conceit of your own that it will disturb your enjoyments, which the King often hath said it shall not.

" Though you commend to the ministers and people the word of the Lord for their rule, yet you did it with a proviso that they have the approbation of the Court, as appears in the same page; and we have great reason both to think and say that the King and his Council and the Church of England understand and follow the rules in God's word as much as this Corporation.

" For the use of the Common Prayer Book: His Majesty doth not impose the use of the Common Prayer Book on any, but he understands that liberty of conscience comprehends every man's conscience as well as any particular, and thinks that all his subjects should have equal rights; and in his letter of June 28, 1662, he requires and charges that all his subjects should have equally an allowance thereof; but why you should put that restraint on his Majesty's subjects that live under his obedience, his Majesty doth not understand that you have any such privileges.

" Concerning ecclesiastical privileges, we suppose you mean sacraments, baptisms, etc. You say we have commended the word of the Lord for our rule therein, referring us to the perusal of the printed law, page 25. We have perused that law, and find that that law doth cut off those privileges which his Majesty will have, and see that the rest of his subjects have."*

* Collections of the Massachusetts Historical Society, Vol. VIII., Second Series, pp. 76, 78, 79.

12

I now resume the narrative of questions as affecting the authority of the Crown and the subjection of the Massachusetts Bay Colony. That colony was the most populous and wealthy of all the New England colonies. Its principal founders were men of wealth and education; the twelve years' tyranny of Charles the First and Laud, during the suspension of Parliament, caused a flow of more than twenty thousand emigrants to Massachusetts Bay, with a wealth exceeding half a million sterling, and among them not less than seventy silenced clergymen. During the subsequent twenty years of the civil war and Commonwealth in England, the rulers of that colony actively sided with the latter, and by the favour and connivance of Cromwell evaded the Navigation Law passed by the Parliament, and enriched themselves greatly at the expense of the other British colonies in America, and in violation of the law of Parliament. In the meantime, being the stronger party, and knowing that they were the favourites of Cromwell, they assumed, on diverse grounds, possession of lands, south, east, north, and west, within the limits of the neighbouring colonies, and made their might right, by force of arms, when resisted; and denied the citizenship of freemen to all except actual members of the Congregational Churches, and punished Dissenters with fine, imprisonment, banishment, and death itself in many instances.

On the restoration of Charles the Second to the throne of his ancestors, it was natural that the various oppressed and injured parties, whether of colonies or individuals, should lay their grievances before their Sovereign and appeal to his protection; and it was not less the duty of the Sovereign to listen to their complaints, to inquire into them, and to redress them if well founded. This the King, under the guidance of his Puritan Councillors, proceeded to do in the most conciliatory and least offensive way. Though the rulers of Massachusetts Bay did not, as did the other New England as well as Southern colonies, recognize and proclaim the King on the announcement of his restoration, but observed a sullen silence until they saw that the monarchy was firmly established; yet the King took no offence at this, but addressed them in terms the most conciliatory, assuring them that he would overlook the past and secure to them the privileges of their Charter, and the continued freedom of their worship, upon the conditions of their taking the oath of allegiance, administer their laws as British subjects, and grant to all their fellow-colonists equal freedom of worship and of conscience with themselves. They professed, as well they might, to receive the King's declaration of oblivion for past offences and irregularities, and promise of perpetuating their original Charter, with feelings of inexpressible gratitude and delight; but they did not publish the King's letter for nearly two years, notwithstanding his command to do so; and when they did publish it, they appended an order that the conditions were not to be acted upon until their further order.

The King's proclamation of pardon of the past, and promise of the future, produced no other effect than a profusion of wordy compliments and a vague intimation of doing as the King required, *as far as their Charter and conscience would permit.* Their policy of proscription and ignoring the Royal authority in their laws and government remaining unchanged, and the complaints of oppressed colonies and individuals multiplying, the adoption of further measures became necessary on the part of the Crown; and it was decided to appoint a Royal Commission, which should be at once a Court of Inquiry and a Court of Appeal, at least in the first instance, reporting the results of their inquiries and their decisions in cases of appeal for the information and final decision of the highest authority in England, to which any dissatisfied party could appeal against the report or decision of the Commissioners. The address or "Petition" to the King, dated 1664, and given above, pp. 153—9, in all its tedious length and verbiage, shows how grossly they misrepresented the character and objects of the Commission, preparatory to resisting and rejecting it, while the King's letter in reply, also given above at length, p. 166, completely refutes their misstatements, and duly rebukes their unjust and offensive insinuations.

On receiving the report of the Commissioners, together with the statements and pretensions of the Massachusetts Bay Court, the King might have employed ships and soldiers to enforce his just and reasonable commands, or have cancelled the Charter, as the conditions of its continuance had not been fulfilled, and have established Massachusetts Bay Plantation as a Royal colony; but he was advised to adopt the milder and more forbearing course of giving them opportunity of answering directly the complaints made against them, and of justifying their acts and laws.   He therefore, in the Royal letter given above, dated April 6, 1666, required them within six months to send five of their number to England to answer and to disprove if they could complaints made against them, and to furnish proof of the professions and statements they had made in their address and petition.   They could no longer evade or delay; they were brought face to face with the authority of King and Parliament; they could adduce nothing but their own assertions in their justification; facts were against their words; they adopted their usual resource to evade all inquiry into their laws and acts by pleading the immunity of their Charter, and refused to send representatives to England.   They wished the King to take their own words alone as proofs of their loyalty to the Crown and equity to their fellow-colonists.   In place of sending representatives to England to meet their accusers face to face and vindicate their acts, they sent two large masts, thirty-four yards long, which they said they desired to accompany with a thousand pounds sterling as a present to his Majesty, but could get no one to lend them that sum, for the purpose of thus expressing their good-will to the King, and of propitiating his favour.   Their language of adulation and profession was most abject, while they implored the Royal clemency for refusing to obey the Royal commands.   Their records state that "11, 7mo., 1666, the General Court assembled on account of a signification from his Majesty requiring the Council of this colony to send five able and meet persons to make answer for refusing jurisdiction to his Commissioners last year; whereof Mr. Richard Bellingham and Mr. Hawthorne to be two of them, whom he requires, on their allegiance, to come by first opportunity.   The Court met and agreed to spend the forenoon of the next day in prayer.

"12, 7mo., 1666.   The Court met and sundry elders, and spent the forenoon in prayer.

"13, 7mo., 1666.   The Court met and the elders were present after lecture and some debate had in Court concerning the duty we owe to his Majesty in reference to his signification."

On the 14th sundry petitions were presented from the "minority" in Boston, Salem, Ipswich, and Newbury, in favour of compliance with the King's requirement; and the subject was debated in Council some days, when, on the 17th, the Court adopted an answer to the " King's signification," containing the following words addressed to the King's Secretary of State, Mr. Morrice:

" We have, in all humility, given our reasons why we *could* not submit to the Commissioners and their mandates the last year, which we understand lie before his Majesty. To the substance thereof we have nothing to add; and therefore can't expect that the ablest persons among us could be in a capacity to declare our case more fully.

" We must therefore commit this our great concernment unto Almighty God, praying and hoping that his Majesty (a prince of so great clemency) will consider the estate and condition of his poor and afflicted subjects at such a time, being in imminent danger, by the public enemies of our nation, by sea and land, and that in a wilderness far remote from relief; wherefore we do in this wise prostrate ourselves before his Majesty, and beseech him to be graciously pleased to rest assured of our loyalty and allegiance *according to our former professions.* Thus with our humble service to your Honour, and earnest prayers to God for his Majesty's temporal and eternal happiness, we remain your Honour's humble servants.

" 17, 7mo., 1666."*

* Danforth Papers, Collections of Massachusetts Historial Society, Vol. VIII., pp. 98, 108, 109, Second Series.

The following particulars are given of the proceedings of the Court at a subsequent meeting on the same subject :

" October 10th, 1666.　The General Court met again, according to adjournment in May last.　At this Court many express themselves very sensible of our condition.　Several earnest for sending, and some against sending. Those for sending none spake out fully that they would have the Governor (Mr. Bellingham) and Major Hawthorne go ; but some will have men go to plead our cause with his Majesty ; to answer what may be alleged against us, alleging reason, religion and our own necessity as forcing us thereto. Others are against it, as being the loss of all, by endangering a *quo warranto* to be brought against our patent, and so to be condemned ; a middle sort would have some go to present the Court's present to his Majesty, of two large masts and a ship's load of masts : and in case any demand were made why the Governor, Major Hawthorne, and others did not appear, to crave his Majesty's favour therein, and to plead with his Majesty, showing how inconsistent it is with our being, for any to be forced to appear to answer in a

But even in their Council, where the "elders" or ministers and their nominees were supreme, both to rule and to persecute, and to maintain which they were plotting and struggling with the intensity of the Papacy of late years against the Government of Italy, there were yet among their number men of distinction, who contended for the rights of the Crown, to decide questions of appeal from the colony, and to appoint a special commission for that purpose, such as Mr. Simon Bradstreet, who had been Governor, and as their Commissioner to England, with Mr. Norton, had obtained the famous letter of Charles the Second, dated 10th of June, 1662, which filled the Court of Massachusetts Bay with inexpressible joy; and Mr. Dudley, son of a former Governor, and himself first Governor appointed by the Crown after the cancelling of the Charter; and Major Dennison, a man of mark, also in their Council.

In Mr. Danforth's notes of the debate on the answer to the King's signification, *Mr. Bradstreet* is reported to have said : "I grant legal process in a course of law reaches us not in an ordinary course; yet I think the King's prerogative gives him power to command our appearance, which, before God and men,

judicial way in England—to answer either appeals or complaints against the country.

"The last proposal is obstructed by sundry, as being ruinous to the whole ; and so nothing can be done, the Governor and some others chiefly opposing it, so as that no orderly debate can be had to know the mind of the Court.

"The Court agreed to send two large masts aboard Capt. Pierce, 34 yards long, and the one 36 and the other 37 inches in diameter, and agreed to levy £1,000 for the payment of what is needful at present ; but is obstructed—none will lend money unless men be sent, others because anything is to be sent ; a return whereof made to the Court, they say they know not what to do more—in case they that have money will not part with it, they are at a stand. Some speak of raising by rate immediately. Others think there is so much dissatisfaction that men are not sent, that it will provoke and raise a tumult ; and in case that it be raised by loan, it will be hardly paid—if consent be not given in their sending men with it, and there be no good effect, which is contingent, and thus we are every way at a stand ; some fearing these things will precipitate our ruin, and others apprehending that to act further will necessitate our ruin."—*Ib.*, pp. 110, 111.

From these notes, which Mr. Danforth made at the time when the proceedings referred to took place, it is plain there were a large number of loyalists even among the Congregationalists, as they alone were eligible to be members of, or to elect to the Court, and that the asserters of independence were greatly perplexed and agitated.

we are to obey." *Mr. Dudley :* " The King's commands pass any-
where—Ireland, Calais, etc.—although ordinary process from
judges and officers pass not.   No doubt you may have a trial at
law when you come to England, if you desire it, and you may
insist upon and claim it.   Prerogative is as necessary as law, and
|it is for the good of the whole that there be always power in
being able to act ; and where there is a right of power, it will
be abused so long as it is in the hands of weak men, and the less
pious the more apt to miscarry ; but right may not be denied
because it may be abused."

After the Court had adopted its answer of refusal to the
King's signification, Mr. Bradstreet said : " I fear we take not a
right course for our safety.   It is clear that this signification is
from his Majesty.   I do desire to have it remembered that I do
dissent, and desire to have it recorded that I dissent, from that
part of it as is an answer to the King's signification." Major
Dennison declared his dissent from the letter to Mr. Morrice, as
not being proportionate to the end desired, and he hoped,
intended, and desired it might be entered—namely, due satisfaction to his Majesty, and the preservation of the peace and liberty
of the colony.*

It is clear from the foregoing facts that the alleged invasion
of chartered rights and privileges put forth by the ruling party
of Massachusetts Bay was a mere pretext to cover the long-
cherished pretensions (called by them " dear-bought rights ")
to absolute independence ; that is, the domination of the Congregationalist Government, to the exclusion of the Crown, to
proscribe from the elective franchise and eligibility to office
all but Congregationalists, and to persecute all who differed
from them in either religious or political opinion, including
their control and suppression of the fredom of the press.†

---

* Danforth Papers, Collections of Massachusetts Historical Society, Vol.
VIII., pp. 99, 100, 108, 109.

† " There had been a press for printing at Cambridge for near twenty
years.   The Court appointed two persons (Captain Daniel Guekins and Mr.
Jonathan Mitchell, the minister of Cambridge), in October, 1662, licensers
of the press, and prohibited the publishing of any books or papers which
should not be supervised by them ;" and in 1668, the supervisors having
allowed the printing " Thomas à Kempis, de *Imitatione Christi*," the Court
interposed (it being wrote by a popish minister, and containing some things

They persisted in the cruel persecution of their Baptist brethren as well as of the Quakers, notwithstanding the King had established the fullest religious liberty by Royal Charter, granted in 1663 to the Colonies of Connecticut and Rhode Island, and had by his letters in 1662 and 1664, and subsequently, forbidden religious persecution and prescribed religious toleration as a condition of the continuance of the Charter in Massachusetts Bay Colony.*

I will give in a note, from the records of their own Court, their persecuting proceedings against certain Baptists in April, 1666, six years after the Restoration.†

less safe to be infused among the people), and therefore they commended to the licensers a more full revisal, and ordered the press to stop in the meantime. (Hutchinson's History of Massachusetts Bay, Vol. I., pp. 257, 258.)

* Even during the Commonwealth in England, the Congregational Government of Massachusetts Bay was one of unmitigated persecution. Mr. Hutchinson, under date of 1655, remarks :

" The persecution of Episcopalians by the prevailing powers in England was evidently from revenge for the persecution they had suffered themselves, and from political considerations and the prevalence of party, seeing all other opinions and professions, however absurd, were tolerated ; but in New England it must be confessed that bigotry and cruel zeal prevailed, and to that degree that no opinion but their own could be tolerated. They were sincere but mistaken in their principles ; and absurd as it is, it is too evident, they believed it to be to the glory of God to take away the lives of his creatures for maintaining tenets contrary to what they professed themselves. This occasioned complaints against the colony to the Parliament and Cromwell, but without success." (History of Massachusetts Bay, Vol. I., p. 189.)

† " Proceedings and sentence of the County Court held at Cambridge, on adjournment, April 17, 1666, against Thomas Goold, Thomas Osburne, and John George (a) (being Baptists):

" Thomas Goold, Thomas Osburne, and John George, being presented by the Grand Jury of this county (Cambridge), for absenting themselves from the public worship of God on the Lord's dayes for one whole year now past, alleged respectively as followeth, viz. :

" Thomas Osburne answered that the reason of his non-attendance was that the Lord hath discovered unto him from His Word and Spirit of Truth, that the society where he is now in communion is more agreeable to the will of God ; asserted that they were a Church, and attended the worship of

(a) Note by Mr. Hutchinson.—"These three persons scrupled at Infant Baptism, separated from the Churches of the country, and with others of the same persuasion with themselves, set up a church in Boston. Whilst Congregationalists in England were complaining of the intolerant spirit of Episcopalians, these Antipædo Baptists in New England had equal reason to complain of the same spirit in the Congregationalists there."

The Puritan historian, Neal, writing under date three years later, 1669, says: "The displeasure of the Government ran very high against the Anabaptists and Quakers at this time. The Anabaptists had gathered one Church at Swanzey, and another at Boston, but the General Court was very severe in putting the laws in execution against them, whereby many honest people were ruined by fines, imprisonment, and banishment, which was the more extraordinary because their brethren in England were groaning under persecution from the Church of England at the same time. Sad complaints were sent over to England every summer of the severity of the Government

God together, and do judge themselves bound to do so, the ground whereof he said he gave in the General Court.

"Thomas Goold answered that as for coming to public worship, they did meet in public worship according to the rule of Christ; the grounds thereof they had given to the General Court of Assistants; asserted that they were a public meeting, according to the order of Christ Jesus, gathered together.

"John George answered that he did attend the public meetings on the Lord's dayes where he was a member; asserted that they were a Church according to the order of Christ in the Gospell, and with them he walked and held communion in the public worship of God on the Lord's dayes."

SENTENCE OF THE COURT.

"Whereas at the General Court in October last, and at the Court of Assistants in September last, endeavours were used for their conviction. The order of the General Court declaring the said Goold and Company to be no orderly Church assembly, and that they stand convicted of high presumption against the Lord and his holy appoyntments was openly read to them, and is on file with the records of this Court.

"The Court sentenced the same Thomas Goold, Thomas Osburne, and John George, for their absenting themselves from the public worship of God on the Lord's dayes, to pay four pounds fine, each of them, to the County order. And whereas, by their own confessions, they stand convicted of persisting in their schismatical assembling themselves together, to the great dishonour of God *and our* profession of his holy name, contrary to the *Act* of the General Order of the Court of October last, prohibiting them therein on the penalty of imprisonment, this Court doth order their giving bond respectively in £20, each of them, for their appearance to answer their contempt at the next Court of Assistants.

"The above named Thomas Goold, John George, and Thomas Osburne made their appeal to the next Court of Assistants, and refusing to put in security according to law, were committed to prison.

"*Vera Copia.*"
"THO. DANFORTH, *Recorder.*"

(Hutchinson's History of Massachusetts Bay, Vol. I., pp. 397—401.)

against the Anabaptists, which obliged the dissenting ministers in London to appear at length in their favour. A letter was accordingly sent over to the Governor of Massachusetts, signed by Dr. Goodwin, Dr. Owen, Mr. Nie, Mr. Caryl, and nine other ministers, beseeching him to make use of his authority and interest for restoring such to their liberty as were in prison on account of religion, and that their sanguinary laws might not be put in execution in future." [Mr. Neal gives the letter, and then proceeds.] " But the excellent letter made no impression upon them ; the prisoners were not released, nor the execution of the laws suspended; nay, so far from this, that ten years after, in the year 1679, a General Synod being called to inquire into the evils that provoked the Lord to bring his judgments on New England, they mention these among the rest, ' Men have set up their thresholds by God's threshold, and their posts by God's post ; Quakers are false worshippers, and such Anabaptists as have risen up among us, in opposition to the Churches of the Lord Jesus, " etc., etc.

" Wherefore it must needs be provoking to God if these things be not duly and fully testified against by every one in their several capacities respectively."*

The present of two large masts and a ship-load of timber ; successive obsequious and evasive addresses ; explanations of agents ; compliance in some particulars with the Royal requirements in regard to the oath of allegiance, and administering the law, so far appeased the King's Government that further action was suspended for a time in regard to enforcing the granting of the elective franchise, eligibility to office, and liberty of worship to other than Congregationalists,† especially as the attention of

---

* Neal's History of New England, Vol. II., Chap. viii., pp. 353, 354, 356.

† " They endeavoured not only by humble addresses and professions of loyalty to appease his Majesty, but they purchased a ship-load of masts (the freight whereof cost them sixteen hundred pounds sterling), and presented them to the King, which he graciously accepted ; and the fleet in the West Indies being in want of provisions, a subscription and contribution was recommended through the colony for bringing in provisions to be sent to the fleet for his Majesty's service, (a) but I find no word of the whole amount. Upon

(a) *Note* by Mr. Hutchinson.—" This was so well received that a letter was sent to the General Court, under the King's sign warrant, dated 21st April, 1669, signifying how well it was taken by his Majesty. So the letter expresses it."

Charles was absorbed by exciting questions at home, by his war with Holland, which he bitterly hated, and his intrigues with France, on which he became a paid dependant.   But the complaints and appeals to the King from neighbouring colonies of the invasion of individual and territorial rights by the Court of Massachusetts Bay, and from the persecuted and proscribed inhabitants of their own colony, awakened at last the renewed attention of the King's Government to the proceedings of the Massachusetts Bay rulers.   The letter which the King was advised to address to them is kind and conciliatory in its tone ; but it shows that while the King, as he had declared in his first letter, addressed to them seventeen years before, recognized the " Congregational way of worship," he insisted on toleration of the worship of Episcopalians, Baptists, etc., and the civil rights and privileges of their members,* denied by these "fathers of

---

the news of the great fire in London, a collection was made through the colony for the relief of the sufferers.   The amount cannot be ascertained." (Hutchinson's History of Massachusetts Bay, Vol. I., pp. 256, 257.)

* The following is a copy of the King's very courteous and reasonable letter :
" Copy of a letter from King Charles II. to the Governor, etc., of the Massachusetts, dated July 24th, 1679.

" CHARLES R.

" Trusty and well beloved—We greet you well.   These our letters are to accompany our trusty and well beloved William Stoughton and Peter Bulkly, Esqres., your agents, who having manifested to us great necessity in their domestic concerns to return back into New England, we have graciously consented thereunto, and the rather because for many months past our Council hath been taken up in the discovery and prosecution of a popish plot, and yet there appears little prospect of any speedy leisure for entering upon such regulation in your affairs as is certainly necessary, not only in respect of our dignity, but of your own perfect settlement.   In the meantime, we doubt not but the bearers thereof, who have demeaned themselves, during their attendance, with good care and discretion, will, from their *own observations*, acquaint you with many important things which may be of such use and advertisement to you, that we might well hope to be prevented, by your applications, in what is expected or desired by us.   So much it is your interest to propose and intercede for the same ; for we are graciously inclined to have all past errors and mistakes forgotten, and that your condition might be so amended as that neither your settlement, or the minds of our good subjects there, should be liable to be shaken and disquieted upon every complaint.   We have heard with satisfaction of the great readiness wherewith our good subjects there have lately offered themselves to the taking of the oath of allegiance, which is a clear manifestation to us that the

American liberty" to the very last; until then, power of proscription and persecution was wrested from them by the cancelling of their Charter.

The chief requirements of this letter were, as stated by Mr. Hutchinson:

" 1. That agents be sent over in six months, fully instructed to answer and transact what was undetermined at that time.

" 2. That freedom and liberty of conscience be given to such persons as desire to serve God in the way of the Church of Eng-

unanswerable defect in that particular was but the fault of a very few in power, who for so long a time obstructed what the Charter and our express commands obliged them unto, as will appear in our gracious letter of the 28th of June (1662), in the fourteenth year of our reign ; and we shall henceforth expect that there will be a suitable obedience in other particulars of the said letter, as, namely, in respect of freedom and liberty of conscience, so as those that desire to serve God in the way of the Church of England be not thereby made obnoxious or discountenanced from their sharing in the government, much less that they or any other of our good subjects (not being Papists) who do not agree in the Congregational way, be by law subjected to fines or forfeitures, or other incapacities for the same, which is a severity to be the more wondered at, whereas liberty of conscience was made one principal motive for your first transportation into those parts ; nor do we think it fit that any other distinction be observed in the making of freemen than that they be men of competent estates, rateable at ten shillings, (a) according to the rules of the place, and that such in their turns be also capable of the magistracy, and all laws made void that obstruct the same. And because we have not observed any fruits or advantage by the dispensation granted by us in our said letter of June, in the fourteenth year of our reign, whereby the number of assistants, settled by our Charter to be eighteen, might be reduced unto the number of ten, our will and pleasure is that the ancient number of eighteen be henceforth observed, according to the letter of the Charter.   And our further will and pleasure is, that all persons coming to any privilege, trust, or office in that colony be first enjoined to take the oath of allegiance, and that all the military commissions as well as the proceedings of justice may run in our royal name.   We are informed that you have lately made some good provision for observing the acts of trade and navigation, which is well pleasing unto us (b) ; and as we doubt not and do expect

(a) *Note* by the historian, Mr. Hutchinson.—They seem to have held out till the last in refusing to admit any to be freemen who were not either Church members, or who did not at least obtain a certificate from the minister of the town that they were orthodox.

(b) *Note* by the historian, Mr. Hutchinson.—This is very extraordinary, for this provision was an act of the colony, declaring that the acts of trade should be in force there.   (Massachusetts History, Vol. I., p. 322.)

land, so as not to be thereby made obnoxious, or discountenanced from their sharing in the government, much less that they, or any other of his Majesty's subjects (not being Papists) who do not agree in the Congregational way, be by law subject to fines or forfeitures or other incapacities.

"3. That no other distinction be observed in making freemen than that they be men of competent estates, rateable at ten shillings, according to the rules of the place, and that such in their turns be capable of the magistracy, and all laws made void that obstruct the same.

"4. That the ancient number of eighteen assistants be observed, as by Charter. (They had been limited to eight or ten.)

"5. That all persons coming to any privilege, trust or office, take the oath of allegiance.

"6. That all military commissions as well as proceedings of justice run in his Majesty's name.

"7. That all laws repugnant to, and inconsistent with, the laws of England for trade, be abolished."*

There were certain injunctions in regard to complaints from neighbouring colonies; but the necessity for such injunctions as those above enumerated, and stated more at large in the King's letter, as stated in note on p. 187, given for the third or fourth time the nineteenth year after the Restoration, shows the disloyal proscriptions and persecuting character of the Government of Massachusetts Bay, and the great forbearance of the King's Government in continuing the Charter while the conditions of its proposed continuance were constantly violated.

Dr. Palfrey speaks of these requirements, and the whole policy

---

that you will abolish all laws that are repugnant to and inconsistent with the laws of trade with us, we have appointed our trusty and well beloved subject, Edward Randolph, Esq., to be our collector, surveyor and searcher not only for the colony, but for all other our colonies in New England, constituting him, by the broad seal of this our kingdom, to the said employments, and therefore recommending him to your help and assistance in all things that may be requisite in the discharge of his trust. Given at our palace of Hampton Court, the 24th day of July, 1679, and in the one and thirtieth year of our reign.

"By his Majesty's Command,
"A. COVENTRY."

* History of Massachusetts Bay, Vol. I., pp. 325, 326.

of the King's Government, as "usurpations" on the chartered
rights of the Massachusetts Bay Colony. But let any reader
say in which of the above seven requirements there is the
slightest " usurpation" on any right of a British subject ; whether
there is anything that any loyal British subject would not
freely acknowledge and respond to ; requirements unhesitatingly
obeyed by all the colonies except that of Massachusetts Bay
alone, and which have been observed by every British Province
of America for the last hundred years, and are observed by the
Dominion of Canada at this day.

Dr. Palfrey, referring to this period (1676—82), says : "Lord
Clarendon's scheme of colonial policy was now ripe," but he
does not adduce a word from Lord Clarendon to show what
that policy was only by insinuations and assertions, and assumes
it to have been the subversion of the rights and liberties of the
Massachusetts Bay Colony. Lord Clarendon, in his letter to
the Governor Endicot, given above, pp. 160, 161, explains his
colonial policy, which was not only to maintain the Charter in
its integrity, but to see that its provisions and objects were not
violated but fulfilled, and that while the Congregational worship
should not be interfered with, the Congregational Government
should not proscribe from the elective franchise and liberty of
worship the members of other Protestant denominations. The
Hon. Robert Boyle, the philosopher and benefactor of New
England, and President of the New England Society for Propagation of the Gospel among the Indians, expressed the same
views with Lord Clarendon, and there is not a shadow of proof
that Lord Clarendon ever entertained any other policy in regard
to New England than that which he expressed in his letter to
Governor Endicot in 1664.

Dr. Palfrey and other New England historians occupy four-
fifths of their pages with accounts of the continental proceedings of the Governments of the Stuarts, and their oppressions
and persecutions of Nonconformists in England, and then
assume that their policy was the same in regard to the New
England Colonies, and that the Massachusetts Bay Colony was
therefore the champion defender of colonial liberties, in denying responsibility to the Imperial Government for its acts, and
refusing the usual oaths, and acts of allegiance to the Throne ;
whereas their *assumptions* (for they are nothing else) are un-

supported by a single fact, and are contradicted, without exception, by the declarations and acts of the Government of Charles
the Second, as well as by those of his royal father.   Language
can hardly exaggerate or reprobate in too strong terms the
cruel persecutions of dissenters from the Established Episcopal
Church in England, by both Charles the First and Charles the
Second ; but the Congregational Government of Massachusetts
Bay exceeded that of the Charleses in proscribing and persecuting dissenters from their Established Congregational Churches
in that colony ; and as well might Messrs. Palfrey, Bancroft, and
other New England historians maintain that, because Congregationalists contended for liberty of worship for themselves in
England, they practised it in regard to those who did not agree
with them in worship in Massachusetts Bay.   The proscription
and persecution of Congregationalists and Baptists by Episcopalian rulers in England were outrivalled by the Congregational rulers in their proscriptions and persecutions of Episcopalians and Baptists in Massachusetts.

It is also assumed by the New England historians referred to
that the King's advisers had intimated the intention of appointing a Governor-General over the Colonies of New England to
see to the observance of their Charters and of the Navigation
Laws ; but wherein did this infringe the rights or privileges of any
Colonial Charter ?   Wherein did it involve any more than right-
ful attention to Imperial authority and interests ?   Wherein
has the appointment or office of a Governor-General of British
North America, in addition to the Lieutenant-Governor of each
province, ever been regarded to this day as an infringement
of the rights and privileges of any Legislature or British subject in the colonies ?   Wherein has the right of appeal by any
colony or party to the Supreme Courts or authorities of England,
against the decisions of local Courts or local executive acts, been
regarded as an infringement of colonial rights, or other than a
protection to colonial subjects ?   When has the right of appeal
by parties in any of the neighbouring States, to the Supreme
Court at Washington, been held to be an invasion of the rights
of such States ?

The rulers of Massachusetts Bay Colony concealed and
secreted their Charter ; they then represented it as containing

provisions which no Royal Charter in the world ever contained ; they represented the King as having abdicated, and excluded himself from all authority over them as a colony or as individuals ; they denied that Parliament itself had any authority to legislate for any country on the western side of the Atlantic ; they virtually claimed absolute independence, erasing the oath of allegiance from their records, proscribing and persecuting all nonconformists to the Congregational worship, invading the territories of other colonies and then maintaining their invasions by military force, denying the authority of Great Britain or of any power on earth to restrict or interfere with their acts. The New England historians referred to are compelled to confess that the Royal Charter contained no such provisions or powers as the rulers of Massachusetts Bay pretended ; yet their narratives and argumentations and imputations upon the British Government assume the truth of the fabulous representations of the Charter, and treat not only every act of the King as royal tyranny, but every suspicion of what the King might do as a reality, and the hostility of the Massachusetts Bay Government as a defence of constitutional rights and resistance of royal despotism. But in these laboured and eloquent philippics against the Government of the Restoration, they seem to forget that the Parliament and Government of the Commonwealth and Cromwell asserted far larger powers over the colonies than did the Government and Parliament of Charles the Second (as is seen by their Act and appointments in their enactments quoted above, pp. 88—90).

The Commonwealth appointed a Governor-General (the Earl of Warwick), Commissioners with powers to remove and appoint Colonial Governors and other local officers ; whereas the Commissioners appointed by Charles the Second had no authority to remove or appoint a single local Governor or other officer, to annul or enact a single law, but to inquire and report ; and even as a Court of Appeal their proceedings and decisions were to be reported for final action in England.

The famous Act of Navigation itself, which ultimately became the chief ground of the American revolutionary war, was passed by the Commonwealth, though, by a collusion between Cromwell and the rulers of Massachusetts Bay, its provisions were evaded in that colony, while rigorously enforced in the other colonies.*

In the first year of Charles the Second this Act was renewed, with some additional provisions.†

But to return to the correspondence between the King's Government and the rulers of Massachusetts Bay. It may be supposed that after the King had promised, in 1662, to forget past offences and continue the justly forfeited Royal Charter upon certain conditions, and that those conditions were evaded by various devices during nearly twenty years, the Royal patience would become exhausted, and that, instead of the gentle instructions and remonstrances which had characterized his former letters, the King would adopt more severe and imperative language. Hence in his next letter, September 30, 1680, to the Governor and Council of the Massachusetts, he commenced in the following words:

"CHARLES R.

"Trusty and well beloved, we greet you well. When by our Royal letter, bearing date the 24th day of July, in the one and thirtieth year of our reign, we signified unto you our gracious

---

* "The people of Massachusetts had always the good-will of Cromwell. In relation to them he allowed the Navigation Law, which pressed hard on the Southern colonies, to become a dead letter, and they received the commodities of all nations free of duty, and sent their ships at will to the ports of continental Europe." (Palfrey's History of New England, Vol. II., Book ii. Chap. x., p. 393.)

† 1660.—The Parliament passed an Act for the general encouragement and increase of shipping and navigation, by which the provisions made in the celebrated Navigation Act of 1651 were continued, with additional improvements. It enacted that no sugar, tobacco, ginger, indigo, cotton, fustin, dyeing woods of the growth of English territories in America, Asia, or Africa, shall be transported to any other country than those belonging to the Crown of England, under the penalty of forfeiture ; and all vessels sailing to the Plantations were to give bonds to bring said commodities to England." (Holmes' American Annals, Vol. I., pp. 314, 315.)

"The oppressive system," says Palfrey, "was further extended by an Act which confined the import trade of the colonists to a direct commerce with England, forbidding them to bring *from* any other or *in* any other than English ships, the products not only of England but of any European state." (History of New England, Vol. II., B. ii., Chap. xi., p. 445.)

Palfrey adds in a note : "Salt for New England fishermen, wines from Madeira and the Azores, and provisions from Scotland and Ireland, were, however, exempted."—*Ib.*

13

inclination to have all past deeds forgotten, setting before you
the means whereby you might deserve our pardon, and commanding your ready obedience to several particulars therein
contained, requiring withall a speedy compliance with the
intimations of your duty given to your late agents during
their attendance here, all which we esteem essential to your
quiet settlement and natural obedience due unto us. We then
little thought that those marks of our grace and favour should
have found no better acceptance among you, but that, before
all things, you should have given preference to the execution
of our commands, when after so many months we come to
understand by a letter from you to one of our principal Secretaries of State, dated the 21st of May last, that very few
of our directions have been pursued by your General Court, the
further consideration of the remaining particulars having been
put off upon insufficient pretences, and even wholly neglecting
your appointment of other agents which were required to be
sent over unto us within six months after the receipt of our
said letters, with full instructions to attend our Royal pleasure
herein in relation to that our Government."

Among other matters, the King " strictly commanded and required " them, " as they tendered their allegiance," to despatch
such agents within three months after their reception of the
order, and with full powers to satisfy his Majesty on the
subjects of complaint; and " he ended the letter," says Mr.
Palfrey, " with a very definite injunction : "

" That the due observance of all our commands above mentioned may not be any longer protracted, we require you, upon
receipt thereof, forthwith to call a General Court, and therein
to read these our letters and provide for our speedy satisfaction,
and in default thereof we shall take the most effectual means to
procure the same. And so we bid you farewell."*

This letter led to the calling of a " Special General Court,"
January, 1681, in which very protracted debates ensued on the
revision of the laws, so long delayed, and the election of agents
to England according to the King's command. Samuel Nowell
and John Richards were elected agents to England, but were
restricted by instructions which forbade conceding anything

* Hutchinson's Collection, etc., pp. 522—525. Palfrey's History of New
England, Vol. III., B. iii., Chap. viii., p. 341.

from their original Charter pretensions, and therefore rendered their agency an insult to the Government and the King, and hastened the catastrophe which they so much dreaded, the cancelling of their Charter.

In the meantime, to appease the displeasure of the Crown, they passed several Acts which had the appearance of obedience to the Royal commands, but which they were careful not to carry into effect.* I will give two or three examples.

They enacted " that the Acts of Trade and Navigation should be forthwith proclaimed in the market-place of Boston by beat of drum, and that all clauses in said Acts relating to this Plantation should be strictly taken notice of and observed." This appears very plausible, and is so quoted by Dr. Palfrey; but he does not add that care was taken that it should not be carried into effect. And to accomplish their purposes, and to assert the subordination of the Royal authority to their own local authority, " they constituted naval *officers*, one for Boston, the other for ' Salem and adjacent parts,' to be commissioned by the Governor, and to exercise powers of a nature to control the Collector appointed in England."†

After nearly twenty years' delay and evasions, they enacted, in 1679, " that the Governor, Deputy Governor, and Magistrates should take the oath of allegiance ' without any reservation,' in

---

* To this there were two or three exceptions. They repealed the penal laws " against keeping Christmas ; " also for punishing with death Quakers returned from banishment ; and to amend the laws relating to heresy and to rebellion against the country.

† Palfrey's History of New England, Vol. III., B. iii., Chap. viii., p. 352.

They usurped authority over New Hampshire and Maine, at the same time that they prevented the execution of the Acts of Trade and Navigation (the 12th and 15th of Charles the Second). Mr. Hutchinson says : " The Massachusetts Government (1670) governed without opposition the Province of New Hampshire and the Province of Maine, and were beginning settlements even further eastward. The French were removed from their neighbourhood on the one side, and the Dutch and Swedes on the other. Their trade was as extensive as they could wish. *No custom-hov·e was established.* The Acts of Parliament of the 12th—15th of King Charles the Second, for regulating the Plantation trade, *were in force;* but the *Governor, whose business it was to carry them into execution, was annually to be elected by the people, whose interest was that they should not be observed!* Some of the magistrates and principal merchants grew very rich." (History of Massachusetts Bay, Vol. I., p. 269.)

the words sent them by his Majesty's orders; but instead of the
'reservation' in their form of oath in former Acts, they virtually
neutralized the oath by an Act requiring a prior preliminary oath
of fidelity to the local Government,* an Act which the Board of
Colonial Plantations viewed as 'derogatory to his Majesty's
honour, as well as defective in point of their own duty.'"

They instructed their agents in England to represent that
there was no colonial law "prohibiting any such as were of the
persuasion of the Church of England." The design of this statement plainly was to impress upon the mind of the King's
Government that there was no obstruction to the worship and
ordinances of the Church of England, and that the elective
franchise and privilege of worship were as open to Episcopalians
as to Congregationalists—the reverse of fact. After repeated
letters from the King in favour of toleration as one of the conditions of continuing their Charter, notwithstanding their past
violation of it, they *professed* to comply with the royal injunctions, but their professed compliance amounted practically to
nothing, as they had evidently intended. The King's Commissioners had said to the Massachusetts Bay Court on this
subject : "For the use of the Common Prayer Book : His Majesty
doth not impose the use of the Common Prayer Book on any ;
but he understands that liberty of conscience comprehends every
man's conscience, as well as any particular, and thinks that all
his subjects should have equal right." To this the Massachusetts Court replied : "Concerning the use of the Common Prayer

* On the very day, October, 1677, that they proposed, in obedience to his
Majesty's command, to pass an order that "the Governor and all inferior
magistrates should see to the strict observation of the Acts of Navigation
and Trade," they made an order "that the law requiring all persons, as well
inhabitants as strangers, that have not taken it, to take the oath of fidelity to
the country, be revived and put in practice throughout the jurisdiction"
(Palfrey, Vol. III., pp. 311—315)—an order intended to counteract the execution of the Acts of Navigation and Trade by the King's Collector, and of
which he complained to England.

"The agents of the colony endeavoured to explain this law to the Board
(of Colonial Plantations in England), and to soften their indignation against
it, but without effect." (*Ib.*, p. 315.) "All persons who refused to take the
oath of fidelity to the country were not to have the privilege of recovering
their debts in Courts of law, nor to have the protection of the Government."
(Truth and Innocency Defended, etc.)

Book and ecclesiastical privileges, our humble addresses to his Majesty have fully declared our main ends, in our being voluntary exiles from our dear native country, which we had not chosen at so dear a rate, could we have seen the word of God warranting us to perform our devotions in that way; and to have the same set up here, we conceive it is apparent that it will disturb our peace in our present enjoyment."*

But afterwards they found it dangerous longer to resist the King's commands, and professed to obey them by providing that those who were not Congregationalists might exercise the elective franchise, provided that, in addition to taking the oath of fidelity to the local Government, and paying a rate which was not paid by one in a hundred, *and obtaining a certificate from the Congregational minister as to their being blameless in words and orthodox in religion, they were then approved by the Court.* The right of franchise was possessed by every member of any Congregational Church, whether he had property or not, or paid rate or not; † not so with any other inhabitant, unless he adduced proof that he had paid rate, produced a certificate of character and of orthodoxy in religion, signed by a Congregational minister, and was approved by the Court. No instance is recorded of any Episcopalian ever having obtained the free-

---

* (Collections of the Massachusetts Historial Society, Second Series, Vol. VIII., pp. 73—78.) The liberty of worship, which they declared had been the object of their emigration to Massachusetts, had never been denied them; had been assured to them by both Charles the First and Charles the Second. The King did not propose to impose the use of the prayer book upon any inhabitant of the colony, but insisted upon freedom of worship for each inhabitant; whereas the Massachusetts Bay Court, under the pretext of liberty of worship for Congregationalists, denied freedom of worship to all others not Congregationalists.

† "This extraordinary law continued in force until the dissolution of the Government; it being repealed in appearance only, (a) after the restoration of King Charles the Second. Had they been deprived of their civil privileges in England by Act of Parliament, unless they would join in communion with the Churches there, it might very well have been the first on the roll of grievances. But such were the requisites for Church membership here, that the grievance is abundantly greater." (Hutchinson's History of Massachusetts Bay, Vol. I., pp. 25, 26.)

(a) *Note* by the historian.—"The minister was to certify that the candidates for freedom were of orthodox principles and of good lives and conversation."

dom of the colony under such conditions ; " nor," as Mr. Hutchinson says, "was there any Episcopal Church in any part of the colony until the Charter was vacated."*

The Court of Massachusetts Bay also instructed their agents in England, in 1682, to represent that "as for Anabaptists, they were now subject to no other penal statutes than those of the Congregational way." But as late as the spring of 1680 the General Court forbade the Baptists to assemble for their worship in a meeting-house which they had built in Boston.† The statement which they instructed their agents to make in England was clearly intended to convey the impression that the Baptist worship was equally allowed with the Congregational worship; but though penalties against individual Baptists may have been relaxed, their worship was no more tolerated than that of the Episcopalian until the cancelling of the Charter.

The same kind of misleading evasion was practised upon the Government in England in regard to the Quakers, as in respect to the Baptists, the Episcopalians, and the elective franchise. The agents of the colony in England were instructed to state that the "severe laws to prevent the violent and impetuous

---

* Hutchinson's History of Massachusetts Bay, Vol. I., p. 431. "The test (that 'no man could have a share in the administration of civil government, or give his voice in any election, unless he was a member of one of the Churches') went a great way towards producing general uniformity. He that did not conform was deprived of more civil privileges than a nonconformist is deprived of by the Test Act in England. Both the one and the other must have occasioned much formality and hypocrisy. The mysteries of our holy religion have been prostituted to mere secular views and advantages."—*Ib.*, p. 432.

† (Palfrey, Vol. III., p. 353, in a note.) Mr. Hildreth states the case as follows : "Encouraged by the King's demand for toleration, construed as superseding the 'by-laws' of the colony, the Baptists ventured to hold a service in their new meeting-house. For this they were summoned before the magistrates, and when they refused to desist the doors were nailed up and the following order posted upon them : 'All persons are to take notice that, by order of the Court, the doors of this house are shut up, and that they are inhibited to hold any meeting therein, or to open the doors thereof without licence from authority, till the General Court take further order, as they will answer the contrary at their peril.' When the General Court met, the Baptists pleaded that their house was built before any law was made to prevent it. This plea was so far allowed that their past offences were forgiven; but they were not allowed to open the house." (History of the United States, Vol. I., Chap. xiv., p. 501.)

intrusions of the Quakers had been suspended;" but they did not say that laws less severe had been substituted, and that fines and imprisonments were imposed upon any party who should be present at a Quakers' meeting. Yet, as late as 1677, the Court of Massachusetts Bay made a law "That every person found at a Quakers' meeting shall be apprehended, *ex officio*, by the con stable, and by warrant from a magistrate or commissioner shall be committed to the House of Correction, and there have the discipline of the house applied to him, and be kept to work, with bread and water, for three days, and then released, or else shall pay five pounds in money as a fine to the country for such offence; and all constables neglecting their duty in not faithfully executing this order, shall incur the penalty of five pounds upon conviction, one-third thereof to the informer."*

They likewise instructed their agents in England to give assurance "That the Acts of Trade, so far as they concerned the colony, should be strictly observed, and that all due encourage-

---

* (Hutchinson's History of Massachusetts Bay, Vol. I., p. 320.) After quoting this law, the historian remarks: "I know of nothing which can be urged in anywise tending to increase the severity of this law, unless it be human infirmity, and the many instances in history of persons of every religion being fully persuaded that the indulgence of any other was a toleration of impiety and brought down the judgments of Heaven, and therefore justified persecution. This law lost the colony many friends."—*Ib.*

The law punishing attendance at Quaker meetings was accompanied by another containing the following clauses :

"Pride, in men wearing long hair like women's hair; others wearing borders of hair, and cutting, curling, and immodest laying out their hair, principally in the younger sort. Grand Jurors to present and the Court to punish all offenders by admonition, fine, or correction, at discretion."

"Excess in apparel, strange new fashions, naked breasts and arms, and pinioned superfluous ribbands on hair and apparel. The Court to fine offenders at discretion."

"A loose and sinful custom of riding from town to town, men and women together, under pretence of going to lectures, but really to drink and revel in taverns, tending to debauchery and unchastity. All single persons, being offenders, to be bound in their good behaviour, with sureties in twenty pounds fine, or suffer fine and imprisonment."—*Ib.*, pp. 320, 321, in a note.

The foregoing pages show the notions and appreciation of the religious rights and liberties by the Massachusetts Bay rulers and legislators in regard to Episcopalians, Baptists, and Quakers. The above quoted clauses of their law passed in 1667, nearly fifty years after the establishment of their government, illustrate their ideas of individual liberty.

ment and assistance should be given to his Majesty's officers and
informers that might prosecute the breaches of said Acts of
Trade and Navigation."* But while as a Court they professed
this in their records and through their agents in England,
officers were elected in the colony who would not execute the
law, and so not a farthing of duties was collected under it
at Massachusetts Bay.

Thus for twenty years the rulers of Massachusetts Bay resisted and evaded the six conditions on which King Charles the

---

* Palfrey, Vol. III., p. 353. Much has been written about these Acts of
Trade and Navigation, as if they were acts of royal despotism and designed
to oppress the colonies for the benefit of England ; whereas they originated
with the Commonwealth, and were designed to benefit the colonies as well as
the mother country. "After the decapitation of Charles I.," says Minot, "the
confused situation of England prevented any particular attention to the colony
until Cromwell's Government. The very qualities which existed in the
character of the inhabitants to render them displeasing to the late King,
operated as much with the Protector in their favour ; and he diverted all
complaints of their enemies against them. Yet he procured the Navigation
Act to be passed by the Parliament, which was a source of future difficulty
to the colony, though it was evaded in New England at first (by Cromwell's
connivance with the rulers of Massachusetts Colony), as they still traded in
all parts and enjoyed a privilege, peculiar to themselves, of importing their
goods into England free of all customs." (Minot's Continuation of the
History of Massachusetts Bay, published according to Act of Congress,
Vol. I., p. 40.)

Mr. Hildreth, referring to the early part of Charles the Second's restoration, says : "As yet the Acts of Trade were hardly a subject of controversy.
The Parliament, which had welcomed back the King, had indeed re-enacted
with additional clauses the ordinance of 1651—an Act which, by restricting
exportations from America to English, Irish, and Colonial vessels, substantially excluded foreign ships from all Anglo-American harbours. To this,
which might be regarded as a benefit to New England ship-owners, a provision
was added still further to isolate the colonies (from foreign countries), the
more valuable colonial staples, mentioned by the name, and hence known as
'enumerated articles,' being required to be shipped exclusively to England
or some English colony. The exportation to the colonies was also prohibited
of any product of Europe, unless in English vessels and from England, except
horses, servants and provisions from Ireland and Scotland. But of the
'enumerated articles' none were produced in New England ; while salt for
fisheries, and wine from Madeira and the Azores, branches of foreign trade
in which New England was deeply interested, were specially exempted from
the operation of an Act which had chiefly in view the more southern
colonies." (Hildreth's History of the United States, Vol. I., Chap. xiv.'
p. 473.)

Second, after his restoration, proposed to overlook and pardon their past offences and perpetuate the Charter given to them by his Royal father; for twenty years the King, without committing a single unconstitutional or oppressive act against them, or without demanding anything which Queen Victoria does not receive, this day, from every colony of the British Empire, endured their evasions and denials of his authority and insults of his Commissioners and officers. In all the despatches of the King's Government to the rulers of Massachusetts Bay, during these twenty years, as the reader of the preceding pages will have seen, the spirit of kindness, and a full recognition of their rights in connection with those of the Crown, were predominant.

This they repeatedly acknowledged in their addresses to the King. They pretended the Royal Charter gave them absolute independence; and on that absurd interpretation and lawless assumption they maintained a continuous contest with the mother country for more than fifty years. Every party in England, and the Commonwealth as well as Royalty, maintained the right of King and Parliament to be the supreme tribunal of appeal and control in America as well as in England; while the rulers of Massachusetts Bay Colony alone, in contradistinction to all the other British colonies in America, denied in short the authority of both King and Parliament, though often amidst wordy professions of personal loyalty to the Throne. Mr. Bancroft well sums up the history of Massachusetts pretensions and intolerance in the sentences: "Massachusetts owned no King but the King of Heaven." "Massachusetts gave franchises to the members of the visible Church," but "inexorably disfranchised Churchmen, Royalists, and all the world's people." "In Massachusetts, the songs of Deborah and David were sung without change; hostile Algonquins like the Canaanites were exterminated or enslaved; and a peevish woman was hanged, because it was written, 'The witch shall die.'"*

No hostile pen ever presented in so few and expressive words the character and policy of the Government of Massachusetts Bay during the whole existence of the first Charter, as is presented in these words of their eulogist Bancroft; and these words express the causes of their contests with the Crown

* History of the United States, Vol. II., Chap. xviii., pp. 461, 462.

and Parliament, of their proscription and persecution of the majority of their fellow-colonists not of their politics or form of worship, and of their dealing at pleasure with the territories of their neighbours,* and the lands and lives of the Indian tribes.

* The following is a specimen of the manner in which they interpreted their Charter to extend their territory. Having interpreted their Charter to exempt themselves from all responsibility to the Crown for their legislation or acts, they devised a new interpretation of their Charter in order to extend their territory to the north and north-east. The Charter limited their territories to three miles of the north bank of the Merrimac. At the end of twenty years they decided that the Charter meant three miles north of the most northern land or elbow of the Merrimac, and then not follow within three miles of the north bank of the river to its mouth, but a straight line east and west, which would give to their Plantation, Maine and a large part of New Hampshire, to the exclusion of the original patentees. When the Royal Commissioners, as directed by the King, came to investigate the complaints on this disputed boundary of territory, they decided against the pretensions of the Massachusetts Bay rulers, and appointed magistrates, etc., to give effect to their decision ; but the authorities of Massachusetts Bay, acknowledging no superior under heaven, resumed control of the territory in dispute as soon as the Commissioners had left the country. Mr. Hildreth says :

" Shortly after the departure of the Royal Commissioners, Leverett, now Major-General of the Colony, was sent to Maine, with three other magistrates and a body of horse, to re-establish the authority of Massachusetts. In spite of the remonstrances of Col. Nichols at New York (the head of the Royal Commission), the new Government lately set up was obliged to yield. Several persons were punished for speaking irreverently of the re-established authority of Massachusetts." (Hildreth's History of the United States, Vol. I., Chap. xiv., pp. 473, 474.) For eleven years the Massachusetts Bay Government maintained this ascendency against all complaints and appeals to England, when in 1677, as Mr. Hildreth says, "After hearing the parties, the Privy Council decided, in accordance with the opinion of the two Chief Justices, that the Massachusetts patent did not give any territory more than three miles distant from the left or north bank of the Merrimac. This construction, which set aside the pretensions of Massachusetts to the province of Maine, as well as to that part of New Hampshire east of the Merrimac, appeared so plain to English lawyers that the agents (of Massachusetts) hardly attempted a word in defence." (History of the United States, Vol. II., Chap. xviii., pp. 496, 497.)

It has been shown that as early as the second year of the civil war in England, the Massachusetts Bay Court passed an Act, in 1643, declaring it a capital crime for any one in their jurisdiction to advocate or support the cause of the King ; some years afterwards they passed an Act forbidding all trade with the other American colonies who would not renounce their allegiance to the King ; in their addresses to the Parliament and Cromwell, in 1651 and 1654, as shown above; they claimed, as a ground of merit for peculiar favour, that they had done their utmost, by devotional and material aid of men and means, in support of the Parliamentary, and afterwards regicide party, from the beginning to the end of the war—so that loyalists as well as churchmen were treated by them as outcasts and aliens—and now, after having begged, in language of sycophantic subserviency, the Royal pardon for the past, and obtained it on certain conditions, they claim the boon but refuse to fulfil the conditions, making all sorts of excuses, promises, and evasions for twenty years—professing and promising one thing in London, doing the opposite in Massachusetts, protracting where they dare not resist, but practically doing to the vacating of the Charter what Mr. Bancroft states in the pregnant sentences above quoted in the text.

CHAPTER VI.

MASSACHUSETTS DURING THE LAST FOUR YEARS OF CHARLES THE SECOND
AND JAMES THE SECOND, FROM 1680 TO 1688—THE IMMEDIATE CAUSES
AND MANNER OF CANCELLING THE FIRST CHARTER.

A CRISIS was now approaching. The state of things shown in
the latter part of the preceding chapter could not be suffered
always to continue. Means must be devised to bring it to an
end.

The Massachusetts Court had sent successive agents to England to explain and to make promises concerning many things
complained of, to crave indulgence and delay in other things
which they could not explain or justify; but they prohibited
their agents, by private instructions, from conceding anything
which the Charter, as they interpreted it, had given them—
namely, absolute independence. But this double game was
nearly played out. Party struggles in England had absorbed
the attention of the King and Cabinet, and caused a public and
vacillating policy to be pursued in regard to Massachusetts; but
the King's Government were at length roused to decisive action,
and threatened the colony with a writ of *quo warranto* in respect to matters so often demanded and as often evaded.

The Massachusetts Court met forthwith, passed an Act to
control the commission of the King's Collector, Edward Randolph, and another Act charging their own newly-appointed
Collector to look strictly after the enforcement of the Acts
of Trade (but in reality to counteract them); repealed another
Act which imposed a penalty for plotting the overthrow of
the Colonial Constitution—an Act levelled against Randolph;
passed another Act substituting the word "Jurisdiction" for
the word "Commonwealth" in their laws. They authorized

their agents merely to lay these concessions before the King, and humbly hoped they would satisfy his Majesty. They also bribed clerks of the Privy Council to keep them informed of its proceedings on Massachusetts affairs, and offered a bribe of £2,000 to King Charles himself. Mr. Hildreth says (1683): "On the appearance of these agents at Court, with powers so restricted, a *quo warranto* was threatened forthwith unless they were furnished with ampler authority. Informed of this threat, the General Court (of Massachusetts), after great debates, authorized their agents to consent to the regulation of anything wherein the Government might *ignorantly,* or *through mistake,* have deviated from the Charter; to accept, indeed, any demands consistent with the Charter (as they interpreted it), the existing Government established under it, and the 'main ends of our predecessors in coming hither,' which main ends were defined by them to be 'our liberties and privileges in matters of religion and worship of God, which you are, therefore, in no wise to consent to any infringement of.' They were authorized to give up Maine to the King, and even to tender him a private gratuity of two thousand guineas. Bribes were quite fashionable at Charles's Court; the King and his servants were accustomed to take them. The Massachusetts agents* had expended considerable sums to purchase a favour, or to obtain information, and by having clerks of the Privy Council in their pay they were kept well informed of the secret deliberations of that body. But this offer (of a bribe of two thousand guineas to the King), unskilfully managed, and betrayed by Cranfield, the lately appointed Royal Governor of New Hampshire, who had advised the magistrates to make it, exposed the Colony to blame and ridicule."†

---

* The Massachusetts Court had applied to Cromwell for permission to use the word "Commonwealth" instead of the word "Plantation," as expressed in their Charter, but were refused. They afterwards adopted it of their own accord.

† Hildreth's History of the United States, Vol. I., Chap. xiv., pp. 505, 506.

Their attempt to bribe the King was not the less bribery, whether Cranfield, for his own amusement, or otherwise to test their virtue, suggested it to them or not. But without any suggestion from Cranfield they bribed the King's clerks from their fidelity in the Privy Council, and bribed others "to obtain favour." The whole tenor of Scripture injunction and morality is against offering as well as taking bribes. After authorizing the employment of

" If a liberty of appeal to England were insisted on, the agents
were 'not to include the colony in any act or consent of theirs,
but to crave leave to transmit the same to the General Court
for their further consideration.' They were 'not to make any
alteration of the qualifications that were required by law, as at
present established, respecting the *admission of freemen.*'"*

It having appeared, on the perusal of the commission of the
Massachusetts agents by Sir Lionel Jenkins, Secretary of State,
that they did not possess the powers required to enable them
to act, they were informed by Lord Radnor that "the Council
had unanimously agreed to report to his Majesty, that unless
the agents speedily obtained such powers as might render them
capable to satisfy in all points, a *quo warranto* should proceed."

"Upon receipt of these advices," says Mr. Hutchinson, "it was
made a question, not in the General Court only, but amongst all
the inhabitants, whether to surrender or not. The opinions of
many of the ministers, and their arguments in support of them,
were given in writing, and in general it was thought better to
die by the hands of others than by their own.† The address was

---

bribery in England to promote their objects, the Court closed their sittings
by appointing " a day for solemn humiliation throughout the colony, to
implore the mercy and favour of God in respect to their sacred, civil, and
temporal concerns, and more especially those in the hands of their agents
abroad." (Palfrey, Vol. III., B. iii., Chap. ix., pp. 374, 375.)

* Palfrey's History of New England, Vol. III., B. iii., Chap. ix., pp.
372, 373.

" The agents of the colony, Messrs. Dudley and Richards, upon their arrival
in England, found his Majesty greatly provoked at the neglect of the colonists not sending before; and in their first letters home they acquainted the
Court with the feelings of the King, and desired to know whether it was
best to hazard all by refusing to comply with his demands, intimating that
they 'seriously intended to submit to the substance.' At that time they had
not been heard before the Council ; but soon after, on presenting the address
which had been forwarded by their hands, they were commanded to show
their powers and instructions to Sir Lionel Jenkins, Secretary of State ; and
on their perusal, finding these powers wholly inadequate, they were informed
by Lord Radnor that the Council had agreed *nem. con.* to report to his
Majesty, that unless further powers were speedily obtained, a *quo warranto*
should proceed in Hilary Term." (Barry's History of Massachusetts, First
Period, Chap. xvii., p. 471. Hutchinson, Vol. I., p. 335.)

† *Note* by the historian Hutchinson.—" The clergy turned the scale for the
last time. The balance which they had held from the beginning, they were
allowed to retain no longer."

agreed upon by the General Court; another was prepared and
sent through the colony, to be signed by the several inhabitants,
which the agents were to present or not, as they thought
proper; and they were (privately) to deliver up the deeds of the
Province of Maine, if required, and it would tend to preserve their
Charter, otherwise not; and they were to make no concessions
of any privileges conferred on the colony by the Charter."*
(That is, according to their interpretation and pretensions.)

" Governor Bradstreet and the moderate party were inclined .
to authorise the agents to receive the King's commands.   The
magistrates passed a vote to that effect.   But all the zeal and
obstinacy of the theocratic party had been roused by the present
crisis—a zeal resulting, as hot zeal often does, in the ultimate
loss of what it was so anxious to save."†

The agents of the colony were not willing to undertake the
defence and management of the question upon the Charter in
Westminster Hall.   The writ of *quo warranto*, which summoned
the Corporation of Massachusetts Bay to defend their acts
against the complaints and charges made against them, was
issued the 27th of June, 1683, and on the 20th of July " It
was ordered by the Privy Council, ' that Mr. Edward Randolph
be sent to New England with the notification of the said *quo
warranto*, which he was to deliver to the said Governor and
Company of the Massachusetts Bay, and thereupon to return to
give his Majesty an account of his proceedings therein.' "‡   This
writ was accompanied by a declaration from the King " that

---

* Hutchinson's History of Massachusetts Bay, Vol. I., pp. 336, 337.
† *Ibid.*
‡ Palfrey's History of New England, Vol. III., B. iii., Chap. ix., p. 374.
Mr. Palfrey, pp. 375, 376, in a note, gives the following abstract of Randolph's
charges presented to the Court : " 1. They assume powers that are not
warranted by the Charter, which is executed in another place than was
intended.   2. They make laws repugnant to those of England.   3. They
levy money on subjects not inhabiting the colony (and consequently not
represented in the General Court).   4. They impose an oath of fidelity to
themselves, without regarding the oath of allegiance to the King.   5. They
refuse justice by withholding appeals to the King.   6. They oppose the Acts
of Navigation, and imprison the King's officers for doing their duty.   7.
They have established a Naval Office, with a view to defraud the customs.
8. No verdicts are ever found for the King in relation to customs, and the
Courts impose costs on the prosecutors, in order to discourage trials.   9.
They levy customs on the importation of goods from England.   10. They do

the private interests and properties of all persons within the colony should be continued and preserved to them, so that no man should receive any prejudice in his freehold or estate ;" also, "that in case the said Corporation of the Massachusetts Bay should, before the prosecution had upon the said *quo warranto*, make a full submission and entire resignation to his pleasure, he would then regulate their Charter (as stated in another place, by adding supplementary clauses) in such a .manner as should be for his service and the good of the colony, without any other alterations than such as he should find necessary for the better support of his Government."*

On the issue of the writ of *quo warranto*, the business of the colony's agents in London was at an end. They returned home, and arrived in Boston the 23rd of October, 1683; and the same week Randolph arrived with the *quo warranto* and the King's accompanying declaration. The announcement of this decisive act on the part of the King produced a profound sensation throughout the colony, and gave rise to the question, "What shall Massachusetts do ?" One part of the colony advocated *submission;* another party advocated *resistance.* The former were called the " Moderate party," the latter the "Patriot party"—the commencement of the two parties which were afterwards known as United Empire Loyalists and Revolutionists.† The Moderate party was led by the memorable Governor Bradstreet, Stoughton, and Dudley, and included a majority of the assistants or magistrates, called the "Upper branch of the Government." The Independence party was headed by the Deputy Governor Danforth, Gookin, and Nowell, and included a majority of the House of Deputies, over whose elections and proceedings the elders or ministers exerted a potent influence.‡

---

not administer the oath of supremacy, as required by the Charter. 11. They erected a Court of Admiralty, though not empowered by Charter. 12. They discountenance the Church of England. 13. They persist in coining money, though they had asked forgiveness for that offence." (Chalmers' Annals, p. 462.)

* *Ib.*, p. 377.

† "From this period (1683) one may date the origin of two parties—the Patriots and Prerogative men—between whom controversy scarcely intermitted, and was never ended until the separation of the two countries." (Minot's History of Massachusetts, etc., Vol. I., p. 51.)

‡ In a Boston town meeting, held January 21, 1684, to consider the King's

Governor Bradstreet and a majority of the assistants, or magistrates, adopted the following resolution :

"The magistrates have voted that an humble address be sent to

declaration, the Rev. Increase Mather, who was then President of Harvard College, and had for twenty years exerted more influence upon the public affairs of Massachusetts than any other man for the same length of time, delivered a speech against submission to the King, which he miscalled " the surrender of the Charter." He said, among other things : " I verily believe we shall sin against the God of heaven if we vote in the affirmative to it. The Scripture teacheth us otherwise. That which the Lord our God hath given us, shall we not possess it ? God forbid that we should give away the inheritance of our fathers. Nor would it be wisdom for us to comply. If we make a full and entire resignation to the King's pleasure, we fall into the hands of men immediately ; but if we do not, we still keep ourselves in the hands of God ; and who knows what God may do for us ?" The historian says that " the effect of such an appeal was wholly irresistible ; that many of the people fell into tears, and there was a general acclamation." (Barry's Colonial History of Massachusetts, Vol. I., pp. 476, 477.)

It is not easy to squeeze as much extravagance and nonsense in the same space as in the above quoted words of Increase Mather. Where was the Scripture which taught them not to submit complaints of their fellow-colonists to their King and his Council, the highest authority in the empire? Both Scripture and profane history furnish us with examples almost without number of usurpers professing that the usurpation and conquest they had achieved was "that which the Lord our God had given" them, and which they should "possess" at all hazards as if it were an "inheritance of their fathers." The "inheritance" spoken of by Mr. Mather was what had been usurped by the rulers of the colony over and above the provisions of their Charter against the rights of the Crown, the religious and political liberties of their fellow-colonists, and encroaching upon the lands of their white and Indian neighbours. Then to submit to the King and Council was to "fall into the hands of men immediately," but to contest with the King in the Courts of Chancery or King's Bench was to "keep themselves in the hands of God," who, it seems, according to Increase Mather's own interpretation, judged him and his adherents unworthy of retaining the "inheritance" of the Charter, the powers and objects of which they had so greatly perverted and abused. The King had expressly declared that the prosecution against the Charter would be abandoned if they would submit to his decision in regard to what had been matters of complaint and dispute between them and their fellow-colonists and Sovereign for more than fifty years, and which decision should be added to the Charter as explanatory regulations, and should embrace nothing affecting their religious liberties or local elective self-government. They refused, and lost their Charter ; Rhode Island and Connecticut submitted, and even resigned their Charters, and were afterwards authorized to resume them, with the privileges and powers conferred by them unimpaired, including the election of their Governors as well as legislators, etc.

14

his Majesty by this ship, declaring that, upon a serious consideration of his Majesty's gracious intimations in his former letters, and
more particularly in his late declaration, that his pleasure and
purpose is only to regulate our Charter in such a manner as
shall be for his service and the good of this his colony, and
without any other alteration than what is necessary for the
support of his Government here, we will not presume to contend
with his Majesty in a Court of law, but humbly lay ourselves
at his Majesty's feet, in submission to his pleasure so declared,
and that we have resolved by the next opportunity to send our
agents empowered to receive his Majesty's commands accordingly.   And, for saving a default for non-appearance upon the
return of the writ of *quo warranto*, that some person or persons
be appointed and empowered, by letter of attorney, to appear
and make defence until our agents may make their appearance
and submission as above.

" The magistrates have passed this without reference to the
consent of their brethren the deputies hereto.

(Signed)   " EDMUND RAWSON, *Secretary.*
" 15th November, 1683."

This resolution was laid before the House of Deputies and
debated by them a fortnight, when the majority of them
adopted the following resolution :

" November 30, 1683.—The deputies consent not, but adhere
to their former bills.

" WILLIAM TERRY, *Clerk.*"*

" They voted instead," says Mr. Hildreth, " an Address to
the King, praying forbearance ; but they authorized Robert
Humphreys, a London barrister and the legal adviser of the
agents, to enter an appearance and to retain counsel, requesting
him ' to leave no stone unturned that may be of service either to
the case itself, or the spinning out of the time as much as possibly
may be.'   No less than three letters were written to Humphreys ;
money was remitted ; but all hopes of defence were futile.
Before the letters arrived in London, a default had already
been recorded.   That default could not be got off, and judgment was entered the next year pronouncing the Charter void."†

* Hutchinson's History of Massachusetts Bay, Vol. I., pp. 338, 339.
† Hildreth's History of the United States, Vol. I., Chap. xiv., p. 507.   The

The manner in which the questions at issue were put to a popular vote in Massachusetts was unfair and misleading; the epithets applied to the "Moderate" or loyal party were offensive and unjust; and the statements of Palfrey, respecting the acts of the King immediately following the vacation of the Charter, are very disingenuous, not to say untrue.

The King had expressly and repeatedly declared that he would not proceed to vacate the Charter if they would submit to his decision on the six grounds mentioned in his first letter to them, June 28, 1662, twenty years before, as the conditions of continuing the Charter, and which they had persistently evaded and resisted; that his decision should be in the form of certain "Regulations" for the future administration of the Charter, and not the vacation of it. Every reader knows the difference between a Royal Charter of incorporation and the Royal instructions issued twenty years afterwards to remedy irregularities and abuses which had been shown to have crept in, and practised in the local administration of the Charter. Yet the ruling party in Massachusetts Bay did not put the question as accepting the King's offers, but as of vacating the Charter. This was raising a false issue, and an avowed imputation and contempt of the King. It is true that Dr. Palfrey and other modern New England historians have said that Charles the Second had from the beginning intended to abolish the Charter; that the "vacation of the Charter was a foregone conclusion." In reply to which it may be said that this is mere assumption, unsupported by facts; that if Charles the Second had wished or intended to vacate the Charter, he had the amplest opportunity and reasons to do so, in the zenith of his popularity and power, when they refused to comply with the conditions on which he proposed to pardon and obliterate the past and continue the Charter, and when they resisted his Commissioners, and employed military force to oppose the exercise of their powers, and set aside their decisions; instead of which he remonstrated with them for more than twenty years, and then gave them long notice and choice to retain the Charter with his "Regu-

notice to the Corporation and Company of Massachusetts to answer to the writ of *quo warranto* was received October, 1683; the final judgment of the Court vacating the Charter was given July, 1685, nearly two years afterwards. (Hutchinson. Vol. I., pp. 337—340.)

lations" on the disputed points, or contest the Charter, as to their observance of it, in a Court of law.   Under the impulse and guidance of violent counsels they chose the latter, and lost their Charter.   In their very last address to the King, they gratefully acknowledged his kindness in all his despatches and treatment of them, contrary to the statements and imputations of modern New England historians; yet they denied him the authority universally acknowledged and exercised by Queen Victoria and English Courts of law over the legislative, judicial, and even administrative acts of every province of the British Empire.   Dr. Palfrey says: " In the Upper branch of the Government there was found at length a *servile* majority;" but " the deputies were prepared for no such *suicide*, though there were not wanting faint hearts and grovelling aims among them."*   At the head of what Dr. Palfrey terms the " servile majority " was the venerable Governor Bradstreet, now more than ninety years of age, the only survivor of the original founders of the colony, who had been a magistrate more than fifty years, more than once Governor, always a faithful and safe counsellor, the agent of the colony in England, and obtaining in June, 1662, the King's letter of pardon—oblivion of the past and promised continuance of the Charter on certain conditions—a letter which the Colonial Court said filled them with inexpressible joy and gratitude (see above, page 141), who then advised them to comply with the King's requirements, and who, after twenty years' further experience and knowledge of public affairs and parties, advises them to pursue the same course for which he is now termed " servile," and ranked with cowards and men of " grovelling aims," advising the colony to commit political " suicide."   The result showed who were the real authors of the " suicide," and Dr. Palfrey forcibly states the result of their doings in the following words:

" Massachusetts, as a body politic, was now no more.   The elaborate fabric, that had been fifty-four years in building, was levelled to the dust.   The hopes of the fathers were found to be mere dreams.   It seemed that their brave struggles had brought no result.   The honoured ally (Massachusetts) of the Protector (Cromwell) of England lay under the feet of Charles the Second.   It was on the Charter granted to Roswell and his

* History of New England, Vol. III., B. iii., Chap. ix., pp. 380, 381.

associates, Governor and Company of Massachusetts Bay, that the structure of the cherished institutions of Massachusetts, religious and civil, had been reared. The abrogation of that Charter swept the whole away. Massachusetts, in English law, was again what it had been before James the First made a grant of it to the Council of New England. It belonged to the King of England, by virtue of the discovery of the Cabots. No less than this was the import of the decree in Westminster Hall. Having secured its great triumph, the Court had no thought of losing anything by the weakness of compassion. The person selected by the King to govern the people of his newly-acquired province was Colonel Piercy Kirk. That campaign in the West of England had not yet taken place which has made the name of Kirk immortal; but fame enough had gone abroad of his brutal character, to make his advent an anticipation of horror to those whom he was appointed to govern. It was settled that he was to be called 'His Majesty's Lieutenant and Governor-General,' and that his authority should be unrestricted."*

This quotation from Dr. Palfrey suggests one or two remarks, and requires correction, as it is as disingenuous in statement as it is eloquent in diction. He admits and assumes the validity of the judicial act by which the Charter was declared forfeited; though the loyalty of this decision was denied by the opposing party in Massachusetts, who denied that any English Court, or that even the King himself, had any authority in Massachusetts to disallow any of its acts or decisions, much less to vacate its Charter, and professed to continue its elections of deputies, etc., and to pass and administer laws as aforetime. Dr. Palfrey's language presents all such pretensions and proceedings as baseless and puerile.

Dr. Palfrey states what is true, that the Massachusetts Government had been the "ally" of Cromwell; but this they had denied in their addresses to Charles the Second. (See above, pp. 153—9.)

It is hardly ingenuous or correct in Dr. Palfrey speaking of Col. Kirk's appointment of the "newly-acquired Province." The office extended over New Hampshire, Maine, and Plymouth as well as Massachusetts; but Kirk never was Governor

---

* Palfrey's History of New England, Vol. III., B. iii., Chap. ix., pp. 394, 395.

of Massachusetts, for before his commission and instructions were completed, all was annulled by the demise of King Charles, which took place the 6th of February, 1685. Mr. Hutchinson says: "Before any new Government was settled, King Charles died. Mr. Blaithwait wrote to the Governor and recommended ɩthe proclaiming of King James without delay. This was done with great ceremony in the high street of Boston (April 20th)."*

Mr. Joseph Dudley, a native of the colony, and one of the two last agents sent to England, was appointed the first Governor after the annulling of the Charter. Mr. Hutchinson says: "The 15th of May (1686), the *Rose* frigate arrived from England, with a commission to Mr. Dudley as President, and divers others, gentlemen of the Council, to take upon them the administration of government." Mr. Dudley's short administration was not very grievous. The House of Deputies, indeed, was laid aside; but the people, the time being short, felt little or no effect from the change. Mr. Stoughton was Mr. Dudley's chief confidant. Mr. Dudley professed as great an attachment to the interest of the colony as Mr. Stoughton, and was very desirous of retaining their favour. A letter from Mr. Mather, then the minister of the greatest influence, is a proof of it.† There was no molestation to the Churches of the colony, but they continued both worship and discipline as before. The affairs of the towns were likewise managed in the same manner as formerly. Their Courts of justice were continued upon the former plan, Mr. Stoughton being at the head of them. Trials were by juries, as usual. Dudley considered himself as appointed to preserve the affairs of the colony from confusion until a Governor

---

* History of Massachusetts Bay, Vol. I., p. 340.

"The Charter fell. This was the last effective act of Charles the Second relative to Massachusetts; for before a new Government could be settled, the monarch was dead. His death and that of the Charter were nearly contemporary." (Barry's History of Massachusetts, First Period, Chap. xvii., p. 478).

† The conclusion of this letter is as follows: "Sir, for the things of my soul, I have these many years hung upon your lips, and ever shall; and in civil things am desirous you may know with all plainness my reasons of procedure, and that they may be satisfactory to you. I am, sir, your servant,

"J. DUDLEY.

"From your own house,
May 17th, '86."

arrived and a rule of administration should be more fully settled.*

The administration of Dudley was only of seven months' duration. "Dudley was superseded by Sir Edmund Andros, who arrived at Boston on the 20th of December (1686), with a commission from King James for the government of New England.† He was instructed to appoint no one of the Council to any offices but those of the least estates and characters, and to displace none without sufficient cause ; to continue the former laws of the country, as far as they were not inconsistent with his commission or instructions, until other regulations were established by the Governor and Council ; to allow no printing press ; to give universal toleration in religion, but encouragement to the Church of England ; to execute the laws of trade, and prevent frauds in Customs.‡ But Andros had other instructions of a more despotic and stringent character ; and being, like King James himself, of an arbitrary disposition, he fulfilled his

* History of Massachusetts Bay, Vol. I., pp. 350, 351, 352. "Though eighteen months had elapsed since the Charter was vacated, the Government was still going on as before. The General Court, though attended thinly, was in session when the new commission arrived. Dudley sent a copy of it to the Court, not as recognizing their authority, but as an assembly of principal and influential inhabitants. They complained of the commission as arbitrary, 'there not being the least mention of an Assembly' in it. expressed doubts whether it were safe for him or them, and thus gloomily dissolved, leaving the government in Dudley's hands." (Hildreth's History of the United States, Vol. II., Chap. xviii., p. 80.)

† Andros was appointed Captain-General and Vice-Admiral of Massachusetts, New Hampshire, Maine, Plymouth, Pemaquid, and Narraganset during pleasure.

‡ (Holmes' Annals, etc., Vol. I., p. 419). Holmes adds : "To support a Government that could not be submitted to from choice, a small military establishment, consisting of two companies of soldiers, was formed, and military stores were transported. The tyrannical conduct of James towards the colonies did not escape the notice and censure of English historians." "At the same time that the Commons of England were deprived of their privileges, a like attempt was made on the colonies. King James recalled their Charters, by which their liberties were secured ; and he sent over Governors with absolute power. The arbitrary principles of that monarch appear in every part of his administration." (Hume's History of England, Act James II.)—Ib., pp. 419, 490.

Hutchinson says : "The beginning of Andros' administration gave great satisfaction. He made high professions as to the public good and the welfare of the people, both of merchants and planters ; directed the judges to adminis-

instructions to the letter. And when his Royal master was dethroned for his unconstitutional and tyrannical conduct, Andros
was seized at Boston and sent prisoner to England, to answer
for his conduct ; but he was acquitted by the new Government,
not for his policy in New England, but because he had acted
according to his instructions, which he pleaded as his justification.*

It is singular that *toleration* in Massachusetts should have
been proclaimed by the arbitrary James, in a declaration above
and contrary to the law for which he received the thanks of the
ministers in that colony, but which resulted in his loss of his
Crown in England.

" James's Declaration of Indulgence was proclaimed (1687),
and now, for the first time, Quakers, Baptists, and Episcopalians
enjoyed toleration in Massachusetts. That system of religious
tyranny, coeval with the settlement of New England, thus
unexpectedly received its death-blow from a Catholic bigot,
who professed a willingness to allow religious freedom to others
as a means of securing it for himself." * * * " Mather, who
carried with him (1689) an address from the ministers, thanking James, in behalf of themselves and their brethren, for his
Declaration of Indulgence arriving in England while King
James was yet in power, had been graciously received by that
monarch. But, though repeatedly admitted to an audience, his
complaints against the Royal Governor (Andros) had produced
no effect. The Revolution intervening, he hastened, with greater
hopes of success, to address himself to the new King, and his
remonstrances prevented, as far as Massachusetts was concerned,
the despatch of a circular letter confirming the authority of all
Colonial officers holding commissions from James II. The
letters actually received at Boston authorized those in authority

---

ter justice according to the custom of the place; ordered the former established
rules to be observed as to rates and taxes, and that all the colony laws not
inconsistent with his commission should be in force." (History of Massachusetts Bay, Vol. I., p. 353).

* " The complaints against Andros, coolly received by the Privy Council,
were dismissed by order of the new King, on the ground that nothing was
charged against the late Governor which his instructions would not fully
justify." (Hildreth's History of the United States, Vol. II., Chap. xviii.,
p. 94.)

to retain provisionally the administration, and directed that Andros and the other prisoners should be sent to England.*

I have now traced the proceedings of the founders and rulers of the Massachusetts Bay Colony during the fifty-four years of their first Charter, with short notices of some occurrences during the three years' reign of James the Second, their revenge not only in his own dethronement, but also on his Governor Andros, for the tyranny which he practised upon them by imprisoning him and his helpers, and by Royal command sending them as prisoners to England, together with the removal of the local officers appointed by Andros and the restoration of their own elected authorities until further instruction from the new King.

There can be no question that the founders of that colony were not only men of wealth, but men of education, of piety, of the highest respectability, of great energy, enterprise, and industry, contributing to the rapid progress of their settlements and increase of their wealth, and stamping the character of their history ; but after their emigration to Massachusetts Bay, and during the progress of their settlements and the organiza-tion and development of their undertakings, their views became narrowed to the dimensions of their own Plantation in govern-ment and trade, irrespective of the interests of England, or of the other neighbour colonies, and their theology and religious spirit was of the narrowest and most intolerant character. They assumed to be the chosen Israel of God, subject to no King but Jehovah, above the rulers of the land, planted there to cast out the heathen, to smite down every dagon of false worship, whether Episcopalian, Presbyterian, Baptist, or Quaker, and responsible to no other power on earth for either their legisla-tive or administrative acts. I will not here recapitulate those acts, so fully stated in preceding pages, and established by evidence of documents and testimony which cannot be success-fully denied. But there are two features of their pretensions and government which demand further remark.

I. The first is the character and narrowness of the foundation on which rested their legislation and government. None but members of the Congregational Churches were eligible to legis-late or fill any office in the colony, or even to be an elector. A

---

* Hildreth's History, etc., Vol. II., Chap. xviii., pp. 83, 93, 94

more narrow-minded and corrupting test of qualification for civil or political office, or for the elective franchise, can hardly be conceived.*   However rich a man might be, and whatever might be his education or social position, if he were not a member of the Congregational Church he was an " alien in the Commonwealth" of the Massachusetts Israel, was ineligible for office, or to be an elector; while his own servant, if a member of the Church, though not worth a shilling, or paying a penny to the public revenue, was an elector, or eligible to be elected to any public office.   The non-members of the Congregational Church were subject to all military and civil burdens and taxes of the State, without any voice in its legislation or administration.   Such was the free (?) Government of Massachusetts Bay, eulogized by New England historians during half a century, until abolished by judicial and royal authority.   What would be thought at this day of a Government, the eligibility to public office and the elective franchise under which should be based on membership in a particular Church?

II. But, secondly, this Government must be regarded as equally unjust and odious when we consider not merely the sectarian basis of its assumptions and acts against the Sovereign on the one hand, and the rights of citizens of Massachusetts and of neighbouring colonies on the other, but the small proportion of the population enfranchised in comparison with the population which was disfranchised.   Even at the beginning it was not professed that the proportion of Congregational Church members to the whole population was more than one to three; in after years it was alleged, at most, not to have been more than one to six.

This, however, is of little importance in comparison with the question, what was the proportion of electors to non-electors in the colony?   On this point I take as my authority the latest

---

* "As a matter of course, this Church test of citizenship did not work well.   The more unscrupulous the conscience, the easier it was to join the Church; and abandoned men who wanted public preferment could join the Church with loud professions and gain their ends, and make Church membership a byeword.   Under the Charter by William and Mary, in 1691, the qualification of electors was then fixed at a ' freehold of forty shillings per annum, or other property of the value of £40 sterling.' " (Elliott's New England History, Vol. I., p. 113.)

and most able apologist and defender of the Massachusetts Government, Dr. Palfrey. He says: "Counting the lists of persons admitted to the franchise in Massachusetts, and making what I judge to be reasonable allowance for persons deceased, I come to the conclusion that the number of freemen in Massachusetts in 1670 may have been between 1,000 and 1,200, or one freeman to every four or five adult males."[*]

The whole population of the colony at this time is not definitely stated, but there was one elector to every "four or five" of the adult "*males.*" This eleven hundred men, because they were Congregationalists, influenced and controlled by their ministers, elected from themselves all the legislators and rulers of Massachusetts Bay Colony in civil, judicial, and military matters, who bearded the King and Parliament, persecuted all who dissented from them in religious worship, encroached upon the property and rights of neighbouring colonies, levied and imposed all the burdens of the State upon four-fifths of their fellow (male) colonists who had no voice in the legislation or administration of the Government. Yet this sectarian Government is called by New England historians a free Government; and these eleven hundred electors—electors not because they have property, but because they are Congregationalists—are called "the people of Massachusetts," while four-fifths of the male population and more than four-fifths of the property are utterly ignored, except to pay the taxes or bear the other burdens of the State, but without a single elective voice, or a single free press to state their grievances or express their wishes, much less to advocate their rights and those of the King and Parliament.

III. Thirdly, from the facts and authorities given in the foregoing pages, there cannot be a reasonable pretext for the statement that the rulers of Massachusetts Bay had not violated both the objects and provisions of the Royal Charter, variously and persistently, during the fifty-four years of its existence; while there is not an instance of either Charles the First or Second claiming a single prerogative inconsistent with the provisions of the Charter, and which is not freely recognized at this day in

---

[*] Palfrey's History of New England, Vol. III., B. iii., Chap. ii., p. 41, in a note.

the Crown and Parliament of Great Britain, by the free inhabitants of every Province of the British Empire. The fact that neither of the Charleses asked for anything more than the toleration of Episcopal worship, never objected to the perfect freedom of worship claimed by the Congregationalists of Massachusetts; and the fact that Charles the Second corresponded and remonstrated for twenty years and more to induce the rulers of Massachusetts Bay to acknowledge those rights of King and Parliament, and their duties as British subjects, shows that there could have been no desire to interfere with their freedom of worship or to abolish the Charter, except as a last resort, after the failure of all other means to restrain the disloyal and oppressive acts of the rulers of that one colony. In contradistinction to the practice of other colonies of New England, and of every British colony at this day, Charles the First and Second were bad kings to England and Scotland, but were otherwise to New England; and when New England historians narrate at great length, and paint in the darkest colours, the persecutions and despotic acts of the Stuart kings over England and Scotland, and then infer that they did or sought to do the same in New England, they make groundless assumptions, contrary to the express declarations and policy of the two Charleses and the whole character and tenor of New England history. The demands of Charles the Second, and the conditions on which he proposed to continue the first Charter in 1662, were every one sanctioned and provided for in the second Royal Charter issued by William and Mary in 1690, and under which, for seventy years, the Government was milder and more liberal, the legislation broader, the social state more happy, and the colony more loyal and prosperous than it had ever been during the fifty-four years of the first Charter. All this will be proved and illustrated in the following chapter.

CHAPTER VII.

The Second Royal Charter ; How Obtained—Massachusetts nearly
Sixty Years under the Second Charter, from 1691 to 1748 ;
to the Close of the First War between England and France,
and the Peace of Aix-la-Chapelle.

I HAVE traced the characteristics of the Government of the
Massachusetts Bay Colony during fifty-four years under its first
Charter, in its relations to the Crown, to the citizens of its own
jurisdiction, to the inhabitants of the neighbouring colonies, and
to the Indians; its denial of Royal authority; its renunciation
of one form of worship and Church polity, and adoption of
another; its denial of toleration to any but Congregationalists,
and of the elective franchise, to four-fifths of the male population; its taxing without representation; its denial of the right
of appeal to the King, or any right on the part of the King or
Parliament to receive appeals, or to the exercise of any super-
vision or means of seeing that "the laws of England were not
contravened" by their acts of legislation or government, while
they were sheltered by the British navy from the actual and
threatened invasion of the Dutch, Spaniards, and French, not
to say the Indians, always prompted and backed by the French,
thus claiming all the attributes of an independent Government,
but resting under the ægis of an Imperial protection to maintain an independence which they asserted, but could not themselves maintain against foreign enemies.

I will now proceed to note the subsequent corresponding facts
of their history during seventy years under the second Royal
Charter.

They averred, and no doubt brought themselves to believe, that with their first Charter, as interpreted by themselves, was bound up their *political life*, or what they alleged to be dearer to them than life, and that in its loss was involved their *political death;* but they made no martial effort to prolong that life, or to save themselves from that premature death.

Mr. Palfrey assigns various reasons for this non-resistance to the cancelling of their Charter; but he omits or obscurely alludes to the real ones.

Dr. Palfrey says: "The reader asks how it could be that the decree by which Massachusetts fell should fail to provoke resistance. He inquires whether nothing was left of the spirit which, when the colony was much poorer, had often defied and baffled the designs of the father of the reigning King. He must remember how times were changed. There was no longer a great patriot party in England, to which the colonists might look for sympathy and help, and which it had even hoped might reinforce them by a new emigration. There was no longer even a Presbyterian party which, little as it had loved them, a sense of common insecurity and common interest might enlist in their behalf. * * * Relatively to her population and wealth, Massachusetts had large capacities for becoming a naval power—capacities which might have been vigorously developed if an alliance with the great naval powers of Continental Europe had been possible. But Holland was now at peace with England; not to say that such an arrangement was out of the question for Massachusetts, while *the rest of New England was more or less inclined to the adverse interest.* Unembarrassed by any foreign war, England was armed with that efficient navy which the Duke of York had organized, and which had lately distressed the rich and energetic Netherlanders; and the dwellings of two-thirds of the inhabitants of Massachusetts stood where they could be battered from the water. They had a commerce which might be molested in every sea by English cruisers. Neither befriended nor interfered with, they might have been able to defend themselves against the corsairs of Barbary in the resorts of their most gainful trade; but England had given them notice, that if they were stubborn that commerce would be dismissed from her protection, and in the circumstances such a notice threatened more than a mere abstinence from aid. The

Indian war had emptied the colonial exchequer. On the other hand, a generation earlier the colonists might have retreated to the woods, but now they had valuable stationary property to be kept or sacrificed. To say no more, the ancient unanimity was broken in upon. Jealousy had risen and grown. * * * Nor was even public morality altogether of its pristine tone. The prospect of material prosperity had introduced a degree of luxury; and luxury had brought ambition and mean longings. Venality had become possible; and clever and venal men had a motive for enlisting the selfish and the stupid, and decrying the generous and wise."*

These eloquent words of Dr. Palfrey are very suggestive, and deserve to be carefully pondered by the reader.

I. In the concluding sentences he tacitly admits that the Government of Massachusetts Bay had become, at the end of fifty-four years, partially at least, a failure in "public morality" and patriotism; yet during that period the Government had been exclusively, in both its legislation and administration, in the hands of one religious denomination, under the influence of its ministers, who were supported by taxation on the whole population, controlled the elections, and whose counsels ruled in all conflicts with the King and Parliament of England. None but a Congregationalist could be a governor, or assistant, or deputy, or judge, or magistrate, or juror, or officer of the army, or constable, or elector, or have liberty of worship. The union of Church and State in Massachusetts was more intimate and intolerant than it had or ever has been in England; and their contests with England in claiming absolute and irresponsible powers under the Charter were at bottom, and in substance, contests for Congregational supremacy and exclusive and proscriptive rule in Church and State—facts so overlooked and misrepresented by New England historians. Yet under this denominational and virtually hierarchical government, while wealth was largely accumulated, the "pristine tone of public morality" declined, and patriotism degenerated into "ambition and venality."

II. It is also worthy of remark, that, according to Dr. Palfrey, had not the spirit of the first generation of the rulers of Massa-

* Palfrey's History of New England, Vol. III., B. iii., Chap. ix., pp. 396—398.

chusetts Bay departed, the war of the American Revolution
would have been anticipated by a century, and the sword would
have been unsheathed, not to maintain the right of representation co-extensive with subjection to taxation, but to maintain
a Government which for half a century had taxed four-fifths
of its citizens without allowing them any representation,
supported the ministers of one Church by taxes on the whole
population, and denied liberty of worship to any but the
members of that one denomination.

III. I remark further, that Mr. Palfrey hints at the two real
causes why the disloyal party (calling itself the "patriotic party")
did not take up arms of rebellion against the mother country.
The one was *disunion* in the colony—"the ancient unanimity
was broken in upon." It has been seen that a majority of the
"Upper branch" of even this denominational Government, and
a large minority of the assembly of deputies, were in favour
of submitting to the conditions which the King had twenty
years before prescribed as the terms of continuing the Charter.
If the defection from disloyalty was so great within the
limits of the denomination, it is natural to infer that it must
have been universal among the four-fifths of the male population
who were denied the rights and privileges of "freemen," yet
subject to all the burdens of the State. Deprived also of all
freedom of the press, and punished by fine and imprisonment
if, even in petitions to the local Legislature for redress of grievances, they complained of the acts of local legislation or government, they could only look to the mother country for deliverance
from local oppression, for liberty of worship and freedom of
citizens. The "ministers" had lost their ascendency even within
the enfranchised circle of their own established churches, while
the great body of the disfranchised Nonconformists could only
regard them as had the Nonconformists in England regarded
Bancroft and Laud. They could assume high perogatives,
arrogate to themselves divine favour and protection, threaten
divine judgments on their adversaries, boast of courage and
power; but they knew that in a trial of strength on the battle-
field their strength would prove weakness, and that they would
be swept from power, and perhaps proscribed and oppressed by
the very victims of their intolerance. The "breaking in upon
ancient unanimity" was but the declining power of a disloyal

Church and State Government of one denomination. A second cause hinted at by Dr. Palfrey why the rulers of Massachusetts Bay did not resort to arms at this time was, that *"the rest of New England was more or less inclined to the adverse interest."* They could command no rallying watchword to combine the other New England colonies against the King, such as they were enabled to employ the following century to combine all the American colonies. "The rest of New England" had found that in the King and Council was their only effectual protection against the aggressions and domination of the rulers of Massachusetts Bay, who denied all right of appeal to the Crown, and denied the right of the Crown to receive and decide upon such appeals. These rulers not only encroached upon the lands of neighbouring colonies, but interfered with their exercise of religious toleration.* The extinction of the pretensions to supremacy and monopoly of power and trade by the rulers of Massachusetts Bay, was the enfranchisement of the other New England Colonies to protection against

* The Plymouth Colony tolerating the proscribed Baptists of Massachusetts Bay, the Court of Massachusetts Bay admonished them in a letter, in 1649, saying "that it had come to its knowledge that divers Anabaptists had been connived at within the Plymouth jurisdiction, and it appeared that the 'patient bearing' of the Plymouth authorities had 'encreased' the same errors ; that thirteen or fourteen persons (it was reported) had been re-baptized at Sea Cunke, under which circumstances 'effectual restriction' was desired, 'the more as the interests of Massachusetts were concerned therein.' The infection of such diseases being so near us, are likely to spread into our jurisdiction, and God equally requires the suppression of error as the maintenance of truth at the hands of Christian magistrates."—*British* (Congregational) *Quarterly Review* for January, 1876, pp. 150, 151.

"The Massachusetts did maintain Punham (a petty Sachem in this province of Rhode Island) twenty years against this colony, and his chief Sachem, and did by armed soldiers besiege and take prisoners Gorton, Hamden, Weeks, Green, and others in this province, and carried them away to Boston, put them in irons, and took eighty head of cattle from them, for all of which they could never obtain any satisfaction. This colony (of Rhode Island) could never be acknowledged (by Massachusetts) for a colony till his Majesty's Charter was published (in 1663), though in the year 1643 they sent over some in England to procure the King's Charter ; but finding that unnatural war begun, and the King gone from London, they took a Charter from the Lords and Commons." (Report of the King's Commissioners, in Hutchinson's Collection of Original Papers relative to the History of Massachusetts Bay, pp. 415, 416.)

15

aggression, and of four-fifths of the male inhabitants of Massachusetts itself to the enjoyment of equal civil and religious liberty.

I think therefore that "ambitions and mean longings," and
even "venality," had quite as much to do on the part of those
who wished to perpetuate the government of disloyalty, proscription, and persecution as on the part of those who desired
to "render unto Cæsar the things that are Cæsar's," and to place
the Government of Massachusetts, like that of the other New
England Colonies, upon the broad foundation of equal and
general franchise and religious liberty.

But to return from this digresssion. After "the fall of the
Charter," November, 1684, the Congregationalists of Massachusetts Bay continued their government for two years, as if nothing had happened to their Charter ; they promptly proclaimed
and took the oath of allegiance to James the Second ; and two
years afterwards sent the celebrated Increase Mather as agent
to England, to thank the King for the Proclamation of Indulgence, which trampled on English laws, and cost the King his
throne, to pray for the restoration of the Charter, and to accuse and
pray for the removal of the King's obnoxious Governor-General
of New England, Sir Edmund Andros. The King received him
very courteously, and granted him several audiences. It would
have been amusing to witness the exchange of compliments between the potent minister of Massachusetts Congregationalism
and the bigoted Roman Catholic King of England ; but though
James used flattering words, he bestowed no favours, did not
relax the rigour of his policy, and retained his Governor of New
England. On the dethronement of James, Dr. Mather paid his
homage to the rising sun of the new Sovereign—professed overflowing loyalty to William and Mary,* and confirmed his professions by showing that his constituents, on learning of the revolution in England, seized and sent prisoner to England, Andros,
the hated representative of the dethroned King. But King

---

* In an audience of King William, obtained by the Duke of Devonshire,
April 28, 1691, Mr. Mather humbly prayed his Majesty's favour to New
England in restoring the old Charter privileges ; adding at the same time
these words : "Sir,—Your subjects there have been willing to venture their
lives to enlarge your dominions ; the expedition to Canada was a great and
noble undertaking. May it please your Majesty also to consider the circumstances of that people, as in your wisdom you have considered the circum-

William did not seem to estimate very highly that sort of loyalty, much less to recognize the Massachusetts assumptions under the old Charter, though he was ready to redress every just complaint and secure to them all the privileges of British subjects.* Mr. Hutchinson says: "Soon after the withdrawal

stances of England and Scotland. In New England they differ from other Plantations; they are called Congregationalists and Presbyterians (a), so that such a Governor as will not suit with the people of New England, may be very proper for other English Plantations." (Neal's History of New England, Vol. II., Chap. xi., pp. 475, 476.)

    * "The Rev. Mr. Increase Mather, Rector of Harvard College, had been at Court in the year 1688, and laid before the King a representation of their grievances, which the King promised in part to redress, but was prevented by the revolution. When the Prince and Princess of Orange were settled on the throne, he, with the rest of the New England agents, addressed their Majesties for the restoring of their Charter, and applied to the Convention Parliament, who received a Bill for this purpose and passed it in the Lower House; but that Parliament being soon dissolved, the Bill was lost." (Neal's History of New England, Vol. II., Chap. xi., p. 474.)

    Mr. J. G. Barry says: "Anxious for the restoration of the old Charter and its privileges, under which the colony had prospered so well, the agent applied himself diligently to that object, advising with the wisest statesmen for its accomplishment. It was the concurrent judgment of all that the best course would be to obtain a reversion of the judgment against the Charter by Act of Parliament, and then apply to the King for such additional privileges as were necessary. Accordingly in the (Convention) House of Commons, *where the whole subject of seizing Charters in the reign of Charles the Second was up, the Charters of New England were inserted with the rest,* and though enemies opposed the measure, it was voted with the rest as a grievance, and that they should be forthwith restored. Thus the popular branch of the Parliament acted favourably towards the colonies; but as the Bill was yet to be submitted to the House of Lords, great pains were taken to interest that branch of the Parliament in the measure; and at the same time letters having arrived giving an account of the proceedings in Boston, another interview was held with the King, before whom, in 'a most excellent speech,' Mr. Mather 'laid the state of the people,' and his Majesty was pleased to signify his acceptance of what had been done in New England, and his intention to restore the inhabitants to their ancient privileges; but 'behold,' adds the narrative, 'while the Charter Bill was depending. the Convention

    (a) This was very ingenious on the part of Dr. Increase Mather to say that the people of New England were called "Presbyterians" as well as "Congregationalists," as the Church of Holland, of which King William as Prince of Orange was Stadtholder, was "Presbyterian." But Dr. Mather did not inform the King that the Presbyterian worship was no more tolerated in Massachusetts than was the Baptist or Episcopalian worship.

of King James, Dr. Mather was introduced to the Prince of
Orange by Lord Wharton, and presented the circular before
mentioned, for confirming Governors being sent to New England.
The 14th of March, Lord Wharton introduced him again to the
King, when, after humbly congratulating his Majesty on his
accession, Dr. Mather implored his Majesty's favour to New
England. The King promised all the favour in his power, but
hinted at what had been irregular in their former government;
whereupon Dr. Mather undertook that upon the first word
they would reform any irregularities they should be advised of,
and Lord Wharton offered to be their guarantee. The King
then said that he would give orders that Sir Edmund Andros
should be removed and called to an account for his mal-
administration, and that the King and Queen should be proclaimed (in Massachusetts) by the former magistrates. Dr.
Mather was a faithful agent, and was unwearied in securing
friends for his country. Besides several of the nobility and
principal commoners, he had engaged the dissenting ministers,
whose weight at that time was far from inconsiderable.*

Dr. Mather's earnestness, ability, and appeals made a favourable impression on the mind of the King, supported as they
were by liberal Churchmen as well as Nonconformists, and also by
the entreaties of the Queen. The King, on the eve of going to
Holland, where he was long detained—which delayed the issuing
of the Massachusetts Charter for twelve months—directed the
Chief Justice, Attorney and Solicitor-Generals to prepare the
draft of a new Charter for Massachusetts. They did so, embodying the provisions of the old Charter, with additional provisions to give powers which had not been given but had been

Parliament was unexpectedly prorogued and afterwards dissolved, and the
Sisyphæan labour of the whole year came to nothing.' All that was obtained
was an order that the Government of the colony should be continued under
the old Charter until a new one was settled ; and a letter from the King was
forwarded to that effect, signed by the Earl of Nottingham, for the delivery
of Sir Edmund Andros and the others detained with him, who were to be sent
to England for trial." (Barry's History of Massachusetts, First Period, Chap.
xviii., pp. 508—510.)

* Hutchinson's History of Massachusetts Bay, Vol. I., pp. 388, 389. But,
in addition, Mr. Mather had the countenance of Archbishop Tillotson and
Bishop Burnet, who had not only received him kindly, but recommended his
applications to the favourable consideration of the King.

usurped in the administration of the old Charter.   The majority
of the King's Council disapproved of this draft of Charter, and
directed the preparation of a second draft.   Both drafts were
sent over to Holland to the King, with the reasons for and
against each; his Majesty agreed with the majority of his
Council in disapproving of the first, and approving of the second
draft of Charter.*

But even before the King and his Council decided upon the
provisions of the new Charter, he determined upon appointing a
Governor for Massachusetts, while meeting their wishes as far
as possible in his selection of the Governor ; for, as Mr. Neal says,
"Two days after he had heard Dr. Mather against continuing
the Governor and officers appointed over Massachusetts by
King James the Second, but restoring the old officers, the King
inquired of the Chief Justice and some other Lords of the

* The King, on starting for Holland, "left orders with his Attorney-General
to draw up a draft of Charter, according as his Majesty expressed in Council,
to be ready for him to sign at his return.   The Attorney-General presented
his draft to the Council Board, June the 8th (1691), which was rejected, and
a new one ordered to be drawn up, which deprived the people of New
England of several essential privileges contained in their former Charter.
Mr. Mather in his great zeal protested against it ; but was told that the agents
of New England were not plenipotentiaries from a foreign State, and therefore must submit to the King's pleasure.   The agents, having obtained a
copy of this Charter, sent over their objections against it to the King, in
Flanders, praying that certain clauses which they pointed out to his Majesty
in their petition might be altered.   And the Queen herself, with her own
royal hand, wrote to the King that the Charter of New England might pass
as it was drawn up by the Attorney-General at first, or be deferred till his
return.   But, after all, it was his Majesty's pleasure that the Charter of New
England should run in the main points according to the second draft ; and
all that the agents could do was to get two or three articles which they
apprehended to be for the good of the country added to it.   The expectations
of the people (of the Congregationalists) of New England were very much disappointed, and their agents were censured as men not very well skilled in the
intrigues of a Court.   It was thought that if they had applied themselves to the
proper persons, and in a right way, they might have made better terms for
their country ; but they acted in the uprightness of their hearts, though the
success did not answer their expectations.   It was debated among them
whether they should accept of the new Charter or stand a trial at law for
reversing the judgment against the old one ; but, upon the advice of some
of the best politicians and lawyers, the majority resolved to acquiesce in the
King's pleasure and accept what was now offered them." (Neal's History of
New England, Vol. II., Chap. xi., pp. 476, 477.)

Council whether, without the breach of law, he might appoint a Governor over New England ? To which they answered that whatever might be the merits of the cause, inasmuch as the Charter of New England stood vacated by a judgment against them, it was in the King's power to put them under that form of government he should think best for them. The King replied, he believed then it would be for the advantage of the people of that colony to be under a Governor appointed by himself ; nevertheless, because of what Dr. Mather had spoken to him, he would consent that the agents of New England should nominate such a person as would be agreeable to the inclinations of the people there ; but, notwithstanding this, he would have Charter privileges restored and confirmed to them."*

It seems to me that King William was not actuated by any theoretical notions of high prerogative, as attributed to him by Messrs. Bancroft and Palfrey, in regard to Massachusetts, but was anxious to restore to that colony every just privilege and power desired, with the exception of the power of the Congregationalists of Massachusetts to prosecute and persecute their fellow-religionists of other persuasions, and of depriving them and other colonists of the right of appeal to the protection of England.† This continued possession of usurped powers by the Congregationalists of Massachusetts, of sole legislation and government under the first Charter, and which they so merci-

* Neal's History of New England, Vol. II., Chap. xi., p. 476.

Massachusetts would doubtless have retained the election of their Governor and their first Charter, as did the colonies of Rhode Island and Connecticut, had her rulers submitted to the conditions on which Charles the Second proposed to continue their Charter. Mr. Hildreth says : " The Charters of Connecticut and Rhode Island never having been formally annulled, and having already been resumed, were pronounced by the English lawyers to be in full force. * * The English lawyers held that the judgment which Massachusetts had persisted in braving was binding and valid in law, until renewed by a writ of error, of which there was little or no hope." (History of the United States, Chap. xviii., pp. 94, 95.)

† " The platform of Church government which they settled was of the Congregational mode, connecting the several Churches together to a certain degree, and yet exempting each of them from any jurisdiction, by way of censure or any power extensive to their own. * * * No man could be qualified to elect or be elected to office who was not a Church member, and no Church could be formed but by a license from a magistrate ; so that the civil and ecclesiastical powers were intimately combined. The clergy were

lessly and disloyally exercised for more than half a century, was manifestly the real ground of their opposition to a new Charter, and especially to the second and final draft of it. Their agent in England, Dr. Increase Mather, who had inflamed and caused the citizens of Boston, and a majority of the popular Assembly of the Legislature, to reject the conditions insisted upon by Charles the Second, and contest in a Court of law the continuance of the first Charter, with their pretensions under it, said that he would rather die than consent to the provisions of the second draft of Charter,* and sent his objections to it to King

consulted about the laws, were frequently present at the passing of them, and by the necessity of their influence in the origination, demonstrated how much the due execution of them depended on their power.

" But the error of establishing one rule for all men in ecclesiastical policy and discipline (which experience has proved cannot be maintained, even in matters of indifference) could not fail of discovering itself in very serious instances as the Society increased. The great body of the English nation being of a different persuasion in this respect, numbers belonging to their Church, who came into the country, necessarily formed an opposition which, as they had the countenance of the King, could not be crushed like those other sectaries. It became a constant subject of royal attention, to allow freedom and liberty of conscience, especially in the use of the Common Prayer, and the rights of sacrament and baptism as thereby prescribed. The law confining the rights of freemen to Church members was at length repealed (in pretence) ; and pecuniary qualifications for those who were not Church members, with good morals and the absurd requisite of orthodoxy of opinion, certified by a clergyman, were substituted in its place. But the great ascendency which the Congregationalists had gained over every other sect made the chance of promotion to office, and the share of influence in general, very unequal, and was, without doubt, one of the most important causes which conspired to the loss of the Charter." (Minot's Continuation of the History of the Province of Massachusetts Bay, etc., Vol. I., Chap. i., pp. 29—31.)

* Mr. Mather was so dissatisfied that he declared that he would sooner part with his life than consent to them. He was told 'the agents of Massachusetts were not plenipotentiaries from a sovereign State ; if they declared they would not submit to the King's pleasure, his Majesty would settle the country, and they might take what would follow.' Sir Henry Ashurst with Mr. Mather withdrew, notwithstanding, their objections against the minutes of Council. The objections were presented to the Attorney-General (Treby), and laid before the Council, and a copy sent to the King in Flanders; but all had no effect. The King approved of the minutes and disliked the objections to them, and the Charter was drawn up by Mr. Blaithwait according to them." (Hutchinson's History of Massachusetts Bay, Vol. I., pp. 409—411.)

William, who was in Holland. The King disapproved of Dr. Mather's objections, and approved of the Charter as revised and as was finally issued, and under which Massachusetts was governed and prospered for three-fourths of a century, notwithstanding the continued opposition of a set of separationists and smugglers in Boston, who had always been the enemies of loyal and liberal government under the first Charter.* But when the new Charter passed the Seals, and the nomination of the first Governor was left to the agent of Massachusetts, Dr. Mather changed his language of protest into that of gratitude. He nominated Sir William Phips ; and on being introduced to the King, at parting, by the Earl of Nottingham, made the following speech :

"Sir, I do, in behalf of New England, most humbly thank your Majesty, in that you have been pleased by a Charter to restore English liberties unto them, to confirm them in their properties, and to grant them some peculiar privileges. I doubt

---

* "A people who were of opinion that their Commonwealth was established by free consent (a); that the place of their habitation was their own ; that no man had a right to enter into their society without their permission ; that they had the full and absolute power of governing all the people by men chosen from among themselves, and according to such laws as they should see fit to establish, not repugnant to those of England (a restriction and limitation which they wholly ignored and violated), they paying only the fifth part of the ore of gold and silver that should be there found for all duties, demands, exactions, and services whatsoever; of course, that they held the keys of their territory, and had a right to prescribe the terms of naturalization to all noviciates; such a people, I say, whatever alterations they might make in their polity, from reason and conviction of their own motion, would not be easily led to comply with the same changes, when required by a king to whom they held themselves subject, and upon whose authority they were dependent only according to their Charter ; and we shall find that their compliance was accordingly slow and occasional, as necessity compelled them to make it." (Minot's Continuation of the History of Massachusetts Bay, Vol. I., pp. 42, 43.)

(a) *Note* by the Author.—The Colony of Plymouth was established in 1620, by free consent, by the Pilgrim Fathers on board of the *Mayflower*, without a Charter ; yet that colony was always tolerant and loyal. But the Colony of Massachusetts Bay was established by the Puritan Fathers in 1629, under the authority of a Royal Charter ; and it was the pretension to and assumption of independent power and absolute government, though a chartered colony, that resulted in their disloyalty to England and intolerance towards all classes of their fellow-colonists not Congregationalists.

not but your subjects will demean themselves with that dutiful affection and loyalty to your Majesty, as that you will see cause to enlarge your Royal favour towards them; and I do most humbly thank your Majesty that you have been pleased to leave to those that are concerned for New England to nominate their Governor."

"Sir William Phips has been accordingly nominated by us at the Council Board. He has done good service to the Crown, by enlarging your dominions and reducing Nova Scotia to your obedience; I know that he will faithfully serve your Majesty to the utmost of his capacity; and if your Majesty shall think fit to confirm him in that place, it will be a further obligation to your subjects there."

"Hereupon Sir William Phips was admitted to kiss his Majesty's hand; and was, by commission under the Broad Seal, appointed Captain-General over the Province of Massachusetts Bay, in New England."*

In the preamble of the Charter, the dates, objects and provisions of previous Charters are recited, and titles to property, etc., acquired under them confirmed; after which it was provided—

1. That there should be "one Governor, one Lieutenant or Deputy Governor, one Secretary of the Province, twenty-eight councillors or members of assembly, to be chosen by popular

---

* Neal's History of New England, Vol. II., pp. 480, 481.

"Sir William Phips was born, of mean and obscure parents, at a small plantation in the eastern part of New England, on the banks of the River Kennebeck, February 2, 1620; his father was a gunsmith, and left his mother a widow, with a large family of small children. William, being one of the youngest, kept sheep in the wilderness until he was eighteen years of age, and was then bound apprentice to a ship carpenter. When he was out of his time he took to the sea, and after several adventures, at last made his fortune by finding a Spanish wreck near Port de la Plata, which got him a great deal of reputation at the English Court, and introduced him into the acquaintance of the greatest men of the nation. Though King James II. gave him the honour of knighthood, yet he always opposed his arbitrary measures, as appears by his refusing the Government of New England when offered to him by a messenger of the abdicated King. Sir William joined heartily in the Revolution, and used his interest at the Court of King William and Queen Mary for obtaining a Charter for his country, in conjunction with the rest of the agents, for which, and his other great services, they nominated him to the King as the most acceptable and deserving person they could think of for Governor."—*Ib.*, pp. 544, 545.

election, and to possess and exercise the general powers of legislation and government."

2. That there should be "liberty of conscience allowed in the worship of God to all Christians (except Papists) inhabiting, or which shall inhabit or be resident within our said province or territory."

3. That " all our subjects should have liberty to appeal to us, our heirs and successors, in case either party shall not rest satisfied with the judgment or sentence of any judicatories or courts within our said province or territory, in any personal action wherein the matter of difference doth exceed the value of three hundred pounds sterling, provided such appeals be made within fourteen days after the sentence or judgment given."

4. That the Governor and General Assembly should have "full power and authority, from time to time, to make, ordain and establish all manner of wholesome and reasonable orders, laws, statutes or ordinances, directions, and instructions, either with penalties or without (so as the same be not repugnant or contrary to the laws of this our realm of England), as they shall judge to be for the good and welfare of our said province or territory."

5. That in the framing and passing of all orders, laws, etc., the Governor should have " a negative voice, subject also to the approbation or disallowance of the King within three years after the passing thereof."

6. That " every freeholder or person holding land within the province or territory, to the annual value of forty shillings, or other estate of fifty pounds sterling, should have a vote in the election of members to serve in the General Court or Assembly."

7. That " the King should appoint, from time to time, the Governor, Lieutenant-Governor, and Secretary of the Province ; but that the Governor, with the advice and consent of the Council or Assistants, from time to time should nominate and appoint Judges, Commissioners of Oyer and Terminer, Sheriffs, Provosts, Marshals, Justices of the Peace," etc.

8. The usual oath of allegiance and supremacy was required to be taken by all persons appointed to office, free from the restrictions and neutralising mutilations introduced into the oath of allegiance by the ecclesiastico-political oligarchy of the Massachusetts Bay Colony under the first Charter.

9. The new Charter also incorporated "*Plymouth* and *Maine, and a tract further east* in the province of Massachusetts." The Plymouth Colony of the Pilgrim Fathers had existed from 1620 to 1690 as a separate Colonial Government, first established by common consent, under seven successive Governors. It now ceased to exist as a distinct Government, to the great regret of its inhabitants, after having been administered tolerantly and loyally for a period of seventy years, as has been narrated above, in Chap. II.

Such is an abstract of the provisions of the second Massachusetts Charter—provisions similar to those which have been incorporated into the constitution and government of every British North American Province for the last hundred years.*

It remains to note how the new Charter was received, and what was the effect of its operation. A faction in Boston opposed its reception, and desired to resume the old contests; but a large majority of the deputies and the great body of the colony cordially and thankfully accepted the new Charter as a great improvement upon the first Charter in terminating their dis-

---

* Modern historians of New England generally speak of the Massachusetts Colony as having been unjustly deprived of its first Charter, after having faithfully observed it for more than half a century, and of having been treated harshly in not having the Charter restored. While Dr. Mather was earnestly seeking the restoration of the Charter at the hands of King William, Mr. Hampden (grandson of the famous John Hampden) consulted Mr. Hooke, a counsellor of note of the Puritan party, and friend of New England. Mr. Hooke stated that "a bare restoration of the Charter of Massachusetts would be of no service at all," as appears both from the Charter itself and the practice of that colony, who have hardly pursued the terms thereof in any one instance, which has given colour to evil-minded men to give them disturbance.

"I. As to the Charter itself, that colony, should they have their Charter, would want—

"1. Power to call a Parliament, or select assembly; for their many thousand freemen have, thereby, an equal right to sit in their General Assembly.

"2. Power to levy taxes and raise money, especially on inhabitants not being of the company, and strangers coming to or trading thither.

"3. They have not any Admiralty.

"4. Nor have they power to keep a Prerogative Court, prove wills, etc.

"5. Nor to erect Courts of Judicature, especially Chancery Courts.

"II. The deficiency of their Charter appears from their practice, wherein

putes and defining their relations with England, in putting an
end to a denominational franchise and tyranny inconsistent
with religious or civil liberty, and in placing the elective franchise, eligibility to office, legislation and government upon the

they have not had respect thereto ; but having used the aforesaid powers
without any grant, they have exercised their Charter powers, also, otherwise
than the Charter directed :

" 1. They have made laws contrary to the laws of England.

" 2. Their laws have not been under their seal.

" 3. They have not used their name of corporation.

" 4. They have not used their seal in their grants.

" 5. They have not kept their General Courts, nor

" 6. Have they observed the number of assistants appointed by the
Charter." (Hutchinson's History of Massachusetts Bay, Vol. I., pp. 410,
411, in a note.)

It is clear from the legal opinion, as has been shown in the foregoing pages,
that the first Puritans of Massachusetts, though only a chartered company, set
up an independent government, paid no attention whatever to the provisions
of the Charter under which they held their land and had settled the colony,
but acted in entire disregard and defiance of the authority, which had granted
their Charter.   Mr. Neal very candidly says : " The old Charter was, in the
opinion of persons learned in the law, defective as to several powers which
are absolutely necessary to the subsistence of the Plantation : for example, it
gave the Government no more power than every corporation in England has ;
power in capital cases was not expressed in it ; it mentioned no House of
Deputies, or Assembly of Representatives ; the Government had thereby no
legal power to impose taxes on the inhabitants that were not freemen (that
is, on *four-fifths* of the male population), nor to erect Courts of Admiralty, so
that if the judgment against this Charter should be reversed, yet if the
Government of New England should exercise the same powers as they had
done before the *quo warranto*, a new writ of *scire facias* might undoubtedly be
issued out against them.   Besides, if the old Charter should have been restored
without a grant of some other advantages, the country would have been very
much incommoded, because the provinces of *Maine* and *New Hampshire* would
have been taken from Massachusetts, and *Plymouth* would have been annexed
to New York, whereby the Massachusetts Colony would have been very much
straitened and have made a mean figure both as to its trade and influence.

" The new Charter grants a great many privileges to New England which
it had not before.   The colony is now made a province, and the General Court
has, with the King's approbation, as much power in New England as the
King and Parliament have in England.   They have all English liberties, and
can be touched by no law, by no tax, but of their own making.   All the
liberties of their religion are for ever secured, and their titles to their lands,
once, for want of some form of conveyance, contested, are now confirmed for
ever." (History of New England, Vol. II., pp. 478, 479.)

broad foundation of public freedom and equal rights to all classes of citizens.*

The influence of the new Charter upon the social state of Massachusetts, as well as upon its legislation and government, was manifestly beneficial. Judge Story observes: "After the grant of the provincial Charter, in 1691, the legislation of the colony took a wider scope, and became more liberal as well as more exact."†

The improved spirit of loyalty was not less conspicuous. Mr. Neal, writing more than twenty years (1720) after the granting of the new Charter, says: " The people of New England are a dutiful and loyal people. * * King George is not known to have a single enemy to his person, family, or government in New England."‡

The influence of the new state of things upon the spirit of

---

* Although a party was formed which opposed submission to the Charter, yet the majority of the Court wisely and thankfully accepted it, and appointed a day of solemn thanksgiving to Almighty God for "granting a safe arrival to His Excellency the Governor and the Rev. Mr. Increase Mather, who have industriously endeavoured the service of the people, and have brought over with them ' a settlement of government, in which their Majesties have graciously given us distinguishing marks of their Royal favour and goodness.' " (Hutchinson's History of Massachusetts Bay, Vol. I., p. 416.)

Judge Story remarks: "With a view to advance the growth of the province by encouraging new settlements, it was expressly provided ' that there should be liberty of conscience allowed in the worship of God to all Christians, except Papists ;' and that all subjects inhabiting in the province, and their children born there, or on the seas going and returning, should have all the liberties and immunities of free and natural subjects, as if they were born within the realm of England. And in all cases an appeal was allowed from the judgments of any Courts of the province to the King in the Privy Council in England, where the matter of difference exceeded three hundred pounds sterling. And finally there was a reservation of the whole Admiralty jurisdiction to the Crown, and of the right to all subjects to fish on the coasts. Considering the spirit of the times, it must be acknowledged that, on the whole, the Charter contains a liberal grant of authority to the province and a reasonable reservation of royal perogative. It was hailed with sincere satisfaction by the colony after the dangers which had so long a time menaced its liberties and peace." (Story's Commentaries on the Constitution of the United States, Vol. I., Book i., Chap. iv., p. 41.)

† *Ib.*, Vol. I., Book i., Chap. iv., p. 45.

‡ History of New England, Vol. II., p. 616.

toleration and of Christian charity among Christians of different denominations, and on society at large, was most remarkable.   In a sermon preached on a public Fast Day, March 22, 1716 (and afterwards published), by the Rev. Mr. Coleman, one of the ministers of Boston, we have the following words :

" If there be any customs in our Churches, derived from our ancestors, wherein those terms of Church communion are imposed which Christ has not imposed in the New Testament, they ought to be laid aside, for they are justly to be condemned by us, because we complain of imposing in other communions, and our fathers fled for the same.   If there ever was a custom among us, whereby communion in our Churches was made a test for the enjoyment of civil privileges in the State, we have done well long since to abolish such corrupt and persecuting maxims, which are a mischief to any free people, and a scandal to any communion to retain.   If there were of old among our fathers any laws enacted or judgments given or executions done according to those laws which have carried too much the face of cruelty and persecution, we ought to be humbled greatly for such errors of our fathers, and confess them to have been sinful ; and blessed be God for the more catholic spirit of charity which now distinguishes us.   Or if any of our fathers have dealt proudly in censuring and judging others who differed from them in modes of worship, let us their posterity the rather be clothed with humility, meekness, and charity, preserving truth and holiness with the laudable zeal of our predecessors " (pp. 20, 21, 22).

The Rev. Dr. Cotton Mather, the distinguished son of the famous Rev. Dr. Increase Mather, but more tolerant than his father, has a passage equally significant and suggestive with that just quoted from Mr. Coleman :

"In this capital city of Boston," says Dr. Cotton Mather, "there are ten assemblies of Christians of different persuasions, who live lovingly and peaceably together, doing all the offices of good neighbourhood for one another in such manner as may give a sensible rebuke to all the bigots of uniformity, and show them how consistent a variety of rites in religion may be with the tranquillity of human society, and may demonstrate to the world that such persecution for conscientious dissents in religion is an *abomination of desolation—*

a thing whereof all wise and just men will say, *cursed be its anger, for it is fierce, and its wrath, for it is cruel.*"*

It is not needful that I should trace the legislation and government of the Province of Massachusetts under the second Charter with the same minuteness with which I have narrated

---

* Fellowship of the Churches : Annexed to the Sermon preached on the Ordination of Mr. Prince, p. 76 ; Boston, 1718 ; quoted in Neal's History of New England, Vol. II., pp. 610, 611.

But the spirit of the old leaven of bigotry and persecution remained with not a few of the old Congregational clergy, who were jealous for the honour of those days when they ruled both Church and State, silenced and proscribed all dissenters from their own opinions and forms of worship. They could not endure any statements which reflected upon the justice and policy of those palmy days of ecclesiastical oligarchy, and were very much stung by some passages in Neal's History of New England. The celebrated Dr. Isaac Watts seems to have been written to on the subject. His letter, apparently in reply, addressed to the Rev. Dr. Cotton Mather, dated February 19, 1720, is very suggestive. The sweet poet and learned divine says :

"Another thing I take occasion to mention to you at this time is my good friend Mr. Neal's History of New England. He has been for many years pastor of a Congregational Church in London—a man of valuable talents in the ministry. I could wish indeed that he had communicated his design to you, but I knew nothing of it till it was almost out of the press. * * He has taken merely the task of an historian upon him. Considered as such (as far as I can judge), most of the chapters are well written, and in such a way as to be very acceptable to the present age.

"But the freedom he has taken to expose the persecuting principles and practices of the first Planters, both in the body of his history and his abridgment of their laws, has displeased some persons here, and perhaps will be offensive there. I must confess I sent for him this week, and gave him my sense freely on this subject. I could wish he had more modified some of his relations, and had rather left out those laws, or in some page had annexed something to prevent our enemies from insulting both us and you on that subject. His answer was, that 'the fidelity of an historian required him to do what he had done;' and he has, at the end of the first and second volumes, given such a character of the present ministers and inhabitants of the country as may justly secure this generation from all scandal ; and that it is a nobler thing to tell the world that you have rectified the errors of your fathers, than if mere education had taught you so large a charity. He told me likewise that he had shown in the preface that all such laws as are inconsistent with the laws of England are, *ipso facto*, repealed by your new Charter. But methinks it would be better to have such cruel and sanguinary statutes as those under the title of ' Heresy' repealed in form, and by the public authority of the nation ; and if the appearance of this book in your

that of Massachusetts Bay under the first Charter.   The successive Governors appointed by England over the province were, upon the whole, men of good sense, and were successful in their administration, notwithstanding the active opposition of a Boston disaffected party that prevented any salary being granted to the Judges or Governor for more than one year at a time. Yet, upon the whole, the new system of government in the Province of Massachusetts was considered preferable to that of the neighbouring colonies of Rhode Island and Connecticut, which retained their old Charters and elected their Governors. Mr. Hutchinson says:

"Seventy years' practice under a new Charter, in many respects to be preferred to the old, has taken away not only all expectation, but all desire, of ever returning to the old Charter. We do not envy the neighbouring Governments which retained and have ever since practised upon their ancient Charters. Many of the most sensible in those Governments would be glad to be under the same Constitution that the Massachusetts Province happily enjoys.*

But Massachusetts and other New England colonies had incurred considerable debts in their wars with the Indians, prompted and aided by the French, who sought the destruction of the English colonies.   But most of these debts were incurred by loans to individual inhabitants and by the issue of paper money, which became greatly depreciated and caused much confusion and embarrassment in the local and Transatlantic trade.†

country shall awaken your General Assembly to attempt to fulfil such a noble piece of service to your country, there will be a happy effect of that part of the history which now makes us blush and be ashamed.

"I have taken the freedom to write a line or two to your most excellent Governor on this subject, which I entreat you to deliver, with my salutation; and I assure myself that Dr. Mather will have a zealous hand in promoting so gracious a work if it may be thought expedient to attempt it." (Collections of the Massachusetts Historical Society, First Series, Vol. V., pp. 200, 201.)

The "glorious work" advised by Dr. Watts was not "attempted," and the "cruel and persecuting statutes passed by the Congregational Court of Massachusetts Bay were never repealed by any "public authority" of that colony, but were tacitly annulled and superseded by the provisions of the "new Charter" of King William and Mary in favour of toleration and civil liberty.

* History of Massachusetts Bay, Vol. I., p. 415.
† The effect of so much paper was to drive all gold and silver out of circu-

At the close of the war between England and France by the peace and treaty of Aix-la-Chapelle, 1749, Mr. Hutchinson thus describes the state of Massachusetts :

"The people of Massachusetts Bay were never in a more easy and happy situation than at the conclusion of the war with France (1749). By the generous reimbursement of the whole charge (£183,000) incurred by the expedition against Cape Breton, the province was set free from a heavy debt in which it must otherwise have remained involved, and was enabled to exchange a depreciating paper medium, which had long been the sole instrument of trade, for a stable medium of silver and gold ; the advantages whereof to all branches of their commerce was evident, and excited the envy of other colonies ; in each of which paper was the principal currency."*

lation, to raise the nominal prices of all commodities, and to increase the rate of exchange on England. Great confusion and perplexity ensued, and the community was divided in opinion, the most being urgent for the issue of more paper money. For this purpose a project was started for a Land-Bank, which was established in Massachusetts, the plan of which was to issue bills upon the pledge of lands. All who were in difficulty advocated this, because they hoped that in the present case they might shift their burdens on to some one else. It was then resisted, and another plan was devised and carried (1714), namely, the issuing of £50,000 of bills of credit by Government, to be loaned to individuals at 5 per cent. interest, to be secured by estates, and to be repaid one-fifth part yearly. This quieted the Land-Bank party for a while. But the habit of issuing bills of credit continued, and was very seductive.

"In 1741, Rhode Island issued £40,000 in paper money, to be loaned to the inhabitants. In 1717, New Hampshire issued £15,000 paper money. In 1733, Connecticut issued £20,000 on the loan system for the first time, Rhode Island made another issue of £100,000." (Elliott's New England History, Vol. II., Chap. xii., p. 230.)

* History of the Province of Massachusetts Bay from 1749 to 1774, p. 1.

CHAPTER VIII.

MASSACHUSETTS AND OTHER COLONIES DURING THE SECOND WAR BETWEEN
GREAT BRITAIN AND FRANCE, FROM THE PEACE OF AIX-LA-CHAPELLE,
1748, TO THE PEACE OF PARIS IN 1763.

BY the peace of Aix-la-Chapelle, France and England retained
their respective possessions as they existed before the war.
Louisburg, which had been captured from the French in 1745
by the skill of the British Admiral Warren, aided most courage-
ously by the Massachusetts volunteers, was therefore restored
to the French, much to the regret and mortification of the New
England colonies, by whom the enterprise against that powerful
and troublesome fortress had first been devised and undertaken.
By the treaty between France and England, the boundaries of
their possessions in America were left undefined, and were to
be settled by Commissioners appointed by the two countries.
But the Commissioners, when they met at Paris, could not agree ;
the questions of these boundaries remained unsettled; and the
French in Canada, with the Indians, nearly all of whom were in
alliance with them, were constantly making aggressions and
committing cruel outrages upon the English colonists in the
back parts of New England, New York, Pennsylvania, and
Virginia, who felt that their only security for life, property,
and liberty was the extinction of French power in America,
and the subjection of the Indians by conquest or conciliation.
The six years which followed the peace of 1748 witnessed
frequent and bloody collisions between the English colonists
and their French and Indian Canadian neighbours, until, in
1756, England formally declared war against France—a war
which continued seven years, and terminated in the extinction
of French power in Canada, and in the enlargement of the

British possessions from Labrador to Florida and Louisiana, and from the Atlantic to the Pacific. This war, in its origin and many scenes of its conflicts and conquests, was an American-Colonial war, and the American colonies were the gainers by its results, for which British blood and treasure had been lavishly expended. In this protracted and eventful conflict, the British Government were first prompted and committed, and then nobly seconded by the colonies, Massachusetts acting the most prominent part.

The last act of the British Government, pursuant to the treaty of Aix-la-Chapelle in 1748, was to restore to the French Government Louisburg, in return for the strongly fortified fort of Madras, which had been wrested from the French by the colonists, assisted by Admiral Warren with a few English ships in 1745; and the first act of the French Government, after the restoration to them of Louisburg, was to prepare for wresting from Great Britain all her American colonies.* They despatched soldiers and all kinds of military stores; encroached upon and built fortresses in the British province of Nova Scotia, and in the provinces of Pennsylvania and Virginia,† and erected a chain of forts, and planted garrisons

* "The French, upon recovering Louisburg, had laid the scheme (the particulars of which shall be exhibited in their due place) for engrossing the whole empire of North America, and in a manner for extirpating the English interest there. Notice of this was, soon after the peace of Aix-la-Chapelle, given to the English Government by their Governors in America, and proper instructions were dispatched to them to resist all encroachments attempted to be made upon the English territories. The Earl of Albemarle (British Ambassador in Paris) had orders from his Court to remonstrate on this occasion; but his remonstrances had so little effect that the French seemed rather encouraged than deterred from their usurpations. The English Governors in America daily sent over complaints of the French encroachments there, which were too little regarded, in hopes of matters being compromised." (Rapin's History of England, Vol. XXI., p. 418.)

† "But their encroachments went further (than Nova Scotia), and this year (1754) they began to make settlements upon the River Ohio, within the limits of the British possessions in the western parts of Virginia. They had likewise committed many hostilities against British subjects in other parts of America."

"All the while the French were multiplying their hostilities and strengthening their usurpations by new recruits of men, money, provisions of all kinds, and ammunition, and some of the best officers in France."

"When the Government of England complained to the French Court of

along the line of the British provinces, from the St. Lawrence to the Ohio river, and thence to the Mississippi.*

The only means at the command of Great Britain to counteract and defeat these designs of France to extinguish the English colonies in America was to prevent them from carrying men, cannon, and other munitions of war hither, by capturing their

those encroachments, the Ministry gave evasive answers, and promised that everything should be amicably adjusted ; but without desisting from their usurpations, which became every day more and more intolerable.   The English, perceiving this, sent general orders to all their Governors in America to repel force by force, and to drive them from all the settlements which they had made contrary to the faith of treaties, and especially along the Ohio." (Rapin's History of England, Vol. XXI., pp. 478—491.)

* "They had been incessantly making settlements upon the English property since the peace of Aix-la-Chapelle, and at last they made a settlement on the western part of Virginia, upon the River Ohio.   Mr. Dinwiddie (Governor of Virginia) having intelligence of this, sent an officer, Major Washington, with a letter to the French commandant there, requiring him to desist, and with orders, if possible, to bring the Indians over to the British interest.   Washington had but indifferent success with the Indians ; and when he arrived with some of the Indians at the French settlements, he found the French by no means inclined to give over their undertaking, and that the Indians, notwithstanding all their fair promises, were much more in their interest than in that of England.   Upon further inquiry it was found that the Indians called the Six Nations, who, by the treaty of Utrecht, were acknowledged to be subject to Great Britain, had been entirely debauched by the French, who had likewise found means to bring over to their interest those vast tracts that lie along the great lakes and rivers to the west of the Apalachian (or Allegany) mountains.

"Having thus got the friendship of those Indians, they next contrived how they could cut them off from all communication with the English, and for that purpose they seized the persons and effects of all the English whom they found trading with the Indians ; and they erected a chain of forts from Canada to Mississippi, to prevent all future communication between the English and those Indians ; at the same time destroying such of the Indians as discovered any affection or regard for the British subjects : so that in a very few years all the eastern as well as the western colonies of Great Britain were in danger of being ruined."—*Ib.*, pp. 290, 291.)

"Though the several provinces belonging to Great Britain, in the neighbourhood of the French encroachments, raised both men and money against them, yet the forms of their legal proceedings in their assemblies were so dilatory that the French always had the start of them, and they surprised a place called Log's Town, belonging to the Virginians, on the Ohio. This was a place of great importance, and the French made themselves masters of the block-house and the truck-house, with skins and other com-

ships thus laden and employed; but the French Government thought that the British Government would not proceed to such extremities, for fear that the former would make war upon the German possessions of the latter, the King of England being the Elector of Hanover. Besides, the proceedings of the French in America were remote and concealed under various pretexts; the French Government could oppose a general denial to the complaints made as to its encroachments on British territory and settlements in the distant wilderness of America; while any attack by England upon French ships at sea would be known at once to all Europe, and excite prejudice against England for such an act in time of peace against a neighbouring nation. The designs and dishonesty of the French Government in these proceedings are thus stated by Rapin:

"Though the French in all their seaports were making the greatest preparations for supporting their encroachments in America, yet the strongest assurances came to England from that Ministry that no such preparations were making, and that no hostility was intended by France against Great Britain or her dependencies. These assurances were generally communicated to the British Ministry by the Duke of Mirepoix, the French Ambassador to London, who was himself so far imposed upon that he believed them to be sincere, and did all in his power to prevent a rupture between the two nations. The preparations, however, were so notorious that they could be no longer concealed, and Mirepoix was upbraided at St. James's with being insincere, and the proofs of his Court's

modities to the amount of £20,000, besides cutting off all the English traders in those parts but two, who found means to escape. About the same time, near 1,000 French, under the command of Monsieur de Carstrecœur, and 18 pieces of cannon, came in 300 canoes from Venango, a fort that they had usurped upon the banks of the Ohio, and surprised an English fort on the forks of the Monongahella. After this, a great many skirmishes happened between the English and the French with various success.

"In the meanwhile, orders came from England to the Governors of the British settlements in America to form a kind of political confederacy, to which every province was to contribute a quota. Though the scheme of political confederacy was the best measure that could be pursued in the situation of the British settlements, yet it had not all the effect that was expected from it." (Rapin's History of England, Vol. XXI., pp. 491, 492.)

double-dealing were laid before him. He appeared to be struck with them ; and complaining bitterly of his being imposed upon, he went in person over to France, where he reproached the Ministry for having made him their tool. They referred him to their King, who ordered him to return to England with fresh assurances of friendship ; but he had scarcely delivered them when undoubted intelligence came that a French fleet from Brest and Rochefort was ready to sail, with a great number of land forces on board. The French fleet, which consisted of twenty-five ships of the line, besides frigates and transports, with a vast number of warlike stores, and between three and four thousand land forces, under Baron Dieskau, were ready to sail from Brest, under Admiral Macnamara. Upon this intelligence, Admiral Holbourne was ordered to reinforce Boscawen with six ships of the line and one frigate ; and a great number of capital ships were put into commission. It was the 6th May (1755) before Macnamara sailed ; but he soon returned with nine of his capital ships, and ordered the rest to proceed under the command of M. Bois de la Mothe.

" When news of so strong a squadron sailing from Brest was confirmed, the people of England grew extremely uneasy for the fate of the squadron under Boscawen and Holbourne ; and it was undoubtedly owing to the bad management of the French that one or both of those squadrons were not destroyed.*

The King, in proroguing Parliament, the 27th of May, 1755, among other things said :

" That he had religiously adhered to the stipulations of the treaty of Aix-la-Chapelle, and made it his care not to injure or

---

* Rapin's History of England, Vol. XXI., pp. 520, 521. Rapin adds :— " While all Europe was in suspense about the fate of the English and French squadrons, the preparations for a vigorous sea war were going on in England with unparalleled spirit and success. Notwithstanding, the French Court still flattered itself that Great Britain, out of tenderness to his Majesty's German dominions, would abstain from hostilities. Mirepoix (the French Ambassador at London) continued to have frequent conferences with the British Ministry, who made no secret that their admirals, particularly Boscawen, had orders to attack the French ships wherever they should meet them ; on the other hand, Mons. de Mirepoix declared that his master would consider the first gun fired at sea, in a hostile manner, as a declaration of war. This menace, far from intimidating the English, animated them to redouble their preparations for war."—*Ib.*, p. 521.

offend any Power whatsoever; but never could he entertain the thoughts of purchasing the name of peace at the expense of suffering encroachments upon, or yielding up, what justly belongs to Great Britain, either by ancient possession or solemn treaties. That the vigour and firmness of his Parliament on this important occasion have enabled him to be prepared for such contingencies as may happen. That, if reasonable and honourable terms of accommodation can be agreed upon, he will be satisfied, and in all events rely on the justice of his cause, the effectual support of his people, and the protection of Divine Providence.*

* Rapin, Vol. XXI., p. 521. It was during this interval that the unfortunate expedition, death, and defeat of General Braddock took place, on the banks of the Ohio river, at Fort du Quesne, afterwards called Pittsburg. "The naval expedition, under Admiral Boscawen, was somewhat more fortunate (than that of Braddock), though far from answering the expectations of the public. He made a prosperous voyage till he came to the banks of Newfoundland, where his rendezvous was; and in a few days the French fleet, under De la Mothe, came to the same station. But the thick fogs which prevail on those coasts, especially at that time of the year, kept the two squadrons from seeing one another; and part of the French squadron escaped up the River St. Lawrence, while some of them went round and got into the same river by the Straits of Belleisle, by a way which had never been attempted before by ships of war. While Boscawen's fleet, however, lay before Cape Race, on the banks of Newfoundland, which was thought to be the proper station for intercepting the enemy, two French ships—the *Alcide*, of 60 guns and 480 men; and the *Lys*, pierced for 64 guns, but mounting only 22, and having eight companies of land forces on board—fell in with the *Dunkirk*, Captain Howe, and the *Defiance*, Captain Andrews, two 60-gun ships of the English squadron, and were, both of them, after a smart engagement, in which Captain (afterwards Lord) Howe behaved with the greatest skill and intrepidity, taken, with about £8,000 on board. Though this action was far from answering the grand destination of the fleet, yet when the news reached England it was of infinite service to the public credit of every kind; as the manner in which it was conducted was a plain proof that the English Government was resolved to observe no further measures with the French, but to take or destroy their ships wherever they could be met with."—*Ib.*, pp. 525, 526.

Yet, in the face of these facts, that the French Government had been encroaching upon the colonies for six years—ever since the treaty of Aix-la-Chapelle; had been transporting soldiers and all the munitions of war to America to exterminate the English colonies; had put to death British subjects; and that complaints of these outrages had been made to England year after year by the Governors and representatives of the Colonies, and that the French Government had at this time, by fair words and false pretences, deceived

This speech to Parliament was delivered a year before war was formally declared between England and France ; and a year before that, in 1754, by royal instructions, a convention of delegates from the Assemblies of the several Colonies was held at Albany, in the Province of New York.   Among other things relative to the union and defence of the Colonies which engaged the attention of this Convention, " a representation was agreed upon in which were set forth the unquestionable designs of the French to prevent the colonies from extending their settle- ments, a line of forts having been erected for this purpose, and many troops transported from France ; and the danger the colonies were in of being driven by the French into the sea, was urged." The representation of the imminent danger to the colonies from the French encroachments probably accele- rated the measures in England which brought on the war with France.*

Mr. Bancroft endeavours again and again to convey the

the Government of England, which had warned the French Government that the English admirals had orders to attack and take all the French ships, public and private, that should be met with at sea; yet, in the face of such facts, Mr. Bancroft, with his habitual hostility to England and endless perver- sions of historical facts, says in 1755 : " France and England were still at peace, and their commerce was mutually protected by the sanctity of treaties. *Of a sudden*, hostile orders were issued to all British vessels of war to take all French vessels, private as well as public," and " eight thousand French seamen were held in captivity. All France resented the perfidy. ' Never,' said Louis the Fifteenth, ' will I forgive the piracies of this insolent nation.' And in a letter to George the Second he demanded ample reparation for the insult to the flag of France by Boscawen, and for the piracies of the English men-of-war, committed in defiance of international law, the faith of treaties, the usages of civilized nations, and the reciprocal duties of kings." (History of the United States, Vol. IV., pp. 217, 218.)

Among the eight thousand French seamen held in captivity were the soldiers destined for America, to invade the British colonies in time of pro- tracted peace and against " the faith of treaties." Mr. Bancroft also ignores the fact that a year before this the Commissioners from the Legislative Assemblies of the several colonies, assembled at Albany, had represented to the British Government the alarming encroachments of the French, and imploring aid, and that the French authorities in America had offered the Indians bounties on English scalps.

* Hutchinson's History of Massachusetts Bay, Vol. III., pp. 21—23.
 " While the Convention was sitting, and attending principally to the frontiers of the colonies, in the western parts, Mr. Shirly (Governor of Massa-

impression that this seven years' war between England and France was a European war, and that the American colonies were called upon, controlled, and attempted to be taxed to aid Great Britain in the contest; yet he himself, in one place, admits the very reverse, and that Great Britain became involved in the war in defence of the American Colonies, as the facts above stated show, and as will appear more fully hereafter. Mr. Bancroft states the whole character and objects of the war, in both America and Europe, in the following words :

"The contest, which had now (1757) spread into both hemispheres, *began in America. The English Colonies, dragging England into their strife,* claimed to advance their frontier, and to include the great central valley of the continent in their system. The *American* question therefore was, shall the continued 'colonization of North America be made under the auspices of English Protestantism and popular liberty, or shall the tottering legitimacy of France, in its connection with Roman Catholic Christianity, win for itself a new empire in that hemisphere? The question of the *European* continent was, shall a Protestant revolutionary kingdom, like Prussia, be permitted to rise up and grow strong within its heart? Considered in its unity as interesting *mankind,* the question was, shall the Reformation, developed to the fulness of Free Inquiry, succeed in its protest against the Middle Age ?

"The war that closed in 1748 had been a mere scramble for advantages, and was sterile of results ; the present conflict, which was to prove a seven years' war, was against the unreformed ; and this was so profoundly true, that all the predictions or personal antipathies of Sovereign and Ministers could not prevent the alliances, collisions, and results necessary to make it so.*

chusetts) was diligently employed in the east, prosecuting a plan for securing the frontiers of Massachusetts Bay."—*Ib.,* p. 25.

"In the beginning of this year (1755) the Assembly of Massachusetts Bay, in New England, passed an Act prohibiting all correspondence with the French at Louisburg ; and early in the spring they raised a body of troops, which was transported to Nova Scotia, to assist Lieutenant-Governor Lawrence in driving the French from the encroachments they had made upon that province." (Hume and Smollett's History of England, Vol. VII., p. 7.)

* History of the United States, Vol. IV., pp. 276, 277.

The object and character of such a war for Protestantism
and liberty, as forcibly stated by Mr. Bancroft himself, was as
honourable to England, as the results of it have been beneficial
to posterity and to the civilization of mankind; yet Mr. Bancroft's sympathies throughout his brilliant but often inconsistent pages are clearly with France against England, the policy
and character of whose statesmen he taxes his utmost ingenuity
and researches to depreciate and traduce, while he admits they
are engaged in the noblest struggle recorded in history.

From 1748 to 1754, the contests in America were chiefly
between the colonists and the French and their Indian allies
(except at sea), and were for the most part unsuccessful on the
part of the colonists, who lost their forts at Oswego and Niagara,
and suffered other defeats and losses. "But in the year 1755,"
says Dr. Minot, "the war in America being now no longer left
to colonial efforts alone, the plan of operations consisted of three
parts. The first was an attack on Fort du Quesne, conducted
by troops from England under General Braddock; the second
was upon the fort at Niagara, which was carried on by American
regulars and Indians (of the Six Nations); and the third was
an expedition against Crown Point, which was supported by
militia from the northern colonies, enlisted merely for that
service."*

The expedition against Fort du Quesne ended in the disgraceful defeat and death of Braddock and one-third of
his men, hundreds of whom were shot down by ambushed
foes whom they never saw. The contemplated attack upon
Niagara was never prosecuted; the expedition against Crown
Point was a failure, and exhaustive of the resources of Massa-

* Minot's History of Massachusetts Bay, Vol. I., p. 228. Dr. Minot adds:
"The whole number assigned for this expedition against Crown Point was
3,700, of which Massachusetts voted to raise 1,560, besides 500 by way of
reinforcement, if judged necessary by the Commander-in-Chief, with the
advice of the Council; and to these 300 more were added after the defeat of
General Braddock. The General Court also voted £600 to be applied
towards engaging the Indians of the Six Nations in the enterprise, and
supporting their families. In short, this became a favourite enterprise both
with the General Court and the people of Massachusetts Bay, not only
because it originated with them, but because it was directed against a
quarter (considering the French in Nova Scotia were subdued and dispersed)
whence they had the most to fear."—*Ib.*, pp. 229, 230.

chusetts; but, as a compensation, Colonel Johnson defeated and took prisoner the French general, Baron Dieskau, for which the King made him a baronet, and the House of Commons voted him a grant of £5,000 sterling.*

The most was made in England as well as the colonies of this decisive victory over a famous French general and his troops, as the year otherwise was disastrous to the English, and "the French, with the assistance of their Indian allies, continued their murders, scalping, capturing, and laying waste the western frontiers of Virginia and Pennsylvania during the whole winter."†

---

* Before Johnson could attack Crown Point, he was himself attacked in his own quarters, at what was called Carrying Place, near Lake George, by Dieskau, at the head of 200 regular troops, 600 Canadians, and 600 savages. Johnson's force consisted of 3,400 provincial soldiers and 300 Indians, "regularly enlisted under the English flag and paid from the English treasury." Among the New England men was Israel Putnam, of Connecticut, then a private soldier, afterwards famous. Mr. Bancroft, as might be expected, depreciates the services of Sir William Johnson in this important and successful battle. But he cannot deny that Johnson selected the most advantageous position for his camp; sent out scouts on all sides, and obtained timely information of the approach of the enemy, and was fully prepared for it; directed the order of battle, in the early part of which he was wounded, causing his removal from the field, when for five hours the provincial soldiers, good marksmen, under their own officers, "kept up the most violent fire that had yet been known in America." The House of Lords, in an address to the King, praised the colonists as "brave and faithful," and Johnson was honoured with a title and money. "But," says Mr. Bancroft, "he did little to gain the victory, which was due to the enthusiasm of the New England men. 'Our all,' they cried, 'depends on the success of this expedition.' 'Come,' said Pomeroy, of Massachusetts, to his friends at home, 'Come to the help of the Lord against the mighty; you that value our holy religion and our liberties will spare nothing, even to the one-half of your estate.' And in all the villages 'the prayers of God's people' went up that 'they might be crowned with victory, to the glory of God ;' *for the war with France seemed a war for Protestantism and freedom.*" (History of the United States, Vol. IV., p. 212.) Dr. Minot justly observes: "Such a successful defence made by the forces of the British colonists against a respectable army, with which the regular troops of France were incorporated, was an honourable instance of firmness, deliberation, and spirit." (History of Massachusetts Bay, Vol. I., p. 254.)

† Hume and Smollett's History of England, Vol. XII., p. 25.

"Thus," says Minot, "ended the transactions of the year 1755—'a year,'

Nor were the years 1756 and 1757 more successful on the part of the English than the year 1755. Some of the principal events are as follows: War was formally declared by England against France in May, and declared by France against England in August. The expenses incurred by Massachusetts and other colonies in the unfortunate Crown Point expedition were compensated by a parliamentary grant of £115,000 sterling.*

The Earl of Loudoun arrived from England as Governor of Virginia, to take command of the British troops in America;

says a well-informed writer of that time, 'never to be forgotten in America.' It opened with the fairest prospects to these distant possessions of the British empire. Four armies were on foot to remove the encroachments of a perfidious neighbour, and our coasts honoured with a fleet for their security, under the command of the brave and vigilant Boscawen. We had everything to hope —nothing to fear. The enemy was dispersed ; and we only desired a proclamation of war for the final destruction of the whole country of New France. But how unlooked-for was the event ! General Winslow (great-grandson of Edward Winslow, one of the patriarchs of the Plymouth Colony), indeed succeeded in Nova Scotia ; but Braddock was defeated ; Niagara and Crown Point remained unreduced ; the savages were let loose from the wilderness ; many thousand farms were abandoned ; the King's subjects inhumanly butchered or reduced to beggary. To all which might be added an impoverishment of finances to a desperate state, the Crown Point expedition having cost, on the part of Massachusetts Bay alone, £76,618 8s. 9½d., besides unliquidated accounts to a large amount for the charge of the sick and wounded, the garrisons at the two forts of William Henry and Edward, and the great stock of provisions laid in for their support." (History of Massachusetts Bay, Vol. I., pp. 259—261.)

* "Mr. Fox, on the 28th of January, presented to the House of Commons a message from the King, desiring them to take into consideration the faithful services of the people of New England and some other parts of North America ; upon which £115,000 were voted, and £5,000 as a reward to Sir William Johnson in particular." (Hume and Smollett's History of England, Vol. XII., p. 42.)

"The sum granted by Parliament was £115,000 sterling, which was apportioned in the following manner : Massachusetts Bay, £54,000 ; Connecticut, £26,000 ; New York, £15,000 ; New Hampshire, £8,000 ; Rhode Island, £7,000 ; New Jersey, £5,000. This money arriving in New York with the troops from England, enabled the Government (of Massachusetts) to pay off by anticipation the sums borrowed of the Commander-in-Chief, and to replenish the public treasury. They had also the satisfaction to find that the Province had not only anticipated the King's expectations in raising men, but had furnished them with provisions, which he had ordered to be found at the national expense." (Minot's History of Massachusetts Bay, Vol. I., p. 288.)

but did little more than consult with the Governors of the
several provinces as to military operations for the ensuing year,
the relations of provincial and regular officers, the amount of
men and means to be contributed by each province for common
defence. He gave much offence by his haughty and imperious
demands for the quartering of the troops in New York and in
Massachusetts.   Additional troops were sent from England,
under Major-General Abercrombie, who superseded the Earl of
Loudoun as Commander-in-Chief.   The fortress at Oswego was
taken and destroyed by the French.*

* "The loss of the two small forts, called Ontario and Oswego, was a considerable national misfortune. They were erected on the south side of the
great Lake Ontario, standing on the opposite sides, at the mouth of Onondaga
river, that discharges itself into the lake, and constituted a port of great
importance, where vessels had been built to cruise upon the lake, which is a
kind of inland sea, and interrupt the commerce as well as the motions and
designs of the enemy. The garrison consisted of 1,400 men, chiefly militia
and new-raised recruits, under the command of Lieutenant-Colonel Mercer,
an officer of courage and experience ; but the situation of the forts was very ill-
chosen ; the materials mostly timber or logs of wood ; the defences wretchedly
contrived and unfurnished ; and, in a word, the place altogether untenable
against any regular approach. Such were the forts which the enemy wisely
resolved to reduce. They assembled a body of troops, consisting of 1,300
regulars, 1,700 Canadians, and a considerable number of Indian auxiliaries,
under the command of the Marquis de Montcalm, a vigilant and enterprising
officer, to whom the conduct of the siege had been entrusted by the Marquis
de Vaudreuil, Governor and Lieutenant-General of New France.   The
garrison having fired away all their shells and ammunition from Fort Ontario,
spiked up the cannon, and, deserting the fort, retired next day across the
river into Fort Oswego, which was even more exposed than the other,
especially when the enemy had taken possession of Fort Ontario, from whence
they immediately began to fire without intermission. Colonel Mercer being
on the 13th killed by a cannon ball, the fort destitute of all cover, the officers
divided in opinion and the garrison in confusion, they next day demanded
capitulation, and surrendered themselves prisoners of war, on condition that
they should be exempted from plunder, conducted to Montreal, and treated
with humanity. These conditions, however, the Marquis did not punctually
observe. The British officers were insulted by the savage Indians, who
robbed them of their clothes and baggage, massacred several of them as they
stood defenceless on parade, and barbarously scalped all the sick people in the
hospital. Finally, Montcalm, in direct violation of the articles as well as
in contempt of common humanity, delivered up above twenty men of the
garrison to the Indians in lieu of the same number they had lost during the
siege ; and in all probability these miserable captives were put to death by

The French, led by Montcalm, took Fort William Henry.*

those barbarians, with the most excruciating tortures, according to the execrable custom of the country.

" The prisoners taken at Oswego, after having been thus barbarously treated, were conveyed in batteaux to Montreal, where they had no reason to complain of their reception ; and before the end of the year they were exchanged. The victors immediately demolished the two forts (if they deserved that denomination), in which they found one hundred and twenty-one pieces of artillery, fourteen mortars, with a great quantity of ammunition, warlike stores and provisions, besides two ships and two hundred batteaux, which likewise fell into their hands." (Hume and Smollett's History of England, Vol. XII., pp. 92—94.)

" The policy of the French was no less conspicuous than the superiority of their arms. Instead of continuing the fort at Oswego, they demolished it in presence of the Indians of the Five Nations, to whom they represented that the French aimed only at enabling them to preserve their neutrality, and therefore destroyed the fortress which the English had erected in their country to overawe them, disdaining themselves to take the same advantage, although put in their hands by the right of conquest." (Minot's History of Massachusetts Bay, Vol. I., pp. 285, 286.)

* Fort William Henry was situated on the southern coast of Lake George, and was built with a view to protect the frontiers of the English colonies— especially New York and Massachusetts. The fortifications were good, defended by a garrison of three thousand men, and covered by an army of four thousand, under the commmand of General Webb, posted at no great distance at Fort Edward. The Marquis de Montcalm had, early in the season, made three different attacks upon Fort William Henry, in each of which he was repulsed by the resolute and courageous garrison. But Montcalm at length assembled all his forces from Crown Point, Ticonderaga, and other parts, amounting to nearly 10,000, including a considerable body of Canadians and Indians; attacked and invested the fort, which sustained the siege from the 3rd to the 9th of August, when, having burst most of their cannon, and expended their own ammunition, and receiving no relief or assistance from General Webb, at Fort Edward, fourteen miles distant, with 4,000 men, Col. Monro surrendered upon the conditions that the garrison should march out with arms, the baggage of the officers and men, and all the usual necessaries of war, escorted by a detachment of French troops to Fort Edward, and interpreters attached to the savages. But, as in the case of the surrender of Oswego, the articles of capitulation were not observed, but were perfidiously broken; the savages fell upon the British troops as they were marched out, despoiled them of their few remaining effects, dragged the Indians in the English service out of their ranks, and assassinated them under circumstances of unheard-of barbarity. Some soldiers with their wives and children are said to have been savagely murdered by these brutal Indians. The greater part of the garrison, however, arrived at Fort Edward under the protection of the French escort. The enemy demolished

The Massachusetts Assembly refused to allow British troops to be quartered upon the inhabitants.*

At the close of the year 1757, the situation of the colonies was alarming and the prospects of the war gloomy. The strong

the fort, carried off the effects, provisions, and everything else left by the garrison, together with the vessels preserved in the lake, and departed without pursuing their success by any other attempt. " Thus ended," continues the historian, "the third campaign in America (1757), where, with an evident superiority over the enemy, an army of 20,000 regular troops, a great number of provincial forces, and a prodigious naval power—not less than twenty ships of the line—we abandoned our allies, exposed our people, suffered them to be cruelly massacred in sight of our troops, and relinquished a large and valuable tract of country, to the eternal reproach and disgrace of the British name." (Hume and Smollett's History of England, Vol. XII., pp. 207—211.)

Mr. Hildreth remarks : "In America, after three campaigns, and extraordinary efforts on the part of the English, the French still held possession of almost all the territory in dispute. They had been expelled indeed from the Bay of Fundy, but they held Louisburg, commanding the entrance to the St. Lawrence, Crown Point, and Ticonderoga, on Lake Champlain ; Frontenac and Niagara, on Lake Ontario; Presque Isle, on Lake Erie; and the chains of forts thence to the head of the Ohio were still in their hands. They had expelled the English from their ancient fort at Oswego, had driven them from Lake George, and compelled the Six Nations to a treaty of neutrality. A devastating Indian war was raging along the whole north-western frontier of the British colonies, and Indian scalping parties penetrated into the very centre of Massachusetts, approached within a short distance of Philadelphia, and kept Maryland and Virginia in constant alarm." (History of the United States, Vol. II., p. 479.)

* " The Massachusetts General Court had provided barracks at the castle for such British troops as might be sent to the province. But some officers (from Nova Scotia) on a recruiting service, finding the distance (three miles) inconvenient, demanded to be quartered in the town. They insisted on the provisions of the Mutiny Act ; but the magistrates to whom they applied denied that Act to be in force in the colonies. Loudoun warmly espoused the cause of his officers ; he declared ' that in time of war the rules and customs must go, and threatened to send troops to Boston to enforce the demand if not granted within 48 hours. To avoid this extremity, the General Court passed a law of their own, enacting some of the principal provisions of the Mutiny Act ; and Loudoun, through Governor Pownall's persuasions, consented to accept this partial concession. The General Court did not deny the power of Parliament to quarter troops in America. Their ground was, that the Act, in its terms, did not extend to the colonies. A similar dispute occurred in South Carolina, where great difficulty was encountered in finding winter quarters for the Royal Americans." (Hildreth's History of the United States, Vol. II., pp. 476, 477.)

statements of Mr. Bancroft are justified by the facts. He says : " The English had been driven from every cabin in the basin of the Ohio; Montcalm had destroyed every vestige of their power within the St. Lawrence. France had her forts on each side of the lakes, and at Detroit, at Mackinaw, at Kaskaskia, and at New Orleans. The two great valleys of the Mississippi and the St. Lawrence were connected chiefly by three well-known routes—by way of Waterford to Fort du Quesne, by way of Maumee to the Wabash, and by way of Chicago to the Illinois. Of the North American continent, the French claimed and seemed to possess twenty parts in twenty-five, leaving four only to Spain, and but one to Britain. Their territory exceeded that of the English twenty-fold. As the men composing the garrison at Fort Loudoun, in Tennessee, were but so many hostages in the hands of the Cherokees, the claims of France to the valleys of the Mississippi and the St. Lawrence seemed established by possession. America and England were humiliated."*

The colonies had shown, by their divided and often antagonistic counsels, their divided resources and isolated efforts, how unable they were to defend themselves even when assisted at some points by English soldiers, commanded by unskilful generals, against a strong and united enemy, directed by generals of consummate skill and courage. The colonies despaired of future success, if not of their own existence, after incurring so heavy expenditures of men and money, and wished England to assume the whole management and expenses of the war.†

---

* Bancroft's History, Vol. IV., p. 267.

† " As the General Court of Massachusetts Bay had been foremost in promoting the Crown Point expedition, and become proportionally exhausted of money, so they lost no time in making such use of the success of the troops in beating off the French as their necessities dictated. They drew up an address to his Majesty, in which they stated their services, and prayed to be relieved from the burden incurred by means of them. They pleaded the precedent of the Cape Breton expedition (for the expenses of which Parliament had compensated them), and prayed that his Majesty would give orders for the support of such forts and garrisons as they hoped to establish, and aid them in the further execution of their designs.

" When the Commander-in-Chief urged upon them to join in the plan of the Assembly of New Jersey, who proposed a meeting of Commissioners from all his Majesty's colonies at New York, to consult what might further

The colonies had done much for their own defence, but they acted as so many petty independent Governments, and could not be brought to combine their resources of men and money in any systematical method, under some central authority, as the same colonies did twenty years later in the American Revolution; and the first proceedings of Abercrombie and Loudoun rendered them powerless to command the confidence and united action of the colonies. General Abercrombie was appointed Commander-in-Chief, to supersede General Shirley, until the arrival of the Earl of Loudoun. Abercrombie landed in New York the 12th of June, with two regiments, and forty German officers, who were to raise and train recruits for Loudoun's Royal American regiment of four thousand—a most impolitic proceeding, which offended and discouraged the colonists. On his arrival at New York he received letters from the shrewd and able Governor of Virginia, Dinwiddie, recommending Washington as "a very able and deserving gentleman," who "has from the beginning commanded the forces of this Dominion. He is much beloved, has gone through many hardships in the service, has great merit, and can raise more men here than any one," and urged his promotion in the British army. But Washington's services and rank were never recognized in the British army. A week after Abercrombie's arrival in New York, he wrote (June 19, 1756) a letter to Governor Colden: "I find you never will be able to carry on anything to any purpose in America, till you have a viceroy or superintendent over all the provinces." He stated that Lord Loudoun's arrival would produce "a great change in affairs."

The 25th of June Abercrombie arrived at Albany, and forthwith insisted that the regular officers should take precedence of the provincial officers, and that the troops should be quartered in private houses, which he accomplished two

be done for the security of his Majesty's territories against the invasion of the French, the same impoverishment constrained the General Court to reply, that the design of securing those territories was what his Majesty alone was equal to project and execute and the nation to support, and that unless they could obtain the relief which they were soliciting of the royal bounty, they should be as far from being able to remove encroachments as to be unable to defend themselves." (Minot's History of Massachusetts Bay, Vol. I., pp. 256, 257.)

17

days afterwards; for on the 27th, "in spite of every subterfuge, the soldiers were at last billeted upon the town," to the great indignation of the Mayor, who wished all the soldiers back again, "for" said he, "we can defend our frontiers ourselves."

The next day after Abercrombie's arrival, Shirley (now relinquishing the office of Commander-in-Chief) informed General Abercrombie of the exposed and unsafe state of Oswego, advising that two battalions be sent forward for its protection; that 200 boats were ready, and every magazine along the passage plentifully supplied. But Abercrombie decided to wait the arrival of Loudoun, who at length reached Albany the 29th of July, and joined Abercrombie in the policy of hesitation and delay, though having 10,000 men at his disposal—the New England regiments, with the provincials from New York and New Jersey, amounting to more than 7,000 men, besides 3,000 soldiers of British regular regiments.

In the meantime the French generals were more active and energetic, taking places of defence between Albany and Oswego, strengthening the defences and garrison of Ticonderaga (then in possession of the French, and called by them Fort Carillon), making a palisaded camp near the mouth of Sandy Creek, close to Oswego, and at length attacking Oswego itself, the enterprising Montcalm making forced marches day and night, marching on foot, living and sleeping like his soldiers, and taking the fort the 9th of August, after a week's siege, capturing 1,600 prisoners, 120 cannon, six vessels of war, 300 boats, stores of ammunition and provisions, and three chests of money.

Loudoun had sufficient forces and time to penetrate to the heart of Canada, had he possessed the qualities of Montcalm; but he preferred to place obstacles to prevent the enemy from attacking him; and after having spent some weeks in busy inactivity at Albany, he dismissed the provincials to their homes, and the regulars to winter quarters.*

---

* A thousand of the regulars were sent to New York, where free quarters for the officers were demanded of the city. Upon its being objected to by the authorities of the city, as contrary to the laws of England and the liberties of America, the Viceroy, Loudoun, replied to the Mayor with an oath, "If you do not billet my officers upon free quarters this day, I'll order here all the troops in North America under my command, and billet them myself upon the city." "So," says Bancroft, "the magistrates got up a subscription,

Loudoun never fought a battle in America; and the only battle in which Abercrombie commanded he kept out of reach of personal danger, was defeated, and retreated* after losing 1,942 men, among whom was General Lord Howe, who had been selected by Pitt to be Commander-in-Chief in America, had not succeeded to it, but had become a favourite with the army and colonists of all classes.

and the officers, who had done nothing for the country but waste its resources, were supported at free quarters during the winter."

The same threats were used, with the same results, to the magistrates of Boston and Philadelphia, to obtain free quarters for the officers.

Bancroft remarks somewhat bitterly : " The arbitrary invasion of private rights and the sanctity of domestic life by the illegal and usurped authority of a military chief, was the great result of the campaign. The frontiers had been left open to the French ; but the tempting example had been given, so dangerous in times of peace, of quartering troops in the principal towns, at the expense of the inhabitants." (History of United States, Vol. IV., pp. 240, 241.)

* The army consisted of between nine and ten thousand provincials—seven thousand raised by Massachusetts—and between six and seven thousand regulars and rangers in the King's pay, where Abercrombie in person was in command.   Lord Howe arrived in Boston from England after the forces had left the Province, and immediately upon his landing began his journey, and joined the army before any action took place.

"This body, the greatest which had ever assembled in arms in America since it was settled by the English, embarked on Lake George the 5th of July, for the French fortress at Ticonderaga (called Carillon by the French), and arrived next day at a cove and landing-place, from whence a way led to the advance guard of the enemy.   Seven thousand men, in four columns, then began a march through a thick wood.   The columns were necessarily broken ; their guides were unskilful ; the men were bewildered and lost ; and parties fell in one upon another.   Lord Howe, the life of the army, at the head of a column, which was supported by light infantry, being advanced, fell in with a party of the enemy, consisting of about four hundred regulars and some Indians.   Many of them were killed, and one hundred and forty-eight taken prisoners.   This, however, was a dearly purchased victory, for Lord Howe was the first who fell on the English side.   The report of his death caused consternation as well as grief through the army, which had placed much confidence in him.

"About five hundred regulars were killed upon the spot, and about one thousand two hundred wounded.   Of the provincials, one hundred were killed, and two hundred and fifty wounded.

"The army still consisted of thirteen or fourteen thousand.   The enemy was much inferior in number.   The retreat, nevertheless, was precipitate. Early in the morning of the 9th the whole army embarked in their boats,

The General Assembly of Massachusetts appropriated out of the public treasury the sum of £250 for erecting a monument to his memory in Westminster Abbey, as a testimony to the sense which the Province had of the services and military virtues of the late Lord Viscount Howe, who fell in the last campaign fighting in the cause of the colonies, and also to express the affection which their officers and soldiers have to his command.

After the disgraceful defeat and still more disgraceful retreat of Abercrombie, the last of the incompetent English generals, General Amherst was appointed Commander-in-Chief, assisted by General Wolfe, and the fortunes of war turned in favour of England and her colonies, and the French power began to wane in America.

This change in the colonies from defeat to victory, from disgrace to honour, from distrust to confidence, from fear to triumph, was owing to a change of councillors and councils in England, and the rousing of the colonies from the shame and defeat of the past to a supreme and combined effort with the English armies for the expulsion of the French from America, and the consequent subjugation and alliance of the Indian tribes, whose hostilities had been all along and everywhere prompted and aided by the French, who paid the Indians large bounties for English scalps.*

and arrived at the other end of the lake in the evening (no enemy pursuing). Provisions, entrenching tools, and many stores of various kinds, fell into the hands of the enemy. The English arms have rarely suffered greater disgrace.

"The ill success of General Abercrombie at Ticonderaga caused his recall. He seemed to expect and desire it. He was succeeded by General Amherst." (Hutchinson's History of Massachusetts Bay, Vol. III., pp. 70—75.)

* "The successes of the French the last year (1757) left the colonies in a gloomy state. By the acquisition of Fort William Henry, they obtained full possession of the Lakes Champlain and George ; and by the destruction of Oswego, they had acquired the dominion of those other lakes which connect the St. Lawrence with the Mississippi. The first afforded the easiest admission from the northern colonies into Canada, or from Canada into those colonies ; the last united Canada to Louisiana. By the continual possession of Fort du Quesne, they preserved their ascendency over the Indians, and held undisturbed possession of all the country west of the Allegany mountains.

"In this adverse state of things, the spirit of Britain rose in full proportion to the occasion ; and her colonies, instead of yielding to despondency, resumed fresh courage, and cheerfully made the preparations for the coming campaign.

"But," says Hutchinson, "in the interval between the repulse at Ticonderaga and the arrival of General Amherst, Colonel Bradstreet (a provincial officer of New York), with 3,000 provincials and 150 regulars, stole a march upon Montcalm, and before he could send a detachment from his army to Lake Ontario by way of the St. Lawrence, went up the Mohawk river. About the 25th of August they arrived at Fort Frontenac; surprised the garrison, who were made prisoners of war; took and destroyed nine small vessels and much merchandise; but having intelligence of a large body of the enemy near, they made haste back to Albany. The men complained of undergoing greater hardship than they had ever undergone before, and many sickened and died from the fatigue of the march.*

After the arrival of Lord Amherst, three expeditions were proposed for the year 1758—the first against Louisburg, the second against Ticonderaga, and the third against Fort du Quesne—all of which were successful

Mr. Pitt had, the last autumn, been placed at the head of a new Administration, which conciliated the contending interests in Parliament ; and while the wisdom of that extraordinary statesman devised great and judicious plans, his active spirit infused new life into all, whether at home or abroad, whose province it was to execute them. In a circular to the Colonial Governors, he assured them of the determination to send a large force to America, to operate by sea and land against the French ; and called upon them to raise as large bodies of men as the number of the inhabitants would allow. The northern colonies were prompt and liberal in furnishing requisite supplies. The Legislature of Massachusetts voted to furnish 7,000 men ; Connecticut, 5,000 ; New Hampshire, 3,000. These troops were ready to take the field very early in May, previous to which time Admiral Boscawen had arrived in Halifax with a formidable fleet, and about 12,000 British troops under the command of General Amherst. The Earl of Loudoun had returned to England, and General Abercrombie, on whom the chief command of the entire forces of the American war had devolved (until the arrival of Lord Amherst), was now at the head of 50,000 men, the most powerful army ever seen in America." (Holmes' Annals of America, Vol. II., pp. 79, 80.)

* History of Massachusetts Bay, Vol. II., p. 74. Holmes gives the following account of this brilliant achievement : " On the proposition of Col. Bradstreet, for an expedition against Fort Frontenac, relinquishing for the present his designs against Ticonderaga and Crown Point, Abercrombie sent that able and gallant officer on this service, with a detachment of 3,000 men, chiefly provincials, and two mortars. Bradstreet having marched to Oswego, embarked on Lake Ontario, and on the evening of the 25th of August landed within a mile of the fort. Within two days his batteries were opened

On the first expedition against Louisburg, Admiral Boscawen sailed from Halifax the 28th of May, with a fleet of 20 ships of the line and 18 frigates, and an army of 14,000 men, under the command of General Amherst, assisted by General Wolfe, and arrived before Louisburg the 2nd of June. The garrison was composed of 2,500 regulars, aided by 600 militia, commanded by the Chevalier de Drucourt, an officer of courage and experience. The harbour was secured by five ships of the line, one 50-gun ship, and five frigates; three of which were sunk across the mouth of the basin. The landing of the troops, artillery, and stores had therefore to be effected some distance from the town, and was extremely difficult and hazardous; but General Wolfe, who led the 2,000 men detached for that purpose, was equal to the occasion, and displayed qualities which designated him as the future conqueror of Quebec. After an obstinate siege from the 8th of June to the 26th of July, the fortress was surrendered at discretion, and the whole of Cape Breton, including St. John Island (since Prince Edward Island), came into possession of Great Britain. The loss on the part of the English was about 400 killed and wounded; the garrison lost upwards of 1,500 men, and the town was reduced to a heap of ruins. The conquerors took 221 pieces of cannon, 16 mortars, and an immense quantity of stores and ammunition, and 5,637 prisoners, including naval officers, sailors, and marines.*

Admiral Boscawen, after taking possession of the Island of St. John, included in the capitulation of Louisburg, sailed with the fleet for England, with General Wolfe, conveying the French prisoners to England, and the trophies of victory. General

within so short a distance that almost every shell took effect; and the French commandant, finding the place untenable, surrendered at discretion. The Indians having previously deserted, the prisoners were but 110. The captors found in the fort 60 pieces of cannon, 16 small mortars, a large number of small arms, a vast quantity of provisions, military stores and merchandise; and nine armed vessels fell into their hands. Col. Bradstreet having destroyed the fort and vessels, and such stores as could not be brought off, returned to the main army." (Annals, Vol. II., p. 83.)

* "The extraordinary rejoicings in England at this victory seemed to revive the honour of the northern British colonies as the former conquerors of Cape Breton. The trophies taken were brought in procession from Kensington to St. Paul's, and a form of thanksgiving was ordered to be used in all the churches." (Minot's History of Massachusetts Bay, Vol. II., p. 38.)

Amherst embarked, with about thirty transports filled with the victorious troops, and encamped on the common at Boston near the end of August, on his march, which he pursued after three days' rest, to the western forts ; for a part of the plan of operations was, after the conquest of Cape Breton, for General Amherst, with 12,000 men, to destroy the enemy's fort at Ticonderaga (so unsuccessfully attacked by Abercrombie the year before), in order to open a way into Canada by the Lakes George and Champlain, and the River Sorell down to Quebec, the capture of which, by advancing up the St. Lawrence, was assigned to the fleet under Admiral Saunders, and to General Wolfe, in command of 9,000 men. It was intended that the armies under Generals Amherst and Wolfe should meet and join in the taking of Quebec; but the junction was not effected, and the two armies operated separately and successfully. The taking of the fortress of Niagara, which was regarded as " the throat of the north-western division of the American continent," was assigned to Brigadier-General Prideaux, aided by Sir William Johnson, who commanded the Provincials and Indians. General Prideaux conducted the expedition and planned the mode of attack ; but on the 19th of July, while walking in his trenches, he was killed by the carelessness of his own gunner in firing a cannon.

" Luckily," says Hutchinson, " for Sir William Johnson, who, as next officer, took the command on Prideaux's death, a body of 1,200 men from Detroit, etc., making an attempt, on the 24th of July, to throw themselves into the fort as a reinforcement, were intercepted and killed, taken, or dispersed, and the next day the garrison capitulated." (History of Massachusetts Bay, Vol. III., p. 77.)

The expedition against the French Fort du Quesne, on the Ohio river, so fatal to General Braddock, was entrusted to General Forbes, with Washington, colonel of the Virginia regulars, as second in command. Forbes, though wasting under the disease of consumption, heroically superintended and endured for three months the difficulties and fatigues of the same line of march pursued by Braddock three years before, leaving Philadelphia in command of 8,000 men early in July, but not reaching Fort du Quesne until late in November. On the evening preceding his arrival, the French garrison, deserted by their Indians, abandoned the fort, and escaped in boats down the Ohio. Hutchinson says: "The expedition for dispossessing the French of Fort du Quesne, near the Ohio, had at first a very unfavourable prospect. The English forces met with a variety of obstructions and discouragements; and when they had advanced to within thirty or forty miles of the fort, they were at a stand deliberating whether they should go forward or not. Receiving intelligence that the garrison was in a weak condition, they pushed on. Upon their arrival at the fort they met with no opposition. The enemy had deserted it, for want of provisions, as was generally believed; and it was added that the provisions intended to supply that fort were destroyed by Bradstreet at Fort Frontenac.* Thus the gallant and laborious exploit of Bradstreet in demolishing Fort Frontenac contributed to the reduction of Fort du Quesne without firing a shot." "The English now took possession of that important fortress, and, in compliment to the popular Minister, called it Pittsburg. No sooner was the English flag erected on it, than the numerous tribes of the Ohio Indians came in and made their submission to the English. General Forbes having concluded treaties with the natives, left a garrison of provincials in the fort and built a block-house near Loyal Hannah, but, worn out with fatigue, he died before he could reach Philadelphia.† In the same month of July that Sir William Johnson dispossessed the French of Niagara, General Amherst took possession of the enemy's lines at Ticonderaga, which the French abandoned after having set fire to the fort. A few days afterwards, in the beginning of August, General Amherst obtained possession of the fort at Crown Point, it having also been abandoned by the French. About the middle of the month General Amherst received information at Crown Point that General Bourlamarque was encamped at Isle aux Noix with 3,500 men and 100 cannon, and that the French had four vessels on the lake under the command of the captain of a man-of-war. He therefore judged it necessary to build a brigantine, a radeau, and a sloop of 16 guns. Such a fleet could not be got ready before the beginning of October; on the 11th of which month General Amherst embarked in batteaux, under the convoy of armed vessels, and proceeded down

---

* History of Massachusetts Bay, Vol. III., p. 75.

† Holmes' Annals, Vol. II., p. 84.

the lake; but encountering cold and stormy weather and contrary winds, he resolved, on the 19th, to return to Crown Point and go into winter quarters. No communications could be opened between the armies of Amherst and Wolfe; but the withdrawal of a great part of the French force from Quebec, to watch and counteract the movements of General Amherst, doubtless contributed to General Wolfe's success. The fleet under Sir Charles Saunders, and the army of five thousand men under General Wolfe, arrived before Quebec the latter part of June, and from that time to the 13th of September a series of daring but unsuccessful attempts were made to get possession of the city. How unyielding perseverance and heroic courage, against apparently insurmountable obstacles, effected the capture of that Gibraltar of America, with the fall of the leaders of both armies in the bloody struggle, has often been vividly described and variously illustrated, which I need not here repeat.

The British and colonial arms were completely successful this year.* Bradstreet destroyed Fort Frontenac; Sir William Johnson captured Niagara; Forbes, aided by Washington, retook Fort du Quesne and named it Pittsburg; Lord Amherst took possession of Ticonderaga and Crown Point; and Wolfe became the conqueror of Quebec. In each of these expeditions the provincial troops rendered essential service. The several provinces were prompted to put forth their utmost efforts from their impending perils by the successive victories of the French and Indians the previous year, and encouraged by the appeal of the Prime Minister, Pitt, who assured them of the strong forces by sea and land from England, and that they would be compensated for the expense they might incur.

The heart of Massachusetts had for many years been set upon the conquest of Canada, both for her own security and for the extension of her northern limits, and she had sacrificed

---

* "The distant and important operations in Canada almost wholly relieved the suffering inhabitants of the frontiers of the Province; and, indeed, by a train of successes, gave a pledge of the future ease and security which was about to spread over all the British colonies. The fall of Crown Point, Ticonderaga, Niagara, and, above all, the capture of Quebec, closed the year with universal rejoicing and well-founded hope that the toils of war would shortly cease throughout the land." (Minot's History of Massachusetts Bay, Vol. II., p. 55.)

much treasure and many lives for that purpose, but had failed in each attempt. The taking of Quebec did not complete the conquest of Canada. On the fall of that city, Montreal became the seat of the French Government; the inhabitants of Canada remained subjects of the King of France; the French military forces within the province, were still very considerable;* and M. de Levi, who succeeded Montcalm as Commander-in-Chief of the army, made a very formidable attempt to recover Quebec.†
On the reduction of that city, the fleet under Sir Charles Saunders returned to England, and General Murray was left in

* " The main body of the French army, which, after the battle of the Plains of Abraham, retired to Montreal, and which still consisted of ten battalions of regulars, had been reinforced by 6,000 Canadian militia and a body of Indians. Here the Marquis de Vaudreuil, Governor-General of Canada, had fixed his head-quarters and determined to make his last stand. For this purpose (after the unsuccessful attempt of M. de Levi to retake Quebec) he called in all his detachments, and collected around him the whole force of the colony." (Holmes' Annals, Vol. II., pp. 98, 99.)

† " In the month of April, when the Upper St. Lawrence was so open as to admit of transportation by water, his artillery, military stores and heavy baggage were embarked at Montreal and fell down the river, under convoy of six frigates; and M. de Levi, after a march of ten days, arrived with his army at Point aux Tremble, within a few miles of Quebec. General Murray, to whom the care of maintaining the English conquest had been entrusted, had taken every precaution to preserve it, but his soldiers had suffered so by the extreme cold of winter, and by the want of vegetables and fresh provisions, that instead of 5,000, the original number of the garrison, there were not at this time above 3,000 men fit for service. With this small but valiant body he resolved to meet him in the field; and on the 28th of April marched out to the Heights of Abraham, where, near Sillery, he attacked the French under M. de Levi with great impetuosity. He was received with firmness; and after a fierce encounter, finding himself outflanked and in danger of being surrounded by superior numbers, he called off his troops and retired into the city. In this action the loss of the English was near 1,000 men, and that of the French still greater. The French general lost no time in improving his victory. On the very evening of the battle he opened trenches before the town; but it was the 11th of May before he could mount his batteries and bring his guns to bear upon the fortifications. By that time General Murray, who had been indefatigable, had completed some outworks, and planted so immense an artillery on its ramparts, that the fire was very superior to that of the besiegers, and in a manner silenced their batteries. A British fleet most opportunely arriving a few days after, M. de Levi immediately raised the siege and precipitately retired to Montreal." (Holmes' Annals, Vol. II., pp. 98, 99.)

command at Quebec with a garrison of 5,000 men, which, during the ensuing winter, owing to the extreme cold, and the want of vegetables and fresh provisions, was reduced to 3,000 men fit for service, when in April M. de Levi, with a superior force, attacked the city, drove General Murray's little army from the Plains of Abraham within the walls, and closely besieged the city, which was relieved, and M. de Levi compelled to raise the siege, by the opportune arrival of the English fleet.

In the meantime, General Amherst was energetically pursuing the most effective measures for the complete extinction of French power in Canada. At the commencement of the year 1760, he applied to the northern colonies for men and means equal to what they had provided for 1759,* and during the winter he made arrangements to bring the armies from Quebec, Lake Champlain, and Lake Ontario, to act against Montreal. Colonel Haviland, by his orders, sailed early in the

---

* "General Amherst made application to Massachusetts for the same number of men for the service of the next year as they had raised the last (1759). *The reduction of Canada was still the object. This alone was found to be a sufficient stimulus to the Assembly, and they needed no other arguments from the Governor. The generous compensations which had been every year made by Parliament not only alleviated the burden of taxes, which otherwise would have been heavy, but by the importation of such large sums of specie increased commerce*, and it was the opinion of some *that the war added to the wealth of the province*, though the compensation did not amount to one-half the charges of government.

"The Assembly, at the session in January, 1760, first granted a large bounty to the men in garrison at Louisburg and Nova Scotia, to encourage them to continue in the service. A vote was then passed for raising 5,000 men more, upon the same encouragement as those of the last year had received. Soon after the Governor received letters from Mr. Pitt making the like requests as had been made by him the last year, and giving the same assurance of compensation. At the beginning of the year the English interest in Canada was in a precarious state. Quebec had been besieged in the spring, after a battle in which General Murray had lost a considerable part of his garrison. Fortunately, Lord Colville (with the English fleet) arrived at a critical time and caused the siege to be raised.

"The danger being over, and there being no probability of any French force from Europe, it seemed agreed that all Canada must fall in the course of the summer. The Massachusetts enlistments went on but slowly. Only 3,300 of the proposed 5,000 men enlisted, and 700 only remained in garrison at Louisburg and Nova Scotia." (Hutchinson's History of Massachusetts Bay, Vol. III., pp. 79, 80.)

spring with a detachment from Crown Point, took possession of the Isle aux Noix, which he found abandoned by the enemy, and proceeded thence to Montreal; while Lord Amherst, with his own division, consisting of about 10,000 regulars and provincials, left the frontier of New York and advanced to Oswego, where he was joined by 1,000 Indians of the Six Nations, under Sir William Johnson. Embarking with his entire army on Lake Ontario, and taking the fort of Isle Royale in his way, he arrived at Montreal, after a difficult and dangerous passage, on the same day that General Murray landed near the place from Quebec. The two generals met with no opposition in disembarking their troops; and by a happy concurrence in the execution of a well-concerted plan, Colonel Haviland joined them with his detachment the next day. The strength of these combined armies, and the masterly disposition made by the commanders, convinced M. de Vaudreuil that resistance would be ineffectual, and he demanded a capitulation; and on the 8th of September, 1760, Montreal, Detroit, Michili-Mackinac, and all other places within the government of Canada, were surrendered to his Britannic Majesty. The destruction of an armament ordered out from France in aid of Canada completed the annihilation of French power on the continent of America.*

But though the conquest of Canada was thus completed, and the American colonies thus secured from the encroachments and dangers which had disturbed their peace and caused

---

* Holmes' Annals, Vol. II., pp. 99, 100. Russell's Europe, Vol. V., Letter 34. General Amherst, in his orders to the army, dated " Camp before Montreal, 8th September, 1760," announces this great event in the following words :

" The general sees with infinite pleasure the successes which have crowned the indefatigable efforts of his Majesty's troops and faithful subjects in North America. The Marquis Vaudreuil has capitulated the troops of France in Canada ; they have laid down their arms, and are to serve no more during the war. The whole country submits to the dominion of Great Britain. The three armies are entitled to the general's thanks on this occasion, and he assures them that he will take the first opportunity of acquainting his Majesty with the zeal and bravery which have always been exerted by the officers and soldiers of the regular and provincial troops, and also by his faithful Indian allies. The general is confident that when the troops are informed that the country is the King's, they will not disgrace themselves by the least appearance of inhumanity or unsolderlike behaviour by taking any plunder ; but that the Canadians, now become British subjects, may feel the good effects of his Majesty's protection."

much sacrifice of life for one hundred and thirty years, yet the war between England and France was not ended, and in 1762 Spain joined France in the war against the former; but the actual scene of the war was chiefly the West Indies, and the series of naval and other battles fought there were successive victories on the part of England. "The progress of the British conquests, which threatened all the distant possessions of the enemy, was arrested by preliminary articles of peace, which were signed and interchanged at Fontainebleau between the Ministers of Great Britain, France, Spain, and Portugal, on the 3rd day of November. On the 10th of February, 1763, a definite treaty was signed at Paris, and soon after ratified."*

The joy was general and intense throughout England and North America at such a conclusion of a seven years' open war, preceded by several years of hostile and bloody encroachments on the settlements of the English provinces by the French and Indians. It was a war prompted and commenced by the colonies, and in which their very existence as well as liberties were involved. No one of the American colonies had a deeper, if as deep a stake in the results of this protracted struggle as the province of Massachusetts; no one had more suppliantly and importunately solicited the aid of money and men from England; and no colony had benefitted so largely in its commerce and resources during the successive years of the contest, as Massachusetts. As early as 1755 (the year before war was formally declared between England and France), the Legislature of Massachusetts adopted an address to the King, in which, after referring to their large expenditure in their unsuccessful expedition

---

* Holmes' Annals, Vol. II., p. 113.

There were still troubles on the borders of some of the provinces with tribes of Indians, but none to excite serious alarm, and hostile Indians were soon brought to submission. The majority of the high-spirited and powerful Cherokee nation spurned every offer of peace; but Lieutenant-Colonel James Grant, in command of the Highlanders and a provincial regiment raised in South Carolina, to act in conjunction with the regular forces, with the addition of some Indian allies—in all about 2,600 men—defeated them, destroyed their towns, magazines and cornfields, and drove them for shelter and subsistence to the mountains, when their chieftains solicited peace.

"This reduction of the Cherokees was among the last humbling strokes given to the power of France in North America." (Heevatt, II., 244--254; quoted in Holmes' Annals, Vol. II., p. 108).

against Crown Point, they stated their services and prayed to be relieved from the burden incurred by means of them. They pleaded the precedent of the Cape Breton invasion (for expenses incurred in which, in 1745, the British Parliament had granted them compensation), and prayed that his Majesty would give orders for the support of such forts and garrisons as they hoped to establish, and aid them in the further execution of their designs. And in another address, adopted in October of the same year, the Massachusetts Court said that the design of securing his Majesty's territories against the invasions of the French was what his Majesty alone was equal to project and execute, and the nation to support; and that unless they could obtain the relief which they were soliciting from the royal bounty, they should be so far from being able to remove encroachments that they would be unable to defend themselves.[*]

Massachusetts having succeeded, with the other colonies, to "drag," as Mr. Bancroft expresses it, "England into a war with France," was thus importunate in soliciting aid and compensation from England for her self-originated expenses, and was so successful in her applications as to make the war a pecuniary benefit as well as a means of securing and enlarging her boundaries; for, in the words of the historian quoted above, in a previous page, "The generous compensations which had been made every year by Parliament not only alleviated the burden of taxes, which otherwise would have been heavy, but, by the importation of such large sums of specie, increased commerce; and it was the opinion of some that the war added to the wealth of the province, though the compensation did not amount to half the charges of the government."[†]

The monies raised by the colonies were expended in them and upon their own citizens—monies passing from hand to hand, and for provisions provided and works done in the colonies; but the large sums appropriated by Parliament for the war in the colonies was so much money abstracted from England, sent across the Atlantic, and added to the resources and wealth of the colonies.

After the close of the war, in 1763, Massachusetts acknow-

[*] Minot's History of Massachusetts Bay, Vol. I., pp. 256, 257.
[†] Hutchinson's History of Massachusetts Bay, Vol. III., p. 79.

ledged her obligations to England for her protection and safety. In an address of both Houses of her Legislature to the Governor that year, they acknowledge that "the evident design of the French to surround the colonies was the immediate and just cause of the war ; that without the protection afforded them during the war, they must have been a prey to the power of France ; that without the compensation made them by Parliament, the burden of the expense of the war must have been insupportable." In their address to the King they make the same acknowledgments, and at the conclusion promise to evidence their gratitude by every expression of duty and loyalty in their power.*

Mr. Otis, afterwards the most eloquent agitator against England, and advocate of independence, at the first town meeting of Boston after the peace, having been chosen chairman, addressed the inhabitants in the following words, which he caused to be printed in the newspapers :

"We in America have certainly abundant reasons to rejoice. The heathen are not only driven out, but the Canadians, much more formidable enemies, are conquered and become our fellow-subjects. The British dominion and power may be said literally to extend from sea to sea, and from the great river to the ends of the earth. And we may safely conclude, from his Majesty's wise administration hitherto, that liberty and knowledge, civil and religious, will be co-extended, improved, and preserved to the latest posterity. No other constitution of civil government has yet appeared in the world so admirably adapted to these great purposes as that of Great Britain. Every British subject in America is of common right, by Act of Parliament, and by the laws of God and nature, entitled to all the essential privileges of Britons. By particular Charters, there are peculiar privileges granted, as in justice they might and ought, in consideration of the arduous undertaking to begin so glorious an empire as British America is rising to. Those jealousies that some weak and wicked minds have endeavoured to infuse with regard to the colonies, had their birth in the blackness of darkness, and it is a great pity they had not remained there for ever. The true interests of Great Britain and her plantations are

---

* Hutchinson's History of Massachusetts Bay, Vol. III., p. 101.

mutual; and what God in His providence has united, let no man dare attempt to pull asunder."*

Such were the official acknowledgments and professed feelings of Massachusetts herself in regard to the conduct of England towards her at the close of the seven years' war with France, which was ratified by the Peace of Paris, 1763, and which secured the American colonies from the hostilities of the French and their Indian allies for more than a hundred years. The language of Massachusetts was but the language of all the American colonies in regard to Great Britain at this period— the language of gratitude and affection.

Down, therefore, to within thirteen years of the American Declaration of Independence, the conduct of England to her American colonies is acknowledged upon the highest authority to have been just and generous.

---

* Hutchinson's History of Massachusetts Bay, Vol. III., pp. 101, 102.

CHAPTER IX.

RELATIONS OF ENGLAND AND THE COLONIES WITH EACH OTHER AND WITH
FOREIGN COUNTRIES.

I. THE position of England in respect to the other European
Powers after the Peace of Paris, 1763.

Mr. Bancroft remarks: "At the peace of 1763, the fame of
England was exalted throughout Europe above that of all
other nations. She had triumphed over those whom she called
her hereditary enemies, and retained half a continent as the
monument of her victories. Her American dominions stretched
without dispute from the Atlantic to the Mississippi, from the
Gulf of Mexico to Hudson's Bay; and in her older possessions
that dominion was rooted firmly in the affections of the colonists
as in their institutions and laws."*

The envy and fears of Europe were excited at this vast
extension of British territory and power, which they regarded
as the foundation of her still more formidable future greatness.
"Her navy, her commerce, and her manufactures had greatly
increased when she held but a part of the continent, and when
she was bounded by the formidable powers of France and Spain.
Her probable future greatness, when without a rival, with a
growing vent for her manufactures and increasing employment
for her marine, threatened to destroy that balance of power

---

* History of the United States, Vol. V., Chap. v., p. 78.
"The Spaniards having taken part in the war, were, at the termination
of it, induced to relinquish to the same Power both East and West Florida
(in exchange for Cuba). This peace gave Great Britain possession of an
extent of country equal in dimensions to several of the kingdoms of Europe."
(Ramsay's Colonial History, Vol. I., Chap. iii., p. 391.)

18

which European sovereigns have for a long time endeavoured to preserve. Kings are republicans with respect to each other and behold with democratic jealousy any one of their order towering above the rest. The aggrandizement of one tends to excite a combination, or at least the wishes of many, to reduce him to the common level. From motives of this kind, the naval superiority of Great Britain was received with jealousy by her neighbours. They were in general disposed to favour any convulsion which promised a diminution of her overgrown power."*

This great increase of the naval and territorial power of Great Britain excited apprehension at home as well as jealousies abroad. Some of her own statesmen and philanthropists entertained doubts as to whether the extent and diversity of her vast territorial acquisitions would add to the strength or happiness of the mother country ; and the policy of centralization and uniformity decided upon, created the discord and hastened the disintegration which reflective minds had apprehended.

II. The position of the American Colonies in regard to England and other nations clearly signalized a system of government which the English statesmen of the times failed to appreciate. The maxim of the King was not merely to reign, but to rule ; and the policy of his Ministers, of successive Administrations, was to enfeeble what was colonial and to strengthen what was imperial ; whereas the extension of colonial territory had brought a large accession of colonial experience and intelligence, which required to be entwined around the throne by the silken cords of kindness and interest, instead of being bandaged to England by 29 Acts of Parliament, every one of which indicated the loss of some sacred birthright or privilege of Englishmen and their posterity as soon as they emigrated from the eastern to the western shores of the Atlantic. Those who emigrated to or were born in America were no less Englishmen than those who remained or were born in England, and were entitled to all the rights and privileges of Englishmen ; among which is the election of representatives who make laws and provide means for their government. The original

* Bancroft's History of the United States, Vol. V., Chap. v., pp. 321, 322.

design of colonization by the British Government was doubtless the extension of its power; the design of English merchants and manufacturers in promoting colonization was obviously the extension of their trade, and therefore their own enrichment; while the design of the colonists themselves, in leaving their native land and becoming adventurers and settlers in new countries, was as manifestly the improvement of their own condition and that of their posterity. As long as the threefold design of these three parties to colonization harmonized, there could be no cause or occasion of collision between them, and they would cordially co-operate in advancing the one great object of growing national greatness by enlarging the commerce and dominions of Great Britain. This was the case in the earlier stages of American colonization. The colonists needed the naval and diplomatic protection of England against foreign invasion, and the manufactures of England for their own wants and conveniences, while England needed the productions of the colonial forests and waters. The colonial trade became a monopoly of England, and its transportation to and from the colonies was confined to English ships and sailors. Even manufactures in the colonies were forbidden, or restricted, as well as their trade with foreign countries, except by way of England; so that the colonies became so many trading ports for English merchandise, and the American traders were little other than factors of English merchants.

However this system of monopoly and restriction might answer the purposes of English merchants and manufacturers, might contribute to build up the mercantile navy of England, and even be politic on the part of Government in colonial infancy, it could not fail ere long to cause friction with the colonies, and was utterly unsuitable to their circumstances as they advanced to manhood.* As the colonies increased in

* "From the first settlement of English America till the close of the war of 1755, the general conduct of Great Britain towards her colonies affords a useful lesson to those who are disposed to colonization. From that era, it is equally worthy of the attention of those who wish for the reduction of great empires to small ones. In the first period, Great Britain regarded the provinces as instruments of commerce. Without the care of their internal police, or seeking a revenue from them, she contented herself with the monopoly of their trade. She treated them as a judicious mother does her

wealth and population, their commerce increased with each
other and with the mother country, and overflowed to the
French and Spanish colonies in the West Indies. Even before
the termination of the war of 1755, a considerable commerce
had been carried on between the British and Spanish colonies;
the latter needed many of the productions and importations of
the former, and the former needed the gold and silver, molasses
and sugar, of the latter. The British colonies sent lumber, fish,
and large quantities of goods imported from England, to the
Spanish colonies, and received chiefly in payment gold and
silver, with which they made remittances to England for the
goods purchased there.* Such was the position of the colonies

dutiful children. They shared in every privilege belonging to her native
sons, and but slightly felt the inconveniences of subordination. Small was
the catalogue of grievances with which even democratic jealousy charged
the parent state, antecedent to the period before mentioned. Till the year
1764, the colonial regulations seemed to have no other object but the common
good of the whole empire. Exceptions to the contrary were few, and had no
appearance of system. When the approach of the colonies to manhood made
them more capable of resisting impositions, Great Britain changed her
ancient system, under which her colonies had long flourished. When policy
would rather have dictated a relaxation of authority, she rose in her demands
and multiplied her restraints." (Ramsay's Colonial History, Vol. I.,
Chap. iii., page 323).

* " This trade, though it did not clash with the spirit of the British navigation laws, was forbidden by their letter. On account of the advantages
which all parties, and particularly Great Britain, reaped from this intercourse, it had long been winked at by persons in power (a); but at the period

(a) Lieutenant-Governor Hutchinson, in a letter to Richard Jackson,
Grenville's Secretary in the Exchequer, September, 1763, says, " The real
cause of the illicit trade in this Province (Massachusetts) has been *the indulgence of the officers of the Customs ;* and we are told that the cause of this
indulgence has been that they are quartered upon for more than their legal
fees, and that without bribery and corruption they must starve."

· As a specimen of this " bribery and corruption," the deposition on oath of
the Deputy Collector of his Majesty's Customs at the port of Salem is given,
to the effect that every time he had been in the office it had been customary
for the Collector to receive of the masters of the vessels entering from Lisbon
casks of wine, boxes of fruit, etc., which was a gratuity for suffering their
vessels to be entered with salt or ballast only, and passing over unnoticed
such cargoes of wine, fruit, etc., which were prohibited to be imported into
his Majesty's plantations ; part of which wine, fruit, etc., the Collector used
to share with Governor Barnard. (Bancroft's History of the United States,
Vol. V., Chap. ix., p. 158, in a note.)

in respect to Great Britain and other European Powers at the peace of Paris in 1763; and such the friendly and affectionate feelings of the colonies towards the mother country down to that period.

III. The treaty of Paris was ratified in February, 1763; and on the 17th of March following, the Chancellor of the Exchequer submitted among the estimates the following item, which was adopted by the Commons:

"Upon account, to enable his Majesty to give a proper compensation to the respective provinces in North America, for the expenses incurred by them in the levying, clothing, and paying of the troops raised by the same, according to the active vigour

before mentioned (1764), some new regulations were adopted by which it was almost destroyed. (a) This was effected by cutters whose commanders were enjoined to take the usual custom-house oaths, and to act in the capacity of revenue officers. So sudden a stoppage of an accustomed and beneficial commerce, by an unusually rigid execution of old laws, was a serious blow to the northern colonies. It was their misfortune that, though they stood in need of vast quantities of British manufactures, their country produced very little that afforded a direct remittance to pay for them. They were therefore under the necessity of seeking elsewhere a market for their produce, and, by a circuitous route, acquiring the means of supporting their credit with the mother country. This they had found by trading with the Spanish and French colonies in their neighbourhood. From them they acquired gold, silver, and valuable commodities, the ultimate profits of which centred in Great Britain. This intercourse gave life to business of every denomination, and established a reciprocal circulation of money and merchandise, to the benefit of all parties concerned. Why a trade essential to the colonies, and which, so far from being detrimental, was indirectly advantageous to Great Britain, should be so narrowly watched, so severely restrained, was not obvious to the Americans. Instead of viewing the parent state, as formerly, in the light of an affectionate mother, they conceived her as beginning to be influenced by the narrow views of an illiberal stepdame."—*Ib.*, pp. 324, 325.

(a) "The sad story of colonial oppression commenced in 1764. Great Britain then adopted regulations respecting her colonies which, after disturbing the ancient harmony of the two countries for about twelve years, terminated in the dismemberment of the empire. These consisted in restricting their former commerce, but more especially in subjecting them to taxation by the British Parliament. By adhering to the spirit of her Navigation Act, in the course of a century the trade of Great Britain had increased far beyond the expectation of her most sanguine sons; but by rigidly enforcing the strict letter of the same in a different situation of public affairs, effects directly the reverse were produced."—*Ib.*, p. 324.

and strenuous efforts of the respective provinces shall be thought by his Majesty to merit, £133,333 6s. 8d."

The several provinces gratefully acknowledged the compensation granted them; of which Massachusetts received the largest share.

This was the last practical recognition on the part of the British Government of the loyal co-operation of the colonies in the war which established the supremacy of Great Britain in North America. From that time forward the instructions, regulations, and measures of the British Government seem to have been dictated by a jealousy of the growing wealth and power of the colonies, and to have been designed to weaken the colonies in order to strengthen the parent state. The policy of the British Administration was undoubtedly to extinguish all military spirit in the colonies, by creating a standing army which the colonies were to support, but wholly independent of them; to discountenance and forbid colonial manufactures, so as to render the colonies entirely dependent upon Great Britain for manufactured goods, hardware, and tools of every description; to destroy their trade with foreign countries by virtually prohibitory duties, so as to compel the colonies to go to the English market for every article of grocery or luxury, in whatever climate or country produced; to restrict the colonial shipping, as well as productions, to British ports alone, and even to tax the trade of the colonies with each other. All the monies arising from the various duties thus imposed were to be paid, not into the provincial treasuries, as heretofore, but into the English exchequer, and to be at the disposal of the British Parliament.

Had the British Government regarded the colonists as Englishmen in their rights and privileges as well as in their duties and obligations; had the British policy been to develop the manufactures and resources of the American colonies equally with those of England, and to leave to their local Legislatures (the only Parliaments in which the colonists had representation by their own election) to legislate on all purely domestic matters, to dispose of all colonial revenues, and to provide for their own protection, as before the war with France, and as is done in the provinces and Dominion of Canada, I doubt not but the American colonies would have remained in heart and policy an integral portion of the British empire, and become the strong right arm of Great Britain in regard to both national resources and national strength. I cannot, therefore, but regard the mistaken policy of the King and his Ministers as the primary cause of the alienation and severance of the American colonies from the mother country.

IV. The proceedings after the peace of Paris, 1763, which caused the alienation of the colonies from Great Britain, commenced on the part of the mother country, towards which, at that time, the language of the colonies was most affectionate and grateful. The first act of the British Government which caused disquiet in the colonies was the rigorous enforcement of the Navigation Act—an Act first passed by the Commonwealth Parliament more than a century before, which had been amended and extended by successive Acts under Charles the Second, which had been beneficial both to the mother country and the colonies, which had given to the naval and mercantile marine of Great Britain their superiority, but which had, in the application of its provisions to the trade between the English, Spanish, and French colonies of America, become almost obsolete by the common consent and practice of colonial governors, custom-house officers, and merchants. But shortly after the treaty of Paris instructions were sent to the colonies, directing the strict enforcement of the Navigation Act. "On the 10th of March, 1764, the House of Commons agreed to a number of resolutions respecting the American trade ; upon which a Bill was brought in, and passed into a law, laying heavy duties on the articles imported into the colonies from the French and other islands of the West Indies, and ordered these duties to be paid in specie into the exchequer of Great Britain. The Americans complained much of this new law, and of the unexampled hardship of being first deprived of obtaining specie, and next being ordered to pay the new duties in specie into the treasury at London, which they said must speedily drain them of all the specie they had. But what seemed particularly hard upon them was a Bill brought in the same session, and passed into a law, ' to *restrain* the currency of paper money in the colonies.'

"At the end of the session the King thanked the House of Commons for the ' wise regulations which had been established to augment the public revenues, to unite the interests of the most distant possessions of his Crown, and to encourage and secure their commerce with Great Britain.'"*

Though the Bill and regulations referred to legalized in a manner the heretofore illicit trade between the colonies and the French and Spanish West India islands, they practically ruined the trade by the burden of duties imposed, and thus distressed and ruined many who were engaged in it.† It is not surprising that

* Prior Documents ; or a Collection of Interesting Authentic Papers relating to the Dispute between Great Britain and America, showing the causes and progress of that misunderstanding from 1764 to 1775, pp. 1, 2 ; London, 1777.

"Four great wars within seventy years had overwhelmed Great Britain with heavy debts and excessive taxation. Her recent conquests, so far from relieving her embarrassments, had greatly increased that debt, which amounted now to £140,000,000, near $700,000,000. Even in the midst of the struggle, in the success of which they had so direct an interest, the military contributions of the colonial assemblies had been sometimes reluctant and capricious, and always irregular and unequal. They might, perhaps, refuse to contribute at all towards a standing army in time of peace, of which they would naturally soon become jealous. It seemed necessary, therefore, by some exertion of metropolitan authority, to extract from the colonies for this purpose a regular and certain revenue." (Hildreth's History of the United States, Vol. II. Chap. xxviii., p. 516.)

This was avowed by the great commoner, Pitt himself, the special friend of America. "In the course of the war between France and England, some of the colonies made exertions so far beyond their equitable quota as to merit a reimbursement from the national treasury ; but this was not universally the case. In consequence of internal discord, together with their greater domestic security, the necessary supplies had not been raised in due time by others of the provincial assemblies. That a British Minister should depend on the colonial assemblies for the execution of his plans, did not well accord with the decisive genius of Pitt ; but it was not prudent, by any innovation, to irritate the colonies during a war in which, from local circumstances, their exertions were peculiarly beneficial. The advantages that would result from an ability to draw forth the resources of the colonies, by the same authority which commanded the wealth of the mother country might, in these circumstances, have suggested the idea of taxing the colonies by authority of the British Parliament. Mr. Pitt is said to have told Dr. Franklin that 'when the war closed, if he should be in the Ministry, he would take measures to prevent the colonies from having a power to refuse or delay the supplies that might be wanted for national purposes,' but he did not mention what those measures should be." (Ramsay's Colonial History, Vol. I., Chap. iii., pp. 320, 321.)

† In the work mentioned in last note, "Prior Documents," etc., extracts

such a policy of restricting both the import and export trade of the colonies to England, apart from the methods of enforcing it, should produce general dissatisfaction in the colonies, and prompt to combinations against such extortion, and for the supply of their own wants, as far as possible independent of English manufactures. Popular meetings were held, and associations were formed in several provinces, pledging their members against purchasing or wearing clothing of English manufacture, and to set about manufacturing woollens, cottons, etc., for themselves, the materials for which they had in great abundance of their own production. Ladies and gentlemen of the wealthiest and most fashionable classes of society appeared in homespun; and merchants pledged themselves to order no more goods from England, and to countermand the orders they had previously given.*

---

of letters are given, showing the effects of the acts and regulations of commerce, even in the West Indies. I give one of these extracts as a specimen :

Extract of a letter from Kingston, in Jamaica, to a merchant in London, dated January 27th, 1765.

" Kingston, which used to be a place of great trade and hurry, is become as still as a desert since we were so wise as to banish our best friends, the Spaniards ; and now the current of that valuable commerce is turned in favour of the French and the Dutch, who have made their ports free, and, taking the advantage of our misconduct, have promised them safety, and so deal with them for all the European goods, upon the same terms as the English did. Were I to depend upon the sale of goods I had from you, I should not be able to remit the money these two or three years."

Extract of a letter from Jamaica, to a friend in London, dated May 12th, 1763:

" We are in the most deplorable state ever known in the island ; the channel through which all the money we had came among us, is entirely stopped up."—*Ib.*, p. 4.

* Prior Documents, etc., pp. 4, 5. Annual Register, Vol VII., Chap. vi.

" The Act which gave rise to these movements and combinations against importing goods from England, passed in the spring of 1764, was known as the 'Sugar Act,' reducing by one-half the duties imposed by the old 'Molasses Act' on foreign sugar and molasses imported into the colonies ; levying duties on coffee, pimento, French and East India goods, and wines from Madeira and the Azores, which hitherto had been free ; and adding iron and lumber to the 'enumerated articles' which could not be exported except to England. This Act was the first Act ever passed by Parliament which avowed the purpose, as it did in its preamble, of ' raising a *revenue* for defraying the expenses of defending, protecting and securing his Majesty's dominions in America.' This Act gave increased jurisdiction to the Admiralty Courts, and provided new and more efficient means for enforcing the collection of the revenue." (Hildreth's History of the United States, Vol. II., Chap. xxviii., pp. 520, 521.)

" In order to remedy the deficiency of British goods, the colonists betook themselves to a variety of domestic manufactures. In a little time large quantities of common cloths were brought to market ; and these, though dearer and of worse quality, were cheerfully preferred to similar articles imported from Britain. That wool might not be wanting, they entered into resolutions to abstain from eating lambs. Foreign elegancies were laid aside. The women were as exemplary as the men in various instances of self-denial. With great readiness they refused every article of decoration for their persons, and of luxury for their tables. These restrictions, which the colonists had voluntarily imposed on themselves, were so well observed, that multitudes of artificers in England were reduced to great distress, and some of their most flourishing manufactories were in a great measure at a stand-still." (Ramsay's Colonial History, Vol. I., Chap. iii., p. 346.)

" This economy became so general at Boston, that the consumption of British merchandise was diminished this year (1764) upwards of £10,000 sterling." (Holmes' Annals, Vol. II., p. 128.)

CHAPTER X.

THE intensity of the flame of colonial dissatisfaction, and
which caused it to burst forth into a conflagration of complaint
and resistance in all the colonies, was the announcement of a
measure to raise a *revenue* in the colonies, by Act of Parliament,
on the very day, March 10th, 1764, that the Bills which bore
so hard on the trade currency of the colonies were passed. Mr.
Grenville, Chancellor of the Exchequer, introduced sundry resolutions relative to the imposition of *stamp duty* in America.
These resolutions affirmed the right, the equity, the policy, and
even the necessity of taxing the colonies.*

* "An American revenue was, in England, a very popular measure. The
cry in favour of it was so strong as to silence the voice of petitions to the
contrary. The equity of compelling the Americans to contribute to the
common expenses of the empire satisfied many, who, without inquiring
into the policy or justice of taxing their unrepresented fellow-subjects,
readily assented to the measures adopted by Parliament for that purpose.
The prospect of easing their own burdens at the expense of the colonists,
dazzled the eyes of gentlemen of landed interest, so as to keep out of their
view the probable consequences of the innovation."

"The disposition to tax the colonies was also strengthened by exaggerated
accounts of their wealth. It was said that the American planters lived in afflu-
ence and with inconsiderable taxes ; while the inhabitants of Great Britain
were borne down by such aggressive burdens as to make a bare existence a
matter of extreme difficulty. The officers who had served in America during
the late war contributed to this delusion. Their observations were founded
on what they had seen in the cities, and at a time when large sums were spent

" The resolutions were not followed this year by any Bill, being only to be held out as an *intention* for next year. They were proposed and agreed to, in a thin House, late at night, and just at the rising, without any debate."* A year from that date, March 10th, 1765, Mr. Grenville introduced his long-expected measure for raising a revenue in the colonies by a duty on stamps—a measure prepared by fifty-five resolutions (in Committee of Ways and Means), on which were based the provisions of the *Stamp Act*, which provided among other things that a tax should be paid on all newspapers, all law papers, all ships' papers, property transfers, college diplomas, and marriage licenses. A fine of £10 was imposed for each non-compliance with the Act, the enforcement of which was not left to the ordinary courts and juries, but to Courts of

by Government in support of fleets and armies, and when American commodities were in great demand. To treat with attention those who came to fight for them, and also to gratify their own pride, the colonists had made a parade of their riches, by frequently and sumptuously entertaining the gentlemen of the British army. These, judging from what they saw, without considering the general state of the country, concurred in representing the colonists as very able to contribute largely towards defraying the common expenses of the empire." (Ramsay's Colonial History, Vol. I., Chap. iii., pp. 332—335.)

* Prior Documents, etc., p. 5.

" The taxes of Great Britain exceeded by £3,000,000 what they were in 1754, before the war ; yet the present object was only to make the colonies maintain their own army. Besides the taxes on trade, which were immediately to be imposed, Mr. Grenville gave notice in the House that it was his intention, in the next session, to bring in a Bill imposing *stamp duties* in America ; and the reasons for giving such notice were, because he understood some people entertained doubts of the power of Parliament to impose internal taxes on the colonies, and because that, of all the schemes which had fallen under his consideration, he thought a Stamp Act was the best. But he was not so wedded to it as to be unwilling to give it up for any one that might appear more eligible ; or if the colonies themselves thought any other mode would be more expedient, he should have no objection to come to it by Act of Parliament. At that time the merits of the question were opened at large. The opponents of the Government were publicly called upon to deny, if they thought it fitting, the right of the Legislature to impose any tax, internal or external, on the colonies ; and not a single member ventured to controvert the right. Upon a solemn question asked in a full House, there was not one negative." (Bancroft's History of the United States, Vol. V., Chap. ix., pp. 186, 187.)

Admiralty without juries, the officers of which were appointed by the Crown, and paid fees out of the fines which they imposed—the informer receiving one-half. The year's notice* of this Bill had given the opportunity of discussing the merits of it on both sides of the Atlantic. The King, at the opening of the session, had presented the colonial question as one of " obedience to the laws and respect for the legislative authority of the kingdom ;" and the Lords and Commons, in reply, declared their intention to pursue every plan calculated for the public advantage, and to proceed therein " with that temper and firmness which will best conciliate and ensure due submission to the laws and reverence for the legislative authority of Great Britain." As it was a money Bill, no petitions were allowed to be presented to the Commons against it. Several members spoke against it, of whom General Conway and Colonel Barré were the principal, both of whom had served in America ;† but the Bill was passed by a majority of five to one. In America, the old, loyal Church of England colony of Virginia led the way in opposition to the Bill, the General Assembly of Burgesses being in session when the news of its having been passed by the British Parliament reached America ; and the resolutions which that Assembly passed covered the

* Mr. Grenville gave the year's notice apparently from motives of kindness and courtesy to the colonies, " in order that the colonies might have time to offer a compensation for the revenues which such a tax might produce. Accordingly, when the agents of these colonies waited upon him to thank him for this mark of his consideration, he told them that he was ready to receive proposals from the colonies for any other tax that might be equivalent in its produce to the stamp tax, hinting withal that their principals would now have it in their power, by agreeing to this tax, to establish a precedent for their being consulted (by the Ministry, we suppose) before any tax was imposed upon them by Parliament.

" Many persons at this side of the water, and perhaps the agents themselves, looked upon this as a humane and generous proceeding. But the colonies seemed to consider it as an affront rather than a compliment. At least not one of them authorized its agent to consent to the stamp duty, or to offer any compensation for it ; and some of them went so far as to send over petitions, to be presented to the King, Lords, and Commons, positively and directly questioning the authority and jurisdiction of Parliament over their properties." (Annual Register, Vol. VIII., Chap. ix., p. 33.)

† See Appendix to this chapter for a summary and review of the speeches of Mr. Charles Townsend and Colonel Barré.

whole ground of colonial opposition to the Stamp Act.* The
Assembly of Virginia sent copies of its resolutions to the
other colonies, and several of their Legislatures adopted the
same or similar resolutions. Two days after adopting the
resolutions, the Governor dismissed the Legislature and ordered
new elections ; but at the new elections all who voted for the
resolutions were re-elected, and all who opposed them were
rejected ; so that the newly-elected Assembly was even more
unanimous against the Stamp Act than the Assembly which
had been dismissed. It was said " the fire began in Virginia ; "

---

* " The province of Virginia took the lead. On the 29th May, 1765, the
House of Burgesses of Virginia adopted the following resolutions :
"Whereas the honourable House of Commons in England have of late
drawn into question how far the General Assembly of this province hath
power to enact laws for levying taxes and imposing duties payable by the
people of this his Majesty's most ancient colony; for settling and ascertaining
the same to all future times, the House of Burgesses of this present General
Assembly have come to the following resolutions :
1. " *Resolved,*—That the first adventurers and settlers of this his Majesty's
colony and dominion of Virginia brought with them, and transmitted to
their posterity, and all other his Majesty's subjects since inhabiting his
Majesty's colony, all the privileges and immunities that have at any time
been held, enjoyed, and possessed by the people of Great Britain.
2. " *Resolved,*—That by the two Royal Charters granted by King James the
First, the colonies aforesaid are declared entitled to all privileges of faithful
liege and natural-born subjects, to all intents and purposes as if they had
been abiding and born within the realm of England.
3. " *Resolved,*—That his Majesty's liege people of this most ancient colony
have enjoyed the right of having been thus far governed by their own
Assembly in the article of taxes and internal police ; and that the same
have never been forfeited, or in any other way yielded up, but have been
constantly recognized by the King and people of Great Britain.
4. " *Resolved,* therefore,—That the General Assembly of this colony, together with his Majesty or his substitute, have, in their representative
capacity, the only exclusive right and power to levy taxes and impositions
upon the inhabitants of this colony ; and that every attempt to vest such
power in any person or persons whatsoever other than the General Assembly
aforesaid, is illegal, unconstitutional, and unjust, and has a manifest tendency to destroy British as well as American freedom." (Prior Documents,
etc., pp. 6, 7.)
These resolutions were introduced by Patrick Henry, in an eloquent and
animated speech, in the course of which the following extraordinary scene
occurred : In an exciting tone he exclaimed, " Cæsar had his Brutus !
Charles the First had his Cromwell ! and George the Third ——" The

" Virginia rang the alarm bell ; " " Virginia gave the signal for
the continent." The petition from the Assembly of New York
was stronger than that from Virginia—" so bold that when it
reached London no one would present it to Parliament." The
remonstrance of Massachusetts was feebler, it having been
modified by the Lieutenant-Governor, Hutchinson, and the
Governor, Barnard. Rhode Island followed New York and
Virginia. The Legislature of Connecticut protested at once
against the stamp tax, and sent decided instructions to their
agent in London to insist firmly upon their rights of taxation
and trial by jury. When the news of these things reached
England, and the colonial agents made their remonstrances,
it was asked, " Will the colonies resist ? " That was not believed
to be possible even by Franklin ; but though no physical
resistance was thought of in any part of America, yet the
opposition to the Stamp Act became increasingly intense among
all classes, from the first announcement of it in May to the
prescribed time of its going into operation, the 1st of November ;
and armed resistance seems to have been viewed as a possible
alternative in the future. It was as yet looked upon as a
contest between the colonists and the Parliament and advisers of
the King, and not with the King himself, to whom ardent
loyalty was professed and no doubt felt. It was at length proposed that a general Congress of representatives of all the
colonies should be held to confer on the measures necessary to
be taken.

The Massachusetts Legislature met the latter part of May,
and recommended, on the 6th of June, the calling of a Congress, to be composed of " Committees from the Houses of
Representatives or Burgesses in the several colonies," to meet
at New York on the first Tuesday of October following, there

Speaker, greatly excited, cried out " Treason ! treason ! " which was re-echoed
from all sides. Then Henry, fixing his eye on the Speaker, and pointing his
finger towards him, raised his voice above the confusion and concluded,
" And George the Third may profit by their example. If this be treason,
make the most of it." (Elliott's History, etc., Vol. II., p. 252.)

Mr Bancroft says : " The resolutions were published in the newspapers
throughout America, and by *men of all parties*—*by Royalists* in office not less
than by the public bodies in the colonies—were received without dispute as
the avowed sentiments of the ' Old Dominion.' " (History of the United
States, Vol. V., Chap. xiii., p. 278.)

to consult "on the difficulties in which the colonies were and must be placed by the late Acts of Parliament levying duties and taxes upon them, and to consider of a general and humble address to his Majesty and the Parliament to implore relief." A circular letter was prepared and sent to the Speakers of the Legislative Assemblies of other colonies; and a Committee was chosen for Massachusetts. On the 7th of October a Congress met at New York, consisting of 28 delegates from the Assemblies of Massachusetts, Rhode Island and Providence Plantations, Connecticut, New York, New Jersey, Pennsylvania, the Delaware counties, Maryland, and South Carolina. The session of this convention or congress lasted three weeks ; the members were found to be of one opinion on the principal subjects discussed. A declaration of the rights and grievances of the colonies was agreed to, in which all the privileges of Englishmen were claimed as the birthright of the colonists, including the right of being taxed only by their own consent. A petition to the King and memorials to each House of Parliament were prepared and adopted. The Assemblies of Virginia, North Carolina, and Georgia were prevented by their Governors from sending representatives to the Congress ; but they forwarded petitions to England similar to those adopted by the Congress.* It is worthy of remark, that, with the exception of Boston, the proceedings of the populace, as well as of the Conventions and Legislative Assemblies, against the Stamp Act, were conducted in a legal and orderly manner, such as to command respect in England as well as in America. But in Boston there had always been a mob, which, under the direction and auspices of men behind the scenes, and opposed to British rule in any form, was ready to come forth as opportunity offered in lawless violence against the authority of the Crown and its officers. In England, eighty years before, mobs were employed to intimidate the Court, Lords, and Commons in passing the Bill of Attainder against Strafford, and against Bishops and Episcopacy. The Rev. Dr. Burgess, the most popular Puritan minister in London at that time, called them his " band-dogs," to be let loose or restrained as occasion required.† Such men as the " band-dogs" of Boston,

---

* Holmes' Annals, Vol. II., page 135. Hildreth's History of the United States, Vol. II., pp. 530, 531.

† Cornelius Burgess, a Puritan minister, used to say of the rabble :

who found a good opportunity for the exercise of their voca-
tion during the discussions of the local Legislature and public
meetings against the Stamp Act, not content with the harmless
acts of patriotism of hanging Lord Bute and Mr. Andrew
Oliver (the proposed distributors of of the stamps) in effigy and
then making bonfires of them, they levelled Mr. Oliver's office
buildings to the ground, and broke the windows and destroyed
most of the furniture of his house. Some days afterwards they
proceeded to the house of William Story, Deputy Registrar of the
Court of Admiralty, and destroyed his private papers, as well
as the records and files of the Court. They next entered and
purloined the house of Benjamin Hallowell, jr., Comptroller of
the Customs, and regaled themselves to intoxication with the
liquors which they found in his cellar. They then, as Mr.
Hildreth says, " proceeded to the mansion of Governor Hutchinson, in North Square. The Lieutenant-Governor and his family
fled for their lives.* The house was completely gutted, and the

---

" These are my band-dogs. I can set them on ; I can fetch them off again."
(Rapin's History of England, Vol. IX., p. 410, in a note.)

    * " On Sunday, 25th August (the day before these riots were renewed),
Dr. Mayhew preached in the west meeting house, from the text, Galatians,
chap. v. verse 12 : ' I would they were even cut off which trouble you.'
Although the sermon was regular enough, the text then seemed significant,
and Hutchinson (History) states that some were excited by it. (Doubtless
the ' Band-dogs' of Dr. M° hew.) At any rate, in the night the bonfires
brought together their crowds, who, grown bold by success, proceeded to
express their hatred against the Admiralty Courts and the Custom-houses
by attacking and damaging the houses of two officers, Story and Hallowell.
In these they found good wines, which served to inflame their blood ; and
then their shout was, ' Hutchinson ! Hutchinson !' A friend hastened to
his house to warn him of his danger. He barred his windows, determined to
resist their fury; but his family dragged him away with them in their flight.
The mob rushed on, and beating down his windows, sacked the house (one
of the finest in Boston) and destroyed everything, even a valuable collection
of books and manuscripts.

" This excess shocked the wise friends of liberty, and in a public meeting
the citizens discovered the destruction, and set their faces against any
further demonstrations of the sort. Rewards were offered for the rioters, and
Mackintosh and some others were apprehended, but were rescued by their
friends ; and it was found impossible to proceed against them." (Elliott's
New England History, Vol. II., pp. 254, 255.)

" Mayhew sent the next day a special apology and disclaimer to Hutchinson.
The inhabitants of Boston, at a town meeting, unanimously expressed their

contents burned in bonfires kindled in the square. Along with Hutchinson's public and private papers perished many invaluable manuscripts relating to the history of the province, which Hutchinson had been thirty years in collecting, and which it was impossible to replace."*   The universal and intense opposi-

abhorrence of these proceedings, and a civil guard was organized to prevent their repetition. Yet the rioters, though well known, went unpunished—a sure sign of the secret concurrence of the mass of the community. Those now committed were revolutionary acts, designed to intimidate—melancholy forerunners of civil war." (Hildreth's History of the United States, Vol. II., Chap. xxviii., p. 528.)

* *Ib.*, p. 527.

1. Lieutenant-Governor Hutchinson, whose house was thus sacked and his valuable papers destroyed, was the historian of his native province of Massachusetts Bay, whom I have quoted so frequently in the present volume of this history. Of his history, Mr. Bancroft, a bitter enemy of Hutchinson's, says :

"At the opening of the year 1765, the people of New England were reading the history of the first sixty years of the Colony of Massachusetts, by Hutchinson. This work is so ably executed that as yet it remains without a rival ; and his knowledge was so extensive that, with the exception of a few concealments, it exhausts the subject. Nothing so much revived the ancestral spirit which a weaving of the gloomy superstitions, mixed with Puritanism, had for a long time overshadowed." (History of the United States, Vol. V., Chap. xi., p. 228.)

2. But though mob violence distinguished Boston on this as well as on other occasions, the opposition was such throughout the colonies, from New Hampshire to Georgia, that all those who had been appointed to receive and distribute the stamps were compelled, by the remonstrances and often threats of their fellow-colonists, to resign the office; and the stamped paper sent from England to the ports of the various provinces was either returned back by the vessel that brought it, or put into a place of safe keeping. "Though the Stamp Act was to have operated from the 1st of November, yet the legal proceedings in Courts were carried on as before. Vessels entered and departed without stamped papers. The printers boldly printed and circulated their newspapers, and found a sufficient number of readers, though they used common paper, in defiance of the Act of Parliament. In most departments, by common consent, business was carried on as though no stamp law existed. This was accompanied by spirited resolutions to risk all consequences rather than submit to use the paper required by the Stamp Act. While these matters were in agitation, the colonists entered into associations against importing British manufactures till the Stamp Act should be repealed. Agreeably to the free constitution of Great Britain, the subject was at liberty to buy, or not to buy, as he pleased. By suspending their future purchases until the repeal of the Stamp Act, the colonists made it the interest of

tion of all ranks in all the colonies (except a few of the office-
holders) was re-echoed and strengthened by opposition and
remonstrances from the merchants and manufacturers in England
and Scotland connected with the American trade.* Parliament
met the 17th December, 1765, when one reason assigned in the

merchants and manufacturers in England to solicit its repeal. They had
usually taken so great a proportion of British manufactures, amounting
annually to two or three millions sterling, that they threw some thousands in
the mother country out of employment, and induced them, from a regard to
their own interest, to advocate the measures wished for by America." (Ramsay's Colonial History, Vol. I., pp. 345, 346).

* " Petitions were received by Parliament from the merchants of London,
Bristol, Lancaster, Liverpool, Hull, Glasgow, etc., and indeed from most of
the trading and manufacturing towns and boroughs in the kingdom. In
these petitions they set forth the great decay of their trade, owing to the laws
and regulations made for America; the vast quantities of our manufactures
(besides those articles imported from abroad, which were enclosed either with
our own manufactures or with the produce of our colonies) which the American trade formerly took off our hands ; by all which many thousand manufacturers, seamen, and labourers had been employed, to the very great
and increasing benefit of the nation. That in return for these exports the
petitioners had received from the colonies rice, indigo, tobacco, naval stores
oil, whale-fins, furs, and lately potash, with other staple commodities, besides
a large balance of remittances by bills of exchange and bullion obtained by
the colonists for articles of their produce, not required for the British market,
and therefore exported to other places.

" That from the nature of this trade, consisting of British manufactures
exported, and of the import of raw material from America, many of them
used in our manufactures, and all of them tending to lessen our dependence
on neighbouring states, it must be deemed of the highest importance in the
commercial system of this nation. That this commerce, so beneficial to the
state, and so necessary to the support of multitudes, then lay under such
difficulties and discouragements, that nothing less than its utter ruin was
apprehended without the immediate interposition of Parliament.

" That the colonies were then indebted to the merchants of Great Britain
to the sum of several millions sterling ; and that when pressed for payment,
they appeal to past experience in proof of their willingness; but declare it is
not in their power at present to make good their engagements, alleging that
the taxes and restrictions laid upon them, and the extension of the jurisdiction of the Vice-Admiralty Courts, established by some late Acts of Parliament, particularly by an Act passed in the 4th year of his present Majesty,
for granting certain duties in the British Colonies and Plantations in America,
and by an Act passed in the 5th year of his Majesty, for granting and applying
certain stamp duties, etc., in said colonies, etc., with several regulations and
restraints, which, if founded in Acts of Parliament for defined purposes, they

Royal speech for calling Parliament together earlier than usual
was the importance of matters which had occurred in America,
all papers connected with which would be laid before them.
After the Christmas recess, the Parliament met the 17th of
January, 1766, when American affairs were again commended
in a speech from the Throne as a principal object of parliamentary
deliberations.   Both Houses, in their replies to the King, showed
that they regarded American affairs in the same important light
as his Majesty; and for more than two months those affairs constituted the principal subject of parliamentary debate, and the
leading topics of conversation among all classes.   The application of the Commons was unwearied; their sittings continued
until after midnight, and sometimes even until morning; the
number of petitions they received, the multitude of papers
and the witnesses they had to examine, occupied much time,
accompanied by continual debates.   The authors of the Stamp
Act were now in opposition, and made most strenuous efforts in
its justification.   The debates turned chiefly on two questions:
1. Whether the Legislature of Great Britain had, or had not,
a right of taxation over the colonies; 2. Whether the late laws,

represent to have been extended in such a manner as to disturb legal commerce and harass the fair trader, and to have so far interrupted the usual,
former and most useful branches of their commerce, restrained the sale of
their produce, thrown the state of the several provinces into confusion, and
brought on so great a number of actual bankruptcies that the former opportunities and means of remittances and payments were utterly lost and taken
from them.

"That the petitioners were, by these unhappy events, reduced to the
necessity of applying to the House, in order to secure themselves and their
families from impending ruin ; to prevent a multitude of manufacturers from
becoming a burden to the community, or else seeking their bread in other
countries, to the irretrievable loss of the kingdom ; and to preserve the
strength of this nation entire, its commerce flourishing, the revenues increasing, our navigation the bulwark of the kingdom, in a state of growth and
extension, and the colonies, from inclination, duty, and interest, attached to
the mother country."

"Such a number of petitions from every part of the kingdom, pregnant
with so many interesting facts, stated and attested by such numbers of people,
whose lives had been entirely devoted to trade, and who must be naturally
supposed to be competent judges of a subject which they had so long and so
closely attended to (besides that it showed the general sense of the nation),
could not fail of having great weight with the House." (Annual Register
for 1766, Vol. IX., Chap. vii., pp. 35, 36.)

especially the Stamp Act, were just and expedient. In the ultimate decision of the first question both parties agreed, and the House affirmed, without a division, "That the Parliament of Great Britain had a right to bind the colonies in all cases whatsoever," without any distinction in regard to taxation. As to the second question, Parliament decided, after very warm and protracted debates, in favour of the total repeal of the Stamp Act. Accordingly two Bills were brought in, pursuant to these resolutions: the one, a declaratory Bill, entitled "An Act for securing the defence of the American colonies of Great Britain," and asserting the right of Parliament to bind the colonies in all cases whatsoever; the other, for the total repeal of the Stamp Act.

[Colonel Barré's celebrated reply to Charles Townsend, and review of it, on the passing of the Stamp Act, will be found in Appendix A. to this chapter; and Lord Chancellor Camden's opinion, and the great commoner Pitt's memorable sayings in the discussion on the *repeal* of the Stamp Act, will be found in Appendix B.]

The Declaratory Act, though avowing the absolute power of Parliament to bind the colonies in all cases whatsoever, and rescinding, as far as an Act of Parliament could, all the declarations and resolutions which had been adopted by the Colonial Assemblies and public meetings against the authority of Parliament, attracted very little attention amid the absorbing interest centred in the Stamp Act, and the universal rejoicings on both sides of the Atlantic at its repeal. The Declaratory Act, as it was called, passed the Commons the beginning of February; and on the 18th of the month, after a vehement discussion, closed by the speeches of Messrs. Grenville and Pitt, the House of Commons, at three o'clock in the morning, repealed the Stamp Act by a majority of 275 to 167. The House of Lords, after warm and protracted discussions, voted for its repeal by a majority of 100 to 71; and three days afterwards, the 18th of March, the royal assent was given to the Act—"An event," says the Annual Register for 1766, "that caused more universal joy throughout the British dominions than perhaps any other that can be remembered."

"Ships in the River Thames displayed their colours, and houses were illuminated all over the city. It was no sooner known in America, than the colonists rescinded their resolutions, and recommenced their mercantile intercourse with the mother country. They presented their homespun clothes to the poor, and imported more largely than ever. The churches resounded with thanksgivings ; and their public and private rejoicings knew no bounds. By letters, addresses, and other means, almost all the colonies showed unequivocal marks of acknowledgment and gratitude. So sudden a calm after so violent a storm is without a parallel in history. By the judicious sacrifice of one law, Great Britain procured an acquiescence in all that remained."*

APPENDIX A. TO CHAPTER X.

DISCUSSION BETWEEN CHARLES TOWNSEND AND COLONEL BARRE IN THE DEBATE ON PASSING THE STAMP ACT, REFERRED TO ON PAGE 293.

It was during the discussion on this Bill that Colonel Barré made the famous retort to Mr. Charles Townsend, head of the Board of Trade. Mr. Townsend made an able speech in support of the Bill and the equity of the taxation, and insisted that the colonies had borne but a small proportion of the expenses of the last war, and had yet obtained by it immense advantages at a vast expense to the mother country. He concluded in the following words:

" And now will these American children, planted by our care,

* Ramsay's Colonial History, Vol. I., p. 348.

" At the same time that the Stamp Act was repealed, the absolute and unlimited supremacy of Parliament was, in words, asserted. The opposers of repeal contended for this as essential. The friends of that measure acquiesced in it, to strengthen their party and make sure of their object. Many of both sides thought that the dignity of Great Britain required something of the kind to counterbalance the loss of authority that might result from her yielding to the clamours of the colonists. The Act for this purpose was called the Declaratory Act, and was, in principle, more hostile to America's rights than the Stamp Act ; for it annulled those resolutions and acts of the Provincial Assemblies in which they had asserted their right to exemption from all taxes not imposed by their own representatives ; and also enacted that the King and Parliament had, and of right ought to have, power to bind the colonies in all cases whatsoever."—*Ib.*, p. 349.

nourished by our indulgence to a degree of strength and opulence, and protected by our arms, grudge to contribute their mite to relieve us from the heavy burden under which we lie ? "

As he sat down, Colonel Barré rose and replied with great energy, and, under the influence of intense excitement, uttered the following impassioned retort to the concluding words of Charles Townsend's speech :

" *They planted by your care !* No ; your oppressions planted them in America. They fled from your tyranny to a then uncultivated, inhospitable country, where they exposed themselves to almost all the hardships to which human nature is liable, and among others to the cruelties of a savage foe—the most subtle, and I will take upon me to say the most formidable of any people upon the face of God's earth ; and yet, actuated by principles of true English liberty, they met all hardships with pleasure, compared with those they suffered in their own country from the hands of those who should have been their friends.

" *They nourished by your indulgence !* They grew by your neglect of them.   As soon as you began to care about them, that care was exercised in sending persons to rule over them, in one department and another, who were perhaps the deputies of deputies to some members of this House, sent to spy out their liberties, to misrepresent their actions, and to prey upon them ; men whose behaviour, on many occasions, has caused the blood of those *sons of liberty* to recoil within them ; men promoted to the highest seats of justice—some who, to my knowledge, were glad, by going to a foreign country, to escape being brought to the bar of a Court of justice in their own.

" *They protected by your arms !* They have nobly taken up arms in your defence ; have exerted a valour amidst their constant and laborious industry, for the defence of a country whose frontier was drenched in blood, while its interior parts yielded all its little savings to your emolument.   And, believe me —remember, I this day told you so—the same spirit of freedom which actuated that people at first will accompany them still. But prudence forbids me to explain myself further. God knows, I do not at this time speak from motives of party heat ; what I deliver are the genuine sentiments of my heart.   However superior to me in general knowledge and experience the respectable body of this House may be, yet I claim to know more of America than most of you, having seen and been conversant in that country. The people, I believe, are as truly loyal as any subjects the King has; but a people jealous of their liberties, and who will vindicate them if ever they should be violated. But the subject is too delicate; I will say no more."

Remarks on the Speeches of Mr. Charles Townsend and Colonel Barré.

Perhaps the English language does not present a more eloquent and touching appeal than these words of Colonel Barré, the utterances of a sincere and patriotic heart. They were taken down by a friend at the time of delivery, sent across the Atlantic, published and circulated in every form throughout America, and probably produced more effect upon the minds of the colonists than anything ever uttered or written. Very likely not one out of a thousand of those who have read them, carried away by their eloquence and fervour, has ever thought of analysing them to ascertain how far they are just or true; yet I am bound to say that their misstatements are such as to render their argument fallacious from beginning to end, with the exception of their just tribute to the character of the American colonists.

The words of Charles Townsend were insulting to the colonists to the last degree, and were open to the severest rebuke. He assumed that because the settlements in America were infant settlements, in comparison with those of the mother country, the settlers themselves were but children, and should be treated as such; whereas the fathers of new settlements and their commerce, the guiding spirits in their advancement, are the most advanced men of their nation and age, the pioneers of enterprise and civilization; and as such they are entitled to peculiar respect and consideration, instead of their being referred to as children, and taxed without their consent by men who, whatever their rank in the society and public affairs of England, could not compare with them in what constituted real manhood greatness. But though Charles Townsend's insulting haughtiness to the American colonists, and his proposal to treat them as minors, destitute of the feelings and rights of grown-up Englishmen, merited the severest rebuke, yet that did not justify the statements and counter-pretensions on which Colonel

Barré founded that rebuke.   Let us briefly examine some of his statements.

1. He says that the oppressions of England planted the settlers in America, who fled from English tyranny to a then uncultivated, inhospitable country.

In reply it may be affirmed, as a notorious fact, that the southern and middle colonies, even to Pennsylvania, were nationalized by the kings of England from their commencement, and were frequently assisted by both King and Parliament.   The Dutch and the Swedes were the fathers of the settlements of New York and New Jersey.   The "Pilgrim Fathers," the founders of the Plymouth colony, did, however, flee from persecution in England in the first years of King James, but found their eleven years' residence in Holland less agreeable than settlement under English rule, or rather English indulgence, in America.   The founders of the Massachusetts Bay settlement were a Puritan section of the Church of England, of which they professed to be devoted members after they embarked for America.   A wealthy company of them determined to found a settlement in America, where they could enjoy the pure worship of the Church of England without the ceremonies enjoined by Archbishop Laud—where they could convert the savage Indians, and pursue the fur and fish trade, and agriculture; but they were no more driven to America by the "tyranny" of England, than the hundreds of thousands of Puritans who remained in England, overthrew the monarchy, beheaded the king, abolished the Church of England, first established Presbyterianism and then abolished it, and determined upon the establishment of Congregationalism at the moment of Cromwell's death.   But those "Puritan Fathers" who came to Massachusetts Bay, actually came under the auspices of a "Royal Charter," which they cherished as the greatest boon conferred upon any people.   But among their first acts after their arrival at Massachusetts Bay was that to abolish the Church of England worship itself, and set up the Congregational worship in its place; to proscribe the Common Prayer Book, and forbid its use even in private families, and to banish those who persisted in its use.   And instead of converting and christianizing the savage heathen—the chief professed object of their emigration, and so expressed in their Royal Charter of

incorporation—they never sent a missionary or established a
school among them for more than twelve years; and then the
first and long the only missionary among the Indians was
John Elliott, self-appointed, and supported by contributions
from England. But during those twelve years, and afterwards,
they slew the Indians by thousands, as the Canaanites and
Amalekites, to be rooted out of the land which God had given
to "the saints" (that is, to themselves), to be possessed and
enjoyed by them. The savage foe, whose arms were bows and
arrows,* were made "formidable" in defence of their homes,
which they had inherited from their forefathers; and if, in
defence and attempted recovery of their homes when driven
from them, they inflicted, after their own mode of warfare,
  cruelties" upon their invaders, yet they themselves were
the greatest sufferers, almost to annihilation.†

* "The aborigines were never formidable in battle until they became
supplied with the weapons of European invention." (Bancroft's History of
the United States, Vol. I., p. 401.)

† The treatment of the Indians by the early New England Puritans is one
of the darkest pages in English colonial history. I have slightly alluded
to it in the preceding pages of this volume. Many passages might be selected
from the early divines of New England, referring to the Indians as the
heathen whom they were to drive out of the land which God had given to
this Israel. I will confine myself to the quotation of a few words from
the late Rev. J. B. Marsden, A.M., noted for his Puritan partialities, in the
two volumes of his *History of the Early and Later Puritans.* But his sense
of Christian justice, tolerance, and humanity revolted at the New England
Puritans' intolerance to each other, and their cruel treatment of the Indians.
Mr. Marsden says:

"The New England Puritans were revered beyond the Atlantic as the
Pilgrim Fathers, the founders of great cities, and of States renowned through the
wide world for wealth, intelligence, and liberty. Their memory is cherished
in England with feelings of silent respect rather than of unmixed admiration;
for their inconsistencies were almost equal to their virtues; and here, while
we respect their integrity, we are not blinded to their faults. A persecuted
band themselves, they soon learned to persecute each other. The disciples
of liberty, they confined its blessings to themselves. The loud champions
of the freedom of conscience, they allowed no freedom which interfered with
their narrow views. Professing a mission of Gospel holiness, they fulfilled it,
but in part. When opposed, they were revengeful; when irritated, fanatical
and cruel. In them a great experiment was to be tried, under conditions
the most favourable to its success; and it failed in its most important point.
The question to be solved was this: How would the Puritans, the hunted,

2. "The colonies being nourished by the indulgence" of
England, assumed by Charles Townsend, is the second ground of
Colonel Barré's retort, who affirmed that the colonies grew by
England's neglect of them, and that as soon as she began to
care for them, that care was exercised in sending persons to
rule over them in one department or another, etc.

persecuted Puritans behave, were they but once free, once at liberty to
carry their principles into full effect? The answer was returned from the
shores of another world. It was distinct and unequivocal. And it was this:
they were prepared to copy the worst vices of their English persecutors, and,
untaught by experience, to imitate their worst mistakes. The severities of
Whitgift seemed to be justified when it was made apparent on the plains of
North America, that they had been inflicted upon men who wanted only the
opportunity to inflict them again, and inflict them on one another." (Marsden's
History of the Early Puritans, Chap. xi., pp. 305, 306.)

After referring to early conflicts between the Puritans and Indians, Mr.
Marsden remarks as follows in regard to the manner in which the Puritans
destroyed the Pequod nation:

"If there be a justifiable cause of war, it surely must be this, when
our territory is invaded and our means of existence threatened. That
the Indians fell upon their enemies by the most nefarious stratagems, or
exposed them, when taken in war, to cruel torments (though such ferocity
is not alleged in this instance), does not much affect the question. They
were savages, and fought white men as they and their fathers had always
fought each other. How then should a community of Christian men have
dealt with them? Were they to contend as savages or civilized men? As
civilized men, or rather as men who had forsaken a land of civilization for
purer abodes of piety and peace? The Pequod war shows how little their
piety could be trusted when their passions were aroused."

"After a week's marching, they came at day-break on the Indian wigwams
and immediately assaulted them. The 'massacre' (so their own chronicler,
Mr. Bancroft, has termed it) spread from one hut to another; for the Indians
were asleep and unarmed. But the work of slaughter was too slow. 'We
must burn them,' exclaimed the fanatic chieftain of the Puritans; and he
cast the first firebrand to windward among their wigwams. In an instant
the encampment was in a blaze. Not a soul escaped. Six hundred Indians,
men, women, and children, perished by the steady hand of the marksman,
by the unresisted broadsword, and by the hideous conflagration.

"The work of revenge was not yet accomplished. In a few days a fresh body
of troops arrived from Massachusetts, accompanied by their minister, Wilson.
The remnants of the proscribed race were now hunted down in their hiding
places; every wigwam was burned; every settlement broken up; every corn-
field laid waste. There remained, says their exulting historian, not a man or a
woman, not a warrior or child of the Pequod name. A nation had disappeared
from the family of men." "History records many deeds of blood equal in

In reply, let it be remembered that three out of the four New England colonies—Plymouth, Rhode Island, and Connecticut—elected their own governors and officers from the beginning to the end of their colonial existence, as did Massachusetts during the first half century of her first Charter, which she forfeited by her usurpations, persecutions, and encroachments upon the rights

ferocity to this ; but we shall seek in vain for a parallel to the massacre of the Pequod Indians. It brought out the worst points in the Puritan character, and displayed it in the strongest light. When their passions were once inflamed, their religion itself was cruelty. A dark, fanatical spirit of revenge took possession, not, as in other men, by first expelling every religious and every human consideration, but, what was infinitely more terrible, by calling to its aid every stimulant, every motive that religion, jaundiced and perverted, could supply. It is terrible to read, when cities are stormed, of children thrown into the flames, and shrieking women butchered by infuriated men who have burst the restraints of discipline. It is a dreadful licence ; and true and gallant soldiers, occur when it may, feel that their profession is disgraced. But this was worse. Here all was deliberately calm ; all was sanctioned by religion. It was no outbreak of mere brutality. The fast was kept ; the Sabbath was observed ; the staff of office, as a sacred ensign, was consecrated by one Christian minister, while another attended upon the marching of soldiery, and cheered them in the murderous design with his presence and his prayers. Piety was supposed not to abhor, but to exult in the exploit. This was true fanaticism. God's word and ordinances were made subservient to the greatest crimes. They were rudely forced and violated, and made the ministers of sin. When the assailants, reeking from the slaughter and blackened with the smoke, returned home, they were everywhere received with a pious ovation. God was devoutly praised, because the first principles of justice, nay, the stinted humanities of war, had been outraged, and unresisting savages, with their wives and children, had been ferociously destroyed." (Marsden's History of the Early Puritans, Chap. xi., pp. 305—311.)

Such was the early Puritan method of fulfilling the Royal Charter to the Massachusetts Company of " Christianizing and civilizing the idolatrous Indians ;" and such is a practical comment upon Colonel Barré's statement as to Indian cruelties.

But the intolerance of the Puritans to each other was as conspicuous as their cruel treatment of the Indians. On this point Mr. Marsden adds :

" The intolerance with which the Puritans had been treated at home might at least have taught them a lesson of forbearance to each other. But it had no such effect. It would almost seem as if, true disciples in the school of the High Commission and Star Chamber, their ambition was to excel their former tyrants in the art of persecution. They imitated, with a pertinacious accuracy, the bad examples of their worst oppressors ; and with far less to excuse them, repeated in America the self-same crimes from which

of others, as I have shown in Chapter VI. of this history; and it has been shown in Chapter VII., on the authority of Puritan ministers, jurists, and historians, that during the seventy years that Massachusetts was ruled under the second Royal Charter, her governors being appointed by the Crown, she advanced in social unity, in breadth and dignity of legislation, and in equity of government, commerce, and prosperity, beyond anything she had enjoyed and manifested under the first Charter—so much so, that the neighbouring colonies would have gladly been favoured with her system of government. It is possible there may have been individual instances of inefficiency, and even failure of character, in some officers of the Government during a period of seventy years, as is the case in all Governments, but such instances were few, if they occurred at all, and such as to afford no just pretext for the rhapsody and insinuations of Colonel Barré on the subject.

3. In the third place, Colonel Barré denied that the colonies had been defended by the arms of England, and said, on the contrary, " they have nobly taken arms in your defence." It is true the colonists carried on their own local contests with the Indians. The northern colonies conceived the idea of driving the French out of America, and twice attacked Quebec for that purpose, but they failed ; and the French and Indians made such encroachments upon them that they implored aid from England " to prevent their being driven into the sea." It was not until England " nobly took up arms" in their behalf, and sent navies and armies for their " defence," that the progress of French arms and Indian depredations were arrested in America, and the colonists were delivered from enemies who had disturbed their peace and endangered their safety for more than a century.

they and their fathers had suffered so much in England. No political considerations of real importance, no ancient prejudices interwoven with the framework of society, could be pleaded here. Their institutions were new, their course was hampered by no precedents. Imagination cannot suggest a state of things more favourable to the easy, safe, and sure development of their views. Had they cherished a catholic spirit, there was nothing to prevent the exercise of the most enlarged beneficence. Their choice was made freely, and they decided in favour of intolerance ; and their fault was aggravated by the consideration that the experiment had been tried, and that they themselves were the living witnesses of its folly." (Marsden's History of the Early Puritans, p. 311.)

At the close of the last French war, the colonies themselves, through their Legislatures, gratefully acknowledged their indebtedness to the mother country for their deliverance and safety, which, without her aid, they said they never could have secured.

APPENDIX B.

Opinions of Mr. Grenville, Mr. Pitt, and Lord Camden (formerly Chief Justice Pratt) on the Stamp Act and its Repeal.

The great commoner, Pitt, was not present in the Commons when the Declaratory and Stamp Acts were passed in 1765; but he was present at one sitting when an address to the King, in reply to a speech from the Throne, relating to opposition in America to the Stamp Act, was discussed, and in which the propriety of repealing that Act was mooted and partially argued. Mr. Pitt held the right of Parliament to impose external taxes on the colonies by imposing duties on goods imported into them, but not to impose internal taxes, such as the Stamp Act imposed. In the course of his speech Mr. Pitt said:

"It is a long time since I have attended in Parliament. When the resolution was taken in the House to tax America, I was ill in bed. If I could have endured to have been carried in my bed, so great was the agitation of my mind for the consequences, I would have solicited some kind hand to have laid me down on this floor, to have borne my testimony against it. It is now an Act that has been passed. I would speak with decency of every act of this House; but I must beg the indulgence to speak of it with freedom.

"As my health and life are so very infirm and precarious, that I may not be able to attend on the day that may be fixed by this House for the consideration of America, I must now, though somewhat unseasonably, leaving the expediency of the Stamp Act to some other time, speak to a point of infinite moment—I mean the right. On a question that may mortally wound the freedom of three millions of virtuous and brave subjects beyond the Atlantic Ocean, I cannot be silent. America being neither really nor virtually represented in Westminster, cannot be held legally, or constitutionally, or reasonably subject to obedience to any money bill of this kingdom. The colonies are, equally with yourselves, entitled to all the natural rights of mankind, and the peculiar privileges of Englishmen; equally bound by the laws, and equally participating in the constitution of this free country. The Americans are the sons, not the bastards, of England. As subjects, they are entitled to the common right of representation, and cannot be bound to pay taxes without their consent. * *

"The Commons of America, represented in their several Assemblies, have ever been in possession of the exercise of this their constitutional right, of giving and granting their own money. They would have been slaves if they had not enjoyed it. * *

"If this House suffers the Stamp Act to continue in force, France will gain more by your colonies than she ever could have done if her arms in the last war had been victorious.

"I never shall own the justice of taxing America internally until she enjoys the right of representation. In every other point of legislation the authority of Parliament is like the north star, fixed for the reciprocal benefit of the parent country and her colonies. The British Parliament, as the supreme gathering and legislative power, has always bound them by her laws, by her regulations of their trade and manufactures, and even in the more absolute interdiction of both. The power of Parliament, like the circulation from the human heart, active, vigorous, and perfect in the smallest fibre of the arterial system, may be known in the colonies by the prohibition of their carrying a hat to market over the line of one province into another; or by breaking down the loom in the most distant corner of the British empire in America; and if this power were denied, I would not permit them to manufacture a lock of wool, or form a horse-shoe or hob-nail. But I repeat the House has no right to lay an internal tax upon America, that country not being represented."

After Pitt ceased, a pause ensued, when General Conway rose and said:

"I not only adopt all that has just been said, but believe it expresses the sentiments of most if not all the King's servants and wish it may be the unanimous opinion of this House."

Mr. Grenville, author of the Stamp Act, now leader of the

opposition, recovering by this time his self-possession, replied
at length to Mr. Pitt. Among other things he said:

" The disturbances in America began in July, and now we
are in the middle of January; lately they were only occurrences;
they are now grown to tumults and riots; they border on open
rebellion; and if the doctrine I have heard this day be confirmed, nothing can tend more directly to produce revolution.
The government over them being dissolved, a revolution will
take place in America.

" External and internal taxation are the same in effect, and
only differ in name. That the sovereign has the supreme legislative power over America cannot be denied; and taxation is a
part of sovereign power. It is one branch of the legislation.
It has been and it is exercised over those who are not and
were never represented. It is exercised over the India
Company, the merchants of London, the proprietors of the
stocks, and over many great manufacturing towns." * *

" To hold that the King, by the concession of a Charter, can
exempt a family or a colony from taxation by Parliament,
degrades the constitution of England. If the colonies, instead
of throwing off entirely the authority of Parliament, had presented a petition to send to it deputies elected among themselves, this step would have evoked their attachment to the
Crown and their affection for the mother country, and would
have merited attention.

"The Stamp Act is but a pretext of which they make use to
arrive at independence. (French report.) It was thoroughly
considered, and not hurried at the end of the session. It passed
through the different stages in full Houses, with only one
division. When I proposed to tax America, I asked the House
if any gentleman would object to the right; I repeatedly asked
it, and no man would attempt to deny it. Protection and
obedience are reciprocal. Great Britain protects America;
America is bound to yield obedience. If not, tell us when they
were emancipated? When they wanted the protection of this
kingdom, they were always ready to ask it. That protection
has always been afforded them in the most full and ample
manner. The nation has run itself into an immense debt to
give it to them; and now that they are called upon to contribute
a small share towards an expense arising from themselves,

they renounce your authority, insult your officers, and break out, I might almost say, into open rebellion.

"The seditious spirit of the colonists owes its birth to the factions in this House. We were told we tread on tender ground; we were told to expect disobedience. What was this but telling the Americans to stand out against the law, to encourage their obstinacy, with the expectation of support from hence? Let us only hold back a little, they would say; our friends will soon be in power.

"Ungrateful people of America! When I had the honour to serve the Crown, while you yourselves were loaded with an enormous debt of one hundred and forty millions sterling, and paid a revenue of ten millions sterling, you have given bounties on their timber, on their iron, their hemp, and many other articles. You have restored in their favour the Act of Navigation, that palladium of British commerce. I offered to do everything in my power to advance the trade of America. I discouraged no trade but what was prohibited by Act of Parliament. I was above giving an answer to anonymous calumnies; but in this place it becomes me to wipe off the aspersion."

When Grenville sat down, several members got up; but the House clamoured for Pitt, who seemed to rise. A point of order was decided in favour of his speaking, and the cry of "Go on, go on!" resounded from all parts of the House. Pitt, addressing the Speaker, said:

"Sir, I have been charged with giving birth to sedition in America. They have spoken their sentiments with freedom against this unhappy Act, and that freedom has become their crime. Sorry I am to hear the liberty of speech in this House imputed as a crime. But the imputation shall not discourage me. It is a liberty I mean to exercise; no gentleman ought to be afraid to exercise it. It is a liberty by which the gentleman who calumniates it might and ought to have profited. He ought to have desisted from his project. The gentleman tells us America is obstinate; America is almost in open rebellion. I rejoice that America has resisted." (At this word the members of the House were startled as though an electric spark had darted through them all.) "I rejoice that America has resisted. If its millions of inhabitants had submitted, taxes would soon have been laid on Ireland; and if ever this nation should have a

20

tyrant for its king, six millions of freemen, so dead to all the feelings of liberty as voluntarily to submit to be slaves, would be fit instruments to make slaves of the rest." * *

" The gentleman tells us of many who are taxed and are not represented—the East India Company, merchants, stockholders, manufacturers. Surely many of these are represented in other capacities. It is a misfortune that more are not actually represented. But they are all inhabitants of Great Britain, and as such are virtually represented. They have connection with those that elect, and they have influence over them.

" Not one of the Ministers who have taken the lead of government since the accession of King William ever recommended a tax like this of the Stamp Act. Lord Halifax, educated in the House of Commons; Lord Oxford, Lord Orford, a great revenue minister (Walpole), never thought of this. None of these ever dreamed of robbing the colonies of their constitutional rights. This was reserved to mark the era of the late Administration.

" The gentleman boasts of his bounties to America. **Are not** these bounties intended finally for the benefit of this kingdom ? If so, where is the peculiar merit to America ? **If they are not,** he has misapplied the national treasures.

" If the gentleman cannot understand the difference between internal and external taxes, I cannot help it. But there is a plain distinction between taxes levied for purposes of *raising revenue* and duties imposed for the *regulation of trade,* for the accommodation of the subject, although in the consequences some revenue may incidentally arise for the latter.

" The gentleman asks when were the colonies emancipated ? I desire to know when they were made slaves ? But I do not dwell upon words. The profits to Great Britain from the trade of the colonies through all its branches is two millions a year. This is the fund that carried you triumphantly through the last war. The estates that were rented at two thousand pounds a year threescore years ago, are at three thousand pounds at present. You owe this to America. This is the price that America pays for your protection ; * and shall a miserable

* It was but just to have added that the trade between England and America was as profitable to America as it was to England, and that the value of prope. ty and rents advanced more rapidly in America than in England.

financier come with a boast that he can fetch a peppercorn into the exchequer to the loss of millions to the nation ?* I dare not say how much higher these profits may be augmented. Omitting the immense increase of people in the northern colonies by natural population, and the emigration from every part of Europe, I am conv. nced the whole commercial system may be altered to advantage." * *

" Upon the whole, I will beg leave to tell the House what is really my opinion. It is that the Stamp Act be repealed absolutely, totally, and immediately ; that the reason for the repeal be assigned, because it was founded on an erroneous principle. At the same time, let the sovereign authority of this country over the colonies be asserted in as strong terms as can be devised, and be made to extend to every point of legislation, that we may bind their trade, confine their manufactures, and exercise every power whatsoever except that of taking their money out of their pockets without their consent.

" Let us be content with the advantage which Providence has bestowed upon us. We have attained the highest glory and greatness. Let us strive long to preserve them for our own happiness and that of our posterity."†

The effect of Pitt's speech was prodigious, combining cogency of argument with fervour of feeling, splendour of eloquence, and matchless oratorical power. The very next day the Duke of Grafton advised the King to send for Pitt ; but the King declined, though in a state of " extreme agitation." Nevertheless, the Duke of Grafton himself sought an interview with Pitt, who showed every disposition to unite with certain members and friends of the liberal Rockingham Administration to promote the repeal of the Stamp Act and the pacification of America ; but it was found that many of the friends and advocates of America did not agree with Pitt in denying the right of Parliament to tax America, though they deemed it inexpedient and

---

* This is a withering rebuke to a conceited though clever young statesman, Lord Nugent, who, in a previous part of the debate, insisted that the honour and dignity of the kingdom obligated them to compel the execution of the Stamp Act, " unless the right was acknowledged and the repeal solicited as a favour," concluding with the remark that " a peppercorn, in acknowledg ment of the right, is of more value than millions without."

† Bancroft's History of the United States, Vol. V., Chap. xxi.

unjust. Pitt could not therefore accept office. Mr. Bancroft remarks: " The principle of giving up all taxation over the colonies, on which the union was to have rested, had implacable opponents in the family of Hardwicke, and in the person of Rockingham's own private secretary (Edmund Burke). ' If ever one man lived more zealous than another for the supremacy of Parliament, and the rights of the imperial crown, it was Edmund Burke.' He was the advocate of ' an unlimited legislative power over the colonies.' ' He saw not how the power of taxation could be given up, without giving up the rest.' ' If Pitt was able to see it, Pitt saw further than he could.' His wishes were very earnest ' to keep the whole body of this authority perfect and entire.' He was jealous of it; he was honestly of that opinion; and Rockingham, after proceeding so far, and finding in Pitt all the encouragement that he expected, let the negotiation drop. Conway and Grafton were compelled to disregard their own avowals on the question of the right of taxation; the Ministry conformed to the opinion, which was that of Charles Yorke, the Attorney-General, and still more of Edmund Burke."*

While the repeal of the Stamp Act was under discussion in the Commons, Dr. Franklin—then Deputy Postmaster-General for America—was summoned to give evidence at the bar of the House. His examination was long and minute. His thorough knowledge of all the subjects, his independence and candour made a deep impression, but he was dismissed from office the day after giving his evidence. Some of the questions and answers are as follows:

Question.—What is your name and place of abode ?

Answer.—Franklin, of Philadelphia.

Q.—Do the Americans pay any considerable taxes among themselves ?

A.—Certainly; many and very heavy taxes.

Q.—What are the present taxes in Pennsylvania levied by the laws of the colony ?

A.—There are taxes on all estates, real and personal; a poll-tax; a tax on all offices, professions, trades, and businesses, according to their profits ; an excise on all wine, rum, and other spirits; and a duty of £10 per head on all negroes imported; with some other duties.

Q.—For what purpose are those taxes levied ?

A.—For the support of the civil and military establishment of the country, and to discharge the heavy debt contracted in the last war.

* History of the United States, Vol. V., Chap. xxi., pp. 397, 398.

Q.—Are not you concerned in the management of the post-office in America?

A.—Yes. I am Deputy Postmaster-General of North America.

Q.—Don't you think the distribution of stamps, by post, to all the inhabitants, very practicable, if there was no opposition?

A.—The posts only go along the sea coasts; they do not, except in a few instances, go back into the country; and if they did, sending for stamps by post would occasion an expense of postage amounting, in many cases, to much more than that of the stamps themselves.

Q.—Are not the colonies, from their circumstances, very able to pay the stamp duty?

A.—In my opinion, there is not gold and silver enough in the colonies to pay the stamp duty for one year.

Q.—Don't you know that the money arising from the stamps was all to be laid out in America?

A.—I know it is appropriated by the Act to the American service; but it will be spent in the conquered colonies, where the soldiers are, not in the colonies that pay it.

Q.—Is there not a balance of trade due from the colonies where the troops are posted, that will bring back the money to the old colonies?

A.—I think not. I believe very little would come back. I know of no trade likely to bring it back. I think it would come from the colonies where it was spent, directly to England; for I have always observed that in every colony the more plenty the means of remittance to England, the more goods are sent for, and the more trade with England carried on.

Q.—What may be the amount of one year's imports into Pennsylvania from Britain?

A.—I have been informed that our merchants compute the imports from Britain to be above £500,000.

Q.—What may be the amount of the produce of your province exported to Britain?

A.—It must be small, as we produce little that is wanted in Britain. I suppose it cannot exceed £40,000.

Q.—How then do you pay the balance?

A.—The balance is paid by our produce carried to the West Indies, and sold in our own island, or to the French, Spaniards, Danes and Dutch; by the same carried to other colonies in North America, as to New England, Nova Scotia, Newfoundland, Carolina and Georgia; by the same carried to different parts of Europe, as Spain, Portugal and Italy. In all which places we receive either money, bills of exchange, or commodities that suit for remittance to Britain; which together with all the profits on the industry of our merchants and mariners, arising in those circuitous voyages, and the freights made by their ships, centre finally in Britain to discharge the balance, and pay for British manufactures continually used in the province, or sold to foreigners by our traders.

Q.—Do you think it right that America should be protected by this country and pay no part of the expense?

A.—That is not the case.   The colonies raised, clothed, and paid, during the last war, nearly 25,000 men, and spent many millions.

Q.—Were not you reimbursed by Parliament ?

A.—We were only reimbursed what, in your opinion, we had advanced beyond our proportion, or beyond what might reasonably be expected from us ; and it was a very small part of what we spent.   Pennsylvania, in particular, disbursed about £500,000, and the reimbursements in the whole did not exceed £60,000.

Q.—You have said that you pay heavy taxes in Pennsylvania ; what do they amount to in the pound ?

A.—The tax on all estates, real and personal, to eighteen-pence in the pound, fully rated ; and the tax on the profits of trades and professions, with other taxes, do, I suppose, make full half-a-crown in the pound.

Q.—Do you not think the people of America would submit to pay the stamp duty if it were moderated ?

A.—No, never, unless compelled by the force of arms.

Q.—What was the temper of America towards Great Britain before the year 1763 ?

A.—The best in the world.   They submitted willingly to the government of the Crown, and paid, in all their courts, obedience to Acts of Parliament. Numerous as the people are in the several old provinces, they cost you nothing in forts, citadels, garrisons, or armies, to keep them in subjection.   They were governed by this country at the expense only of a little pen, ink and paper.   They were led by a thread.   They had not only a respect, but an affection for Great Britain, for its laws, its customs and manners, and even a fondness for its fashions, that greatly increased the commerce.   Natives of Britain were always treated with particular regard ; to be an Old-England-man was of itself a character of some respect, and gave a kind of rank among us.

Q.—And what is their temper now ?

A.—Oh ! very much altered.

Q.—Did you ever hear the authority of Parliament to make laws for America questioned till lately ?

A.—The authority of Parliament was allowed to be valid in all laws, except such as should levy internal taxes.   It was never disputed in levying duties to regulate commerce.

Q.—In what light did the people of America use to consider the Parliament of Great Britain ?

A.—They considered the Parliament as the great bulwark and security of their liberties and privileges, and always spoke of it with the utmost respect and veneration.   Arbitrary ministers, they thought, might possibly at times attempt to oppress them ; but they relied on it, that the Parliament on application would always give redress.   They remembered with gratitude a strong instance of this, when a Bill was brought into Parliament, with a clause to make royal instructions laws in the colonies, which the House of Commons would not pass, and it was thrown out.

Q.—And have they not still the same respect for Parliament ?

A.—No ; it is greatly lessened.

Q.—To what causes is that owing ?

A.—To a concurrence of causes ; the restraints lately laid on their trade by which the bringing of foreign gold and silver into the colonies was prevented ; the prohibition of making paper money among themselves, and then demanding a new and heavy tax by stamps ; taking away at the same time trial by juries, and refusing to see and hear their humble petitions.

Q.—Don't you think they would submit to the Stamp Act if it was modified, the obnoxious parts taken out, and the duty reduced to some particular of small moment ?

A.—No ; they will never submit to it.

Q.—What is your opinion of a future tax, imposed on the same principle of that of the Stamp Act ; how would the Americans receive it ?

A.—Just as they do this. They would not pay it.

Q.—Have not you heard of the resolutions of this House, and of the House of Lords, asserting the right of Parliament relating to America, including a power to tax the people there ?

A.—Yes ; I have heard of such resolutions

Q. What will be the opinion of the Americans on those resolutions ?

A.—They will think them unconstitutional and unjust.

Q.—Was it an opinion in America before 1763, that the Parliament had no right to levy taxes and duties there ?

A.—I never heard any objection to the right of levying duties to regulate commerce ; but a right to levy internal taxes was never supposed to be in Parliament, as we are not represented there.

Q.—You say the colonies have always submitted to external taxes, and object to the right of Parliament only in levying internal taxes ; now, can you show that there is any kind of difference between the two taxes to the colony on which they may be laid ?

A.—I think the difference is very great. An external tax is a duty levied on commodities imported ; that duty is added to the first cost, and other charges on the commodity, and when it is offered for sale, makes a part of the price. If the people do not like it at that price, they refuse it ; they are not obliged to pay it. But an internal tax is forced from the people without their consent, if not levied by their own representatives. The Stamp Act says we shall have no commerce, make no exchange of property with each other ; neither purchase, nor grant, nor recover debts ; we shall neither marry nor make our wills unless we pay such and such sums, and thus it is intended to extort our money from us, or ruin us by the consequences of refusing to pay it.

Q.—But supposing the internal tax or duty to be levied on the necessaries of life imported into your colony, will not that be the same thing in its effects as an internal tax ?

A.—I do not know a single article imported into the northern colonies, but what they can either do without or make themselves.

Q.—Don't you think cloth from England absolutely necessary to them ?

A.—No, by no means absolutely necessary ; with industry and good management, they may very well supply themselves with all they want.

Q.—Considering the resolution of Parliament as to the right, do you think, if the Stamp Act is repealed, that the North Americans will be satisfied?

A.—I believe they will.

Q.—Why do you think so?

A.—I think the resolutions of right will give them very little concern, if they are never attempted to be carried into practice. The colonies will probably consider themselves in the same situation in that respect with Ireland; they know you claim the same right with regard to Ireland, but you never exercise it. And they may believe you never will exercise it in the colonies, any more than in Ireland, unless on some very extraordinary occasion.

Q.—But who are to be the judges of that extraordinary occasion? Is not the Parliament?

A.—Though the Parliament may judge of the occasion, the people will think it can never exercise such right till representatives from the colonies are admitted into Parliament, and that, whenever the occasion arises, representatives will be ordered.

Q.—Did the Americans ever dispute the controlling power of Parliament to regulate the commerce?

A.—No.

Q.—Can anything less than a military force carry the Stamp Act into execution?

A.—I do not see how a military force can be applied to that purpose.

Q.—Why may it not?

A.—Suppose a military force sent into America, they will find nobody in arms; what are they then to do? They cannot force a man to take stamps, who refuses to do without them. They will not find a rebellion; they may indeed make one.

Q.—If the Act is not repealed, what do you think will be the consequences?

A.—A total loss of the respect and affection the people of America bear to this country, and of all the commerce that depends on that respect and affection.

Q.—How can the commerce be affected?

A.—You will find that, if the Act is not repealed, they will take very little of your manufactures in a short time.

Q.—Is it in their power to do without them?

A.—I think they may very well do without them.

Q.—Is it their interest not to take them?

A.—The goods they take from Britain are either necessaries, mere conveniences, or superfluities. The first, as cloth, etc., with a little industry they can make at home; the second they can do without, till they are able to provide them among themselves; and the last, which are much the greatest part, they will strike off immediately. They are mere articles of fashion, purchased and consumed because the fashion in a respected country, but will now be detested and rejected. The people have already struck off, by general agreement, the use of all goods fashionable in mournings, and many thousand pounds worth are sent back as unsaleable.

Q.—Suppose an Act of internal regulations connected with a tax, how would they receive it ?

A.—I think it would be objected to.

Q.—Then no regulation with a tax would be submitted to ?

A.—Their opinion is, that when aids to the Crown are wanted, they are to be asked of the several Assemblies, according to the old-established usage, who will, as they always have done, grant them freely ; and that their money ought not to be given away without their consent by persons at a distance, unacquainted with their circumstances and abilities. The granting aids to the Crown is the only means they have of recommending themselves to their Sovereign, and they think it extremely hard and unjust that a body of men, in which they have no representation, should make a merit to itself of giving and granting what is not its own, but theirs, and deprive them of a right they esteem of the utmost value and importance, as it is the security of all their other rights.

Q.—But is not the post-office, which they have long received, a tax as well as a regulation ?

A.—No ; the money paid for the postage of a letter is not of the nature of a tax ; it is merely a *quantum meruit* for a service done ; no person is compellable to pay the money if he does not choose to receive the service. A man may still, as before the Act, send his letter by a servant, a special messenger, or a friend, if he thinks it cheaper and safer.

Q.—But do they not consider the regulations of the post-office, by the Act of last year, as a tax ?

A.—By the regulations of last year, the rate of postage was generally abated near thirty per cent. through all America ; they certainly cannot consider such abatement as a tax.

Q.—If an excise was laid by Parliament, which they might likewise avoid paying, by not consuming the articles excised, would they then object to it ?

A.—They would certainly object to it, as an excise is unconnected with any service done, and is merely an aid which they think ought to be asked of them, and granted by them if they are to pay it, and can be granted for them by no others whatsoever, whom they have not empowered for that purpose.

Q.—You say they do not object to the right of Parliament in levying duties on goods to be paid on their importation ; now, is there any kind of difference between a duty on the importation of goods and an excise on their consumption ?

A.—Yes, a very material one ; an excise, for the reasons I have just mentioned, they think you can have no right to levy within their country. But the sea is yours ; you maintain by your fleets the safety of navigation in it, and keep it clear of pirates ; you may have therefore a natural and equitable right to some toll or duty on merchandise carried through that part of your dominions, towards defraying the expense you are at in ships to maintain the safety of that carriage.

Q.—Supposing the Stamp Act continued and was enforced, do you imagine that ill-humour will induce the Americans to give as much for worse manufactures of their own, and use them preferably to better ones of yours ?

A.—Yes, I think so. People will pay as freely to gratify one passion as another—their resentment as their pride.

Q.—What do you think a sufficient military force to protect the distribution of the stamps in every part of America ?

A.—A very great force ; I can't say what, if the disposition of America is for a general resistance.

Q.—If the Stamp Act should be repealed, would not the Americans think they could oblige the Parliament to repeal every external tax law now in force ?

A.—It is hard to answer questions of what people at such a distance will think.

Q.—But what do you imagine they will think were the motives of repealing the Act ?

A.—I suppose they will think that it was repealed from a conviction of its inexpediency ; and they will rely upon it that, while the same expediency subsists, you will never attempt to make such another.

Q.—What do you mean by its inexpediency ?

A.—I mean its inexpediency on several accounts : the poverty and inability of those who were to pay the tax, the general discontent it has occasioned, and the impracticability of enforcing it.

Q.—If the Act should be repealed, and the Legislature should show its resentment to the opposers of the Stamp Act, would the colonies acquiesce in the authority of the Legislature ? What is your opinion they would do ?

A.—I don't doubt at all that if the Legislature repeal the Stamp Act, the colonies will acquiesce in the authority.

Q.—But if the Legislature should think fit to ascertain its right to levy taxes, by any Act levying a small tax, contrary to their opinion, would they submit to pay the tax ?

A.—The proceedings of the people in America have been considered too much together. The procedings of the Assemblies have been very different from those of the mobs, and should be distinguished, as having no connection with each other. The Assemblies have only peaceably resolved what they take to be their rights ; they have taken no measures for opposition by force ; they have not built a fort, raised a man, or provided a grain of ammunition in order to such opposition. The ringleaders of riots they think ought to be punished ; they would punish them themselves if they could. Every sober, sensible man would wish to see rioters punished, as otherwise peaceable people have no security of person or estate. But as to an internal tax, how small soever, levied by the Legislature here on the people there, while they have no representatives in this Legislature, I think it will never be submitted to. They will oppose it to the last. They do not consider it as at all necessary for you to raise money on them by your taxes, because they are, and always have been, ready to raise money by taxes among themselves, and to grant large sums, equal to their abilities, upon requisition from the Crown. They have not only granted equal to their abilities, but during all the last war they granted far beyond their abilities, and beyond their proportion with this country, you yourselves being judges, to the amount of many hundred thousand pounds ; and this they did freely and readily, only on a sort of promise from the Secretary of State that it should be recommended to Parliament to make them compensation. It was accordingly recommended to Parliament, in the most honourable manner, for them. America has been greatly misrepresented and abused here, in papers and pamphlets and speeches, as ungrateful, unreasonable, and unjust in having put this nation to immense expense for their defence, and refusing to bear any part of that expense. The colonies raised, paid, and clothed near 25,000 men during the last war—a number equal to those sent from Britain, and far beyond their proportion ; they went deeply into debt in doing this, and all their taxes and estates are mortgaged, for many years to come, for discharging that debt. The Government here was at that time very sensible of this. The colonies were recommended to Parliament. Every year the King sent down to the House a written message to this purport : That his Majesty, being highly sensible of the zeal and vigour with which his faithful subjects in North America had exerted themselves in defence of his Majesty's just rights and possessions, recommended it to the House to take the same into consideration, and enable him to give them a proper compensation. You will find those messages on your journals every year of the war to the very last, and you did accordingly give £200,000 annually to the Crown, to be distributed in such compensation to the colonies. This is the strongest of all proofs that the colonies, far from being unwilling to bear a share of the burden, did exceed their proportion ; for if they had done less, or had only equalled their proportion, there would have been no room or reason for compensation. Indeed, the sums reimbursed them were by no means adequate to the expense they incurred beyond their proportion ; but they never murmured at that : they esteemed their Sovereign's approbation of their zeal and fidelity, and the approbation of this House, far beyond any other kind of compensation ; therefore there was no occasion for this Act to force money from an unwilling people. They had not refused giving money for the purposes of the Act ; no requisition had been made ; they were always willing and ready to do what could reasonably be expected from them, and in this light they wish to be considered.

Q.—But suppose Great Britain should be engaged in a war in Europe, would North America contribute to the support of it ?

A.—I do think they would, as far as their circumstances would permit. They consider themselves as a part of the British empire, and as having one common interest with it ; they may be looked on here as foreigners, but they do not consider themselves as such. They are zealous for the honour and prosperity of this nation, and, while they are well used, will always be ready to support it, as far as their little power goes.

Q.—Do you think the Assemblies have a right to levy money on the subject there, to grant to the Crown ?

A.—I certainly think so ; they have always done it.

Q.—Would they do this for a British concern ; as, suppose, a war in some part of Europe that did not affect them ?

A.—Yes, for anything that concerned the general interest. They consider themselves as a part of the whole.

Q.—What is the usual constitutional manner of calling on the colonies for aids ?

A.—A letter from the Secretary of State.

Q.—Is this all you mean—a letter from the Secretary of State ?

A.—I mean the usual way of requisition—in a circular letter from the Secretary of State, by his Majesty's command, reciting the occasion, and recommending it to the colonies to grant such aids as became their royalty and were suitable to their abilities.

Q.—Did the Secretary of State ever write for money for the Crown ?

A.—The requisitions have been to raise, clothe, and pay men, which cannot be done without money.

Q.—Would they grant money alone if called on ?

A.—In my opinion they would, money as well as men, when they have money or can make it.

Q.—What used to be the pride of the Americans ?

A.—To indulge in the fashions and manufactures of Great Britain.

Q.—What is now their pride ?

A.—To wear their old clothes over again, till they can make new ones.*

* Prior Documents, pp. 64—81.

CHAPTER XI.

AUTHORITY OF PARLIAMENT OVER THE BRITISH COLONIES.

BEFORE proceeding with a summary statement of events which followed the repeal of the Stamp Act, I think it proper to state the nature and extent of the authority of Parliament over the colonies, as interpreted by legislative bodies and statesmen on both sides of the Atlantic. Mr. Bancroft well remarks:

"It is the glory of England that the rightfulness of the Stamp Act was in England itself a subject of dispute. It could have been so nowhere else. The King of France taxed the French colonies as a matter of course; the King of Spain collected a revenue by his own will in Mexico and Peru, in Cuba and Porto Rico, and wherever he ruled. The States-General of the Netherlands had no constitutional doubt about imposing duties on their outlying colonies. To England exclusively belongs the honour that between her and her colonies the question of right could arise; it is still more to her glory, as well as to her happiness and freedom, that in that contest her success was not possible. Her principles, her traditions, her liberty, her constitution, all forbade that arbitrary rule should become her characteristic. The shaft aimed at her new colonial policy was tipped with a feather from her own wing."*

In the dispute which took place in 1757 between the Legislative Assembly of Massachusetts and the Earl of Loudoun as to the extension of the Mutiny Act to the colonies, and the passing of an Act by the local Legislature for the billeting of the troops, as similar in its provisions as possible to those of the Mutiny Act—so that it was accepted by the Earl of Loudoun— the Massachusetts Assembly vindicated their motives for deny-

---

* History of the United States, Vol. V., Chap. xx., pp. 366, 367.

ing the application of the Mutiny Act to the colonies, and for providing quarters for the military by an Act of their own, yet recognizing the legitimate authority of Parliament, in a message to Governor Barnard containing the following words :

" We wish to stand perfectly right with his lordship (the Earl of Loudoun), and it will be a great satisfaction to us if we may be able to remove his misapprehension of the spring and motives of our proceedings. His lordship is pleased to say that we seem willing to enter into a dispute upon the necessity of a provincial law to enforce a British Act of Parliament.

" We are utterly ignorant as to what part of our conduct could give occasion for this expression. The point in which we were obliged to differ from his lordship was the extent of the provision made by Act of Parliament for regulating quarters, We thought it did not reach the colonies. *Had we thought it did reach us, and yet made an Act of our own to enforce it, there would have been good grounds for his lordship's exception;* but being fully persuaded that the provision was never intended for us, what better step could we take than, agreeable to the twentieth section of the Articles of War, to regulate quarters as the circumstances of the province require, but still as similar to the provisions made in England as possible ? And how can it be inferred from thence that we suppose a provincial Act necessary to enforce an Act of Parliament ?

" We are willing, by a due exercise of the powers of civil government (and we have the pleasure of seeing your Excellency concur with us), to remove, as much as may be, all pretence of necessity of military government. Such measures, we are sure, will never be disapproved by the Parliament of Great Britain, *our dependence upon which we never had a desire or thought of lessening.* From the knowledge your Excellency has acquired of us, you will be able to do us justice in this regard.

" In our message to your Excellency, which you transmitted to his lordship, we declared that the Act of Parliament, the extent of which was then in dispute, as far as it related to the Plantations, had always been observed by us.

" *The authority of all Acts of Parliament which concern the colonies, and extend to them, is ever acknowledged in all the*

Courts of law, and made the rule in all judicial proceedings in the province. There is not a member of the General Court, we know no inhabitant within the bounds of the Government, that ever questioned this authority.

" *To prevent any ill consequences which may arise from an opinion of our holding such principles, we now utterly disavow them, as we should readily have done at any time past if there had been occasion for it;* and we pray that his lordship may be acquainted therewith, that we may appear in a true light, and that no impressions may remain to our disadvantage."*

This is a full and indefinite recognition of the supreme authority of Parliament, even to the providing of accommodation for the soldiers ; and such was the recognition of the authority of Parliament throughout the colonies. " It was generally allowed," says Dr. Ramsay, " that as the planting of colonies was not designed to erect an independent Government, but to extend an old one, the parent state had a right to restrain their trade in every way which conduced to the common emolument. They for the most part considered the mother country as authorized to name ports and nations to which alone their merchandise should be carried, and with which alone they should trade ; but the novel claim of taxing them without their consent was universally reprobated as contrary to their natural, chartered, and constitutional rights. In opposition to it, they not only alleged the general principles of liberty, but ancient usage. During the first hundred and fifty years of their existence they had been left to tax themselves and in their own way." "In the war of 1755, the events of which were fresh in the recollection of every one, the Parliament had in no instance attempted to raise either men or money in the colonies by its own authority. As the claim of taxation on one side and the refusal on the other were the very hinges on which the revolution turned they merit a particular discussion."†

The only exception to the authority of Parliament over the colonies was levying *internal* taxes. A marked distinction was made between *external* and *internal* taxes. It was admitted upon all hands that the Parliament had the constitutional right

---

* Hutchinson's History of Massachusetts Bay, Vol. III., Chap. i., pp. 65, 66.
† Colonial History, Vol. I., pp. 327, 328.

to impose the former, but not the latter. The Tory opposition in the British Parliament denied the distinction between *external* and *internal* taxes, and maintained that if Parliament had the right to impose the one they had equally the right to impose the other; but the advocates of American rights maintained the distinction between *external* and *internal* taxation; and also Dr. Franklin, in his evidence at the bar of the House of Commons, in February, 1766, which I have quoted at length above, as the best exposition of the colonial side of the questions at issue between England and America. I will here reproduce two questions and answers on the subject now under consideration:

Q.—"You say they do not object to the right of Parliament, in levying duties on goods, to be paid on their importation; now, is there any kind of difference between a duty on the importation of goods and an excise on their consumption?"

A.—"Yes, a very material one; an excise, for the reasons I have just mentioned, they think you can have no right to levy within their country. But the sea is yours; you maintain by your fleets the safety of navigation in it, and keep it clear of pirates; you may have therefore a natural and equitable right to some toll or duty on merchandise carried through that part of your dominions, towards defraying the expense you are at in ships to maintain the safety of that carriage."

Q.—"Does this reasoning hold in the case of a duty laid on the produce of their lands exported? And would they not then object to make a duty?"

A.—"If it tended to make the produce so much dearer abroad as to lessen the demand for it, to be sure they would object to such a duty; *not to your right of levying it*, but they would complain of it as a burden, and petition you to lighten it."

It will be observed that in these words of Dr. Franklin there is the fullest recognition of the right of Parliament to impose duties on all articles imported into, or exported from, the colonies; the only exception was the levying direct or *internal* taxes for the purposes of revenue, the right to impose which was held, and we think justly held, to belong to the representative Legislatures elected by the colonists themselves. Such also were the views of the two great statesmen, Pitt and Burke, who with such matchless eloquence advocated the rights of the colonies—whose speeches have become household words in America, and are found in all their school books. Mr. Pitt, in a speech which I have quoted at length in a previous chapter, said expressly:

"Let the sovereign authority of this country over the colonies be asserted in as strong terms as can be devised, and be made to extend to every point of legislation whatsoever, that we may bind their trade, confine their manufactures, and exercise every power except that of taking their money out of their pockets without their consent."

Mr. Pitt therefore advocated the repeal of the Stamp Act with all his fiery eloquence and energy, saying that he rejoiced that the colonists had resisted that Act—not by riots or force of arms, but by every constitutional mode of resistance, in the expression of public opinion against an unjust and oppressive measure. Mr. Pitt's speech has been quoted by American writers, and inserted in American school books, to justify the resistance of America to England in the revolution which was declared in 1776; but his speech was delivered, and the Act against which it was delivered was repealed, ten years before. The United Empire Loyalists were as much opposed to the Stamp Act as any other colonists, and rejoiced as heartily at its repeal.

Edmund Burke was the appointed agent of the province of New York, and no member of the House of Commons equalled him in the eloquent and elaborate advocacy of the popular rights of the colonies. Extracts from his speeches have been circulated in every form, and in unnumbered repetition in American periodicals and school books; but what he said as to the authority of Parliament over the colonies has not found so wide a circulation in America. In advocating the repeal of the Stamp Act, in his celebrated speech on *American taxation*, Mr. Burke said:

"What is to become of the Declaratory Act, asserting the entireness of British legislative authority, if we abandon the practice of taxation? For my part, I look upon the rights stated in that Act exactly in the manner in which I viewed them on its very first proposition, and which I have often taken the liberty, with great humility, to lay before you. I look, I say, on the imperial rights of Great Britan, and the privileges which

21

the colonists ought to enjoy under those rights, to be just the most reconcilable things in the world. The Parliament of Great Britain sits at the head of her extensive empire in two capacities: one, as the local Legislature of this island, providing for all things at home, immediately, and by no other instrument than the executive power; the other, and I think her nobler capacity, is what I call her *imperial character*, in which, as from the throne of heaven, she superintends all the several inferior Legislatures, and guides and controls them all, without annihilating any. As all these Provincial Legislatures are only co-ordinate with each other, they ought all to be subordinate to her, else they can neither preserve mutual peace, nor hope for mutual justice, nor effectually afford mutual assistance. It is necessary to coerce the negligent, to restrain the violent, and to aid the weak and deficient, by the overruling plenitude of its power. She is never to intrude into the place of the others while they are equal to the common ends of their institution. But in order to enable Parliament to answer all these ends of provident and beneficent superintendence, her powers must be boundless. The gentlemen who think the powers of Parliament limited, may please themselves to talk of requisitions. But suppose the requisitions are not obeyed? What! Shall there be no reserved power in the empire to supply a deficiency which may weaken, divide, and dissipate the whole? We are engaged in war; the Secretary of State calls upon the colonies to contribute; some would do it; I think most would cheerfully furnish whatever is demanded. One or two, suppose, hang back, and, easing themselves, let the stress of the draft be on the others—surely it is proper that some authority might legally say, 'Tax yourselves for the common supply, or Parliament will do it for you.' This backwardness was, as I am told, actually the case of Pennsylvania, for some short time towards the beginning of the last war, owing to some internal dissensions in the colony. But whether the act were so, or otherwise, the case is equally to be provided for by a competent sovereign power. But then this ought to be no ordinary power, nor ever used in the first instance. This is what I meant when I have said at various times that I consider the power of taxing in Parliament as an instrument of empire, and not as a means of supply."*

* Speech on American taxation.

CHAPTER XII.

SUMMARY OF EVENTS FROM THE REPEAL OF THE STAMP ACT, MARCH, 1766, TO THE END OF THE YEAR.

THE universal joy caused in both Great Britain and America by the repeal of the Stamp Act foreshadowed a new era of unity and co-operation between the mother country and the colonies. But though trade and commerce resumed their activity, and mutual expressions of respect and affection characterized the correspondence, private and official, between England and America, the rejoicings of re-union were soon silenced, and mutual confidence, if restored at all, soon yielded to mutual suspicion. The King regretted the repeal of the Stamp Act as "a fatal compliance" which had "wounded the majesty" of England, and planted "thorns under his own pillow." He soon found a pretext for ridding himself of the Ministers who had influenced the Parliament, and compelled himself to adopt and sanction that measure, and to surround himself with Ministers, some of whom sympathized with the King in his regrets, and all of whom were prepared to compensate for the humiliation to America in the repeal of the Stamp Act, by imposing obligations and taxes on the colonies in other forms, under the absolute authority of Parliament affirmed in the Declaratory Act, and which the Americans had fondly regarded as a mere salvo to English pride, and not intended for any practical purpose. Mr. Pitt had rested his opposition to the Stamp Act upon the distinction between *external* and *internal* taxes, as did Dr. Franklin in his evidence at the bar of the House of Commons; the opposition and the protesting Lords denied the distinction; and when Dr. Franklin was asked—

"Does the distinction between internal and external taxes

exist in the Charter ?" he answered: " No, I believe not;" and being asked, " Then may they not, by the same interpretation, object to the Parliament's right of external taxation ?" he answered: " They never have hitherto. Many arguments have been lately used here to show them that there is no difference, and that if you have no right to tax them internally, you have no right to tax them externally, or make any other law to bind them. At present they do not reason so, but in time they may possibly be convinced by these arguments."*

I now proceed to give a summary statement of the events between Great Britain and the colonies which followed the repeal of the Stamp Act, March 19th, 1766.

Within ten days of its passing, the Act repealing the Stamp Act was officially transmitted to America by General Conway †·

* In the House of Lords, Lord Mansfield, replying to Lord Camden, said : " The noble lord who quoted so much law, and denied the right of the Parliament of Great Britain to levy *internal* taxes upon the colonies, allowed at the same time that *restrictions upon trade and duties upon the ports were legal.* But I cannot see any real difference in this distinction ; for I hold it to be true, that a tax laid in any place is like a pebble falling into and making a circle in a lake, till one circle produces and gives motion to another, and the whole circumference is agitated from the centre. A tax on tobacco, either in the ports of Virginia or London, is a duty laid upon the inland Plantations of Virginia, a hundred miles from the sea, wherever the tobacco grows." (Quoted in Bancroft's History of the United States, Vol. V., p. 411.) Mr. Grenville argued in the same strain in the House of Commons, and the Americans, as apt pupils, soon learned by such arguments to resist *external* as they had successfully resisted *internal* taxes.

† General Conway, as leader of the House of Commons, moved the resolution for the repeal of the Stamp Act, and also moved the resolution for the Declaratory Bill. Colonel Barre moved an amendment to strike out from the resolution the words " in all cases whatsoever." He was seconded by Pitt, and sustained by Beckford. " Only three men, or rather Pitt alone, ' debated strenuously the rights of America' against more than as many hundred ; and yet the House of Commons, half-conscious of the fatality of its decision, was so awed by the overhanging shadow of coming events that it seemed to shrink from pronouncing its opinion. Edmund Burke, eager to add glory as an orator to his just renown as an author, argued for England's right in such a manner that the strongest friends of power declared his speech to have been ' far superior to that of every other speaker ;' while Grenville, Yorke, and all the lawyers ; the temperate Richard Hussey, who yet was practically for humanity and justice ; Blackstone, the commentator on the laws of England, who still disliked internal taxation of America by Parliament, filled many hours with solemn arguments for England's unlimited

then Secretary of State for America, who accompanied them with a circular to the several Governors, in which, while he firmly insisted upon a proper reverence for the King's Government, endeavoured affectionately to allay the discontents of the colonists.   When the Governor of Virginia communicated this letter to the House of Burgesses, they unanimously voted a statue to the King, and the Assembly of Massachusetts voted a letter of thanks to Mr. Pitt and the Duke of Grafton.

But in addition to the circular letter to the several Governors, counselling forgetfulness and oblivion as to the disorders and contentions of the past, General Conway wrote a separate letter to Governor Barnard, of Massachusetts, in which he said : " Nothing will tend more effectually to every conciliating purpose, and there is nothing, therefore, I have in command more earnestly to require of you, than that you should exert yourself in *recommending* it strongly to the Assembly, that full and ample compensation be made to those who, from the madness of the people, have suffered for their acts in deference to the British Legislature."   This letter was but a *recommendation*, not a *command* or *requisition*, to the Legislature, and seems to have been intended as an instruction to Governor Barnard alone ; but he, now indulging his personal resentments as well as haughty spirit, represented the letter of General Conway as a *command* and *requisition* founded on " justice and humanity," and that the authority from which it came ought to preclude all doubts about complying with it, adding, " Both the business and the time are most critical—let me entreat you to recollect yourselves, and to consider well what you are about. Shall the private interests, passions, or resentments of a few

supremacy.   They persuaded one another, and the House, that the Charters which kings had granted were, by the unbroken opinions of lawyers, from 1689, subordinate to the good-will of the Houses of Parliament ; that Parliament, for a stronger reason, had power to tax—a power which it had been proposed to exert in 1713, while Harley was at the head of the Treasury, and again at the opening of the Seven Years' War." * *

" So the watches of the long winter's night wore away, and at about four o'clock in the morning, when the question was called, less than ten voices, some say five, or four, some said but three, spoke out in the minority ; and the resolution passed for England's right to do what the Treasury pleased with three millions of freemen in America." (Bancroft's History of the United States., Vol. V., pp. 415—417.)

men deprive the whole people of the great and manifold advantages which the favour and indulgence of their King and his Parliament are now preparing for them ? Surely after *his Majesty's commands* are known, the very persons who have created the prejudices and prepossessions I now endeavour to combat will be the first to remove them."

The opposition to the Stamp Act, which the Governor interpreted as "prejudices and prepossessions which he now endeavoured to combat," had been justified by the King and Parliament themselves in rejecting it ; and he thus continued to make enemies of those whom he might have easily conciliated and made friends. The Assembly answered him in an indignant and sarcastic tone, and charged him with having exceeded the authority given in Secretary Conway's letter ; concluding in the following words :

" If this *recommendation,* which your Excellency terms a *requisition,* be founded on so much justice and humanity that it cannot be controverted—if the *authority* with which it is introduced should preclude all disputation about complying with it, we should be glad to know what freedom we have in the case ?

" In answer to the questions which your Excellency has proposed with seeming emotion, we beg leave to declare, that we will not suffer ourselves to be in the least influenced by party animosities or domestic feuds, let them exist where they may ; that if we can possibly prevent it, this fine country shall never be ruined by any person ; that it shall be through no default of ours should this people be deprived of the great and manifest advantages which the favour and indulgence of our most gracious Sovereign and his Parliament are even now providing for them. On the contrary, that it shall ever be our highest ambition, as it is our duty, so to demean ourselves in public and in private life as shall most clearly demonstrate our loyalty and gratitude to the best of kings, and thereby recommend his people to further gracious marks of the royal clemency and favour

" With regard to the rest of your Excellency's speech, we are constrained to observe, that the general air and style of it savours more of an act of grace and pardon than of a parliamentary address to the two Houses of Assembly ; and we most sincerely wish your Excellency had been pleased to reserve it, *if needful,* for a proclamation."

It was thus that fresh seed of animosity and hostility was sown between Governor Barnard and the Massachusetts Assembly, and sown by the Governor himself, and the growth of which he further promoted by refusing to confirm the choice of Mr. Hancock, whom the Assembly had elected as their Speaker, and refused to sanction six of their twenty-eight nominations to the Council, because they had not nominated the four judges of the Supreme Court and the Crown officers. Hence the animosity of their reply to his speech above quoted. But as the Governor had, by the Charter, a veto on the election of Speaker and Councillors, the Legislature submitted without a murmur.

But in the course of the session (six months after the Governor's speech upon the subject), the Assembly passed an Act granting compensation to the sufferers by the late riots, the principal of whom were the Lieutenant-Governor, the Collector of Customs, and the appointed Distributor of Stamps. The Act was accompanied by a declaration that it was a free gift of the Province, and not an acknowledgment of the justice of their claim ; it also contained a provision of amnesty to the rioters. The Act was agreed to by the Council and assented to by the Governor ; but it was disallowed by the King on the advice of the English Attorney and Solicitor General, because, as alleged, it assumed an act of grace which it belonged to the King to bestow, through an act of oblivion of the evils of those who had acted unlawfully in endeavouring to enforce the Stamp Act, which had been passed by the British Parliament the same year. The Massachusetts Assembly ordered that their debates should henceforth be open to the public.

The Legislature of New York also passed an Act granting compensation to those who had suffered a loss of property for their adherence to the Stamp Act, but stated it to be a free gift.

Before the close of 1766, dissatisfaction and distrust were manifest in several colonies, and apprehensions of other encroachments by the British Parliament upon what they held to be their constitutional rights. Even the General Assembly of Virginia, which had in the spring session voted a statue to the King, and an obelisk to Mr. Pitt and several other members of Parliament, postponed, in the December following, the final consideration of the resolution until the next session. The Virginia

press said: " The Americans are hasty in expressing their gratitude, if the repeal of the Stamp Act is not, at least, a tacit
compact that Great Britain will never again tax us;" and
advised the different Assemblies, without mentioning the proceedings of Parliament, to enter upon their journals as strong
declarations of their own rights as words could express.*

The Assembly of New York met early in 1766, in the best
spirit; voted to raise on Bowling Green an equestrian statue to
the King, and a statue of William Pitt—"twice the preserver
of his country."

" But the clause of the Mutiny or Billeting Act (passed in
1765, in the same session in which the Stamp Act was passed),
directing Colonial Legislatures to make specific contributions
towards the support of the army, placed New York, where the
head-quarters were established, in the dilemma of submitting
immediately and unconditionally to the authority of Parliament, or taking the lead in a new career of resistance. The
rescript was in theory worse than the Stamp Act. For how
could one legislative body command what another legislative
body should enact ? And viewed as a tax it was unjust, for it
threw all the burden of the colony where the troops chanced to
be collected. The requisition of the General, made through the
Governor, 'agreeably to the Act of Parliament,' was therefore
declared to be unprecedented in its character and unreasonable
in its amount; yet in the exercise of the right of free deliberation, everything asked for was voted, except such articles as
were not provided in Europe for British troops which were in
barracks."†

---

* Allen's History of the American Revolution, Vol. I., Chap. v., p. 101.
Bancroft's History of the United States, Vol. VI., Chap. xxv., p. 6.

† Bancroft's History of the United States, Vol. VI., Chap. xxv., pp. 15, 16.

" The colonies were required, at their own expense, to furnish the troops
quartered upon them by Parliament with fuel, bedding, utensils for cooking,
and various articles of food and drink. To take off the edge from this bill,
bounties were granted on the importation of lumber and timber from the
plantations ; coffee of domestic growth was exempted from additional duty ;
and iron was permitted to be carried to Ireland." (Barry's History of Massachusetts, Second Period, Chap. x., p. 295.)

CHAPTER XIII.

EVENTS OF 1767—A NEW PARLIAMENT—FIRST ACT AGAINST THE PRO-
VINCE OF NEW YORK—BILLETING SOLDIERS ON THE COLONIES.

A NEW House of Commons was elected in 1766, less favourable to the colonies than the preceding one; and one of the
first acts of the new Parliament was founded on the intelligence
received from New York, that the Assembly had refused to
comply with all the requirements of the Billeting Act in providing for his Majesty's troops which had been quartered upon
that province.*

A Bill was introduced by Mr. Grenville, the object of which
was to restrain the Assembly and Council of New York from
passing any Act until they had complied with the requisitions of the Billeting Act. Though the Bill was introduced by the leader of the opposition, it received the
countenance and support of Ministers (Pitt being Premier,
though absent through illness), "who regarded it as a measure
at once dignified and forbearing." The Bill passed with little
opposition; the Legislature of New York was at once frightened
into immediate compliance, though the feeling with which it
was done may be easily conceived. The effect, however, in other

---

* "This affair being brought before the House occasioned many debates, and
some vigorous measures were proposed. June 15th, a Bill was passed by
which the Governor, Council, and Assembly of New York were prohibited
from passing or assenting to any Act of Assembly for any purpose whatsoever, till they had in every respect complied with all the terms of the Act
of Parliament. This restriction, though limited to one colony, was a lesson
to them all, and showed their comparative inferiority, when brought in question with the supreme legislative power." (Annual Register for 1767, Vol.
X., p. 48.)

colonies, was not only to excite fears and dissatisfaction, but to call forth public expressions of hostile sentiment, regarding the Act as an infringement of their chartered privileges ; and they argued that if the legislative powers of so loyal a colony as New York could be thus suspended, they had little security for their own privileges guaranteed to them by Charter.*

On the 26th of January, while the House of Commons, in Committee of Supply, was considering the estimate for the garrison and land forces in the colonies, Mr. Grenville took the opportunity of expressing his dissatisfaction with the repeal of the Stamp Act, and insisted upon the necessity of relieving England from the burden, which should be borne by the colonies, and which, with contingencies, exceeded £400,000. Mr. Charles Townshend, then Chancellor of the Exchequer, replied that " the Administration has given its attention to give relief to Great Britain from bearing the whole expense of securing, defending, and protecting America and the West India islands. I shall bring into the House some propositions that I hope may tend, in time, to ease the people of England upon this head,

---

* The carrying into effect of the Billeting Act in Boston is thus stated by Mr. Holmes :

" An Act had been passed by Parliament, the same session in which the Stamp Act was passed, that obliged the Colonial Assemblies to provide quarters for the soldiers, and furnish them with fire, beds, candles, and other articles at the expense of the colonies. The jealousy of Massachusetts was awakened by the attempt of the Governor to execute this law. In June an addition was made to the British troops at the castle, in the harbour of Boston, and the Governor requested that provision be made by the Assembly for their support. After due deliberation, the House resolved that such provision be made for them while they remain here, as has been heretofore usually made for his Majesty's regular troops when occasionally in the province. The caution with which this resolution was drawn shows how reluctant the Assembly were to have a military force placed in the province ; and how careful neither to yield any portion of their legislative rights, nor to furnish a precedent for the repetition of a measure equally obnoxious and dangerous to the colonists. The suspension of the power of legislation in New York justly excited alarm throughout all the colonies ; for it was perceived that every Colonial Assembly would, by parity of reasoning, be put on their trial for good behaviour, of which the British Ministry would be the judge. Richard Henry Lee, of Virginia, said, 'An Act for suspending the Legislature of that province hangs, like a flaming sword, over all our heads, and requires by all means to be removed.'" (Annals, etc., Vol. II., p. 149.)

and yet not be heavy in any manner upon the people in the colonies. *I know the mode by which a revenue may be drawn from America without offence.*" He was applauded from all sides of the House, and continued : " I am still a firm advocate for the Stamp Act, for its principle, and for the duty itself ; only the heats which prevailed made it an improper time to press it. I laugh at the absurd distinction between internal and external taxes. I know of no such distinction. It is a distinction without a difference. It is perfect nonsense. If we have a right to impose the one, we have a right to impose the other. The distinction is ridiculous in the opinion of everybody except the Americans."* In conclusion, laying his hand on the table in front of him, he declared to the House, " England is undone if this taxation of America is given up."† Grenville demanded Townsend to pledge himself to his declaration of obtaining a revenue from the colonies ; and did so promptly amid the applause of the House. In June, Townshend proceeded to redeem his pledge, and for that purpose brought successively three Bills into the House, all of which were passed by nearly unanimous votes.

" The first of these Bills, in the preamble, declared an American revenue expedient, and promised to raise it by granting

---

* The Americans took the Chancellor of the Exchequer at his word, the plain and logical inference from which was, that if it was unlawful to impose *internal* taxes, it was equally unlawful to impose *external* taxes. The colonies had unanimously denied the lawfulness of *internal* taxes imposed by Parliament, and in that denial had been sustained by the opinions of Lord Camden, Pitt, and other English statesmen, and virtually by the repeal of the Stamp Act itself. Henceforth they resisted the imposition by Parliament of external as well as internal taxes.

† Referring to the applause of the Commons which greeted Townshend's utterances of his intention to draw a revenue from the colonies, Mr. Bancroft says : " The loud burst of rapture dismayed Conway, who sat in silent astonishment at the unauthorized but premeditated rashness of his presumptuous colleague. The next night the Cabinet questioned the insubordinate Minister ' how he had ventured to depart on so essential a point from the profession of the whole Ministry ;' and he browbeat them all. ' I appeal to you,' said he, turning to Conway, ' whether the House is not bent on obtaining a revenue of some sort from the colonies ?' Not one of the Ministry then in London (Pitt being absent and ill) had sufficient authority to advise his dismission, and nothing less could have stopped his measures." (History of the United States, Vol. VI., Chap. xxvii., pp. 47—49.)

duties on glass, red and white lead, painters' oil and paper, and threepence a pound on tea—all English productions except the last—all objects of taxation in the colonies. The exportation of tea to America was encouraged by another Act which allowed a drawback for five years of the whole duty payable on importation into England.'* The preamble of the Bill stated that the duties are laid for the better support of the government and the administration of the colonies. One clause of the Act enabled the King, by sign manual, to establish a general civil list for each province of North America, with any salaries, pensions, or appointments his Majesty might think proper. The Act also provided, after all such ministerial warrants under the sign manual "as are thought proper and necessary" shall be satisfied, the residue of the revenue shall be at the disposal of the Parliament.†

* "The colonists had been previously restrained from manufacturing certain articles for their own consumption. Other Acts confined them to the exclusive use of British merchandise. The addition of duties put them wholly in the power and discretion of Great Britain. 'We are not,' said they, 'permitted to import from any nation other than our own parent state, and have been, in some cases, restrained by her from manufacturing for ourselves; and she claims a right to do so in every instance which is incompatible with her interest. To these restrictions we have hitherto submitted; but she now rises in her demands, and imposes duties on those commodities, the purchasing of which elsewhere than in her own market her laws forbid, and the manufacturing of which for her own use she may, at any moment she pleases, restrain. Nothing is left for us to do but to complain and pay.'" (Ramsay's Colonial History, Vol. I., Chap. iii., pp. 351, 352.)

† "Townshend opened the debate with professions of candour, and the air of a man of business. Exculpating alike Pennsylvania and Connecticut, he named as the delinquent colonies—Massachusetts, which had invaded the King's perogative by a general amnesty, and in a message to its Governor had used expressions derogatory to the authority of Parliament; Rhode Island, which had postponed but not refused to indemnify the sufferers by the Stamp Act; and New Jersey, which had evaded the Billeting Act, but had yet furnished the King's troops with every essential thing to their perfect satisfaction. Against these colonies it was not necessary to institute severe proceedings. But New York, in the month of June last, besides appointing its own Commissary, had limited its supplies to two regiments, and to those articles only which were provided in the rest of the King's dominions, and in December had refused to do more.

"It became Parliament not to engage in controversy with its colonies, but to assert its sovereignty without uniting them in a common cause. For

2. The second Bill, intended to ensure the execution of the first, authorized his Majesty to appoint a Board of Commissioners of Customs to reside in the colonies, to give them such orders and instructions from time to time as his Majesty might think proper. This Board of Customs had its seat at Boston; its duty was to see to the strict enforcement of the revenue laws in America, and it was authorized to make as many appointments as the Commissioners might think fit, and to pay the appointees what sums they pleased, and were not accountable for their malconduct, though they were authorized to seize vessels suspected of having goods which had not been duly entered.*

this end he proposed to proceed against New York, and against New York alone. To levy a local tax would be to accept a penalty in lieu of obedience. He should, therefore, move that New York, having disobeyed Parliament, should be restrained from any legislative act of its own till it should comply.

"He then proceeded to advocate the establishment of a Board of Commissioners of the Customs, to be stationed in America.

"'Our right of taxation,' he continued, 'is indubitable ; yet, to prevent mischief, I was myself in favour of repealing the Stamp Act. But there can be no objection to port duties on wine, oil, and fruits, if allowed to be carried to America directly from Spain and Portugal ; on glass, paper, lead, and colours ; and especially on tea. Owing to the high charges in England, America has supplied itself with tea by smuggling it from the Dutch possessions ; to remedy this, duties hitherto levied upon it in England are to be given up, and a specific duty collected in America itself.'"

" The American revenue, it was further explained, was to be placed at the disposal of the King for the payment of his civil officers.

" This speech, pronounced with gravity and an air of moderation by an orator who was the delight of the House, implied a revolution in favour of authority. The Minister was to have the irresponsible power of establishing, by sign manual, a general civil list in every American province, and at his pleasure to grant salaries and pensions, limited only by the amount of the American revenue. The proposition bore on its face the mark of owing its parentage to the holders and patrons of American offices ; and yet it was received in the House with general favour. Richard Jackson was not regarded when he spoke against the duties themselves, and foretold the mischief that would ensue." (Bancroft's History of the United States, Vol. VI., Chap. xxix., pp. 75—77.)

" The Commissioners, from the first moment of their institution, had been an eyesore to the people of Boston. This, though partly owing to their active zeal in detecting smugglers, principally arose from the association which existed in the minds of the inhabitants between the Board of Customs and an American revenue. The Declaratory Act of 1766, the Revenue Act of 1767

3. A third Bill, in Mr. Charles Townshend's scheme for the taxation of the colonies, was for the establishment in America of *Courts of Vice-Admiralty*—at Halifax, Boston, Philadelphia, and Charleston—Courts in which the colonists were deprived of the right of trial by jury, which were invested with authority to seize and transport accused persons to England to be tried there—Courts of which the officers and informers were paid out of the proceeds of sales of confiscated goods, and in proportion to their amounts, and were therefore personally interested in confiscating as many goods as possible, and from their decisions there was no appeal except to England—a process not only tedious, but ruinously expensive, even if successful, of which there could be little hope.

In connection with these three Acts (the operations and effects of which Charles Townshend did not live to see),* the navy and military in America were commanded, not as a defence against foreign or even Indian invasions, but as Custom-house guards and officers, to enforce the payment of taxes on the

together with the pomp and expense of this Board, so disproportionate to the small income of the present duties, conspired to convince not only the few who were benefitted by smuggling, but the great body of enlightened freemen, that further and greater impositions of parliamentary taxes were intended. In proportion as this opinion gained ground, the inhabitants became more disrespectful to the executive officers of the revenue, and more disposed, in the frenzy of patriotism, to commit outrages on their persons and property. The constant bickering that existed between them and the inhabitants, together with the steady opposition given by the latter to the discharge of the official duties of the former, induced the Commissioners and friends of an American revenue to solicit the protection of a regular force at Boston. In compliance with their wishes, his Majesty ordered two regiments and some armed vessels to repair thither for supporting and assisting the officers of Customs in the execution of their duty." (Ramsay's Colonial History, Vol. I., Chap. iii., pp. 355, 356.)

* His Revenue Act, and the two subsequent Acts to give it effect, produced an excitement throughout the American colonies that will be noticed hereafter. Mr. Bancroft remarks : "They would nullify Townshend's Revenue Act by consuming nothing on which he had laid a duty, and avenge themselves on England by importing no more British goods. At the beginning of this excitement (September, 1767), Charles Townshend was seized with fever, and after a short illness, during which he met danger with the unconcerned levity that had marked his conduct of the most serious affairs, he died at the age of forty-one, famed alike for incomparable talents and extreme instability." (History of the United States, Vol. VI., p. 98.)

colonists. The very next day after the King had given the royal sanction to the system of Courts of Admiralty in America, "orders were issued directly to the Commander-in-Chief in America, that the troops under his command should give their assistance to the officers of the revenue for the effectual suppression of the contraband trade. Nor was there delay in following up the new law, to employ the navy to enforce the Navigation Acts. To this end Admiral Colville, the naval Commander-in-Chief on the coasts of North America, from the River St. Lawrence to Cape Florida and the Bahama Islands, became the head of a new corps of revenue officers. Each captain of his squadron had Custom-house commissions, and a set of instructions from the Lords Commissioners of the Admiralty for his guidance; and other instructions were given them by the Admiral, to enter into the harbours or lie off the coasts of America; to qualify themselves, by taking the usual Custom-house oaths, to do the office of Custom-house officers; to seize such persons as were suspected by them to be engaged in illicit trade."*

The effect of these acts and measures was to create universal dissatisfaction throughout the colonies, as they were not even in pretence for the regulation of trade, but for the purpose of raising a parliamentary revenue in America, and therefore differed not in principle from the tax imposed by the Stamp Act. "The colonists contended that there was no real difference between the principle of these new duties and the Stamp Act. They were both designed to raise a revenue in America, and in the same manner. The payment of the duties imposed by the Stamp Act might have been evaded by the total disuse of stamped paper, and so might the payment of these duties by

---

* Bancroft's History of the United States, Vol. V., Chapter ix., pp. 161, 162. Mr. Bancroft adds:

"The promise of large emoluments in case of forfeiture stimulated their natural and irregular vivacity to enforce laws which had become obsolete, and they pounced upon American property as they would have gone to war in quest of prize-money. Even at first their acts were equivocal, and they soon came to be as illegal as they were oppressive. There was no redress. An appeal to the Privy Council was costly and difficult; and besides, when it so happened, before the end of the year, that an officer had to defend himself on an appeal, the suffering colonists were exhausted by the delay and expense, while the Treasury took care to indemnify their agent."—*Ib.*, p. 162.

the total disuse of those articles on which they were laid; but in neither case without great difficulty. The Revenue Act of 1767 produced resolves, petitions, addresses, remonstrances, similar to those with which the colonists opposed the Stamp Act. It also gave rise to a second association for suspending further importations of British manufactures till those offensive duties should be taken off."*

The year 1767 closed with enlarging and multiplying associations to dispense with the use of goods of British manufacture, the appointment of Lord North to succeed Charles Townshend as Chancellor of the Exchequer, and of the Earl of Hillsborough to succeed the Earl of Shelburne as Secretary of State for the Colonies. Lord North had voted for the Stamp Act and against its repeal; and Lord Hillsborough was less indulgent to the colonies than Lord Shelburne.

---

* Ramsay's Colonial History, Vol. I., Chapter iii., pp. 352, 353.

"Towards the last of October, the inhabitants of Boston, 'ever sensitive to the sound of liberty,' assembled in a town meeting, and voted to dispense with a large number of articles of British manufacture, which were particularly specified; to adhere to former agreements respecting funerals; and to purchase no new clothing for mourning. Committees were appointed to obtain subscribers to this agreement, and the resolves were sent in to all the towns of the province and abroad to other colonies. The 20th of the ensuing month (20th of November, the time when the Acts went into operation) passed without tumult. Placards were exhibited and effigies were set up, but the people in general were quiet. Otis (the most popular man in Boston), at a town meeting *held to discountenance riot*, delivered a speech in which he recommended caution, and advised that no opposition should be made to the new duties. ' The King has a right,' said he, ' to appoint officers of the Customs in what manner he pleases and by what denominations; and to resist his authority will but provoke his displeasure.' Such counsel was displeasing to the zealous, but it was followed." (Barry's History of Massachusetts, Vol. II., Chapter xi., pp. 340, 341.)

CHAPTER XIV.

EVENTS OF 1768—PROTESTS AND LOYAL PETITIONS OF THE COLONISTS
AGAINST THE ENGLISH PARLIAMENTARY ACTS FOR RAISING REVENUE
IN THE COLONIES.

THE meetings and protests against the Revenue Acts and
petitions for their repeal, which began in the autumn of 1767,
increased throughout the colonies in 1768. In January, the
General Assembly of Massachusetts voted a temperate and
loyal petition to the King,* and letters urging the rights of the
province, addressed to Lord Shelburne, General Conway, the
Marquis of Rockingham, Lord Camden, and the Earl of Chatham. The petition and these letters were all to the same effect.
The petition to the King was enclosed to Denis de Berdt, a
London merchant (who was appointed agent for the colony),
with a long letter of instructions. All these papers are pervaded with a spirit of loyalty, and ask for nothing more than
the enjoyment of the rights and privileges which they had
ever possessed and enjoyed down to the year after the peace of
Paris in 1763.

---

* The following are the concluding paragraphs of this petition to the King,
dated 20th January, 1768:

"With great sincerity permit us to assure your Majesty, that your subjects
of this province ever have and will continue to acknowledge your Majesty's
High Court of Parliament as the supreme legislative power of the whole
empire, the superintending authority of which is clearly admitted in all
cases that can consist with the fundamental rights of nature and the constitution, to which your Majesty's happy subjects in all parts of your empire conceive they have a just and equitable claim.

"It is with the deepest concern that your humble suppliants would
represent to your Majesty, that your Parliament, the rectitude of whose

22

In addition to these representations and letters sent to England, the Massachusetts General Assembly adopted, on the 11th of February, and sent a circular letter to the Speakers of the respective Houses of Burgesses of the other American provinces. In this ably-written letter there is no dictation or assumption of authority, but a statement of their representations to England, and a desire for mutual consultation and harmonious action. They say: "This House hope that this letter will be candidly considered in no other light than as expressing a disposition freely to communicate their mind to a sister colony, upon a common concern, in the same manner as they would be glad to receive the sentiments of your or any other House of Assembly on the continent."

As this letter was the first step to the union of the American colonies, and was followed by results that culminated in the War of Independence, it may be proper to give such extracts from it as will show its character and design; in neither of which do I

intentions is never to be questioned, has thought proper to pass divers Acts imposing taxes on your Majesty's subjects in America, with the sole and express purpose of raising a revenue. If your Majesty's subjects here shall be deprived of the honour and privilege of voluntarily contributing their aid to your Majesty in supporting your government and authority in the province, and defending and securing your rights and territories in America, which they have always hitherto done with the utmost cheerfulness : if these Acts of Parliament shall remain in force, and your Majesty's Commons in Great Britain shall continue to exercise the power of granting the property of their fellow-subjects in this province, your people must then regret their unhappy fate in having only the name left of free subjects.

" With all humility we conceive that a representation of your Majesty's subjects of this province in the Parliament, considering their local circumstances, is utterly impracticable. Your Majesty has heretotore been graciously pleased to order your requisitions to be laid before the representatives of your people in the General Assembly, who have never failed to afford the necessary aid to the extent of their ability, and sometimes beyond it ; and it would be ever grievous to your Majesty's faithful subjects to be called upon in a way that should appear to them to imply a distrust ot their most ready and willing compliance.

" Under the most sensible impressions of your Majesty's wise and paternal care for the remotest of your faithful subjects, and in full dependence on the royal declarations in the Charter of this province, we most humbly beseech your Majesty to take our present unhappy circumstances under your Royal consideration, and afford us relief in such manner as in your Majesty's great wisdom and clemency shall seem meet." (Prior Documents, etc., pp. 175—7

find anything which I think is inconsistent with the principles and spirit of a loyal subject. The general principles on which they rested their claims to the rights and privileges of British subjects are stated as follows :

"The House have humbly represented to the Ministry their own sentiments : That his Majesty's High Court of Parliament is the supreme legislative power over the whole empire. That in all free States the constitution is fixed ; and as the supreme legislative derives its power and authority from the constitution, it cannot overleap the bounds of it without destroying its foundation. That the constitution ascertains and limits both sovereignty and allegiance ; and therefore his Majesty's American subjects, who acknowledge themselves bound by the ties of allegiance, have an equitable claim to the full enjoyment of the fundamental rules of the British constitution. That it is an essential, unalterable right in nature, ingrafted into the British constitution as a fundamental law, and ever held sacred and irrevocable by the subjects within the realm, that what a man hath honestly acquired is absolutely his own, which he may freely give, but cannot be taken from him without his consent. That the American subjects may, therefore, exclusive of any consideration of Charter rights, with a decent firmness adapted to the character of freemen and subjects, assert this natural constitutional right.

"It is moreover their humble opinion, which they express with the greatest deference to the wisdom of the Parliament, that the Acts made there, imposing duties on the people of this Province, *with the sole and express purpose of raising a revenue,* are infringements of their natural and constitutional rights; because, as they are not represented in the British Parliament, his Majesty's Commons in Great Britain by those Acts grant their property without their consent."

Then, after showing the impracticability, on various grounds, of the representation of the colonies in the British Parliament, on which account local subordinate Legislatures were established, that the colonists might enjoy the inalienable right of representation, the circular letter proceeds :

"Upon these principles, and also considering that were the right in the Parliament ever so clear, yet for obvious reasons it would be beyond the rule of equity, that their constituents should be taxed on the manufactures of Great Britain here, in addition to the duties they pay for them in England, and other advantages arising to Great Britain from the Acts of Trade, this House have preferred a humble, dutiful, and loyal petition to our most gracious Sovereign, and made such representation to his Majesty's Ministers as they apprehend would tend to obtain redress.

"They have also submitted to consideration, whether any people can be said to enjoy any degree of freedom if the Crown, in addition to its undoubted authority of constituting a Governor, should appoint him such a stipend as it shall judge proper, without the consent of the people, and at their expense and whether, while the judges of the land and other civil officers hold not their commissions during good behaviour their having salaries appointed for them by the Crown, independent of the people, hath not a tendency to subvert the principles of equity and endanger the happiness and security of the subjects.

"In addition to these measures, the House have wrote a letter to their agent, Mr. De Berdt, the sentiments of which he is directed to lay before the Ministry, wherein they take notice of the hardship of the Act for Preventing Mutiny and Desertion, which requires the Governor and Council to provide enumerated articles for the King's marching troops, and the people to pay the expense; and also the commission of the gentlemen appointed Commissioners of Customs to reside in America, which authorizes them to make as many appointments as they think fit, and to pay the appointees what sums they please, for whose malconduct they are not accountable." ❊ *

"These are the sentiments and proceedings of this House; and as they have too much reason to believe that the enemies of the colonies have represented them to his Majesty's Ministers and the Parliament as factious, disloyal, and having a disposition to make themselves independent of the mother country, they have taken occasion, in the most humble terms, to assure his Majesty and his Ministers that, with regard to the people of this province, and, as they doubt not, of all the colonies, the charge is unjust.

"The House is fully satisfied that your Assembly is too generous and enlarged in sentiment to believe that this letter proceeds from an ambition of taking the lead, or dictating to other Assemblies; they freely submit their opinion to the judgment of others, and shall take it kind in your House to point out to them anything further that may be thought necessary.

"This House cannot conclude without expressing their firm confidence in the King, our common Head and Father, that the united and dutiful supplications of his distressed American subjects will meet with his Royal and favourable acceptance.

"SIGNED BY THE SPEAKER."

This circular letter of the Massachusetts Assembly was exceedingly displeasing to the British Ministry, and called forth two letters from the Earl of Hillsborough, who had succeeded the Earl of Shelburne as Principal Secretary of State for the Colonies.

One of these letters was a circular addressed through the Governor to the General Assemblies of each of the several colonies. This letter is dated "Whitehall, April 21, 1768" The first paragraph is as follows:

"GENTLEMEN,—I have his Majesty's commands to transmit to you the enclosed copy of a letter from the Speaker of the House of Representatives of the colony of Massachusetts Bay, addressed by order of that House to the Speaker of the Assembly of each colony upon the continent of North America; as his Majesty considers this measure to be of a most dangerous and factious tendency, calculated to inflame the minds of his good subjects in the colonies, to promote an unwarrantable combination, and to excite and encourage an open opposition to and denial of the authority of Parliament, and to subvert the true principles of the constitution, it is his Majesty's pleasure that you should, immediately upon the receipt hereof, exert your utmost influence to defeat this flagitious attempt to disturb the public peace, by prevailing upon the Assembly of your province to take no notice of it, which will be treating it with the contempt it deserves."

This most ill-advised letter of Lord Hillsborough had the very opposite effect from that which he had hoped and intended. It increased the importance of the Massachusetts House of Representatives in the estimation of other colonies, and produced responses of approval from most of their General Assemblies.

The Speaker of the House of Burgesses of Virginia, in a

letter to the Speaker of the House of Representatives of Massachusetts, dated Virginia, May 9, 1768, says:

"The House of Burgesses of this colony proceeded, very soon after they met, to the consideration of your important letter of the 11th of February, 1768, written in the name and by the order of the House of Representatives of your province; and I have received their particular direction to desire you to inform that honourable House that they applaud them for their attention to American liberty, and that the steps they have taken thereon will convince them of their opinion of the fatal tendency of the Acts of Parliament complained of, and of their fixed resolution to concur with the other colonies in their application for redress.

"After the most deliberate consultation, they thought it their duty to represent to the Parliament of Great Britain that they are truly sensible of the happiness and security they derive from their connection with and dependence upon Great Britain, and are under the greatest concern that any unlucky incident should interrupt that salutary harmony which they wish ever to subsist. They lament that the remoteness of their situation often exposes them to such misrepresentations as are apt to involve them in censures of disloyalty to their Sovereign, and the want of proper respect to the British Parliament; whereas they have indulged themselves in the agreeable persuasion, that they ought to be considered as inferior to none of their fellow-subjects in loyalty and affection.

"They do not affect an independency of their parent kingdom, the prosperity of which they are bound to the utmost of their abilities to promote, but cheerfully acquiesce in the authority of Parliament to make laws for preserving a necessary dependence and for regulating the trade of the colonies. Yet they cannot conceive, and humbly insist it is not essential to support a proper relation between the mother country and colonies transplanted from her, that she should have a right to raise money from them without their consent, and presume they do not aspire to more than the natural rights of British subjects when they assert that no power on earth has a right to impose taxes on the people, or take the smallest portion of their property, without their consent given by their representatives in Parliament. This has ever been considered as the chief pillar of the constitution. Without this support no man can be said to have the least shadow of liberty, since they can have no property in that which another can by right take from them when he pleases, without their consent."

After referring to the antiquity and grounds of their rights as British subjects, and to the fact of their not being represented in Parliament, of the impracticability of being so, and "the oppressive Stamp Act, confessedly imposing internal taxes, and the late Acts of Parliament giving and granting certain duties in the British colonies, mainly tending to the same end," the Virginia House of Burgesses proceed as follows:

"The Act suspending the legislative power of New York, they consider as still more alarming to the colonists, though it has that single province in view. If the Parliament can compel them to furnish a single article to the troops sent over, they may by the same rule oblige them to furnish clothes, arms, and every other necessary, even the pay of the officers and soldiers—a doctrine replete with every mischief, and utterly subversive of all that is dear and valuable. For what advantage can the people of the colonies derive from their right of choosing their own representatives, if those representatives, when chosen, were not permitted to exercise their own judgments— were under a necessity (on pain of being deprived of their legislative authority) of enforcing the mandates of the British Parliament?

"They trust they have expressed themselves with a firmness that becomes freemen pleading for essential rights, and with a decency that will take off every imputation of faction or disloyalty. They repose entire confidence in his Majesty, who is ever attentive to the complaints of his subjects, and is ever ready to relieve their distress; and they are not without hopes that the colonies, united in a decent and regular opposition, may prevail on the new House of Commons to put a stop to measures so directly repugnant to the interests both of the mother country and her colonies."

The day after these proceedings by the House of Burgesses, the Governor of Virginia dissolved them.

The House of Representatives of New Jersey, after gratefully acknowledging the receipt of the Massachusetts circular, observe:

"The freedom with which the House of Representatives of

the Massachusetts Bay have communicated their sentiments upon a matter of so great concern to all the colonies, hath been received by this House with that candour the spirit and design of your letter merits. And at the same time that they acknowledge themselves obliged to you for communicating your sentiments to them, they have directed me to assure you that they are desirous to keep up a correspondence with you, and to unite with the colonies, if necessary, in further supplications to his Majesty to relieve his distressed American subjects."

Answers to the Massachusetts circular from the Houses of Representatives of Connecticut, of Georgia, and of Maryland, were given to the same effect. The Maryland House of Representatives, in addition to the answer to the Speaker of the House of Representatives, presented an address to Governor Sharpe, of Maryland, in reply to the letter of Lord Hillsborough. Their address is dated June 23rd, 1768, and contains the following words:

"In answer to your Excellency's message of the 20th, we must observe, that if the letter from the Speaker of the House of Representatives of the colony of Massachusetts Bay, addressed to and communicated by our Speaker to this House, be the same with the letter, a copy of which you are pleased to intimate hath been communicated to the King's Ministers, it is very alarming to find, at a time when the people of America think themselves aggrieved by the late Acts of Parliament imposing taxes on them for the sole and express purpose of raising a revenue, and in the most dutiful manner are seeking redress from the Throne, any endeavours to unite in laying before their Sovereign what is apprehended to be their just complaint, should be looked upon 'as a measure of most dangerous and factious tendency, calculated to inflame the minds of his Majesty's good subjects in the colonies, and to promote an unwarrantable combination, to excite and encourage an open opposition to and denial of the authority of Parliament, and to subvert the true principles of the constitution.'

"We cannot but view this as an attempt in some of his Majesty's Ministers to suppress all communication of sentiments between the colonies, and to prevent the united supplications of America from reaching the royal ear. We hope the conduct of this House will ever evince their reverence and respect for the laws, and faithful attachment to the constitution; but we cannot be brought to resent an exertion of the most undoubted constitutional right of petitioning the Throne, or any endeavours to procure and preserve a union of the colonies, as an unjustifiable attempt to revive those distractions which it is said have operated so fatally to the prejudice of both the colonies and the mother country. We have the warmest and most affectionate attachment to our most gracious Sovereign, and shall ever pay the readiest and most respectful regard to the just and constitutional power of the British Parliament; but we shall not be intimidated by a few sounding expressions from doing what we think is right."*

Thus the unconstitutional assumptions and despotic instructions of Lord Hillsborough to the Legislative Assemblies of the several colonies were manfully and in a moderate and loyal spirit repelled by them, in the clear knowledge of the constitutional rights of Englishmen, whether resident in America or England. But while Lord Hillsborough foolishly and vainly dictated to the several colonies to treat the colony of Massachusetts with contempt, he advanced a step further in his would-be domination over Massachusetts itself by directing Governor Barnard to order the House of Representatives, under a threat of dissolution, to rescind the resolution which they had adopted to send the circular to the representative Assemblies of other colonies. Lord Hillsborough, in a letter to the Governor of Massachusetts Bay, dated April 22nd, 1768, said:

"It is the King's pleasure, that so soon as the General Court is again assembled, at the time prescribed by the Charter, you should require of the House of Representatives, in his Majesty's name, to rescind the resolution which gave birth to the circular letter from the Speaker, and to declare their disapprobation thereof, and dissent to that rash and hasty proceeding." "But if, notwithstanding the apprehensions which may justly be entertained of the ill-consequences of a continuance of this factious spirit, which seems to have influenced the resolutions of the Assembly at the conclusion of the last session, the new Assembly should refuse to comply with his Majesty's reasonable expectation, it is the King's pleasure that you should immediately

* Prior Documents, etc., p. 210.

dissolve them, and transmit to me, to be laid before his Majesty, an account of their proceedings thereupon, to the end that his Majesty may, if he thinks fit, lay the whole matter before his Parliament, that such provisions as shall be found necessary may be made to prevent for the future a conduct of so extraordinary and unconstitutional a nature."*

If it was unwise for Lord Hillsborough to write letters to the Governors of the several colonies to induce their Assemblies to treat with silent contempt the circular letter of the Massachusetts Assembly, it was absurd for him to order that Assembly to rescind its resolution to send a letter which had been sent, and acted upon, and answered—a resolution and letter, indeed, of a preceding House of Assembly. But the new House of Assembly, after long deliberation and discussion, refused, by a majority of 92 to 17, to rescind the obnoxious resolution of the late House of Assembly, and at the same time prepared and addressed to Lord Hillsborough an elaborate letter in vindication of their proceedings. The House was, of course, forthwith *dissolved.*

Lord Hillsborough's letter produced discontent not only in Massachusetts, but in all the American provinces. It, in effect, denied the right of consultation and petition to the colonists; for, as was said by Dr. Franklin, " a demand attended with a penalty of dissolution seemed a command, not a requisition, leaving no deliberative or discretionary power in the Assembly; and the ground of its being a petition to the King, guarded with a most explicit declaration of the supreme legislative power of Parliament, it wore the severe and dreadful appearance of a penal prohibition against petitioning. It was, in effect, saying you shall not even presume to complain, and reducing them below the common state of slavery, in which, if men complain with decency, they are heard unless their masters happen to be monsters. It warmed moderation into zeal, and inflamed zeal into rage. Yet still there appeared a disposition to express their grievances in humble petitions. All the Assemblies on the continent, in answer to a requisition of similar import to that already mentioned, asserted the right of the subject to petition for redress of grievances. They joined

---

* Prior Documents, etc.

in petitions stating the imposition of taxes upon them without their consent, and the abolition of juries in revenue cases, as intolerable grievances, from which they prayed relief."*

It is singular and proper to observe that the Massachusetts Assembly were now complaining, and justly complaining, of the denial of their right of petition, and of being taxed without their own consent, when more than a century before their forefathers had not only denied the right of religious worship according to their conscience to Baptists, Presbyterians, and Episcopalians, but the right of petition for the redress of grievances to both the local Legislature and the King and Parliament, and seized their private papers and fined and imprisoned them for attempting thus to petition ; denied to four-fifths of the inhabitants of Massachusetts Bay the right of franchise itself, because they were not certified members of the Congregational Church ; taxed them for half a century without allowing them any representation in the Legislature that taxed them, and then fined and imprisoned those of them who complained by petition of thus being taxed without representation, as well as being denied the freedom of religious worship

But though the General Assembly of Massachusetts Bay were now receiving a part of the measure which their preceding General Assemblies had meted out in full measure to four-fifths of their own fellow-citizens during more than half of the previous century, yet that does not make Lord Hillsborough's letter the less unconstitutional and tyrannical, nor the conduct and vindication of the House of Representatives of Massachusetts Bay less manly and justifiable. The Governor of the colony and his abettors had represented constitutional opposition and remonstrances against single Acts of Parliament, and of the Ministers of the day, as disloyalty to the King and treasonable resistance to lawful authority, and had already pursued such a course of action as to create a pretext for bringing soldiers and ships of war to the city, and consequent hostility and collisions between citizens and the soldiery, so as apparently to justify the suspension of the constituted legislative authorities in Massachusetts Bay, and enable the governors, judges, and executive officers to obtain large salaries

* Prior Documents, etc., p. 262.

and perquisites out of the colonists for present gratification and future residence and expenditure in England.

Massachusetts was at that time the most populous and the most wealthy colony in America, and Boston was the port of the largest trade; and though the House of Representatives there had not used stronger language in its remonstrances to Parliament and petitions to the King than the House of Representatives of Virginia (the next most populous colony), or Pennsylvania, or New York, or Maryland, or New Jersey, or Connecticut, or Rhode Island, yet the British Ministry determined to establish the newly-asserted parliamentary power in America by making an example of Massachusetts and of the port of Boston. There was the appointed seat of the English Board of Commissioners of Customs, attended by a *posse* of officers whose haughtiness and taunts and threats contributed not a little to irritate those with whom they had intercourse.

Three circumstances occurred which tended to increase the popular irritation, and hasten the approaching crisis—the seizure and detention of a sloop, the stationing of soldiers in the city, and pressing of seamen contrary to law.

As to the seizure of the vessel, accounts differ. Dr. Holmes, in his Annals, says:

"The laws of trade had been hitherto greatly eluded, but the Commissioners of the Customs were now determined that they should be executed. On the arrival of the sloop *Liberty*, laden with wines from Madeira, belonging to Mr. John Hancock, an eminent merchant of Boston, the tidesman, Thomas Kirk, went on board, and was followed by Captain Marshall, who was in Mr. Hancock's employ. On Kirk's refusing several proposals made to him, Marshall with five or six others confined him below three hours, during which time the wine was taken out. The master entered some pipes next morning; but the sloop was seized for a false entry, and removed from the wharf under the guns of the *Romney* man-of-war. The removal of the sloop was highly resented, as implying apprehension of a rescue, and every method was taken to interrupt the officers in the execution of their business; and many persons determined to be revenged. A mob was soon collected; and Mr. Harrison, the collector, Mr. Hallowell, the comptroller, Mr. Irving, the inspector of imports and exports, and a son of the collector, very narrowly escaped with their lives. The mob proceeded to the houses of the collector and comptroller, and having broken their windows, and those of the inspector-general, they next took and dragged the collector's (pleasure) boat through the town and burned it on the common. These outrages induced the Custom-house officers to take refuge, first on board the *Romney* man-of-war and afterwards in Castle William."*

On the other hand, Dr. Franklin states the affair as follows:

"On the 10th of June a seizure was made of a sloop fastened to the wharf, by an armed force, and the seizure carried by violence to the man-of-war. That this seizure was made with every circumstance of violence and insult which could irritate a mob, is proved by the oaths of thirteen eye-witnesses whose credibility has never been impeached. Unhappily, the irritation succeeded but too well. The collector and comptroller who made the seizure in that manner were treated with great indignity and personal injury by the mob."†

Another circumstance, productive of more intense and general excitement, if possible, and which transpired very shortly after the seizure and detention of the sloop *Liberty*, was the impressment of some seamen belonging to the town by the captain of the man-of-war *Romney*. This was done, as alleged, in violation of an Act of Parliament for the encouragement of trade to America—6 Anne, chap. xxvii., section 9—which says:

"No mariner or other person who shall serve on board, or be retained to serve on board, any privateer or trading ship or vessel that shall be employed in any port of America, nor any mariner or person being on shore in any port thereof, shall be

* American Annals, etc., Vol II., pp. 157, 158; the authority given is Gordon, Vol. I., pp. 168—172. Dr. Ramsay gives a similar account of the affair in his Colonial History, Vol. I., Chap. iii., p. 355.

† Prior Documents, pp. 262, 263.

Dr. Franklin adds in a note: "That the seizure was unjust, is plain from this, that they were obliged to restore the vessel, after detaining her a long time, not being able to find any evidence to support a prosecution. The suits for enormous sums against a number of persons, brought in the Court of Admiralty, being found insupportable, were, after long continuance, to the great expense and trouble of these persons, dropt by a declaration of the King's advocate that his Majesty would prosecute no further; but the prosecuted could obtain no costs or damages, for so is the law."—*Ib.*, p. 263.

liable to be impressed or taken away by any officer or officers belonging to her Majesty's ships of war." To prevent the tumults which were feared from such a flagrant and dangerous infraction of the law, a legal town-meeting was called, in which the inhabitants assembled petitioned the Governor to interpose and prevent such outrages upon the rights and liberties of the people; but the Governor declined to interfere—stated that he had no control over his Majesty's ships of war—that he would, however, use his utmost endeavours to get the impressing of men for the King's ships of war so regulated as to avoid all the inconveniences to the town which the petitioners apprehended.

In the midst of these excitements and discontents, so threatening and dangerous without some form of expression, many of the peace-loving and respectable inhabitants of Boston urged the Governor to convene the Legislature, but he refused without a command from the King. The select men of Boston then proposed to the several towns and townships of the colony the election of a Convention, to meet in Boston the 22nd of September, "to deliberate on constitutional measures to obtain redress of their grievances." Ninety-six towns and eight districts elected delegates to the Convention, which sat four days; "disclaimed any legislative authority, petitioned the Governor, made loyal professions, expressed their aversion to standing armies, to tumults and disorders, their readiness to assist in suppressing riots and preserving the peace; recommended patience and good order; and after a short session dissolved."[*]

The day before the close of this Convention, it was announced that three men-of-war and transports had arrived at Boston harbour with about 900 troops, and the fleet next day came to anchor near Castle William. The Commissioners of Customs and their friends had solicited the stationing of a regular force in the town.

"The ships having taken a station which commanded the town, the troops, under cover of the cannon of the ships, landed without molestation, and to the number of 700 men marched, with muskets charged and bayonets fixed, martial music, and

* Holmes' Annals, etc., Vol. II., p. 158.

the usual military parade, into the common. In the evening the Select Men of Boston were required to quarter the regiments in the town ; but they absolutely refused. A temporary shelter, however, in Faneuil Hall was permitted to one regiment that was without camp equipage. The next day the State House, by the order of the Governor, was opened for the reception of the soldiers; and after the quarters were settled, two field pieces with the main guard were stationed just in its front. Everything was calculated to excite the indignation of the inhabitants. The lower floor of the State House, which had been used by gentlemen and merchants as an exchange ; the representatives' chamber, the Court-house, Faneuil Hall—places with which were associated ideas of justice and freedom, as well as of convenience and utility—were now filled with regular soldiers. Guards were placed at the doors of the State House, through which the Council must pass in going to their own chamber. The common was covered with tents. The soldiers were constantly marching and countermarching to relieve the guards. The sentinels challenged the inhabitants as they passed. The Lord's day was profaned, and the devotion of the sanctuary was disturbed by the sound of drums and other military music. There was every appearance of a garrisoned town. The colonists felt disgusted and injured, but not overawed, by the obtruded soldiery. After the troops had obtained quarters, the Council were required to provid' barracks for them, agreeably to Act of Parliament, but they resolutely declined any measure which might be construed into submission to that Act. Several large transports arrived at Boston from Cork, having on board part of the 64th and 65th British regiments, under Colonels MacKay and Pomeroy ; the object of which was to protect the revenue officers in the collection of duties.*

---

* Holmes' Annals, etc., Vol. II., pp. 153, 150.

The Boston *American Gazette*, under the head of "A Journal of Transactions in Boston," says, September 30th, 1768 : "Early this morning a number of boats were observed round the town, making soundings, etc. At three o'clock in the afternoon, the *Launceston*, of 40 guns ; the *Mermaid*, of 28 ; the *Glasgow*, 20 ; the *Beaver*, 14 ; *Senegal*, 14 ; *Bonetta*, 10, and several armed schooners, which, together with the *Romney*, of 60 guns, and the other ships of war before in the harbour, all commanded by Captain Smith, came up to town, bringing with them the 14th Regiment, Colonel Dalrymple, and the 29th Regiment, Colonel Carr, none having been disembarked at Castle

Such was the state of things in Massachusetts and in other colonies at the close of the year 1768.

Island ; so that we now behold Boston surrounded, in a time of profound peace, with about fourteen ships of war, with springs on their cables, and their broadsides to the town. If the people of England could but look into the town, they would smile to see the utmost good order and observance of the laws, and that this mighty armament has no other rebellion to subdue than what has existed in the brain and letters of the inveterate G——r B——d (Governor Barnard), and the detested Commiss (Commissioners) of the Board of Cust—s (Customs). What advantage the Court of Versailles may take of the present policy of the British Ministry can be better determined hereafter." (pp. 177, 178.)

CHAPTER XV.

Events of 1769—Unjust Imputations of Parliament on the Loyalty of the Colonists, and Misrepresentations of their Just and Loyal Petitions.

The earliest proceedings of this year in regard to the American colonies took place in the British Parliament. In all the resolutions, protests, addresses, and petitions which had been adopted by American Assemblies and at town meetings, asserting the exclusive right of the colonists to tax themselves, and against taxation without representation by the British Parliament, they professed heartfelt loyalty to the King, and disclaimed all views of independence; while in England the Parliament asserted unlimited supremacy in and over the colonies, and the Royal speeches, as well as the resolutions and addresses adopted by the Lords and Commons, represented the colonies as being in a state of disobedience to law and government, adopting measures subversive of the constitution, and manifesting a disposition to throw off all allegiance to the mother country. The House of Lords passed resolutions censuring the resolutions and proceedings of the Massachusetts House of Representatives, pronouncing the election of deputies to sit in Convention, and the meeting of that Convention at Boston, daring insults to his Majesty's authority, and audacious usurpations of the powers of Government; yet, as has been seen, that Convention expressly disclaimed any assumption of government, and simply expressed the grievances complained of, prayed for their redress, declared their loyalty to the King, and recognition of the supreme authority of Parliament according to the constitution, and quietly dissolved. But the House of Commons declared con-

23

currence in the resolutions of the Lords; and both Houses, in their address to the King, endorsed the measures of his Ministers, declared their readiness to give effectual support to such further measures as might be found necessary to execute the laws in Massachusetts Bay, and prayed his Majesty "to direct the Governor (Barnard) to take the most effectual methods for procuring the fullest information touching all treason or misprision of treason within the Government since the 30th day of December, 1767, and to transmit the same, together with the names of the persons who were most active in the commission of such offences, to one of the Secretaries of State, in order that his Majesty might issue a special commission for inquiring, hearing and determining the said offences, *within the realm of Great Britain*, pursuant to the provision of the statute of the 35th of Henry the Eighth."

The holding of town-meetings and their election of deputies, etc., were as much provided for in the provincial laws as the meeting and proceedings of the House of Representatives, or as are the meetings and proceedings of town, and township, and county municipal councils in Canada. The wholesale denunciations of disloyalty and treason against the people of a country was calculated to exasperate and produce the very feelings imputed; and the proposal of the two Houses of Parliament to make the Governor of Massachusetts Bay a detective and informer-general against persons opposed to his administration and the measures of the British Ministry, and the proposition to have them arrested and brought 3,000 miles over the ocean to England, for trial before a special commission, for treason or misprision of treason, show what unjust, unconstitutional, and foolish things Parliaments as well as individuals may sometimes perpetrate. Nothing has more impressed the writer, in going through this protracted war of words, preliminary to the unhappy war of swords, than the great superiority, even as literary compositions, much more as State documents, of the addresses and petitions of the Colonial Assemblies, and even public meetings, and the letters of their representatives, when compared with the dispatches of the British Ministry of that day and the writings of their partizans.

The resolutions and joint address of the Houses of Parliament, which were adopted in February, reached America in

April, and gave great offence to the colonists generally instead of exciting terror, especially the part of the address which proposed bringing alleged offenders from Massachusetts to be tried at a tribunal in Great Britain. Massachusetts had no General Assembly at that time, as Governor Barnard had dissolved the last Assembly, and the time prescribed by the Charter for calling one had not arrived; but the House of Burgesses of the old, loyal Church of England colony of Virginia took the state of all the colonies into serious consideration, passed several resolutions, and directed their Speaker to transmit them without delay to the Speakers of the Assemblies of all the colonies on the continent for their concurrence. In these resolutions the House of Burgesses declare—" That the sole right of imposing taxes on the inhabitants of this colony is now, and ever hath been, legally and constitutionally vested in the House of Burgesses, with consent of the Council, and of the King or his Governor for the time being; that it is the privilege of the inhabitants to petition their Sovereign for redress of grievances, and that it is lawful to procure the concurrence of his Majesty's other colonies in dutiful addresses, praying the Royal interposition in favour of the violated rights of America; that all trials for treason, misprision of treason, or for any felony or crime whatsoever, committed by any persons residing in any colony, ought to be in his Majesty's courts within said colony, and that the seizing of any person residing in the colony, suspected of any crime whatsoever committed therein, and sending such person to places beyond the sea to be tried, is highly derogatory of the rights of British subjects, as thereby the inestimable privilege of being tried by jury from the vicinage, as well as the liberty of producing witnesses on such trial, will be taken away from the accused."

The House agreed also to an address to his Majesty, which stated, in the style of loyalty and real attachment to the Crown, a deep conviction that the complaints of the colonists were well founded. The next day Lord Botetourt, the Governor of Virginia, dissolved the House in the following words : " Mr. Speaker and Gentlemen of the House of Burgesses, I have heard of your resolves, and augur ill of their effects. You have made it my duty to dissolve you ; and you are dissolved accordingly."

The Assembly of South Carolina adopted resolutions similar to those of Virginia, as did the Lower House of Maryland and the Delaware counties, and the Assembly of North Carolina, and was on that account dissolved by Governor Tyron. Towards the close of the year, the Assembly of New York passed resolutions in concurrence with those of Virginia. The members of the House of Burgesses of Virginia, and of the Assembly of North Carolina, after their dissolution, met as private gentlemen, chose for moderators their late Speakers, and adopted resolutions against importing British goods. This was followed by other colonies, and the non-importation agreement became general. Boston had entered into the non-importation agreement as early as August, 1768, which was soon after adopted in Salem, the city of New York, and the province of Connecticut; but the agreement was not generally entered into until after the Virginia resolutions. "The meetings of non-importation associations were regularly held in the various provinces. Committees were appointed to examine all vessels arriving from Britain. Censures were freely passed on such as refused to concur in these associations, and their names were published in the newspapers as enemies of their country. The regular Acts of the Provincial Assemblies were not so much respected and obeyed as the decrees of these Committees."*

Governor Barnard could not delay calling the General Assembly of Massachusetts beyond the time prescribed by the Charter for its meeting in May; and when it met, its first act was to

---

* Ramsay's Colonial History, Vol. I., Chapter iii., p, 359.

The following are the resolutions subscribed by the merchants and traders of New York, dated 27th August, 1768 :

I. That we will not send for from Great Britain, either upon our own account or on commission, this fall, any other goods than what we have already ordered.

II. That we will not import any kind of merchandise from Great Britain, either on our own account or on commission, or any otherwise, nor purchase from any factor or others, any kind of goods imported from Great Britain directly, or by way of any of the other colonies, or by way of the West Indies, that shall be shipped from Great Britain after the first day of November, until the forementioned Acts of Parliament, imposing duties on paper, glass, etc., be repealed; except only the articles of coals, salt, sailcloth, wool, card-wool, grindstones, chalk, lead, tin, sheet-copper, and German steel.

III. We further agree not to import any kind of merchandise from

appoint a Committee to wait on the Governor, and represent to him " that an armament by sea and land investing this metropolis, and a military guard with cannon pointed at the door of the State House, where the Assembly is held, are inconsistent with the dignity and freedom with which they have a right to deliberate, consult, and determine," and added, " They expect that your Excellency will, as his Majesty's representative, give effectual orders for the removal of the above-mentioned forces by sea and land out of this port, and the gates of this city, during the session of the said Assembly." The Governor answered : " Gentlemen, I have no authority over his Majesty's ships in this port, or his troops within this town, nor can I give any orders for the removal of the same." The House persisted in declining to do business while surrounded with an armed force, and the Governor at length adjourned it to Cambridge.

On the 9th of July the Governor sent a message to the House with accounts of expenditures already incurred in quartering his Majesty's troops, desiring funds for their payment, and requiring a provision for the quartering of the troops in the town and on Castle Island, "according to Act of Parliament." The next day, among other things, the House passed the following resolutions :

" That a general discontent on account of the Revenue Acts, an expectation of the sudden arrival of a military power to enforce said Acts, an apprehension of the troops being quartered upon the inhabitants, the General Court (or Assembly) dissolved, the Governor refusing to call a new one, and the people almost

Hamburg and Holland, directly from thence, nor by any other way whatsoever, more than we have already ordered, except tiles and bricks.

IV. We also promise to countermand all orders given from Great Britain, or since the 16th instant, by the first conveyance; ordering those goods not to be sent, unless the forementioned duties are taken off.

V. And we further agree, that if any person or persons subscribing hereto shall take any advantage, by importing any kind of goods that are herein restricted, directly or indirectly, contrary to the true intent and meaning of this agreement, such person or persons shall by us be deemed enemies to their country.

VI. Lastly, we agree, that if any goods shall be consigned or sent over to us, contrary to our agreement in this subscription, such goods so imported shall be lodged in some public warehouse, there to be kept under confinement until the forementioned Acts be repealed.

reduced to a state of despair, rendered it highly expedient and necessary for the people to convene their (town) committees to associate (in convention), consult, and advise the best means to promote peace and good order ; to present their united complaints to the Throne, and jointly to pray for the Royal interposition in favour of their violated rights ; nor can this procedure possibly be illegal, as they expressly disclaim all governmental acts.

" That the establishment of a standing army in this colony, in time of peace, is an invasion of national rights.

" That a standing army is not known as a part of the British constitution.

" That sending an armed force into the colony, under pretence of assisting the civil authority, is highly dangerous to the people, unprecedented and unconstitutional."

On the 12th of July the Governor sent a message to the House requesting an explicit answer to his message of the 6th, as to whether the House would or would not make provision for quartering the troops. After anxious deliberation, the unusually full House of 107 members present unanimously answered :

"As representatives, by the Royal Charter and the nature of our trust, we are only empowered to grant such aids as are reasonable, of which we are free and independent judges, at liberty to follow the dictates of our own understanding, without regard to the mandates of another. Your Excellency must, therefore, excuse us in this express declaration that as we cannot, consistently with our honour or interest, and much less with the duty we owe to our constituents, so we shall never make provision for the purposes mentioned in your messages."

Governor Barnard rejoined, in his last words to the Assembly, " To his Majesty, and if he pleases to his Parliament, must be referred your invasion of the rights of the Imperial sovereignty. By your own acts you will be judged. Your publications are plain and explicit, and need no comment." And he prorogued the Assembly until the 10th day of January, 1770. He wrote to Lord Hillsborough : " Their last message exceeds everything." Three weeks afterwards, the 1st of August, unexpectedly to himself, Barnard was recalled. He had expected to be appointed Governor of Virginia ; but on his arrival in England he found that the British Ministers had promised the London-American merchants that they would never employ him again in America.* He answered the purposes of the corrupt Ministerial oligarchy in England, to mislead the Sovereign on one hand and oppress the colonists on the other. But for him there would have been no ships of war or military sent to Boston; no conflicts between the citizens and soldiers; probably no revolutionary war. Barnard's departure from Boston was signalized by the ringing of bells, and firing of cannon, and bonfires at night. He was succeeded in the government by Lieutenant-Governor Hutchinson, a man who had rendered great service to his native country by his History, and his labours in the Legislature for ten years, but who had become extremely unpopular by his secret support of the English Revenue Acts and duplicate policy of Barnard, whom he at length equalled in avarice and deception, and greatly excelled in ability.

One of the most effective and least objectionable means of obtaining the repeal of the Revenue Acts was the agreement not to purchase or import goods of British manufacture or goods imported from British ports. At best the revenues arising from the operation of these Acts would not amount to £20,000 a year. They were maintained in England as a badge of the absolute authority of Parliament; they were resisted in America as a badge of colonial independence of taxation—without repre-

---

* The following is the portrait which Mr. Bancroft has drawn of the character of Barnard, and I cannot deny its accuracy :

" Trained as a wrangling proctor in an Ecclesiastical Court, he had been a quarrelsome disputant rather than a statesman. His parsimony went to the extreme of meanness; his avarice was insatiable and restless. So long as he connived at smuggling, he reaped a harvest in that way; when Grenville's sternness inspired alarm, it was his study to make the most money out of forfeitures and penalties. Professing to respect the Charter, he was unwearied in zeal for its subversion, declaring his opposition to taxation by Parliament, he urged it with all his power. Asserting most solemnly that he had never asked for troops, his letters reveal his perpetual importunity for ships of war and an armed force. His reports were often false—partly with design, partly from the credulity of panic. He placed everything in the most unfavourable light, and was ready to tell every tale and magnify trivial rumours into acts of treason. He was despondent when conciliation prevailed in England. The officers of the army and navy despised him for his cowardice and duplicity, and did not conceal their contempt." (History of the United States, Vol. VI., Chap. xli., p. 291.)

sentation. There was no crime, political or moral, in refusing to buy goods of any kind, much less goods burdened with what they considered unlawful duties. Mr. Bancroft remarks:

" The agreement of non-importation originated in New York, where it was rigidly carried into effect. No acrimony appeared; every one, without so much as a single dissentient, approved of the combination as wise and legal; persons in the highest stations declared against the Revenue Acts, and the Governor wished their repeal. His acquiescence in the association for coercing that repeal led the moderate men among the patriots of New York to plan a union of the colonies in an American Parliament (similar to that which now exists in the Dominion of Canada), preserving the Governments of the several colonies, and having the members of the General Parliament chosen by their respective Legislatures. They were preparing the greatest work of their generation, to be matured at a later day. Their confidence of immediate success assisted to make them alike disinclined to independence and firm in their expectation of bringing England to reason by suspending their mutual trade.

" The people of Boston, stimulated by the unanimity and scrupulous fidelity of New York, were impatient that a son of Barnard, two sons of Hutchinson, and about five others, would not accede to the agreement. At a great meeting of merchants in Faneuil Hall, Hancock proposed to send for Hutchinson's two sons, hinting, what was true, that the Lieutenant-Governor was himself a partner with them in their late extraordinary importations of tea. As the best means of coercion, it was voted not to purchase anything of the recusants. Subscription papers to that effect were carried around from house to house, and everybody complied."

" A letter from New York next invited Boston to extend the agreement against importing indefinitely, until every Act imposing duties should be repealed; and on the 17th (of October), by the great influence of Molineux, Otis, Samuel Adams, and William Cooper, this new form was adopted."* The opposition

* History of the United States, Vol. VI., Chap. xlii., pp. 308, 309, 311. For the first non-importation resolutions adopted by the merchants of New York, see note on page 356.

" The trade between Great Britain and her colonies on the continent of

in Boston to the reception of goods from England became so general and determined, that even Governor Hutchinson quailed before it, and the soldiers stood silent and inactive witnesses of it.   Mr. Bancroft says:

"Early in October (1769), a vessel laden with goods, shipped by English houses themselves, arrived in Boston.   The military officers had been speculating on what would be done, and Colonel Dalrymple stood ready to protect the factors.   But his assistance was not demanded.   Hutchinson permitted the merchants to reduce the consignees to submission, and even to compel an English adventurer to re-embark his goods.   One and another of the Boston recusants yielded; even the two sons of Hutchinson himself, by their father's direction, gave up 18 chests of tea, and entered fully into the (non-importation) agreement.   Four still held out, and their names, with those of the two sons of Hutchinson, whose sincerity was questioned, stood recorded as infamous on the journals of the town of Boston.   On the 15th another ship arrived; again the troops looked on as bystanders, and witnessed the complete victory of the people.[*]

But in the following month, November, a new turn was given to public thought, and new feelings of joy were inspired throughout America, by a dispatch from Lord Hillsborough to the King's personal friend, Lord Botetourt, Governor of Virginia, promising the repeal of the obnoxious Revenue Acts, and to impose no further taxes on the colonies.   Lord Hillsborough says:

"I can take upon me to assure you, notwithstanding information to the contrary from men with factious and seditious

America, on an average of three years (from 1766 to 1769), employed 1,078 ships and 28,910 seamen.   The value of goods exported from Great Britain on the same average was £3,370,900; and of goods exported from the colonies to Great Britain and elsewhere £3,924,606."   (Holmes' Annals, etc., Vol. II., p. 162.)

[*] History of the United States, Vol. VI., Chap. xlii., p. 311.

"To the military its inactivity was humiliating.   Soldiers and officers spoke of the people angrily as rebels.   The men were rendered desperate by the firmness with which the local magistrates put them on trial for every transgression of the provincial laws.   Arrests provoked resistance.   'If they touch you, run them through the bodies,' said a captain of the 29th Regiment to his soldiers, and he was indicted for the speech."—*Ib.*, p. 314.

views, that his Majesty's present Administration have at no time entertained a design to propose to Parliament to lay any further taxes upon America for the purpose of raising a revenue; and that it is at present their intention to propose, the next session of Parliament, to take off the duties upon glass, paper and colours, upon consideration of such duties having been laid contrary to the true principles of commerce." Lord Hillsborough further informed Lord Botetourt that "his Majesty relied upon his prudence and fidelity to make such explanation of his Majesty's measures as would tend to remove prejudices and to re-establish mutual confidence and affection between the mother country and the colonies."

In Lord Botetourt's address to the Virginia Assembly, transmitting a copy of the dispatch, he said:

"It may possibly be objected that as his Majesty's present Administration are not immortal, their successors may be inclined to attempt to undo what the present Ministers shall have attempted to perform; and to that objection I can give but this answer: that it is my firm opinion that the plan I have stated to you will certainly take place, and that it will never be departed from; and so determined am I for ever to abide by it, that I will be content to be declared infamous if I do not, to the last hour of my life, at all times, in all places, and upon all occasions, exert every power with which I either am, or ever shall be, legally invested, in order to obtain and maintain for the continent of America that satisfaction which I have been authorized to promise this day by the confidential servants of our gracious Sovereign, who, to my certain knowledge, rates his honour so high, that he would rather part with his crown than preserve it by deceit."

These assurances were received by the Virginians with transports of joy, viewing them as they did as abandoning, never to be resumed, the design of raising a revenue in America by Act of Parliament. The General Assembly of Virginia, in reply to Lord Botetourt's address, thus expressed themselves:

"We are sure our most gracious Sovereign, under whatever changes may happen in his confidential servants, will remain immutable in the ways of truth and justice, and that he is incapable of deceiving his faithful subjects; and we esteem your lordship's information not only as warranted, but even sanctified by the Royal word."[*]

It was understood and expected on all sides that the unproductive tax on tea would be repealed with the other articles enumerated in the Revenue Acts. Such was the wish of Governor Botetourt; such was the advice of Eden, the newly appointed Lieutenant-Governor of Maryland; Colden, who now administered the government of New York, on account of the death of More, assured the Legislature of the greatest probability that the late duties imposed by authority of Parliament, so much to the dissatisfaction of the colonies, would be taken off the ensuing session.[†]

"Thus," says Mr. Bancroft, "all America confined its issue with Great Britain to the single question of the Act imposing a duty on tea." "Will not a repeal of all other duties satisfy the colonists?" asked one of the Ministerial party of Franklin in London. And he frankly answered, 'I think not; it is not the sum paid in the duty on tea that is complained of as a burden, but the principle of the Act expressed in the preamble.' This faithful advice was communicated to the Ministry; but what effect could it produce when Hillsborough administered the colonies, with Barnard for his counsellor?"[‡]

---

[*] Quoted from Ramsay's Colonial History, Vol. I., Chap. iii., pp. 363, 364.

[†] Bancroft's History, Vol. VI., Chap. xlii., pp. 315, 316.

"The general tendency to conciliation prevailed. Since the merchants of Philadelphia chose to confine their agreement for non-importation to the repeal of Townshend's Act, the merchants of Boston, for the sake of union, gave up their more extensive covenant, and reverted to their first stipulations. The dispute about the Billeting Act had ceased in New Jersey and Pennsylvania; the Legislature of New York, pleased with the permission to issue colonial bills of credit, disregarded the appeal from Macdougall to the betrayed inhabitants of that city and colony, and sanctioned a compromise by a majority of one. South Carolina was commercially the most closely connected with England. The annual exports from Charleston reached in value about two and a quarter millions of dollars, of which three-fourths went directly or indirectly to England. But however closely the ties of interest bound Carolina to England, the people were high-spirited; and, notwithstanding the great inconvenience to their trade, they preserved in the strict observance of their (non-importation) association, looking with impatient anxiety for the desired repeal of the Act complained of."—*Ib.*, pp. 317, 318.

[‡] History of the United States, Vol. VI., Chap. xlii., p. 318.

CHAPTER XVI.

EVENTS OF 1770—AN EVENTFUL EPOCH—EXPECTATIONS OF RECONCILIA-
TION AND UNION DISAPPOINTED.

THIS was the year of bloody collision and parliamentary decision, which determined the future relations between Great Britain and the American colonies. Dr. Ramsay observes:

"From the Royal and Ministerial assurances given in favour of America in 1769, and the subsequent repeal in 1770 of five-sixths of the duties which had been imposed in 1767, together with the consequent renewal of the mercantile intercourse between Great Britain and her colonies, many hoped that the contention between the two countries was finally closed. In all the provinces, excepting Massachusetts, appearances seemed to favour that opinion. Many incidents operated there to the prejudice of that harmony which had begun elsewhere to return. Stationing a military force among them was a fruitful source of uneasiness. The royal army had been brought thither with the avowed design of enforcing submission to the mother country. Speeches from the Throne and addresses from both Houses of Parliament had taught them to look upon the inhabitants of Massachusetts as a factious, turbulent people, who aimed at throwing off all subordination to Great Britain. They, on the other hand, were accustomed to look upon the soldiery as instruments of tyranny, sent on purpose to dragoon them out of their liberties.

"Reciprocal insults soured the tempers, and mutual injuries embittered the passions of the opposite parties. Some fiery spirits, who thought it an indignity to have troops quartered among them, were constantly exciting the townspeople to quarrel with the soldiers.

"On the 2nd of March, 1770, a fray took place near Mr. Gray's ropewalk, between a private soldier of the 20th Regiment and an inhabitant. The former was supported by his comrades, the latter by the ropemakers, till several on both sides were involved in the consequences. On the 5th a more dreadful scene was presented. The soldiers when under arms were pressed upon, insulted and pelted by the mob, armed with clubs, sticks, and snowballs covering stones. They were also dared to fire. In this situation, one of the soldiers, who had received a blow, in resentment fired at the supposed aggressors. This was followed by a single discharge from six others. Three of the inhabitants were killed and five were dangerously wounded. The town was immediately in commotion. Such were the temper, force, and number of the inhabitants, that nothing but an engagement to remove the troops out of the town, together with the advice of moderate men, prevented the townsmen from falling on the soldiers. Capt. Preston, who commanded, and the party who fired on the inhabitants, were committed to jail, and afterwards tried. The captain and six of the men were acquitted. Two were brought in guilty of manslaughter (and were lightly punished). *It appeared on the trial that the soldiers were abused, insulted, threatened, and pelted before they fired.* It was also proved that only seven guns were fired by the eight prisoners. These circumstances induced the jury to give a favourable verdict. The result of the trial reflected great honour on John Adams and Josiah Quincy, the counsel for the prisoners (promising young lawyers and popular leaders), and also on the integrity of the jury, who ventured to give an upright verdict in defiance of popular opinion."*

* Colonial History, Vol. I. Chap. iii., pp. 364, 365.

Several American historians have sought to represent the soldiers as the first aggressors and offenders in this affair. The verdict of the jury refutes such representations. The accuracy of Dr. Ramsay's statements given above cannot be fairly questioned ; he was a member of South Carolina Legislature, an officer in the revolutionary army during the whole war, and a personal friend of Washington. Mr. Hildreth says : " A weekly paper, the 'Journal of the Times,' was filled with all sorts of stories, some true, but the greater part false or exaggerated, *on purpose to keep up prejudice against the soldiers. A mob of men and boys,* encouraged by the sympathy of the inhabitants, *made a constant practice to insult and provoke them.* The result to be expected soon

A further hindrance to returning harmony in Massachusetts, as in the other colonies, was another ill-judged act of the British Ministers in making the Governor and judges wholly indepen-

followed. After numerous fights with straggling soldiers, a serious collision at length took place : a picket guard of eight men, *provoked beyond endurance by words and blows*, fired into a crowd, killed three persons and dangerously wounded five others." " The story of the ' Boston massacre,' for so it was called, exaggerated into a ferocious and unprovoked assault by brutal soldiers on a defenceless people, produced everywhere intense excitement. The officer and soldiers of the picket guard were indicted and tried for murder. They were defended, however, by John Adams and Josiah Quincy, two young lawyers, the most zealous among the popular leaders: and so clear a case was made in their behalf, that they were all acquitted except two, who were found guilty of manslaughter and slightly punished." (History of the United States, Chap. xxix., pp. 554, 555, 556.)

Dr. Holmes states that " the soldiers were pressed upon, insulted by the populace, and dared to fire ; one of them, who had received a blow, fired at the aggressors, and a single discharge from six others succeeded. Three of the inhabitants were killed and five dangerously wounded. The town was instantly thrown into the greatest commotion. The drums beat to arms, and thousands of the inhabitants assembled in the adjacent streets. The next morning Lieutenant-Governor Hutchinson summoned a Council ; and while the subject was in discussion, a message was received from the town, which had convened in full assembly, declaring it to be their unanimous opinion 'that nothing can rationally be expected to restore the peace of the town, and prevent blood and carnage, but the immediate removal of the troops.' On an agreement to this measure, the commotion subsided. Captain Preston, who commanded the party of soldiers, was committed with them to jail, and all were afterwards tried. The captain and six of the men were acquitted. Two were brought in guilty of manslaughter. The result of the trial reflected great honour on John Adams and Josiah Quincy, the counsel for the prisoners, and on the integrity of the jury." (Annals, etc., Vol. II., pp. 166, 167.)

How much more honourable and reliable are these straightforward statements of those American historians of the times, and the verdict of even a Boston jury, than the sophistical, elaborate, and reiterated efforts of Mr. Bancroft, in the 43rd and 44th chapters of his History, to implicate the soldiers as the provoking and guilty causes of the collision, and impugning the integrity of the counsel for the prosecution, the court, and the jury.

In the Diary of J. Adams, Vol. II., p. 229, are the following words :

" Endeavours had been systematically pursued for many months by certain busy characters to excite quarrels, rencounters, and combats, single or compound, in the night, between the inhabitants of the lower class and the soldiers, and at all risks to enkindle an immortal hatred between them."— (Quoted by Mr. Hildreth, Vol. II., p. 409, in a note.)

dent of the province in regard to their salaries, which had always
been paid by the local Legislature in annual grants, but which
were now, for the first time, paid by the Crown. The House of
Assembly remonstrated against this innovation, which struck at
the very heart of public liberty, by making the administrator
of the government, and the courts of law, wholly independent
of the people, and wholly dependent on the Crown, all holding
their offices during pleasure of the Crown, and depending upon
it alone for both the amount and payment of their salaries, and
that payment out of a revenue raised by taxing the people
without their consent.

The House addressed the Governor and judges to know
whether they would receive their salaries as heretofore, by
grants of the Legislature, or as stipends from the Crown.
Three out of the four judges announced that they would
receive their salaries as heretofore, by grants from the local
Legislature; but Governor Hutchinson and Chief Justice Oliver
announced that they would receive their salaries from the
Crown. They therefore became more and more odious to the
inhabitants, while the discussion of the new question of the
relations of the Executive and Judiciary to the people, upon
the grounds of public freedom and the impartial administration
of justice, greatly increased the strength of the opposition
and the importance of the local House of Representatives
as the counterpart of the House of Commons, and as guardians
of the rights of the people.

At an early period of Canadian history, the salaries of governors and judges were determined and paid by the Crown,
out of what was called a casual and territorial revenue, independent of the representatives of the people, and the judges
held their places during pleasure; but after much agitation, and
a determined popular struggle of several years, a civil list for
both the governors and judges was agreed upon and voted by
the Legislature. The tenure of the offices of judges was made
that of good behaviour, instead of pleasure; and executive
councillors and heads of departments were made dependent upon
the confidence of the Legislature, with the control of revenues
of every kind raised in the country; since which time there
have been peace, loyalty, and progress throughout the provinces
of the Canadian Dominion.

To turn now to the affairs of the colonies as discussed and decided upon in the British Parliament, which met the 9th of January, 1770. The King, in opening Parliament, expressed his regret that his endeavours to tranquillize America had not been attended with the desired success, and that combinations had been formed to destroy the commercial connection between the colonies and the mother country. The opposition in both Houses of Parliament dwelt strongly on the prevailing discontents, both in England and in the colonies. Ministers, admitting these discontents, imputed them to the spirit of faction, the speeches and writings of agitators, and to petitions got up and circulated by their influence. Lords Camden and Shelburne resigned, disapproving of the policy of the Administration, as did soon after, on the 28th of January, 1770, the Duke of Grafton, First Lord of the Treasury, and was succeeded by Lord North as Chancellor of the Exchequer. Lord Chatham, after an absence of two years, recovered sufficiently to make his clarion voice once more heard in the councils of the nation against official corruption, and in defence of liberty and the rights of the colonies, the affairs of which now occupied the attention of Parliament. The British manufacturers and merchants who traded to America had sustained immense losses by the rejection of their goods, through the non-importing associations in America, and apprehended ruin from their continuance, and therefore petitioned Parliament, stating their sufferings and imploring relief. On the 5th of March Lord North introduced a Bill into the Commons for the repeal of the whole of the Act of 1767, which imposed duties on glass, red lead, paper, and painters' colours, but retaining the preamble, which asserted the absolute authority of Parliament to bind the colonies in all cases whatsoever, and retaining, as an illustration of that authority, the clause of the Act which imposed a duty on tea. He said:—" The articles taxed being chiefly British manufactures, ought to have been encouraged instead of being burdened with assessments. The duty on tea was continued, for maintaining the parliamentary right of taxation. An impost of threepence in the pound could never be opposed by the colonists, unless they were determined to rebel against Great Britain. Besides, a duty on that article, payable in England, and amounting to nearly one shilling in the pound, was taken off on its exportation to America; so that the inhabitants of the colonies saved ninepence in the pound. The members of the opposition, in both Houses, advocated the repeal of the clause on tea, and predicted the inefficiency of the Bill should that clause be retained, and repeated the arguments on the injustice and inexpediency of taxing America by Act of Parliament; but the Bill was carried by a large majority, and assented to by the King on the 12th of April."

The repeal of the obnoxious port duties of 1767 left no pretence for retaining the duty on *tea* for raising a *revenue*, as the tea duty, at the highest computation, would not exceed £16,000 a year; and when Lord North was pressed to relinquish that remaining cause of contention, he replied:

"Has the repeal of the Stamp Act taught the Americans obedience? Has our lenity inspired them with moderation? Can it be proper, while they deny our legal right to tax them, to acquiesce in the argument of illegality, and by the repeal of the whole law to give up that honour? No; the most proper time to exert our right of taxation is when the right is refused. To temporize is to yield; and the authority of the mother country, if it is now unsupported, will in reality be relinquished for ever. A total repeal cannot be thought of till America is prostrate at our feet."

Governor Pownall, who had spent many years in America, and had preceded Barnard as Governor of Massachusetts, moved an amendment, to include the repeal of the duty on tea as well as on the articles included in the original motion of Lord North. In the course of his speech in support of the amendment he said:

"If it be asked whether it will remove the apprehensions excited by your resolutions and address of the last year, for bringing to trial in England persons accused of treason in America? I answer, no. If it be asked, if this commercial concession would quiet the minds of the Americans as to the political doubts and fears which have struck them to the heart throughout the continent? I answer, no; so long as they are left in doubt whether the Habeas Corpus Act, whether the Bill of Rights, whether the Common Law as now existing in England, have any operation and effect in America, they cannot be satisfied. At this hour they know not whether the civil constitu-

24

tion be not suspended and superseded by the establishment of a military force. The Americans think that they have, in return to all their applications, experienced a temper and disposition that is unfriendly—that the enjoyment and exercise of the common rights of freemen have been refused to them. Never with these views will they solicit the favour of this House; never more will they wish to bring before Parliament the grievances under which they conceive themselves to labour. Deeply as they feel, they suffer and endure with alarming silence. For their liberty they are under no apprehensions. It was first planted under the auspicious genius of the constitution, and it has grown up into a verdant and flourishing tree; and should any severe strokes be aimed at the branches, and fate reduce it to the bare stock, it would only take deeper root, and spring out more hardy and durable than before. They trust to Providence, and wait with firmness and fortitude the issue."

The statements of Governor Pownall were the result of long observation and experience in America, and practical knowledge of the colonists, and were shown by results to be true to the letter, though treated with scorn by Lord North, and with aversion by the House of Commons, which rejected his amendment by a majority of 242 to 204.

The results of the combinations against the use of British manufactures were illustrated this year by the candidates for the degree of Bachelor of Arts at Harvard College appearing dressed in black cloth manufactured wholly in New England. The general plan of non-importation of English manufactured goods was now relinquished on the repeal of the duties imposed upon them; but the sentiment of the principal commercial towns was against the importation of any tea from England. An association was formed not to drink tea until the Act imposing the duty should be repealed. This was generally agreed to and observed throughout the colonies.

But the retaining of threepence in the pound on tea did not excite so much hostility in the colonies against the Parliament as might have been expected. The Act of Parliament was virtually defeated, and the expected revenue from tea failed because of the resolution of the colonial associations of the people to use no tea, and of the merchants to import none on which the duty was charged. The merchants found means to smuggle, from countries to which the authority of Great Britain did not extend, a sufficient supply of tea for the tea-drinking colonists. Thus the tea-dealers and tea-drinkers of America exercised their patriotism and indulged their taste—the one class making an additional threepence a pound on tea by evading the Act, and the other class enjoying the luxury of tea as cheap as if no tea duty Act of Parliament existed, and with the additional relish of rendering such Act abortive. ' The facilities for smuggling tea, arising from the great extent of the American coasts, and the great number of harbours, and the universality of the British anti-tea associations, and the unity of popular sentiment on the subject, rendered the Act of Parliament imposing the duty a matter of sport rather than a measure of oppression even to the most scrupulous, as they regarded the Act unconstitutional, and every means lawful and right by which the obnoxious Act could be evaded and defeated. It is probable that, in the ordinary course of things, the Act would have become practically obsolete, and the relations of the colonies to the mother country have settled down into quietness and friendliness, but for another event, which not only revived with increased intensity the original question of dispute, but gave rise to other occurrences that kindled the flame of the American revolution. That event was the agreement between the Ministry and the East India Company, which interfered with the natural and ordinary channels of trade, and gave to that Company a monopoly of the tea trade of America. From the diminished exportation of tea from England to the colonies, there were, in warehouses of the British East India Company, seventeen millions of pounds of tea for which there was no demand. Lord North and his colleagues were not willing to lose the expected revenue, as small as it must be at last from their American Tea Act, and the East India Company were unwilling to lose the profits of their American tea trade.

An agreement was therefore entered into between the Ministry and the Company, by which the Company, which was authorized by law to export their tea free of duty to all places whatsoever, could send their tea cheaper to the colonies than others who had to pay the exceptionable duty, and even cheaper than before it had been made a source of revenue; "for the duty taken off it when exported from Great Britain was greater than that to be paid for it on its importation into the colonies. Confident of success in finding a market for their tea, thus reduced in its price, and also of collecting a duty on its importation and sale in the colonies, the East India Company freighted several ships with teas for the different colonies, and appointed agents (or consignees) for its disposal." This measure united both the English and American merchants in opposition to it upon selfish grounds of interest, and the colonists generally upon patriotic grounds. "The merchants in England were alarmed at the losses that must come to themselves from the exportations of the East India Company, and from the sales going through the hands of consignees. Letters were written to colonial patriots, urging their opposition to the project. The (American merchants) smugglers, who were both numerous and powerful, could not relish a scheme which, by underselling them and taking a profitable branch of business out of their hands, threatened a diminution of their gains. The colonists were too suspicious of the designs of Great Britain to be imposed upon.

"The cry of endangered liberty once more excited an alarm from New Hampshire to Georgia. The first opposition to the execution of the scheme adopted by the East India Company began with the American merchants. They saw a profitable branch of their trade likely to be lost, and the benefits of it transferred to a company in Great Britain. They felt for the wound that would be inflicted on their country's claim of exemption from parliamentary taxation; but they felt, with equal sensibility, for the losses they would sustain by the diversion of the streams of commerce into unusual channels. Though the opposition originated in the selfishness of the merchants, it did not end there. The great body of the people, from principles of the purest patriotism, were brought over to second their wishes. They considered the whole scheme as calculated to seduce them into an acquiescence with the views of Parliament for raising an American revenue. Much pains were taken to enlighten the colonists on this subject, and to convince them of the eminent hazard to which their liberties were exposed.

"The provincial patriots insisted largely on the persevering determination of the parent state to establish her claim of taxation by compelling the sale of tea in the colonies against the solemn resolutions and declared sense of the inhabitants, and that at a time when the commercial intercourse of the two countries was renewed, and their ancient harmony fast returning. The proposed vendors of the tea were represented as revenue officers, employed in the collection of an unconstitutional tax imposed by Great Britain.   The colonists contended that, as the duty and the price of the commodity were inseparably blended, if the tea were sold every purchaser would pay a tax imposed by the British Parliament as part of the purchase money."[*]

[*] Ram:ay's Colonial History, Vol. I., Chap. iii., pp. 370—372.

CHAPTER XVII.

EVENTS OF 1771, 1772, 1773—THE EAST INDIA COMPANY'S TEA REJECTED
IN EVERY PROVINCE OF AMERICA—RESOLUTIONS OF A PUBLIC MEET-
ING IN PHILADELPHIA THE MODEL FOR THOSE OF OTHER COLONIES.

BY this unprecedented and unjustifiable combination between
the British Ministry and East India Company to supersede the
ordinary channels of trade, and to force the sale of their tea in
America, the returning peace and confidence between Great
Britain and the colonies was arrested, the colonial merchants of
both England and America were roused and united in opposition to the scheme, meetings were held, associations were
formed, and hostility throughout all the colonies became so
general and intense, that not a chest of the East India Company's tea was sold from New Hampshire to Georgia, and only
landed in one instance, and then to rot in locked warehouses.
In all cases, except in Boston, the consignees were prevailed
upon to resign; and in all cases except two, Boston and Charleston, the tea was sent back to England without having been
landed. At Charleston, South Carolina, they allowed the tea
to be landed, but not sold; and it rotted in the cellars of the
store-houses. At Philadelphia, the consignees were forced to
resign and send the tea back to England.* At New York they
did the same. At Portsmouth, New Hampshire, they sent the

---

* The resolutions adopted by a meeting of the inhabitants of Philadelphia,
on the 18th of October, 1773, afford a specimen of the spirit of all the colonies,
and the model of resolutions adopted in several of them, even Boston. They
were as follows:

"1. That the disposal of their own property is the inherent right of freemen; that there can be no property in that which another can, of right, take

tea away to Halifax. At Boston the consignees were the sons
of Hutchinson, the Governor, and he determined that it should
be landed and sold; while the mass of the people, led by committees of the "Sons of Liberty," were equally determined that
the tea should not be landed or sold.

As this Boston tea affair resulted in the passing of two Acts
of Parliament—the Bill for closing the port of Boston, and the
Bill for suspending the Charter and establishing a new constitution of government for Massachusetts—and these were followed
by an American Congress and a civil war, I will state the
transactions as narrated by three American historians, agreeing
in the main facts, but differing in regard to incidental circumstances.

Dr. Ramsay narrates the general opposition to the scheme of
the East India Company, and that at Boston in particular, in
the following words:

"As the time approached when the arrival of the tea ships

from us without our consent ; that the claim of Parliament to tax America
is, in other words, a claim of right to levy contributions on us at pleasure.

" 2. That the duty imposed by Parliament upon tea landed in America is a
tax on the Americans, or levying contributions on them without their consent.

" 3. That the express purpose for which the tax is levied on the Americans,
namely, for the support of government, administration of justice, and defence
of his Majesty's dominions in America, has a direct tendency to render Assemblies useless, and to introduce arbitrary government and slavery.

" 4. That a virtuous and steady opposition to this Ministerial plan of governing America is absolutely necessary to preserve even the shadow of liberty,
and is a duty which every freeman in America owes to his country, to
himself, and to his posterity.

" 5. That the resolution lately entered into by the East India Company,
to send out their tea to America, subject to the payment of duties on its
being landed here, is an open attempt to enforce this Ministerial plan, and a
violent attack upon the liberties of America.

" 6. That it is the duty of every American to oppose this attempt.

" 7. That whosoever shall, directly or indirectly, countenance this attempt,
or in anywise aid or abet in unloading, receiving, or vending the tea sent or
to be sent out by the East India Company, while it remains subject to the
payment of a duty here, is an enemy to his country.

" 8. That a Committee be immediately chosen to wait on those gentlemen
who it is reported are appointed by the East India Company to receive and
sell said tea, and request them, from a regard to their own character, and the
peace and good order of the city and province, immediately to resign their
appointments." (Ramsay's Colonial History, Vol. I., pp. 372, 373.)

might be soon expected, such measures were adopted as seemed most likely to prevent the landing of their cargoes. The tea consignees appointed by the East India Company were in several places compelled to relinquish their appointments, and no others could be found hardy enough to act in their stead. The pilots in the River Delaware were warned not to conduct any of the tea ships into their harbour. In New York, popular vengeance was denounced against all who would contribute in any measure to forward the views of the East India Company. The captains of the New York and Philadelphia ships, being apprised of the resolution of the people, and fearing the consequence of landing a commodity charged with an odious duty, in violation of their declared public sentiments, concluded to return directly to Great Britain without making any entry at the Custom-house.

" It was otherwise in Massachusetts. The tea ships designed for the supply of Boston were consigned to the sons, cousins, and particular friends of Governor Hutchinson. When they were called upon to resign, they answered that 'it was out of their power.' The Collector refused to give a clearance unless the vessels were discharged of dutiable articles. The Governor refused to give a pass for the vessels unless properly qualified for the Custom-house. The Governor likewise requested Admiral Montague to guard the passages out of the harbour, and gave orders to suffer no vessels, coasters excepted, to pass the fortress from the town without a pass signed by himself. From a combination of these circumstances the return of the tea vessels from Boston was rendered impossible. The inhabitants then had no option but to prevent the landing of the tea, to suffer it to be landed and depend on the unanimity of the people not to purchase it; to destroy the tea, or to suffer a deep-laid scheme against their sacred liberties to take effect. The first would have required incessant watching, by night as well as by day, for a period of time the duration of which no one could compute. The second would have been visionary to childishness, by suspending the liberties of a growing country on the self-denial and discretion of every tea-drinker in the province. They viewed the tea as the vehicle of an unconstitutional tax, ar.d as inseparably associated with it. To avoid the one, they resolved to destroy the other. About seventeen persons, dressed as Indians, repaired to the tea ships, broke open 342 chests of tea, and, without doing any other damage, discharged their contents into the water.

" Thus, by the inflexibility of the Governor, the issue of this business was different at Boston from what it was elsewhere. The whole cargoes of tea were returned from New York and Philadelphia; that which was sent to Charleston was landed and stored, but not offered for sale. Mr. Hutchinson had repeatedly urged Government to be firm and persevering. He could not, therefore, consistently with his honour, depart from a line of conduct he had so often and so strongly recommended to his superiors. He also believed that the inhabitants would not dare to perfect their engagements, and flattered himself that they would desist when the critical moment arrived.

" Admitting the rectitude of the American claims of exemption from parliamentary taxation, the destruction of the tea by the Bostonians was warranted by the great law of self-preservation; for it was not possible for them by any other means to discharge the duty they owed to their country.

" The event of this business was very different from what had been expected in England. The colonists acted with so much union and system, that there was not a single chest of any of the cargoes sent out by the East India Company sold for their benefit."*

The Rev. Dr. Holmes, in his Annals of America, says:

" The crisis now approached when the colonies were to decide whether they would submit to be taxed by the British Parliament, or practically support their own principles and meet the consequences. One sentiment seems to have pervaded the entire continent. The new Ministerial plan was universally considered as a direct attack on the liberties of the colonists, which it was the duty of all to oppose. A violent ferment was everywhere excited; the Corresponding Committees were extremely active; and it was very generally declared that whoever should, directly or indirectly, countenance this dangerous invasion of their rights, is an enemy to his country. The East India Company, confident of finding a market for their tea, reduced as it now was in its price, freighted several ships to the colonies with that

* Ramsay's Colonial History, Vol. I., Chap. iii., pp. 373—375.

article, and appointed agents for the disposal of it. Some cargoes were sent to New York, some to Philadelphia, some to Charleston (South Carolina), and three to Boston. The inhabitants of New York and Philadelphia sent the ships back to London, 'and they sailed up the Thames to proclaim to all the nation that New York and Pennsylvania would not be enslaved.' The inhabitants of Charleston unloaded the tea and stored it in cellars, where it could not be used, and where it finally perished.

"The inhabitants of Boston tried every measure to send back the three tea ships which had arrived there, but without success. The captains of the ships had consented, if permitted, to return with their cargoes to England; but the consignees refused to discharge them from their obligations, the Custom-house to give them a clearance for their return, and the Governor refused to grant them a passport for clearing the fort. It was easily seen that the tea would be gradually landed from the ships lying so near the town, and that if landed it would be disposed of, and the purpose of establishing the monopoly and raising a revenue effected. To prevent this dreaded consequence, a number of armed men, disguised like Indians, boarded the ships and threw their whole cargoes of tea into the dock."*

A more circumstantial and graphic account of this affair is given by Mr. J. S. Barry, in his History of Massachusetts, in the following words:

"On Sunday, November 28, 1773, one of the ships arrived, bringing one hundred and fourteen chests of tea. Immediately the Select Men held a meeting; and the Committee of Correspondence obtained from Rotch, the owner of the vessel, a promise not to enter it until Tuesday. The towns around Boston were summoned to meet on Monday; 'and every friend to his country, to himself, and to posterity,' was desired to attend, 'to make a united and successful resistance to this last, worst, and most destructive measure of administration.'

"At an early hour (Monday, November 29) the people gathered, and by nine o'clock the concourse was so great that Faneuil Hall was filled to overflowing. A motion to adjourn to

---

* Holmes' Annals, etc., Vol. II., pp. 181, 182.

the Old South Meeting-house, the 'Sanctuary of Freedom,' was made and carried; and on reaching that place, Jonathan Williams was chosen Moderator, and Hancock, Adams, Young, Molineux, and Warren, fearlessly conducted the business of the meeting. At least five thousand persons were in and around the building, and but one spirit animated all. Samuel Adams offered a resolution, which was unanimously adopted, 'That the tea should be sent back to the place from whence it came, at all events, and that no duty should be paid on it.' The consignees asked time for consideration, and 'out of great tenderness' their request was granted. To prevent any surprise, however, a watch of twenty-five persons, under Edward Proctor, was appointed to guard the ship during the night.

"The answer of the consignees was given in the morning (November 30); and after declaring that it was out of their power to send back the teas, they expressed their readiness to store them until otherwise advised. In the midst of the meeting the Sheriff of Suffolk entered, with a proclamation from the Governor, warning the people to disperse; but the message was received with derision and hisses, and a unanimous vote not to disperse. The master and owner of the ship which had lately arrived were then required to attend; and a promise was extorted from them that the teas should be returned without landing or paying a duty. The factors of two other vessels which were daily expected were next summoned, and similar promises were given by them; upon which the meeting, after voting to carry into effect, 'at the risk of their lives and properties,' their former resolves, quietly dissolved.

"After this dissolution, the Committee of Correspondence of Boston and its vicinity held meetings daily, and gave such directions as circumstances required. The other ships, on their arrival, anchored beside the *Dartmouth* (Rotch's vessel), that one guard might serve for all; and the inhabitants of a number of towns, at meetings convened for the purpose, promised to aid Boston whenever their services should be needed. At the end of twenty days the question must be decided, and if the teas were landed all was lost. As the crisis drew near the excitement increased. Hutchinson was confident that no violent measures would be taken. The wealth of Hancock and others seemed sufficient security against such measures. But the people had counted the cost, and had determined to risk all rather than be slaves.

"The eventful day (December 16) at last dawned; and two thousand from the country, besides the citizens of Boston, assembled in the Old South Meeting-house at ten o'clock, to decide what should be done. It was reported that Rotch, the owner of the *Dartmouth*, had been refused a clearance; and he was immediately instructed to 'protest against the Custom-house, and apply to the Governor for his pass.' But the Governor had stolen to his residence at Milton, and at three o'clock in the afternoon Rotch had not returned. What should be done? 'Shall we abide by our resolutions?' it was asked. Adams and Young were in favour of that course; Quincy, distinguished as a statesman and patriot, advised discretion; but the people cried, 'Our hands have been put to the plough; we must not look back;' and the whole assemblage of seven thousand persons voted unanimously that the tea should not be landed.

"Darkness in the meantime had settled upon the town, and in the dimly-lighted church the audience awaited the return of Rotch. At a quarter before six he made his appearance, and reported that the Governor had refused him his pass. 'We can do no more to save the country,' said Samuel Adams; and a momentary silence ensued. The next instant a shout was heard at the door; the war-whoop sounded; and forty or fifty men, disguised as Indians, hurried along to Griffin's Wharf, posted guards to prevent intrusion, boarded the ships, and in three hours' time had broken and emptied into the sea three hundred and forty-two chests of tea. So great was the stillness, that the blows of the hatchets as the chests were split open were distinctly heard. When the deed was done, every one retired, and the town was as quiet as if nothing had occurred."*

---

* Barry's History of Massachusetts, Second Period, Chap. xiv., pp. 470—473.

The historian adds: "The Governor was in a forlorn state, and was unable to keep up even a show of authority. Every one was against him. The Houses were against him. 'The superior judges were intimidated from acting,' and 'there was not a justice of the peace, sheriff, constable, or peace-officer in the province who would venture to take cognizance of any breach of law against the general bent of the people.'"—*Ib.*, 473, 474.

The foregoing threefold narrative presents substantially the American case of destroying the East India Company's tea by the inhabitants of Boston. The account by Mr. Bancroft is more elaborate, digressive, dramatic, and declamatory, but not so consecutive or concise as the preceding. Governor Hutchinson, who had advised the very policy which now recoiled upon himself, corroborates in all essential points the narrative given above. He states, however, what is slightly intimated above by Dr. Ramsay, that the opposition commenced by the merchants against the monopoly of the East India Company, rather than against the tax itself, which had been paid without murmuring for two years, and that the parliamentary tax on tea was seized upon, at the suggestion of merchants in England, to defeat the monopoly of the East India Company, and to revive and perpetuate the excitement against the British Parliament which had been created by the Stamp Act, and which was rapidly subsiding. Governor Hutchinson says:

"When the intelligence first came to Boston it caused no alarm. The threepenny duty had been paid the last two years without any stir, and some of the great friends to liberty had been importers of tea. The body of the people were pleased with the prospect of drinking tea at less expense than ever. The only apparent discontent was among the importers of tea, as well those who had been legal importers from England, as others who had illegally imported from Holland, and the complaint was against the East India Company for monopolizing a branch of commerce which had been beneficial to a great number of individual merchants. And the first suggestion of a design in the Ministry to enlarge the revenue, and to habituate the colonies to parliamentary taxes, was made from England; and opposition to the measure was recommended, with an intimation that it was expected that the tea would not be suffered to be landed."*

The Committees of Correspondence in the several colonies soon availed themselves of so favourable an opportunity for promoting their great purpose. It soon appeared to be their

---

* Governor Hutchinson, in a note, referring to the mercantile English letters which contained the suggestion not to allow the landing of the tea of the East India Company, says:

"These letters were dated in England the beginning of August, and were

general determination, that at all events the tea should be sent
back to England in the same ships which brought it.   The
first motions were at Philadelphia (Oct. 18th), where, at a meeting
of the people, every man who should be concerned in unlading,

received in America the latter end of September and the beginning of
October."

Mr. Bancroft states as follows the causes and circumstances of this disastrous tea agreement between the British Ministry and East India Company :

" The continued refusal of North America to receive tea from England
had brought distress upon the East India Company, which had on hand,
wanting a market, great quantities imported in the faith that that agreement
(in the colonies, not to purchase tea imported from England) could not hold.
They were able to pay neither their dividends nor their debts; their stock
depreciated nearly one-half ; and the Government must lose their annual payment of four hundred thousand pounds.

" The bankruptcies, brought on partly by this means, gave such a shock to
credit as had not been experienced since the South Sea year, and the great
manufacturers were sufferers.   The directors came to Parliament with an
ample confession of their humbled state, together with entreaties for assistance
and relief, and particularly praying that leave might be given to export
tea free of all duties to America and to foreign ports.   Had such leave
been granted in respect of America, it would have been an excellent commercial regulation, as well as have restored a good understanding to every part
of the empire.   Instead of this, Lord North proposed to give to the Company
itself the right of exporting its teas.   The existing law granted on their exportation to America a drawback of three-fifths only of the duties paid on importation.   Lord North now offered to the East India Company a drawback of
the whole.   Trecothick, in the committee, also advised to take off the import
duty in America of threepence the pound, as it produced no income to the
revenue; but the Ministry would not listen to the thought of relieving
America from taxation.   ' Then,' added Trecothick in behalf of the East
India Company, ' as much or more may be brought into revenue by not
allowing a full exemption from the duties paid here.'   But Lord North refused to discuss the right of Parliament to tax America, insisting that no
difficulty could arise; that under the new regulation America would be able
to buy tea from the Company at a lower price than from any other European
nation, and that men will always go to the cheapest market.

" The Ministry was still in its halcyon days; no opposition was made even
by the Whigs; and the measure, which was the King's own, and was
designed to put America to the test, took effect as law from the 10th day of
May, 1773.   It was immediately followed by a most carefully prepared
answer from the King to petitions from Massachusetts, announcing that he
' considered his authority to make laws in Parliament of sufficient force and
validity to bind his subjects in America, in all cases whatsoever, as essential
to the dignity of the Crown, and a right appertaining to the State, which it
was his duty to preserve entire and inviolate ;' that he therefore ' could not

receiving, or vending the tea, was pronounced an enemy to his country. This was one of the eight resolves passed at the meeting. The example was followed by Boston, November 3rd.*

Then follows Governor Hutchinson's account of the meetings and gatherings in Boston ; the messages and answers between their Committees and the consignees, Custom-house officers, and the ultimate throwing of the tea into the dock, substantially as narrated in the preceding pages, together with his consultations with his Council, and his remarks upon the motives and conduct of the parties opposed to him. He admits that his Council was opposed to the measures which he proposed to suppress the meetings of the people ; he admits the universal hostility of the people of Boston and of the neighbouring towns to the landing of the tea ; that " while the Governor and Council were sitting on the Monday, in the Council Chamber, and known to be consulting upon means for preserving the peace of the town, several thousands of inhabitants of Boston and other towns were assembled in a public meeting-house at a small distance, in direct opposition and defiance. He says he " sent the Sheriff with a proclamation, to be read in the meeting, bearing testimony against it as an unlawful assembly, and requiring the Moderator and the people present forthwith to separate at their peril. Being read, a general hiss followed, and then a question whether they would surcease further proceedings, as the Governor required, which was determined in the negative, *nemine contradicente.*"

It may be asked upon what legal or even reasonable ground had Governor Hutchinson the right to denounce a popular meeting which happened at the same time that he was holding a council, or because such meeting might entertain and express

---

but be greatly displeased with the petitions and remonstrance in which that right was drawn into question,' but that he 'imputed the unwarrantable doctrines held forth in the said petitions and remonstrance to the artifices of a few.' All this while Lord Dartmouth (the new Secretary of State for the Colonies, successor to Lord Hillsborough) ' had a true desire to see lenient measures adopted towards the colonies,' not being in the least aware that he was drifting with the Cabinet towards the very system of coercion against which he gave the most public and the most explicit pledges." (History of the United States, Vol. VI., pp. 453—460.)

   * See these resolutions, in a note on pp. 374, 375.

views differing from or in defiance of those which he was proposing to his Council?

Or, what authority had Governor Hutchinson to issue a proclamation and send a Sheriff to forbid a public meeting which the Charter and laws authorized to be called and held, as much as the Governor was authorized to call and hold his Council, or as any town or township council or meeting may be called and held in any province of the Dominion of Canada? It is not surprising that a public meeting "hissed" a command which was as lawless as it was powerless. The King himself would not have ventured to do what Governor Hutchinson did, in like circumstances; and British subjects in Massachusetts had equal civil rights with British subjects in England.

Governor Hutchinson admits that the public meeting was not only numerous, but composed of all classes of inhabitants, and was held in legal form; and his objection to the legality of the meeting merely because persons from other towns were allowed to be present, while he confesses that the inhabitants of Boston at the meeting were unanimous in their votes, is the most trivial that can be conceived. He says:

"A more determined spirit was conspicuous in this body than in any former assemblies of the people. It was composed of the lowest, as well, and probably in as great proportion, as of the superior ranks and orders, and all had an equal voice. No eccentric or irregular motions, however, were suffered to take place—all seemed to have been the plan of but a few—it may be, of a single person. The 'form' of town meeting was assumed, the Select Men of Boston, town clerks, etc., taking their usual places; but the inhabitants of any other town being admitted, it could not assume the name of a 'legal meeting of any town.'" (A trivial technical objection.)

Referring to another meeting—the last held before the day on which the tea was thrown into the sea—Governor Hutchinson states:

"The people came into Boston from the adjacent towns within twenty miles, from some more, from others less, as they were affected; and, as soon as they were assembled (November 14th, 1773), enjoined the owner of the ship, at his peril, to demand of the Collector of Customs a clearance for the ship, and appointed ten of their number a committee to accompany him, and adjourned for two days to receive the report. Being reassembled (at the end of the two days), and informed by the owner that a clearance was refused, he was enjoined immediately to apply to the Governor for a pass by the Castle. He made an apology to the Governor for coming upon such an errand, having been compelled to it, and received an answer that no pass ever had been, or lawfully could be, given to any vessel which had not first been cleared at the Custom-house, and that upon his producing a clearance, such pass would immediately be given by the naval officer."

Governor Hutchinson knew that the Custom-house could not give the clearance without the landing of the tea and payment of the duty provided for; he knew that the Custom-house had been applied to in vain to obtain a clearance. His reference of the owner to the Custom house was a mere evasion and pretext to gain time and prevent any decisive action on the part of the town meeting until the night of the 16th, when the 20 days after the entry of the ships would have expired, and the Collector could seize the cargoes for non-payment of duties, place it in charge of the Admiral at the Castle, and sell it under pretence of paying the duties. He says : "The body of the people remained in the meeting-house until they had received the Governor's answer; and then, after it had been observed to them that, everything else in their power having been done, it now remained to proceed in the only way left, and that the owner of the ship having behaved like a man of honour, no injury ought to be offered to his person or property, the meeting was declared to be dissolved, and the body of the people repaired to the wharf and surrounded the immediate actors (who were 'covered with blankets, and making the appearance of Indians') as a guard and security until they had finished their work. In two or three hours they hoisted out of the holds of the ships three hundred and forty-two chests of tea, and emptied them into the sea. The Governor was unjustly censured by many people in the province, and much abused by the pamphlet and newspaper writers in England, for refusing his pass, which it is said would have saved the property thus destroyed; but he would have been justly censured if he had granted it. He was bound, as all the Governors were, by oath, faithfully to observe the

25

Acts of Trade, and to do his endeavour that the statute of King
William, which established a Custom-house, and is particularly mentioned in the Act, be carried into execution."

In Governor Hutchinson's own statement and vindication of
his conduct, he admits that the meetings of the people were
lawfully called and regularly conducted; that they were
attended by the higher as well as lower classes of the people;
that they exhausted every means in their power, deliberately
and during successive days, to have the tea returned to England
without damage, as was done from the ports of New York and
Philadelphia; and that by his own acts, different from those of
New York, Pennsylvania, and South Carolina, whose Governors
were subject to the same oaths as himself, the opposers of taxation by the British Parliament were reduced to the alternative
of defeat, or of throwing the tea in question into the sea, as
the Governor had effectually blocked up every possible way to
their having the tea returned to England. Governor Hutchinson does not pretend to the technical scrupulousness of his oath,
applicable to ordinary cases, binding him to write to the Admiral
to guard the tea by an increased number of armed vessels in the
channel of the harbour, and to prevent any vessel from passing
out of the harbour for sea, without his own permit; nor does
he intimate that he himself was the principal partner in the
firm, nominally in the name of his sons, to whom the East
India Company had principally consigned as agents the sale of
the tea in question; much less does he say that in his letters to
England, which had been mysteriously obtained by Dr. Franklin, and of the publication of which he so strongly and justly
complained, he had urged the virtual deprivation of his country
of its constitution of free government by having the Executive
Councillors appointed and the salaries of the governor, judges,
secretary, and attorney and solicitor-generals paid by the
Crown out of the taxes of the people of the colony, imposed
by the Imperial Parliament. Governor Hutchinson had rendered great service to his country by his History, and as a
public representative, for many years in its Legislature and
Councils, and was long regarded as its chief leader; but he had
at length yielded to the seductions of ambition and avarice,
and became an object of popular hatred instead of being, as he

had many years been, a popular idol.   He had sown the seed of which he was now reaping the fruits.

It is not surprising that, under such circumstances, Governor Hutchinson's health should become impaired and his spirits depressed, and that he should seek relief from his burdens and vexations by a visit to England, for which he applied and obtained permission, and which proved to be the end of his government of Massachusetts; for General Gage was appointed to succeed him as Governor, as well as Commander-in-Chief of the King's forces in America.

In reviewing the last few months of Mr. Hutchinson's government of Massachusetts, it is obvious that his ill-advised policy and mode of proceeding—arising, no doubt, in a great measure, from his personal and family interest in speculation in the new system of tea trade—was the primary and chief cause of those proceedings in which Boston differed from New York, Philadelphia, and Charleston in preventing the landing of the East India Company's tea.   Had the authorities in the provinces of New York and Pennsylvania acted in the same way as did the Governor of Massachusetts, it cannot be doubted that the same scenes would have been witnessed at Charleston, Philadelphia, and New York as transpired at Boston. The eight resolutions which were adopted by the inhabitants of Philadelphia, in a public town meeting, on the 8th of October, as the basis of their proceedings against the taxation of the colonies by the Imperial Parliament, and against the landing of the East India Company's tea, were adopted by the inhabitants of Boston in a public town meeting the 3rd of November.   The tea was as effectually prevented from being landed at the ports of New York and Philadelphia as it was at the port of Boston, and was as completely destroyed in the damp cellars at Charleston as in the sea water at Boston.*

* "In South Carolina, some of the tea was thrown into the river as at Boston." (English Annual Register for 1774, Vol. XVII., p. 50.)

CHAPTER XVIII.

THE year 1774 commenced, among other legacies of 1773,
with that of the discontent of all the colonies,* their unanimous rejection of the East India tea, stamped with the
threepenny duty of parliamentary tax, as the symbol of the
absolutism of King and Parliament over the colonies.   The
manner of its rejection, by being thrown into the sea at Boston,
was universally denounced by all parties in England.   The
accounts of all the proceedings in America against the admission
of the East India tea to the colonial ports, were coloured by the
mediums through which they were transmitted—the royal
governors and their executive officers, who expected large
advantages from being assigned and paid their salaries by the
Crown, independent of the local Legislatures ; and the consignees
of the East India Company, who anticipated large profits from
their monopoly of its sale.   Opposition to the tea duty was
represented as "rebellion"—the assertors of colonial freedom
from imperial taxation without representation were designated
"rebels" and "traitors," notwithstanding their professed loyalty

---

* " The discontents and disorders continue to prevail in a greater or less
degree through all the old colonies on the continent.   The same spirit
pervades the whole.   Even those colonies which depended most upon the
mother country for the consumption of their productions entered into similar
associations with the others ; and nothing was to be heard of but resolutions
for the encouragement of their own manufactures, the consumption of home
products, the discouragement of foreign articles, and the retrenchment of all
superfluities. (English Annual Register for 1774, Vol. XVII., p. 45.)

to the Throne and to the unity of the empire, and that their utmost wishes were limited to be replaced in the position they occupied after the peace of Paris, in 1763, and after their unanimous and admitted loyalty, and even heroism, in defence and support of British supremacy in America.

" Intelligence," says Dr. Holmes, " of the destruction of the tea at Boston was communicated on the 7th of March (1774), in a message from the Throne, to both Houses of Parliament. In this communication the conduct of the colonists was represented as not merely obstructing the commerce of Great Britain, but as subversive of the British Constitution. Although the papers accompanying the Royal message rendered it evident that the opposition to the sale of the tea was common to all the colonies; yet the Parliament, enraged at the violence of Boston, selected that town as the object of its legislative vengeance. Without giving the opportunity of a hearing, a Bill was passed by which the port of Boston was legally precluded from the privilege of landing and discharging, or of lading or shipping goods, wares, and merchandise; and every vessel within the points Aldeston and Nahant was required to depart within six hours, unless laden with food or fuel.

" This Act, which shut up the harbour of Boston, was speedily followed by another, entitled 'An Act for Better Regulating the Government of Massachusetts,' which provided that the Council, heretofore elected by the General Assembly, was to be appointed by the Crown; the Royal Governor was invested with the power of appointing and removing all Judges of the Courts of Common Pleas, Commissioners of Oyer and Terminer, the Attorney-General, Provost-Marshal, Justices, Sheriffs, etc.; town meetings, which were sanctioned by the Charter, were, with few exceptions, expressly forbidden, without leave previously obtained of the Governor or Lieutenant-Governor, expressing the special business of said meeting, and with a further restriction that no matters should be treated of at these meetings except the electing of public officers and the business expressed in the Governor's permission; jurymen, who had been elected before by the freeholders and inhabitants of the several towns, were to be all summoned and returned by the sheriffs of the respective counties; the whole executive government was taken out of the hands of the people, and the nomination of all important officers invested in the King or his Governor.

"In the apprehension that in the execution of these Acts riots would take place, and that trials or murders committed in suppressing them would be partially decided by the colonists, it was provided by another Act, that if any persons were indicted for murder, or any capital offence, *committed in aiding the magistracy*, the Governor might send the person so indicted to another county, or to Great Britain, to be tried.

"These three Acts were passed in such quick succession as to produce the most inflammatory effects in America, where they were considered as forming a complete system of tyranny. 'By the first,' said the colonists, 'the property of unoffending thousands is arbitrarily taken away for the act of a few individuals; by the second, our chartered liberties are annihilated; and by the third, our lives may be destroyed with impunity.'"*

The passing of these three Bills through Parliament was attended in each case with protracted and animated debates.

The first debate or discussion of American affairs took place on the 7th of March, in proposing an address of thanks to the King for the message and the communication of the American papers, with an assurance that the House would not fail to exert every means in their power of effectually providing for objects so important to the general welfare as maintaining the due execution of the laws, and for securing the just dependence of the colonies upon the Crown and Parliament of Great Britain.

In moving this address to pledge Parliament to the exertion of every means in its power, Mr. Rice said: "The question now brought to issue is, whether the colonies are or are not the colonies of Great Britain." Lord North said, "Nothing can be done to re-establish peace, without additional powers from Parliament." Nugent, now Lord Clare (who had advocated the Stamp Act, if the revenue from it should not exceed a peppercorn, as a symbol of parliamentary power), entreated that there might be no divided counsels. Dowdeswill said: "On the

* Holmes' Annals, etc., Vol. II., pp. 185, 186. These three Bills were followed by a fourth, legalizing the quartering of the troops on the inhabitants in the town of Boston.

repeal of the Stamp Act, all America was quiet; but in the following year you would go in pursuit of your peppercorn—you would collect from peppercorn to peppercorn—you would establish taxes as tests of obedience. Unravel the whole conduct of America; you will find out the fault is at home." Pownall, former Governor of Massachusetts and earnest advocate of American rights, said: "The dependence of the colonies is a part of the British Constitution. I hope, for the sake of this country, for the sake of America, for the sake of general liberty, that this address will pass with a unanimous vote." Colonel Barré even applauded the good temper with which the subject had been discussed, and refused to make any opposition. William Burke, brother of Edmund Burke, said: "I speak as an Englishman. We applaud ourselves for the struggles we have had for our constitution; the colonists are our fellow-subjects; they will not lose theirs without a struggle." Wedderburn, the Solicitor-General, who bore the principal part in the debate, said: "The leading question is the dependence or independence of America." The address was adopted without a division.*

On the 14th of March, Lord North explained at large his American policy, and opened the first part of his plan by asking leave to bring in a Bill for the instant punishment of Boston. He stated, says the Annual Register, "that the opposition to the authority of Parliament had always originated in the colony of Massachusetts, and that colony had been always instigated to such conduct by the irregular and seditious proceedings of the town of Boston: that, therefore, for the purpose of a

* Bancroft's History of the United States, Vol. VI., Chap. lii., pp. 502—510. Mr. Bancroft says:

"The next day letters arrived from America, manifesting no change in the conduct of the colonies. Calumny, with its hundred tongues, exaggerated the turbulence of the people, and invented wild tales of violence. It was said at the palace, and the King believed, that there was in Boston a regular committee for tarring and feathering; and that they were next, to use the King's expression, 'to pitch and feather' Governor Hutchinson himself. The press was also employed to rouse the national pride, till the zeal of the English people for maintaining English supremacy became equal to the passions of the Ministry. Even the merchants and manufacturers were made to believe that their command of the American market depended on the enforcement of the British claim of authority."—*Ib.*, p. 511.

thorough reformation, it became necessary to begin with that
town, which by a late unpardonable outrage had led the way to
the destruction of the freedom of commerce in all parts of
America: that if a severe and exemplary punishment were
not inflicted on this heinous act, Great Britain would be wanting
in the protection she owed to her most peaceable and meritorious
subjects: that had such an insult been offered to British property in a foreign port, the nation would have been called upon
to demand satisfaction for it.

" He would therefore propose that the town of Boston should
be obliged to pay for the tea which had been destroyed in their
port: that the injury was indeed offered by persons unknown
and in disguise, but that the town magistracy had taken no
notice of it, had never made any search for the offenders, and
therefore, by a neglect of manifest duty, became accomplices in
the guilt: that the fining of communities for their neglect in
punishing offences committed within their limits was justified
by several examples.   In King Charles the Second's time, the city
of London was fined when Dr. Lamb was killed by unknown
persons.   The city of Edinburgh was fined and otherwise punished for the affair of Captain Porteous.   A part of the revenue
of the town of Glasgow had been sequestered until satisfaction
was made for the pulling down of Mr. Campbell's house.
These examples were strong in point for such punishments.
The case of Boston was far worse.   It was not a single act
of violence; it was a series of seditious practices of every
kind, and carried on for several years.

" He was of opinion, therefore, that it would not be sufficient
to punish the town of Boston by obliging her to make a pecuniary satisfaction for the injury which, by not endeavouring to
prevent or punish, she has, in fact, encouraged; security must be
given in future that trade may be safely carried on, property protected, laws obeyed, and duties regularly paid.   Otherwise the
punishment of a single illegal act is no reformation.   It would
be therefore proper to take away from Boston the privilege of
a port until his Majesty should be satisfied in these particulars,
and publicly declare in Council, on a proper certificate of the
good behaviour of the town, that he was so satisfied.   Until
this should happen, the Custom-house officers, who were now
not safe in Boston, or safe no longer than while they neglected

their duty, should be removed to Salem, where they might exercise their functions."*

The Bill passed the first reading without discussion. At the second reading, Mr. Byng alone voted no, though there was considerable discussion. "Mr. Bollan, the agent for the Council of Massachusetts Bay, presented a petition, desiring to be heard in behalf of said Council and other inhabitants of Boston; but the House refused to receive the petition."†

At the third reading, the Lord Mayor of London presented a petition in behalf of several natives and inhabitants of North America then in London. "It was drawn," says the Annual Register, "with remarkable ability." The petitioners alleged that "the proceedings were repugnant to every principle of law

---

* Annual Register for 1774, Vol. XVII., pp. 62, 63. "At the first introduction, the Bill was received with very general applause. The cry raised against the Americans, partly the natural effect of their own acts, and partly of the operations of Government, was so strong as nearly to overbear the most resolute and determined in the opposition. Several of those who had been the most sanguine favourers of the colonies now condemned their behaviour and applauded the measure as not only just but lenient (even Colonel Barré). He said: 'After having weighed the noble lord's proposition well, I cannot help giving it my hearty and determined approval.' Others, indeed (as Dowdeswill and Edmund Burke), stood firmly by their old ground. They contented themselves, in that stage of the business, with deprecating the Bill; predicting the most fatal consequences from it, and lamenting the spirit of the House, which drove on or was driving on to the most violent measures, by the mischiefs produced by injudicious counsels; one seeming to render the other necessary. They declared that they would enter little into a debate which they saw would be fruitless, and only spoke to clear themselves from having any share in such fatal proceedings."—*Ib.*, pp. 164, 165.

† Annual Register for 1774, Vol. XVII., p. 65, which adds: "This vote of rejection was heavily censured. The opposition cried out at the inconsistency of the House, who but a few days ago received a petition from this very man, in this very character; and now, only because they chose to exert their power in acts of injustice and contradiction, totally refuse to receive anything from him, as not duly qualified. But what, they asserted, made this conduct the more unnecessary and outrageous was, that at that time the House of Lords were actually hearing Mr. Bollan on his petition, as a person duly qualified, at their bar. 'Thus,' said they, 'this House is at once in contradiction to the other and to itself.' As to the reasons given against his qualifications, they are equally applicable to all American agents; none of whom are appointed as the Minister now requires they should be, and thus this House cuts off communication between them and the colonies whom they are assisting by their acts."

and justice, and under such a precedent no man in America could enjoy a moment's security; for if judgment be immediately to follow on accusation against the people of America, supported by persons notoriously at enmity with them, the accused unacquainted with the charges, and from the nature of their situation utterly incapable of answering and defending themselves, every fence against false accusation will be pulled down.

" They asserted that law is executed with as much impartiality in America as in any part of his Majesty's dominions. They appealed for proof of this to the fair trial and favourable verdict in the case of Captain Preston and his soldiers.

" That in such a case the interposition of parliamentary power was full of danger and without precedent. The persons committing the injury were unknown. If discovered, the law ought first to be tried. If unknown, what rule of justice can punish the town for a civil injury committed by persons not known to them?

" That the instances of the cities of London, Edinburgh, and Glasgow were wholly dissimilar. All these towns were regularly heard in their own defence. Their magistrates were of their own choosing (which was not the case of Boston), and therefore they were more equitably responsible. But in Boston the King's Governor has the power, and had been advised by his Council to exert it; if it has been neglected, he alone is answerable."* In conclusion, the petitioners strongly insisted on the injustice of the Act, and its tendency to alienate the affections of America from the mother country.

The petition was received, but no particular proceedings took place upon it.

" The Bill passed the House on the 25th of March, and was carried up to the Lords, where it was likewise warmly debated; but, as in the Commons, without a division. It received the Royal assent on the 31st of March.†

---

* Annual Register for 1774, Vol. XVII., pp. 65, 66.

† *Ib.*, p. 67.

The Bill underwent a more full and fair discussion in the House of Lords than in the House of Commons. The amiable Lord Dartmouth, then Secretary of State for the Colonies, "a man that prayed," desired lenient measures, called what passed in Boston " commotion," not open "rebellion.

Dr. Ramsay remarks : " By the operation of the Boston Port Act, the preceding situation of its inhabitants and that of the East India Company was reversed. The former had more reason to complain of the disproportinate penalty to which they were indiscriminately subjected, than the latter of that outrage on their property, for which punishment had been inflicted. Hitherto the East India Company were the injured party ; but from the passing of this Act the balance of injury was on the opposite side. If wrongs received entitled the former to reparation, the latter had a much stronger title on the same ground. For the act of seventeen or eighteen individuals, as many thousands were involved in one general calamity.*

But Lord Mansfield said, " What passed in Boston is the last overt act of high treason, proceeding from our own lenity and want of foresight. It is, however, the luckiest event that could befall this country, for all may now be recovered. Compensation to the East India Company I regard as no object of the Bill. The sword is drawn, and you must throw away the scabbard. Pass this Act, and you will be past the Rubicon. The Americans will then know that we shall not temporize any longer ; if it passes with a tolerable unanimity, Boston will submit, and all will end in victory without carnage." The Marquis of Rockingham and the Duke of Richmond warmly opposed the measure, as did Lords Camden and Shelburne, the latter of whom proved the tranquil and loyal condition in which he had left the colonies on giving up their administration.

* Colonial History, Vol. I., Chap. iv., p. 379.

" The inhabitants of Boston, distinguished for politeness and hospitality no less than for industry and opulence, were sentenced, on the short notice of twenty days, to a deprivation of the means of subsistence. The rents of land-holders ceased, or were greatly diminished. The immense property in stores and wharves was rendered in a great measure useless. Labourers and artificers, and many others employed in the numerous occupations created by an extensive trade, shared the general calamity. Those of the people who depended on a regular income, and those who earned their subsistence by daily labour, were equally deprived of the means of support. Animated, however, by the spirit of freedom, they endured their privations with inflexible fortitude. Their sufferings were soon mitigated by the sympathy and relieved by the charity of the other colonists. Contributions were everywhere raised for their relief. Corporate bodies, town meetings, and provincial conventions sent them letters and addresses applauding their conduct and exhorting them to perseverance. The inhabitants of Marblehead (which was to be the seaport instead of Boston) generously offered the Boston merchants the use of their harbour, wharves, warehouses, and their personal attendance, on the lading or unlading of their goods, free of all expense. The inhabitants of Salem (the newly appointed capital) concluded an address

Shortly after the passing of the Boston Port Bill, the second Bill was brought into Parliament, entitled "An Act for the Better Regulating of the Government of the Province 'of Massachusetts Bay." This Bill was brought in on the 28th of March, three days before the Royal assent was given to the Boston Port Bill. As the town of Boston had received no notice of the Bill which closed its port, and had therefore no opportunity to vindicate its conduct or rights, so the Province received no notice of the Bill which changed its system of government, which abrogated so much of its Charter as gave to its Legislative Assembly the choice of the Council; abolished town meetings, except for the choice of town officers, or on the special permission of the Governor, which gave to the Crown the appointment and removal of the sheriffs, and to the sheriffs the selection of the juries, which had hitherto been elected by the people. After an animated debate, led by Dunning in opposition, the Bill passed the Commons by a vote of more than three to one.

The third penal Bill brought in and passed was said to have been specially recommended by the King himself. It authorized, at the discretion of the Governor, the removal for trial to Nova Scotia or Great Britain of all magistrates, revenue officers, or soldiers indicted for murder or other capital offence. Mr. Bancroft says: "As Lord North brought forward this wholesale Bill of indemnity to the Governor and soldiers, if they should trample upon the people of Boston and be charged with murder, it was noticed that he trembled and faltered at every word; showing that he was the vassal of a stronger will than his own, and vainly struggled to wrestle down the feelings which his nature refused to disavow."[*]

Colonel Barré, who had supported the Boston Port Bill, said: "I execrate the present measure; you have had one meeting of

to Governor Gage in a manner that reflected great honour on their virtue and patriotism. 'By shutting up the port of Boston,' they said, 'some imagine that the course of trade might be turned hither, and to our benefit; but nature, in the formation of our harbour, forbids our becoming rivals in commerce with that convenient mart; and were it otherwise, we must be dead to every idea of justice, lost to all feelings of humanity, could we indulge one thought to seize on wealth and raise our fortunes on the ruins of our suffering neighbours.'" (Holmes' Annals, etc., Vol. II., pp. 187, 188.)

[*] History of the United States, Vol. VI., Chap. lii., pp. 525, 526.

the colonies in Congress. You may soon have another. The Americans will not abandon their principles; for if they submit they are slaves." The Bill passed the Commons by a vote of more than four to one.

The fourth Bill legalized the quartering of troops within the town of Boston.

The question now arises, What were the effects of these measures upon the colonies? We answer, the effects of these measures were the very reverse of what had been anticipated and predicted by their advocates in England, both in and out of Parliament. The general expectation in England was that they would not be resisted in America; that Boston and Massachusetts would submit; that if they should not submit, they would be isolated from the other provinces, who would not identify themselves with or countenance the extreme proceedings of Boston and of Massachusetts. These measures had been adopted by the Government and Parliament of Great Britain in the months of March and April, and were to take effect the 1st of June. In the two following months of May and June, America spoke, and twelve colonies out of thirteen (Georgia alone excepted) protested against the measures of the British Parliament, and expressed their sympathy with Boston and Massachusetts. Boston itself spoke first, and instead of submitting, as had been predicted by Lords Mansfield and others, held a town meeting as soon as they received intelligence of the passing of the Boston Port Bill, at which resolutions were passed expressing their opinion of the impolicy, injustice, inhumanity and cruelty of this Act, from which they appealed to God and to the world; also inviting other colonies to join with them in an agreement to stop all imports and exports to and from Great Britain and Ireland and the West Indies until the Act should be repealed."*

---

* Marshall's Colonial History, Chap. xiv., p. 405.

" As soon as the Act was received, the Boston Committee of Correspondence, by the hand of Joseph Warren, invited eight neighbouring towns to a conference ' on the critical state of public affairs.' On the 12th, at noon, Metcalf Bowler, the Speaker of the Assembly of Rhode Island, came before them with the cheering news that, in answer to a recent circular letter from the body over which he presided, all the thirteen Governments were pledged to union. Punctually at the hour of three in the afternoon of that day, the

Mr. Bancroft, remarks :

"The merchants of Newburyport were the first who agreed to suspend all commerce with Britain and Ireland. Salem, also, the place marked out as the new seat of government, in a very full town meeting, and after unimpassioned debates, decided almost unanimously to stop trade, not with Britain only, but even with the West Indies. If in Boston a few cravens proposed to purchase a relaxation of the blockade by quailing before power, the majority were beset by no temptation so strong as that of routing at once the insignificant number of troops who had come to overawe them. But Samuel Adams, while he compared their spirit to that of Sparta or Rome, was ever inculcating patience as the characteristic of a true patriot ; and the people having sent forth their cry to the continent, waited self-possessed for voices of consolation."*

committees from the eight villages joined them in Faneuil Hall, the cradle of American liberty, where for ten years the freemen of the town had debated the great question of justifiable resistance. Placing Samuel Adams at their head, and guided by a report prepared by Joseph Warren of Boston, Gardener of Cambridge, and others, they agreed unanimously on the injustice and cruelty of the Act by which Parliament, without competent jurisdiction, and contrary as well to natural right as to the laws of all civilized states, had, without a hearing, set apart, accused, tried and condemmed the town of Boston." (Bancroft's History of the United States, Vol. VII., Chap. i., pp. 35, 36.)

* History of the United States, Vol. VII., Chap. x., pp. 38, 39.

Referring to General Gage's arrival at Boston, as Commander-in-Chief of the continent as well as successor to Hutchinson as Governor of Massachusetts, Mr. Bancroft says :

"On the 17th of May, Gage, who had remained four days with Hutchinson at Castle William, landed at Long Wharf amidst salutes from ships and batteries. Received by the Council and civil officers, he was escorted by the Boston cadets, under Hancock, to the State House, where the Council presented a loyal address, and his commission was proclaimed with three volleys of musketry and as many cheers. He then partook of a public dinner in Faneuil Hall. A hope still lingered that relief might come through his intercession. But Gage was neither fit to reconcile nor to subdue. By his mild temper and love of society, he gained the good-will of his boon companions, and escaped personal enmities ; but in earnest business he inspired neither confidence nor fear. Though his disposition was far from being malignant, he was so poor in spirit and so weak of will, so dull in his perceptions and so unsettled in his opinions, that he was sure to follow the worst advice, and vacillate between smooth words of concession and merciless

In the meantime, according to the provisions of the Charter, the Legislature of Massachusetts, the last Wednesday in May, proceeded to nominate the twenty-eight councillors. Of these, General Gage negatived the unprecedented number of thirteen, including all the popular leaders nominated. He laid nothing before the General Assembly but the ordinary business of the province; but gave notice that the seat of government would be removed to Salem the 1st of June, in pursuance of the Act for Closing the Port of Boston.

The Legislature reassembled, according to adjournment, at Salem the 7th day of June,* after ten days' prorogation, and on the 9th the Council replied to the Governor's speech at the opening of the session. Their answer was respectful, but firmly and loyally expressive of their views and feelings. They declared their readiness " on all occasions cheerfully to co-operate with his Excellency" in every step tending to " restore harmony" and " extricate the province from their present embarrassments," which, in their estimation, were attributable to the conduct of his " two immediate predecessors." They at the same time affirmed that " the inhabitants of the colony claimed no more than the rights of Englishmen, without diminution or abridgment ;" and that these, " as it was their indispensable duty, so would it be their constant endeavour to maintain to the utmost of their power, in perfect consistence with the truest loyalty to the Crown, the just prerogatives of which they should ever be zealous to support." To this address the Governor replied in the following bitter words: " I cannot receive this address, which contains indecent reflections on my predecessors, who have been tried and honourably acquitted by

severity. He had promised the King that with four regiments he would play the lion, and troops beyond his requisition were hourly expected. His instructions enjoined upon him the seizure and condign punishment of Samuel Adams, Hancock, Joseph Warren, and other leading patriots ; but he stood in such dread of them that he never so much as attempted their arrest."
—*Ib.*, pp. 37, 38.

* But before the prorogation, which took place the 28th of May, the Assembly desired the Governor to appoint the 1st day of June as a day of fasting and prayer ; but he refused, assigning as a reason, in a letter to Lord Dartmouth, that " the request was only to give an opportunity for sedition to flow from the pulpit."

the Lords of the Privy Council, and their conduct approved by the King. I consider this address as an insult upon his Majesty and the Lords of the Privy Council, and an affront to myself."

The answer of the Assembly was very courteous, but equally decided with that of the Council. They congratulated his Excellency on his safe arrival, and declared that they "honoured him in the most exalted station of the province, and confided in him to make the known Constitution and Charter the rule of his administration;" they "deprecated the removal of the Court to Salem," but expressed a hope that "the true state of the province, and the character of his Majesty's subjects in it, their loyalty to their Sovereign and their affection for the parent country,* as well as their invincible attachment to their just rights and liberties, would be laid before his Majesty, and that he would be the happy instrument of removing his Majesty's displeasure, and restoring harmony, which had been long interrupted by the artifices of interested and designing men."

The House of Representatives, after much private consultation among its leading members, proceeded with closed doors to the consideration and adoption, by a majority of 92 to 12, of resolutions declaring the necessity of a general meeting of all the colonies in Congress, "in order to consult together upon the present state of the colonies, and the miseries to which they are and must be reduced by the operation of certain Acts of Parliament respecting America; and to deliberate and determine upon wise and proper measures to be by them recommended to all the colonies for the recovery and establishment of their just rights and liberties, civil and religious, and the restoration of union and harmony between Great Britain and the colonies, most ardently to be desired by all good men." They elected

---

* "The people of Massachusetts were almost exclusively of English origin. Beyond any other colony they loved the land of their ancestors; but their fond attachment made them only the more sensitive to its tyranny. To subject them to taxation without their consent was robbing them of their birthright; they scorned the British Parliament as a 'Junta of the servants of the Crown rather than the representatives of England.' Not disguising to themselves their danger, but confident of victory, they were resolved to stand together as brothers for a life of liberty." (Bancroft's History of the United States, Vol. VII., Chap. i., p. 38).

five gentlemen to represent Massachusetts to the proposed Congress.

The House also proceeded with all expedition to draw up a declaration of their sentiments, to be published as a rule for the conduct of the people of Massachusetts. "This declaration," says Dr. Andrews, "contained a repetition of grievances; the necessity they were now under of struggling against lawless power; the disregard of their petitions, though founded on the clearest and most equitable reasons; the evident intention of Great Britain to destroy the Constitution transmitted to them from their ancestors, and to erect upon its ruins a system of absolute sway, incompatible with their disposition and subversive of the rights they had uninterruptedly enjoyed during the space of more than a century and a half. Impelled by these motives, they thought it their duty to advise the inhabitants of Massachusetts to throw every obstruction in their power in the way of such evil designs, and recommended as one of the most effectual, a total disuse of all importations from Great Britain until an entire redress had been obtained of every grievance.

"Notwithstanding the secrecy with which this business was carried on," continues Dr. Andrews, "the Governor was apprized of it; and on the very day it was completed, and the report of it made to the House (and adopted), he dissolved the Assembly, which was the last that was held in that colony agreeably to the tenor of the Charter."*

---

* History of the War with America, France and Spain, and Holland, commencing in 1775, and ending in 1783. By John Andrews, LL.D., in four volumes, with Maps and Charts. London : Published by his Majesty's Royal Licence and Authority, 1788. Vol. I., pp. 137, 138.

A more minute and graphic account of the close of this session of the Massachusetts Court or Legislature is as follows :

"On the appointed day the doors were closed and the subject was broached ; but before any action could be taken in the premises, a loyalist member obtained leave of absence and immediately dispatched a messenger to Gage, to inform him of what was passing. The Governor, in great haste, sent the Secretary to dissolve the Court. Finding the door locked, he knocked for admission, but was answered, that 'The House was upon very important business, which when they had finished, they would let him in.' Failing to obtain an entrance, he stood upon the steps and read the proclamation in the hearing of several members and others, and after reading it in the Council Chamber, returned. The House took no notice of this message, but proceeded with their business ; and, by a vote of 117 to 12, having determined that a Committee should be appointed to meet, as soon as may be, the Committees that are or shall be appointed by the several colonies on this continent to consult together upon the present state of the colonies, James Bowdoin, Thomas Cushing, Samuel Adams, John Adams, and Robert Treat Paine were selected for that purpose, and funds were provided for defraying their expenses." (Barry's History of Massachusetts, Second Period, Chap. xiv., pp. 484, 485.)

CHAPTER XIX.

1774, UNTIL THE MEETING OF THE FIRST GENERAL CONGRESS IN
SEPTEMBER.

THE responses to the appeals of Boston and the proposals of
the Assembly of Massachusetts, for a meeting of Congress
of all the colonies, were prompt and general and sympathetic
beyond what had been anticipated; and in some colonies
the expressions of approval and offers of co-operation and
assistance preceded any knowledge of what was doing, or had
been done, in Massachusetts.

In Virginia the House of Burgesses were in session when the
news arrived from England announcing the passing by the
British Parliament of the Boston Port Bill; and on the 26th of
May the House resolved that the 1st of June, the day on which
that Bill was to go into effect, should be set apart by the
members as a day of fasting, humiliation, and prayer, "devoutly
to implore the Divine interposition for averting the heavy
calamities which threatened destruction to their civil rights,
and the evils of a civil war, and to give them one heart
and one mind to oppose, by all just and proper means,
every injury to American rights." On the publication of this
resolution, the Governor (the Earl of Dunmore) dissolved the
House. But the members, before separating, entered into an association and signed an agreement, to the number of 87, in which,
among other things, they declared "that an attack made on one
of their sister colonies, to compel submission to arbitrary taxes,
was an attack made on all British America, and threatened ruin
to the civil rights of all, unless the united wisdom of the whole
be applied in prevention." They therefore recommended to

their Committee of Correspondence to communicate with the
several Committees of the other provinces, on the expediency
of appointing deputies from the different colonies, to meet
annually in Congress, and to deliberate on the common interests
of America. This measure had already been proposed in town
meetings, both in New York and Boston. The colonies, from
New Hampshire to South Carolina inclusive, adopted this
measure; and where the Legislatures were not in session, elections were made by the people.*

While there was a general agreement of sentiment throughout the colonies in favour of a Congress or Convention of all
the colonies to consult on common rights and interests, and to
devise the best means of securing them, there was also a corresponding sympathy and liberality for the relief of the inhabitants of Boston, who were considered as suffering for the
maintenance of rights sacred to the liberties of all the colonies,
as all had resisted successfully the landing of the tea, the badge
of their enslavement, though all had not been driven by the
Governor, as in the case of Massachusetts, to destroy it in order
to prevent its being landed. Yet even this had been done to
some extent both in South Carolina and New York.

The town of Boston became an object of interest, and its
inhabitants subjects of sympathy throughout the colonies of
America. All the histories of those times agree " that as soon
as the true character of the Boston Port Act became known in
America, every colony, every city, every village, and, as it were,

---

* Marshall's History of the American Colonies, Chap. xiv., pp. 403, 407.
" Resolutions were passed in every colony in which Legislatures were
convened, or delegates assembled in Convention, manifesting different
degrees of resentment, but concurring in the same great principles. All
declared that the cause of Boston was the cause of British America ; that
the late Acts respecting that devoted town were tyrannical and unconstitutional ; that the opposition to this unministerial system of oppression ought
to be universally and perseveringly maintained; that all intercourse with the
parent country ought to be suspended, and domestic manufactures encouraged ; and that a General Congress should be formed for the purpose
of uniting and guiding the Councils and directing the efforts of North
America.
" The Committees of Correspondence selected Philadelphia for the place,
and the beginning of September as the time, for the meeting of this important Council."—Ib., pp. 409, 410.

the inmates of every farm-house, felt it as a wound of their affections. The towns of Massachusetts abounded in kind offices. The colonies vied with each other in liberality. The record kept at Boston shows that 'the patriotic and generous people' of South Carolina were the first to minister to the sufferers, sending early in June two hundred barrels of rice, and promising eight hundred more. At Wilmington, North Carolina, the sum of two thousand pounds currency was raised in a few days; the women of the place gave liberally. Throughout all New England the towns sent rye, flour, peas, cattle, sheep, oil, fish; whatever the land or hook and line could furnish, and sometimes gifts of money. The French inhabitants of Quebec, joining with those of English origin, shipped a thousand and forty bushels of wheat. Delaware was so much in earnest that it devised plans for sending relief annually. All Maryland and all Virginia were contributing liberally and cheerfully, being resolved that the men of Boston, who were deprived of their daily labour, should not lose their daily bread, nor be compelled to change their residence for want. In Fairfax county, Washington presided at a spirited meeting, and headed a subscription paper with his own gift of fifty pounds. A special chronicle could hardly enumerate all the generous deeds. Cheered by the universal sympathy, the inhabitants of Boston 'were determined to hold out and appeal to the justice of the colonies and of the world;' trusting in God that 'these things should be overruled for the establishment of liberty, virtue and happiness in America.'"*

It is worthy of inquiry, as to how information could be so rapidly circulated throughout colonies sparsely settled over a territory larger than that of Europe, and expressions of sentiment and feeling elicited from their remotest settlements? For, as Dr. Ramsay says, "in the three first months which followed the shutting up of the port of Boston, the inhabitants of the colonies, in hundreds of small circles as well as in their Provincial Assemblies and Congresses, expressed their abhorrence of the late proceedings of the British Parliament against Massachusetts; their concurrence in the proposed measure of appointing deputies for a *General* Congress; and their willing-

* Bancroft's History of the United States, Vol. VII., pp. 72—75.

ness to do and suffer whatever should be judged conducive to the establishment of their liberties."* "In order to understand," says the same author, "the mode by which this flame was spread with such rapidity over so great an extent of country, it is necessary to observe that the several colonies were divided into counties, and these again subdivided into districts, distinguished by the names of towns, townships, precincts, hundreds, or parishes. In New England, the subdivisions which are called towns were, by law, bodies corporate ; had their regular meetings, and might be occasionally convened by their officers. The advantages derived from these meetings, by uniting the whole body of the people in the measures taken to oppose the Stamp Act, induced other provinces to follow the example. Accordingly, under the Association which was formed to oppose the Revenue Act of 1767, Committees were established, not only in the capital of every province, but in most of the subordinate districts. Great Britain, without designing it, had, by her two preceding attempts at American revenue, taught her colonies not only the advantage but the means of union. The system of Committees which prevailed in 1765, and also in 1767, was revived in 1774. By them there was a quick transmission of intelligence from the capital towns through the subordinate districts to the whole body of the people ; a union of counsels and measures was effected, among widely disseminated inhabitants."†

It will be observed that the three Acts passed by Parliament in

---

* Colonial History, Vol. I., Chap. v., p. 398.

† Ib., pp. 395, 396.

" It is, perhaps, impossible for human wisdom to contrive any system more subservient to these purposes than such a reciprocal exchange of intelligence by Committees of Correspondence. From want of such a communication with each other, and consequently of union among themselves, many States have lost their liberties, and more have been unsuccessful in their attempts to regain them after they were lost.

" What the eloquence and talents of Demosthenes could not effect among the States of Greece, might have been effected by the simple device of Committees of Correspondence. The few have been enabled to keep the many in subjection in every age from the want of union among the latter. Several ot the provinces of Spain complained of oppression under Charles the Fifth, and in transports of rage took arms against him ; but they never consulted or communicated with each other. They resisted separately, and were, therefore, separately subdued."—Ib., p. 396.

respect to Massachusetts, and the fourth, for quartering soldiers in towns, changed the Charter of the province, and multiplied the causes of difference between Great Britain and the colonies. To the causes of dissatisfaction in the colonies arising from the taxing of them assumed by Parliament (now only threepence a pound on tea), the arrangement with the East India Company and the Courts of Admiralty, depriving the colonists of the right of trial by jury, were now added the Boston Port Bill, the Regulating Act, the Act which essentially changed the chartered Constitution of Massachusetts, and the Act which transferred Government officers accused of murder, to be removed to England. Mr. Bancroft justly observes that "the Regulating Act complicated the question between America and Great Britain. The country, under the advice of Pennsylvania, might have indemnified the East India Company, might have obtained by importunity the repeal of the tax on tea, or might have borne the duty, as it had borne that on wine; but Parliament, after ten years of premeditation, had exercised the power to abrogate the laws and to change the Charter of a province without its consent; and on this arose the conflict of the American Revolution."*

* Bancroft's History of the United States, Vol. VII., Chap. viii., p. 97.

The authority of this new Act was never acknowledged in Massachusetts. Of the 36 Legislative Councillors nominated by the Crown, one-third of them declined to accept the appointment, and nearly all who did accept were soon compelled, by the remonstrances and threats of their neighbours, to resign. So alarmed was Governor Gage, that after he had summoned the new Legislature to meet him at Salem, he countermanded his summons by proclamation; but which was considered unlawful, and the Assembly met, organized itself, and passed resolutions on grievances, and adopted other proceedings to further the opposition to the new Act and other Acts complained of.

Even the Courts could not be held. At Boston the judges took their seats, and the usual proclamations were made; when the men who had been returned as jurors, one and all, refused to take the oath. Being asked why they refused, Thomas Chase, one of the petit jury, gave as his reason, "that the Chief Justice of the Court stood impeached by the late representatives of the province." In a paper offered by the jury, the judges found their authority disputed for further reasons, that the Charter of the province had been changed with no warrant but an Act of Parliament, and that three of the judges, in violation of the Constitution, had accepted seats in the new Council. The Chief Justice and his colleagues repairing in a body to the Governor, represented the impossibility of exercising their office in Boston or in any other part of the province; the army was too small for their protection; and besides, none would act as jurors. Thus the authority of the new Government, as established by Act of Parliament, perished in the presence of the Governor, the judges and the army.—*Ib.*, pp. 111, 112.

The English historian, Dr. Andrews, remarks on this subject :

" The list of the new (Legislative) Council appointed by the Crown consisted of thirty-six members. But twelve of the number declined their commissions, and most of those who accepted were speedily obliged to resign them in order to save their property and persons from the fury of the multitude. The judges newly appointed experienced much the same treatment. All the inferior officers of the Courts of Judicature, the clerks, the juries, and all others concerned, explicitly refused to act under the new laws. In some places the populace shut up the avenues to the court-houses; and upon being required to make way for the judges and officers of the court, they declared that they knew of no court nor establishment in the province contrary to the ancient usages and forms, and would recognize none.

" The former Constitution being thus destroyed by the British Legislature, and the people refusing to acknowledge that which was substituted in its room, a dissolution of all government necessarily ensued. The resolution to oppose the designs of Great Britain produced occasionally some commotions; but no other consequences followed this defect of government. Peace and good order remained everywhere throughout the province, and the people demeaned themselves with as much regularity as if the laws still continued in their full and formal rigour." (Andrews' History of the War, Vol. I., pp. 145, 146.)

CHAPTER XX.

THE GENERAL CONGRESS OR CONVENTION AT PHILADELPHIA, SEPTEMBER
AND OCTOBER, 1774.

THE word Congress, in relation to the United States, is synonymous with the word Parliament in Great Britain, signifying the
Legislature of the nation at large; but before the revolution
the word Congress was used, for the most part, as synonymous
with Convention—a voluntary meeting of delegates elected by
towns or counties for certain purposes. A meeting of delegates
from the several towns of a county was called a *Congress*, or
Convention of such county; a meeting of delegates of the
several towns of a province was called a Provincial Congress, or
Convention; and a meeting of *delegates* of the several County
Conventions in the several provinces was called a *General* or
Continental Congress, though they possessed no *legal* power, and
their resolutions and addresses were the mere expressions of
opinion or advice.

Such was the Continental Congress that assembled in Philadelphia the 5th of September, 1774—not a legislative or executive body possessing or assuming any legislative or executive
power—a body consisting of fifty-five delegates elected by the
representatives of twelve out of the thirteen provinces—Georgia,
the youngest and smallest province, not having elected delegates.
The sittings of this body, or Congress, as it was called, continued
about eight weeks, and its proceedings were conducted with all
the forms of a Legislative Assembly, but with closed doors,
and under the pledge of secrecy, until dissolved by the authority
of the Congress itself.

Each day's proceedings was commenced with prayer by some

minister.   Mr. Peyton Randolph, Speaker of the House of Burgesses of Virginia, was elected President, and Mr. Charles Thompson, of Pennsylvania, was chosen Secretary.

After deciding upon the mode of conducting the business, it was resolved, after lengthened discussion, that each colony should be equal in voting—each colony having one vote, whatever might be the number of its delegates.

This Congress consisted of the assembled representatives of the American colonies, and truly expressed their grievances, opinions, and feelings.   As the proceedings were with closed doors, the utterances of individuals were not reported; but in the reported results of their deliberations there is not an opinion or wish expressed which does not savour of affection to the mother country and loyalty to the British Constitution.   Down to this ninth or last year of the agitation which commenced with the passing of the Stamp Act, before bloody conflicts took place between British soldiers and inhabitants of Massachusetts, there was not a resolution or petition or address adopted by any Congress, or Convention, or public meeting in the colonies, that contained a principle or sentiment which has not been professed by the loyal inhabitants of British America, and which is not recognized at this day by the British Government and enjoyed by the people in all the provinces of the Dominion of Canada.

The correctness of these remarks will appear from a summary of the proceedings of this Continental Congress, and extracts from its addresses, which will show that the colonies, without exception, were as loyal to their constitutional sovereign as they were to their constitutional rights,* though in royal

---

* The royal historian, Andrews, states :

"The delegates were enjoined, by the instructions they had received from their constituents, solemnly to acknowledge the sovereignty of Great Britain over them, and their willingness to pay her the fullest obedience, as far as the constitution authorized her to demand it ; they were to disclaim all notions of separating from her ; and to declare it was with the deepest regret they beheld a suspension of that confidence and affection which had so long, and so happily for both, subsisted between Great Britain and her colonies.

"But they were no less carefully directed at the same time to assert the rights transmitted to them by their ancestors.   These rights they would never surrender, and would maintain them at all perils.   They were entitled to all the privileges of British subjects, and would not yield to the unjust pretensions of Parliament, which, in the present treatment of the colonies,

messages and ministerial speeches in Parliament their petitions
and remonstrances were called treason, and the authors of them
were termed rebels and traitors.　The principal acts of this
Congress were a Declaration of Rights; an address to the
King; an address to the people of Great Britain; a memorial
to the Americans; a letter to the people of Canada,　Non-importation and non-exportation agreements were adopted and
signed by all the members; and Committees of Vigilance were
appointed.

"Then on the 26th of October, the 'fifty-five' separated and
returned to their homes, determined, as they expressed it, 'that
they were themselves to stand or fall with the liberties of
America.' " *

Among the first important acts of this Congress was the
declaration of colonial rights, grievances, and policy.　As this
part of their proceedings contains the whole case of the colonies
as stated by their own representatives, I will give it, though
long, in their own words, in a note.†　This elaborate and ably

had violated the principles of the constitution and given them just occasion
to be dissatisfied and to rise in opposition.　Parliament might depend this
opposition would never cease until those Acts were wholly repealed that had
been the radical cause of the present disturbances." (Andrews' History of
the War with America, Spain and Holland, from 1775 to 1783, pp. 156, 157.)

* Elliott's New England History, Vol. II., Chap. xvi., p. 289.

"Washington and Lee believed the non-importation and exportation
agreements would open the eyes of England ; but Patrick Henry agreed
with John and Samuel Adams in believing that *force* must decide it, and,
like them, was ready to meet any emergency."—*Ib.*

"The New York Legislature at once repudiated the doings of the Congress ; but elsewhere it met with a hearty response."—*Ib.*, p. 290.

† " Whereas, since the close of the last war, the British Parliament, claiming a power, of right, to bind the people of America by statutes in all cases
whatsoever, hath in some Acts expressly imposed taxes on them ; and in
others, under various pretences, but in fact for the purpose of raising a
revenue, hath imposed rates and duties payable in these colonies, established
a Board of Commissioners with unconstitutional powers, and extended the
jurisdiction of Courts of Admiralty, not only for collecting the said duties,
but for the trial of causes merely arising within the body of a county :

" And whereas, in consequence of other statutes, judges, who before held
only estates at will in their offices, have been made dependent on the Crown
alone for their salaries, and standing armies kept in times of peace :

" And whereas it has lately been resolved in Parliament, that by force of a
statute made in the thirty-fifth year of the reign of King Henry VIII.,

written paper does not appear to contain a sentiment of treason, nor anything which the members of the Congress had not a right to express and complain of as British subjects; while they

colonists may be transported to England and tried there upon accusations for treasons, and misprisions and concealments of treasons committed in the colonies, and by a late statute such trials have been directed in cases therein mentioned:

"And whereas, in the last session of Parliament, three statutes were made— one entitled, 'An Act to discontinue, in such manner and for such time as are therein mentioned, the landing and discharging, lading or shipping of goods, wares, and merchandise, at the town, and within the harbour of Boston, in the province of Massachusetts Bay, in North America;' another entitled, 'An Act for the better regulating the Government of the Province of Massachusetts Bay, in New England;' and another Act entitled, 'An Act for the impartial administration of justice, in the cases of persons questioned for any act done by them in the execution of the law, or for the suppression of riots and tumults, in the province of the Massachusetts Bay, in New England;' and another statute was then made, 'for making more effectual provision for the government of the province of Quebec,' etc.—all which statutes are impolitic, unjust, and cruel, as well as unconstitutional, and most dangerous and destructive of American rights:

"And whereas assemblies have been frequently dissolved, contrary to the rights of the people, when they attempted to deliberate on grievances; and their dutiful, humble, loyal, and reasonable petitions to the Crown for redress have been repeatedly treated with contempt by his Majesty's Ministers of State; the good people of the several colonies of New Hampshire, Massachusetts Bay, Rhode Island and Providence Plantations, Connecticut, New York, New Jersey, Pennsylvania, New Castle, Kent and Sussex on Delaware, Maryland, Virginia, North Carolina, and South Carolina, justly alarmed at the arbitrary proceedings of Parliament and Administration, have severally elected, constituted, and appointed deputies to meet and sit in General Congress, in the city of Philadelphia, in order to obtain such establishment as that their religion, laws, and liberties may not be subverted; whereupon the deputies so appointed being now assembled, in a full and free representation of these colonies, taking into their most serious consideration the best means of attaining the ends aforesaid, do in the first place, as Englishmen, what their ancestors in like cases have usually done, for asserting and vindicating their rights and liberties, DECLARE, that the inhabitants of the English colonies in North America, by the immutable laws of nature, the principles of the English Constitution, and the several charters or compacts, have the following rights:

"Resolved, N. C. D. 1st, That they are entitled to life, liberty, and property; and they have never ceded to any sovereign power whatever a right to dispose of either without their consent.

"Resolved, N. C. D. 2nd, That our ancestors, who first settled these colonies, were, at the time of their emigration from the mother country, entitled to all

explicitly recognized in Parliament all the authority which could be constitutionally claimed for it, and which was requisite for British supremacy over the colonies, or which had ever been exercised before 1764.

the rights, liberties, and immunities of free and natural-born subjects within the realm of England.

" Resolved, N. C. D. 3rd, That by such emigration they by no means forfeited, surrendered, or lost any of those rights, but that they were, and their descendants now are, entitled to the exercise and enjoyment of all such of them as their local and other circumstances enabled them to exercise and enjoy.

" Resolved, 4th, That the foundation of English liberty and of all free government is a right in their people to participate in their Legislative Council; and as the English colonists are not represented, and from their local and other circumstances cannot properly be represented in the British Parliament, they are entitled to a free and exclusive power of legislation in their several Provincial Legislatures, where their right of representation can alone be preserved, in all cases of taxation and internal polity, subject only to the negative of their Sovereign, in such manner as has been heretofore used and accustomed. But from the necessity of the case, and a regard to the mutual interest of both countries, we cheerfully consent to the operation of such Acts of the British Parliament as are *bona fide* restrained to the regulation of our external commerce, for the purpose of securing the commercial advantages of the whole empire to the mother country, and the commercial benefits of its respective members ; excluding every idea of taxation, internal or external, for raising a revenue on the subjects in America without their consent.

" Resolved, N. C. D. 5th, That the respective colonies are entitled to the common law of England, and more especially to the great and inestimable privilege of being tried by their peers of the vicinage, according to the course of that law.

" Resolved, 6th, That they are entitled to the benefit of such of the English statutes as existed at the time of their colonization ; and which they have, by experience, respectively found to be applicable to their several local and other circumstances.

" Resolved, N. C. D. 7th, That these his Majesty's colonies are likewise entitled to all the immunities and privileges granted and confirmed to them by Royal Charters, or secured by their several codes of Provincial laws.

" Resolved, N. C. D. 8th, That they have a right peaceably to assemble, consider of their grievances, and petition the King ; and that all prosecutions, prohibitory proclamations, and commitments for the same, are illegal.

" Resolved, N. C. D. 9th, That the keeping a standing army in these colonies, in times of peace, without the consent of the Legislature of the colony in which such army is kept, is against law.

" Resolved, N. C. D. 10th, It is indispensably necessary to good government, and rendered essential by the English constitution, that the constituent

On the 1st of October, the Congress, after long consideration. unanimously resolved—

"That a loyal address to his Majesty be prepared, dutifully requesting the Royal attention to the grievances which alarm and distress his Majesty's faithful subjects in North America,

branches of the Legislature be independent of each other ; that, therefore, the exercise of legislative power in several colonies, by a Council appointed, during pleasure, by the Crown, is unconstitutional, dangerous, and destructive to the freedom of American legislation.

"All and each of which the aforesaid deputies, in behalf of themselves and their constituents, do claim, demand, and insist on, as their indubitable rights and liberties ; which cannot be legally taken from them, altered or abridged by any power whatever, without their own consent, by their representatives in their several Provincial Legislatures.

"In the course of our inquiry, we find many infringements and violations of the foregoing rights, which, from an ardent desire that harmony and mutual intercourse of affection and interest may be restored, we pass over for the present, and proceed to state such Acts and measures as have been adopted since the last war, which demonstrate a system formed to enslave America.

"Resolved, N. C. D., That the following Acts of Parliament are infringements and violations of the rights of the colonies ; and that the repeal of them is essentially necessary, in order to restore harmony between Great Britain and the American colonies, viz. :

"The several Acts of 4 Geo. III. chaps. 15 and 34—5 Geo. III. chap. 25 —6 Geo. III. chap. 52—7 Geo. III. chap. 41 and chap. 46—8 Geo. III. chap. 22, which imposed duties for the purpose of raising a revenue in America, extend the power of the Admiralty Courts beyond their ancient limits ; deprive the American subject of trial by jury ; authorize the judge's certificate to indemnify the prosecutor from damages that he might otherwise be liable to ; requiring oppressive security from a claimant of ships and goods seized, before he shall be allowed to defend his property, and are subversive of American rights.

"Also 12 Geo. III. chap. 24, intituled 'An Act for the better securing his Majesty's dockyards, magazines, ships, ammunition, and stores,' which declares a new offence in America, and deprives the American subject of a constitutional trial by a jury of the vicinage, by authorizing the trial of any person charged with the committing of any offence described in the said Act, out of the realm, to be indicted and tried for the same in any shire or county within the realm.

"Also the three Acts passed in the last session of Parliament, for stopping the port and blocking up the harbour of Boston, for altering the Charter and Government of Massachusetts Bay, and that which is intituled 'An Act for the better administration of justice,' etc.

"Also, the Act passed in the same session for establishing the Roman Catholic religion in the province of Quebec, abolishing the equitable system and entreating his Majesty's gracious interposition to remove such grievances, and thereby to restore to Great Britain and the colonies that harmony so necessary to the happiness of the British empire, and so ardently desired by all America."

This address or petition, like all the papers emanating from this Congress, was written with consummate ability.[*] "In this petition to the King, the Congress begged leave to lay their grievances before the Throne. After a particular enumeration of these, they observed that they wholly arose from a destructive system of colony administration adopted since the conclusion of the last war. They assured his Majesty that they had made such provision for defraying the charges of the administration of justice, and the support of civil government, as had been judged just, and suitable to their respective circumstances; and that for the defence, protection, and security of the colonies, their militia would be fully sufficient in time of peace; and in case of war, they were ready and willing, when constitutionally required, to exert their most strenuous efforts in granting supplies and raising forces. They said, "We ask but for peace, liberty, and safety. We wish not a diminution of the prerogative; nor do we solicit the grant of any new right in our favour. Your royal authority over us, and our connection with Great

of English laws, and erecting a tyranny there, to the great danger (from so total a dissimilarity of religion, law, and government) of the neighbouring British colonies, by the assistance of whose blood and treasure the said country was conquered from France.

"Also, the Act passed in the same session for the better providing suitable quarters for officers and soldiers in his Majesty's service in North America.

"Also, that the keeping a standing army in several of these colonies, in time of peace, without the consent of the Legislature of that colony in which such army is kept, is against law.

"To these grievous Acts and measures, Americans cannot submit; but in hopes their fellow-subjects in Great Britain will, on a revision of them, restore us to that state in which both countries found happiness and prosperity, we have for the present only resolved to pursue the following peaceable measures: 1. To enter into a non-importation, non-consumption, and non-exportation agreement or association; 2. To prepare an address to the people of Great Britain, and a memorial to the inhabitants of British America; and 3. To prepare a loyal address to his Majesty, agreeable to resolutions already entered into." (Marshall's American Colonial History, Appendix IX., pp. 481—485.)

[*] See the Earl of Chatham's remarks on page 423.

Britain, we shall always carefully and zealously endeavour to support and maintain."* They concluded their masterly and touching address in the following words:

"Permit us, then, most gracious Sovereign, in the name of all your faithful people in America, with the utmost humility, to implore you, for the honour of Almighty God, whose pure religion our enemies are undermining; for your glory, which can be advanced only by rendering your subjects happy and keeping them united; for the interest of your family, depending on an adherence to the principles that enthroned it; for the safety and welfare of your kingdom and dominions, threatened with almost unavoidable dangers and distresses, that your Majesty, as the loving Father of your whole people, connected by the same bonds of law, loyalty, faith, and blood, though dwelling in various countries, will not suffer the transcendent relation formed by these ties to be farther violated in certain expectation of efforts that, if attained, never can compensate for the calamities through which they must be gained."†

Their address to the people of Great Britain is equally earnest and statesmanlike. Two or three passages, as samples, must suffice. After stating the serious condition of America, and the oppressions and misrepresentations of their conduct, and their claim to be as free as their fellow-subjects in Great Britain, they say:

"Are not the proprietors of the soil of Great Britain lords of their own property? Can it be taken from them without their consent? Will they yield it to the arbitrary disposal of any men or number of men whatsoever? You know they will not.

"Why then are the proprietors of the soil of America less lords of their property than you are of yours; or why should they submit it to the disposal of your Parliament, or any other Parliament or Council in the world, not of their election? Can the intervention of the sea that divides us cause disparity of rights; or can any reason be given why English subjects who

* Ramsay's Colonial History, Vol. I., p. 418.

† "The Committee which brought in this admirably well-drawn and truly conciliatory address were Mr. Lee, Mr. John Adams, Mr. Johnston, Mr. Henry, Mr. Rutledge, and Mr. Dickenson. The original composition has been generally attributed to Mr. Dickenson." (Marshall's American Colonial History, Chap. xiv., p 419, in a note.)

live three thousand miles distant from the royal palace should enjoy less liberty than those who are three hundred miles distant from it? Reason looks with indignation on such distinctions, and freemen can never perceive their propriety."

They conclude their address to their fellow-subjects in Great Britain in the following words:

"We believe there is yet much virtue, much justice, and much public spirit in the English nation. To that justice we now appeal. You have been told that we are seditious, impatient of government, and desirous of independence. Be assured that these are not facts, but calumnies. Permit us to be as free as yourselves, and we shall ever esteem a union with you to be our greatest glory and our greatest happiness; and we shall ever be ready to contribute all in our power to the welfare of the empire. We shall consider your enemies as our enemies, and your interest as our own.

"But if you are determined that your Ministers shall wantonly sport with the rights of mankind; if neither the voice of justice, the dictates of law, the principles of the Constitution, nor the suggestions of humanity can restrain your hands from shedding human blood in such an impious cause, we must then tell you that we will never submit to be hewers of wood and drawers of water to any Ministry or nation in the world.

"*Place us in the same situation that we were at the close of the late war, and our former harmony will be restored.*"

The address of the members of this Congress to their constituents is a lucid exposition of the several causes which had led to the then existing state of things, and is replete with earnest but temperate argument to prove that their liberties must be destroyed, and the security of their persons and property annihilated, by submission to the pretensions of the British Ministry and Parliament. They state that the first object of the Congress was to unite the people of America, by demonstrating the sincerity and earnestness with which reconciliation had been sought with Great Britain upon terms compatible with British liberty. After expressing their confidence in the efficacy of the passive commercial resistance which had been adopted, they conclude their address thus:

"Your own salvation and that of your posterity now depend upon yourselves. You have already shown that you entertain

27

a proper sense of the blessings you are striving to retain.
Against the temporary inconveniences you may suffer from a
stoppage of trade, you will weigh in the opposite balance the
endless miseries you and your descendants must endure from
an established arbitrary power." * * *

"Motives thus cogent, arising from the emergency of your
unhappy condition, must excite your utmost diligence and zeal
to give all possible strength and energy to pacific measures
calculated for your relief. But we think ourselves bound in
duty to observe to you, that the schemes agitated against the
colonies have been so conducted as to render it prudent that you
should extend your views to mournful events, and be in all
respects prepared for every contingency. Above all things, we
earnestly entreat you, with devotion of spirit, penitence of
heart, and amendment of life, to humble yourselves, and implore
the favour of Almighty God; and we fervently beseech His
Divine goodness to take you into His gracious protection."

The letters addressed to the other colonies not represented in
the Congress require no special reference or remark.

After completing the business before them, this first General
Congress in America recommended that another Congress should
be held in the same place on the tenth day of the succeeding
May, 1775, "unless redress of their grievances should be previously obtained," and recommending to all the colonies "to
choose deputies as soon as possible, to be ready to attend at that
time and place, should events make their meeting necessary."

I have presented an embodiment of the complaints, sentiments,
and wishes of the American colonies in the words of their
elected representatives in their first General Congress. I have
done so for two reasons: First, to correct as far as I can the
erroneous impression of thousands of English and Canadian
readers, that during the ten years' conflict of words, before the
conflict of arms, between the British Ministry and Parliament
and Colonies, the colonists entertained opinions and views
incompatible with subordination to the mother country, and
were preparing the way for separation from it. Such an opinion
is utterly erroneous. Whatever solitary individuals may have
thought or wished, the petitions and resolutions adopted by the
complaining colonists during these ten years of agitation
breathe as pure a spirit of loyalty as they do of liberty; and

in no instance did they ask for more, or as much, as the inhabitants of the provinces of the Canadian Dominion this day enjoy.

My second reason for thus quoting the very words of the declarations and petitions of the colonists is to show the injustice with which they were represented and treated by the British Ministry, Parliament, and press in England.

It was hoped by the Congress that their address to the people of England would have a happy influence in favour of the colonies upon the public mind, and tell favourably on the English elections, which took place the latter part of the year 1774; but the elections were suddenly ordered before the proceedings of the Congress could be published in England. The elections, of course, resulted adversely to the colonies; and the new Parliament was more subservient to the Ministry against the colonies than the preceding Parliament.*

This new Parliament met the 30th day of November, when the King was advised to inform them, among other things, "that a most daring spirit of resistance and disobedience to the laws unhappily prevailed in the province of Massachusetts, and had broken forth in fresh violences of a very criminal nature; that these proceedings had been countenanced and encouraged in his other colonies; that unwarrantable attempts had been made to obstruct the commerce of his kingdom by unlawful combinations; and that he had taken such measures and given such orders as he judged most proper and effectual for carrying

---

* "Some time before the proceedings of Congress reached England, it was justly apprehended that the non-importation agreement would be one of the measures they would adopt. The Ministry, apprehending that this event, by distressing the trading and manufacturing towns, might influence votes against the Court in the election of a new Parliament, which was, of course, to come on in the succeeding year, suddenly dissolved the Parliament and immediately ordered a new one to be chosen. It was their design to have the whole business of elections over before the inconveniences of non-importation could be felt. The nation was thus surprised into an election. Without knowing that the late American acts had driven the colonies into a firm combination to support and make common cause with the people of Massachusetts, a new Parliament was returned, which met thirty-four days after the proceedings of Congress were first published in Philadelphia, and before they were known in Great Britain. This, for the most part, consisted either of the former members, or of those who held similar sentiments." (Ramsay's Colonial History, Vol. I., Chap. vi., p. 424.)

into execution the laws which were passed in the last session of the late Parliament relative to the province of Massachusetts."*

Answers were adopted in both Houses of Parliament re-echoing the sentiments of the Royal Speech, but not without vehement debates. There was a considerable minority in both Lords and Commons that sympathised with the colonies, and condemned the Ministerial policy and the Acts of the previous Parliament complained of. In the Commons, the Minister was reminded of the great effects he had predicted from the American acts. "They were to humble that whole continent without further trouble; and the punishment of Boston was to strike so universal a panic in all the colonies that it would be totally abandoned, and instead of obtaining relief, a dread of the same fate would awe the other provinces to a most respectful submission."† But the address, re-echoing the Royal Speech for coercion, was adopted by a majority of two to one.

In the Lords a similar address was passed by a large majority ; but the Lords Richmond, Portland, Rockingham, Stamford, Torrington, Ponsonby, Wycombe, and Camden entered upon the journals a protest against it, which concluded in the following memorable words :

"Whatever may be the mischievous designs or the inconsiderate temerity, we wish to be known as persons who have disapproved of measures so injurious in their past effects and future tendency, and who are not in haste, without inquiry or information, to commit ourselves in declarations which may precipitate our country into all the calamities of civil war."‡

Before the adjournment of the new Parliament for the Christmas holidays, the papers containing the proceedings of the Continental Congress at Philadelphia reached England. The first impression made by them is said to have been in favour of America. The Ministry seemed staggered, and their opposers triumphed in the fulfilment of their own predictions as to the effects of Ministerial acts and policy in America. The Earl of Dartmouth, Secretary of State for the Colonies, after a day's perusal of these papers, said that the petition of the Congress to the King (of which extracts have been given above)

* Ramsay's Colonial History, Vol. I., Chap. vi., pp. 424, 425.

† Ib., p. 425.

‡ Ib., p. 425.

was a decent and proper one. He cheerfully undertook to present it to the King; and reported afterwards that his Majesty was pleased to receive it very graciously, and would lay it before his two Houses of Parliament. From these favourable circumstances, the friends of conciliation anticipated that the petition of the Colonial Congress would be made the basis of a change of measures and policy in regard to the colonies. But these hopes were of short duration.

CHAPTER XXI.

THE RE-ASSEMBLING OF PARLIAMENT—LETTERS FROM COLONIAL GOVER-
NORS, REVENUE AND MILITARY OFFICERS, AGAINST THE COLONISTS
OPPOSED TO THE MINISTERIAL POLICY—THE MINISTRY, SUPPORTED
BY PARLIAMENT, DETERMINE UPON CONTINUING AND STRENGTHENING
THE COERCIVE POLICY AGAINST THE COLONIES.

ON the re-assembling of Parliament in January, 1775, a
number of papers were produced from governors, and revenue
and military officers in America, which contained various statements adverse to the proceedings and members of the Congress,
and the opposition to the coercive Acts of Parliament.

Ministers and their supporters were pleased with these papers,
which abetted their policy, lauded and caressed their authors,
and decided to concede nothing, and continue and strengthen
the policy of coercion.

On the 20th of January, the first day of the re-assembling of
the Lords, Lord Dartmouth laid the papers received from
America before the House. The Earl of Chatham, after an
absence of two years, appeared again in the House with restored
health, and with all his former energy and eloquence. He
moved:

"That a humble address be presented to his Majesty, most
humbly to advise and beseech him that, in order to open the
way toward a happy settlement of the dangerous troubles in
America, by beginning to allay ferments and soften animosities
there, and above all for preventing, in the meantime, any
sudden catastrophe at Boston, now suffering under daily irritation of an army before their eyes, posted in their town, it may
graciously please his Majesty that immediate orders may be
despatched to General Gage for removing his Majesty's forces

from the town of Boston as soon as the rigours of the season and other circumstances indispensable to the safety and accommodation of said troops may render the same practicable."

Lord Chatham advocated his motion in a very pathetic speech, and was supported by speeches by the Marquis of Rockingham, Lords Shelburne and Camden, and petitions from merchants and manufacturers throughout the kingdom, and most prominently by those of London and Bristol. But the motion was negatived by a majority of 68 to 13.

In the course of his speech Lord Chatham said:

"Resistance to your acts was as necessary as it was just; and your imperious doctrine of the omnipotence of Parliament and the necessity of submission will be found equally impotent to convince or to enslave.

"The means of enforcing the thraldom are as weak in practice as they are unjust in principle. General Gage and the troops under his command are penned up, pining in inglorious inactivity. You may call them an army of safety and of guard, but they are in truth an army of impotence; and to make the folly equal to the disgrace, they are an army of irritation.

"But this tameness, however contemptible, cannot be censured; for the first drop of blood shed in civil and unnatural war will make a wound that years, perhaps ages, may not heal. * * The indiscriminate hand of vengeance has lumped together innocent and guilty; with all the formalities of hostility, has blocked up the town of Boston, and reduced to beggary and famine thirty thousand inhabitants. * *

"When your lordships look at the papers transmitted to us from America—when you consider their decency, firmness, and wisdom, you cannot but respect their cause, and wish to make it your own. For myself, I must avow that in all my reading —and I have read Thucydides, and have studied the master-states of the world—for solidity of reason, force of sagacity, and wisdom of conclusion under a complication of difficult circumstances, no nation or body of men can stand in preference to the General Congress of Philadelphia. The histories of Greece and Rome give us nothing equal to it, and all attempts to impose servitude upon such a mighty continental nation must be vain. We shall be forced ultimately to retract; let us retract while we can, not when we must. These violent Acts must be repealed; you will repeal them; I pledge myself for it, I stake my reputation upon it, that you will in the end repeal them. Avoid, then, this humiliating necessity. With a dignity becoming your exalted station, make the first advance towards concord, peace, and happiness; for that is your true dignity. Concession comes with better grace from superior power, and establishes solid confidence on the foundations of affection and gratitude. Be the first to spare; throw down the weapons in your hand.

"Every motive of justice and policy, of dignity and of prudence, urges you to allay the ferment in America by a removal of your troops from Boston, by a repeal of your Acts of Parliament, and by demonstrating amiable dispositions towards your colonies. * * If the Ministers persevere in thus misadvising and misleading the King, I will not say that the King is betrayed, but I will pronounce that the kingdom is undone; I will not say that they can alienate the affections of his subjects from his Crown, but I will affirm that, the American jewel out of it, they will make the Crown not worth his wearing."*

The Earl of Suffolk, with whining vehemence, assured the House that, in spite of Lord Chatham's prophecy, the Government was resolved to repeal not one of the Acts, but to use all possible means to bring the Americans to obedience; and after declaiming violently against their conduct, boasted as "having been one of the first to advise coercive measures."

Ex-Lord Chancellor Camden excelled every other speaker, except Lord Chatham, in the discussion; he declared in the course of his speech:

"This I will say, not only as a statesman, politician, and philosopher, but as a common lawyer: My lords, you have no right to

---

* When the words of Lord Chatham were reported to the King, his Majesty was "stung to the heart," and was greatly enraged, denouncing Lord Chatham as an "abandoned politician," "the trumpet of sedition," and classified him with Temple and Grenville as "void of gratitude." The King repelled and hated every statesman who advised him to conciliate the colonists by recognising them as having the rights of British subjects. He was the prompter of the most violent measures against them, and seemed to think that their only rights and duties were to obey whatever he might command and the Parliament declare.

tax America; the natural rights of man, and the immutable laws of nature, are all with that people.   King, Lords, and Commons are fine-sounding names, but King, Lords, and Commons may become tyrants as well as others.   It is as lawful to resist the tyranny of many as of one.   Somebody once asked the great Selden in what book you might find the law for resisting tyranny.   'It has always been the custom of England,' answered Selden, 'and the custom of England is the law of the land.' "

After several other speeches and much recrimination, and a characteristic reply from Lord Chatham, his motion was rejected by a majority of sixty-eight to eighteen; but the Duke of Cumberland, the King's own brother, was one of the minority.   The King triumphed in what he called "the very handsome majority," and said he was sure "nothing could be more calculated to bring the Americans to submission."   The King's prediction of "submission" was followed by more united and energetic resistance in the colonies.

But Lord Chatham, persevering in his efforts of conciliation, notwithstanding the large majority against him, brought in, the 1st of February, a Bill entitled "A Provisional Act for Settling the Troubles in America, and for Asserting the Supreme Legislative Authority and Superintending Power of Great Britain over the Colonies."   The Bill, however, was not allowed to be read the first time, or even to lie on the table, but was rejected by a majority of sixty-four to thirty-two—a contempt of the colonists and a discourtesy to the noble mover of the Bill without example in the House of Lords.

In the meantime, petitions were presented to the Commons from various towns in England, Scotland, and Ireland, by manufacturers and merchants connected with the colonial trade. On the 23rd of January, Alderman Hayley presented a petition from the merchants of the City of London trading to America, stating at great length the nature and extent of the trade, direct and indirect, between Great Britain and America, and the immense injury to it by the recent Acts of Parliament, and praying for relief; but this petition was conveyed to the "Committee of Oblivion," as were petitions from the merchants of Glasgow, Liverpool, Norwich and other towns, on American affairs.   These petitions, together with their advocates in both Houses of Parliament, showed that the oppressive

policy and abuse of the Americans were the acts of the
Ministry of the day, and not properly of the English people.

On the 26th of January, Sir George Saville offered to present
a petition from Dr. Franklin, Mr. Bollan, and Mr. Lee, stating
that they had been authorized by the American Continental
Congress to present a petition from the Congress to the King,
which his Majesty had referred to that House, and that they
were able to throw great light upon the subject; they therefore
prayed to be heard at the bar in support of the petition. After
a violent debate the petition was rejected by a majority of 218
to 68.*

Lord North, on the 2nd of February, moved that the House
resolve itself into Committee on an address to his Majesty,
thanking him for having communicated to the House the several
papers relating to the present state of the British colonies, and
from which " we find that a part of his Majesty's subjects in

---

* Dr. Franklin had been Postmaster-General for America. When he
assumed the office the expenditure exceeded the receipts by £3,000 a year ;
under his administration the receipts gradually increased so as to become
a source of revenue. The day after his advocacy of the American petitions
before the Privy Council, he was dismissed from office. Referring to the
manner in which American petitions and their agents were treated by the
British Government, Dr. Franklin expressed himself as follows, in a letter
to the Hon. Thomas Cushing, Speaker of the House of Representatives of
Massachusetts :

"When I see that all petitions and complaints of grievances are so
odious to Government that even the mere pipe which conveys them becomes
obnoxious, I am at a loss to know how peace and union is to be maintained
or restored between the different parts of the empire. Grievances cannot be
redressed unless they are known ; and they cannot be known but through
complaints and petitions. If these are deemed affronts, and the messengers
punished as offenders, who will henceforth send petitions ? and who will
deliver them ? It has been thought a dangerous thing in any State to
stop up the vent of griefs. Wise governments have therefore generally
received petitions with some indulgence even when but slightly founded.
Those who think themselves injured by their rulers are sometimes, by
a mild and prudent answer, convinced of their error. But where complaining is a crime, hope becomes despair." (Collections of Massachusetts Historical Society.)

[Yet the Government of Massachusetts, under the first Charter, pronounced petitions a crime, and punished as criminals those who petitioned
against the governmental acts which denied them the right of worship or
elective franchise because they were non-Congregationalists.]

the province of Massachusetts Bay have proceeded so far as to resist the authority of the Supreme Legislature ; that a *rebellion* at this time actually exists within the said province ; and we see, with the utmost concern, that they have been countenanced and encouraged by unlawful combinations and engagements entered into by his Majesty's subjects in several other colonies, to the injury and oppression of many of their innocent fellow-subjects resident within the kingdom of Great Britain and the rest of his Majesty's dominions. This conduct on their part appears to us the more inexcusable when we consider with how much temper his Majesty and the two Houses of Parliament have acted in support of the laws and constitution of Great Britain ; to declare that we can never so far desert the trust reposed in us as to relinquish any part of the sovereign au thority over all his Majesty's dominions which by law is invested in his Majesty and the two Houses of Parliament, and that the conduct of many persons, in several of the colonies, during the late disturbances, is alone sufficient to convince us how necessary this power is for the protection of the lives and fortunes of all his Majesty's subjects ; that we ever have been and always shall be ready to pay attention and regard to any real griev-ances of any of his Majesty's subjects, which shall, in a dutiful and constitutional manner, be laid before us ; and whenever any of the colonies shall make proper application to us, we shall be ready to afford them every just and reasonable indulgence ; but that, at the same time, we consider it our indispensable duty humbly to beseech his Majesty to take the most effectual measures to enforce due obedience to the laws and authority of the Supreme Legislature ; and that we beg leave, in the most solemn manner, to assure his Majesty that it is our fixed resolu-tion, at the hazard of our lives and properties, to stand by his Majesty against all rebellious attempts, in the maintenance of the just rights of his Majesty and the two Houses of Parlia-ment."*

I have given Lord North's proposed address to the King at length, in order that the reader may understand fully the policy of the Government at that eventful moment, and the statements on which that policy was founded.

---

* Parliamentary Register for 1775, p. 134.

In relation to this address several things may be observed:
1. There is not the slightest recognition in it that the American
colonists have any constitutional rights whatever; they are
claimed as the absolute property of King and Parliament, irrespective of local Charters or Legislatures. 2. It is alleged that
Parliament always had been and would be "ready to pay attention to any *real* grievances of any of his Majesty's subjects
which shall, *in a dutiful and constitutional manner*, be laid
before us," when "we shall be ready to afford them every just
and reasonable *indulgence*." Yet every one of the hundreds
of petitions which had been sent from the colonies to England
for the previous ten years, complaining of grievances, was
rejected, under one pretext or another, as not having been
adopted or transmitted in "a dutiful and constitutional manner."
If a Legislative Assembly proceeded to prepare a petition of
grievances to the King, the King's Governor immediately dissolved the Assembly; and when its members afterwards met
in their private capacity and embodied their complaints, their
proceedings were pronounced unlawful and seditious. When
township, county, and provincial conventions met and expressed
their complaints and grievances in resolutions and petitions,
their proceedings were denounced by the Royal representatives
as unlawful and rebellious; and when elected representatives
from all the provinces (but Georgia) assembled in Philadelphia
to express the complaints and wishes of all the provinces, their
meeting was declared unlawful, and their petition to the King
a collection of fictitious statements and rebellious sentiments,
though more loyal sentiments to the King, and more full recognition of his constitutional prerogatives were never expressed
in any document presented to his Majesty. When that petition
of the Continental congregation was presented to the Earl
of Dartmouth, the head of the Colonial Department, he said
it was a decent and proper document, and he would have
pleasure in laying it before the King, who referred it to the
House of Commons; yet Lord North himself and a majority
of his colleagues, backed by a majority of the House of
Commons, rejected that petition, refused to consider its statements and prayers, but instead thereof proposed an address
which declared one of the colonies in a state of rebellion,
abetted by many in other colonies, advised military force

against the colonies, and assured the King that they would stand by his Majesty "at the hazard of their lives and properties, against all rebellious attempts" to maintain the assumed rights of his Majesty and the two Houses of Parliament over the colonies. Yet not one of them ever afterwards risked a hair of his head in the war which they advised to maintain such rights.

3. It was also as insulting and provoking to the colonists as it was unjust, impolitic, and untrue, to assert that a rebellion "existed in one province of America, and was encouraged by many persons in other colonies;" when not an act of rebellion existed in any colony, but dissatisfaction, meetings to express sentiments and adopt petitions founded upon their declining and agreeing not to buy or drink tea, or buy or wear clothes of English manufacture, until English justice should be done to them—all which they had a right as British subjects to do, and for doing which those were responsible who compelled them to such self-denying acts in the maintenance of constitutional rights which are now recognised as such, at this day, throughout all the colonies of the British empire.

It is not surprising that Lord North's motion and statements were severely canvassed in the House of Commons. Mr. Dunning, in reply to Lord North, "insisted that America was not in rebellion, and that every appearance of riot, disorder, tumult, and sedition the noble lord had so carefully recounted arose not from disobedience, treason, or rebellion, but was created by the conduct of those whose views were to establish despotism." The Attorney-General (Thurlow) argued strongly against Mr. Dunning's position that the Americans were not in rebellion, and affirmed the contrary. General Grant said "he had served in America, knew the Americans well, and was certain they would not fight; they would never dare to fight an English army; they did not possess any of the qualifications necessary to make good soldiers; and that a very slight force would be more than sufficient for their complete reduction. He repeated many of their commonplace expressions, ridiculed their enthusiasm in religion, and drew a disagreeable picture of their manners and ways of living."

Mr. Fox entered fully into the question; pointed out the injustice, the inexpediency, the folly of the motion; prophesied defeat on one side of the water, and ruin and punishment on

the other. He said, among other things, "The reason why the
colonies objected to taxes by Parliament for revenue was, that
such revenue, in the hands of Government, took out of the hands
of the people that were to be governed that control which
every Englishman thinks he ought to have over the Government to which his rights and interests are entrusted." He
moved an amendment to omit all the motion but the three first
lines, and to substitute: "But deploring that the information
which they (the papers) had afforded served only to convince
the House that the measures taken by his Majesty's servants
tended rather to widen than to heal the unhappy differences
which had so long subsisted between Great Britain and
America, and praying a speedy alteration of the same."

A long debate ensued; after which the House divided on Mr.
Fox's amendment, which was lost by a majority of 304 to 105.
Lord North's motion was then adopted by a majority of 296 to
106.

Thus was war *virtually* proclaimed by the British Ministry
of the day and the Parliament (not by the people) of Great
Britain against the colonies.

On the 6th of February the report of Lord North's address
was made to the House, when Lord John Cavendish moved to
recommit the proposed address agreed to in the Committee. He
strongly recommended the reconsideration of a measure which
he deemed fraught with much mischief. He commented on
the proposed address; thought it improper to assert that
rebellion exists; mentioned the insecurity created by the Act
changing the Government of Massachusetts Bay; said the
inhabitants knew not for a moment under what Government
they lived.

A long discussion ensued. On the side of absolute prerogative,
and of subduing the colonies to it by military force, spoke Mr.
Grenville, Captain Harvey, Sir William Mayne, Mr. Stanley, Mr.
Adam, Mr. Scott, the Solicitor-General (Wedderburn, who
grossly insulted Dr. Franklin before the Privy Council), Mr.
Mackworth, and Mr. Sawbridge. For the recommitting the ad-
dress, and in favour of a conciliatory policy towards the colonies,
spoke, besides Lord John Cavendish, the mover, Mr. Lumley, the
Lord Mayor of London, Rt. Hon. T. Townshend, Mr. Jolyffe, Lord
Truham, Governor Johnstone, Mr. Burke, and Colonel Barré.

A conference was held between the Lords and Commons, and the address was made the joint address of both Houses of Parliament and presented to the King the 9th of February; to which the King replied as follows:

"My Lords and Gentlemen,—I thank you for this very dutiful address, and for the affectionate and solemn assurances you give me of your support in maintaining the just rights of my crown and of the two Houses of Parliament; and you may depend on my taking the most speedy and effectual measures for enforcing due obedience to the laws and authority of the Supreme Legislature. When any of my colonies shall make a proper and dutiful application, I shall be ready to concur with you in affording them every just and reasonable indulgence; and it is my ardent wish that this disposition on our part may have a happy effect on the temper and conduct of my subjects in America."

The "disposition" of "indulgence," shown by Parliament was simply the enforcement of its declaratory Act of absolute power to bind the colonies in all cases whatsoever, and "the proper and dutiful application of any colony" was simply a renunciation of all they had claimed as their constitutional rights—a penitent prayer of forgiveness for having avowed and maintained those rights, and of submitting all their rights and interests to the absolute and merciful consideration of the King and his Parliament, and that in the presence of the parliamentary enactments and royal institutions of the previous ten years. During those years, the Parliament, with royal consent, had passed acts to tax the colonies without representation, ignoring their own representative Legislatures; had imposed duties on goods imported, to be enforced by Courts which deprived the colonists of the privilege of trial by jury; had made by Act of Parliament, without trial, the city of Boston not only responsible for tea destroyed by seventeen individuals, but blocked up its port not only until the money was paid, but until the city authorities should give guarantee satisfactory to the King that the tea and other revenue Acts should be enforced —a proceeding unprecedented and unparalleled in the annals of British history. Even in more arbitrary times, when the cities of London, Glasgow, and Edingurgh were made responsible for property lawlessly destroyed within their limit, it was only until after trial in each case, in which those cities had an opportunity of defence, and in neither case was the trade of the city prohibited and destroyed. But the British Ministry and Parliament proceeded still further by superseding the most essential provisions of the Charter of the Province of Massachusetts, and changing its whole constitution of government—a high-handed act of arbitrary government which had not been attempted by either Charles the First or Charles the Second in regard to the same colony; for when charges were brought, in 1632, against the Massachusetts authorities, for having violated the Charter, Charles the First appointed a commission, gave the accused a trial, which resulted in their acquittal and promised support by the King; and when they were accused again in 1634, the King did not forthwith cancel their Charter, but issued a second commission, which, however, never reported, in consequence of the commencement of the civil war in England, which resulted in the death of the King. Then, in the restoration, when charges were preferred, by parties without as well as within the province, against the Government of Massachusetts, King Charles the Second appointed a commission to examine into the complaints, and at length tested their acts by trial in the highest courts of law, and by whose decision their first Charter was cancelled for repeated and even habitual violations of it. But without a trial, or even commission of inquiry, the King and Parliament changed the constitution of the province as well as extinguished the trade of its metropolis.

CHAPTER XXII.

1775 CONTINUED—PARLIAMENT PROCEEDS TO PASS AN ACT TO PUNISH ALL
THE NEW ENGLAND COLONIES FOR SYMPATHISING WITH MASSACHU-
SETTS, BY RESTRICTING THEIR TRADE TO ENGLAND AND DEPRIVING
THEM OF THE NEWFOUNDLAND FISHERIES.

THE British Ministry and both Houses of Parliament do not
seem to have been satisfied with having charged Massachusetts
and its abettors with rebellion, and determined to punish the
recusant province and its metropolis accordingly, but they proceeded, during the same session, even to punish the other New
England provinces for alleged sympathy with the town of
Boston and the province of Massachusetts. The very day after
the two Houses of Parliament had presented their joint address
to the King, declaring the existence of "rebellion" in the
province of Massachusetts, abetted by many persons in the other
provinces, Lord North introduced a Bill into the Commons to
restrain the trade and commerce of the provinces of New
Hampshire, Massachusetts, Rhode Island, and Connecticut, to
Great Britain and Ireland and the British Islands in the West
Indies, and to prohibit those provinces from carrying on any
fishery on the banks of Newfoundland. Lord North assigned
as the reason for this Bill that the three other New England
colonies "had aided and abetted their offending neighbours,
and were so near them that the intentions of Parliament would
be frustrated unless they were in like manner comprehended
in the proposed restraints." The Bill encountered much opposition in both Houses, but was passed by large majorities.

Shortly after passing this Bill to restrain the trade of the
New England colonies and to prohibit them the fisheries of

28

Newfoundland, as well as from trading with foreign countries, intelligence reached England that the middle and southern colonies were countenancing and encouraging the opposition of their New England brethren, and a second Bill was brought into Parliament and passed for imposing similar restraints on the colonies of East and West Jersey, Pennsylvania, Maryland, Virginia, South Carolina, and the counties on the Delaware. It is singular to note in this Bill the omission of New York, Delaware, and North Carolina. It was probably thought that the omission of these colonies would cause dissension among the colonies ; but the three exempted provinces declined the distinction, and submitted to the restraints imposed upon the other colonies.

Much was expected by Lord North and his colleagues from the General Assembly of New York, which had not endorsed the proceedings of the first Continental Congress, held in Philadelphia the previous September and October ; but at the very time that the British Parliament was passing the Act which exempted New York from the disabilities and punishments inflicted on its neighbouring colonies, north and south, the Legislative Assembly of New York was preparing a petition and remonstrance to the British Parliament on the grievances of all the colonies, not omitting the province of Massachusetts. This petition and remonstrance of the General Assembly of New York was substantially a United Empire document, and expressed the sentiments of all classes in the colonies, except the Royal governors and some office-holders, as late as May, 1775. The following extracts from this elaborate and ably-written address will indicate its general character. The whole document is given in the Parliamentary Register, Vol. I., pp. 473—478, and is entitled "The Representation and Remonstrance of the General Assembly of the Colony of New York, to the Honourable the Knights, Citizens, and Burgesses of Great Britain, in Parliament assembled." It commences as follows :

"Impressed with the warmest sentiments of loyalty and affection to our most gracious Sovereign, and zealously attached to his person, family, and government, we, his Majesty's faithful subjects, the representatives of the ancient and loyal colony of New York, behold with the deepest concern the unhappy disputes subsisting between the mother country and her colonies.

Convinced that the grandeur and strength of the British empire, the protection and opulence of his Majesty's American dominions, and the happiness and welfare of both, depend essentially on a restoration of harmony and affection between them, we feel the most ardent desire to promote a cordial reconciliation with the parent state, which can be rendered permanent and solid only by ascertaining the line of parliamentary authority and American freedom on just, equitable, and constitutional grounds. To effect these salutary purposes, and to represent the grievances under which we labour, by the innovations which have been made in the constitutional mode of government since the close of the last war, we shall proceed with that firmness which becomes the descendants of Englishmen and a people accustomed to the blessings of liberty, and at the same time with the deference and respect which is due to your august Assembly to show—

" That from the year 1683 till the above-mentioned period the colony has enjoyed a Legislature consisting of three distinct branches—a Governor, Council, and General Assembly; under which political frame the representatives of the people have uniformly exercised the right of their civil government and the administration of justice in the colony.

" It is therefore with inexpressible grief that we have of late years seen measures adopted by the British Parliament subversive of that Constitution under which the people of this colony have always enjoyed the same rights and privileges so highly and deservedly prized by their fellow-subjects in Great Britain—a Constitution in its infancy modelled after that of the parent state, in its growth more nearly assimilated to it, and tacitly implied and undeniably recognised in the requisitions made by the Crown, with the consent and approbation of Parliament.

" An exemption from internal taxation, and the exclusive right of providing for the support of our own civil government and the administration of justice in this colony, we esteem our undoubted and inalienable rights as Englishmen; but while we claim these essential rights, it is with equal pleasure and truth we can declare, that we ever have been and ever will be ready to bear our full proportion of aids to the Crown for the public service, and to make provision for the necessary purposes, in as ample and adequate a manner as the circumstances of the colony will admit. Actuated by these sentiments, while we address ourselves to a British House of Commons, which has ever been so sensible of the rights of the people, and so tenacious of preserving them from violation, can it be a matter of surprise that we should feel the most distressing apprehensions from the Act of the British Parliament declaring their right to bind the colonies in all cases whatsoever ?—a principle which has been actually exercised by the statutes made for the sole and·express purpose of raising a revenue in America, especially for the support of Government, and other usual and ordinary services of the colonies.

" The trial by a jury of the vicinage, in causes civil and criminal arising within the colony, we consider as essential to the security of our lives and liberties, and one of the main pillars of the Constitution, and therefore view with horror the construction of the statute of the 35th of Henry the Eighth, as held up by the joint address of both Houses of Parliament in 1769, advising his Majesty to send for persons guilty of treasons and misprisions of treasons in the colony of Massachusetts Bay, in order to be tried in England ; and we are equally alarmed at the late Act empowering his Majesty to send persons guilty of offences in one colony to be tried in another, or within the realm of England. * * *

" We must also complain of the Act of the 7th of George the Third, chapter 59th, requiring the Legislature of this colony to make provision for the expense of supplying troops quartered amongst us, with the necessaries prescribed by that law; and holding up by another Act a suspension of our legislative powers till we should have complied, as it would have included all the effects of a tax, and implied a distrust of our readiness to contribute to the public service.

" Nor in claiming these essential rights do we entertain the most distant desire of independence of the parent kingdom. We acknowledge the Parliament of Great Britain necessarily entitled to a supreme direction and government over the whole empire, for a wise, powerful, and lasting preservation of the great bond of union and safety among all the branches; their authority to regulate the trade of the colonies, so as to make it subservient to the interest of the mother country, and to prevent its being injurious to the other parts of his Majesty's dominions. * * *

"Interested as we must consider ourselves in whatever may affect our sister colonies, we cannot help feeling for the distresses of our brethren in the Massachusetts Bay, from the operation of the several Acts of Parliament passed relative to that province, and of earnestly remonstrating in their behalf. At the same time, we also must express our disapprobation of the violent measures that have been pursued in some of the colonies, which can only tend to increase our misfortunes and to prevent our obtaining redress.

"We claim but a restoration of those rights which we enjoyed by general consent before the close of the last war; we desire no more than a continuation of that ancient government to which we are entitled by the principles of the British Constitution, and by which alone can be secured to us the rights of Englishmen. Attached by every tie of interest and regard to the British nation, and accustomed to behold with reverence and respect its excellent form of government, we harbour not an idea of diminishing the power and grandeur of the mother country, or lessening the lustre and dignity of Parliament. Our object is the happiness which we are convinced can only arise from the union of both countries. To render this union permanent and solid, we esteem it the undoubted right of the colonies to participate in that Constitution whose direct aim is the liberty of the subject; fully trusting that your honourable House will listen with attention to our complaints, and redress our grievances by adopting such measures as shall be found most conducive to the general welfare of the whole empire, and most likely to restore union and harmony amongst all its different branches.

"By order of the General Assembly,

"JOHN CRUGER, *Speaker.*

"Assembly Chamber, City of New York, the 25th day of March, 1775."

This representation and remonstrance having been presented to the House of Commons, Mr. Burke moved, the 15th of May, that it be brought up. He said "he had in his hand a paper of importance from the General Assembly of the Province of New York—a province which yielded to no part of his Majesty's dominions in its zeal for the prosperity and unity of the empire, and which had ever contributed as much as any, in its proportion, to the defence and wealth of the whole." "They never had before them so fair an opportunity of putting an end to the unhappy disputes with the colonies as at present, and he conjured them in the most earnest manner not to let it escape, as possibly the like might never return. He thought this application from America so very desirable to the House, that he could have made no sort of doubt of their entering heartily into his ideas, if Lord North, some days before, in opening the budget, had not gone out of his way to make a panegyric on the last Parliament, and in particular to commend as acts of lenity and mercy those very laws which the Remonstrance considers as intolerable grievances."

" Lord North spoke greatly in favour of New York, and said he would gladly do everything in his power to show his regard to the good behaviour of that colony; but the honour of Parliament required that no paper should be presented to that House which tended to call in question the unlimited rights of Parliament."

" Mr. Fox said the right of Parliament to tax America was not simply denied in the Remonstrance, but was coupled with the exercise of it. The exercise was the thing complained of, not the right itself. When the Declaratory Act was passed, asserting the right in the fullest extent, there were no tumults in America, no opposition to Government in any part of that country; but when the right came to be exercised in the manner we have seen, the whole country was alarmed, and there was an unanimous determination to oppose it. The right simply is not regarded; it is the exercise of it that is the object of opposition. It is this exercise that has irritated and made almost desperate several of the colonies. But the noble lord (Lord North) chooses to be consistent, and is determined to make them all alike. The only province that was moderate, and in which England had some friends, he now treats with contempt. What will be the consequence when the people of this moderate province are informed of this treatment? That representation which the cool and candid of this moderate province had framed with deliberation and caution is rejected—is not suffered to be presented—is not even to be read by the clerk. When they hear this they will be inflamed, and hereafter be as distinguished by their violence as they have hitherto been by their moderation. It is the only method they can take to regain the esteem and confidence of their brethren in the other colonies who have been offended at their moderation. Those who refused to send deputies to the Congress (at Philadelphia), and trusted to Parliament, will appear ridiculous in the eyes of all America. It will be proved that those who distrusted and defied Parliament had made a right judgment, and those who relied upon its moderation and clemency had been mistaken and duped ; and the consequence of this must be, that every friend the Ministers have in America must either abandon them, or lose all credit and means of serving them in future."

"Governor *Johnstone* observed that when Mr. Wilkes had formerly presented a petition full of matter which the House did not think to enter into, they did not prevent the petition being brought up, but separated the matter which they thought improper from that which they thought ought to be heard. The House might make use of the same selection here. Ministers have long declared they wished for a dutiful application from one of the colonies, and now it is come they treat it with scorn and indignity. Mr. Cornwall had said it came only from twenty-six individuals. These twenty-six are the whole Assembly. When the question to adopt the measures recommended by the Congress was negatived by a majority of one only in this Assembly of twenty-six individuals, the Ministers were in high spirits, and these individuals were then represented as all America."

Lord North's amendment to reject the petition was adopted by a majority of 186 to 67.*

"After having been foiled in the House of Commons," says the royal historian, " it now remained to be decided whether that colony's representations would meet with a more gracious reception in the House of Lords. But here the difficulty was still greater than in the other House. The dignity of the peerage was said to be insulted by the appellation under which it had been presumed to usher those representations into that Assembly. They were styled a Memorial; such a title was only allowable

* Parliamentary Register, Vol. I., pp. 467—473.

in transactions between princes and states independent of each other, but was insufferable on the part of subjects. The answer was that the lowest officer in the service had a right to present a memorial, even to his Majesty, should he think himself aggrieved; with much more reason might a respectable body present one to the House of Lords. But, exclusive of the general reason that entitled so important a colony to lay such a paper before them, the particular reason of its fidelity, in spite of so many examples of defection, was alone a motive which ought to supersede all forms, and engage their most serious attention to what it had to propose.

"After sundry arguments of the same nature, the question was determined against hearing the Memorial by forty-five peers to twenty-five.

"When the rejection of these applications was announced to the public, a great part of the nation expressed the highest discontent. They now looked forward with dejection and sorrow at the prospect of mutual destruction that lay before them, and utterly gave up all other expectations."*

It might be supposed that such a rejection of the petition of

---

* Dr. Andrews' History of the War with America, Spain, and Holland, Vol. I., pp. 275, 276.

" The Ministerial objections were that it was incompatible with the dignity of the House to suffer any paper to be presented that questioned its supreme authority. Particular notice was taken at the same time that the title of Petition did not accompany this paper ; it was called a Representation and Remonstrance, which was not the usual nor the proper manner of application to Parliament. This singularity alone was sufficient to put a negative on its presentation.

" To this it was replied, that the times were so dangerous and critical that words and forms were no longer deserving of attention. The question was whether they thought the colony of New York was worthy of a hearing ? No colony had behaved with so much temperateness and discretion. Notwithstanding the tempestuousness of the times, and the general wreck of British authority, it had yet preserved a steady obedience to Government. While every other colony was bidding defiance to Britain, this alone submissively applied to her for redress of grievances. Was it consistent with policy, after losing the good-will of all the other colonies, to drive this, through a needless and punctilious severity, into their confederacy against this country ? Could we expect, after such a treatment, that this colony could withstand the arguments that would be drawn from our superciliousness to induce it to relinquish a conduct which was so ill requited ?"—Ib., p. 274.

the most loyal colony in America would end the presentation
of petitions on the part of the colonies to the King and Parliament, and decide them at once either to submit to the extinction
of their constitutional rights as British subjects, or defend them
by force.   But though they had, both separately and unitedly,
declared from the beginning that they would defend their
rights at all hazards, they persisted in exhausting every possible
means to persuade the King and Parliament to desist from such
a system of oppression, and to restore to them those rights which
they enjoyed for more than a century—down to the close of
the French war in 1763.

CHAPTER XXIII.

1775 CONTINUED—THE SECOND CONTINENTAL CONGRESS IN AMERICA.

SIX MONTHS after the General Assembly of New York adopted its Memorial, and four months after its rejection by both Houses of Parliament, the second Continental Congress met, in the month of September, at Philadelphia.

This Assembly consisted of fifty-five members, chosen by twelve colonies. The little colony of Georgia did not elect delegates, but promised to concur with the sister colonies in the effort to maintain their rights to the British Constitution. Many of the members of this Assembly were men of fortune and learning, and represented not only the general sentiments of the colonies, but their wealth and respectability.* "The

* " Each of the three divisions by which the colonies were usually designated—the New England, the Middle, and the Southern Colonies—had on the floor of Congress men of a positive character. *New England* presented in John Sullivan, vigour; in Roger Sherman, sterling sense and integrity; in Thomas Cushing, commercial knowledge; in John Adams (afterwards President of the United States), large capacity for public affairs; in Samuel Adams (no relation to John Adams), a great character with influence and power to organize. The *Middle* Colonies presented in Philip Livingston, the merchant prince of enterprise and liberality; in John Jay, rare public virtue, juridical learning, and classic taste; in William Livingston, progressive ideas tempered by conservatism; in John Dickenson, "The Immortal Farmer," erudition and literary ability; in Cæsar Rodney and Thomas McKean, working power; in James Duane, timid Whigism, halting, but keeping true to the cause; in Joseph Galloway, downright Toryism, seeking control, and at length going to the enemy. The *Southern* Colonies presented in Thomas Johnson, the grasp of a statesman; in Samuel Chase, activity and boldness; in the Rutledges, wealth and accomplishment; in Christopher Gadsden, the genuine American; and in the Virginia delegation—

object, as stated in the credentials of the delegates, and especially in those of the two most powerful colonies of Massachusetts and Virginia, was to obtain the redress of grievances, and to restore harmony between Great Britain and America, which, it was said, was desired by all good men. It was the conviction that this might be done through a Bill of Rights, in which the limits of the powers of the colonies and the mother country might be defined."*

Some three weeks after the assembling of Congress, before the end of September, a petition to the King was reported, considered, and adopted. This petition was addressed to the King, in behalf of the colonists, beseeching the interposition of the Royal authority and influence to procure them relief from their afflicting fears and jealousies, excited by the measures pursued by his Ministers, and submitting to his Majesty's consideration whether it may not be expedient for him to be pleased to direct some

---

an illustrious group—in Richard Bland, wisdom ; in Edmund Pendleton, practical talent ; in Peyton Randolph, experience in legislation ; in Richard Henry Lee, statesmanship in union with high culture ; in Patrick Henry, genius and eloquence ; in Washington, justice and patriotism. 'If,' said Patrick Henry, 'you speak of solid information and sound judgment, Washington unquestionably is the greatest man of them all.' Those others who might be named were chosen on account of their fitness for the duties which the cause required. Many had independent fortunes. They constituted a noble representation of the ability, culture, political intelligence, and wisdom of twelve of the colonies." (Frothingham's Rise of the Republic of the Twelve States, pp. 360, 361.)

* *Ib.*, pp. 363, 364.

After preliminary proceedings, Congress decided to appoint a Committee to state the rights of the colonies, the instances in which those rights had been violated, and the most proper means to obtain their restoration ; and another Committee to examine and report upon the statutes affecting the trade and manufactures of the colonies. On the same day, Samuel Adams, in answer to the objection to opening the session with prayer, grounded on the diversity of religious sentiment among the members, said he could hear prayer from any man of piety and virtue, who was a friend of the country, and moved that Mr. Duché, an Episcopalian, might be desired to read prayers for the Congress the following morning. The motion prevailed. "The Congress sat with closed doors. Nothing transpired of their proceedings except their organization and the rule of voting (each province having an equal vote). The members bound themselves to keep their doings secret until a majority should direct their publication."—*Ib.*, pp. 364, 365.

mode by which the united applications of his faithful colonists to the Throne may be improved into a happy and permanent reconciliation; and that in the meantime measures be taken for preventing the further destruction of the lives of his Majesty's subjects,* and that such statutes as more immediately distress any of his Majesty's colonies be repealed. "Attached to your Majesty's person, family, and government," concludes this address of the Congress, "with all the devotion that principle and affection can inspire, connected with Great Britain by the strongest ties that can unite societies, and deploring every event that tends in any degree to weaken them, we solemnly assure your Majesty that we not only most ardently desire that the former harmony between her and these colonies may be restored, but that a concord may be established between them upon so firm a basis as to perpetuate its blessings, uninterrupted by any future dissensions, to succeeding generations in both countries." This petition was read in Parliament the 7th of December, 1775, at the request of Mr. Hartley, with several other petitions for pacification; but they were all rejected by the House of Commons.†

* The battles of Lexington and Bunker's Hill had occurred some months before the adoption of this petition.

† Holmes' Annals, Vol. II., p. 232.

Richard Penn, late Governor of Pennsylvania, was chosen by Congress to go to Great Britain, with directions to deliver their petition to the King himself, and to endeavour, by his personal influence, to procure its favourable reception; but Mr. Penn, though from the city whose Congress had twice assembled, a man distinguished in the colony for moderation and loyalty, and the appointed agent of the Congress, was not asked a question, even when he presented the American petition to the Secretary of State for the Colonial Department, and the King refused to see him.—*Ib.*, pp. 231, 232.

"Two days after the delivery of a copy of the petition of Congress, the King sent out a proclamation for *suppressing rebellion and sedition.* It set forth that many of his subjects in the colonies had proceeded to open and avowed rebellion by arraying themselves to withstand the execution of the law, and traitorously levying war against him. 'There is reason,' so ran its words, 'to apprehend that such rebellion hath been much promoted and encouraged by the traitorous correspondence, counsels, and comfort of divers wicked and desperate persons within our realm.' Not only all the officers, civil and military, but all the subjects of the realm were therefore called upon to disclose all traitorous conspiracies, and to transmit to one of the Secretaries of State 'full information of all persons who should be found carrying on correspondence with, or in any manner or degree aiding or abetting the persons now in open arms and rebellion against the Government within any of the colonies

The answer of the King to the respectful and loyal constitutional petition of Congress was to proclaim the petitioners "rebels," and all that supported them "abettors of treason."*

in North America, in order to bring to condign punishment the authors, perpetrators, and abettors of such traitorous designs.'

"The proclamation, aimed at Chatham, Camden, Barré, and their friends, and the boldest of the Rockingham party, even more than against the Americans, was read, but not with the customary ceremonies, at the Royal Exchange, where it was received with a general hiss."

"The irrevocable publication having been made, Penn and Arthur Lee were 'permitted' on the 1st of September to present the original of the American petition to Lord Dartmouth, who promised to deliver it to the King; but on their pressing for an answer, 'they were informed that as it was not received on the throne, no answer would be given.' Lee expressed sorrow at the refusal, which would occasion so much bloodshed; and the deluded Secretary answered: 'If I thought it would be the cause of shedding one drop of blood, I should never have concurred in it." (Bancroft's History of the United States, Vol. VIII., Chap. xlix., pp. 132, 133.)

Yet "on the 23rd of August Lord Dartmouth wrote to General Howe, who (Aug. 2, 1775) superseded General Gage as the Commander of the British army, that there was 'no room left for any other consideration but that of proceeding against the twelve associated colonies in all respects with the utmost rigour, as the open and avowed enemies of the State.'" (Frothingham's Rise of the American Republic, p. 446.)

* "In the meantime (beginning of October) Richard Penn hastened to England with the second petition. The King was now continually occupied with American affairs. He directed that General Gage should be ordered 'instantly to come' over, on account of the battle of Bunker Hill; thought Admiral Graves ought to be recalled from Boston 'for doing nothing,' and completed the arrangements for the employment of Hanoverians in America. Impatient at the delay of the Cabinet in acting upon the proclamation agreed upon, he put this in train by ordering one to be framed and submitted, August 18th, to Lord North, and fixed the day for its promulgation. He was confirmed in his extreme views by General Haldimand, fresh from America, who reported that 'nothing but force could bring the colonies to reason,' and that it would be dangerous to give ear to any proposition they might submit. The King was convinced that it would be better 'totally to abandon the colonies' than 'to admit a single shadow' of their doctrines (a). Five days

(a) A private letter by Captain Collins, lately arrived from London, says that "on the 19th of August General Haldimand was closeted with his Majesty two hours, giving him a state of the American colonies; and that in the course of the conversation his Majesty expressed his resolution in these memorable words: 'I am unalterably determined, at every hazard, and at the risk of every consequence, to compel the colonies to absolute submission.'"

The first day of November brought to the Continental Congress this proclamation, together with the intelligence that the British army and navy were to be largely increased, and that German mercenary soldiers from Hanover and Hesse had been hired, as it was found impossible to obtain soldiers in England to fight against their fellow-subjects in America.* On the same day the intelligence was received from General Washington, in Massachusetts, of the burning of Falmouth (now Portland).†

after penning these words, he issued (August 23rd) a proclamation for suppressing rebellion and sedition. (The purpose of this fatal proclamation is given in the sub-note.)

This proclamation, unlike Lord North's plan, ignored the colonies as political unities. It is levelled against individuals in rebellion, and all within the realm who should aid them." (Frothingham's Rise of the American Republic, pp. 444—446. Donne's Correspondence of Geo. III.)

* "In the autumn of this year (1775), General Gage repaired to England, and the command of the British army devolved on Sir William Howe. The offer of this command had been first made to General Oglethorpe, his senior officer, who agreed to accept the appointment on the condition that the Ministry would authorize him to assure the colonies that justice should be done to them. This veteran and patriotic General declared at the same time that he knew the people of America well ; that they never would be subdued by arms, but that their obedience would be ever secured by doing them justice." (Holmes' Annals, Vol. II., p. 235.)

"The Earl of Effingham, who in his youth had been prompted by military genius to enter the army, and had lately served as a volunteer in the war between Russia and Turkey, finding that his regiment was intended for America, renounced the profession which he loved, as the only means of escaping the obligation of fighting against the cause of freedom. This resignation gave offence to the Court, and was a severe rebuke to the officers who did not share his scruple ; but at London the Common Hall, in June, thanked him publicly as 'a true Englishman ;' and the guild of merchants in Dublin addressed him in the strongest terms of approbation." (Bancroft's History of the United States, Vol. VII., Chap. xxxiii. pp. 343, 344.)

† "In compliance with a resolve of the Provincial Congress to prevent Tories from conveying out their effects, the inhabitants of Falmouth, in the north-eastern part of Massachusetts, had obstructed the loading of a mast ship. The destruction of the town was determined on as a vindictive punishment. Captain Mowat, detached for that purpose with armed vessels by Admiral Graves, arrived off the place on the evening of the 17th of October. He gave notice to the inhabitants that he would give them two hours 'to remove the human species,' at the end of which time a red pendant would be hoisted at the maintop-gallant mast-head ; and that on the least resistance, he should be freed from all humanity dictated by his orders or his inclination.

The simultaneous intelligence of the treatment of the second
petition of Congress, the Royal proclamation, the increase of
the army and navy, the employment of seventeen thousand
Hanoverians and Hessian mercenaries to subdue America, and
the burning of Falmouth, produced a great sensation in Congress

Upon being inquired of by three gentlemen who went on board his ship for
that purpose respecting the reason of this extraordinary summons, he
replied that he had orders to set on fire all the seaport towns from Boston to
Halifax, and that he supposed New York was already in ashes. He could
dispense with his orders, he said, on no terms but the compliance of the
inhabitants to deliver up their arms and ammunition, and their sending on
board a supply of provisions, four carriage guns, and the same number of
the principal persons in the town as hostages; that they should engage not to
unite with their country in any opposition to Britain; and he assured them
that on a refusal of these conditions he would lay their town in ashes within
three hours. Unprepared for the attack, the inhabitants by entreaty obtained
the suspension of an answer until morning, and employed this interval in
removing their families and effects. Considering opposition as unavailing,
they made no resistance. The next day, Captain Mowat commenced a
furious cannonade and bombardment; and a great number of people standing
on the heights were spectators of the conflagration, which reduced many of
them to penury and despair; 139 dwelling-houses and 278 stores were burnt.
Other seaports were threatened with conflagration, but escaped; Newport,
on Rhode Island, was compelled to stipulate for a weekly supply, to avert it."
(Holmes' Annals, Vol. II., pp. 219, 220.)

Mr. Bancroft's account of this transaction is as follows: "In the
previous May, Mowat, a naval officer, had been held prisoner for a few hours
at Falmouth, now Portland; and we have seen Linzee, in a sloop of war,
driven with loss from Gloucester. It was one of the last acts of Gage to plan
with the Admiral how to wreak vengeance on the inhabitants of both those
ports. The design against Gloucester was never carried out; but Mowat, in
a ship of sixteen guns, attended by three other vessels, went up the harbour of
Portland, and after a short parley, at half-past nine on the morning of the
16th of October, he began to fire upon the town. In five minutes several
houses were in a blaze; parties of marines had landed, to spread the conflagration by hand. All sea-going vessels were burned except two, which
were carried away. The cannonade was kept up till after dark. St. Paul's
Church, the public buildings, and about one hundred and thirty dwelling-
houses, three-fourths of the whole, were burned down; those that remained
standing were shattered by balls and shells. By the English account the
destruction was still greater. At the opening of a severe winter, the inhabitants were turned adrift in poverty and misery. The wrath of Washington was justly kindled as he heard of these 'savage cruelties,' this new
'exertion of despotic barbarity.'" (History of the United States, Vol. VIII.,
Chap. xlvii., p. 113.)

and throughout the colonies.   Some of the New England members of the Congress, especially John and Samuel Adams, had
long given up the idea of reconciliation with England, and had
desired independence.   This feeling was, however, cherished by
very few members of the Congress; but the startling intelligence caused many members to abandon all hope of reconciliation with the mother country, and to regard independence as
the only means of preserving their liberties.   Yet a large
majority of the Congress still refused to entertain the proposition of independence, and awaited instructions from their constituents as to what they should do in these novel and painful
circumstances.   In the meantime the Congress adopted energetic
measures for the defence of the colonies, and the effectiveness
of their union and government.   In answer to applications from
South Carolina and New Hampshire for advice on account of
the practical suspension of their local Government, Congress
"recommended" each province "to call a full and free representation of the people, and that the representatives, if they
think it necessary, establish such a form of government as in
their judgment will best promote the happiness of the people,
and most effectually secure peace and good-will in the province
*during the continuance of the present dispute between Great
Britain and the colonies.*   The province of Massachusetts had
refused to acknowledge any other local Government than that
which had been established by the Royal Charter of William
and Mary, and which had never been cancelled by any legal
proceedings; and they continued to elect their representatives,
and the representatives met and appointed the Council, and
acted under it, as far as possible, irrespective of General Gage
and the officers of his appointment.

The colonies were a unit as to their determination to defend
by force and at all hazards their constitutional rights and
liberties as British subjects; but they were yet far from being
a unit as to renunciation of all connection with England and
the declaration of independence.   The Legislature of Pennsylvania was in session when the news of the rejection of the
second petition of Congress and the King's proclamation arrived,
and when fresh instructions were asked from constituents of the
members of Congress; and even under these circumstances,
Mr. Dickenson, " The Immortal Farmer," whose masterly letters

had done so much to enlighten the public mind of both England and America on the rights of the colonies and the unconstitutional acts of the British Administration and Parliament, repelled the idea of separation from England. The Legislature of Pennsylvania continued to require all its members to subscribe the old legal qualification which included the promise of allegiance to George the Third ; "so that Franklin," says Bancroft, "though elected for Philadelphia, through the Irish and Presbyterians, would never take his seat. Dickenson had been returned for the county by an almost unanimous vote." The Legislature, on the 4th of November, elected nine delegates to the Continental Congress. Of these, one was too ill to serve ; of the rest, "Franklin stood alone as the unhesitating champion of independence ; *the majority remained to the last its opponents.* On the 9th, Dickenson reported and carried the following instructions to the Pennsylvania delegates : 'We direct that you exert your utmost endeavours to agree upon and recommend such measures as you shall judge to afford the best prospect of obtaining redress of American grievances, and restoring that union and harmony between Great Britain and the colonies so essential to the welfare and happiness of both countries. Though the oppressive measures of the British Parliament and Administration have compelled us to resist their violence by force of arms, yet we strictly enjoin you, that you, in behalf of this colony, dissent from and utterly reject any propositions, should such be made, that may cause or lead to a separation from our mother country, or a change of the form of this government.' The influence of the measure was wide. Delaware was naturally swayed by the example of its more powerful neighbour ; the party of the proprietary of Maryland took courage ; in a few weeks the Assembly of New Jersey, in like manner, held back the delegates of that province by an equally stringent declaration."* After stating that the Legislature of Pennsylvania, before its adjournment, adopted rules for the volunteer battalions, and appropriated eighty thousand pounds in provincial paper money to defray the expenses of military preparation, Mr. Bancroft adds, that "extreme discontent led the more determined to expose through the press the trimming

---

* Bancroft's History United States, Vol. VIII., Chap. xlix., pp. 138, 139.

of the Assembly; and Franklin encouraged Thomas Paine, an emigrant from England of the previous year, who was master of a singularly lucid and attractive style, to write an appeal to the people of America in favour of independence."* "Yet the men of that day had been born and educated as subjects of a king; to them the House of Hanover was a symbol of religious toleration, the British Constitution another word for the security of liberty and property under a representative government. They were not yet enemies of monarchy; they had as yet turned away from considering whether well-organized civil institutions could not be framed for wide territories without a king; and in the very moment of resistance they longed to escape the necessity of a revolution. Zubly, a delegate from Georgia, a Swiss by birth, declared in his place 'a republic to be little better than a government of devils;' shuddered at the idea of separation from Britain as fraught with greater evils than had yet been suffered."†

---

* In this appeal of Paine's, *monarchy* was for the first time attacked in America, except by the rulers of the Massachusetts colony, under the first Charter. Some of Paine's words were, that "In the early ages of the world, mankind were equals in the order of creation; the heathen introduced the government of kings, which the will of the Almighty, as declared by Gideon and the prophet Samuel, expressly disapproved. To the evil of monarchy we have added that of hereditary succession; and as the first is a lessening of ourselves, so the second might put posterity under the government of a rogue or a fool. Nature disapproves it, otherwise she would not so frequently turn it into ridicule. England since the Conquest hath known some few good monarchs, but groaned beneath a much larger number of bad ones." "In short, monarchy and succession have laid not England only, but the world, in blood and ashes." (Bancroft's History of the United States, Vol. VIII., Chap. xlix., pp. 236, 237.)

† But though Mr. Dickenson had done more than any other man in America to vindicate colonial rights and expose the unconstitutional character of the acts of the British Ministry and Parliament, he was opposed to a declaration of independence, like a majority of the colonists; yet he advocated resistance by force against submission to the Boston Port Bill, and the suspension of the Massachusetts Charter, and both without a trial, as in similar cases even under the despotic reigns of Charles the First and Second. Mr. Bancroft blames Mr. Dickenson severely for the instructions of the Pennsylvania Legislature to its nine delegates in the Continental Congress in October, 1775; but, writing under the date of the previous May, Mr. Bancroft says: "Now that the Charter of Massachusetts had been impaired, Dickenson did not ask merely relief from parliamentary taxation; he required

The exact time when the minds of the leading men in the colonies, and the colonists, began to undergo a transition from the defence of their constitutional liberties as British subjects to their security by declaring independence of Great Britain, seems to have been the receipt of the intelligence of the scornful rejection of the second petition of Congress, and of the King's proclamation, putting the advocates of colonial rights out of the protection of the law, by declaring them rebels, and requiring all public officers, civil and military, to apprehend them with a view to their punishment as such. Some individuals of eminence in the colonies had previously despaired of reconciliation with England, and had regarded Independency as the only hope of preserving their liberties, but these were the exceptions: the leaders and colonists generally still hoped for reconciliation with England by having their liberties restored, as they were recognized and enjoyed at the close of the French war in 1763. They had regarded the King as their Father and Friend, and laid all the blame upon his Ministers and Parliament, against whose acts they appealed to the King for the protection of their rights and liberties. But it gradually transpired, from year to year, that the King himself was the real prompter of these oppressive acts and measures, and though long discredited,* yet when the King ostentatiously announced himself as the champion of the Parliament and its acts, his determination to enforce by the whole power of the realm, the absolute submission of the colonies; and when all this intelligence, so often repeated and doubted, was confirmed by the

security against the encroachments of Parliament on charters and laws. The distinctness with which he spoke satisfied Samuel Adams himself, who has left on record that the Farmer was a thorough Bostonian." (History of the United States, Vol. VII., Chap. xxxvi., p. 377.)

* As late as May, 1775, after the bloody affair of Concord and Lexington, Mr. Bancroft remarks :

" The delegates of New England, especially those from Massachusetts, could bring no remedy to the prevailing indecision (i.. the Continental Congress), for they suffered from insinuations that they represented a people who were republican in their principles of government and fanatics in religion, and they wisely avoided the appearance of importunity or excess in their demands.

" As the delegates from South Carolina declined the responsibility of a decision which would have implied an abandonment of every hope of peace, there could be no efficient opposition to the policy of *again seeking the restora-*

issue of the Royal proclamation, which it was known and admitted that the King himself had urged and hastened, the most sanguine advocates and friends of reconciliation were astounded and began to despair; and the idea of independence was now boldly advocated by the press.

In 1773, Dr. Franklin said to the Earl of Chatham, "I never heard from any person the least expression of a wish for separation." In October, 1774, Washington wrote, "I am well satisfied that no such thing as independence is desired by any thinking man in America; on the contrary, that it is the ardent wish of the warmest advocates for liberty that peace. and tranquillity, on constitutional grounds, may be restored, and the horrors of civil discord prevented." Jefferson stated, "Before the 19th of April, 1775 (the day of General Gage's attack on Concord, and the Lexington affair), I never heard a whisper of a disposition to separate from Great Britain." And thirty-seven days before that wanton aggression of General. Gage,* John Adams, in Boston, published:

"That there are any who pant after independence is the greatest slander on the Province." Sparks, in a note entitled "American Independence," in the second volume of the Writings

tion of American liberty through the mediation of the King. This plan had the great advantage over the suggestion of an immediate separation from Britain, that it could be boldly promulgated, and was *in harmony with the general wish; for the people of the continent,* taken collectively, *had not as yet ceased to cling to their old relations with their parent land;* and so far from scheming independence, now that independence was become inevitable, they postponed the irrevocable decree and still longed that the necessity for it might pass by." (History of the United States, Vol. VII., Chap. xxxvi., pp. 376, 377.)

* Lord Dartmouth (the Secretary of State for the Colonies) said: "The attempts of General Gage at Concord are fatal. By that unfortunate event the happy moment of advantage is lost."

"The condemnation of Gage was universal. Many people in England were from that moment convinced that the Americans could not be reduced, and that England must concede their independence. The British force, if drawn together, could occupy but a few insulated points, while all the rest would be free; if distributed, would be continually harassed and destroyed in detail.

"These views were frequently brought before Lord North. That statesman was endowed with strong affections, and was happy in his family, in his fortune and abilities; in his public conduct, he and he alone among Ministers was sensible to the reproaches of remorse; and he cherished the sweet feel-of Washington, remarks: "It is not easy to determine at what precise date the idea of independence was first entertained by the principal persons in America." Samuel Adams, after the events of the 19th of April, 1775, was prepared to advocate it. Members of the Provincial Congress of New Hampshire were of the same opinion. President Dwight, of Yale College (Travels in New England and New York, Vol. I., p. 159), says: "In the month of July, 1775, I urged in conversation with several gentlemen of great respectability, firm Whigs, and my intimate friends, the importance and even necessity of a declaration of independence on the part of the colonies, but found them disposed to give me and my arguments a hostile and contemptuous, instead of a cordial reception. These gentlemen may be considered as the representatives of the great body of thinking men of this country." In the note of Sparks are embodied the recollections of Madison, Jay, and others, and the contemporary statements of Franklin and Penn. They are in harmony with the statements and quotations in the text, and sustain the judgment of Dr. Ramsay (History of South Carolina, Vol. I., p. 164), who says: "Till the rejection of the second petition of Congress, the reconciliation with the mother country was the unanimous wish of the Americans generally."*

When Washington heard of the affair of Concord and Lexington, April 19, 1775, he wrote, in his own quiet residence at Mount Vernon, "Unhappy is it to reflect that a brother's sword should be sheathed in a brother's breast, and that the once happy and peaceful plains of America are to be either drenched with blood or inhabited by slaves. Sad alternative! But, can a virtuous man hesitate in his choice?" Mr. Bancroft says: "The reply to Bunker Hill from England reached Washington before the end of September (1775); and the manifest determination of the Ministers to push the war by sea and land, with the utmost vigour, removed from his mind every doubt of the necessity of independence. Such also was the conclu-

ings of human kindness. Appalled at the prospect, he wished to resign. But the King would neither give him release, nor relent towards the Americans. How to subdue the rebels was the subject of consideration." (Bancroft's History of the United States, Vol. VII., Chap. xxxiii., pp. 345, 346.)

* Frothingham's Rise of the American Republic, p. 453, in a note.

sion of Greene; and the army was impatient when any of the chaplains prayed for the King."*

It was thus that King George the Third, by his own acts, lost the confidence and affection of his loyal subjects in America, and hastened a catastrophe of which he had been repeatedly and faithfully warned, and which none deprecated more generally and earnestly than the leaders and inhabitants of the American colonies; but who determined, and openly declared their determination in every petition to the King and Parliament for ten years, that, if necessary, at all hazards, they would maintain and defend their constitutional rights as Englishmen.

Now, at the close of the year 1775, and before entering upon the eventful year of 1776, when the American colonies adopted the Declaration of Independence, let us recapitulate the events which thus brought the mother country and her colonial offspring face to face in armed hostility.

1. No loyalty and affection could be more cordial than that of the American colonies to England at the conquest of Canada from the French, and the peace of Paris between Great Britain and France in 1763. Even the ancient and traditional disaffection of Massachusetts to England had dissolved into feelings of gratitude and respect and avowed loyalty. Indeed, loyalty and attachment to England, and pride in the British Constitution, was the universal feeling of the American colonies at the close of the war which secured North America to England, and for the triumphant termination of which the American colonies had raised and equipped no less than twenty-five thousand men, without whose services the war could not have been accomplished.

---

* History of the United States, Vol. VIII., Chap. xlvii., p. 108.

In November, 1775, Jefferson wrote to a refugee : " It is an immense misfortune to the whole empire to have a king of such a disposition at such a time. We are told, and everything proves it true, that he is the bitterest enemy we have ; his Minister is able, and that satisfies me that ignorance or wickedness somewhere controls him. Our petitions told him, that from our King there was but one appeal. After colonies have drawn the sword, there is but one step more they can take. That step is now pressed upon us by the measures adopted, as if they were afraid we would not take it. There is not in the British Empire a man who more cordially loves union with Great Britain than I do ; but by the God that made me, I will cease to exist before I yield to a connection on such terms as the British Parliament propose ; and in this I speak the sentiments of America."—*Ib.*, p. 143.

2. The first five years of the war with France in America had been disastrous to Great Britain and the colonies, under a corrupt English Administration and incompetent generals; but after the accession of the Earl of Chatham to the Premiership the tide of war in America turned in favour of Great Britain by the appointment of able generals—Amherst and Wolfe— and Admiral Boscawen and others, and by adopting constitutional methods to develop the resources of the colonies for the war; and in two years the French power was crushed and ceased to exist in America. When the Crown, through its Prime Minister, made requisition to the Colonial Legislatures for money and men, as was the usage in England, the Colonial Legislatures responded by granting large sums of money, and sending into the field more than twenty thousand soldiers, who, by their skill, courage, and knowledge of the country, and its modes of travel and warfare, constituted the pioneers, skirmishers, and often the strongest arm of the Britsh army, and largely contributed in every instance to its most splendid victories. Their loyalty, bravery, and patriotism extracted grateful acknowledgments in both Houses of Parliament, and even from the Throne; while the colonies as cordially acknowledged the essential and successful assistance of the mother country. At no period of colonial history was there so deep-felt, enthusiastic loyalty to the British Constitution and British connection as at the close of the war between France and England in 1763. But in the meantime George the Third, after his accession to the throne in 1760, determined not only to *reign over* but to *rule* his kingdom, both at home and abroad. He ignored party government or control in Parliament; he resolved to be his own Prime Minister—in other words, to be despotic; he dismissed the able and patriotic statesmen who had wiped off the disgrace inflicted on British arms and prestige during the five years of the French and Indian war in the American colonies, and had given America to England, and called men one after another to succeed them, who, though in some instances they were men of ability, and in one or two instances were men of amiable and Christian character, were upon the whole the most unscrupulous and corrupt statesmen that ever stood at the head of public affairs in England, and the two Parliaments elected under their auspices were the most

venal ever known in British history. The King regarded as a
personal enemy any member of Parliament who opposed his
policy, and hated any Minister of State (and dismissed him as soon
as possible) who offered advice to, instead of receiving it from,
his Royal master and implicitly obeying it ; and the Ministers
whom he selected were too subservient to the despotism and
caprices of the Royal will, at the frequent sacrifice of their
own convictions and the best interests of the empire.

For more than a hundred years the colonies had provided for
and controlled their own civil, judicial, and military administration of government, and when the King required special
appropriations of money and raising of men during the Seven
Years' War, requisitions were made by his Ministers in his
name, through the Governors, to the several Provincial Legislatures, which responded with a liberality and patriotism that
excited surprise in England at the extent of their resources in
both money and men. But this very development of colonial
power excited jealousy and apprehensions in England, instead
of sympathy and respect, and within a twelvemonth after the
treaty of Paris, in 1763, the King and his Ministers determined
to discourage and crush all military spirit and organization in
the colonies, to denude the Colonial Legislatures of all the attributes of British constitutional free government, by the British
Government not only appointing the Governors of the colonies,
but by appointing the members of one branch of the Legislature, by appointing Judges as well as other public officers to
hold office during the pleasure of the Crown, and fixing and
paying their salaries out of moneys paid by colonists, but levied
not by the Colonial Legislatures, but by Acts of the British
Parliament, contrary to the usage of more than a century ; and
under the pretext of *defending* the colonies, but really for the
purpose of ruling them ; proposing an army of 20 regiments of
500 men each, to be raised and officered in England, from the
penniless and often worse than penniless of the scions and relatives of Ministers and members of Parliament, and billeted upon
the colonies at the estimated expense of £100,000 sterling a
year, to be paid by the colonies out of the proceeds of the
Stamp and other Acts of Parliament passed for the purpose of
raising a revenue in the colonies for the support of its civil and
military government.

No government is more odious and oppressive than that which has the mockery of the form of free government without its powers or attributes. An individual despot may be reached, terrified, or persuaded, but a despotic oligarchy has no restraint of individual responsibility, and is as intangible in its individuality as it is grasping and heartless in its acts and policy. For governors, all executive officers, judges, and legislative councillors appointed from England, together with military officers, 20 regiments all raised in England, the military commanders taking precedence of the local civil authorities, all irresponsible to the colonists, yet paid by them out of taxes imposed upon them without their consent, is the worst and most mercenary despotism that can be conceived. The colonists could indeed continue to elect representatives to one branch of their Legislatures; but the Houses of Assembly thus elected were powerless to protect the liberties or properties of their constituents, subject to abuse and dissolution in case of their remonstrating against unconstitutional acts of tyranny or advocating rights.

Such was the system passionately insisted upon by King George the Third to establish his absolute authority over his colonial subjects in America, and such were the methods devised by his venal Ministers and Parliament to provide places and emoluments for their sons, relatives, and dependents, at the expense of the colonists, to say nothing of the consequences to the virtue of colonial families from mercenary public officers and an immoral soldiery.

The American colonies merited other treatment than that which they received at the hands of the King and Parliament from 1763 to 1776; and they would have been unworthy of the name of Englishmen, and of the respect of mankind, had they yielded an iota of the constitutional rights of British subjects, for which they so lawfully and manfully contended. What the old colonies contended for during that eventful period was substantially the same as that which has been demanded and obtained during the present century by the colonies of the Canadian Dominion, under the names of "local self-government" or "responsible government," and which is now so fully enjoyed by them. Had Queen Victoria reigned in England instead of George the Third, there would have been no Declaration of Independence, no civil war in America, but the thirteen American provinces would have remained as affectionately united to the mother country, and as free as are the provinces of the Canadian Dominion at this day.

George the Third seems to me to have been, before and during the American Revolution, the worst Sovereign for the colonies that ever occupied the throne of England; but after and since that revolution he was the best of Sovereigns for the remaining British colonies of North America. He learned lessons during that revolution which essentially changed his character as the ruler of colonies, though I am not aware that he ever formally confessed the change through which he had passed. It is therefore quite reconcilable that he should be regarded by the old American colonies, now the United States, as a tyrant, while his name is revered and loved by the colonists of the Canadian Dominion as the Father of his people.

CHAPTER XXIV.

1775 AND BEGINNING OF 1776—PREPARATION IN ENGLAND TO REDUCE THE COLONISTS TO ABSOLUTE SUBMISSION—SELF-ASSERTED AUTHORITY OF PARLIAMENT.

THE eventful year of 1775—the year preceding that of the American Declaration of Independence—opened with increased and formidable preparations on the part of England to reduce the American colonies to absolute submission. The ground of this assumption of absolute power over the colonies had no sanction in the British Constitution, much less in the history of the colonies; it was a simple declaration or declaratory Bill by the Parliament itself, in 1764, of its right to bind the colonies in all cases whatsoever, and no more a part of the British Constitution than any declaration of Parliament in the previous century of its authority over the monarchy and the constitution and existence of the House of Lords. Assuming and declaring an authority over the American colonies which Parliament had never before, and which it has never since exercised, and which no statesman or political writer of repute at this day regards as constitutional, Parliament proceeded to tax the colonies without their consent, to suspend the legislative powers of the New York Legislature, to close the port of Boston, to annul and change all that was free in the Charter Government of Massachusetts, to forbid the New England colonies the fisheries of Newfoundland, and afterwards to prohibit to all the colonies commerce with each other and with foreign countries; to denounce, as in the Royal Speech to Parliament of the previous October, as "rebellion," remonstrances against and opposition to these arbitrary and cruel enactments; to appeal to Holland and Russia (but in vain) for the aid of foreign soldiers, and to hire of German blood-trading princes seventeen thousand mercenary soldiers to butcher British subjects in the colonies, even to liberate slaves for the murder of their masters, and to employ savage Indians to slaughter men, women, and children.

All this was done by the King and his servants against the colonies before the close of the year 1775, while they still disclaimed any design or desire for independence, and asked for nothing more than they enjoyed in 1763, after they had given the noblest proof of liberality and courage, to establish and maintain British supremacy in America during the seven years' war between England and France, and enjoyed much less of that local self-government, immunity, and privilege which every inhabitant of the Canadian Dominion enjoys at this day.

During that French war, and for a hundred years before, the colonists had provided fortresses, artillery, arms, and ammunition for their own defence; they were practised marksmen, far superior to the regular soldiery of the British army, with the character and usages of which they had become familiar. They offered to provide for their own defence as well as for the support of their civil government, both of which the British Government requires of the provinces of the Canadian Dominion, but both of which were denied to the old provinces of America, after the close of the seven years' war with France. The King and his Ministers not only opposed the colonies providing for their own defence, but ordered the seizure of their magazines, cannon, and arms. General Gage commenced this kind of provocation and attack upon the colonists and their property; seized the arms of the inhabitants of Boston; spiked their cannon at night on Fort Hill; seized by night, also, 13 tons of colonial powder stored at Charleston; sent by night an expedition of eight hundred troops, twenty miles to Concord, to seize military provisions, but they were driven back to Lexington with the loss of 65 killed and 180 wounded, and on the part of the colonists 50 killed and 34 wounded. This was the commencement of a bloody revolution, and was soon followed by the battle of Bunker's Hill, in which, "on the part of the British," says Holmes, "about 3,000 men were engaged in this action; and their killed and wounded amounted to 1,054. The number of

Americans in this engagement was 1,500; and their killed, wounded, and missing amounted to 453."*

In each of these conflicts the attack was made and the first shot was fired on the part of the British troops.   Of this, abundant evidence was forthwith collected and sent to England. It was carefully inculcated that in no instance should the colonists attack or fire the first shot upon the British troops; that in all cases they should act upon the defensive, as their cause was the defence of their rights and property; but when attacked, they retaliated with a courage, skill, and deadly effect that astonished their assailants, and completely refuted the statements diligently made in England and circulated in the army, that the colonists had no military qualities and would never face British troops.†

* Annals, etc., Vol. II., p. 211.   The annalist adds in a note, that "Of the British 226 were killed and 828 wounded ; 19 commissioned officers being among the former, and 70 among the latter.   Of the Americans, 139 were killed and 314 wounded and missing.   The only provincial officers of distinction lost were General Joseph Warren, Col. Gardner, Lieut.-Col. Parker, and Messrs. Moore and McClany."

† The royal historian, Andrews, gives the following or English account of the battle of Bunker's Hill, together with the circumstances which preceded and followed it :

(PRELIMINARY STATEMENTS.)

"On the 12th of June (1775), a proclamation was issued by the British Government at Boston, offering a pardon, in the King's name, to all who laid down their arms and returned to their homes and occupations.   Two persons only were excepted—Mr. Samuel Adams and Mr. John Hancock—whose guilt was represented as too great and notorious to escape punishment.   All who did not accept of this offer, or who assisted, abetted, or corresponded with them, were to be deemed guilty of treason and rebellion, and treated accordingly. By this proclamation it was declared that as the Courts of Judicature were shut, martial law should take place, till a due course of justice could be re-established.

"But this act of Government was as little regarded as the preceding.   To convince the world how firmly they were determined to persevere in their measures, and how small an impression was made by the menaces of Britain, Mr. Hancock, immediately after his proscription, was chosen President of the Congress.   The proclamation had no other effect than to prepare people's minds for the worst that might follow.

The reinforcements arrived from Britain ; the eagerness of the British military to avail themselves of their present strength, and the position of the Provincials, concurred to make both parties diligent in their prepara-

About the same time that General Gage thus commenced war upon the people of Massachusetts, who so nobly responded in defence of their constitutional rights, Lord Dunmore, Governor of Virginia, committed similar outrages upon the traditionally loyal Virginians, who, as Mr. Bancroft says, " were accustomed to associate all ideas of security in their political rights with

tion for action. It was equally the desire of both: the first were earnest to exhibit an unquestionable testimony of their superiority, and to terminate the quarrel by one decisive blow ; the others were no less willing to come to a second engagement (the first being that of Concord and Lexington), from a confidence they would be able to convince their enemies that they would find the subjugation of America a much more difficult task than they had promised themselves.

" Opposite to the northern shore of the peninsula upon which Boston stands, lies Charleston, divided from it by a river (Mystic) about the breadth of the Thames at London Bridge. Neither the British nor Provincial troops had hitherto bethought themselves of securing this place. In its neighbourhood, a little to the east, is a high ground called Bunker's Hill, which overlooks and commands the whole town of Boston.

" In the night of the 16th of June, a party of the Provincials took possession of this hill, and worked with so much industry and diligence, that by break of day they had almost completed a redoubt, together with a strong intrenchment, reaching half a mile, as far as the River Mystic to the east. As soon as discovered they were plied with a heavy and incessant fire from the ships and floating batteries that surrounded the neck on which Charleston is situated, and from the cannon planted on the nearest eminence on the Boston side.

" This did not, however, prevent them from continuing their work, which they had entirely finished by mid-day, when it was found necessary to take more effectual methods to dislodge them.

" For this purpose a considerable body was landed at the foot of Bunkers Hill, under the command of General Howe and General Pigot. The first was to attack the Provincial lines, the second the redoubt. The British troops advanced with great intrepidity, but on their approach were received with a fire behind from the intrenchments, that continued pouring during a full half hour upon them like a stream. The execution it did was terrible ; some of the brave stand oldest officers declared that, for the time it lasted, it was the hottest service they had ever seen. General Howe stood for some moments almost alone, the officers and soldiers about him being nearly all slain or disabled ; his intrepidity and presence of mind were remarkable on this trying occasion.

" General Pigot, on the left, was in the meantime engaged with the Provincials who had thrown themselves into Charleston, as well as with the redoubt, and met with the same reception as the right. Though he conducted his attack with great skill and courage, the incessant destruction made among the

the dynasty of Hanover, and had never, even in thought, desired to renounce their allegiance. They loved to consider themselves an integral part of the British empire. The distant life of landed proprietors, in solitary mansion-houses, favoured independence of thought; but it also generated an aristocracy, which differed widely from the simplicity and equality of New England. Educated in the Anglican Church, no religious zeal had imbued them with a fixed hatred of kingly power; no deep-seated antipathy to a distinction of ranks, no theoretic

troops threw them at first into some disorder; but General Clinton coming up with a reinforcement, they quickly rallied and attacked the works with such fury that the Provincials were not able to resist them, and retreated beyond the neck of land that leads into Charleston.

"This was the bloodiest engagement during the whole war. The loss of the British troops amounted in killed and wounded to upwards of 1,000. Among the first were 19, and among the last 70 officers. Colonel Abercrombie, Major Pitcairn, of the Marines, and Majors Williams and Spenlowe, men of distinguished bravery, fell in this action, which, though it terminated to the advantage of the King's forces, cost altogether a dreadful price.

"The loss on the Provincial side, according to their account, did not exceed 500. This might be true, as they fought behind intrenchments, part of which were cannon proof, and where it was not possible for the musketry to annoy them. This accounts no less for the numbers they destroyed, to which the expertness of their marksmen chiefly contributed. To render the dexterity of these completely effectual, muskets ready loaded were handed to them as fast as they could be discharged, that they might lose no time in reloading them, and they took aim chiefly at the officers. * * *

"The great slaughter occasioned on the left of the British troops, from the houses in Charleston, obliged them to set fire to that place. The Provincials defended it for some time with much obstinacy, but it was quickly reduced to ashes; and when deprived of that cover, they were immediately compelled to retire.

"But notwithstanding the honour of the day remained to the British troops, the Americans boasted that the real advantages were on their side. They had, said they, so much weakened their enemies in this engagement, as to put an entire stop to their operations. Instead of coming forth and improving their pretended victory, they did not dare to venture out of the trenches and fortifications they had constructed round Boston.

"The only apparent benefit gained by the troops was that they kept possession of the ground whereon Charleston had stood; they fortified it on every side, in order to secure themselves from the sudden attacks that were daily threatened from so numerous a force as that which now invested Boston. * * *

"The Provincials, on the other hand, to convince the troops how little their success had availed them, raised intrenchments on a height opposite

zeal for the introduction of a republic, no speculative fanaticism drove them to a restless love of change. They had, on the contrary, the greatest aversion to a revolution, and abhorred the dangerous experiment of changing their form of government without some absolute necessity.*

But the Virginians, like all true loyalists, were "loyal to the people's part of the Constitution as well as to that which pertains to the Sovereign."† To intimidate them, Dunmore issued

Charleston, intimating to them that they were ready for another Bunker's Hill business whenever they thought proper, and were no less willing than they to make another trial of skill.

" Their boldness increased to a degree that astonished the British officers, who had, unhappily, been taught to believe them a contemptible enemy, averse to the dangers of war, and incapable of the regular operations of an army. The skirmishes were now renewed in Boston Bay. The necessities of the garrison occasioned several attempts to carry off the remaining stock of cattle and other articles of provision the islands might contain. But the Provincials, who were better acquainted with the navigation of the bay, landed on these islands, in spite of the precaution of the numerous shipping, and destroyed or carried off whatever could be of use; they even ventured so far as to burn the light-house, situated at the entrance of the harbour, and afterwards made prisoners of a number of workmen that had been sent to repair it, together with a party of marines that guarded them." (Dr. Andrews' History of the Late War, etc., Vol. I., Chap. xiii., pp. 300—306, published under royal authority in 1785.)

* History of the United States, Vol. VII., Chap. xxv., pp. 271, 272.

† The Secretary of State had instructed Lord Dunmore to call the Assembly together, in order to submit to them a "conciliatory proposition," as it was called, which Lord North had introduced into Parliament—a proposition calculated to divide the colonies, and then reduce each of them to servitude; but the colonies saw the snare, and every one of them rejected the insidious offer. Lord Dunmore, in obedience to his instructions, assembled for the last time the Virginia House of Burgesses in June, 1775, to deliberate and decide upon Lord North's proposition. But while the Burgesses were deliberating upon the subject submitted to them, Lord Dunmore, agitated by his own fears, left with his family the seat of government, and went on board a ship of war. The House of Burgesses, however, proceeded in their deliberations ; referred the subject to a Committee, which presented a report prepared by Mr. Jefferson, and adopted by the House, as a final answer to Lord North's proposal. They said, " Next to the possession of liberty, they should consider a reconciliation as the greatest of human blessings, but that the resolution of the House of Commons only changed the form of oppression, without lightening its burdens ; that government in the colonies was instituted not for the British Parliament, but for the colonies them-

proclamations, and threatened freeing the slaves against their masters. On the night of the 20th of April he sent a body of marines, in the night, to carry off a quantity of gunpowder belonging to the colony, and stored in its magazine at Williamsburg. As soon as this arbitrary seizure of the colony's property became known, drums sounded alarm throughout the city of Williamsburg, the volunteer company rallied under arms, and the inhabitants assembled for consultation, and at their request the Mayor and Corporation waited upon the Governor and asked him his motives for carrying off their powder privately "by an armed force, particularly at a time when they were

selves; that the British Parliament had no right to meddle with their Constitution, or to prescribe either the number or the pecuniary appointments of their officers; that they had a right to give their money without coercion, and from time to time; that they alone were the judges, alike of the public exigencies and the ability of the people; that they contended not merely for the mode of raising their money, but for the freedom of granting it; that the resolve to forbear levying pecuniary taxes still left unrepealed the Acts restraining trade, altering the form of government of Massachusetts, changing the government of Quebec, enlarging the jurisdiction of Courts of Admiralty, taking away the trial by jury, and keeping up standing armies; that the invasion of the colonies with large armaments by sea and land was a style of asking gifts not reconcilable to freedom; that the resolution did not propose to the colonies to lay open a free trade with all the world; that as it involved the interests of all the other colonies, they were in honour bound to share one fate with them; that the Bill of Lord Chatham on the one part, and the terms of Congress on the other, would have formed a basis for negotiation and a reconciliation; that leaving the final determination of the question to the General Congress, they will weary the King with no more petitions—the British nation with no more appeals." "What then," they ask, "remains to be done?" and they answer, "That we commit our injuries to the justice of the even-handed Being who doeth no wrong."

When the Earl of Shelburne read Mr. Jefferson's report, he said: "In my life I was never more pleased with a State paper than with the Assembly of Virginia's discussion of Lord North's proposition. It is masterly. But what I fear is, that the evil is irretrievable."

"At Versailles, the French Minister, Vergennes, was equally attracted by the wisdom and dignity of the document. He particularly noticed the insinuation that a compromise might be effected on the basis of the modification of the Navigation Acts; and saw so many ways opened of settling every difficulty, that it was long before he could persuade himself that the infatuation of the British Ministry was so blind as to neglect them all." (Bancroft's History of the United States, Vol. VII., Chap. xxxvii., pp. 386—388.)

30

apprehensive of an insurrection among their slaves;" and they demanded that the powder should be forthwith restored.

Lord Dunmore first answered evasively; but learning that the citizens had assembled under arms, he raged and threatened. He said: "The whole country can easily be made a solitude; and by the living God, if any insult is offered to me, or to those who have obeyed my orders, I will declare freedom to the slaves, and lay the town in ashes."*

Lord Dunmore at the same time wrote to the English Secretary of State: "With a small body of troops and arms, I could raise such a force among *Indians, Negroes,* and other persons, as would soon reduce the refractory people of this colony to obedience.'

Yet, after all his boasting and threats, the value of the powder thus unlawfully seized was restored to the colony. Lord Dunmore, agitated with fears, as most tyrants are, left the Government House from fear of the people excited by his own conduct towards them, and went on board of the man-of-war ship *Tower,* at York (about 12 miles from Williamsburg, the capital of the Province), thus leaving the colony in the absolute possession of its own inhabitants, giving as a reason for his flight, his apprehension of "falling a sacrifice to the daringness and atrociousness, the blind and unmeasurable fury of great numbers of the people;" and the assurance of the very people whom he feared as to his personal safety and that of his family, and the repeated entreaties of the Legislative Assembly that he

---

* Bancroft's History of the United States, Vol. VII., Chap. xxv., p. 276.

"The offer of freedom to the negroes came very oddly from the representative of the nation which had sold them to their present masters, and of the King who had been displeased with the colony for its desire to tolerate that inhuman traffic no longer ; and it was but a sad resource for a commercial metropolis, to keep a hold on its colony by letting loose slaves against its own colonists."—*Ib.*, p. 276.

"Dunmore's menace to raise the standard of a servile insurrection and set the slaves upon their masters, with British arms in their hands, filled the South with horror and alarm. Besides, the retreat of the British troops from Concord raised the belief that the American forces were invincible ; and the spirit of resistance had grown so strong, that some of the Burgesses appeared in the uniform of the recently instituted provincial troops, wearing a hunting shirt of coarse linen over their clothes, and a woodman's axe by their sides."
—*Ib.*, pp. 384, 385.

would return to land, with assurance of perfect safety from injury or insult, could not prevail upon Lord Dunmore to return to the Government House, or prevent him from attempting to govern the ancient Dominion of Virginia from ships of war. He seized a private printing press, with two of its printers, at the town of Norfolk, and was thus enabled to issue his proclamations and other papers against the inhabitants whom he had so grossly insulted and injured.*

"In October" (1775), says Bancroft, "Dunmore repeatedly landed detachments to seize arms wherever he could find them. Thus far Virginia had not resisted the British by force. The war began in that colony with the defence of Hampton, a small village at the end of the isthmus between York and James rivers. An armed sloop had been driven on its shore in a very violent gale; its people took out of her six swivels and other stores, made some of her men prisoners, and then set her on fire. Dunmore blockaded the port; they called to their assistance a company of "Shirtmen," as the British called the Virginia regulars, from the hunting shirt which was their uniform, and another company of minute men, besides a body of militia.

"On the 26th Dunmore sent some of the tenders close into Hampton Roads to destroy the town. The guard marched out to repel them, and the moment they came within gunshot, George Nicholas, who commanded the Virginians, fired his musket at one of the tenders; it was the first gun fired in Virginia against the British. His example was followed by his party. Retarded by boats which had been sunk across the Channel, the British on that day vainly attempted to land.

---

* "Meantime, Dunmore, driven from the land of Virginia, maintained command of the water by means of a flotilla composed of the *Mercury*, of 24 guns; the *Kingfisher*, of 16; the *Otter*, of 14, with other ships and light vessels, and tenders which he had engaged in the King's service. At Norfolk, a town of about 6,000 inhabitants, a newspaper was published by John Holt. About noon on the last day of September (1775), Dunmore, finding fault with its favouring (according to him) 'sedition and rebellion,' sent on shore a small party, who, meeting with no resistance, seized and brought off two printers and all the materials of the printing office, so that he could publish from his ship a Gazette on the side of the King. The outrage, as we shall see, produced retaliation." (Bancroft's History of the United States, Vol. VIII., Chap. lv., pp. 220, 221.)

The following night the Culpepper riflemen were despatched to the aid of Hampton; and William Woodford, Colonel of the 2nd Regiment of Virginia, was sent by the Committee of Safety from Williamsburg to take the direction. The next day the British, having cut their way through the sunken boats, renewed the attack; but the riflemen poured upon them a heavy fire, killing a few and wounding more. One of the tenders was taken, with its armament and seven seamen; the rest were with difficulty towed out of the creek. The Virginians lost not a man. This was the first battle of the revolution in the ancient Dominion, and its honours belonged to the Virginians."*

In consequence of this failure of Lord Dunmore to burn the town of Hampton, he proclaimed martial law and freedom to the slaves. The English Annual Register states that, " In

* Bancroft's History of the United States, Vol. VIII., Chap. lv., pp. 221, 222.

The English Annual Register of 1776 states as follows the policy of Lord Dunmore, culminating in the successful defence of Hampton and the repulse of his ships :

" Whether Lord Dunmore expected that any extraordinary advantages might be derived from an insurrection of the slaves, or that he imagined there was a much greater number of people in the colony who were satisfied with the present system of government than really was the case (*a mistake, and an unfortunate one, which, like an epidemical distemper, seems to have spread through all our official departments in America*)—upon whatever grounds he proceeded, he determined, though he relinquished his government, not to abandon his hopes, nor entirely to lose sight of the country which he had governed. He, accordingly, being joined by those friends of government who had rendered themselves too obnoxious to the people to continue with safety in the country, as well as by a number of runaway negroes, and supported by the frigates of war which were upon the station, endeavoured to establish such a marine force as would enable him, by means of the noble rivers, which render the most valuable parts of that rich country accessible by water, to be always at hand and ready to profit by any favourable occasion that offered.

" Upon this or some similar system he by degrees equipped and armed a number of vessels of different kinds and sizes, *in one of which he constantly resided, never setting his foot on shore but in a hostile manner.* The force thus put together was, however, *calculated only for depredation,* and never became equal to any essential service. The former, indeed, was in part a matter of necessity; for as the people on shore would not supply those on board with provisions or necessaries, they must either starve or provide them by force. * * These proceedings occasioned the sending of some detachments of the new-raised forces of the colonists to protect their coasts, and from these ensued a small, mis-

consequence of the repulse (at Hampton) a proclamation was issued (Nov. 7th) by the Governor, dated on board the ship *William*, off Norfolk, declaring, that as the civil law was at present insufficient to prevent and punish treason and traitors, martial law should take place, and be executed throughout the colony; and requiring all persons capable of bearing arms to repair to his Majesty's standard, or to be considered as traitors." He also declared all indentured servants, negroes, and others, appertaining to rebels, who were able and willing to bear arms, and who joined his Majesty's forces, to be free.

"The measure for emancipating the negroes," continues the Annual Register, "excited less surprise, and probably had less effect, from its being so long threatened and apprehended, than if it had been more immediate and unexpected. It was, however, received with the greatest horror in all the colonies, and has been severely condemned elsewhere, as tending to loosen the bands of society, to destroy domestic security, and encourage the most barbarous of mankind to the commission of the most horrible crimes and the most inhuman cruelties; that it was confounding the innocent with the guilty, and exposing those who were the best of friends to the Government, to the same loss of property, danger, and destruction with the most incorrigible rebels."*

chievous, predatory war, incapable of affording honour or benefit, and in which, at length, every drop of water and every necessary was purchased at the price or risk of blood.

"During this state of hostility, Lord Dunmore procured a few soldiers from different parts, with whose assistance an attempt (Oct. 25th) was made to burn a post town in an important situation called Hampton. It seems the inhabitants had some previous suspicion of the design, for they had sunk boats in the entrance of the harbour and thrown such other obstacles in the way as rendered the approach of the ships, and consequently a landing, impracticable on the day when the attack was commenced. The ships cut a passage through the boats in the night, and began to cannonade the town furiously in the morning; but at this critical period the townspeople were relieved from their apprehensions and danger by the arrival of a detachment of rifle and minute men from Williamsburg, who had marched all night to their assistance. These, joined with the inhabitants, attacked the ships so vigorously with their small arms that they were obliged precipitately to quit their station, with the loss of some men and of a tender, which was taken." (Annual Register, Vol. XIX., Fourth Edition, pp. 26, 27.)

. * English Annual Register, Vol. XIX.

It will be observed in Lord Dunmore's proclamation, as also in the English Register, and I may add in General Stedman's History of the American War, and in other histories of those times, the terms "rebels," "treason," and "traitors" are applied to those who, at that time, as in all previous years, disclaimed all desire of separation from England, and only claimed those constitutional rights of Englishmen to which they were as lawfully entitled as the King was to his Crown, and very much more so than Lord Dunmore was entitled to the authority which he was then exercising; for he had been invested with authority to rule according to the Constitution of the colony, but he had set aside the Legislature of the colony, which had as much right to its opinions and the expression of them as he had to his; he had abandoned the legal seat of government, and taken up his residence on board a man-of-war, and employed his time and strength in issuing proclamations against people to whom he had been sent to govern as the representative of a *constitutional* sovereign, and made raids upon their coasts, and burned their towns. In truth, Lord Dunmore and his abettors were the real "rebels" and "traitors," who were committing "treason" against the constitutional rights and liberties of their fellow-subjects, while the objects of their hostility were the real loyalists to the Constitution, which gave to the humblest subject his rights as well as to the Sovereign his prerogatives.

Lord Dunmore, from his ship of war, had no right to rule the rich and most extensive colony in America. He had abandoned his appointed seat of government, and he became the ravager of the coasts and the destroyer of the seaport towns of the ancient dominion. This state of things could not long continue. Lord Dunmore could not subsist his fleet without provisions; and the people would not sell their provisions to those who were seeking to rob them of their liberties and to plunder their property. The English Annual Register observes:

"In the meantime, the people in the fleet were distressed for provisions and necessaries of every sort, and were cut off from every kind of succour from the shore. This occasioned constant bickering between the armed ships and boats, and the forces that were stationed on the coast, particularly at Norfolk. At length, upon the arrival of the *Liverpool* man-of-war from

England, a flag was sent on shore to put the question " whether they would supply his Majesty's ships with provisions ?" which being answered in the negative, and the ships in the harbour being continually annoyed by the fire of the rebels from that part of the town which lay next the water, it was determined to dislodge them by destroying it.   Previous notice being accordingly given to the inhabitants that they might remove from danger, the first day of the New Year (1776) was signalized by the attack, when a violent cannonade from the *Liverpool* frigate, two sloops of war, and the Governor's armed ship the *Dunmore*, seconded by parties of sailors and marines, who landed and set fire to the nearest houses, *soon produced the desired effect, and the whole town was reduced to ashes.*"*

Mr. Bancroft eloquently observes : " In this manner the Royal Governor burned and laid waste the best town in the oldest and

---

* British Annual Register, Vol. XIX., p. 31.

Mr. Bancroft's account of this barbarous conflagration is as follows :

" New Year's day, 1776, was the saddest day that ever broke on the women and children then in Norfolk ; warned of their danger by the commander of the squadron, there was for them no refuge.   The *Kingfisher* was stationed at the upper end of Norfolk ; a little below her, the *Otter ;* Below, in the *Liverpool*, anchored near the middle of the town ; and next him lay the *Dunmore ;* the rest of the fleet was moored in the harbour.   Between three and four in the afternoon, the *Liverpool* opened its fire upon the borough ; the other ships immediately followed the example, and a severe cannonade was begun from about sixty pieces of cannon.   Dunmore then himself, as night was coming on, ordered out several boats to burn warehouses on the wharves ; and hailed to Belew to set fire to a large brig which lay in the dock. All the vessels of the fleet, to show their zeal, sent great numbers of boats on shore to assist in spreading the flames along the river ; and as the buildings were chiefly of pine wood, the conflagration, favoured by the wind, spread with amazing rapidity, and soon became general.   Women and children, mothers with little ones in their arms, were seen by the glare running through the shower of cannon balls to get out of their range.   Two or three persons were hit ; and the scene became one of extreme horror and confusion. Several times the British attempted to land, and once to bring cannon into the street ; but they were driven back by the spirit and conduct of the Americans.   The cannonade did not abate till ten at night ; after a short pause it was renewed, but with less fury, and was kept up till two the next morning.   The flames, which had made their way from street to street, raged for three days ; till four-fifths, or, as some computed, nine-tenths of the houses were reduced to ashes and heaps of ruins." (History of the United States, Vol. VIII., Chap. lvi., pp. 230, 231.)

most loyal colony of England, to which Elizabeth had given a name, and Raleigh devoted his fortune, and Shakspeare and Bacon and Herbert foretokened greatness; a colony where the people themselves had established the Church of England, and where many were still proud of their ancestors, and in the day of the British Commonwealth had been faithful to the line of kings."*

* History of the United States, Vol. VIII., Chap. lvi., p. 231.

The English Annual Register observes : " Such was the fate of the unfortunate town of Norfolk, the most considerable for commerce in the colony, and so growing and flourishing before these unhappy troubles, that in the two years from 1773 to 1775, the rents of the houses increased from £8,000 to £10,000 a year. However just the cause, or urgent the necessity, which induced this measure, it was undoubtedly a grievous and odious task to a Governor to be himself the principal actor in burning and destroying the best town in his government.

" Nor was the situation of other Governors in America much more eligible than that of Lord Dunmore. In South Carolina, Lord William Campbell, having as they said, entered into a negotiation with the Indians for coming in to the support of the Government in that province, and having also succeeded in exciting a number of those back settlers whom we have heretofore seen distinguished in the Carolinas, under the title of Regulators, to espouse the same cause, the discovery of these measures, before they were ripe for execution, occasioned such a ferment among the people, that he thought it necessary to retire from Charleston on board a ship of war in the river, from whence he returned no more to the seat of his government.

" Similar measures were pursued in North Carolina (with the difference that Governor Martin was more active and vigorous in his proceedings), but attended with as little success. The Provincial Congress, Committees, and Governor were in a continual state of the most violent warfare. Upon a number of charges, particularly of fomenting a civil war, and exciting an insurrection among the negroes, he was declared an enemy to America in general, and to that colony in particular, and all persons were forbidden from holding any communication with him. These declarations he answered with a proclamation of uncommon length, which the Provincial Congress resolved to be a false, scandalous, scurrilous and seditious libel, and ordered it to be burned by the hands of the common hangman.

" As the Governor expected, by means of the back settlers, as well as of the Scotch inhabitants and Highland emigrants, who were numerous in the province, to be able to raise a considerable force, he took pains to fortify and arm his palace at Newburn, that it might answer the double purpose of a garrison and a magazine. Before this could be effected, the moving of some cannon excited such a commotion among the people that he found it necessary to abandon the palace and retire on board a sloop-of-war in Cape Fear river. The people upon this occasion discovered

When Washington learned the fate of the rich emporium of his own "country," for so he called Virginia, his breast heaved with waves of anger and grief. "I hope," said he, "this and the threatened devastation of other places will unite the whole country in one indissoluble band against a Government which seems lost to every sense of virtue and those feelings which distinguish a civilized people from the most barbarous savages."

Thus the loyal churchmen of Virginia received the same treatment from Lord Dunmore as did the republican Congregationalists of Massachusetts from General Gage. The loyal Presbyterians of the two Carolinas experienced similar treatment from Governors Campbell and Martin, as stated by the English Annual Register, in the preceding note. The three Southern Governors each fled from their seats of government and betook themselves to ships of war; while Gage was shut up in Boston until his recall to England.

The Southern colonies, with those of New England, shared the same fate of misrepresentation, abuse, and invasion of their rights as British subjects; the flames of discontent were spread through all the colonies by a set of incompetent and reckless Governors, the favourites and tools of perhaps the worst Administration and the most corrupt that ever ruled Great Britain. All the colonies might adopt the language of the last address of the Assembly of Virginia: "We have exhausted every mode of application which our inventions could suggest, as proper and promising. We have decently remonstrated with Parliament; they have added new injuries to the old. We have wearied the King with our supplications; he has not deigned to answer them. We have appealed to the native honour and justice of the British nation; their efforts in our favour have been hitherto

---

powder, shot, ball, and various military stores and implements which had been buried in the palace garden and yard. This served to inflame them exceedingly, every man considering it as if it had been a plot against himself in particular.

"The Provincial Congress published an address to the inhabitants of the British empire, of the same nature with those we have formerly seen to the people of Great Britain and Ireland, containing the same professions of loyalty and affection, and declaring the same earnest desire of a reconciliation." (English Annual Register, Vol. XIX., pp. 31—33.)

ineffectual." At the meeting of Parliament, October 26th, 1775, the King was advised to utter in the Royal speech the usual denunciation against the colonies, but the minority in Parliament (led by Mr. Fox, Mr. Burke, General Conway, and Lord John Cavendish) discussed and denied the statements in the Royal speech, and exhibited the results of the Ministerial warfare against the colonies at the close of the year 1775, the year before the Declaration of Independence. "In this contest," says the Annual Register of 1776, "the speech was taken to pieces, and every part of it most severely scrutinized. The Ministers were charged with having brought their Sovereign into the most disgraceful and unhappy situation of any monarch now living. Their conduct had already wrested the sceptre of America out of his hands. One-half of the empire was lost, and the other thrown into a state of anarchy and confusion. After having spread corruption like a deluge through the land, until all public virtue was lost, and the people were inebriated with vice and profligacy, they were then taught in the paroxysms of their infatuation and madness to cry out for havoc and war. History could not show an instance of such an empire ruined in such a manner. They had lost a greater extent of dominion in the first campaign of a ruinous civil war, which was intentionally produced by their own acts, than the most celebrated conquerors had ever acquired in so short a space of time.

"The speech was said to be composed of a mixture of assumed and false facts, with some general undefined and undisputed axioms, which nobody would attempt to controvert. Of the former, that of charging the colonies with aiming at independence was severely reprehended, as being totally unfounded, being directly contrary to the whole tenor of their conduct, to their most express declarations both by word and writing, and to what every person of any intelligence knew of their general temper and disposition.* But what they never intended, we

---

* General Conway said : " The noble lord who has the direction of the affairs of this country tells you that the Americans aim at Independence. I defy the noble lord, or any other member of this House, to adduce one solid proof of this charge. He says : ' The era of 1763 is the time they wish to recur to, because such a concession on our part would be, in effect, giving up their dependence on this country.' I would ask the noble lord,

may drive them to. They will, undoubtedly, prefer independence to slavery. They will never continue their connection with this country unless they can be connected with its privileges. The continuance of hostility, with the determined refusal of security for these privileges, will infallibly bring on separation.

"The charge of their making professions of duty and proposals of reconciliation only for the insidious purpose of amusing and deceiving, was equally reprobated. It was insisted that, on the contrary, these had from the beginning told them honestly, openly and bravely, without disguise or reserve, and declared to all the world, that they never would submit to be arbitrarily taxed by any body of men whatsoever in which they were not represented. They did not whisper behind the door, nor mince the matter; they told fairly what they would do, and have done, if they were unhappily urged to the last extremity. And that though the Ministers affected not to believe them, it was evident from the armament which they sent out that they did; for however incompetent that armament has been to the end, nobody could admit a doubt that it was intended to oppose men in arms, and to compel by force, the incompetence for its purposes proceeding merely from that blind ignorance and total misconception of American affairs which had operated upon the Ministers in every part of their conduct.

"The shameful accusation," they said, " was only to cover that wretched conduct, and, if possible, to hide or excuse the disgrace and failure that had attended all their measures. Was any other part of their policy more commendable or more successful? Did the cruel and sanguinary laws of the preceding session answer any of the purposes for which they were proposed? Had they in any degree fulfilled the triumphant predictions, had they kept in countenance the overbearing vaunts

Did the people of America set up this claim previous to the year 1763 ? No; they were then peaceful and dutiful subjects. They are still dutiful and obedient. (Here was a murmur of disapprobation.) I repeat my words I think them so inclined ; I am sure they would be so, if they were permitted. The acts they have committed arise from no want of either. They have been forced into them. Taxes have been attempted to be levied on them ; their Charters have been violated, nay, taken away ; administration has attempted to coerce them by the most cruel and oppressive laws."

of the Minister? They have now sunk into the same nothing-
ness with the terrors of that armed force which was to have
looked all America into submission. The Americans have faced
the one, and they despise the injustice and iniquity of the
other. * * *

"The question of rebellion was also agitated; and it was
asserted that the taking up of arms in the defence of just
rights did not, according to the spirit of the British Constitution, come within that comprehension. It was also asserted
with great confidence, that notwithstanding the mischiefs which
the Americans had suffered, and the great losses they had sustained, they would still readily lay down their arms, and return
with the greatest good-will and emulation to their duty, if candid and unequivocal measures were taken for reinstating them
in their former rights; but that this must be done speedily,
before the evils had taken too wide an extent, and the animosity and irritation arising from them had gone beyond a
certain pitch.

"The boasted lenity of Parliament was much lauded. It was
asked whether the Boston Port Bill, by which, without trial or
condemnation, a number of people were stripped of their commercial property, and even deprived of the benefit of their real
estates, was an instance of it? Was it to be found in the
Fishery Bill, by which large countries were cut off from the use
of the elements, and deprived of the provision which nature had
allotted for their sustenance? Or was taking away the Charter
and all the rights of the people without trial or forfeiture the
measure of lenity from which such applause was now sought?
Was the indemnity held out to military power lenity? Was it
lenity to free soldiers from a trial in the country where the
murders with which they should stand charged, when acting
in support of civil and revenue officers, were committed, and
forcing their accusers to come to England at the pleasure of a
governor?" * * *

"The debate in the House of Lords was rendered particularly
remarkable by the unexpected defection of a noble duke (Duke
of Grafton) who had been for some years at the head of the
Administration, had resigned of his own accord at a critical
period, but who had gone with the Government ever since, and
was at this time in high office. The line which he immediately

took was still more alarming to the Administration than the act of defection. Besides a decisive condemnation of all their acts for some time past with respect to America, as well as of the measures now held out by the speech, he declared that he had been deceived and misled upon that subject; that by the with-holding of information, and the misrepresentation of facts, he had been induced to lend his countenance to measures which he never approved; among those was that in particular of coercing America by force of arms, an idea the most distant from his mind and opinions, but which he was blindly led to give a support to from his total ignorance of the true state and disposition of the colonies, and the firm persuasion held out that matters would never come to an extremity of that nature; that an appearance of coercion was all that was required to establish a reconciliation, and that the stronger the Government appeared, and the better it was supported, the sooner all disputes would be adjusted."

"He declared that nothing less than a total repeal of all the American laws which had been passed since 1763 could now restore peace and happiness, or prevent the most destructive and fatal consequences—consequences which could not even be thought of without feeling the utmost degree of grief and horror; that nothing could have brought him out in the present ill state of his health but the fullest conviction of his being right—a knowledge of the critical situation of his country, and a sense of what he owed to his duty and to his conscience; that these operated so strongly upon him, that no state of indisposi-tion, if he were even obliged to come in a litter, should pre-vent his attending to express his utmost disapprobation of the measures which were now being pursued, as well as of those which he understood from the lords in office it was intended still to pursue. He concluded by declaring that if his nearest relations or dearest friends were to be affected by this question, or that the loss of fortune, or of every other thing which he most esteemed, was to be the certain consequence of his present conduct, yet the strong conviction and compulsion operating at once upon his mind and conscience would not permit him to hesitate upon the part which he should take.

"The address was productive of a *protest* signed by *nineteen* lords, in which they combat the civil war as unjust and impolitic in its principles, dangerous in its contingent and fatal in its final consequences.   They censured the calling in of foreign forces to decide domestic quarrels as disgraceful and dangerous. They sum up and conclude the protest by declaring: 'We cannot, therefore, consent to an address which may deceive his Majesty and the public into a belief of the confidence of this House in the present Ministers, who have deceived Parliament, disgraced the nation, lost the colonies, and involved us in a civil war against our clearest interests, and upon the most unjustifiable grounds wantonly spilling the blood of thousands of our fellow-subjects.' "*

* Annual Register, Vol. XIX., Chap. ix., pp. 57, 58, 63, 69, 70, 74, 75.

CHAPTER XXV.

THE ASSEMBLING OF CONGRESS, MAY 10TH, 1776, AND TRANSACTIONS
UNTIL THE DECLARATION OF INDEPENDENCE, THE 4TH OF JULY.

IT was under the circumstances stated in the preceding
chapter, the General Congress, according to adjournment the
previous October, re-assembled in Philadelphia the 10th of May,
1776. The colonies were profoundly convulsed by the transactions which had taken place in Massachusetts, Virginia, North
and South Carolina, by the intelligence from England, that
Parliament had, the previous December, passed an Act to increase the army, that the British Government had largely
increased both the army and navy, and on failure of obtaining
sufficient recruits in England, Scotland, and Ireland, had nego-
tiated with German p·inces, who traded in the blood of their
down-trodden subjects, for seventeen thousand Hanoverian
and Hessian mercenaries, to aid in reducing the American
colonies to absolute submission to the will of the King and
Parliament of Great Britain. It was supposed in England that
the decisive Act of Parliament, the unbending and hostile attitude of the British Ministry, the formidable amount of naval
and land forces, would awe the colonies into unresisting and
immediate submission; but the effect of all these formidable
preparations on the part of the British Government was to
unite rather than divide the colonies, and render them more
determined and resolute than ever to defend and maintain their
sacred and inherited rights and liberties as British subjects.

The thirteen colonies were a unit as to what they understood
and contended for in regard to their British constitutional rights
and liberties—namely, the rights which they had enjoyed for

more than a century—the right of taxation by their own elected representatives alone, the right of providing for the support of their own civil government and its officers—rights far less extensive than those which are and have long been enjoyed by the loyal provinces of the Canadian Dominion.   There were, indeed, the Governors and their officers, sent from England—the favourites and needy dependents of the British Ministry and Parliament, sent out to subsist upon the colonists, but were not of them, had no sympathy with them, nor any influence over them except what they had over their dependents and the families with whom they had formed connections.   They were noisy and troublesome as a *faction*, but not sufficient in numbers or influence to constitute a *party*, properly speaking.

There was like unity among the colonies in regard to the *defence* and *support* of the rights and liberties which they claimed.   There was, indeed, doubt on the part of a few, and but a few, comparatively, as to the wisdom and expediency of taking arms and meeting the King's officers and troops in the field of battle in support of their rights; but all agreed that they should defend themselves and their property when attacked by the King's troops, whether attacked by the King's orders or not; for they held that their title to their property and constitutional rights was as sacred and divine as that of the King to his throne.*

* "The theory that the popular leaders were playing a game of hypocrisy may be tested in the case of Washington, whose sterling patriotism was not more conspicuous than his irreproachable integrity.   The New York Provincial Congress, in an address to him (June 26th, 1775), on his way from Philadelphia to the American camp around Boston, say that accommodation with the mother country was 'the fondest wish of each American soul.' Washington, in reply, pledged his colleagues and himself to use every exertion to re-establish peace and harmony.   'When we assumed the soldier,' he said, ' we did not lay aside the citizen ; and we shall most sincerely rejoice with you in that happy hour when the establishment of American liberty on the most solid and firm foundations shall enable us to return to our private stations, in the bosom of a free, peaceful, and happy country.'(a)   There was no incompatibility in the position of military leader of a great uprising with a desire to preserve the old political ties.   When the Barons of Runnymede,

(a) "The London Chronicle of August 8th, 1775, has the speech of the New York Provincial Congress, and the reply of Washington of the 26th of June, 1775."

The question of questions with the General Congress on its assembling in May, 1776, was what measures should be adopted for the defence of their violated and invaded rights, and upon what grounds should that defence be conducted ? For the first time in the General Congress was it proposed to abandon the ground on which they had vindicated and maintained their rights as British subjects in their several Legislatures and Conventions for eleven years, and successfully defended them by force of arms for more than one year, or to avow entire separation from the mother country, and declare absolute independence as the ground of maintaining their rights and liberties ?

There had long been some prominent men who held republican sentiments, and some newspapers had in 1775 mooted the idea of separation from the mother country. Such views prevailed widely in Massachusetts; there had always been a clique of Congregational Republicans and Separationists in Boston, from the days of Cromwell. They looked back upon the halcyon days when none but Congregationalists could hold office—civil, judicial, or military—or even exercise the elective franchise, and the disclaimers of any earthly king ; and though the separation from the mother country and renunciation of monarchical government was carefully avoided in the official documents of Massachusetts, as it was disclaimed in the strongest terms in the official papers of other colonies, yet the sentiment of hostility to monarchy and of separation from England was artfully inculcated in resolutions, addresses, etc., prepared by Samuel Adams, and sent forth from the Massachusetts Conven-

---

surrounded by their retainers, wrested from King John the great Charter, they meant not to renounce their allegiance, but simply to preserve the old government. Though an act of apparent rebellion, yet it was in the strictest sense an act of loyalty. So the popular leaders, in their attitude of armed resistance, were loyal to what they conceived to be essential to American liberty. They were asserting the majesty of constitutional law against those who would have destroyed it, and thus were more loyal to the Constitution than was George III. There really is no ground on which justly to question the sincerity of declarations like those of Congress and Washington. They aimed at a redress of grievances ; and the idea was quite general, of a Bill of Rights, or an American Constitution, embodying the conditions on which the integrity of the empire might be preserved. This was their last appeal for a settlement on such a basis." (Frothingham's Rise of the Republic of the United States, Chap. xi., pp. 438, 439.)

tion.* He was a man of blameless life (no relation to John Adams)—a rigid religionist of the old Massachusetts Puritan stamp—a hater of England and of British institutions, able and indefatigable in everything that might tend to sever America from England, in regard to which his writings exerted a powerful influence. He was the Corypheus of the Separatist party in Boston, the Chairman of the Committee of Correspondence, and wrote the Massachusets circulars to other colonies.

It was only early in May, 1776, that the question of independence was discussed in the General Congress. The Congress *recommended* those colonies whose Governors had left their governments, or were declared disqualified on account of their oppressive and cruel conduct, to form governments for themselves. This, however, was not understood as a declaration of independence, but a temporary measure of necessity, to prevent anarchy and confusion in the colonies concerned. This proceeding was immediately followed by a more comprehensive measure intended to feel the pulse of the colonies on the subject of independence.

" The Congress had waited with considerable patience, and some anxiety, the result of the late session of Parliament; they had forborne to do anything which might not be justified upon the fair principles of self-defence, until it appeared that the Ministry was resolved that nothing short of the most abject submission should be the price of accommodation. Early in May, therefore, the Congress adopted a measure intended to sound the sentiments of the colonies on the subject of independence. They stated the rejection of their petitions, and the employment of foreign mercenaries to reduce them to obedience, and concluded by declaring it expedient that all the colonies should proceed to the establishment of such a form of government as

---

* Mr. Bancroft, writing under date of October, 1775, says : "The Americans had not designed to establish an independent government; of their leading statesmen it was the desire of Samuel Adams alone; they had all been educated in the love and admiration of constitutional monarchy; and even John Adams and Jefferson so sincerely shrank back from the attempt at creating another government in its stead, that, to the last moment, they were most anxious to avert a separation, if it could be avoided without a loss of their inherited liberties." (History of the United States, Vol. VIII., Chap. li., p. 161.)

their representatives might think most conducive to the peace and happiness of the people. This preamble and resolution were immediately forwarded; and in a few days afterwards Richard Henry Lee, of Virginia, gave notice to the Congress that he should, on an appointed day, move for a *Declaration of Independence.* This was accordingly done, but the consideration of the question was postponed until the 1st of July— *so timid, so wavering, so unwilling to break the maternal connection were most of the members.**

It is clear that, so far from the Declaration of Independence being the spontaneous uprising of the colonies, as represented by so many American historians, that when it was first mooted in Congress the majority of the General Congress itself were startled at it, and were opposed to it. " On the 15th day of May, only four of the colonies had acted definitely on the question of independence. North Carolina had authorized her delegates to concur with the delegates from the other colonies 'in declaring independency;' Rhode Island had commissioned hers ' to join in any measures to secure American rights;' in Massachusetts, various towns had pledged themselves to maintain any declaration on which Congress might agree; and Virginia had given positive instructions to her delegates that Congress should make a declaration of independence. These proceedings were accompanied with declarations respecting a reservation to each colony of the right to form its own government, in the adjustment of the power universally felt to be necessary, and which

---

* Allan's American Revolution, Vol. I., pp. 342, 343.

" The interval was employed in unceasing exertions by the friends of independence to prepare the minds of the people for the necessity and advantages of such a measure. The press teemed with essays and pamphlets, in which all the arts of eloquence were used to ridicule the prejudices which supported an attachment to the King and Government of England. Among the numerous writers on this momentous question, the most luminous, the most eloquent, and the most forcible was *Thomas Paine.* His pamphlet entitled ' Common Sense' was not only read, but understood, by everybody; and those who regard the independence of the *United States* as a blessing will never cease to cherish the remembrance of *Thomas Paine.* Whatever may have been his subsequent career—in whatever light his religious principles may be regarded—it should never be forgotten that *to him, more than to any single individual, was owing the rapid diffusion of those sentiments and feelings which produced the act of separation from Great Britain.*"—*Ib.,* pp. 343, 344.

was to be lodged in a new political unit, designated by the terms, 'Confederation,' 'Continental Constitution,' and 'American Republic.' "*

"On the 7th of June, Richard Henry Lee, in behalf of the Virginia delegates, submitted in Congress resolves on independence, a confederation, and foreign alliances. His biographer says that 'tradition relates that he prefaced his motion with a speech,' portraying the resources of the colonies and their capacity for defence, dwelling especially on the bearing which an independent position might have on foreign Powers, and concluded by urging the members so to act, that the day might give birth to an American Republic. The motion was:—

"'That these united colonies are, and of right ought to be, free and independent States, that they are absolved from all allegiance to the British Crown, and that all political connection between them and the State of Great Britain is and ought to be totally dissolved.'

"'That it is expedient forthwith to take the most effectual measures for forming foreign alliances.'

"'That a plan of confederation be prepared and transmitted to the respective colonies for their consideration and approbation.'

"John Adams seconded the motion. The Journal of Congress says, 'that certain resolutions respecting independency being moved and seconded, they were postponed till to-morrow morning,' and that 'the members were enjoined to attend punctually at ten o'clock in order to take the same into their consideration. Jefferson says the reason of postponement was that the House were obliged to attend to other business. The record indicates that no speech was made on that day.

"The next day was Saturday. John Hancock, the President, was in the chair; and Charles Thompson was the Secretary. The resolves were immediately referred to a Committee of the Whole, in which Benjamin Harrison presided—the confidential correspondent of Washington, and subsequently Governor of Virginia. They were debated with animation until seven o'clock in the evening, when the President resumed the chair, and reported that the Committee had considered the matter referred

* Frothingham's Rise of the Republic of the United States, p. 512.

to them, but, not having come to any decision, directed him to move for leave to sit again on Monday.

"In Congress, on Monday, Edward Rutledge moved that the question be postponed three weeks. The debate on this day continued until seven o'clock in the evening. Not a single speech of any member is known to be extant. Jefferson at the time summed up the arguments used by the speakers during both days. The result may be given in his words : ' It appearing, in the course of the debates, that the colonies of New York, New Jersey, Pennsylvania, Delaware, Maryland, and South Carolina were not yet matured for falling from the parent stem, but that they were fast advancing to that state, it was thought most prudent to wait awhile for them. It was agreed in Committee of the Whole to report to Congress a resolution, which was adopted by a vote of seven colonies to five, and this postponed the resolution on independence to the 1st day of July ; and ' in meanwhile, that no time be lost, a Committee be appointed to prepare a declaration in conformity to it.' On the next day a Committee was chosen for this purpose by ballot : Thomas Jefferson, of Virginia ; John Adams, of Massachusetts ; Benjamin Franklin, of Pennsylvania ; Roger Sherman, of Connecticut ; and Robert R. Livingstone, of New York. [Such was the Committee that prepared the Declaration of Independence.] On the 12th a Committee of one from each colony was appointed to report the form of confederation, and a Committee of five to prepare a plan of treaties to be proposed to foreign Powers.

"When Congress postponed the vote on independence, the popular movement in its favour was in full activity. Some of the members left this body to engage in it. Others promoted it by their counsel."*

"On the day agreed upon for the consideration of Mr. Lee's motion, the 1st of July, Congress resolved itself into a Committee of the Whole ; the debates on the question were continued with great warmth for *three days*. It had been determined to take the vote by *colonies* ; and as a master-stroke of policy, the author of which is not known to history, it had been proposed and agreed, that *the decision on the question, whatever might be*

* Frothingham's Rise of the Republic of the United States, Chap. xi., pp. 513—517.

the state of the votes, should appear to the world as the unanimous voice of the Congress. On the first question [of independence], *six* colonies were in the affirmative, and *six* in the negative—*Pennsylvania* being without a vote by the equal division of her delegates. In this state of the business, it appears, on the authority of evidence afterwards adduced before Parliament, that Mr. *Samuel Adams* once more successfully exerted his influence; and that one of the delegates of Pennsylvania was brought over to the side of independence. It is more probable, however, that the influence of Mr. Adams extended no further than to procure that one of the dissenting members withdraw from the House; and that the vote of Pennsylvania was thus obtained."*

It is thus seen that the Declaration of Independence, so far

* Allan's American Revolution, Chap. xii., pp. 344, 345.

" The question before the Committee was the portion of the *motion relating to independence*, submitted by the Virginia delegates on the 7th of June. The New York members read their instructions, and were excused from voting. Of the three delegates from Delaware, Rodney was absent, Read in the negative, and thus the vote of that colony was lost. South Carolina was in the negative ; and so was Pennsylvania, by the votes of Dickenson, Willing, Morris, and Humphries, against those of Franklin, Morton, and Wilson. Nine colonies—New Hampshire, Connecticut, Massachusetts, Rhode Island, New Jersey, Maryland, Virginia, North Carolina, Georgia—voted in the affirmative. The Committee rose, the President resumed the chair, and Harrison reported the resolution as having been agreed to. Edward Rutledge, of South Carolina, said that were the vote postponed till next day, he believed that his colleagues, though they disapproved of the resolution, would then join in it for the sake of unanimity. The final question, in accordance with this request, was postponed until the next day ; but it was agreed to go into Committee on the draft of the Declaration.

" On the 2nd July, probably fifty members were present in Congress. After disposing of the business of the morning, it resumed the resolution *on independence*, and probably without much debate proceeded to vote. McKean sent an express to Rodney, at Dover, which procured his attendance, and secured the vote of Delaware in the affirmative ; while the same result was reached for Pennsylvania by Dickenson and Morris absenting themselves, and allowing Franklin, Wilson, and Morton to give the vote against Willing and Humphries. The South Carolina delegates concluded to vote for the measure. Thus twelve colonies united in adopting the following resolution :

" 'That these united colonies are, and of right ought to be, free and independent States ; that they are absolved from all allegiance to the British Crown, and that all political connection between them and the State of

from being the spontaneous uprising of the American colonies, was the result of months of agitation by scarcely a dozen leaders in the movement, by canvassing at public meetings, and of delegates elected by them, not excelled by any political and nearly balanced parties in England or Canada in a life and death struggle for victory. In this case, the important question was to be decided by some fifty members of Congress; and when the first vote was given, after many weeks of popular agitation, and three days of warm discussion in Congress, there was a tie—six colonies for and six against the Declaration of Independence—after which a majority of one was obtained for the Declaration, by inducing the absence of certain members opposed to it; and then, when a majority of votes was thus obtained, others were persuaded to vote for the measure *"for the sake of unanimity,"* though they were opposed to the measure itself.

It has indeed been represented by some American historians,

Great Britain is, and ought to be, totally dissolved.'" (Frothingham's Rise of the Republic of the United States, Chap. xi., pp. 537, 538.)

On the adoption of this resolution, continues the same historian, " Congress went immediately into Committee of the Whole to consider the draft of a Declaration of Independence, or the form of announcing the fact to the world. During the remainder of that day, and during the sessions of the 3rd and 4th, the phraseology, allegations, and principles of this paper were subjected to severe scrutiny. Its author relates : ' The pusillanimous idea that we had friends in England worth keeping terms with still haunted the minds of many. For this reason, those passages which conveyed censure on the people of England were struck out, lest they should give them offence. The clause, too, reprobating the enslaving of the inhabitants of Africa was struck out in complaisance to South Carolina and Georgia, who had never attempted to restrain the importation of slaves, and who, on the contrary, wished to continue it. Our northern brethren also, I believe, felt a little tender under these censures ; for though their people had very few slaves themselves, yet they had been pretty considerable carriers of them to others.' (Memoirs of Jefferson, i. 15.) The striking out of the passage declaring the slave trade ' piratical warfare against human nature itself,' was deeply regretted by many of that generation. Other alterations were for the better, making the paper more dispassionate and terse, and—what was no small improvement—more brief and exact. On the evening of the 4th the Committee rose, when Harrison reported the Declaration as having been agreed upon. It was then adopted by twelve States, unanimously." [That is, by the majority of the delegates of twelve provinces, and, of course, *reported* as " unanimous," according to previous agreement.]—*Ib.*, p. 539.

that the vote of Congress for Independence was *unanimous ;* but the fact is far otherwise. As the vote was taken by *colonies,* and not by the majority of the individual members present, as in ordinary legislative proceedings, the majority of the delegates from each colony determined the vote of that colony ; and by a previous and very adroit proposal, an agreement was entered into that the *vote of Congress should be published to the world as* UNANIMOUS, however divided the votes of members on the question of Independence might be ; and on this ground the signatures of those who had opposed it, as well as of those who voted in favour of it, were ultimately affixed to the Declaration, though it was published and authenticated by the signatures of the President, John Hancock, of Massachusetts, and Charles Thompson, of Philadelphia, as Secretary.

The Declaration of Independence, as thus adopted, is as follows :

" A Declaration by the Representatives of the United *States* of America, in Congress assembled :

" When, in the course of human events, it becomes necessary for one people to dissolve the political bands which have connected them with another, and to assume among the powers of the earth the separate and equal station to which the laws of nature and nature's God entitle them, a decent respect to the opinions of mankind requires that they should declare the causes which impel them to such separation.

" We hold these truths to be self-evident: that all men are created equal ; that they are endowed by their Creator with certain unalienable rights, that among these are life, liberty, and the pursuit of happiness , that to secure these rights, governments are instituted among men, deriving their just powers from the consent of the governed; and whenever any form of government becomes destructive of these ends, it is the right of the people to alter or abolish it, and to institute a new government, laying its foundation on such principles, and organizing its powers in such form, as to them shall seem most likely to effect their safety and happiness. Prudence, indeed, would dictate that governments long established should not be changed for light and transient causes ; and accordingly, all experience hath shown that mankind are more inclined to suffer, while evils are sufferable, than to right themselves by abolishing the forms to which they are accustomed ; but when a long train of abuses and usurpations, pursuing invariably the same object, evinces a design to reduce them under absolute despotism, it is their right, it is their duty to throw off such government, and to provide new guards for their future security. Such has been the patient sufferance of these colonies, and such is now the necessity which constrains them to alter their former systems of government. The history of the present King of Great Britain is a history of repeated injuries and usurpations ; all having in direct object the establishment of an absolute tyranny over these States : to prove this, let facts be exhibited to a candid world.

" He has refused his assent to laws the most wholesome and necessary for the public good.

" He has forbidden his Governours to pass laws of immediate and pressing importance, unless suspended in their operations till his assent should be obtained ; and when so suspended, he has utterly neglected to attend to them.

" He has refused to pass other laws, for the accommodation of large districts of people, unless those people would relinquish the rights of representation in the Legislature ; a right inestimable to them, and formidable to tyrants only.

" He has called together legislative bodies at places unusual, uncomfortable, and distant from the depositories of their public records, for the sole purpose of fatiguing them into compliance with his measures.

" He has dissolved Representative Houses repeatedly, for opposing, with manly firmness, his invasion on the rights of the people.

" He has refused, for a long time after such dissolution, to cause others to be elected, whereby the legislative powers, incapable of annihilation, have returned to the people at large for their exercise—the State remaining, in the meantime, exposed to all the dangers of invasion from without, and convulsions within.

" He has endeavoured to prevent the population of these States ; for that purpose obstructing the laws for naturalization of foreigners, refusing to pass others to encourage their migrations hither, and raising the conditions of new appropriations of lands.

" He has obstructed the administration of justice, by refusing his assent to laws for establishing judiciary powers.

" He has made judges dependent on his will alone for the tenure of their offices, and the amount and payment of their salaries.

" He has erected a multitude of new offices, and sent hither swarms of officers, to harass our people and eat out their substance.

" He has kept among us, in times of peace, standing armies, without the consent of our Legislatures.

" He has affected to render the military independent of, and superior to, the civil power.

" He has combined with others to subject us to a jurisdiction foreign to our Constitution, and unacknowledged by our laws, giving his assent to their pretended acts of legislation.

" For quartering large bodies of armed troops among us.

" For protecting them, by a mock trial, from punishment for any murders which they should commit on the inhabitants of these States.

" For cutting off our trade with all parts of the world.

" For imposing taxes on us without our consent.

" For depriving us, in many cases, of the benefit of trial by jury.

" For transporting us beyond seas, to be tried for pretended offences.

" For abolishing the free system of English laws in a neighbouring Province, establishing therein an arbitrary government, and enlarging its bounda.ies so as to render it at once an example and fit instrument for introducing the same absolute rule into these colonies.

" For taking away our Charters, abolishing our most valuable laws, and altering fundamentally the forms of our governments.

" For suspending our own Legislatures, and declaring themselves invested with power to legislate for us in all cases whatsoever.

" He has abdicated government here, by declaring us out of his protection, and waging war against us.

" He has plundered our seas, ravaged our coasts, burnt our towns, and destroyed the lives of our people.

" He is at this time transporting large armies of foreign mercenaries to complete the work of death, desolation, and tyranny, already begun with ₊circumstances of cruelty and perfidy scarcely paralleled in the most barbarous ages, and totally unworthy the head of a civilized nation.

" He has constrained our fellow-citizens, taken captive on the high seas, to bear arms against their country, to become the executioners of their friends and brethren, or to fall themselves by their hands.

" He has excited domestick insurrections amongst us, and has endeavoured to bring on the inhabitants of our frontiers the merciless Indian savages, whose known rule of warfare is undistinguished destruction of all ages, sexes, and conditions.

" In every stage of these oppressions we have petitioned for redress in the most humble terms : our repeated petitions have been answered only by repeated injury.   A prince whose character is thus marked by every act which may define a tyrant, is unfit to be the ruler of a free people.

" Nor have we been wanting in attention to our British brethren.   We have warned them, from time to time, of attempts by their Legislature to extend an unwarrantable jurisdiction over us ; we have reminded them of the circumstances of our emigration and settlement here ; we have appealed to their native justice and magnanimity ; and we have conjured them, by the ties of our common kindred, to disavow these usurpations, which would inevitably interrupt our connection and correspondence.   They too have been deaf to the voice of justice and consanguinity.   We must, therefore, acquiesce in the necessity which denounces our separation, and hold them, as we hold the rest of mankind, enemies in war, in peace friends.

" We therefore, the representatives of the United States of America, in General Congress assembled, appealing to the Supreme Judge of the world for the rectitude of our intentions, do, in the name and by the authority of the good people of these colonies, solemnly publish and declare, that these United Colonies are, and of right ought to be, Free and Independent States ; and that they are absolved from allegiance to the British Crown ; and that all political connection between them and the State of Great Britain is, and ought to be, totally dissolved; and that, as free and independent States, they have full power to levy war, conclude peace, contract alliances, establish commerce, and to do all other acts and things which independent States may of right do. And for the support of this Declaration, with a firm reliance on the protection of Divine Providence, we mutually pledge to each other our lives, our fortunes, and our sacred honour."

Note.—This Declaration will be discussed in the next chapter.

CHAPTER XXVI.

Declaration of Independence Discussed.

THE foregoing chapters bear ample testimony how heartily I have sympathized with our elder brother colonists of America, in their conception and manly advocacy and defence of their constitutional rights as British subjects ; how faithfully I have narrated their wrongs and advocated their rights, and how utterly I have abhorred the despotic conduct of George the Third, and of his corrupt Ministers and mercenary and corrupted Parliament, in their unscrupulous efforts to wrest from the American colonists the attributes and privileges of British freemen, and to convert their lands, with their harbours and commerce, into mere plantations and instruments to enrich the manufacturers and merchants of England, and provide places of honour and emolument for the scions and protegees of the British aristocracy and Parliament. But I cannot sympathize with, much less defend, the leaders of the old American colonists in the repudiating what they had professed from their fore-fathers ; in avowing what they had for many years denied ; in making their confiding and distinguished defenders in the British Parliament—the Chathams, Camdens, Sherburnes, the Foxes, Burkes, and Cavendishes—liars in presence of all Europe ; in deliberately practising upon their fellow-colonists what they had so loudly complained of against the King and Parliament of Great Britain; in seeking the alliance of a Power which had sought to destroy them for a hundred years, against the land of their forefathers which had protected them during that hundred years, and whose Administration had wronged and sought to oppress them for only twelve years.

After many years of anxious study and reflection, I have a strong conviction that the Declaration of American Independence, in 1776, was a great mistake in itself, a great calamity to America as well as to England, a great injustice to many thousands on both sides of the Atlantic, a great loss of human life, a great blow to the real liberties of mankind, and a great impediment to the highest Christian and Anglo-Saxon civilization among the nations of the world.

In this summary statement of opinion—so contrary to the sentiments of American historians and to popular feeling in the United States—I mean no reflection on the motives, character, patriotism, and abilities of those great men who advocated and secured the adoption of the Declaration of Independence in the General Congress of 1776. I believe America has never produced a race of statesmen equal in purity of character, in comprehensiveness of views, in noble patriotism and moral courage, to "the Fathers of the American Revolution." Their discussions of public questions, during the eleven years which preceded the Declaration of Independence, evince a clearness of discernment, an accuracy of statement, a niceness of distinction, a thorough knowledge of the principles of government, and the mutual relation of colonies and the parent State, elegance of diction, and force of argument, not surpassed in discussions of the kind in any age or country; their diplomatic correspondence displays great superiority in every respect over the English statesmen of the day, who sought to oppress them; the correspondence of Washington with General Gage commanded alike the admiration of Europe and the gratitude of America; the memorials and other public papers transmitted to England by the American Congress, and written by Jay and other members, drew forth from the Earl of Chatham, in the House of Lords, January 20th, 1775, the following eulogy: "When your lordships look at the papers transmitted to us from America—when you consider their decency, firmness, and wisdom, you cannot but respect their cause, and wish to make it your own. For myself, I must avow that in all my reading— and I have read Thucydides, and have studied and admired the master States of the world—for solidity of reason, force of sagacity, and wisdom of conclusion under a complication of difficult circumstances, no nation or body of men can stand in preference to the General Congress at Philadelphia. The histories of Greece and Rome give us nothing equal to it, and all attempts to impose servitude upon such a mighty continental nation must be vain."

" We shall be forced ultimately to retract ; let us retract while we can, not when we must. These violent Acts must be repealed ; you will repeal them ; I pledge myself for it, I stake my reputation on it, that you will in the end repeal them."

(Those violent Acts were repealed three years afterwards.)

When the Earl of Shelburne read the reply, written by Jefferson, of the Virginia Legislature, to Lord North's proposition, his Lordship said: " In my life, I was never more pleased with a State paper than with the Assembly of Virginia's discussion of Lord North's proposition. It is masterly. But what I fear is that the evil is irretrievable."

Among the statesmanlike productions of that period, the correspondence of Franklin, the masterly letters of Dickenson, the letters and State papers of Samuel and John Adams, Jay and Livingstone, and of many others, exhibit a scholarly race of statesmen and writers of whom any nation or age might be proud.

But it must not be forgotten that the education of every one of these great men, and their training in public affairs, was under English constitutional government, for which every one of them (except Samuel Adams) expressed their unqualified admiration, and to which they avowed their unswerving attachment to within twelve months of the declaration of independence. Though the United States can boast of many distinguished scholars and politicians and jurists, I believe American democracy has never produced a generation of scholarly, able, and stainless statesmen, such as those who had received the whole of their mental, moral, and political training when America formed a part of the British empire.

It is not surprising, indeed, that the major part (for they were not unanimous) of so noble and patriotic a class of statesmen should, by the wicked policy and cruel measures against them by the worst administration of government that ever ruled England, be betrayed into an act which they had so many years disavowed. Placing, as they rightly did, in the foreground the civil and religious liberties of Englishmen as the first ingredient of the elements of political greatness and social progress, they became exasperated into the conviction that the last and only effective means of maintaining those liberties was to sever their connection with England altogether, and declare their own absolute independence. We honour the sentiments and courage which prompted them to maintain and defend their liberties; we question not the purity and patriotism of their motives in declaring independence as the means of securing those liberties; but we must believe that, had they maintained the integrity of their professions and positions for even a twelvemonth longer, they would have achieved all for which they had contended, would have become a free and happy country, as Canada now is, beside the mother country and not in antagonism to her, maintaining inviolate their national life and traditions, instead of forming an alliance for bloody warfare with their own former and their mother country's hereditary enemics.

It was unnatural and disgraceful for the British Ministry to employ German mercenaries and savage Indians to subdue the American colonists to unconditional obedience; but was it less unnatural for the colonists themselves to seek and obtain the alliance of the King of France, whose government was a despotism, and who had for a hundred years sought to destroy the colonists, had murdered them without mercy, and employed by high premiums the Indians to butcher and scalp men, women, and children of the colonists—indeed, to "drive them into the sea," and to exterminate them from the soil of America? Yet with such enemies of civil and religious liberty, with such enemies of their own liberties, and even their existence as Anglo-Saxons, the colonists sought and obtained an alliance against the mother country, which had effectually, and at an immense expenditure, defended them against the efforts of both France and Spain to destroy them. Had the American colonists maintained the position and professions after 1776, as they had maintained them before 1776, presenting the contrast of their own integrity and unity and patriotism to the perfidious counsels, mercenary and un-English policy of the British Ministry and Parliament, they would have escaped the disastrous defeats and bloodshed of 1777-8, and would have repeated the victories which they had gained over the English soldiers in 1775 and the early part of 1776. Unprepared and sadly deficient in arms and ammunition, they repulsed the regular English soldiers sent against them at Concord, at Lexington, at Bunker's Hill; they had shut up as prisoners the largest English army ever sent to New England, and, though commanded by such generals as Howe and Clinton, compelled their evacuation of the city of Boston. In the Southern States they had routed the English forces, and had compelled the Governors of Virginia and South and North Carolina to take refuge on board of English men-of-war. Before the declaration of independence, the colonists fought with the enthusiasm of Englishmen for Englishmen's rights, and the British soldiers fought without heart against their fellow-subjects contending for what many of both the soldiers and officers knew to be rights dear to all true Englishmen; but when the Congress of the American colonies declared themselves to be no longer Englishmen, no longer supporters of the constitutional rights of Englishmen, but separationists from England, and seeking alliance with the enemies of England, then the English army felt that they were fighting against enemies and not fellow-subjects, and fought with an energy and courage which carried disaster, in almost every instance, to the heretofore united but now divided colonists, until France and Spain came to their assistance.

With these preliminary and general remarks, we proceed to state more specifically the grounds on which we regard, as a calamity to the interests of true liberty and of civilization, the change of position, policy, and principles avowed by the General Congress in the Declaration of Independence, 1776.

I. The Declaration of Independence was a renunciation of all the principles on which the General Congress, Provincial Legislatures, and Conventions professed to act from the beginning of the contest. The foregoing pages present abundant testimony and illustration how earnestly, how constantly, how unanimously the American colonists expressed their attachment to the mother country and to the principles of the British Constitution—how indignantly they repelled, as an insult and a slander, every suspicion and statement that they meditated or desired *independence*, or that they would ever consent to sever the ties of their connection with the mother country and the glorious principles of her constitution of government.

In the same Congress of 1775, by which Washington was

appointed Commander-in-Chief, the higher departments of the army were organized. Bills of credit to the amount of three millions were emitted to defray the expenses of the war, and after the battles of Lexington and Bunker's Hill, while the English army were shut in Boston by the Provincial volunteers, a declaration was signed by Congress, justifying their proceedings, but disdaining any idea of separation from England. They say, "We are reduced to the alternative of choosing an unconstitutional submission to the tyranny of irritated Ministers, or resistance by force. The latter is our choice. We have counted the cost of this contest, and find nothing so dreadful as voluntary slavery. Honour, justice, and humanity forbid us tamely to surrender that freedom which we received from our gallant ancestors, and which our innocent posterity have a right to receive from us. * *

"With hearts fortified with these animating reflections, we most solemnly, before God and the world, *declare* that, exerting the utmost energy of those powers which our beneficent Creator hath graciously bestowed upon us, the arms we have been compelled by our enemies to assume, we will, in defiance of every hazard, with unabating firmness and perseverance, employ for the preservation of our liberties ; being with one mind resolved to die freemen rather than to live slaves.

" Lest this declaration should disquiet the minds of our friends and fellow-subjects in any part of the empire, *we assure them that we mean not to dissolve that union which has so long and so happily subsisted between us, and which we sincerely wish to see restored.* Necessity has not yet driven us to that desperate measure, or induced us to excite any other nation to war against them. *We have not raised armies with ambitious designs of separating from Great Britain, and of establishing independent States.* We fight not for glory or for conquest. We exhibit to mankind the remarkable spectacle of a people attacked by unprovoked enemies, without any imputation or even suspicion of offence. They boast of their privileges and civilization, and yet proffer no milder conditions than servitude or death.

" In our native land, in defence of the freedom that is our birthright, and which we ever enjoyed until the late violation of it, for the protection of our property acquired solely by the

32

honest industry of our forefathers and ourselves, against violence actually offered, we have taken up arms. We shall lay
them down when hostilities shall cease on the part of the
aggressors, and all danger of their being renewed shall be removed, and not before."*

"Amidst these hostile operations, the voice of peace was yet
heard—allegiance to the King was still acknowledged, and a
lingering hope remained that an accommodation was not impossible. Congress voted a petition to his Majesty, replete with
professions of duty and attachment; and addressed a letter to
the people of England, conjuring them, by the endearing appella-
tions of 'friends, countrymen, and brethren,' to prevent the
dissolution of 'that connection which the remembrance of
former friendships, pride in the glorious achievements of common
ancestors, and affection for the heirs of their virtues had heretofore maintained.' *They uniformly disclaimed any idea of
independence, and professed themselves to consider union with
England, on constitutional principles,* as the greatest blessing
which could be bestowed on them."†

It is needless to multiply authorities and illustrations; the
whole tenor of the history of the colonies, as presented in the
preceding chapters of this volume, evinces their universal appreciation of the principles of the British Constitution and their
universal attachment to union with the mother country.‡

* Judge Marshall's History of the American Colonies, Chap. XIV.,
pp. 449—451.

† *Ib.,* p. 457.

‡ "The commencement of hostilities on the 19th of April, 1775, exhibited
the parent State in an odious point of view. But, nevertheless, at that
time, and for a twelvemonth after, a majority of the colonists wished for no
more than to be re-established as subjects in their ancient rights. Had
independence been their object, even at the commencement of hostilities,
they would have rescinded the associations which have been already mentioned, and imported more largely than ever. Common sense revolts at the
idea that colonists, unfurnished with military stores and wanting manufactures of every kind, should, at the time of their intending a serious struggle
for independence, by a voluntary agreement, deprive themselves of the
obvious means of procuring such foreign supplies as their circumstances
might make necessary. Instead of pursuing a line of conduct which might
have been dictated by a wish for independence, they continued their exports
for nearly a year after they ceased to import. This not only lessened the
debts they owed to Great Britain, but furnished additional means for carry-

Even in the spring of 1776, after months of agitation by advocates of separation in various colonies, a majority of the delegates in Congress were for weeks opposed to separation; and it required long preparation to familiarize the minds of its advocates to separation, and to reconcile any considerable number of colonists to hostile severance from the land of their forefathers. It may easily be conceived what must have been the shock to a large part, if not a majority, of the colonists, to have burst upon them, after weeks' secret session of Congress, a declaration which, under the term Independence, renounced all the principles and associations in which they had been educated, which they had often avowed and held dear from their ancestors, which proclaimed their mother country their enemy, and denounced connection with her a crime. Such a renunciation of the past, and wrenching from it, could not otherwise than weaken the foundations of society and the obligation of oaths, as may be seen by a comparison in these respects of the sacredness of laws and oaths, and their administration in America before and since the revolution.

II. The Declaration of Independence was a violation of good faith to those statesmen and numerous other parties in England who had, in and out of Parliament, supported the rights and character of the colonies during the whole contest. They had all done so upon the ground that the colonists were contending for the constitutional rights of Englishmen; that they intended and desired nothing more. On the ground that the colonists, like the barons of Runnymede, were contending for the sacred rights of Englishmen, and relying on the faith of their declaration that Englishmen they would ever remain, their cause was patriotically espoused and nobly vindicated in England by Lords Chatham, Camden, Shelburne, the Duke of Richmond, and others in the House of Lords; by Messrs. Burke and Fox, Lord John Cavendish, Mr. Dunning (afterwards Lord Ashburton), and others in the House of Commons; and by cor-

ing on war against themselves. To aim at independence, and at the same time to transfer their resources to their enemies, could not have been the policy of an enlightened people. It was not till some time in 1776 that the colonists began to take other ground, and contend that it was for their interest to be for ever separated from Great Britain." (Dr. Ramsay's History of the United States, Vol. II., Chap. xii., pp. 158, 159.)

porations of cities and towns, and multitudes out of Parliament. Lord Mahon, in the sixth volume of his History of England (pp. 35—37), relates that before the Earl of Chatham introduced his famous "Provincial Bill for Settling Troubles in America," and supported it by his masterly speeches in the Lords, he sent for Dr. Franklin, the principal representative of the colonists, to consult him and ascertain from him distinctly whether there was any tendency or danger of the American colonies separating from England, and was assured by Dr. Franklin that there was not the least feeling in that direction; that the American colonies were universally loyal to connection with the mother country, and desired and contended for nothing more than the constitutional rights of Englishmen.[*]

It was not till after this assurance, and it was under this conviction and with this object, that the Earl of Chatham delivered those appeals in behalf of America which electrified the British public, and gave tone to the subsequent debates in both Houses of Parliament. These eloquent and unanswerable defences of British rights, invaded and denied in regard to the persons of the American colonists, were delivered in 1775 and the early part of 1776; but scarcely had their echoes died away on the waves of the Atlantic, when news came from America

---

[*] Lord Mahon says: "In framing this measure, he sought the aid and counsel of Dr. Franklin. Already, in the month of August preceding, they had become acquainted, through the mediation of Lord Stanhope, who carried Dr. Franklin to Hayes (the residence of Lord Chatham). Lord Chatham had then referred to the idea which began to *prevail in England, that America aimed at setting up for herself as a separate State. The truth of any such idea was loudly denied by Dr. Franklin.* 'I assured his lordship,' Dr. Franklin said, 'that having more than once travelled almost from one end of the continent to the other, and kept a great variety of company, eating and drinking and conversing with them freely, I never had heard from any person, drunk or sober, the least expression of a wish for separation, or hint that such a thing would be advantageous to America. * * In fine, Lord Chatham expressed much satisfaction in my having called upon him, *and particularly in the assurances I had given him that America did not aim at independence.*'" (Works, Vol. V., p. 7, ed. 1844.)

The Earl of Chatham's last speech was an appeal against the separation of the American colonies from England, and his last words were : "My lords, I rejoice that the grave has not closed upon me ; that I am still alive to lift up my voice against the dismemberment of this ancient and most noble monarchy." (Bancroft, Vol. IX., p. 495.)

that the Congress, so warmly eulogized in the British Parliament for its fidelity to English connection, as well as to the
rights of England, had, after a secret session of two months,
renounced all connection with England, and all acknowledgment of its authority and principles of government, thus fulfilling the statements and predictions of the parliamentary
enemies of American rights, and presenting their advocates,
Chatham, Camden, Burke, etc., as liars and deceivers before the
British nation and in the face of all Europe. The Ministerial
party triumphed; the advocates of colonial rights were con-
founded, and their influence in and out of Parliament was
paralyzed. The power of the corrupt Ministers who had been
oppressing the colonies for ten years, was tottering to their fall :
they had played their last card; they had exhausted their
credit; they had staked their existence on the truth of the
statements they had made, and the accomplishment of the
measures they had adopted; their measures had failed; they
saw that half-armed colonists had everywhere repulsed the
picked English generals and soldiers; their statements as to
the intentions and principles of the colonists would have also
been falsified had the Congress in 1776 adhered to the declaration of principles and avowal of purposes which it had made
in 1775; the friends of American rights would have been
triumphant, in and out of Parliament, in England, and 1777
would doubtless have witnessed the overthrow of the corrupt
British Ministry, the constitutional freedom of the American
colonies in connection with the unity of the empire, instead of
seven years' bloody warfare, the destruction of the national life
and of the oneness of the Anglo-Saxon race.

III. But the Declaration of Independence on the part of its
authors was not only a violation of good faith to the statesmen and others in England who had advocated the constitutional rights of the colonists, it was also a violation both of
good faith and justice to their colonial fellow-countrymen who
continued to adhere to connection with the mother country upon
the principles professed in all times past by the separationists
themselves.*

* " In the beginning of the memorable year 1776, there was a public opinion
in favour of independence in New England, and but little more than individual preferences for it in the Middle or Southern colonies. So deeply

The adherents of connection with England had, with the exception of certain office-holders and their relations, been as earnest advocates of colonial rights as had the leaders of the separation. The opponents of the constitutional rights of the colonies, in the colonies, were few and far between—not numerous enough to form a party, or even to be called a party. The Congress of 1775 declared the colonies to be "a unit" in their determination to defend their rights, but disdained the idea of separation from the mother country; and Mr. John Adams stated at the same time: "All America is united in sentiment. When a masterly statesman, to whom America has erected a statue in her heart for his integrity, fortitude, and perseverance in her cause, invented a Committee of Correspondence in Boston, did not every colony, nay, every county, city, hundred, and town upon the whole continent adopt the measure as if it had been a revelation from above? Look over the resolves of the colonies for the past year; you will see that one understanding governs, one heart animates the whole."*

Such were the sentiments and feelings of America in resisting the innovations upon their rights of a British Ministry, while they denied the idea of separation from the mother country as a calumny; and such were the grounds on which millions in England and Scotland, in and out of Parliament, supported them.†

seated was the affection for the mother country, that it required all the severe acts of war, directed by an inexorable Ministry and the fierce words from the throne, to be made fully known throughout America before the *majority* of the people could be persuaded to renounce their allegiance and assume the sovereignty. Jefferson says that Samuel Adams was constantly holding caucuses with distinguished men, in which the measures to be pursued were generally determined upon, and their several parts were assigned to the actors who afterwards appeared in them." (Frothingham's Rise of the Republic of the United States, pp. 468, 469.)

"Though that measure (independence), a few months before, was not only foreign from their wishes, but the object of their abhorrence, the current suddenly became so strong in its favour that it bore down all opposition. The multitude was hurried down the stream; but some worthy men could not easily reconcile themselves to the idea of an eternal separation from a country to which they had long been bound by the most endearing ties." (Ramsay's History of the United States, Vol. II., pp. 161, 162.)

* Quoted by Bancroft, Vol. VII., p. 234.

† "Millions in England and Scotland" (said John Adams, who nominated

When, therefore, the Congress at Philadelphia voted, by a majority of one or two, but declaring that their vote should be published as unanimous, to renounce all the professions of the past of connection with the mother country, to declare her their enemy, and to avow eternal separation from her, it may be easily conceived how a large portion of the colonists would feel that their confidence had been betrayed; that the representations they had made to English statesmen would bear the stamp of untruth; that their hopes had been blasted, and that they were now to be treated as rebels and traitors for adhering to the faith of their forefathers; for, as Mr. Allan remarks, the Declaration of Independence " left no neutrals. He who was not for independence, unconditional independence, was an enemy."* Thus the many tens of thousands of colonists who adhered to the faith of their forefathers, and the traditions and professions of their own personal history, were, by a single act of Congress, declared "enemies" of their country, " rebels," and even "traitors," because they would not renounce their oath of allegiance, and swear allegiance to a self and newly-created authority, to relinquish the defence of the rights of Englishmen for the theory of republican independence, adherence to which had been advocated by the Chathams and Burkes in the British Parliament, in preference to the new doctrines propounded by the leaders in the Philadelphia Congress, for maintaining the unity and life of a great nation rather than dismember and destroy it. Was it doing as one would be done by? Was it not a violation of good faith, and hard treatment, for men to be declared by a new tribunal criminals in July, for maintaining what all had held to be loyal and patriotic in January? All the arguments and appeals of the Northern States against the separation of the

Washington as Commander-in-Chief, and was afterwards President of the United States)—" millions in England and Scotland think it unrighteous, impolitic, and ruinous to make war upon us ; and a Minister, though he may have a marble heart, will proceed with a desponding spirit. London has bound her members under their hands to assist us ; Bristol has chosen two known friends of America ; many of the most virtuous of the nobility and gentry are for us, and among them a St. Asaph, a Camden, and a Chatham ; the best bishop that adorns the bench, as great a judge as the nation can boast, and the greatest statesman it ever saw." (Bancroft's History of the United States, Vol. VII., Chap. xxi., p. 235.)

* History of the American Revolution, Vol. I., Chap. xiii., p. 353.

Southern States from the Republic, as destructive of the life of
the nation, in the recent civil war of 1864—1869, were equally
strong, on the same ground, against the separation of the
American colonies from the mother country in the civil war of
1776—1783. The United Empire Loyalists of that day were,
as the conservators of the life of the nation, against the dismemberment of the empire, as are the Americans of the Northern
States of the present day the conservators of the life of their
nation in opposing the dismemberment of the Republic.

IV. But this is not all. This Declaration of the 4th of July,
1776, was the commencement of persecutions, proscriptions, and
confiscations of property against those who refused to renounce
the oaths which they had taken, as well as the principles and
traditions which had, until then, been professed by their persecutors and oppressors as well as by themselves. The declaration
of independence had been made in the name and for the professed purposes of liberty; but the very first acts under it
were to deprive a large portion of the colonists not only of
liberty of action, but liberty of thought and opinion—to extract
from them oaths and declarations which could not have been
sincere, and which could have been little better than perjuries,
for the sole purpose of saving life, liberty, or property. They
were a numerous and intelligent portion of the community;
were equally interested in the welfare of the country as their
assailants, instead of being designated by every epithet of
opprobrium, and denied the freedom of opinion and privileges
of citizenship.* Mr. Elliott remarks :—

"The Tories comprised a large number, among whom were
many rich, cultivated, and kindly people ; these last, above all,

* It was the plea then, as it had and has always been in all tyranny,
whether wielded by an individual or an oligarchy or a committee, whether
under the pretext of liberty or of order, to persecute all dissenting parties,
under profession of preventing division and promoting unity. But the true
friends of liberty, even in perilous times, have always relied upon the justice
of their principles and excellence of their policy and measures for support
and success, and not upon the prison, the gallows, and the impoverishment
of the dissenters by plunder. The Congress itself had declared to England
that the " colonists were a unit" in behalf of liberty ; but their own enactments and proceedings against the Loyalists refuted their own statements.
Even in England, tyrannical and corrupt as was the Government at the time,
and divided as were both Parliament and people, and assailed by foreign

needed watching, and were most dangerous. In looking over the harsh treatment of the Tories by the rebels, it should be remembered that a covert enemy is more dangerous than an open one, and that the Tories comprised both of these. Many men of property and character in Massachusetts were in favour of England, partly from conviction and partly from fear. That large and often cultivated class called "Conservatives," who hold by the past rather than hope for the future, and are constitutionally timid, feared change; they were naturally Tories. Most of the Episcopalians in New England (though not in Virginia) opposed the revolutionary movements. They had felt the oppression and contempt of the New England Congregationalists, and looked to the English Government and the English Church for help. But in Virginia, where they were strong, this was not so; and there the Episcopalians were among the warmest asserters of the rights of man."

" In New York there was at first a very large proportion of Tories; in 1776, not less than twelve hundred and ninety-three persons, in the County of Queen's alone, professed themselves subjects to the King. In Suffolk County, eight hundred enrolled themselves as King's militia."

" In New Jersey, Governor Franklin, son of Benjamin Franklin, led the King's friends, and was active against the Americans until it became necessary to put him in confinement. The war carried on between Tories and Whigs was more merciless than any other, and more cruel and wanton than that of the Indians."

and domestic enemies, the proceedings of both Houses of Parliament were open to the public ; every member was not only free to express his opinions, but those opinions were forthwith published to the world, and every man throughout the kingdom enjoyed freedom of opinion. It was reserved for the American Congress, while professing to found liberty, to conduct its proceedings in secret for eleven years, to suppress the freedom of the press and individual freedom of opinion, and to treat as criminals those who dissented from its acts of policy. The private biography and letters of the principal actors in the American revolution, published during the present century, show (with the exception of Washington and very few others) that individual ambition had quite as much to do in the contest of separation from the mother country as patriotic love of constitutional liberty, which, even at this day, in the United States, is not comparable with that of Great Britain—some of the ablest American writers being judges.

" Laws were made in Rhode Island against all who supplied the enemy with provisions, or gave them information.

" In Connecticut the Tories were not allowed to speak or write against Congress or the Assembly.

" In Massachusetts a man might be banished unless he would swear fealty to the cause of liberty.

" Severe laws were also passed against the Tories in New Hampshire, New York, New Jersey, and Virginia, and in nearly all the colonies now seaboard States.

" John Jay thought the Confiscation Act of New York inexcusable and disgraceful."*

Mr. Hildreth remarks: " Very serious was the change in the legal position of the class known as Tories—in many of the States a very large minority, and in all, respectable for wealth and social position. Of those thus stigmatized, some were inclined to favour the utmost claims of the mother country; but *the greater part, though determined to adhere to the British connection, yet deprecated the policy which had brought on so fatal a quarrel.* This loyal minority, especially its more conspicuous members, as the warmth of political feeling increased, had been exposed to the violence of mobs, and to all sorts of personal indignities, in which private malice or a wanton and violent spirit of mischief had been too often gratified under

---

* Elliott's New England History, Vol. II., Chap. xxvii., pp. 369—375.

" A large number of the merchants in all the chief commercial towns of the colonies were openly hostile, or but coldly inclined to the common cause. General Lee, sent to Newport (Rhode Island) to advise about throwing up fortifications, *called the principal persons among the disaffected before him, and obliged them by a tremendous oath to support the authority of Congress.* The Assembly met shortly after, and passed an Act subjecting to death, with confiscation of property, all who should hold intercourse with or assist the British ships. But to save Newport from destruction it presently became necessary to permit a certain stated supply to be furnished to the British ships from that town." (Hildreth's History of the United States, Vol. III., Chap. xxxii., p. 102.)

" In the Middle colonies the unwillingness to separate from Great Britain was greater than in the colonies either to the North or South. One reason probably was, that in this division were the towns of New York and Philadelphia, which greatly profited by their trade to England, and which contained a larger proportion of English and Scotch merchants, who, with few exceptions, were attached to the royal cause." (Tucker's History of the United States, Vol. I., p. 150.)

the guise of patriotism. By the recent political changes, Tories and suspected persons became exposed to dangers from the law as well as from mobs. Having boldly seized the reins of government, the new State authorities claimed the allegiance of all residents within their limits, and under the lead and recommendation of Congress, those who refused to acknowledge their authority, or who adhered to their enemies, were exposed to severe penalties, confiscation of property, imprisonment, banishment, and finally death."*

Thus was a large minority of the most wealthy and intelligent (their wealth and intelligence making them the greater criminals) inhabitants of the colonies, by the act of a new body not known to the Constitutions of any of their provinces, reduced to the alternative of violating their convictions, consciences, and oaths, or being branded and treated as enemies of their country, deprived not only of the freedom of the press and of speech, but made criminals for even neutrality and silence, and their property confiscated to defray the expenses of a war upon themselves. Had Congress, in July, 1776, maintained the principles and objects it avowed even in the autumn of 1775, there would have been no occasion of thus violating good faith and common justice to the large minority of the colonies; there is every reason to believe that there would have been a universal rallying, as there had been the year before, in defence of the constitutional rights of Englishmen and the unimpaired life of the empire; there would have been a far larger military force of enthusiastic and patriotic volunteers collected and organized to defend those rights than could ever afterwards be embodied to support independence; there would have been a union of the friends of constitutional liberty on both sides of the Atlantic; good faith would have been

---

* History of the United States, Vol. III., Chap. xxxiii., pp. 137, 138.

On the 18th of June, 1776, about two weeks before adopting the Declaration of Independence, Congress "Resolved,—That no man in these colonies charged with being a Tory, or unfriendly to the cause of American liberty, be injured in his person or property, unless the proceeding against him be founded on an order of Congress or Committee," etc. But this resolution amounted practically to nothing. It seems to have been intended to allay the fears and weaken the opposition of loyalists, but contributed nothing for their protection, or to mitigate the cruel persecutions everywhere waged against them.

kept on both sides, and the "millions in England and Scotland," sustained by the millions in America, instead of being abandoned by them in the very crisis of the contest in the mother country, would have achieved in less than a twelvemonth a victory for freedom, for civilization, and for humanity, far beyond what had been accomplished in the English Revolution of 1688.

V. The Declaration of Independence was the commencement of weakness in the army of its authors, and of defeats in their fields of battle. The Declaration has been announced as the birth of a nation, though it was actually the dismemberment of a nation. It was hailed with every demonstration of joy and triumph on the part of those who had been prepared for the event, and no efforts were spared on the part of those who had advocated independence in the army, in the Congress, and in the provinces, to accompany the circulation of the Declaration with every enthusiastic expression of delight and anticipated free government, in which, of course, they themselves would occupy the chief places of profit and power. But this enthusiasm, notwithstanding the glowing descriptions of some American historians, was far from being general or ardent. Lord Mahon says: "As sent forth by Congress, the Declaration of Independence having reached the camp of Washington, was, by his orders (as commanded by Congress), read aloud at the head of every regiment. There, as in most other places, it excited much less notice than might have been supposed." An American author of our own day (President Reed), most careful in his statements, and most zealous in the cause of independence, observes that "No one can read the private correspondence of the times without being struck with the slight impression made on either the army or the mass of the people by the Declaration."*

The Adjutant-General, in his familiar and almost daily letters to his wife, does not even allude to it. But though there was little enthusiasm, there were some excesses. At New York a party of soldiers, with tumultuary violence, tore down and beheaded a statue of the King which stood upon Broadway,

---

* Life and Correspondence of President Reed, Vol. I., p. 195. Washington, however, in his public letter to Congress (unless Mr. Jared Sparks has *improved* this passage), says that the troops had testified their "warmest approbation." (Writings, Vol. III., p. 457.)

having been erected only six years before. Washington, greatly to his honour, did not shrink from the duty of rebuking them next day, in his General Orders, for their misdirected zeal.*

Within a few weeks after the Declaration of Independence, Washington's army, composed of forces raised before that Declaration, consisted of 27,000 men—a larger army than he was ever after able to assemble, and more than twice as large as he commanded within a few months afterwards.

It has been seen with what readiness, zeal, and enthusiasm thousands and tens of thousands of volunteers offered their services during the year 1775, and the first part of the year 1776, in defence of British liberty, in union with the friends of civil liberty and defenders of American liberty in England; but when, after the Declaration of the 4th of July, 1776, the cause became one of Congressional liberty instead of British liberty, of separation from the mother country instead of union with it, of a new form of government instead of one to which they had sworn allegiance, and which they had ever lauded and professed to love,—then, in these novel circumstances, the provincial army dwindled from day to day by desertions, as well as from other causes, and recruiting its ranks

---

* Lord Mahon's History of England from the Peace of Utrecht, Vol. VI., Chap. liv., pp. 161, 162.

Lord Mahon adds : "It was at this inauspicious juncture, only a few hours after independence had been proclaimed in the ranks of his opponents, that the bearer of the pacific commission, Lord Howe, arrived off Sandy Hook. He had cause to regret most bitterly both the delay of his passage and the limitation of his powers. He did not neglect, however, whatever means of peace were still within his reach. He sent on shore a declaration, announcing to the people the object of his mission. He despatched a friendly letter, written at sea, to Dr. Franklin, at Philadelphia. But when Franklin's answer came it showed him wholly adverse to a reconciliation, expressing in strong terms his resentment of the 'atrocious injuries' which, as he said, America had suffered from 'your unformed and proud nation.' Lord Howe's next step was to send a flag of truce, with another letter, to Washington. But here a preliminary point of form arose. Lord Howe, as holding the King's commission, could not readily acknowledge any rank or title not derived from his Majesty. He had therefore directed his letter to 'George Washington, Esq.' On the other hand, Washington, feeling that, in his circumstances, to yield a punctilio would be to sacrifice a principle, declined to receive or open any letter not addressed to him as General. Thus at the very outset this negotiation was cut short."—*Ib.*, pp. 162, 163.

could only be effected by bounties in money and the promise of
lands; the uninterrupted victories of the colonists during the
twelve months previous to the Declaration of Independence
were succeeded by uninterrupted defeats during the twelve
months succeeding it, with the exception of the brilliant and
successful surprise raids which Washington made upon *Trenton* and *Princeton*. But these exploits were wholly owing to
Washington's skill, and sleepless energy, and heroic courage,
with feeble forces, in contrast to the lethargy and self-indul-
gence of the English officers on the one hand and the inactivity
of Congress on the other.

The first trial of strength and courage between the English
and revolutionary forces took place in August, a few weeks
after the Declaration of Independence, in the battle of Long
Island, in which Washington's army was completely defeated;
New York and all New Jersey soon fell into the hands of the
British. For this success General Howe received the honour of
knighthood, as did General Carlton for similar success in
Canada—the one becoming Sir William Howe, and the other
Sir Guy Carlton; but neither did much afterwards to merit
the honour. The English officers seemed to have anticipated a
pastime in America instead of hard fighting and severe service,
and the German mercenaries anticipated rich plunder and
sensual indulgence.

In the autumn and winter following Washington's defeat at
Long Island and forced evacuation of New York, and indeed of
New Jersey, Sir William Howe buried himself in self-indul-
gent inactivity for six months in New York; while a portion
of his army sought quarters and plunder, and committed brutal
acts of sensuality, in the chief places of New Jersey. Loyalty
seems to have been the prevalent feeling of New Jersey on the
first passing of the King's troops through it.*

This is stated on unquestionable authority (see the previous
note); scarcely any of the inhabitants joined the American

---

* After the battle of Long Island and the evacuation of New York, " six
thousand men, led by Earl Cornwallis, were landed on the Jersey side. At
their approach the Americans withdrew in great haste to Fort Lee, leaving
behind their artillery and stores. Washington himself had no other alternative than to give way with all speed as his enemy advanced. He fell back
successively upon Brunswick, upon Princeton, upon Trenton, and at last to

retreating army, while numbers were daily flocking to the royal army. But within twelve months, when that royal army passed through the same country, on the evacuation of Philadephia by Sir Henry Clinton (Sir William Howe having returned to England), the inhabitants were universally hostile,

the Pennsylvania side of the Delaware. To all these places, one after another, did Lord Cornwallis, though slowly, and with little vigour, pursue him.

" This fair province of the Jerseys, sometimes called the Garden of America, did not certainly on this occasion prove to be its bulwark. The scene is described as follows by one of their own historians, Dr. Ramsay: ' As the retreating Americans marched through the country, scarcely one of the inhabitants joined them, while numbers were daily flocking to the royal army to make their peace and obtain protection. They saw on the one side a numerous, well-appointed, and full clad army, dazzling their eyes with their elegance of uniforms ; on the other a few poor fellows who, from their shabby clothing, were called ragamuffins, fleeing for their safety. Not only the common people changed sides in this gloomy state of public affairs, but some of the leading men in New Jersey and Pennsylvania adopted the same expedient.'

" Yet it is scarcely just to the Americans to ascribe, with Dr. Ramsay, their change of sides to nothing beyond their change of fortune. May we not rather believe that a feeling of concern at the separation, hitherto suppressed in terror, was now first freely avowed—that in New Jersey, and not in New Jersey alone, an active and bold minority had been able to overrule numbers much larger, but more quiescent and complying ?

" Another remark made by the same historian might, as history shows, be extended to other times and countries besides his own. The men who had been the vainest braggarts, the loudest blusterers in favour of independence, were now the first to veer around or to slink away. This remark, which Dr. Ramsay makes only four years afterwards, is fully confirmed by other documents of earlier date, but much later publication, by the secret correspondence of the time. Thus writes the Adjutant-General : 'Some of our Philadelphia gentlemen, who came over on visits, upon the first cannon went off in a violent hurry. Your noisy Sons of Liberty are, I find, the quietest in the field.' Thus again Washington, with felicitous expression, points a paragraph at the ' chimney-corner heroes.'

" At this period the effective force under Washington had dwindled down to four thousand men.

" The Congress at this juncture, like most other public assemblies, seemed but slightly affected by the dangers which as yet were not close upon them. On the 11th of December they passed some resolutions contradicting, as false and malicious, a report that they intended to remove from Philadelphia. They declared that they had a higher opinion of the good people of these States than to suppose such a measure requisite, and that they would not instead of being universally loyal, as the year before. The royal historian says:

" In setting out on this dangerous retreat, the British general clearly perceived that it would be indispensably necessary to provide for all possible contingencies. *His way lay entirely through an enemy's country, where everything was hostile in the extreme, and from whence no assistance or help of any sort was to be expected.*"*

The causes of this change in the feelings of the inhabitants of the Jerseys, in the space of a few months, in regard to the British army and mother country, will be a subject of future inquiry; but, in the meantime, the manifest failure of the revolutionary army to maintain its position during the twelve months following the Declaration of Independence, its declining numbers, and the difficulty of recruiting its ranks, show that the act of violent severance from the mother country did not spring from the heart and intellect of the colonists, but from a portion of them which had obtained all the resources of material and military power, under the profession of defending their rights as British subjects, with a view to ultimate reconciliation and union with the mother country ; but had used their advantages to declare severance from the mother country, to excite hatred against it, and establish themselves in sovereignty over America. Referring to the state of the colonies toward the close of 1777, the latest American historian, Mr. Frothingham, says :

" This was a period of great political languor. The burden of the war was severely felt. The blaze of freedom, it was said, that burst forth at the beginning had gone down, and numbers, in the thirst for riches, lost sight of the original object. (Inde-

---

leave the city of Philadelphia 'unless the last necessity shall direct it.' These resolutions were transmitted by the President to Washington, with a request that he would publish them to the army in General Orders. Washington, in reply, excused himself from complying with that suggestion. In thus declining it, he showed his usual sagacity and foresight ; for on the very next day after the first resolution, the Congress underwent a sudden revulsion of opinion, and did not scruple to disperse in all haste, to meet again the 20th of the same month, not at Philadelphia, but at Baltimore." (Lord Mahon's History of England, etc., Vol. VI., Chap. liv., pp. 189—193.)

 * Dr. Andrews' History of the American War, etc., Vol. III., Chap. xxxv., p. 111.

pendent Chronicle, March 12, 1778.) 'Where,' wrote Henry
Laurens (successor to John Hancock as the President of the
Congress) to Washington, 'where is virtue, where is patriotism
now, when almost every man has turned his thoughts and attention to gain and pleasures?'" (Letter, November 20, 1778.)*

VI. The Declaration of Independence was the avowed expedient and prelude to a sought-for alliance with France and Spain
against the mother country, notwithstanding they had sought for
a hundred years to extirpate the colonists, and had been prevented from "driving them into the sea" by the aid of the army
and navy and vast expenditure of the mother country.

It seems difficult to reconcile with truthfulness, fairness, and
consistency, the intrigues and proposed terms of alliance between the leaders of Congress and the King of France. These
intrigues commenced several months before the Declaration of
Independence, when the authors of it were disclaiming any wish
or design to separate from England, and their desire for reconciliation with the mother country by a recognition of their
rights as they existed in 1763. As early as December, 1775,
six months before the Declaration of Independence, a Congress
Secret Committee of Correspondence wrote to Arthur Lee, in
London (a native of Virginia, but a practising barrister in
London), and Charles Dumas, at the Hague, requesting them
to ascertain the feeling of European Courts respecting America,
enjoining "great circumspection and secrecy."† They hoped
most from France; but opposition was made in Congress when
it was first suggested to apply for aid to the ancient enemy
both of the colonies and England. Dr. Zubly, of Georgia, said:
" A proposal has been made to apply to France and Spain. I
apprehend the man who would propose it (to his constituents)
would be torn to pieces like De Witt." Within three months
after the utterance of these words in Congress, M. de Bouvouloir, agent of the French Government, appeared in Philadelphia,
held secret conferences with the Secret Committee, and assured
them that France was ready to aid the colonies on such conditions as might be considered equitable. These conferences were

---

* Frothingham's Rise of the American Republic, Chap. xii., p. 572.
† The Life of Arthur Lee (I., p. 53) contains the letter to Lee, copied from
the original MSS. in the handwriting of Franklin, dated December 12, 1775,
and signed by Franklin, Dickenson. and Jay.

33

so secret that De Bouvouloir says that "the Committee met him at an appointed place after dark, each going to it by a different road."*

A few weeks later, the Secret Committee appointed Silas Deane commercial agent to Europe (March 3), to procure military supplies, and to state to the French Minister, Count Vergennes, the probability of the colonies totally separating from England; that France was looked upon as the power whose friendship they should most desire to cultivate; and to inquire whether, in case of their independence, France would acknowledge it, and receive their Ambassadors.

In April, 1776, three months before the Declaration of Independence, the inquiry was made of Franklin, "When is the Continental Congress by general consent to be formed into a Supreme Legislature?" He replied, "Nothing seems wanting but that general consent. The novelty of the thing deters some; the doubt of success, others; *the vain hope of reconciliation, many.* Every day furnishes us with new causes of increasing enmity, and new reasons for *wishing an eternal separation;* so that there is a rapid increase of the *formerly small party* who were for an independent government."*

From these words of Dr. Franklin, as well as from the facts stated in the preceding pages, it is clear the Declaration of Independence was not the spontaneous voice of a continent, as represented by many American historians, but the result of a persistent agitation on the part of the leaders in Congress, and their agents and partizans in the several provinces, who *now* represented every act of the corrupt Administration in England as the act of the *nation,* and thus sought to alienate the affections of the colonists from the mother country. Upon Dr. Franklin's own authority, it is clear that he was opposed to any reconciliation with England and in favour of an "eternal separation" months before the Declaration of Independence; that the party "for an independent government" were "the formerly small party," but had "a rapid increase," which Dr. Franklin and his friends knew so well how to promote, while they amused and deceived the friends of the unity of the

* Frothingham's Rise of the American Republic, Chap. xi., p. 488.
* Franklin to Josiah Quincy, April 15, 1776. Sparks' Works, Vol. VIII., p. 181.

empire, in both England and America, by professing an earnest desire for reconciliation with the mother country.

The same double game was played against England by the French Government and the secret leaders of the American Congress, the latter professing a desire for reconciliation with England, and the former professing the warmest friendship for England and disapprobation of the separation of the colonies from England, while both parties were secretly consulting together as to the means of dismembering the British empire. "It was," says Dr. Ramsay, "evidently the interest of France to encourage the Americans in their opposition to Great Britain; and it was true policy to do this by degrees, and in a private manner, lest Great Britain might take the alarm. It is certain that Great Britain was amused with declarations of the most pacific disposition on the part of France, at the time the Americans were liberally supplied with the means of defence; and it is equally certain that this was the true line of policy for promoting that dismemberment of the British empire which France had an interest in accomplishing. It was the interest of Congress to apply to the Court of France, and it was the interest of France to listen to their application."*

The application for alliance with France to war with England

* History of the United States, Vol. II., Chap. xv., pp. 242, 243.

The same historian observes : " On the 11th of June, Congress appointed a Committee to prepare a plan of a treaty to be proposed to foreign powers. The discussion of this novel subject engaged their attention till the latter end of September. Congress having agreed on the plan of the treaty which they intended to propose to the King of France, proceeded to elect commissioners to solicit its acceptance. Dr. Franklin, Silas Deane, and Thomas Jefferson were chosen. The latter declining to serve, Arthur Lee, who was then in London, and had been very serviceable to his country in a variety of ways, was elected in his room. It was resolved that no member should be at liberty to divulge anything more of these transactions than ' that Congress had taken such steps as they judged necessary for obtaining foreign alliances.' "—*Ib.*, pp. 242, 243.

It is worthy of remark, that although Dr. Franklin consented to act as one of the commissioners to France, he opposed the application itself ; for he himself wrote a few months afterwards as follows : " I have never yet changed the opinions I gave in Congress, that a virgin state should preserve a virgin character, and not go about suitoring for alliances, but wait with decent dignity for the applications of others. I was overruled, perhaps for the best." (Works, Vol. VIII., p. 209.)

was far from being the voice of America. The fact that it was under discussion in Congress three months before it could be carried, shows how strong must have been the opposition to it in Congress itself, and how vigorous and persevering must have been the efforts to manipulate a majority of its members into acquiescing in an application for arms, money, and men to a Government which was and had always been the enemy of civil and Protestant liberty—which had hired savage Indians to butcher and scalp their forefathers, mothers, and children, without regard to age or sex, and which had sought to destroy their very settlements, and drive them into the sea, while the British Government had preserved them from destruction and secured to them the American continent. It is easy to conceive how every British heart in America must have revolted at the idea of seeking to become brother warriors with the French against the mother country. Nor was the proceeding known in America until America was committed to it, for the Congress made itself a secret conclave ; its sittings were held in secret ; no divisions were allowed to be recorded ; its debates were suppressed ; its members were sworn to secrecy ; the minorities had no means of making known their views to the public ; it was decided by the majority that every resolution published should be reported as having been adopted *unanimously*, though actually carried by the slenderest majority. The proceedings of that elected Congress, which converted itself into a secret conclave, were never fully known until the present century, and many of them not until the present age, by the biographies of the men and the private correspondence of the times of the American Revolution. The United Empire Loyalists of those times were not permitted to speak for themselves, and their principles, character and acts were only known from the pens of their adversaries. Had the heart of America been allowed to speak and act, there would have been no alliance of America, France, and Spain against England ; the American colonies would have achieved their own noblest freedom unstained by future bloodshed, and untainted by so unnatural an alliance ; the Anglo-Saxon race and language would have been one, and greatly more advanced than it now is in the cause of the world's freedom and civilization.

History has justly censured, in the severest language, the

conduct of Lord North's Administration for employing German mercenaries to aid in maintaining the assumed prerogative of King and Parliament in the colonies; but was it less censurable and more patriotic for the administrative leaders in Congress to engage French and Spanish forces, both at sea and land, to invade Great Britain and her possessions, and to unite with Republicans for the dismemberment of the British empire?

END OF VOL. I.